Find the Perfect Gift

Visit these sites for help in finding the unusual gifts for every occasion. Need help keeping track of special gift-giving dates? Sign up for e-mail reminders of when gifts and cards are due at Memotome.com (`memotome.com`), a free service that's really handy.

Unusual Gift Sites

URL	Site Name	Description
bestmonthlyclubs.com	bestmonthlyclubs.com	The gift that keeps on giving! Pick a theme, such as cookies, chocolate, jellies and more, and a package containing those items will be sent each month.
vanmorevanities.com	Vanmore Vanities	Give a an inexpensive Vanigram, a laminated card displaying a custom phrase that's sent with an adorable stuffed bear.
metmuseum.org/store	The Met Store	The Metropolitan Museum of Art's Store holds everything an art lover adores. An art kit filled with supplies will delight budding artists.
statue.com	Statue.com	From life-size to desk-size, the statues from Statue.com will make someone happy.
bubbles.com	Ebubbles	The best in bath and body products awaits you at Ebubbles.
cozycashmere.com	Cozy Cashmere	The perfect baby gift, this elegant, soft cashmere blanket is ideal for crib or stroller.
bulkcandystore.com	Bulk Candy Store	Send a variety of sweets to the good people in your life from one of the sweetest places on the Internet.
claxtonfruitcake.com	Claxton Fruit Cake	The name "Claxton" is practically synonymous with fruit cakes filled with sweet fruit, raisins and nuts. Fruit cake lovers will start grinning as soon as the box arrives.
bigtopbarkery.com	Big Top Barkery	Canine friends always enjoy treats from this bakery just for dogs. For an extraspecial treat, send a "Pawty in a Box."

For Dummies: Bestselling Book Series for Beginners

2005 Online Shopping Directory For Dummies®

Tips for Smart Shopping

Follow these simple tips to maximize your shopping experience and stay safe.

- ✔ **Know what you're buying.** Read the product description carefully before you submit your order. Is the product the right size, the right color and shape? Verifying the details now will save time and money in the future.

- ✔ **Be aware of the total cost of the purchase.** Expensive shipping charges, fees for gift-wrapping, and applicable taxes can add up fast.

- ✔ **Don't pay for your purchase with cash.** The best way to pay for online purchases is by credit card (not debit or check cards) or a service like PayPal. Although problems are unlikely, if you have a dispute down the road you'll have the credit card company on your side.

- ✔ **Get familiar with the merchant.** You've got to feel comfortable about the business from which you're buying before you make your purchase. If you're dealing with an unfamiliar vendor and you want to know more about the merchant, send an e-mail message or contact the business by phone. Reputable merchants will be happy to answer all of your questions.

- ✔ **Look for security on the merchant's Web site.** A merchant who takes credit cards should provide some assurance that the transaction is safe. If you're not sure or not comfortable, shop elsewhere.

- ✔ **Guard your privacy.** Read the merchant's Privacy Policy carefully. Always remember that you don't need to answer intrusive or personal questions that aren't relative to your buying experience at a Web site.

- ✔ **Check for satisfaction or product guarantees before you order.** Of course you don't expect to be disappointed! However, a vendor who offers a no questions asked—money back guarantee is much easier to deal with if the product you purchased is defective.

Save Money on Books

EveryBookstore.com (ebs.allbookstores.com) is a book lovers dream. After you've entered the book title or ISBN number, this amazing site searches through most Web bookstores and presents you with a list of sites that offer the book. Prices and shipping costs are displayed, and you can buy the book directly from the EveryBookstore.com site. You can also search on author or keywords. Good deal!

Wiley, the Wiley Publishing logo, For Dummies, the Dummies Man logo, the For Dummies Bestselling Book Series logo and all related trade dress are trademarks or registered trademarks of John Wiley & Sons, Inc. and/or its affiliates. All other trademarks are property of their respective owners.

For Dummies: Bestselling Book Series for Beginners

2005 Online Shopping Directory

FOR

DUMMIES®

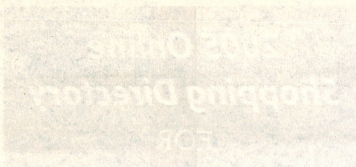

2005 Online Shopping Directory FOR DUMMIES®

by Barbara Kasser and Frank Fiore

WILEY

Wiley Publishing, Inc.

2005 Online Shopping Directory For Dummies®

Published by
Wiley Publishing, Inc.
111 River Street
Hoboken, NJ 07030-5774

WILEY

About the Authors

Barbara Kasser is a network administrator for a major specialty chemical company. In her spare time, she is the Team Leader Coordinator for the Boca Raton Community Emergency Response Team. Barbara is the author of several books, including *Internet Shopping Yellow Pages*, *Practical Internet*, *Using the Internet, 4th Edition* and *Netscape Navigator, Browsing and Beyond*. Barbara also co-authored *Internet Explorer 4, One Step at a Time*.

Growing up, Barbara dreamed of being a librarian. She now considers herself an Internet librarian and is thrilled to share her Internet knowledge with her co-workers, friends, and readers. An Internet user since its earliest days, Barbara has watched the online world grow and change. In the office, she uses the Internet for everything from research to communication. At home, Barbara and her family can't imagine life without the Internet. They use it for everything from casual chatting to business purposes.

Frank Fiore is an eBusiness expert and accomplished author of six eBusiness books: *Successful Affiliate Marketing for Merchants*, *e-Marketing Strategies*, *The Complete Idiot's Guide to Starting an Online Business*, *Dr. Livingston's Online Shopping Safari Guidebook*, *Tech TVs Starting an Online Business*, and *How to Succeed in Sales Using Today's Technology*. He is the Online Shopping Guide for About.com and a prolific writer of eBusiness features on Informit.com. In addition to his writing endeavors, he has appeared on numerous TV and radio talk shows discussing online shopping and the future of eCommerce and teaches college level courses on eMarketing. He lives in Paradise Valley, Arizona, with his wife and their Scottish sheepdog.

Dedication

From Barbara: To my dear friend Bea, who is always there when I need her.

From Frank: To Dudley, Hennasea, and Bristol

Authors' Acknowledgments

It takes a lot of people and effort to produce any book, especially one like this. My deepest thanks to the great team at Wiley, including the proofers, artists, layout team, and indexer, who worked so hard to transform my plain text into this finished book. To Sarah Hellert, a great editor and Paula Lowell, the copy editor, thanks for working so tirelessly to get everything done on time. To Tom Heine for shepherding the process along.

My friend Spot who kept me company all through the long dark nights deserves a hug too.

Of course, I need to thank David Fugate and all the folks at Waterside Productions. I don't know if I could ever write another book without your help.

I also want to thank the people who helped me when I was so crunched for time. Marivi Iglesias, Kate Chase, Wendy Willard, and Keeley Smith were calm, cool, and collected and helped me finish the book. My husband Bill Kasser turned into a great writer during the project. I don't know what I would have done without his help.

Finally, my friends and family deserve lots of credit. Ken, thanks for calling and checking up on me. Richard, thanks for giving up your Mom for most of your vacation. I know I'm not always the easiest person to live with when I'm working on a book!

Publisher's Acknowledgments

We're proud of this book; please send us your comments through our online registration form located at dummies.com/register/.

Some of the people who helped bring this book to market include the following:

Acquisitions, Editorial, and Media Development

Project Editor: Sarah Hellert

Acquisitions Editor: Tom Heine

Copy Editor: Paula Lowell

Editorial Manager: Robyn Siesky

Editorial Assistant: Adrienne D. Porter

Cartoons: Rich Tennant (the5thwave.com)

Production

Project Coordinator: Erin Smith

Layout and Graphics: Denny Hager, Joyce Haughey, Stephanie D. Jumper, Barry Offringa, Lynsey Osborn, Jacque Roth, Julie Trippetti

Proofreaders: Laura Albert, Vicki Broyles, David Faust, John Greenough, Brian H. Walls

Indexer: Sherry Massey

Special Help: Teresa Artman, Leah Cameron, Rebecca Huehls, Richard Meyer, Linda Morris, Kathie Rickard

---

Publishing and Editorial for Technology Publishing

Richard Swadley, Vice President and Executive Group Publisher

Barry Pruett, Vice President and Publisher, Visual/Web Graphics

Andy Cummings, Vice President and Publisher, Technology Dummies

Mary Bednarek, Executive Acquisitions Director, Technology Dummies

Mary C. Corder, Editorial Director, Technology Dummies

Publishing for Consumer Dummies

Diane Graves Steele, Vice President and Publisher

Joyce Pepple, Acquisitions Director

Composition Services

Gerry Fahey, Vice President of Production Services

Debbie Stailey, Director of Composition Services

Contents at a Glance

Table of Contents

Introduction

●●

"*V*eni, Vidi, VISA." I came, I saw, I did a little shopping.

That's the way it was back in 1997 — in the "early days" of online shopping. I remember how enthused I was about shopping on the Net, limited as it was at that time. I expressed my enthusiasm to a colleague who flared his nostrils and said, "Online shopping will never catch on."

Seven years and a number of dot-com busts later, online shopping has finally caught on and has grown leaps and bounds with each year, setting new sales records every shopping season. Much has changed in those seven years. That's why *2005 Online Shopping Directory For Dummies* is a must-have if you're going to safely and successfully shop the World Wide Web.

As more and more consumers come online each and every day, a fast-growing number of them are being hooked on the selection, convenience, and bargains they find online. The online retailers range from discount stores to auctions, from well-known brick-and-mortar stores to niche boutiques, from stores that sell internationally to mom-and-pop establishments that sell out of their homes. Consumers have found that shopping these stores online is fun, easy, and surprising — and saves both time and money. Online shopping has blossomed into a billion-dollar industry with shopping sites numbering in the tens of thousands and offering millions of products to you, the everyday consumer.

Which poses a problem. How do you find what you want?

When online shopping first got started back in the old days, you could easily bookmark in your Web browser every shopping site that existed and you knew what each one sold. Doing so is impossible today. What sometimes seems even more impossible is finding a particular product that you want. Even though shopping search engines have improved over the years, they still have a long way to go toward meeting the needs of the online shopper.

For example, if you search for the words *cell phone* in one of the better shopping search engines like Froogle, you get over 800,000 results. If you want to be more specific by trying *Motorola cell phone,* you get almost 200,000 listings. Even if you know what type of Motorola cell phone you want and search for *Motorola cell phone V66*, you still get over 6,000 results!

Obviously, searching for products via a search engine isn't a very efficient way to shop online. After all, online shopping is supposed to save you money *and* time. That's what this *For Dummies* book will do for you. Pure and simple, this guide to online shopping can not only help you save money, but also save you time — and we all know that time is money.

But *2005 Online Shopping Directory For Dummies* is something more. It's a source of the information you need to be not just an online shopper, but also a successful online consumer.

About This Book

The web has a reputation for being as difficult to navigate as the jungle. You've probably heard the online shopping horror stories about stolen credit card numbers, sites that work slowly or not at all, and about those that love to sneak a piece of spyware onto your computer to track where you go and what you see — or worse, that install a nasty little virus that can turn your computer to digital mush.

Well, set your fears aside.

The listings in this book are jam-packed with information about what an online merchant sells, how they ship, what they charge, and how easy the site is to navigate. There's one important online shopping maxim that I abide by, and it's actually posted right above my computer. Really. I'll read it to you.

"An informed online shopper is a successful online shopper."

So what does that mean? It means that information is king when shopping online. Information is what *2005 Online Shopping Directory For Dummies* will give you, not only on hundreds and hundreds of online shopping sites that I have personally visited and reviewed, but also the nuts-and-bolts knowledge needed to make your online shopping experience safe, easy, profitable, and fun!

The shopping sites chosen to grace the listings in this book may sometimes surprise you. You may notice that some very well known retailers are left out, and other, unknown retailers are included. Many of the well-known sites missing in this collection are so well known that you could easily find them on your own. After all, you're not a real dummy. Others are brand-name manufacturers selling direct, whose products can be bought through other retailers, and I saw their sites as duplicates. Techno-elegant but slow-loading and confusing sites were excluded altogether. I wanted to guide you to shopping sites that were unique and unusual in both product and category — hard to find but useful in their distinctiveness. Hopefully, the result is a remarkable collection of the big, the small — and yes, even the "ugly" (see Uglis.com in Chapter 5).

The end result is this book. In it I list and review merchants who sell merchandise from A (Apparel) to Z (Zantrex). I also throw in some unusual shopping sites for merchandise that you thought you would never need, and virtual products made of electrons that you can purchase and download straight to your computer.

But people do not live by merchandise alone. We also shop for services.

So, this book offers a selection of shopping sites that offer services, too. Some you use every day, others you may not have thought of using. They range from limo drivers to veterinarians, accountants to personal assistants, and financial advisors to wedding planners.

Finally, a completely different world of shopping has become a mainstay today in the online world — trading with your fellow natives. I'm talking about the hundreds of classified and auction sites on the Web. Auction sites like eBay have given the online shopper the opportunity to buy products directly from people like you and me. Classifieds sites offer merchandise for sale similar to what you would find in your local newspaper.

To make the shopping sites listed in this book useful to you, they're organized into categories that reflect the kinds of products and services you buy every day. The following sections describe these categories.

Antiques, crafts, and collectibles

Got a yen for collecting Beanie Babies or animation art? Or perhaps antiques are your bag? Or maybe you enjoy the artwork of the masters, or consider yourself the next Picasso? Whatever your aesthetic or collecting interests, the shopping sites listed in the Antiques, Crafts, and Collectibles category can fill your need.

Apparel

Supposedly, clothes make the person. The listings in the Apparel category supply you with just about everything you need to stylishly project or effectively protect your temple of the soul. The listings cover men's wear, women's wear, kid's wear, as well as swimsuits and clothing categories that may be new to you.

Auctions and classifieds

Going once, going twice, SOLD! Online auctions are the hottest thing to hit the Internet since e-mail. If you're looking for that matching thermos to go with your childhood Roy Rogers lunch box, or just a good deal on a set of snow tires for your 1957 Ford Edsel — and anything in between — you can find it at one of the sites listed in the Auctions and Classifieds category.

Babies and children

That little bundle of joy also comes with your needing a bundle of money. The Babies and Children category shows you where to spend it. These shopping sites can set you up quickly in baby clothes, supplies, and furniture. As your babies grow on through toddlerhood and into happy little children, you'll find at these shopping sites everything you need to clothe, entertain, and educate them — and keep them safe.

Computers and consumer electronics

If it blinks, buzzes, flashes, or computes, then the shopping sites listed in the Computers and Consumer Electronics category sell it. These sites can supply your battery-powered, techno-needs with almost every conceivable electronic product offered for sale today. If you're looking for computer items, video, audio, telephones, or just some nifty electronic gadgets, these shopping sites offer electronic nirvana.

Drinks

Wet your whistle! That's what you'll do at the Drink category sites. Whether you're looking for wine, beer, coffee, tea, or soft drinks, these shopping sites let you belly up to the bar.

Entertainment

The Entertainment sites offer books, magazines, music, videos, games, concert tickets, restaurant reservations, and education — whatever you need to keep yourself and your family entertained.

Flowers and gifts

"Say it with flowers," as the ad goes. But you can also say it with the special and unique gift shops that the Web has to offer. Be it a romantic gift, something for a special occasion, or something personalized, you can share your feelings with special items offered in the Flowers and Gifts category.

Food

Live to eat, or eat to live? Whatever your epicurean eating philosophy, the stores in the Food category offer a wide variety of foodstuffs for the omnivore, carnivore, or herbivore within us — plus a good after-dinner cigar.

Health and beauty

Beauty may be in the eye of the beholder, and healthy is as healthy does, but the Health and Beauty shopping sites take themselves seriously when offering you products that make you shine from the inside out. You'll find products that meet your personal hygiene, beauty, fitness, medication, and sexual care needs.

Home and garden

Sprucing up your pad has never been easier when shopping at the Home and Garden sites. From home appliances to fancy furnishings, these stores are your online sources for home improvement and work savers. If you like to garden, give your green thumb a helping hand with the gardening products offered from these online stores.

International

Shop the world! That's what the word *World* in the World Wide Web promises. It's true. You can shop actual stores in faraway lands for exotic and practical products that you can't get at home. The International shopping sites show you how.

Malls and megastores

If it's a selection you want, then the Malls and Megastores sites are the one-stop shops to find it. These online malls and megastores can fill your shopping list — and your shopping cart — in a hurry. With a one-click purchase, you can optimize your time and your shipping charges.

Office supplies

You can outfit your office or home office with a few mouse clicks at the Office Supplies sites. You can find pencils, pens, paper, paperclips, folders, computer supplies, office equipment, and even furniture.

Outdoors

There's nothing like the fresh smell of the great outdoors. But to enjoy communing with nature, you're going to need more than Walden's Pond. The shopping sites in the Outdoor category can outfit you with everything you need to enjoy your stay in the great outdoors.

Pets

The Pets sites offer you items to help you feed, supply, secure, help, entertain, or train your pet, whether your pet walks, crawls, flies, or swims.

Seasonal and holidays

Holidays and seasonal events require their own type of shopping sites. The stores in the Seasonal category cater to the unique products needed to make your celebration of these holidays rewarding.

Sports, hobbies, and crafts

Free time. Do we really have any left? Make the most of what free time you do have with a hobby or sport. Whether you prefer team, outdoor, water, or solo sports, the Sports and Hobbies shopping sites can provide everything you need to enjoy the sporting life. If you're more of the armchair type, hobby supplies and activities are available from these online stores for you, too.

Transportation

Getting around town has never been easier, and the shopping sites in the Transportation category offer cars, bikes, or motorcycles to send you on your merry way. You can even get help financing and insuring your vehicle of choice. If you already have a way to travel, and just need accessories, you can find them at these sites, too.

Travel

Plan your next trip in your slippers. Using the online stores in the Travel category, you can book your flight, rent your car, and reserve a room all at the same time. Find that exotic vacation package or plan that next perfect cruise. Then shop these stores to equip yourself with the travel gear you need.

Zany fun

Besides the traditional products and services found online these days, you can find a whole different category of products for purchase that are, well, zany to say the least. Look to the Zany fun online stores for the unusual product that, up to now, you thought you could live without.

Conventions Used in This Book

A word about some of the different kinds of type you'll be seeing as you peruse through this *For Dummies* book. Translating into print the technology of the Web is not easy. After all, we are bound by an offline world where a simple tap on a word in a book doesn't get us to a destination in cyberspace. So, whenever you see a Web site mentioned in a sentence, you will see the actual URL (Universal Resource Locator — the name of the Web site in Internetese) in `courier font` (without the usual http:// or www) in parentheses right after the name of the site.

For example, a great megastore to shop at is Amazon (`amazon.com`) for products galore.

Foolish Assumptions

In writing *2005 Online Shopping Directory For Dummies* I had to make a number of foolish assumptions. I spell them out here so you're not confused when you're ready to shop.

- ✔ You have a computer (a PC, or a Mac, if you're of the other religious persuasion).
- ✔ You have access to the Internet.
- ✔ You want to buy online.
- ✔ You have a credit card. (Having one is not essential to shop, and some sites cannot process credit cards — but I highly recommend using one online — more of that later in Part I.)
- ✔ You're comfortable about using that credit card online (if you're not now, this *For Dummies* guide assuages your fears later).

There you go. If I've assumed correctly, then you're ready to partake of the fabulous world of online shopping — a virtual banquet of merchandise and services ready for your consumption.

Icons Used in This Book

Now and then throughout the first few chapters of this book, you're going to see a series of small icons. These icons alert you to brief sentences or paragraphs that contain tips, warnings, technical jargon, or specific things to keep in mind when shopping online.

This icon points out some quick ideas on how to save time when shopping online.

I might have to get a little technical once in a while in order to describe a particular point about online shopping. This icon alerts you to that fact.

Don't worry. Don't slam the book shut and run screaming from the room when you come to one of these icons. They're just a friendly warning on what to keep in mind or to avoid when shopping online.

These are important rules to remember every time you shop online. Think of them as shopping commandments.

How This Book Is Organized

2005 Online Shopping Directory For Dummies is divided into three parts. Part I fills you in on what the wonderful world of online shopping is about and how to make your shopping excursions safe, easy, profitable, and fun. Part II is where you get down to business. You'll find an ensemble of online shopping sites ready for you to shop. Part III is the Part of Tens — some quick and easy ten-part rules to use as a guide when shopping online.

Part I: Online Shopping Overview

The online shopping world is one crazy bazaar of products and services. But how do you make sense out of it? Just what does it mean to be an online shopper and what should you be aware of when shopping online? How do you choose a merchant? How do you protect yourself from scams and unscrupulous retailers? What about buying from individuals who hawk their wares on the many online auction sites and classified ads that pepper the Web? Are they safe to buy from? How do you know? How do you protect your purchase in any case? The chapters of Part I cover all of this information and more.

Part II: Online Shopping Sites

Whether you want to buy or just "window shop," the almost 1,500 listings in Part II direct you to some of the best and most unique shopping sites on the Web today. The listings are organized by category and standardized on a set of evaluation criteria that gives a quick thumbnail sketch of the retailer and what to expect from its store. Here's something you won't find in those other online shopping directories — Shopping Excursions. Included in many of the chapters is a brief Shopping Excursion that shows you how to go about making a particular purchase on the Web in that category. For example, "Buying a New Car Online" at the end of Chapter 22 leads you through the process and directs you to Web sites that will help you choose a car, buy it, finance it, and insure it. Shopping Excursions like these pull together all the information provided in this book and directs it at a particular shopping objective.

Part III: The Part of Tens

Part III provides a quick checklist of what you need to know in several categories to make your shopping excursions secure, time-saving, and profitable, It also shows you how to solve a purchase problem if one arises, as well as how to find the best product for your needs. Keep this Part of Tens by your computer when shopping the World Wide Web, and your shopping excursions will be safe and successful.

How to Use This Book

Each shopping category chapter includes in its introduction a description of the category, tips for buying products and services in that category, shopping resources and tools, and the keywords the shopping sites are listed under.

You can do what we all love to do — window shop. Pick one of the categories and leisurely browse through the listings and see what catches your attention. Then visit that shopping site and perhaps find a treasure that you didn't even know existed or a gift for someone who has everything.

Understanding the site listings

Let's face it, giving each of the hundreds of merchants listed here a thorough and detailed review would create a book thousands of pages long, not to mention the risk to one's health just picking it up! So the thumbnail reviews had to be a concise, informative description of what the merchant sells and how.

Company URL

The URL is the Web site address of the online merchant. To visit the site, just type the URL into your browser's address bar. In the sample listing, the URL is **19dollareyeglasses.com** (by the way, notice that the URL is not the same name as the company name, which sometimes happens). To open the merchant's Web site, type **19dollareyeglasses.com**. If the site opens correctly, then you're in! If your browser says that the site can't be found, don't give up. Type the following into your browser — **www.19dollareyeglasses.com**. One way or the other should work.

★ The Star icon

Some sites are just head and shoulders above the rest. We can shop on the Web for just about anything we see in the real world, but there's more on the Web than what your local merchants or standard online retailers offer. That's the beauty of online shopping. The star icon next to the company URL identifies a unique retailer for the category, a retailer selling a unique product, a retailer selling a normal product in a unique way, or perhaps a retailer offering shopping information that is a great help in making a buying decision.

Company name

Most of the time the company name doesn't differ from the company URL, but sometimes it does. That's why the Company Name and URL indexes in this book are so useful. The company name is also often the name that shows up on your credit card statement.

Company phone number

If the retailer has a toll-free number, I list it; if not, I give the company's local number. If a company can't be reached by phone, that information is also provided. Obviously, a phone number is useful if you have questions about the product or service the retailer offers or about the retailer itself.

Company e-mail address

Another way to reach a retailer is through its e-mail address. Most of the time, the e-mail address listed is for either customer service or the sales department. Like the company phone number, a retailer's e-mail address is useful if you have questions. If no e-mail address is available, I also list that information.

Keywords

The keywords give you a quick study of what type of products the retailer offers at its store. I explain what they signify in the introduction of each chapter of the listings, and they can appear in more than one chapter. This feature enables you to search in the Keyword Index and find retailers who sell that product or service, no matter what category they appear in.

Short review

The review gives you some background information on the site — who the retailer is, what kinds of products are offered at the site, how you can buy the merchandise, and any unique services or site features you can take advantage of as an online shopper. I also provide little nuggets of information or advice about the site, as needed.

Vital five

You'll notice five icons at the end of the list. They represent my ratings for Price, Selection, Service, Convenience, and Security, on a scale of 1 to 3, with 1 being a low score and 3 being a high score. These are the five criteria you should consider when deciding to buy from a Web merchant.

Understanding the Vital Five icons

Every online shopper needs a quick litmus test for finding out who a retailer is, what this retailer offers the online consumer, and how well the company services and protects its customers. The Vital Five icons show you at a glance all about an online merchant. Each category is rated from 1 to 3. *Note:* All Vital Five categories may not apply to every retailer. However, the more icons within each category, the higher the rating for that category.

We'll go into the Vital Five in more detail in Part I. But for now, here's what they can mean in a listing:

Price: This category's rating indicates whether the average price of what a merchant sells is low, medium, or high — or if they are a discounter, every-day retailer, or a seller of high-end goods or services.

Selection: This category's rating indicates whether a merchant's selection is adequate (one icon), good (two icons), or excellent (three icons) for its category.

Convenience: The Convenience rating indicates how easily a consumer can purchase an item from the site and how many convenient services the merchant offers the shopper (one icon equals adequate, two equals good, or three equals excellent). The criteria used are a description and/or picture of the product or service, multiple payment options, ease of purchase, a site search engine, a FAQ (Frequently Asked Questions) page, the availability of gift certificates or gift-wrapping, and/or a Preferred Shopper Club.

Service: In the Service category, I rate the level of customer service with one to three icons indicating adequate, good, or excellent. The criteria I used are whether an e-mail confirming the order is sent out, whether the total of the order is given before the credit card information is taken, whether an estimated ship date is given, whether a date shipped notification is sent via e-mail, and whether the site offers 100 percent customer satisfaction guarantee. I also take into account shipping and handling costs (flat-rate shipping or shipping rate based on carrier rates) and availability of special shipping, such as APO/FPO shipping, overnight shipping, and/or international shipping.

Security: The Security rating of one to three icons indicating adequate, good, or excellent lets you know whether the site offers protection of a customer's purchase (secure credit card system), whether a privacy statement is posted, and whether the site has a third-party endorsement (such as from the BBB).

Where to Go from Here

A universe of shopping is available to you today, and this directory of online shopping sites lists the best in the world. So, start your computer, open the book, and shop till you drop!

Part I
Online Shopping Overview

The 5th Wave — By Rich Tennant

"Since we began online shopping, I just don't know where the money's going."

In this part . . .

Products and services and downloads — oh my!

When you shop the world online, you quickly realize you're not in Kansas anymore. When you search the many shopping directories on the Web, you're confronted with a blooming, buzzing confusion of shopping possibilities. How do you choose? Which are the best? How do you separate the hype from the truth? How do you protect yourself?

And besides, just what is online shopping anyway?

These questions and a whole lot more are answered in Part I. So turn the page to get started.

Chapter 1

Shopping the Global Superstore

. . . .

. . . .

You've heard the hype about online shopping. You may have even dabbled in it a bit — purchasing a small gift here or an airline ticket there. But have you really given thought to the possibility of buying online just about everything you may need?

Well you can. The hype is true. The shopping opportunities online are big — really big. You can buy almost anything you can think of from the rapidly growing digital marketplace called the World Wide Web — and you can do it 24 hours a day, 7 days a week, 365 days a year — in your fuzzy slippers.

What Is Online Shopping, Anyway?

You can think of online shopping as, well, the shopper's nirvana.

Okay, maybe *nirvana* is a bit much. However, what else can free you from the earthly constraints of both time and space, provide you with a universe of products and services that you never thought existed, and enable merchandise to miraculously appear on your doorstep with a simple click of your mouse?

But it's not all peaches and cream in this shopping land of milk and honey. In the words of that great philosopher and sportsman, Yogi Berra, "If you don't know where you're going, you just might get there." Picking a merchant, choosing a product, and slapping down your credit card can be a recipe for disaster if you haven't done your homework.

Remember the axiom from the Introduction of this book? "An informed online shopper is a successful online shopper." So many online purchases go bad for the simple reason that the online shopper didn't do the proper research before entering his or her credit card number into the order form.

Stepping through the Buying Process

So how do people make a decision to buy? Well, in fact, we make a lot of little decisions that all add up to whether we've made a purchase we're happy with. In the real world we sense a need either through advertisements on TV, radio, newspapers, or magazines. Or we may see something a friend has or while window-shopping in the mall. After we decide to purchase a certain product or service, we start looking for a place to buy it. We may have a favorite store in mind, or a store recommendation from a friend, or be swayed by a retailer's advertisement.

In concert with your choice of merchants, you may consider which one can offer you the best "deal" on your chosen product. However, the best deal may not necessarily mean the best price. If the product needs little explanation before the sale or support after the sale, like a book, CD, or video game, the cheapest price will suffice. But if you're buying a diamond or a car, you'll need an education up front to make the proper buying decision. And after you make the purchase, you want guarantees, warranties, or service after the sale. All of these items may add to the price of the product or service.

If time is infinite, we never seem to have enough of it. In the real world all the factors discussed previously could turn into a real chore involving a lot of time and effort wandering from store to store looking for the best deal, or even just getting educated. But on the Web, the decision-making and educating process is much different. Yes, you still need to go through the process but it is far less time consuming and even fun.

So how do you find the information online you need to make an informed buying decision? Who do you turn to? Where do you start? Ah, young grasshopper. The journey of a million miles starts with but a single step. And that first step in becoming an informed shopper is knowing exactly what you want.

Choosing the goods

You heard *The DaVinci Code* was a great book. You decide to buy it. No problem. Decision made. But suppose you're in the market for a digital camera.

Unless you know the exact make and model, and are certain you'll be happy with it, you need to do a lot a research if you're going to make a successful purchase.

Luckily for you, the Web shines when it comes to offering just this sort of information. The Web is basically an information storehouse. You can find information on just about anything made today. You can find sites offering professional product reviews or sites with reviews of products by other shoppers like you (and nearly all the reviews are free) that can help you make the proper product or service purchasing decision. Chapter 29 covers several online product review sites, but here are a few of the best.

Utilizing product reviews

For unbiased, objective product reviews, check out these three popular sites — Consumer Reports, ConsumerSearch, and CNET.

The granddaddy of all product review organizations is Consumer Reports. This independent, nonprofit testing and information organization has been in existence since 1936. It has an online site at `consumerreports.org` that mirrors its prestigious magazine. The only downside is that the site isn't free. But if you want the best of a certain item, then this site can help you find it.

On the other hand, ConsumerSearch.com (`consumersearch.com`) is free to use. Even though it's not as popular or esteemed as Consumer Reports, this organization offers an extensive list of product reviews for your examination. At this site, product reviews are analyzed and then ranked for your use.

If you're a denizen of the universe of electronics and want unbiased reviews on computers, personal assistants, digital cameras, cell phones, camcorders, TVs, and home theaters, then CNET.com (`cnet.com`) is your choice of destinations for reviews on these types of products. You can even find reviews of wireless plans and Internet service providers on the site.

Reading consumer reviews

Some of the best opinions you can get on products you're interested in buying are those of your fellow shoppers. Two sites listing consumer opinions are Epinions and RateItAll.com.

Epinions (`epinions.com`) is a reliable source of product insight from consumers offering unbiased advice, in-depth product evaluations, and personalized recommendations. And what about the disgruntled consumer who may not be giving his or her opinion in a fair and balanced light? Epinions tries its best to highlight the people behind the reviews so that you know exactly whom to trust.

An example of an epinion on a brand of microwave might be as follows:

I cannot sing the praises of this microwave loudly enough. Mine has been going strong for the past three years and I don't know what I would do without it.

Or maybe one like this:

If you are in the market for a new microwave like we are, your money would be better spent on a different model.

Another site for a wide and diverse selection of reviews is RateItAll.com (`rateitall.com`). Think of RateItAll.com as a consumer coffee house where you can find, share, and seek opinions on many products. This organization offers consumer opinions on not only products, but retailers, too. You get double your times' worth using this site.

Getting the goods

If the Web's one thing, it's a virtual wealth of merchant choices. That's why this book is so valuable to you, the online shopper. I've done the picking for you on hundreds of merchants in dozens of shopping categories. But suppose you find a merchant that has a product you're looking for but isn't covered in the listings, or perhaps you saw it mentioned in a newspaper, TV, or radio ad. How do you know the merchant is legitimate and safe to buy from?

The Web comes to the rescue again.

A number of reliable information sites track and review merchants on the Web. Chapter 27 offers a list of them, but one of the best is BizRate.com.

Researching a merchant

BizRate.com (`bizrate.com`) is one of the oldest and well-known merchant review sites. It was one of the first organizations to rate online merchants. The ratings are obtained from actual consumers who have just made a purchase at an online retailer; data is collected from more than one million online buyers each month. When the order is completed, the customer is asked to rate the shopping experience and the merchant. After a few weeks, the customer is sent an e-mail questionnaire asking whether he or she is satisfied with the purchase and if not, why. This information is stored as a review on the BizRate.com site.

Because the merchants that BizRate.com rates are all members of BizRate.com, a good thumbnail description of each store it rates is supplied, including a brief description of the store, full contact information, and a list of its features and services.

At BizRate.com you might see reviews like this:

Awesome experience. Everything is great. The tech support is first rate. They have my business for life. Perfect!

Or maybe one like this:

The JVC CD Recorder I ordered was a complete lemon. The plastic bag surrounding the machine was not sealed — it was probably a product returned for repair!

Either way, you get the information you're looking for.

Using the Vital Five to choose a merchant

Everyone is looking for a good deal when buying a product or service. But if the deal looks too good to be true, it probably is.

You may be tempted to grab that deal before it goes away. But here's some good advice: Another good deal is always coming down the pike. You may miss a lot of Queen Marys but all it takes is to catch one Titanic and you're left with the sinking feeling that you made a poor buying decision. That's why the Vital Five of *2005 Online Shopping Directory For Dummies* — Price, Selection, Convenience, Service, and Security — are so important to making an informed buying decision.

When it comes to the Price category, you can find a wide range of prices on products and within categories on the Web. Discount stores and outlet stores sell brand-name merchandise at low, low prices. At the other extreme are stores that sell high-end and expensive luxury goods. A large number of small one-of-a-kind boutiques exist that sell their wares at specialty prices. And some retailers sell products and services at the suggested retail prices or at a small discount.

Keep in mind that the low price you see may not reflect the best deal for that product or service on the Web. The best price may not be the *shipped* price. Be sure to check out what the shipping and handling fees are when buying from a merchant. That 30 percent off list price may be added back into the shipped price of the product — and then some.

As for Selection, unless the merchant offers a product not easily found elsewhere on the Web, look for retailers who have a wide and deep selection of the product they sell. Being able to compare products at a single site saves shopping time, which is one of the most important reasons to shop the Web.

The Convenience factor refers to how easy it is to purchase from a merchant and how many convenient services the merchant offers the shopper. For example, how easy is it to use the site? Do you arrive at the storefront and find yourself confronted and confused by a hundred different pieces of information? Is what the retailer sells presented to you in an easy-to-understand manner? Can you easily navigate the shopping site? Can you find what you're looking for without clicking through endless Web pages?

A good indication of a well-designed online store is this: If you can reach the Buy button of a product you came to purchase in three to four mouse clicks, then the merchant has done a good job of designing his or her Web store.

Other convenience factors to look for at a merchant's Web store are good descriptions of the product or service that answers your questions and, if a product, at least one picture of it. See whether the merchant offers multiple payment options, an easy-to-use shopping cart, a site search engine, and — very important for ease of use — a FAQ (Frequently Asked Questions) page. Finally, look for convenience services like gift certificates or gift-wrapping, or a Preferred Shopper Club where you can get additional discounts the next time you visit the merchant.

Service for the online consumer is another vital component to take into consideration. The level of customer service offered the online shopper is very important because it offers a way to get answers to questions before you buy as well as a way to get answers to your questions after you buy. A merchant should offer you multiple ways to contact it. Look for phone and fax numbers, a complete mailing address, and an e-mail address. The more ways you can contact the merchant, the better chance you'll have of answering product and shipping questions before the sale, resolving customer service problems after the sale, or just checking on the status of your order. Keep in mind, however, that some small mom-and-pop stores only have an e-mail address. Consider this when making your purchase.

Make sure the merchant gives you a complete *shipped price* for the product you want to buy *before* you give out your credit card number. The last thing you want is a surprise at the end of your order.

Other service factors to look for are information on order confirmations and status updates of your order. These services are normally done with a confirmation e-mail after the sale and periodic e-mails alerting you to the status and shipping date of your purchase. Merchants should also offer a 100 percent satisfaction guarantee and be willing to take back the product with no questions asked. There may be some exceptions to this rule, such as for customized products or underwear and bathing suits. For these items, the merchant should offer some kind of partial refund or a store credit.

Also check out the company's shipping policies. What are the costs? Does the company have a flat rate for shipping products or a shipping rate based on carrier rates? Does it ship to APO/FPO addresses? Is overnight shipping or international shipping available? You should ask these questions and have them answered before you place your order.

Finally, there are the security concerns. These come in three flavors — credit card security, privacy issues, and third-party endorsements. If you place an order online and enter your credit card number onto an online form, you want to make sure that the information you entered is encrypted when it is sent over the Web. Also, you want to know what personal information the merchant is collecting from you and how it plans to use it. I cover this information in more detail in the next chapter.

Many sites have a third-party endorsement on how they do business and how they deal with their customers. The most popular of these third-party endorsers is the BBB or Better Business Bureau (bbbonline.com).

Two more popular third-party endorsers are BizRate (bizrate.com) and WebAssured (webassured.com). I discussed BizRate and the evaluations of their member merchants available to the consumer earlier in this chapter. A merchant endorsed by WebAssured promises a high standard of conduct in dealing with customers. Web sites carrying the WebAssured seal promise that customers get whatever they order.

There you are. You're now an informed online shopper. Use the product and merchant review sites before you shop, keep the Vital Five in mind when you shop, and your shopping excursions will be both rewarding and fun.

Chapter 2

Shopping Securely Online

· ·

In This Chapter

▶ Protecting your personal information

▶ Protecting your credit card number

▶ Securing your computer from spyware

· ·

*O*nline shopping can be a shopper's paradise. However, snakes lurk in this garden of paradise, and if you're not careful, they will separate you from your hard-earned money and even invade your privacy.

The two biggest fears of consumers when they shop online are privacy concerns and credit card security. So what can you do to protect yourself? First, you have to know what information is collected about your visits and purchases by online merchants, and whether and how the merchant protects this information. Second, you need to understand the pros and cons of buying on the Web as well as how your credit card information is secured and protected when being transmitted over the Internet. Finally, unscrupulous retailers are not the only ones who may use your personal information. Visiting non-eCommerce sites poses an even bigger risk to your personal privacy and may damage your computer.

I start this chapter by discussing something near and dear to all of our hearts — our personal information and how it's used when we visit or buy from an online merchant.

Protecting Your Personal Information

Our personal privacy is very important to us, and if you're like most people, you protect it as much as you can. Still, if you've been on the Internet for any length of time you have most probably been assaulted by junk e-mail —

otherwise known as spam — offering everything from diet pills to the seedier products on the Web. Where do these companies get your e-mail address? You didn't give it to them — or did you?

If you have a personal home page with your e-mail address on it, or if you've ever posted a message on a Usenet discussion board or subscribed to an online newsletter, the chances are excellent that the e-mail address you posted or voluntarily gave was picked up by spammers. These spammers use e-mail harvesting programs to find e-mail addresses to add to their mailing lists. The best way to avoid this type of spam is to not post your e-mail address on a Web page or partake in the open and public discussion groups that are on Usenet.

Giving out your information

Your personal information has been gathered other ways (whether you gave it voluntarily or not), such as when you visit and/or buy from an online merchant. Notice that I said *visit* and not just *buy*. A certain amount of information is gathered on you every time you visit any kind of Web site.

When you visit a Web site you involuntarily supply information about your computer. The site's computer collects information on your computer. This computer may automatically collect information about your computer configuration, such as your browser type, operating system, IP address, or ISP domain name. The computer may gather navigational and click-stream data that shows what pages you visited and how long you may have used various features on the site.

You can do little to stop this kind of information being collected when you visit a Web site. The good news is that this information does not reveal or can't be associated with your personal identity. Most sites use this information to evaluate, improve, and enhance the site for the benefit of all users.

Another way of involuntarily providing information is through the use of cookies. Cookies created by a Web site are small data files stored by your browser in your computer when you visit a site. Most browsers automatically accept cookies. Cookies permit a Web site or a merchant to recognize you and avoid burdensome and repetitive requests for identical information. The bad news is that these cookies can be used to track your browsing on the Web.

The good news is that cookies from one site cannot be read by other sites, and you can change your browser settings to refuse cookies altogether.

This information you involuntarily give when visiting a Web site cannot be matched to your personal identity. It's the information you voluntarily give an organization that can impinge on your privacy, if what you give and how the organization uses it is not spelled out in a site's privacy policy.

Keeping your information private

Privacy on the Web has become a big issue with consumers over the last few years. In some surveys, it ranks ahead of credit card security concerns.

This concern by consumers forced the FTC to issue a mandate that organizations and merchants that collect personal information must tell visitors to their site what personal information they collect, how they collect it, and how they plan to use it.

Today, many Web sites that collect personal information from the public have a privacy statement posted somewhere on their Web site. Normally, a link to their privacy policy is found at the bottom of the home page. If you can't find it there, then check the site's About Us page or the Help page.

Now, just because a merchant has a privacy policy doesn't automatically mean your privacy is protected. What the privacy policy tells you is what information is collected and how the company plans to use it. The company can state flat-out that it'll use your information to send advertising e-mails to you, or rent or sell your name to other organizations.

That's why you have to *read* the privacy policy!

The privacy policy hopefully isn't written in legalese and can be understood by the average person. It should contain at least the following information:

- ✔ **Cookies:** Will they be installed on your computer?

- ✔ **Personal information:** This is the information the merchant needs to process your order such as your name, address, phone number, and credit card number.

- ✔ **Demographic information and personal preferences:** The merchant may ask you for demographic information such as your gender, age, or income level or your preferences, such as your personal likes and dislikes, your favorite color, and taste in music and books. I don't recommend your giving this kind of information to the merchant unless you're getting something valuable in return. For example, in return for this information you're made a preferred customer and are given discounts on future purchases. Even then, be selective as to the information you provide.

✔ **The use of your personal information:** How will this company use your personal information? Does it reserve the right to send you unsolicited promotional e-mails?

✔ **Disclosure of your personal information:** Will the company sell, trade, or rent your personal information to other organizations?

Read the privacy policy and decide for yourself whether this merchant is one you want to do business with.

One last danger to avoid when protecting your personal information: Beware of *phishing!* It's a sneaky way of getting you to reveal your credit card number, bank account numbers, and any other sensitive personal information that can enable scammers to steal your personal identity.

Here's how it works: You may receive in your e-mail a cleverly disguised message that appears to be from a reputable company like Citibank, eBay, or PayPal, or even from a merchant that you purchased a product from. The scammers have no idea if you have had any relationship with the companies they're posing as. That's why it's called phishing. A typical bogus e-mail may request the recipient to "confirm" personal information. Does this trick work? Believe it or not, a surprisingly large number of people fall for it and in the process hand over their identities.

Protecting Your Credit Card

Remember these letters — SSL. These three letters certify that your credit card information is encrypted when sent over the Internet.

To understand what SSL is, we have to get a little technical.

You know you're using an SSL technology when you see `https://` — notice the s at the end of the http, rather than `http://`. In addition, if you're using a browser that recognizes SSL — and most do, including Netscape Navigator, Microsoft Internet Explorer, AOL's version 3, and Spyglass, among others — you'll also see a see a symbol, such as a lock, that signifies that you're on a secure page. Any information you enter on such a page is encrypted at your browser, sent over the public Internet in encrypted form, and then de-encrypted on the merchant's computer.

But these technical indicators only show up when you start to place your order. How do you find out whether the site's secure when you're trying to decide to shop there? The merchant tells you, via a Security or a Security & Privacy navigational link. Other times you can find the information on the site's Help or FAQ pages. If the site is secure for credit card orders, the merchant will let you know. If you can't find any mention of security, assume the site is not secure.

Staying under Spyware's Radar

The new kid on the Internet block is a threat to your computer and personal privacy. It's called by many names — spyware, adware, hijackware, and parasiteware — but the end result is the same. These programs can ruin your online experience, slow your computer to a crawl, and even change your system settings. But that's not the worst of it. They can also report your computing behavior to others, serve up ads you may or may not want, or change your browser's startup and search pages.

Where do they come from and how do they get on your computer? They are normally attached to free software that you download, and you may not be aware that they are running on your computer.

One survey estimated that 90 percent — yep, that's 90 percent — of personal computers have some kind of spyware on them. If you have a form of spyware on your computer, your PC will continuously "call home," using your Internet connection to send information about you and your surfing habits to some remote location on the Web.

So what do you do about the problem? Download a couple of spyware-removal programs. Two good ones are Ad-aware and Spybot, and they're free! To search for and remove unwanted adware and spyware, just download these two programs from Download.com (`download.com`) and run them.

Just as with your anti-virus program, you must keep your spyware-removal programs up-to-date for them to be effective.

The best way to fight spyware is to avoid it altogether. Keep these tips in mind when surfing the Net:

✔ Keep your operating system and browser up to date. Vendors frequently update their software with fixes and patches of known security flaws in their software — flaws that spyware takes advantage of.

✔ Stay out of "bad" neighborhoods. Don't go wandering around Web sites with questionable content, such as adult sites, or that offer free downloads of hacked music and software. These free download sites often add on the spyware programs that attach themselves to your computer.

✔ If you arrive at a Web site that asks you for permission to download a program that allows you to view the site better, just say no. Some programs are fine, such as Macromedia's popular Shockwave plug-in for viewing Flash animations. But others can download a piece of spyware onto your computer.

✔ Adjust your browser settings to decline the installation of Active X or Java programs on your computer. In IE, choose Tools⇨Options⇨ Security. At this point, you can adjust your settings. Keep in mind that if you increase security above Medium, some Web sites may not work properly.

✔ Check out the free piece of software you want before you download it. Surf on over to Google, type in the name of the free software along with the words *adware* or *spyware*. Read the information on the Web site and pay close attention to the licensing agreement that will appear as part of the installation routine.

Remaining Vigilant

Maintaining your personal privacy and the security of your personal information on the Web is your job. No one can or will do it for you. Keep the tips provided in this chapter in mind. Stay informed, and when in doubt, ask questions. The old adage of "buyer beware" goes double on the Web.

Chapter 3

Buying from Your Fellow Netizens

. . . .

In This Chapter

▶ Learning what to buy from individuals

▶ Learning how to buy from individuals

▶ Protecting your purchase

. . . .

You can easily see that the world of online shopping offers you a universe of products from a wide selection of merchants. But are you aware of the alternative universe of products that are offered for sale from your fellow Netizens? I'm talking about the many online auctions and classified ads that inhabit the Web. The array of products that they offer the online consumer matches those of the average online retailer, and in many cases, offer products that you either can't find at an online merchant, or the same products at lower prices.

Sounds great, right? There is a catch, though. Buying safely from an unknown individual, and getting a sweet deal instead of a sour one, requires a different buying strategy than the ones discussed so far in the book. This virtual flea market has its own unique set of rules you must follow.

For proof, look at the annual Top Ten Consumer Complaint Categories list from the Federal Trade Commission (`ftc.gov/opa/2004/01/top10.htm`). Online auctions makes the list every year. Does that mean that you shouldn't take advantage of this alternative shopping paradise of products offered for sale by individuals? Of course not. If you follow the simple rules explained in this chapter, you can safely and successfully buy from your fellow Netizens.

Doing Your Homework

You may be tired of hearing this already, but you must do your homework before you buy! This rule applies doubly when you buy from individuals on the Web.

More often then not, a purchase from an individual goes bad because the buyer didn't know what he or she was buying and/or how the transaction was to take place. Before you buy, you must know exactly what you're buying and how you're going to pay for it. Individuals are not retailers; therefore, the guarantees, warrantees, return privileges, and purchase protections that you would have with a standard online retailer are few and far between when buying from individuals on the Web, whether you make the purchase through a well-known auction site like eBay or by answering a classified ad on Yahoo!

Figuring out what you're buying

This lack of the aforementioned items means that you have to ask questions — lots of questions — and you won't find the answers in a 100-words classified ad or a brief listing on an auction site. What kind of questions should you ask? At the minimum, you should ask the following:

- What exactly is being sold?
- How will the item be shipped? Will it be insured? By you or the seller?
- How will the item be paid for?
- When will the item be shipped?
- If the item doesn't work or if you're not satisfied with it, can you return it?
- What is the seller's full contact information?

You can probably ask many detailed questions depending upon the type of product you are interested in buying. But when you're trying to figure out what exactly is being sold, remember that the information provided in the ad or listings will most certainly be slim. For example, if what you want to buy is a computer item, will it work in your computer? If it's a part or add-on to an item you have, like a car or a piece of electronic equipment, will the item work or be compatible with it?

And how about the condition of the merchandise? Is it new and factory sealed? Never been opened? Not even for a quick peek? Is it new but the box has been opened, but it's never been used? Is it still in the original factory box with all documentation and packing material? If not, why? And if it's used, how old is it? What is the physical and working condition of the product? Keep asking questions until you're satisfied that the product is what you want.

I suggest that if you're going take the opportunity to purchase from an online auction site, drop by your local bookstore or surf on over to Amazon.com and pick up a copy of *eBay For Dummies*. This book can give you the lowdown on bidding strategies, buyers' rights, and auction lingo, as well as how to make your purchases at eBay — and other auction sites — safe and profitable.

Knowing whom you buy from

In addition to figuring out what you're buying, you also need to find out from whom you're buying, and that's where things get a bit sticky. In the words of Butch Cassidy, "Who are those guys?" Whether you buy from an established auction site like eBay or a classified ad, you're buying from an individual, not an e-mail address. Finding out who the buyer is and where he or she is located is very important. You need to have full contact information on him or her that includes the seller's home address, home and work telephone numbers, and cell phone number, if any. Having this information helps to ensure you can contact him or her, as well as makes it easier to report the person to the auction site if the transaction fails because of the seller.

You can confirm the seller's information through directory assistance in the seller's city.

Finding out an item's worth

One of the biggest mistakes consumers make when buying from an online auction site is overpaying for a product. I'm not referring to overbidding, where you're caught up in the heat of the auction. If you're bidding on a product, know what the thing is really worth.

This again is where the Internet comes to the rescue. If you're bidding on antique or collectible merchandise, use the Google (google.com) search engine to search on the item name. Do a general search using the company name and descriptive terms, such as "Johnson ironstone china pitcher." You may not find your specific item, but you may find something similar that can give you an idea of what the item you want is worth. When you bid on retail products, use the different comparison shopping agents like mySimon (mysimon.com) and Shopping.com (shopping.com) to get a feel for what an item may cost.

Getting the item shipped

Even though you're the buying and the seller is doing the shipping, you should find out how the seller plans to ship your product. Remember, you're not dealing with a standard retail store. You're entirely dependant upon an individual like yourself. Just think of the last box of home-baked cookies you received that arrived as a pile of crumbs.

Be sure to ask the seller two questions: First, will the product be packed properly to prevent its being damaged in transit? And second, will it be insured against damage or loss (sometimes the seller offers this option to you; in other words, you pay for the insurance)? You're probably asking yourself why you should care how the item is packed if it's insured. Here's why: Packages do get damaged or lost, even when they're shipped by the big, well-known shipping companies. Even if your package is insured, if the shipping company determines that the package was not packed properly, then it will not pay the claim. If the shipping company does not pay the claim, your seller might not replace it — and you're out your money.

Paying for the item

"In God we trust; all others pay cash." This little axiom may be fine for the seller, but it could cause a huge problem for you, the buyer, when purchasing from individuals. It all boils down to trust. Do you trust the person you're buying from? Or if you have little information, how much in dollars are you willing to risk in a transaction with someone unknown to you? If you're unwilling to take any risk whatsoever, then use the payment strategies discussed next.

The key to reducing your risk is to confirm that what you bought is what you ordered before you lose control of your payment. That means you should make sure you receive and examine the product before the seller takes possession of your money. One way to check is to purchase the merchandise COD (cash on delivery). With this method you know you have received a product from the seller. The downside is that the postman or UPS guy normally will not let you open the box before you pay for it. Shipping a brick is just as easy as shipping a modem.

A much better way to get 100 percent security is to use an Internet escrow service — one that has been around for a while and has a good reputation.

An escrow service acts like a trustworthy third-party — a trusted intermediary. You give the escrow company your credit card number to pay for the merchandise you ordered. The escrow company notifies the seller to ship the merchandise to you with a return receipt addressed to the escrow service. After the escrow service receives the receipt, you typically have a day or two to confirm that the merchandise you received is what you ordered. The escrow service then forwards your money to the seller. If you didn't receive what you ordered, or if the product is damaged in shipment, you can refuse to accept it and the escrow company will refund your money. The process is straight and simple, and your purchase is protected.

Escrow.com (`escrow.com`) is an escrow service company that has a good reputation as well as longevity. Escrow.com is fully licensed and accredited as an escrow company and is subject to compliance with all applicable escrow regulations of the State of California. You can find others on the Web, too. However, with any escrow company, always use a credit card when paying for a product using an escrow service. Do NOT wire money, send a check of any kind, or use a debit card to the escrow company. If something goes wrong with the deal or if the escrow company becomes disreputable, you always have control of your money on a credit card. Just call your bank and it will reverse the charges for you.

A seller insisting on using a particular escrow service, one that you don't know of or can't find reliable information on, could be a sign of a scam. Escrow scams have happened in the past, and you can be sure more will happen in the future. If you suspect a scam, propose an alternative escrow company, one that you know and are comfortable with. If the seller refuses, he or she could very well be a scam artist.

Keeping Records

Be sure to save all copies of e-mail correspondence between you and the seller. Save a copy of the posted ad, shipping papers, receipts and labels, and notes regarding phone calls. Save all personal information such as addresses and phone numbers. And save all of this information for at least a year. Do so for many reasons, such as safe trading, tax information, and other contingencies. Treat each transaction like you do your income tax. If you're in doubt about whether to save a bit of information concerning a transaction, by all means, save it!

Part II
Online Shopping Sites

The 5th Wave · By Rich Tennant

"Oh, that there's just something I picked up as a grab bag special from the 'Curiosities' Web Page."

In this part . . .

Congratulations! You're now ready to shop the World Wide Web.

Use what you learned in Part I to enjoy the fruits of what the virtual marketplace has to offer — and purchase what you see with confidence. So fire up your computer and launch your virtual shopping window on a world of products, services, and information available to you with just a click of your mouse. You'll be amazed at what you can buy from the comfort of your own home.

Chapter 4

Antiques, Art, and Collectibles: Building Your Private Collection

. . . .

*O*ne of the most interesting things about human beings is their desire to collect things. People have many reasons for collecting. For some, it's the thrill of the hunt, of tracking down that special antique or the rare autograph of a sports star. For others, it's the joy of ownership that drives them to purchase one more item. No two people have the same two reasons for keeping a collection. The old saying "One man's trash is another man's treasure" really is correct.

Your collection can be as small as a single painting or piece of sculpture or can contain antique posters or photographs. Maybe you collect antiques, sports memorabilia, or stuffed bears. Your collection can have great monetary value, beauty, or both, or it can be made up of homely items that have meaning to only you.

Fortunately, the Internet is a collector's dream. You can find anything for sale online, and sometimes you can sell some of the stuff you've already collected to make room for more. You're not limited to the fine art at your local galleries or what's for sale at the swap meet at the fairgrounds or high school. Your private collection is global now. Hold on to your hat! You're off on a seven-continent buying trip.

Don't be fooled by art forgers. If a site says a painting or piece of artwork is original, ask for proof before you buy. Visit The Art of the Fake Exhibition at the Internet Public Library (`ipl.org/div/kelsey`) for a fascinating look at selected Egyptian artifacts — both real and fake that have been exhibited in museums around the world.

Key Word Index

Antiques

The Antiques store sites sell merchandise that's old and generally expensive. You can search for anything big, like furniture, to something small, like jewelry.

Collectibles

The Collectibles sites offer a medley of items. A collectible can be anything that folks collect, such as pottery, glassware, tableware, ceramics, or toys. Does it have value? You decide.

Fine Art

Artifacts, original paintings in any medium, and valuable pieces of art belong in the Fine Art keyword category. Most of the Fine Art sites are online galleries.

Memorabilia

The Memorabilia sites sell everything from clothes worn by Hollywood stars to toys given out by fast-food chains.

Museum Store

After you tour a museum, you can shop elbow-to-elbow with your other tour members for museum reproductions, cards, and other mementos. I show you the best Museum Store sites, but leave the annoying crowds behind.

Photography

Whether it's in digital format, black-and-white, color, sepia, or with or without a frame, the collection of photographs sold at the Photography sites is spectacular.

Posters

Shop at the Poster sites for posters in every imaginable color, subject, and size.

Sculpture

Big, small, indoor, outdoor — if you want sculpture you'll find it at the sites marked with the Sculpture keyword.

a1sculptures.com
PhotoframesPlus.com

866-944-5623
sales@photoframesplus.com

Sculpture

The sculptures at PhotoframesPlus.com are perfect for either desktop or shelf. Categorized by Golf, The Classics, Aquatic Wildlife Collection, Stock Market Series, Limited Edition, and Base and Sphere, each sculpture is no more than twelve inches high. Some come with clocks. Expect to pay anywhere between $50 and $200, depending on the sculpture you select. Shipping is usually next day. The site ships internationally.

abbottandcostellocollectibles.com
Abbott & Costello Comedy Collectibles

818-558-3799
accollectibles@aol.com

Memorabilia

The story behind Abbott & Costello Comedy Collectibles is almost as interesting as the incredible memorabilia sold at its site, which is dedicated to the slapstick team who entertained audiences for decades. The site is owned by Chris Costello, daughter of Lou Costello. She launched the site after a squabble with the Abbot and Costello Fan Club. Warring A&C factions notwithstanding, viewing the collection of videos, posters, CDs, and notecards assembled in honor of the famous comedy duo is fascinating. Don't miss the limited edition Collecticritter Bears. (There's even one for Groucho Marx.)

absolutelyvintage.net
Absolutely Vintage

No phone number listed
jvejewel@aol.com

Antiques • Collectibles

If rummaging through vintage jewelry is your passion, you'll spend hours on the carefully arranged Absolutely Vintage site. The only problem is that just as you get to the end of a well-worded description and are salivating over the digital photo of the brooch, earrings, necklace, or bracelet, you'll see that hateful word: SOLD. The vintage jewelry moves fast at Absolutely Vintage, and it's easy to see why. Collections are arranged by theme such as Cameo Classics, Butterfly Bonanza, and so on. PayPal is accepted at this site, and the company ships internationally.

afterimagegallery.com
Afterimage Gallery

877-868-5462
images@afterimagegallery.com

Photography • Posters

If you're near Dallas, Texas, visit Afterimage Gallery for a look at its extensive collection of photographs — over 32,000 in all. Over two million people per year visit the gallery's online location. Unfortunately, the entire collection of photographs is not available for purchase. In fact, it's hard to tell the complete list of merchandise because the on-site link leads to "A Selection of Prints and Books." Browse the selection, but don't be deterred if you don't see what you want. There's a good chance your selection is located in a warehouse or back room of the gallery. Call or send an e-mail to make sure.

alamy.com
Alamy Images

+44 (0)1235 844600
customerservices@alamy.com

Photography

Alamy Images houses over one million traditionally licensed and royalty-free images from broad categories such as business and lifestyles to specific sporting events. As a licensed Alamy user, you will have access to the image library. Using the site's convenient search tools, you can locate the images you want and then download them to your computer with the Easy Download Tool that's included with your subscription. Also included is Alamy's custom Interpolation Service, which allows you to increase the resolution of your pictures without any quality loss. You'll be billed for your downloads once every thirty days.

★ allposters.com
AllPosters.com

888-654-0143
orders@allposters.com

Posters

If there's an image you've always wanted to see in poster form, there's a good chance you'll find it at AllPosters.com. The site carries hundreds of thousands of posters and art prints, and provides framing and mounting services, too. AllPosters.com "is dedicated to bringing customers the best selection of posters and art prints in the world." From the customer's perspective, it appears this company is making good on this lofty promise. International shipping makes the service even better.

 Recommended   Price   Selection   Convenience   Service   Security

almostoriginals.com
Almost Originals

888-236-7862
info@almostoriginals.com

Fine Art • Posters

Sure, it would be easy to think that what's done by the family-run Almost Originals site is almost counterfeiting, but they call it "fine quality canvas art reproductions" so we will, too. The process works like this: You buy a paper print. This company lifts the ink off the paper and applies it to canvas with a UV protective coating. You get an almost original painting on canvas. Pretty cool, eh? You choose your print from thousands of in-stock prints, or just let the company know if you want a custom job. Almost Originals has been in the transfer business for over twenty years and is really good at what it does.

★ antiquejewelryexch.com
Antique Jewelry Exchange

800-809-4190
tymlessgem@antiquejewelryexch.com

Antiques • Collectibles

Jason and Heidi are waiting for you over at The Antique Jewelry Exchange Online Shop. You'll be treated to a collection of over 7,500 pieces of exquisite rarities and jewels. Start your visit by checking out the Jewel of the Day. You'll be able to make a great deal, provided you get there early. The best way to shop at The Antique Jewelry Exchange Online Shop is to browse through the Product List. When you see a piece that interests you, click it to display the picture and product description. Sign up for the site's e-mail newsletter and enter to win a T-shirt.

antiquejewelryforsale.com
Antique Jewelry For Sale.com

212-944-2534
stephen@antiquejewelryforsale.com

Antiques • Collectibles

Page after page of diamonds, emeralds, rubies, and other gorgeous gemstones. Are these antique pieces the real thing? According to the seller, Stephen Herdemian, the answer is "yes." He's a renowned jeweler who prides himself on his honesty. As stated on the site, "If Steve says a certain piece is from the 1920s, it is. Every piece of jewelry offered on this website is without question the age that it is stated to be." If you have any questions about a piece, you're invited to call or e-mail Steve. Have jewelry to sell? Steve may be interested; details are at the site.

art.com
Art.com
800-952-5592
support@art.com
Posters

Two young college friends started Art.com back in 1997. Through smart business sense, good customer service, and, of course, great products, the Art.com now offers customers a whopping "1.4 trillion combinations" with convenience, speed, and value. Shop here for posters and framed prints on just about any topic you can dream of. Frames are optional, but strongly advisable. You won't find better or more inexpensive frames anywhere. Check out The Limited Edition Galleries for works from new and exciting artists. On a budget? Unframed posters in the Clearance section are often under $5 apiece.

Artbazaar.co.uk
Art Bazaar
No phone number listed
customerservice@artbazaar.co.uk
Fine Art

"Why buy a print or a poster, when you can afford an original?" Absolutely no reason at all is the obvious answer, when you're shopping at this British-based art site. The artworks here are clever, edgy, and brightly colored. They practically burst through the computer screen and light up the room around you. Delivery for United Kingdom buyers is handled by courier and costs £10. U.S. and other buyers need to contact the site prior to purchase to make delivery arrangements.

artisat.com
Artisat.com
No phone number listed
virtual_curator@artisat.com
Fine Art • Photography • Posters • Sculpture

Artisat.com showcases original artwork from Asia. The service provides a service to Asian artists who were having difficulty finding a global market for their work, and it enables customers like you and me to connect with unknown artists. Prices are displayed conveniently in U.S. dollars. Choose your work from the following medium: Watercolors, Oils and Acrylics, Chalk and Pastel, Pencils and Charcoal, Pen and Ink, Etching and Prints, Photography, and Mixed Media. Add artworks to a virtual portfolio as you shop. If you have any questions, e-mail them to the Virtual Curator for answers within a day or so.

 Recommended   Price   Selection   Convenience   Service   Security

artnet.com
Artnet
212-497-9700
info@artnet.com
Fine Art

If you're serious about buying fine art on the Internet, Artnet is an important stop. The site has links to hundreds of galleries and individual artists. Serious buyers can research the Fine Arts Auctions Database, which contains over two million illustrated fine art auction records spanning more than twelve years from most of the major auction houses around the world. The site works best if you think of it as a stepping-stone to the finest galleries and dealers. You'll be able to buy a limited selection of art directly from Artnet.

artstall.com
Artstall.com
9122-2818520
webmaster@artstall.com
Fine Art • Sculpture

Artstall.com hails from Mumbai, India. (Mumbai was known as Bombay until 1997.) The site is set up as a virtual gallery with shopping, an art café, library, services, and, of course, a variety of paintings in many different styles and colors. If you're wondering whether a painting will "go" with your wall color, click the handy color palette to change the background, and get a reasonable idea of how the painting will look in your home. Artstall.com ships internationally; no matter where you are, your original Indian artwork will be delivered to your door.

barewalls.com
Barewalls.com
877-227-3925
help@barewalls.com
Posters

This site leaves no excuse for bare walls. Whether you're looking for your home, office, dorm room, or a special place, you're sure to find the print or poster that will be perfect on that wall. You'll also find the perfect frame. Barewalls.com allows you to select framing options and mats and view an image of the finished product before you buy. The site provides volumes of useful information about artists, art, and decorating. The offerings range from photography to paintings with poster subjects, as well as magazine covers. With so much to choose from, your walls won't be bare for long.

bauerboys.com
bauerboys.com
760-327-2717
gmcd@bauerboys.com
Antiques • Collectibles

Bright and cheerful Fiesta pottery makes up the bulk of collection at this site that's devoted to pottery and antique American dinnerware. Bauerboys.com carried both current and vintage pieces of the popular collectible. However, the company has decided to limit its future stock to only vintage Fiestaware. If you see a current piece you like, don't delay! Be aware that the return policy at this site is tricky. Make it easy on yourself — don't try to return something unless it arrives in damaged condition.

beverlyfactor.com
Beverly Factor Photography
949-673-2555
bfactor@beverlyfactor.com
Photography • Posters

Beverly Factor is an underwater photographer who has traveled the globe photographing the mysterious world below the ocean's surface. Her signature works include images of the underworld and exotic wildlife. Beverly's stunning photographs can be purchased as photographic or canvas prints. Photographic prints are made on Fujichrome print material, mounted on acid-free foam-core backing board, and matted with a three-inch acid-free archival mat in black or white. Canvas prints have the look of an oil painting and are mounted directly on the canvas. All works are numbered and signed.

carenschiro.com
Caren Schiro Sculpture LLC
No phone number listed
E-mail form on site
Sculpture

Caren Schiro lives and works in the Southwest. She sculpts in bronze and pewter. Her love of her surroundings, and particularly of nature, is evident in her work. Her sculpture has been compared to three-dimensional Arizonan Norman Rockwell. She completes the work down to the last detail. For example, her sculpture of a cowboy boot is so realistic that you might be tempted to try it on your foot! That's actually the goal of this incredible artist. She designs her sculptures to be touched and held. Learn about the lost wax process she uses to create her bronze and pewter sculptures, and buy one for your collection at the site.

 Recommended   Price   Selection   Convenience   Service   Security

★ carouselstore.com
The Carousel Store
866-394-6253
E-mail form on site
Collectibles

Carousels were common during the early 1900s. Although you won't find too many left today, the carousel left behind its own art form. Working with a legendary carousel restorer and builder named Dan Horenberger, the owners of The Carousel Store have put together an incredible collection of collectible carousel art. "The Carousel Store's goal is simple: Offer the largest selection of carousel-related items to lovers of carousels." Shop the site for the complete line of American Classic carousel animals. The animals range from a small replica of a carousel horse to a full-sized carousel horse.

★ castle-bryher.co.uk
Castle Bryher Ltd.
No phone number listed
enquiries@castle-bryher.com
Antiques • Collectibles

Of course, if you're an antique collector in the south of England, you already know that Castle Bryher Ltd. sells antique and collectible ceramics. You've probably seen them at a number of antique and collectors' centers and perhaps purchased a few treasures from this company's incredible stock. If you're like the rest of us, this site is your first introduction to Castle Bryher Ltd.'s huge collection. Search by manufacturer and then deepen the search to Item Type (for example, "Cats") or by theme (for example, "Chintz") or any combination of these criteria. Items can be shipped outside the U.K.

ccgallery.com
CC Gallery
No phone number listed
cbf@ccgallery.com
Fine Art • Photography

You may be tempted to call the hand-colored pictures at CC Gallery "tintographs" if you're new to the art form. It works like this: The artist (in this case, the talented Carol Luther) develops black-and-white photographic images and then applies varying layers of color using oils and pencils. The results are soft, almost three-dimensional, and very compelling. Each finished work is slightly different, because each work is done to order. You'll be ordering a real one-of-a kind artwork if you decide to take a chance. Stained glass is also available from this site.

celebritygift.com
CelebrityGift.com

800-660-0566
sales@celebritygift.com

Memorabilia

From classic film stars to today's Hollywood and sports legends, CelebrityGift. com has a remembrance about just about everyone who's ever done any-thing notable. The site even offers a collection of memorabilia devoted to American Presidents. The memorabilia varies from photographs and posters to playing cards and themed merchandise such as mugs and shirts. Not everything sold at this site is signed or authentic. Shop by Departments or use the handy Search feature to locate the star or famous name you want. Volume discounts can be arranged; contact the site for details.

chisholm-poster.com
Chisholm Larsson Gallery

212-741-1703
info@chisholm-poster.com

Posters

Vintage posters are the name of the game at this hip New York gallery. The Chisholm Larsson Gallery site holds 27,000 posters, mostly of foreign films. Unfortunately, you can't browse a complete online catalog or search a com-prehensive category. Use the slick search engine that enables you to fill in lots of information to locate the poster you want and take your chances that you'll find all the posters that match your criteria. Even if you don't find the exact poster you came for, you'll come away a winner. The posters at this site are detailed, elegant, and lovely.

directiques.com
Directiques

800-578-2687
E-mail form on site

Collectibles

Casual browsers and serious collectors will both come away happy from a trip to Directiques. The site has something for everyone interested in col-lectibles. Experienced dealers and first-timers can set up shop and offload stock, while buyers can expect to find great deals. Unfortunately, the site doesn't offer a centralized shopping cart. Each dealer handles the com-merce at his or her table and most of the time you'll complete transactions by e-mail. The site also serves as a resource for related services such as appraisers or restorers.

 Recommended   Price   Selection   Convenience   Service   Security

doubletakeart.com
Doubletake Gallery
763-567-2233
info@doubletakeart.com
Fine Art

Doubletake Gallery is a true fine art consignment gallery. The artworks accepted for display at Doubletake are by internationally recognized artists and are owned by people from across the United States. The works in the gallery change frequently, but you'll find works by many well-known artists. (On a recent visit I found paintings by Thomas McKnight and Salvador Dali.) Almost everything here sells considerably below retail. You'll need to follow the e-mail link to contact the seller directly, because the site doesn't offer online buying. To sell fine art in your own collection, check out the related information at the site.

easystreetantiques.com
Easy Street Antiques
877-515-6264
cchell@easystreetantiques.com
Antiques • Collectibles

Easy Street Antiques has been selling antiques and collectibles on the Internet since 1997 and seems to have figured out some of the problems of dealing with such a difficult commodity. Browsing at this site has a homey, comfortable feeling, thanks, to the clear pictures and detailed descriptions of the items up for sale. Shop the site for glassware, kitchen pottery glass and primitives, aluminum giftware, and holiday items. Don't miss the antique textiles and linens, including collectible hankies, tablecloths, pillowcases, towels, lace, scarves, fabrics, and blankets.

egallery.com
The Electric Gallery
800-276-0495
E-mail form on site
Fine Art

The works of over two hundred artists are displayed in The Electric Gallery, and the list keeps growing. Each wing of the gallery features different types of artwork. The Amazon Project displays the works of the young artists from the Usko-Ayar Amazonian School of Painting, while professionals who used a variety of styles and media to create their art have paintings in the Still Life wing. There's even a special section to meet the artists. Prices are high, but a special under $250 section makes original paintings affordable for everyone.

elite-art.com
Elite-Art.com
858-513-1703
info@elite-art.com

Fine Art • Sculpture

Fine art on the Internet? Absolutely! One look at this site will convince you that Elite-Art has gathered the works from the world's best art collections and put them on display for your approval. Select from the following categories: Realism, Impressionism, Modernism, Expressionism, Surrealism, Abstract, Naïve, City and Nature, Figurative, Still Life, Nude Art, Replicas, Metal and Sculpture, and Photography. Detailed information about each artist is available. Pricing on the works is flexible. Some works are priced through a reverse auction process, where bidders can suggest their own price.

fabulousfoilprints.com
Fabulous Foil Prints
No phone number listed
info@fabulousfoilprints.com

Posters

How about a real conversation piece? A poster done on foil is bound to grab the attention of anyone walking by. Choose your subject from a wide variety of categories, including dragons, fairies, unicorns, American Indians, American eagles, old-fashioned shops, cats, dogs, horses, and many more. The foil printing process gives a different look to the posters, almost making them appear three dimensional. As you look away you'll swear the poster subject is alive. This effect has been created on purpose after years of careful study to perfect the process. You can read the scientific explanation at the site.

fastfoodtoys.com
Aunt Linda's Toys
419-332-3901
auntlinda@fastfoodtoys.com

Collectibles • Memorabilia

Linda Gegorski is the creative genius behind Aunt Linda's Toys. An avid collector herself, she was the founder of the national McDonald's Collectors Club in 1990. She has collected McDonald's toys and memorabilia for over 25 years. Shop here for all the great giveaways that were included in Happy Meals and other promotions over the years. The site doesn't have a search function so you'll need to browse page by page. Unfortunately, no pictures of the items are on the site. E-mail your order to Aunt Linda when you find what you want. International shipping is available.

 Recommended   Price   Selection   Convenience   Service   Security

fishermanswidow.com
The Fisherman's Widow

877-732-8697
admin@fishermanswidow.com

Collectibles

Ships ahoy! Collectors will find a great collection of nautical-themed merchandise at The Fisherman's Widow. Whether you have an established collection or are just starting one, you're sure to find the perfect items at this site. Barometers, books and logs, compasses, hourglasses, and ships' wheels are great looking and dress up your home. For something really different, check out the display boats. Each one is a showpiece. Most orders from The Fisherman's Widow ship within 24 hours, and complete satisfaction is guaranteed. Gift wrapping is available, as well as an opportunity to join the e-mail mailing list to receive news about upcoming sales and new stock.

★ globalgallery.com
Global Gallery

888-456-2254
curator@globalgallery.com

Posters

Finally! An elegant and efficient site that makes finding art as simple as child's play. Using a specially designed search engine, known as the Power Search Interface, you can search through thousands of posters and prints in a few seconds. However, if you have slightly more time, browsing through the categories and ogling the art is more fun. Visit the Knowledge Center for information on art history and the art world that will amaze you and your friends. In a hurry? Use the Quick Search to find that perfect poster or print.

guggenheim.org
Guggenheim Museum Store

800-329-6109
sales@guggenheim.org

Museum Store • Posters

Getting to the Guggenheim online store takes a few clicks, but don't give up — it's worth it! You'll find a breathtaking collection of posters and prints from the Guggenheim Museum's global exhibitions and permanent collection. Prices are so reasonable for the unframed posters that you'll swear you're shopping in a discount store. The online museum store also carries a great selection of books, scarves and ties, and T-shirts and hats. Online purchases get a discount at checkout.

guild.com
GUILD.com

877-344-8453
art-info@guild.com

Collectibles • Fine Art • Photography • Sculpture

The vision behind THE GUILD is to bring high-quality original art to people in their homes. The term "art" is used loosely; art can be a painting, a piece of jewelry, a mug, or a mirror made by a skilled artist or craftsman. GUILD.com offers over 8,000 original paintings, prints, photographs, sculptures, and works in the fine craft media of glass, ceramics, fiber, metal, and wood. Each listing in the online catalog contains information about the artist. Shop by art type, price range, or artist. If you like a particular piece, send it to your friend on a free e-postcard, courtesy of GUILD.com.

★ heritagephotographs.com
Heritage Photographs

603-456-2159
manager@heritagephotographs.com

Photography • Posters

Heritage Photographs specializes in vintage photograph and graphic image reproductions. Prior to display, each image is digitally captured, restored, sized, and color toned. The images are grouped by categories, making it easy to find the era and subject you want. The images have been carefully chosen; don't be surprised to feel an instant bond with some of the subjects of the pictures. Purchase more than one image for a price break. If you desire, you can have any image blown up to poster size. Get free JPEGs and clip art, even if you don't choose to buy.

historicfotos.com
Fleet Irvine Photomurals

530-343-0865
historicfotos@historicfotos.com

Photography • Posters

The photographs at this vintage photo site are eloquent snapshots of time gone by. For the most part, the subjects look natural and unaware that they're being photographed. Although the site houses the entire collection of the photographer, only a few themes are on sale online at any given time. Each week a new picture is eligible for extra discounts. Photographs are available in 8 × 10 and 11 × 14 inches. All photographs are hand-printed, sepia-toned, and mounted in a double, hand-beveled mat ready to place in a standard size frame. Frames are available as well. Murals of up to 4 × 8 feet can be obtained.

 Recommended   Price   Selection   Convenience   Service   Security

home.att.net/~deerliteful
Deerliteful

201-707-4241
happy-memories@worldnet.att.net

Antiques • Collectibles

The Deerliteful site is loaded with deer. You can find deer-themed antiques as well as other deer collectibles and crafts. The deer appear in various shapes, colors, and positions on china, pottery, porcelain and glassware figurines, planters, lamps, jewelry, textiles, and unique handicrafts. The detailed catalog shows pictures and descriptions so you'll have a good idea of what you're ordering. Good news for softies: "We do not carry items made from antlers, taxidermy, or deerskin, nor items with a hunting theme" is displayed prominently at the site.

houseinthecountry.com
House in the Country

800-276-0495
E-mail form on site

Posters

If you're a retailer, interior designer or decorator, own a furniture store or can prove that you're not just an average customer, do I have a deal for you! A House in the Country offers incredible unframed art prints to the wholesale trade. The selection is amazing and prices are way below retail. This company also offers beautiful hardwood frames in several rich finishes. In order to purchase from the site, you'll need to qualify for a wholesale password, which means you must intend to resell the prints or use them for visual displays in a legitimate business. You'll score some great art if you qualify. Be sure to include "www" to access this site.

jonheck.com
Jon Heck Photographs

609-485-0893
jonheck@aol.com

Photography

Jon Heck is an ordinary guy who has a great eye behind the camera. His color shots of landscapes and seascapes are so powerful that you'll swear you can feel the sunlight or smell the tang of the ocean. The photos in his Dead Trees collection are both emotional and aloof. Jon's work is affordable, so you can afford to buy a few photographs while you're here. New customers get 25 percent off the first order, and he offers a free giveaway every month.

logsart.com
Logsart.com
888-856-4775
inquiries@logsart.com
Photography • Posters

Dress up your walls and preserve your savings at Logsart.com. You'll find thousands of quality fine art prints, photographs, and posters along with unique finished art products. Standard pricing is 25 percent below retail stores. Wholesale customers who can prove that they are reselling the artwork, or using it for display purposes, are entitled to special wholesale pricing. However, everyday customers who take advantage of Logsart's specials will find near-wholesale pricing on many popular posters and prints. Shipping is $8.50 on U.S. poster orders with free shipping on orders more than $75.

lovejoyjewelry.com
LoveJoy Jewelry
540-348-4284
customer-service@lovejoy.com
Antiques • Collectibles

Estate, antique, and one-of-a-kind pieces are the order of the day at Lovejoy Jewelry. E. Susan Kellogg, who fell in love with jewelry as a teenager, runs the site. Shop her site for bracelets, brooches, rings, earrings, necklaces, and more. Navigating the site and finding what you want is easy. Pictures are sometimes fuzzy, but the well-written descriptions help bridge the gap. Prices are generally reasonable. Purchases are handled through PayPal.

metmuseum.org/store
The Met Store
800-468-7386
customer.service@metmuseum.org
Museum Store • Posters • Sculpture

Visitors to The Metropolitan Museum of Art's store are in for a treat. The items for sale at this site have been carefully selected and produced by a team of art historians, designers, and master craftspeople. Reproductions bear close resemblance to the originals, and all products sold at The Met Store are first rate. You'll find posters, wood art panels, and framed prints. Also available are stationery and calendars. Want to create your own masterpiece? Buy an art kit, filled with supplies. Get something from the line of clothing and accessories to show your love of the Met. Browse the full catalog at the site.

 Recommended   Price   Selection   Convenience   Service   Security

minerva-antiques.co.uk
Minerva Antiques International

44 020 8691 2221
enquiry@minerva-antiques.co.uk

Antiques

Whether you need one antique accent piece or enough antiques to decorate a house or commercial establishment, Minerva Antiques International is the place to start your English antique shopping expedition. The site is set up as a virtual shop: Customers wander from room to room in a virtual floor plan to see the available selection. Prices are in pounds, but a handy currency converter at the site helps with the details. Call for shipping outside the U.K. The site has links to other antique sites in England as well as to the "Greenwich Gateway," a superdirectory for the area.

mingwrecks.com
Nanhai Marine Archaeology

609 41 31 002
sten@tm.net.my

Fine Art

The story told on the pages of this site is positively captivating! According to the information, Nanhai Marine Archaeology is a Malaysian-based company specializing in the search for historical shipwrecks and underwater excavation. The company claims to be offering pottery and Asian art that has been excavated from 11th–19th century (Song dynasty to Ming dynasty) shipwrecks in the South China Sea. This company asserts that all the proper paperwork is in place for you to purchase and receive these priceless treasures. Is it true? You should investigate before you buy. However, the story makes for fascinating reading on a dull night.

mixedgreens.com
Mixed Greens

212-331-8888
info@mixedgreens.com

Fine Art • Photography • Sculpture

Mixed Greens is an art gallery in New York City. The online gallery features relatively affordable works by 30 contemporary artists. If you're in a hurry to purchase what you see, you can buy immediately. Otherwise, you can indulge in the site's Online Collection. Here, after you create an identity, you can add and discard works to your personal collection, meet the artists, and build (virtual) worth. It's fun and free. Of course, Mixed Greens hopes that all this collecting will make you want to own for real what you've selected in your pretend collection.

momastore.org
MoMA Online Store
800-447-6662
orderservices@moma.org
Museum Store • Posters

MoMA, short for Museum of Modern Art, presents some spectacular works of art that double as watches, personal accessories, toys, and kitchen tools. You'll find examples from the history of twentieth-century design, as well as some of the latest designs that have been accepted into the museum's extensive collection. The poster collection in the online shop is stunning. Browse through the store's categories or search for a particular piece or designer. Join MoMA online and receive a discount on purchases made at the site.

museumofbadart.org
The Museum Of Bad Art
781-444-6757
moba@museumofbadart.org
Museum Store • Photography • Posters

Yes, these folks are serious. There really is a Museum of Bad Art in Needham, Massachusetts, and you could visit the gallery there. You're better off to view the Museum of Bad Art online and pick up a few mementos at the site. A CD of the collection is available (in Mac format only), showing the gallery's 28 rooms. You'll also find a selection of reproduction posters, paintings, and photographs that hang in the gallery. Send them as gifts or hang them proudly at home. It's all done tongue in cheek, of course. Join MoBA and get the latest bad art news.

nancysteinbockposters.com
Nancy Steinbock Vintage Posters
800-438-1577
nancy@nancysteinbockposters.com
Posters

Nancy Steinbock Vintage Posters is famous in the art world for her stellar collection of posters. The posters offered at this site are from the 1880s to 1950s. You won't find a reproduction offered for sale; every poster is guaranteed to be original. Of notable interest are the mini-posters in the Affiches Illustrees section. The posters, actually stone lithographs, were printed in Paris by Imp. Chaix, who also printed "Les Maitre de l'Affiche." These original prints were executed in 1896. E-mail for a quote on the prices.

 Recommended   Price   Selection   Convenience   Service   Security

★ nga.gov/shop
National Gallery of Art

800-697-9350
mailorder@nga.gov

Museum Store • Posters

The National Gallery of Art is the home to one of the most comprehensive art collections in the world. Longs lines of visitors enjoy the paintings, sculpture, decorative arts, and works on paper that highlight artists from the Middle Ages to the present. The Gallery's online shop sells jewelry, reproductions, and stationery based on the National Gallery's permanent collection and exhibitions. The Children's Shop offers toys and books kids of all ages will enjoy. Finish your shopping trip with an online tour of the Gallery.

nicholsonprints.com
NicholsonPrints.com

No phone number listed
nipr@cnicholson.com

Photography • Posters

The work of photographer Chris Nicholson is featured at NicholsonPrints.com. The gallery features a display of his work. Choose your prints from images of New England autumn color, seals, kangaroos, lighthouses, golf courses, Australian Outback deserts, butterflies, and more. The Americana section is especially poignant. Small thumbnail pictures of each print are displayed in the gallery; click one to enlarge it and view it in greater detail. NicholsonPrints.com does not take credit cards, so you'll need to use PayPal when you order online.

nightowlbooks.com
NightOwlBooks

703-590-2966
who@nightowlbooks.com

Posters

Don't let the name of this site fool you. The night owl doesn't give a hoot about books. It's movie posters he's after, and not the mainstream ones either! Shop at this site for vintage movie posters that date from the 1930s to the 1980s. Thousands of them are in stock, from first-run movies to deplorable bombs. Cult movie posters run a close second, with just about every movie between 1950 and 1980 represented. Westerns, Blaxploitation flicks, martial arts favorites, and Elvis movies get a share of the movie poster spotlight.

noguchi.org
The Isamu Noguchi Garden Museum

718-721-2308
akari@noguchi.org

Fine Art • Museum Store

Isamu Noguchi was born in 1904, and continued making sculpture, furniture, and art accessories until his death in 1988. His sixty-year career touched the face of history. Visit the museum dedicated to this talented artist and buy some of the furniture and art that made him famous. Much of the furniture is custom, and although it can be ordered online, further input from you will be required later on. For example, you'll need to choose colors and fabrics for the fabulous freeform sofa and ottoman. Items like the signature Knife and Fork flatware set that was designed by Noguchi in 1952 are available for instant delivery.

★ novica.com
NOVICA

877-266-8422
service@novica.com

Collectibles • Fine Art • Sculpture

Suppose you assembled a team of craftsmen, artisans, and incredibly creative and talented people from around the world, and asked them to re-create the treasures from their respective countries. In the end, you would spend time and money and, chances are, you would have been better shopping at NOVICA in the first place. NOVICA combs the globe finding handmade treasures and prices them fairly. Whether you're looking for an original painting from India, a sculpture from Brazil, or a small trinket from anywhere, NOVICA has you covered. Shop by category or click the map to shop by region.

★ oilpaintingsforless.com
Oil Paintings For Less

818-957-1274
info@oilpaintingsforless.com

Fine Art

Oil Paintings For Less is easy to recommend. You can choose your painting from many categories, including Flowers and Still Lifes, Ships and Boats, Houses, Mountains and Trees, Landscapes, and more. The paintings are one-of-a-kind works. When a painting is sold, it is removed from the site. A unique virtual onsite framing service enables you to see what your painting will look like in the various quality frames carried by Oil Paintings For Less. This service gives the site an element of fun.

oldplank.com
Antiques on Old Plank Road

630-971-0500
webstore@oldplank.com

Antiques

If you're in the vicinity of Westmont, Illinois, the bricks-and-mortar location of Antiques on Old Plank Road should be your first shopping choice. The rest of us will have to make do with the online location, but you won't hear too many complaints. This site is so well done that you can practically smell the furniture polish. The site features both antique furniture *and* reproductions, so you don't need to worry too much about that devilish thing called a budget. Shipping charges can mount up, so consider the cost before you order a beautiful armoire or claw-footed chest, for example.

paintingsdirect.com
PaintingsDIRECT.com

212-504-8151
customersupport@paintingsdirect.com

Fine Art • Photography

Claiming it's "the easiest way find and buy original paintings," PaintingsDIRECT.com awaits your visit. The site features artwork from artists all around the world. This company deals directly with the artists. When you order from PaintingsDIRECT.com, a company representative contacts the artist and works with him or her to deliver the painting to you. This very customized process guarantees the authenticity of the paintings and the best service possible. While you're shopping, send your friend an Artcard. The cards are beautiful and free to send.

patentmuseum.com
PatentMuseum.com

414-383-5260
patentmuseum@aol.com

Collectibles

You couldn't have invented a better gift for a creative genius! The PatentMuseum.com sells reproductions of patents issued by the United States Patent and Trademark Office. Cruising through the site's category search provides a mini-history lesson. Who knew, that Joseph Glidden patented his Barbed Wire Fence in 1874 or Mary Phelps Jacob received a patent on the design of a Brassiere in 1914? Not all patents issued by the office are listed on the site, so you'll have to be content with what you find. All told though, the certificates are inexpensive and make great collectibles.

Pendemonium.com
Pendemonium

888-372-2050
sam@pendemonium.com

Antiques • Collectibles

In our technology-driven world it is rare when we have time to take pen in hand and slow our thoughts to the speed at which we can write legibly. Such is the joy of writing with a fountain pen. If you enjoy fountain pens and vintage writing instruments, a visit to Pendemonium.com is a must. Fountain pens have a great history. Pendemonium has a selection of the Parker and Sheaffer pens that were the writing tools of choice for earlier generations. Other brands such as Waterman and Pelikan are represented, too. A visit is a must for the pen collector and recommended for anyone else.

★ photonewyork.com
photoNewYork.com

212-569-8282
E-mail form on site

Memorabilia • Photography • Posters

New York: The city that never sleeps. The images that make this city so fascinating are captured at photoNewYork.com. Find posters, prints, and photographs, arranged in easy-to-find categories, such as Historical, Classical, Celebrity, and so on. The inventory changes daily, so don't wait if you see something you like. The Functional Art category offers images of the city on lamps and furniture that are both decorative and functional. The Memorabilia section offers an impressive collection of current signed sports gear. Art for 9/11, a best-selling category, sells the images we'll never forget.

photos-now.net
Photos-Now.net

No phone number listed
webmaster@photos-now.net

Photography

Anyone who's tried to design a professional Web site or work with Web graphics has encountered this problem sooner or later: The free graphics on the Net just don't cut it. Clip art, images with fuzzy edges, or super-imposed heads and so on tend to make an otherwise well-designed Web site look unpolished and unprofessional. Photos-Now.net rises to the rescue with the service it offers. For a monthly fee, you have access to around 8,000 downloadable royalty-free photos and graphic backgrounds. Visit the site, browse through the photo catalog, and decide whether the service is right for you.

 Recommended   Price   Selection   Convenience   Service Security

⭐ picassomio.com
PicassoMio.com

877-212-5879
customer@picassomio.com

Fine Art • Photography • Posters • Sculpture

With locations on both sides of the Atlantic, PicassoMio has received high marks from critics and buyers as a great place to discover and buy contemporary art. Why? For one thing, PicassoMio partners with respected galleries, dealers, artists to bring you fine art, sculpture, photography, and more. For another, this company can also provide you with an Independent Party Authenticity Endorsement with your purchase of a PicassoMio artwork. Of course, the third reason is that the works found at the site are stunning. Come and see for yourself.

pietrasantart.com
PietrasantArt.com

818-446-0900
sales@pietrasantart.com

Sculpture

Pietrasanta is a small town in Italy known for its marbleworks. If you can't get there this year, you're in luck! PietrasantArt.com is offering artworks and beautiful sculptures direct from the Gift Shop and the Art Shop. Before you buy, be sure to take a look at the shipping information. Phrases like "We won't be held responsible for any damages occurred during transportation" might be off-putting to some nervous buyers. However, if you're willing to take a chance, check out the amazing marble statues offered at this site. Prices are shown in lira, with rough dollar equivalents.

postergroup.com
Postergroup.com

866-897-1525
E-mail form on site

Posters

Postergroup.com started small. The founder, Mickey Ross, picked up a few vintage posters during a trip to Europe. Those posters became the base for his collection. Soon, collecting original vintage posters was his hobby and then his passion, which grew into a thriving business that serves you and me. Postergroup.com offers over 2,500 original vintage posters from all four corners of the globe. The posters are suitable for hanging in a personal residence or displaying in a public place, like a restaurant or office building. Posters come in all sizes and some are priced below $250.

printsellers.com
PrintSellers.com
800-669-7843
info3@printsellers.com
Collectibles • Photograph

Our view of the world keeps changing. And so does the way we map it. The "real" antique maps are worth a fortune, if they're even still available. The folks at PrintSellers.com sell reproductions of antique maps. That way, you don't need to worry about spilling coffee on your priceless image of Captain Bligh's view of the Sandwich Islands, and your reproduction copy has more color and life than the original. "Many of our clients claim our artists' reproductions surpass the originals in quality, color, and design," say the site owners. You'll also find reproductions of historical photographs and some books.

★ prosportsmemorabilia.com
Pro Sports Memorabilia
888-950-5399
service@prosportsmemorabilia.com
Memorabilia

Pro Sports Memorabilia distributes authentic sports collectibles. The products sold at this site are licensed by the NFL, NBA, NHL, and MLB. You'll find signed jerseys, helmets, mugs, photos, posters, and more. Expect to see current stars and vintage stars; it's not unusual for a Pittsburgh Steelers jersey from the Steel Curtain era of the seventies to be mixed in with one from last year's team! Pro Sports Memorabilia obtains all of its sports signatures from paid athlete appearances and signings. The signatures are authentic.

pushposters.co.uk
PushPosters.com
44-141-951-4460
sales@pushposters.co.uk
Posters

PushPosters.com, based in Scotland, sells music-themed merchandise. Performers from A to Z are represented with a variety of posters, fan wear, tour books, and flags. Most of the performers are rock musicians, and several are European or out of the mainstream. Check out the posters in the Limited Edition series; in addition to their unique beauty, these posters might be valuable art some day. Prices at the site are shown in pounds, euros, and dollars, making it easy for international visitors to shop without the need for calculators. Shipping is global.

 Recommended   Price   Selection   Convenience   Service   Security

★ raabcollection.com
Raab Collection

610-446-6193
raab@raabautographs.com

Memorabilia

Looking for a slice of history? You'll find it at this site. You may become so fascinated that you find yourself coming back for more! The Raab Collection offers autographs, historically significant letters, documents, manuscripts, and autographs from American and foreign history. The collection includes items from presidents and authors, kings and soldiers, impressionists and physicists, composers and the Founding Fathers, and covers every era from the Middle Ages to the present day. The credentials of Steven Raab, the founder, are on the site, along with his professional affiliations.

retrojunction.com
RetroJunction.com

866-738-7650
sales@retrojunction.com

Collectibles • Memorabilia

The fun and funky 50s and 60s come alive again at RetroJunction.com. An eclectic collection of clocks, toys, lunchboxes, retro radios and phones, tin signs, posters and fabric, and more is available at this kitschy site. Many of the items are reproductions of the original products. While this ensures that they'll work better than their "real" counterparts, you may want to take a pass if authenticity is desired. Still, it's fun to have a princess phone with rotary dial and a jukebox (with hidden CD player) on your desk.

rockandrollgallery.com
Rock and Roll Gallery.com

310-659-0441
chris@rockandrollgallery.com

Photography

Rock and Roll Gallery.com sells photographs of the legends of rock-and-roll music. The site has hundreds of photos ready for purchase. However, unless you're a real die-hard fan or enjoy watching page after page of nameless performers appear on the screen, the site's limiting navigation tools impede progress before too long. Skip the useless category searches and type the name of the performer or group you would like to find. (On a recent visit, I tried Elvis Presley, Kiss, and Cher.) You'll see applicable photos in a few seconds. The virtual frame shows how your photo will look in a frame.

roslynherman.com
Roslyn Herman & Co.

718-846-3496
info@roslynherman.com

Memorabilia

There's an old saying that says something like one man's junk is another man's treasure. That adage is certainly proven true at this site, where people pay big money to buy anything and everything simply because it was previously owned by a celebrity. The stock is ever changing, but might include a shirt owned by Sly Stallone, a tie owned by Burt Lancaster, and a ring worn by Jennifer Aniston. All items feature a certificate of authenticity.

rrauction.com
R&R Enterprises Autograph Auction

800-937-3880
danette@rrauction.com

Memorabilia

A celebrity autograph is a valuable commodity and fun to collect. Each month, R&R Enterprises Autograph Auction sells about 2,000 autographs in an auction format. You'll need to register at the site and get a personal number. Then you'll browse through the monthly catalog and view the names up for bids in the following categories: Presidents and First Ladies, Notable and Notorious, Military, Space and Aviation, Art and Literature, Animation and Comic Art, Music, Entertainment, and Sports. You enter your bid in the on-site bid box and try to win the autographs you want. Details are at the site.

rubylane.com
Ruby Lane

415-864-4563
info1@rubylane.com

Antiques • Collectibles • Fine Art

In concept, Ruby Lane seems like a really good idea: a virtual brick-paved street with many charming independent shops offering quality antiques, collectibles, fine art, jewelry, and handcrafted items from around the world. Unfortunately, the navigation and search feature of Ruby Lane makes it difficult to zero in on specific items unless you know exactly what you want. That said, if you have time to browse, you can find some very unusual items in a variety of price ranges. Also on the plus side, Ruby Lane's centralized shopping cart enables you to pick and choose items from store to store and pay just once when you're ready to leave.

 Recommended   Price   Selection   Convenience   Service   Security

salvadordalimuseum.org/shop
The Salavador Dali Museum
No phone number listed
support@salvadordalimuseum.org
Museum Store • Posters

If you love the work of the famous artist Salvador Dali, you'll enjoy The Salavador Dali Museum online store. The melting clock, perhaps Dali's most familiar icon, is available as a travel clock. Many of Dali's paintings in the museum are available in posters and framed formats ready to hang. You'll also find a collection of clever clothes, called "Dali Wear." The tin plates and cocktail napkins add a touch of the surreal to any gathering. The rest of the collection is not to be missed.

sculpturedecor.com
Artisan House Sculptures
888-205-8560
artisan@cerzanstudio.com
Sculpture

A sculpture collection for your walls is a great investment and makes it easy to decorate your home. At Artisan House Sculptures, a staff of craftsman and an apprentice handcraft each piece to re-create the artist's original concept. The metals are formed, cast, welded, brazed, and finished exquisitely. The intent of the artist is the key. Throughout the creation of the sculpture, that intent is looked to as the "standard of excellence." Choose a sculpture from the Abstract, Contemporary, Nautical, or Southwestern categories. Freestanding floor sculptures and table-top sculptures are also available. Free shipping is included on all metal sculptures.

shop.louvre.fr
The Louvre Online Shop
No phone number listed
E-mail form on site
Museum Store • Sculpture

The Louvre's online shop is run by The Réunion des Musées Nationaux. The RMN manages a number of sites: shop.louvre.fr, musee-orsay.fr, and a general-type store at museesdefrance.com. Although some people complain about the hoity-toity attitude of the French, they couldn't be more oriented towards customer service at this site. Prices are listed in both Eurodollars and U.S. dollars, and a helpful section of links at the bottom of each page of merchandise leads to related merchandise at the sister sites. The site offers up a great selection of items, most of it elegant and refined. Shipping anywhere is never a problem.

speedyartonline.com
SpeedyArtOnline.com
888-395-2577
No e-mail address listed
Fine Art

How fast do you want it? SpeedyArtOnline.com understands that you don't want to wait for weeks for your painting to be packed and shipped. After you've browsed through the 3,000 oil paintings and frames available at this site and made your selection, you want your artwork yesterday. So SpeedyArtOnline.com promises to ship your order within 24 hours if you live in the United States. To show how serious this company is, it'll ship for free! If you live outside the U.S., you'll get the same great service, but you'll have to pay a nominal fee for shipping. Still a great fast deal!

spiart.com
Southern Photographic Images
No phone number listed
E-mail form on site
Photography

Southern Photographic Images is a new gallery that specializes in the reproduction and sale of fine photographic art. Its introductory exhibition is a showing and sale of the works of Fonville Winans. The stunning black-and-white photos chronicle Louisiana's rich cultural heritage. Most of the photographs capture scenes of Baton Rouge and the small fishing village of Grand Isle. The images are reproduced on photographic paper from negatives made from the artist's original prints and mounted in acid-free mats. Sizes from 5×7 inches to 16×20 inches are available as silver-gelatin prints on heavy-fiber, multi-contrast paper.

starrynightantiques.com
Starry Night Antiques
877-515-6264
susan_starr@verizon.net
Antiques • Collectibles • Memorobilia

Starry Night Antiques specializes in antique American and European furnishings and accessories. Because the online catalog is an extension of the merchandise in the Ellicott City, Maryland, store, there's no telling what treasure you'll find. You may find porcelain, pottery, crystal, glassware, jewelry, furniture, rare books, and more. Or, you may find that nothing is available and you need to check back tomorrow. Look every few days or so — you'll agree the time is well spent.

 Recommended   Price   Selection   Convenience   Service   Security

starvedartists.com
The Starved Artists
No phone number listed
suggestions@starvedartists.com

Photography

The Starved Artists site is an Internet community that showcases the works of new and emerging photographers. You'll find photos for sale that you won't find anywhere else on the Web. Although the artists are responsible for selling their own work, use the site's master Search engine to find what you want. Enter a keyword and you'll see all related photographs. Or browse through the Artist's Stores if you have more time. The Starved Artists site handles all purchase transactions. If you're a budding photographer with works to sell, read the details at the site about opening your own store here.

statue.com
Statue.com
618-692-1121
gloria@statue.com

Sculpture

Sure, you could send to faraway Greece or Italy, wait forever, and then, if you were really lucky, receive your marble statue in one piece. There's a better way to buy the statues you want — order them from Statue.com! Although the statues here are made from MARBLECast, an in-house blended marble material, they look identical to ones made entirely from marble. Ancient reproductions and animal statues are the biggest sellers. The wall reliefs and friezes are stunning. The Christ Consolator, at 10 feet tall, is the largest statue at the site. It's available by special order only.

stoneroads.com
StoneRoads.com
888-511-4545
orders@stoneroads.com

Collectibles

Want to own or collect something really beautiful? Visit Stoneroads.com for hand-painted decorative ceramic pottery. Each piece is like a work of art, with brilliant colors, soft hues, and floral designs. The pottery is actually tin-glazed earthenware. It comes from all over the world. In fact, it's called by many names, depending on the country from which it originated. Choose pieces from Spain, Portugal, Italy, or the United States. Learn more about the fascinating history of this affordable collectible and decide which piece you'll add to your new or existing collection.

thealcove.com
The Alcove
800-438-9527
info@thealcove.com
Collectibles

What's better than a collection of stuffed bears? (I have one myself.) Nothing, perhaps, other than a collection of stuffed dogs or cats by A Breed Apart. Or maybe dolls from designers like Heidi Plusczok, Alexandra Koukinova, or Adora. Alternatively, you might decide on a collection of fine art, including paintings and lithographs. Whatever you choose, The Alcove has what you need. Its comprehensive bear collection includes all the Steiff animals, including those that are hard to find. The site is easy to navigate, and you'll be pleased with the easy-to-read descriptions. So pleased, in fact, you may decide to start another collection.

theantiquescompany.com
The Antiques Company
No e-mail address listed
antiques@theantiquescompany.com
Antiques

The Antiques Company is entirely Internet-based. Because it doesn't have to pay rent or stay shut up in a shop, it can afford to spend the necessary time and money to find the finest stitched samplers, silk pictures, steins, and Majolica pottery and present them to you. Thumbnail pictures of the items for sale are displayed in the catalog; click one to enlarge the view. See an expensive piece that you can't live without? Not to worry; an installment plan can be negotiated.

theartifact.com
The Artifact
888-965-0001
info@theartifact.com
Fine Art • Museum Store

"Own a Piece of History . . . Give a Piece of History." Whichever you choose, you can do it at The Artifact. Fine art, artifacts and museum reproductions, as well as historical and classical jewelry are for sale here. The items are grouped by period for easy searching; for example, Ancient Greek and Roman, Asian, Oriental and Hindu, and Pre-Columbian and American. Of course, you can use the site's Search function to locate what you want. The Artifact's shipping policy makes it easy to buy: Low fixed-price shipping is under $7 for the first item and $4 for each additional item.

 Recommended   Price   Selection   Convenience   Service   Security

★ theartofbronze.com
The Art of Bronze
877-365-4438
sales@theartofbronze.com
Sculpture

Make an investment in the future with a statue from The Art of Bronze. This company features works of art by artists such as Remington, Moreau, Kauba, and others. Each unique statue from this site is mounted on a marble base with an engraved plaque with the sculpture and artist name. The Art of Bronze will engrave your name on the back of the statue, creating a family heirloom. Shop here with confidence — it claims the U.S. Government as one of its current customers! Your order may take several days; the Art of Bronze won't ship until your sculpture is perfect.

thecameocollection.com
The Cameo Collection
574-533-4070
cameos@thecameocollection.com
Antiques • Collectibles

What's your cameo IQ? Do you know that most popular cameos today are carved from seashells? This tradition began around the fifteenth century and was made popular by Queen Victoria. However, although women wear cameos now, in the past men wore them, too. The Emperor Napoléon wore a cameo to his own wedding and founded a school in Paris to teach the art of cameo-carving to young apprentices. Read more about these amazing pieces of jewelry and buy one or two for your own collection at The Cameo Collection.

theorigins.com
theOrigins
415-821-6110
customerservice@theorigins.com
Collectibles • Fine Art • Sculpture

theOrigins takes itself seriously. More than just a site to sell art items and collectibles, it is one of the few commerce sites that professes to have a mission and a purpose that don't involve making a profit. The site operates with the idea that cultural heritage is preserved through artistic traditions. "Every piece we offer has been created through artistic traditions handed down for generations, or is a reproduction of a famous work of cultural art." If this sounds like mumbo-jumbo to you, ignore the rhetoric and enjoy the incredible collection of art, artifacts, and sculpture assembled from around the world.

thomaskinkade.com
Thomas Kinkade

877-853-4732
E-mail form on site

Collectibles • Fine Art

Thomaskinkade.com is the official site for Thomas Kinkade, Painter of Light. The prolific painter's fine art collection is arranged by subject, so you can discover your treasure in no time flat. The painter's charming commentary appears next to each painting, making the purchase a very personal experience. Further personalize your choice with a special frame. If you're after a collectible, trinket, or special gift, you'll find a wide variety of choices with some that won't take too big a bite out of your wallet. Sign up for a free newsletter at the site or join the Thomas Kinkade Collectors' Society.

tias.com
Tias.com

888-653-7883
info@tias.com

Antiques • Collectibles

Tias.com is the leaseholder for over 1,000 small antique and collectible shops. Think of shopping at this site as like going to huge, online flea market — some of the stalls are worthless, some are overpriced, but in between the losers are some real gems that you wouldn't find anywhere else. Use the Tias search function if you're looking for a specific item. Otherwise, click the link to Shops and then stroll through the list. Currently, there's no central checkout, so you'll need to buy as you go.

toysplus.com
We're Dreamin2

800-960-0040
dreamin2@toysplus.com

Collectibles

Collectors of Angel Hugs Plus, Baby Gund, and Baby Gund Plus, Precious Moments, Dreamsicles, and all similar collectibles will love this site. We're Dreamin2 is simple and easy to navigate, making shopping a breeze. The product lines are conveniently listed down the side. Click the one you want or search by brand or theme. If you're looking for a specific item, use We're Dreamin2's handy search feature. Hard-to-find and discontinued product lines are carried here, making this simple site a shopping gem.

 Recommended   Price   Selection   Convenience   Service   Security

★ uniquities-archant.com
Uniquities Architectural Antiques

403-228-9221
info@uniquities-archant.com

Collectibles

The collectibles from this site won't fit on a shelf or remain behind glass. Uniquities carries all manner of architectural antiques and garden statuary, specializing in an impressive inventory of ancient stone and iron. You'll find an incredible collection of urns, stained glass, and eccentricities. The owners travel to the U.K. four times a year on buying trips to replenish the amazing stock. The site is located in Canada but ships internationally. You may want to call and arrange shipping on some of the heavier items.

ustradediscount.com
U.S. Trade Discount

239-598-3431
E-mail form on site

Memorabilia

If you're a lover of the music scene, you won't want to pass up the opportunity to hold a piece of it in your hands. U.S. Trade Discount offers autographed guitars and other signed collectibles by music industry greats. On a recent visit, signed guitars from Bon Jovi, Alicia Keyes, and Willie Nelson were available, along with a host of other big stars. You can also find autographed microphones, albums, gloves, and more. The site has a great search feature that's especially useful for gifts. Enter the name of the music personality and, if desired, the amount you want to spend, and what's available is displayed.

vintagevending.com
Vintage Vending

888-242-6633
No e-mail address on site

Collectibles • Memorabilia

Vintage Vending is a blast from the past. In fact, the self-bestowed title of "The Web's Retro Planet" seems to jibe perfectly with the huge volume of kitschy items hanging around this site. Expect to find accessories, furniture, and home furnishings from the 1920s through the 1960s, with an emphasis on the 1950s. Many of the items for sale at the site are reproductions. For example, the furniture — chairs, booth sets, pub sets — is new and can be ordered in your choice of colors. A few old pieces are mixed in with the stock, so read the descriptions carefully if you want the real deal.

whk-antiques.com
WHK Antiques
44 (0)1625 434126
info@whk-antiques.com
Antiques • Collectibles • Fine Art

Shop at WHK Antiques for English and Staffordshire pottery and figurines. Some of the pieces shown in the online catalog are quite old, dating back to over 100 years and more, while others are from more recent times. Most pieces are displayed with clear photographs. Prices are shown in both pounds (the site is in the U.K.) and U.S. dollars and include international shipping. If you order, please be aware that the catalog doesn't always reflect availability because the owners also maintain a store. They'll send you a confirmation and a full condition report before they proceed with the final order details.

worldbronzes.com
The World of Bronzes
818-446-0900
sales@worldbronzes.com
Sculpture

Not everyone can afford bronze sculptures by famous artists. However, The World of Bronzes specializes in the reproduction of beautiful pieces of sculpture. For a fraction of the cost of the original piece (if it was even available), you can have a bronze statue replica of the works of Rodin, Remington, Mene, Kauba, and other famous artists. The World of Bronzes certifies that its statues are authentic reproductions of the original works. It also certifies that all sculptures are made with the lost wax process of casting, and skilled artists complete all final hand detailing.

world-wide-art.com
World Wide Art
800-518-8453
questions@world-wide-art.com
Posters

Admittedly, this site is not one of the more robust poster sites on the Internet. So why include it? World Wide Art offers its customers a feature you simply don't see too often anymore — layaway! Here's how it works: Find the poster you want and pay 40 percent of the total amount due. (All layaways require a credit card on file for monthly billing.) Next month and each subsequent month, 10 percent of the total amount will be charged monthly to the credit card on file. Monthly statements will be mailed with the credit card receipt. When your poster is paid off, it's mailed to you.

 Recommended   Price   Selection   Convenience   Service   Security

wotoandwife.bc.ca
Woto and Wife Antiques

250 286 1291
info@wotoandwife.bc.ca

Antiques

Woto and his wife are real characters! They scour the countryside in Vancouver looking for Victorian treasures to sell to you and me. On any given day, the stock can change but two things are always consistent at this site: Prices are fair, and the level of service is high. When you find what you like on the online catalog, you'll have to call and place your order (there is no online ordering at this time). Shipping is international and only Canadian residents pay sales tax.

wowart.net
Wow Art

678-464-3504
services@wowart.net

Fine Art

Does the thought of owning an original Van Gogh excite you? How about an original work of art from Cezanne, Degas, Manet, or just about any other painter you can name. Of course, fine art like this would be astronomically expensive, if you could even find it for sale. That's where Wow Art comes in. They offer reproductions of original works that are so detailed that you'll be hard-pressed to tell the difference. The team of Wow Art artists works diligently to re-create each picture, brush stroke by stroke. The online catalog reads like an art history textbook and prices are low. Amaze your friends and business colleagues with your "original" Wow Art paintings.

yesterjewels.bigstep.com
Yesterjewels

No phone number listed
bonnie@yesterjewels.com

Collectibles

Costume jewelry is fun because you change your look without breaking the bank. The owner of Yesterjewels is committed to providing a great experience for her many clients. She works full time to replenish her stock of vintage jewelry and handbags and describes each item with love and care on the site. You'll find an eclectic collection here that changes according to the whim of the customers and what's available on the open market. Items that appear early in the morning may be gone in the afternoon; the pages are updated throughout the day when possible.

Starting an Antiques and Collectibles Business

The popularity of PBS's *Antiques Road Show* has made many people think of starting an antique and collectible business. How about you? Visit the official Antiques Roadshow site and take a virtual tour of the set at pbs.org/wgbh/pages/roadshow/virtual/index.html. The tour is fun and gives you a feel for what the job might entail.

If you decide you want to become an antiques collector, you'll be welcomed to an ever-growing club. Lots of folks are having fun while buying and selling antiques and collectibles. Some people are even managing to turn a profit!

Before you jump into the collecting business, you should know a few things. Buying and selling is a complex business. In order to be successful, you must learn to be an expert in your chosen collecting field, authenticate each item, and become an expert evaluator.

Choose an area of specialization that interests you, and is one in which you have some experience. Strive to become an expert in that field. Dictionary.com (dictionary.com) defines "expert" as "a person with a high degree of skill in or knowledge of a certain subject." The best way to become an expert in the collectible business is to learn from respected collectors. Meet Ralph and Terry Kovel at Kovel Online (kovel.com). The Kovels have authored several books on collecting and are recognized as foremost experts in the collectibles world.

Visit the online auctions at eBay (ebay.com) and Yahoo! Auctions (auctions.yahoo.com) to get a feel for what items in your specialty cost. You don't want to overpay when you buy and undercharge when you sell. Old and Sold Antiques Auction and Marketplace (oldandsold.com) is another great place for beginners. The site is a virtual community for collectors with articles, message boards, and ongoing auctions.

When you finally buy your first items, make sure you've gotten what you paid for. Beginning collectors sometimes get excited over a "rare" find that is actually an ordinary piece. Appraisal Day.com (appraisalday.com/services.htm) and Ask the Appraiser (collectingchannel.com/ata/cesATEIndex.asp?ref=33) provide online and regular U.S. mail appraisals in the fields of fine art, antiques, and collectibles for a nominal fee.

Now it's time to make some money. If you've gotten attached to those first items you bought, you'll have a hard time selling them. Just do it! Set up a table at a local flea market or tag sale and gauge the reaction of your customers. Of course, you can establish an online presence as well with GoAntiques (goantiques.com) or whybidmore (whybidmore.com).

As soon as you make a sale, invest in some new items. Your second buying trip will be easier. This time, you'll know what to look for and might even snag a great deal. In turn, sell these new items and go out and do it again.

Good Luck with your new business venture. With a little perseverance, you'll be known as the expert in your field!

Chapter 5

Apparel: Dressing for Work and Play

● ●

*B*ecause our bodies require a variety of clothing and accessories for an even greater variety of circumstances and moods, this chapter covers shopping for apparel. Whether you just want to find a pair of jeans, locate a trendy T-shirt, or assemble an entire wardrobe, you can find the products you're looking for at these online stores.

Within these listings, both men and women will find a variety of clothing stores offering casual and formal attire for weekends and workdays, work and recreation, for nights out and days in, and those special occasions. They have you "covered." You find underwear to outerwear; tops to bottoms; T-shirts to suit coats; caps to footwear; and clothing for the big, short, and tall.

Last, but not least, you mustn't forget to accessorize! So, I've included shopping sites for jewelry, ties, belts, sunglasses, watches, hats, and anything else you'll need to complete your look.

Here are some Web sites that can help you on sizing:

- ✔ **Men's Tops/Bottoms:** vickerey.com/sizechartm.html
- ✔ **Women's Tops/Bottoms:** universaloverall.com/Women_Size.htm
- ✔ **Men's and Women's Shoes:** shoedini.com/pop_shoesizingcharts.htm
- ✔ **European Size Charts Men/Women:** usatourist.com/english/tips/sizes.html
- ✔ **Bra Fitting Guide:** apennyearned.co.uk/bra-fitting-guide.html

You can check these sites out for women's and men's fashion tips:

- ✔ **Men's Fashion Tips:** about.com/cs/menstips
- ✔ **Women's Fashion Tips:** saviodsilva.net/life/37.htm
- ✔ **Hey, guys! Read This Before Buying Her Clothes:** fashion.about.com/cs/menstips/bb/buyforher.htm
- ✔ **Men's Style Guide:** askandyaboutclothes.com/How%20to%20Look%20Your%20Best/Introduction.htm

Key Word Index

Accessories

These shopping sites have you covered — from head to toe. You'll find stores that sell caps and hats, ties and scarves, as well as belts and purses.

Athletic

These stores offer the clothing that you exercise or play sports in. It's no longer a fashion faux pas to wear athletic wear out and about.

Career

The stores with this keyword offer clothes that make the man — and the woman.

Casual

Casual is just that — comfortable clothing to relax in around the house or to wear when you're not attending work (unless it's causal day). In these stores, you can find sportswear, streetwear, and jeans.

Designer

If you enjoy wearing someone else's name on your clothing, then these shopping sites are for you. Be prepared to pay extra for the privilege.

Eyewear

You'll always look cool in designer eyewear. The stores with this keyword offer a wide selection of styles, name brands, and sunglasses.

Footwear

No shoes, no service? No problem. These stores can outfit you with tennis and dress shoes, saddles and flip-flops, and the hosiery and socks that go with them.

Formal

Shop at stores listed with this keyword, and you'll be "puttin' on the Ritz." They offer a fine selection of classy tuxedos for men and beautiful gowns and dresses for women.

Jewelry

You can find a nice selection of body adornment, from charm bracelets to gemstones, at online stores with this keyword.

Outerwear

These sites offer coats, jackets, windbreakers, and raingear — all you need to protect yourself from the elements in style.

Sleepwear

You can still be fashionable even in your sleep. Stores with this keyword offer all-around comfortable sleepwear for both men and women.

Specialty

The stores that sport this keyword carry clothing for the big and tall, short and small, wedding and maternity fashions, specialty work clothes, and custom-made clothing that fits you to a T.

Swimwear

Just add water! The stores with this keyword offer both men and women the latest styles to wear around the pool or at the beach.

Underwear

A good foundation is the basis of good fashion and comfortable clothing. Stores that sport this keyword offer both standard and designer underwear for men and women.

Vintage

Are the 1960s coming back? They could be if these stores have their way. Pay a visit to these online stores for vintage and funky clothing.

Watches

These stores offer watches from the utilitarian Timex to the expensive Rolex — and some at discount prices.

1worldsarongs.com
1World Sarongs

888-727-6647
customerservice@1worldsarongs.com
Specialty

What's your sarong IQ? Most of us don't know much about this versatile garment. However, after reading about the multiple uses of this interesting garment, you many want to order one (or two) for yourself. 1World Sarongs has the largest selection of sarongs on the Web — in fact, they have thousands of them. They sell sarongs made from all over the world, and many of their unique designs are available exclusively through them. When you visit, check out their awesome beads, sparkling jewelry, and one-of-a-kind folk art.

abercrombie.com
Abercrombie & Fitch

888-856-4480
E-mail form on site

Accessories • Athletic • Casual • Outerwear • Sleepwear • Underwear

Way back when, Abercrombie & Fitch supplied outdoor gear and supplies to adventurers like Teddy Roosevelt, Robert Peary, and Ernest Hemingway. Now the brand is hot on high school and college campuses. The online store doesn't have the loud music heard at its mall counterpart, but it carries all the same great clothes for men and women. Accessories, like belts, totes, caps, and casual shoes round out the collection. Don't miss the A&F Sales room. Clothes that were so popular yesterday are selling for a fraction of their original price today.

ae.com
American Eagle Outfitters

888-232-4535
custserv@ae.com

**Accessories • Athletic • Casual • Sleepwear •
Swimwear • Underwear • Watches**

American Eagle Outfitters targets the 15 to 25 age group with T-shirts, polo shirts, cargo shorts, and jeans. There are also plenty of other good looking casual clothes and accessories on this site. Couple that with an ever changing selection of underwear, swimwear, outerwear, and shoes and you have an easy-to-navigate site that young people flock to in droves. Hey, even if you aren't in the target age group, someone you know probably is. Rather than puzzle over what a person might like the next time a holiday or birthday rolls around, send an AE Gift Card — you can get one at the site.

 Recommended  Price   Selection   Convenience   Service   Security

aldenshop.com
The Alden Shop
800-273-7463
info@aldenshop.com
Footwear

"Recognized worldwide as the premier men's dress shoe," Alden offers classic men's shoes, dress and casual, in fine Cordovan leather. This leather is distinctive and will take on a shine and patina if you take care of your shoes. Quality doesn't come cheap. Be prepared to pay hundreds of dollars for these fine shoes. The site offers a large range of shoe sizes — from A and AAA to E and EEE. An international size conversion chart at the site enables international visitors to find the shoes they need.

★ alexblake.com
Alex Blake.com
866-469-3338
info@alexblake.com
Footwear

Hosiery is one of those funny things you don't think about much. That is, until the day you can't find the pair of socks or panty hose you need to complete your outfit. Fortunately, Alex Blake.com makes it easy to stay one leg up on the problem. At this site, you can shop for the brand, style, size, and color of hosiery in the quantities that you need. Alex Blake specializes in hosiery of all kinds — Ankle Length, Argyle, Capri, Control Top, Fishnet, Footie Loafer Sock, Footless, Knee High, Lightweight, Matte, Novelty, Opaque, Pantyhose, and Reinforced Toe — and at affordable prices. Join the Hosiery Club, and when you buy twelve pairs, you get the next pair of hosiery free.

allenedmonds.com
Allen Edmonds
877-817-7615
eservice@allenedmonds.com
Accessories • Footwear

In today's disposable society, a company like Allen-Edmonds stands out. Their high quality men's shoes are made to last a lifetime. Each shoe is crafted by hand in a unique 212-step process. Select your Allen-Edmonds shoe by style, occasion, or color or enter your size and width and see what's available. Your Allen-Endmond shoes are bound to become your favorite footwear. Don't worry when they become a bit worn. Use the company's unique recrafting service. Send them back in the free Recraft pack and in a few short weeks, your shoes will be returned to you, almost as good as new. Details are at the site.

★ alljacketsallthetime.com
All Jackets All theTime
800-434-4729
support@cctaylor.com
Outerwear

Jackets — and nothing but jackets! This site lives up to its name by selling outstanding jackets, coats, and parkas all year, every season, every day. You name the type of jacket, and there's a 99 percent chance this site offers it. Add an unconditional money-back guarantee and you have the makings for a pain-free shopping experience. Although the site caters primarily to men, women can find pea coats, cashmere sweaters, and London Fog raincoats.

★ americanfit.com
AmericanFit.com
201-653-9466
tailor@americanfit.com
Career • Casual • Specialty

What a fabulous idea! AmericanFit.com says, "Don't Throw a Fit get your Pants Custom FIT." The folks who run this site know how hard it is to get pants that fit. For not much more than department store prices, they'll make you a custom pair of pants. You can send them a pair of your best-fitting pants and they'll copy the size and shape. Or send them your measurements and a personal pattern will be created just for you. In a hurry? Choose your pants and then fill out the onscreen form with your measurements. No matter how you choose to do it, you'll be thrilled with the results. International shipping is available.

annacris.com
Anna Cris
800-281-2662
info@annacris.com
Specialty

Anna Cris Maternity is a good place to find quality maternity clothing for both casual and business wear. It sells brand-name apparel plus its own line of clothing that includes contemporary and casual maternity fashion, and maternity business/career suits. The site also offers maternity lingerie, tall maternity clothes, nursing clothes, and maternity fitness clothes. In addition to the clothing, you can find gifts and accessories for the pregnant mother, gift certificates, and baby accessories.

★ Recommended   Price   Selection   Convenience   Service   🔒 Security

anntaylor.com
Ann Taylor

800-342-5266
E-mail form on site

Accessories • Career • Casual • Footwear • Outerwear

Ann Taylor's clothing for women has always been known for its grace and style, and their online store reflects those qualities perfectly. You can shop by category of clothing or by outfit. Shop for formal and casual work clothing, weekend casual clothing, and clothing for special occasions. The site also offers a special section of clothing for petite sizes. Want to visit an Ann Taylor retail store? The site's handy store locator will speed you on your way.

anthropologie.com
Anthropologie

800-309-2500
service@anthropologie.com

Accessories • Casual • Sleepwear • Outerwear

Anthropologie gets the inspiration for its clothing and home decor styles off the beaten path. Their credo is that icons of everyday life in other countries become beautiful works of art in our own. They sell unique products that are, per their company story, "carefully developed to reflect the spirit of the culture" where they were found. The exquisite women's clothes sold at Anthropologie are stunning. Even Anthropologie's accessories — bags and jewelry — and their shoes are unique. Don't miss the sale items for a chance to save big dollars on one-of-a-kind items.

anyknockoff.com
AnyKnockOff.com

877-856-5199
info@anyknockoff.com

Accessories • Eyewear • Jewelry • Watches

So Dior, Fendi, Gucci, Cartier, and other designer labels are well out of your price range. No matter, because there's AnyKnockOff.com, a team of experienced and passionate professionals who believe that trends in fashion are too expensive and transitory to warrant paying an excessive amount of money. What this means is that you can get expensive, look-alike jewelry, handbags, and sunglasses for pennies on the dollar. So you know, you're not getting illegal imitations sold to you by the Internet equivalent of a sleazy guy in a dark raincoat! The items are "inspired by" the original designers. In some cases the differences are obvious; in other cases, even the most seasoned shopper would have a hard time telling the original from the items sold at this site.

⭐ apeainthepod.com
A Pea In The Pod

877-273-2763
E-mail form on site
Specialty

A Pea In The Pod is an online retailer for maternity clothes whose pitch line is "Maternity Redefined" — and it is. Now you can say *style* even while you're pregnant — if you have the bucks. A Pea In The Pod is where models and television and movie celebrities shop to meet their apparel needs of those nine months and still stay chic. You can find designer labels, classic attire, casual, special occasion, and intimate apparel at this classy site.

athleta.com
Athleta

888-322-5515
E-mail form on site
Athletic

If you're a woman into fitness and sports, then this online retailer offers everything you need from athletic wear to workout wear. In addition to all the products they offer from companies like Patagonia, Marmot, and Adidas, Athleta also designs its own outdoor and running apparel as well as a fitness line. If you're looking for athletic pants in tall and short sizes, this site offers them. When you're done shopping, read the Sports Tips at the site to stay on top of your game.

attivousa.com
Attivo USA

No phone number listed
cs@attivousa.com
Underwear

Attívo USA claims the lowest prices on men's underwear on the Web — guaranteed. The prices are very good for what they sell. And what they sell are unique, fashionable briefs, boxers, boxer briefs, bikinis, and jock straps. The selection isn't great, but what this site offers is not easy to find at your local mall. If you get tired of shopping, try the UnderGames and UnderWordFinds to entertain yourself between shopping excursions.

 Recommended   Price   Selection  Convenience   Service   Security

bananarepublic.com
Banana Republic

888-277-8953
E-mail form on site

Accessories • Career • Casual • Designer • Footwear • Jewelry • Outerwear • Sleepwear • Swimwear

Since its beginning in 1978, Banana Republic has grown into one of the nation's largest apparel retailers. From selling just casual clothing with a safari look, they are now a full-service apparel retailer for both men and women. If you're trying for a casual yet professional look at work, then check out Banana Republic's Wear to Work. The program is a guide to help you dress for work with style. The program includes Wear to Work departments featuring styling tips and the latest trends for both formal and casual work environments.

barenecessities.com
Bare Necessities

877-728-9272
info@barenecessities.com

Footwear • Sleepwear • Underwear

Although the Bare Necessities site looks like an online store for women, it's for men, too. Its selection of undergarments for men is almost as complete as that for women. Shopping is a breeze. Choose your product and then use the drop-down menus to select size, color, and quantity. The site covers all the bases — bra sizing help, fitting tips, gift suggestions, and quick links to brand-name merchandise. Don't forget to check out the sales and specials section for added cost savings.

bebe.com
Bebe

877-232-3777
askus@bebe.com

Accessories • Casual • Footwear • Outerwear • Swimwear

Are you a Bebe woman? The look at Bebe is hip and sophisticated, with just a hint of sexuality. Generally body-conscious women between the ages of 18 and 35 do best at Bebe, although there are no hard and fast rules. The site makes navigation a snap. Use the helpful menu at Bebe to find the item you're shopping for — tops, bottoms, dresses, outerwear, shoes, and so on. There's even a category for sales items. Sign up for Bebe promotions and special offers at the site. You'll be the first to know when you can score a good deal on a hip outfit.

betseyjohnson.com
BetseyJohnson.com

877-464-3293
customerservice@betseyjohnson.com

Casual • Designer • Footwear • Outerwear

A fashion mogul since the 1960s, designer Betsey Johnson designs clothes that meet the fashion needs of the time. Her fellow designers presented her with the Timeless Talent Award in 1999 (created specially for her) to recognize her impact on the fashion world. Now you can purchase Betsey's original designs at BetseyJohnson.com. Shop at her site for a seasonal selection of dresses, coats, tops, and bottoms. Scope out the accessories, such as bags and shoes. The look is definitely distinctive. Be prepared to dig down deep for anything you order; Betsey's original designs do not come cheap!

bigdogs.com
Big Dogs

800-642-3647
internetcustomerservice@bigdogs.com

Athletic • Casual • Outerwear • Swimwear • Underwear

"Run with the big dogs or stay on the porch!" Now that's a store with attitude. That attitude is apparent in the high quality, reasonably priced activewear and accessories for men, women, and children of all ages produced by Big Dogs Sportswear. The comfortable clothes are designed to be worn over and over and feature fun graphics and distinctive colors. If you're new to the brand, start with some boxer shorts or a T-shirt. You'll be back for more!

★ bigtalldirect.com
BigTallDirect.com

800-214-9686
customerservice@bigtalldirect.com

Specialty

With over 13,000 big and tall products for men in its database, BigTallDirect.com is definitely worth a look. Many of the top brands are offered at this site, such as Axis, Columbia, Cutter & Buck, Foxfire, Greg Norman, Levi's, Nautica, Polo Jeans, Savane, Tommy Hilfiger, and Wrangler. There's no skimping on the selection either. The site offers dress shirts, Hawaiian shirts, jackets, knit and sport shirts, sweaters, and T-shirts. Slacks, jeans, and shorts are also available in dress or athletic wear. They also carry a nice selection of underwear, neckties, belts, and other accessories for the bigger guy.

 Recommended   Price   Selection   Convenience   Service   Security

birkenstockexpress.com
Birkenstock Express

800-451-1459
E-mail form on site

Footwear

If you have the bucks, they have the sandals, the clogs, and the shoes. Birkenstock created a curved shoe that reflects the true shape of the human foot. The shoe started as a healthy alternative to street shoes and soon became the choice of the 1960s crowd. Today, Birkenstock offers more than 400 styles of sandals, clogs, and shoes that are available in a wide range of materials, colors, and sizes. You can buy from the entire line today at their online store.

bluenile.com
Blue Nile

800-242-2728
service@bluenile.com

Jewelry • Watches

At Blue Nile, you can find education and guidance — two things needed to make your jewelry shopping easy and successful. Learn the four Cs of buying a diamond — Cut, Clarity, Color, and Carat. Blue Nile diamond and jewelry consultants have years of experience, and they don't work on commission. They are ready to answer all your questions. You can even build your own engagement ring. They offer over 20,000 round diamonds that they can set in a ring ranging in price from under $400 to (gulp!) over $180,000. They also sell pearls, gemstones, and other fine jewelry.

★ bridesave.com
BrideSave.com

800-321-4696
president@bridesave.com

Specialty

Looking for wedding gowns? Lots of wedding gowns? Then BrideSave.com is the place for you. Not only can you find over 2,500 wedding gowns to choose from, but BrideSave.com is also the world's leading online wedding apparel destination. Its goal is to provide complete one-stop shopping for the bride-to-be by striving to provide the most current selection, the most complete size range, the best prices, and the largest variety of styles. Take a minute to check out the wedding tips and honeymoon travel service too.

brooksbrothers.com
Brooks Brothers

800-274-1815
E-mail form on site

Career • Footwear • Formal • Outerwear • Specialty • Underwear

Rank has its privileges, and this store is one the top-ranking establishments in the retail clothing industry. They've been around long enough to earn their rank, since 1818, in fact. Those who have worn their high-class threads include U.S. presidents, famous actors, and explorers. Whether you're at the country club or a formal affair; man, woman or child; or big or tall; Brooks Brothers has the look for you. Match up those qualities with their service and convenience, and you can't go wrong buying from this online store.

bss.com
Batik Shirt Shop

603-934-2358
rkell@bss.com

Casual

In some fashion quarters, T-shirts get a bad rap. They're not really seen as "stylish." But that's not true for all T-shirts. Take the batik T-shirt. The word batik (pronounced "ba-teek") is Indonesian and means "wax writing." The stylish T-shirts this online retailer offers will go with any "dressy-casual" outfit. What else can these designs be but artwear: the twin Celtic fairies intertwined in a batik diamond design, or a not-so-fierce dragon resting on a Celtic knot. The prices are very reasonable for a work of art.

★ buy4lesstuxedo.com
Buy4lessTuxedo.com

888-660-3342
E-mail form on site

Accessories • Formal

I don't know about you, but I've always wondered whether it was right to wear a cummerbund and vest simultaneously. Also, which end of the cummerbund points up? These questions and more about wearing a tuxedo are answered for you in Buy4lessTuxedo.com's FAQ/Tuxedo 101. But information is not all you get here. You also can buy some of the finest tuxedos from brand-name designers at discount prices. Its product search engine is one of the best I've seen. You can search by color, style, lapel, buttons, fabric, price, and designer at the same time — with a lowest price guarantee.

 Recommended　 Price　 Selection　 Convenience　 Service　Security

cafeshops.com/heatherart
Heather Art

877-809-1659
E-mail form on site

Casual

Meet Heather, a graphic designer who has accumulated a fair amount of artwork over the years, including digital, photographic, and mixed media such as acrylic paintings, watercolors, and drawings — all created by her. She puts that art on some high-quality T-shirts. Space Dude, Guitar Dude, and Goaty Goats are just a few of her off-center graphics and pictures that appear on her T-shirts and make them unique. Shop here for Heather's quirky art on shirts, posters, prints, and more.

casualmale.com
Casual Male

800-767-0319
info@casualmale.com

Accessories • Career • Casual • Footwear • Outerwear • Specialty • Underwear

Finding not only the right fit, but also clothing that's stylish and doesn't break your wallet can be hard for larger men. Casual Male does both. They offer their own line of quality clothing, and they also sell name brands such as Dockers, Levi's, Geoffrey Beene, Ocean Pacific, Polo Jeans Co., New Balance, Sketchers, and Deer Stags for the big or tall man.

chadwicks.com
Chadwick's

800-677-0340
E-mail form on site

Accessories • Athletic • Career • Casual • Designer • Footwear • Outerwear • Specialty • Swimwear

Looking for department store clothes for women at reduced prices? Chadwick's is your site! An offshoot of the popular Chadwick's of Boston catalog, this site offers hundreds of products at savings of 20–50 percent off what you'd expect to pay in the mall. Best of all, the variety is extensive. The site offers a wide range of sizes and styles and also carries matching accessories. Brides can find beautiful wedding gowns at the online bridal boutique. Stylish maternity wear is available too. Visit the clearance center to save an additional 70 percent over already reduced prices.

chantelrenee.com
Chantel Renee

516-695-0788
E-mail form on site

Specialty

Chantel Renee makes it fun to be pregnant! The clothes here are kicky and fun, and showcase moms-to-be. Clothes are built for comfort as well as looks, with soft, non-binding belly bands. The items here are arranged by season, making it easy to coordinate an entire pregnancy in a few shopping trips. Within each season, items are coordinated by color. It's easy to pair pants and sweaters in Ravishing Red, for example. Check out the fun stuff section for laughs and giggles just for pregnant women. If you're unhappy with your purchase, it can be returned or exchanged for a new item.

cheaptux.com
CheapTux.com

888-245-0148
E-mail form on site

Accessories • Formal

CheapTux.com offers tuxedos, men's formal wear, tuxedo shirts, and more for all occasions including tuxedos for wedding and prom tuxedos. In a breezy style guaranteed to make you smile, the site explains its philosophy: "A tuxedo is nothing more than a black suit." Accordingly, the formal clothing at this site is priced reasonably. You can get a complete tuxedo package — a jacket, trousers, shirt, cummerbund, and tie — starting as low as $139.95 with free shipping. If you're looking for something more upscale, you'll find designer tuxedos from Neil Allyn, Geoffrey Beene, and Fumagalli at discounted prices. Read the Q & A's at the site for some lessons in formal etiquette.

coolibar.com
Coolibar

800-926-6509
service@coolibar.com

Accessories • Casual • Specialty • Swimwear

The name *Coolibar* comes from a eucalyptus tree found in the harsh Australian outback, and like the tree, Coolibar's UV protection clothing provides protection from the sun's damaging ultraviolet rays. This online retailer offers the only sun-protective clothing, hats, and swimwear recommended by the Skin Cancer Foundation. So, if you're tired of applying and reapplying sunscreen when you go outside, consider Coolibar's UV protection clothing. It's stylish and costs little more than regular clothing.

 Recommended   Price   Selection   Convenience   Service   Security

coyotees.com
Coyote Graphics

800-791-2799
mike@coyotees.com

Casual

Tired of the same old T-shirts, with sports team logos or rude sayings emblazoned on the front? Coyote Graphics creates shirts that advertise the wonders of nature. Artist and nature lover Michael Boardman creatively designs each of the site's colorful and educational wildlife garments. He travels the world to study and draw animals in their own natural environments. The artwork on shirts by Coyote Graphics has been used fundraising for wildlife. Pricing is reasonable for these high quality cotton shirts. Go ahead and make a "real" fashion statement and order a shirt (or two) from this site.

★ cufflinks.com
Cufflinks.com

877-283-3565
info@cufflinks.com

Accessories

When you're getting dressed up, you need some classy cufflinks to go with that shirt with the French cuffs. Cufflinks.com sells a wide selection of cuffs for every occasion. They offer cufflinks from David Donahue, Nancy and Rise, Abba, Kenneth Cole, and many other top designers. Categories include cufflinks for weddings, cufflinks with precious and semi-precious stones, sport cufflinks, career, and hobby- and animal-related cufflinks, just to name a few. They also offer the cool and unique, such as the watch cufflink and the compass cufflink.

★ cyberswim.com
CyberSwim

800-291-2943
service@cyberswim.com

Swimwear

Women who want to look "ten pounds lighter in ten seconds" can slip into one of CyberSwim's suits. Its swimwear — called the MiracleSuit — uses a patented blend of fabric that delivers three times the holding power of ordinary swimsuits. You get maximum control, without sacrificing comfort. Added to that, CyberSwim has a great selection of swimsuits to satisfy any woman's taste. You can find styles and sizes to flatter every figure. You can even search by figure-enhancing swimsuit features, from waist-minimizing designs to leg-elongating styles.

dadshats.com
Dad's Hats.com

888-323-7428
service@dadshats.com

Accessories

You might think that these days wearing hats is out of style. But if you are one of those men who think a snappy hat tops off a classy fashion statement, then Dad's has your hat. This site sells the finest selection and quality of classic and contemporary men's hats and caps. The site is organized well for finding the hat that you want. In addition to shopping by brand and style, you can shop by season, which is a plus. Have you seen the latest Kangol caps? Kangol hats and caps are enjoying a new popularity these days, thanks to a rapper named LL Cool J. Read the story at the site of how he revitalized the Kangol brand back in 1984, and then order one of these nifty hats for yourself.

danier.com
Danier Leather

877-932-6437
comments@danier.com

Accessories • Casual • Outerwear • Specialty

Got leather? Danier Leather does. Lots of it. Danier can offer customers exceptional value in addition to outstanding quality because there's never a middleman to pay. Don't know a lot about the care of your leather product? No problem. Danier's online cleaning guide tells you how best to care for your leather or suede garment using its cleaning products. And get this: If you have a question that's not answered there, you can ask the online customer service expert.

denimexpress.com
Denim Express

866-438-3364
customerservice@denimexpress.com

Casual • Specialty

Look at the wide selection of brands that Denim Express sells, and you know they have to have your jeans. No fancy story here, or fancy site for that matter. Just the straight scoop on what you need to know to order your brand-name pair of jeans. Simply choose a brand, a style or fit, pick your size from the drop-down menu, select a color, and you're done. In just a matter of days, you'll be walking around in those new jeans knowing you did it without the hassle of visiting the mall.

 Recommended   Price   Selection   Convenience   Service   Security

⭐ designeroutlet.com
Designer Outlet

800-923-9915
doutlet@aol.com

Accessories • Casual • Designer • Footwear • Jewelry • Outerwear • Specialty

When you hear overstock, you think bargain. That's what you get at the Designer Outlet. This site was created by female fashion industry executives to provide you with a new way to shop for designer overstocks for men, women, toddlers, and children. DesignerOutlet.com offers the finest quality overstock goods — items like watches, scarves, clothing, and more — from top designers and manufacturers at greatly reduced prices. They do not sell any irregular or damaged merchandise. A 100 percent satisfaction guarantee, gift certificates, designer labels, international shipping, and plus sizes for women make this online retailer a find for the bargain hunter.

⭐ diamondsonweb.com
Diamonds on the Web

888-968-8810
E-mail form on site

Jewelry

Another diamond store? Yes, but Diamonds on the Web is different. Here's the deal. You buy a loose diamond at discounted prices. Why? This company buys all its diamonds directly from the source, so no additional third-party fees are involved. Then you select a setting for your diamond. The setting service is free. But these diamonds are not ordinary. They're laser-inscribed for your protection, which means the diamonds you buy are all graded by the GIA, EGL, or AGS, and the certificate number is laser inscribed on the girdle of the diamond. You can upgrade your diamond at any time, and a credit will be applied for the full amount you paid, for the lifetime of the diamond. Try to do that with your new car.

drjays.com
Dr.Jay's.com
888-437-5297
service@drjays.com

Casual • Footwear • Outerwear • Specialty • Underwear

The Dr. Jay's legacy began in 1975 with the opening of its first store in the South Bronx section of New York. Since that time, Dr. Jay's has been the name to turn to for urban fashion. Shop at Dr.Jay's.com for the hip looks seen on rappers and rockers. Brands like Avirex, Hustler, and Kangol lead the way for men, while women can find fashions by Fila, J.Lo, and Playboy. Boutique NYC sizzles with the hottest looks on the street. Check out the photos of people just like you and me dressed in Dr. Jay's fashions, and fit yourself with a new set of threads.

★ ebags.com
eBags.com
800-820-6126
E-mail form on site

Accessories

In the 1960s, people used to say, "What's your bag?" Well, whatever it is, eBags has it. It sells all kinds of bags. In fact, eBags is the world's largest online retailer of bags and accessories. It offers handbags, luggage, laptop cases, backpacks, duffle bags, and urban gear such as music packs. You can shop by these categories or by the amount of money you want to spend. If you find a better price for your chosen bag, eBags will match that price with its 110 percent guarantee. Groovy!

ecowool.com
Ecowool
64-9-425-7449
E-mail form on site

Casual • Footwear • Outerwear

Have you ever heard of ecowool? From New Zealand, products made from this miracle wool fiber are thermal, fire-retardant, and easy care. More importantly, because they're made from New Zealand merino wool, the products made of ecowool provide absolute comfort in all four seasons and are soft, light, and luxurious. Shop at ecowool for women's boots, coats, and jackets. Ecowool provides an on-site exchange rate calculator and offers free worldwide shipping and a no quibble 100 percent satisfaction guarantee. Definitely worth a look.

 Recommended   Price   Selection    Convenience   Service   Security

epicmenswear.com
Epic Menswear

203-389-7514
emenswear@snet.net

Casual • Career • Outerwear

Choosing a well-made pair of trousers is like money in the bank. It improves your equity! That's Epic's view on the clothing it sells for the big and tall man. Epic is committed to making the large and extra-large man look good. Its selection is chosen for quality, fit, and styling, all the way through to waist size 70 inches. Epic guarantees your satisfaction 100 percent. It also offers a new line of T-shirts that keep you cool, dry, and odor-free. That's "big" news for any man.

europacouture.com
EuropaCouture.com

412-973-1311
service@europacouture.com

Accessories • Casual • Footwear • Formal • Outerwear • Sleepwear

Haute couture — you know it when you see it. You'll see it at EuropaCouture.com, and at discount prices. EuropaCouture.com offers several categories of apparel, including dresses, suits, formals, coats, and furs. You can also find handbags, shoes, lingerie, and accessories, all to meet your desire for upscale fashion. While at this site, check out Club Europa. It's free to join, and you can earn rebate certificates on the products you buy from EuropaCouture.com.

★ exofficio.com
Ex Officio

800-644-7303
info@exofficio.com

Casual • Specialty

If you're getting bugged by bugs, then Ex Officio offers a solution. This online retailer sells a unique line of apparel called BUZZ OFF Insect Shield Insect Repellent Apparel. Its clothing has proven to be extremely effective against mosquitoes, ticks, and other annoying and potentially disease-carrying insects. A complete outfit of BUZZ OFF apparel will enable you to enjoy the outdoors without the nuisance of applying nasty insect-repellent lotions and sprays. You'll repel more than insects. They've also included 30+ UV sun protection in this apparel.

fabric8.com
Fabric8
888-554-4321
orders@fabric8.com

Accessories • Casual • Outerwear

Looking for an online boutique that features really exciting-looking clothes? You've come to the right place! Fabric8 has been called "The Best Way To Shop SF Without Leaving Home." Its boutique features "unique, quality goods by urban independent designers." The clothing on this site is funky, urban, "street chic" for him and her. The clothing is carefully selected from North American companies. You get free shipping when ordering three or more items. The site ships internationally.

fanwear.com
Fanwear
877-326-9327
fanwear2@aol.com

Athletic • Casual • Outerwear

If you're a sports fan, you love to show your team's colors. Fanwear can fix you right up. It's a snap to find your favorite sports team and buy apparel that shows your support of it. Fanwear sells only officially licensed NFL, NHL, NBA, and MLB jerseys, hats, jackets, T-shirts, and sweatshirts for adults and kids. If you have the team, this site has the apparel. Fanwear will match any competitor's prices. Read all the details and purchase with confidence.

fashiondig.com
Fashion Dig
866-327-4344
custservice@fashiondig.com

Accessories • Casual • Footwear • Outerwear • Sleepwear

Fashion Dig offers a shopping experience you don't have everyday. Shop for women's and men's vintage apparel by the decade! Yep, that's right, you can shop through the years for apparel starting at the turn of the century to the present — and shop for a wide variety of apparel categories to boot. Check out The Fashion Dig Style Galleries while you're there. They feature the looks of twentieth-century style with archival images and interesting facts about the history of fashion.

 Recommended   Price   Selection   Convenience   Service   Security

fitigues.com
Fitigues.com
800-235-9005
catalog@fitigues.com
Casual

Fitigues offers clothing that's comfortable and has style: These are clothes you can live in. If you're looking for casual clothes for working out and hanging out, then shop at this site. You can shop for men's, women's, and kid's casual apparel in the standard online shopping manner, or you can shop its virtual catalog by "thumbing" your way through the pages, and, if you see something you like, placing it in your shopping cart for purchase.

★ fitmaternity.com
Fit Maternity & Beyond
888-961-9100
info@fitmaternity.com
Specialty

Fit Maternity is on a mission: to help pregnant woman enjoy exercising with the proper fitness maternity wear. Almost every study relating to pregnancy and exercise concludes that exercise is not only safe during pregnancy but also healthy for both mother and child. You won't find trendy, stylish clothing at Fit Maternity & Beyond, but what you will find is solid, comfortable clothing to help women "exercise at whatever level they feel comfortable during and after their pregnancy." This site offers a wide selection of fitness clothing, underwear, swimsuits, and maternity aids.

flipfloptrunkshow.com
FlipFlopTrunkShow.com
888-544-7404
guru@flipfloptrunkshow.com
Footwear

Question: Do you know what a thong, slide, or mule is in women's footwear? If not, FlipFlopTrunkShow will quickly educate you. (Answer: different styles of sandals). FlipFlopTrunkShow is serious about sandals. This company believes that thongs, slides, and mules are not just for summer anymore and can be worn with a bathing suit or an evening gown. Its sandals are both cute, original, and yes, always stylish. Its designer shop matches the great look of its sandals with handbags, belts, and T-shirts. This site is a fun place to shop.

florsheim.com
Florsheim

800-843-7463
customer.service@florsheim.com

Accessories • Footwear • Formal

Florsheim has been selling men's shoes since 1892. The company was formed around the idea of producing exceptional men's shoes, and that ideal is still very much in evidence today. You can search and shop its proprietary designs in all categories of shoes — dress, refined casual, casual, tuxedo, and boots. You can also search its inventory by size or keyword. Besides its own line of shoes, Florsheim sells shoes from Imperial, FLS, and Comfortech — and the stylish Nunn Bush line. Remember to "polish off" your purchase with genuine Florsheim accessories.

Fossil.com
Fossil

866-379-2824
E-mail form on site

Accessories • Casual • Eyewear • Outerwear •Watches

The name Fossil may bring ancient artifacts to mind, but the products this company sells are very "today." For example, an exciting hi-tech watch called the Fossil WristNet combines with the MSN Direct service, to deliver everything from the weather to your next appointment, tailored to your interests and location, all at a glance of your wrist. (See the site for complete details.) Of course, you can choose from the other more mundane category of watches, too. Fossil has also become a source for casual apparel, jackets, sunglasses, and accessories like wallets, belts, and bags for men and women.

freshpair.com
Fresh Pair

866-373-7472
customercare@freshpair.com

Footwear • Sleepwear • Specialty • Underwear

Did you know that everywhere you look the fashion-aware are sporting hot lingerie as their day-to-day (or evening) wear? And that nothing is sexier than the hot look of chemise with jeans? You can find out these facts and more than just a fresh pair of undies at Fresh Pair. Online help and expert advice on what size to pick, what to wear, and insights into styles and trends make this retailer a first stop to shop for your head-to-toe brand-name underwear. Fresh Pair didn't forget the sleepwear and undergarments for big and tall men and full-figured women, either.

 Recommended   Price   Selection   Convenience   Service Security

gap.com
The Gap

888-906-1104
E-mail form on site

Accessories • Casual • Footwear • Outerwear • Specialty • Underwear

Can you imagine life without The Gap? The site carries all the great styles and fashions you can find at your local Gap store. The merchandise at the site is seasonal and is available for men, women, girls, boys, and babies. Search the site by department or enter a keyword to go directly to the item you want. Use the site to track the balance on Gap gift cards you've received, or order a gift card for someone else. The Gap offers simple style and comfort for all members of the family.

gemplers.com
Gempler's

800-382-8473
customerservice@gemplers.com

Specialty

The Internet probably isn't the first place you turn for work clothes, but that's because you don't know about Gempler's. You'll find a comprehensive collection of apparel for folks who work out-of-doors, including hats, gloves, boots, a complete line of coveralls, brand name coveralls, shirts, jeans, and more. Because the clothes here are the "real deal," they're built to last and will stand up to years of hard wear. While you're shopping, take some time to read about the other products sold by Gempler's. You'll learn a lot about farming and turn management, and may be able to apply what you've learned to caring for your lawn or garden.

guess.com
GUESS.com

877-444-8377
E-mail form on site

Accessories • Athletic • Casual • Designer • Footwear • Jewelry • Watches

GUESS is one of the most recognizable brands in the world. It came to prominence in the 1970s when the Marciano brothers took previously utilitarian denim jeans and raised them to the level of a fashion statement. The GUESS site remains true to its roots with fashionable denim for men, women, and children. It also reflects the company's broader tastes with tops, accessories, watches, and shoes. Returns? Online purchases can be returned at GUESS retail stores. GUESS.com is both fashionable and convenient.

⭐ hatsinthebelfry.com
Hats In the Belfry

888-999-4287
hats@hatsinthebelfry.com

Accessories

Hats should be fun, and not just for dressy occasions or to keep the sun off your head. This online retailer, Hats In the Belfry, puts the fun back into wearing hats. It sells all kinds of men's hats, ladies' hats, caps and berets, seasonal hats, custom hats, crazy hats, funny Hats, Indiana Jones hats, Kangol caps, Stetson hats, Kaminski hats, and Tilley hats and caps. It even sells Easter hats, fall and winter hats — I can go on and on but you get the idea. The site even supplies a size chart for that perfect fit. Hats off, I say!

hatxpress.com
HatXpress.com

519-654-2719
info@hatxpress.com

Accessories

If it's the season to wear a hat, HatXpress has the hat for you. This online store is organized by men and ladies' hats by season (Spring and Fall). It carries men's dress and ladies' Chanterelle hats, and men's and ladies' sport and leisure hats. HatXpress.com remembers the kids, too. The site has a fun selection of hats with an attitude, like the Nasty, Creeper, Scrub, Hheader, and Rock Me hats. Finally, an extensive hat guide and sizing chart are on the site to help you pick out the right style and size hat for you.

hicksfurs.com
Hicks Furs

905-545-3911
sherrie@hicksfurs.com

Accessories • Formal • Outerwear

Fur fashions come and go, and if you have an old fur coat taking up space in your closet, why not refurbish it? Hicks Furs can restyle your old fur coat. This company specializes in recycling old fur coats into fashionable new fur coats, fur-lined trench coats, jackets, sweaters and vests, heirloom teddy bears, pillows, purses, hats, massage mitts, and more. The site offers an online catalog, but no online ordering, so you have to call to place your order and get options for shipping.

 Recommended   Price   Selection   Convenience   Service 🔒 Security

hipundies.com
HipUndies.com

866-625-2999
hipservice@hipundies.com

Underwear

Though a bit pricey, HipUndies.com's underwear for women is, indeed, hip. As the saying goes, you get what you pay for. The site offers a great collection of lingerie from Cosabella, Eberjey, Hanky Panky, Samantha Chang, and more. It also carries fun cotton pajamas from Nick & Nora, The Cat's Pajamas (known for their sushi pajamas), and Bedhead PJs. Need to send a gift? HipUndies.com has a great selection — you'll find camisoles, slippers, and pajamas. Send a heated microwaveable herbal aromatherapy neck wrap shaped like a dog or cat to help a friend relieve some stress.

★ hksilk.com
Hong Kong Silk Company

800-525-2950
care@hksilk.com

Accessories • Sleepwear • Underwear

Mmm, the feel of silk. Now you can purchase that feel online at — where else — the Hong Kong Silk Company. (Actually, the company is not in Hong Kong, but outside of Philadelphia!) This company is a direct importer and wholesaler of fine silks from Asia. It claims that its efficient business model allows it to pass the savings on to you. It sells silk garments, including silk pajamas, robes, briefs, and boxers for men and panties and thongs for women. The company also sells beautiful silk scarves for both sexes. What's intriguing about the store, however, is the price of the products — they are very affordable.

hollisterco.com
Hollister Co.

866-681-3116
clubcali@hollisterco.com

Accessories • Athletic • Casual • Footwear • Swimwear • Underwear

This site transports you to Southern California and its youth focused beach culture. Welcome to Club Cali, where the surf's always up, the sun always shines, and people look good in their Hollister clothes. Shop here for the double entendre T-shirts Hollister is famous for (called graphic T's), as well as polo shirts, cargo shorts, pants, and accessories like bags and shoes. If you enjoy the music playing at the site, don't worry. It's for sale too, on a CD. If only real life could be as uncomplicated as life at Club Cali.

hushpuppies.com
Hush Puppies

800-545-2425
E-mail form on site

Footwear

Shop at this site for casual shoes from Hush Puppies. You'll find fun, comfortable styles that take the wearer from work to weekends. Navigation is a breeze at the Hush Puppies site. Use the helpful menu to find the category you're shopping for — men, women, kids, or slippers. When you see a shoe you like, use the convenient zoom and pan feature to view the shoe from all dimensions. (Really neat!) Make a great deal on some comfy Hush Puppies at the online Outlet Store.

internationalmale.com
International Male

800-293-9333
service@internationalmale.com

Accessories • Career • Casual • Footwear • Outerwear • Underwear

Many years ago, more than I like to count, I saw my first International Male catalog. I knew this company was going places. Now imitated, it created distinctive designs that just say "cool." International Male's clothing for men only is unique and designed to suit you whether your look is straightlaced and buttoned-down or exciting and eclectic. International Male provides great ways to save to loyal customers with its IM Advantage and IM Advantage Gold Clubs. Each offers free shipping and other perks. Find out which club is right for you at the site.

★ italianbraceletcharms.com
Italian Bracelet Charms

401-398-0972
admin@italianbraceletcharms.com

Accessories

Italian charm bracelets are the latest fashion fad to our shores. These bracelets and charms are a hit with the younger female set, and you can find them in malls throughout the country. This online retailer, Italian Bracelet Charms, does an excellent job providing a wide selection of Italian bracelets at reasonable prices. Besides the bracelets and charms, the site provides a sizing chart, advice on caring for and cleaning your charms, and a three-step, easy-to-use process to help you chose and buy your charm bracelet — select, add, and assemble. Simple.

 Recommended   Price   Selection   Convenience   Service   Security

jcrew.com
J. Crew

800-562-0258
service@jcrew.com

Accessories • Athletic • Career • Casual • Footwear • Outerwear • Swimwear • Underwear

J. Crew presents classic designs with modern attitude for men and women. You can find chinos and seersucker men's pants or a simple basic black silk faille dress. There are also cargo shorts and low rise jeans. Men's shirts and women's tops reflect a unique mix of modern and traditional styling that works perfectly. This is just the site for the traditionalist to modernize his or her wardrobe. It can also be the site where the young person can graduate to some grown-up fashion without losing a sense of youthful exuberance.

jewelswarehouse.com
Jewels Warehouse

877-444-5393
sales@jewelswarehouse.com

Jewelry

Having a site organized to help you shop in different ways is always a plus. Jewels Warehouse lets you shop by products, category, or price — or you can use the keyword site search engine to find something that you don't readily see available. You naturally have lots of questions when buying expensive jewelry, so during working hours a live representative is available to speak with online. If that isn't enough, you can use an online Learning Center to learn how to buy a diamond. Just remember the four Cs — Cut, Carat, Clarity, and Color.

justmysize.com
Just My Size

800-261-5902
E-mail form on site

Athletic • Footwear • Sleepwear • Swimwear • Underwear

Finding good-fitting undergarments isn't always easy for full-figured women. That's why Just My Size is a lifesaver. This site has your size, from X to 6X and 14W to 40W. These folks claim to be specialists in plus-size fashions — in apparel, intimates, and hosiery — and understand your needs and wants. The bras, panties, shapewear, sleepwear, workout wear, and swimwear are tastefully presented. Finding your size is a snap using their pull-down menus on each product page.

know-him.com
Know Him

No phone listed
E-mail form on site

Athletic • Casual

Holy Moses — a shopping sight for Christian casual apparel! The Know Him company's goal is to reach the Christian community with sportswear that leaves an impression of quality, uniqueness, and fashion while spreading the good news of Jesus Christ. You have to admit, this site offers some unique T-shirts and sweatshirts for the young Christian set that you won't find at more secular stores. So if you like to wear your heart, and faith, on your T-shirts, then this shopping site is for you.

landsend.com
Lands' End

800-963-4816
E-mail form on site

Athletic • Career • Casual • Footwear • Outerwear • Sleepwear • Swimwear

Lands' End started out selling racing sailboat equipment, duffle bags, rain suits, sweaters, and other clothing. It has evolved into a premier casual clothing store for men, women, and kids (sailboat equipment no longer carried). As a direct merchant, Lands' End works directly with mills and manufacturers, eliminating the markups of middlemen and thus passing the savings on to you. The company's selection is far and wide, and if you have a question, you can use its excellent live customer service.

leathergoodsconnection.com
Leather Goods Connection

706-776-9171
info@leathergoodsconnection.com

Accessories

Remember those leather shops you visited where the smell emanating throughout the store perked up your nose? You can get the same feeling at Leather Goods Connection. If you're looking for quality, soft, custom-made designer leather and willing to pay the price, then this online retailer has your bag. The goods sold here are custom-crafted one at a time. You can find handbags, backpacks, handmade harness leather belts, fanny packs, men's and women's calf skin leather wallets, Italian leather wallets, or whatever custom-made leather accessories you have been looking for and couldn't find elsewhere.

 Recommended   Price   Selection   Convenience   Service   Security

⭐ legweardirect.com
LegwearDirect.com

877-534-3472
customerservice@legweardirect.com

Footwear

What if you could buy the very same brand-name hosiery sold under designer labels in the finest department stores and lingerie shops around the country for about half the price? Well, LegwearDirect.com manufactures many of the high-quality tights, socks, and other fashion legwear sold under designer labels in department stores. These items are the same high quality, the same height of style, but carry the LegwearDirect.com label instead. Because you're not paying to see a designer label, at LegwearDirect.com you'll pay less — direct from the manufacturer.

⭐ llbean.com
L.L. Bean

800-441-5713
E-mail form on site

Accessories • Casual • Footwear • Outerwear • Swimwear

Back in 1912, Leon Leonwood (L.L.) Bean opened his first, small retail store. Of course, you and I know that establishment as the retail giant L.L. Bean. Although the face of the company has changed over the years, its unwavering commitment to quality and customer satisfaction continues to make it a favorite with loyal customers. Shops online for casual clothing, active wear, outerwear, footwear and accessories for men, women, and children. The apparel is well made and backed by L.L. Bean's 100% guarantee. If you're not satisfied with your purchase, return it for a complete refund. You'll also find outdoor gear and equipment and luggage and travel items for sale at the site.

maidenform.com
Maidenform

888-888-9328
orders@maidenform.com

Underwear

In the words of Maidenform, "it all starts with a good foundation." You couldn't ask for a better retailer site to build that foundation. Maidenform has a long reputation for quality and price, and it shows on its site. One of the better values of the site is the "What to wear" section. Use this handy guide to pick the ideal undergarment for anything you wear. When you're wearing the right thing underneath, your clothes are bound to look and feel better. You can use a "Fit yourself" size form to help you select the most comfortable bra for you.

⭐ makingitbigonline.com
Making It Big

877-644-1995
customerservice@bigwomen.com

Athletic • Casual • Career • Footwear • Swimwear • Underwear

If you can't find your size at other women's plus-size sites, then try Making It Big. It sells women's blouses and shirts, dresses and skirts, activewear and swimwear, pants and shorts, jackets and ensembles, and prints — and you can have most in custom colors. Items that feature their color wheel are available for custom dyeing so you can have both your size and color. If you don't know your correct size, you can call them. They'll help you with that, too.

⭐ maternitymall.com
Maternity Mall

800-466-6223
E-mail form on site

Specialty

If you're looking for a wide selection of maternity clothes for just about any occasion and use, then Maternity Mall has it all. Dresses, shirts, skirts, shorts, tops, bottoms, career, sleepwear, swimwear — it's all here for the women with child. An added plus to this site is the encyclopedic information on pregnancy and infant care. They offer expert advice and maternity tools, including articles that offer information on pregnancy, tracking your pregnancy, and fetal development week by week. This is a top-notch site for apparel and information.

menswearhouse.com
Men's Wearhouse

877-986-9669
E-mail form on site

Accessories • Career • Casual • Designer • Footwear • Formal • Outerwear • Specialty

"You'll love the way you look!" That's the promise of the Men's Wearhouse. This company has you covered from head to toe. You'll find dress suits, shoes, slacks, accessories, and business casual. The Men's Wearhouse compensated for trend towards the less formal workplace with its line of business casual clothes that were comfortable but still professional. Read the articles on dressing right, like "Dress for Success," "Casual Know-How," and "How to Tie a Tie" for important information that can help you look like a million bucks.

 Recommended Price Selection Convenience Service Security

napoleonstailor.com
Napoleon's Tailor

800-233-9522
info@napoleonstailor.com

Career • Casual • Formal • Outerwear • Underwear

Napoleon's Tailor carries a full line of casual and dress wear for men 5'8" or under. The clothes here are designed to give shorter men the same silhouette and proportionate fit that taller men find with their clothing. Trousers can be hemmed and sleeves can be rolled up, but the look is never right. Regular-sized sweaters that come down past the hips on a shorter man look plain silly! That's why buying clothes designed to fit make sense. The site sells shirts, jackets, pants, and outerwear. Prices are reasonable and the service is great.

nordstrom.com
Nordstrom

888-282-6060
E-mail form on site

Accessories • Athletic • Career • Casual • Footwear • Outerwear • Sleepwear • Swimwear

You can either get rich finding the gold or selling the picks and shovels. When John W. Nordstrom went to find his fortune in the Alaskan Gold Rush, he made it selling the picks and shovels. He translated that success into the retail emporium we know as Nordstrom. Today Nordstrom is one of the best-known names in apparel. Instead of categorizing departments by merchandise, Nordstrom created fashion departments that fit individuals' lifestyles. The fashion specialty chain offers renowned services, generous size ranges, and a selection of the finest apparel, shoes, and accessories for the entire family.

norwaysweaters.com
Norway Sweaters

905-545-3911
sales2004@norwaysweaters.com

Casual

Here's an MBA research project that worked. Norway Sweaters, run by two former MBA classmates, sells the finest quality traditional Norwegian wool ski sweaters for men and women. Here's the best part: You don't have to go to Norway to get them. The sweaters are as traditional as you can get. Each sweater has original Norwegian designs, including the pewter clasps. Norway Sweaters offers a full money-back guarantee, and the company is based in the U.S. for easy shipping and returns. These sweaters are original designs, so be prepared to pay the price.

⭐ oddballshoe.com
Oddball Shoe Company
800-884-4046
oddball@oddballshoe.com

Footwear

What's so odd about this retailer is the shoe sizes it offers. The Oddball Shoe Company specializes in big shoes for big feet — large size shoes, boots, and sandals starting from men's size 12 and going up — way up! It gets even better. Right on the front page you can search for your odd-sized shoe by style, color, size, width, or by brand. Like many footwear sites, this one offers a size chart to help you decide on your shoe, and if you have any friends with big feet, you can buy gift certificates, as well. This is a unique store for unique customers — but sorry, all the shoes are for men only.

oldnavy.com
Old Navy
800-653-6289
E-mail form on site

Accessories • Athletic • Casual • Footwear • Outerwear • Sleepwear • Specialty • Swimwear • Underwear

The tabs across the top of Old Navy's homepage say it all. Clothing for men, women, boys, girls, baby boys, baby girls, and maternity. This store is a family affair at family prices. The clothing is inexpensive, simple, trendy, and casual. You can mix and match tops and bottoms with ease and find outerwear to match. Another nice touch is the ability to view and shop right from the latest ad. Read the ad and then shop the site. Shopping here is easy and fast, and you'll be ready for more sooner than you think.

onehanesplace.com
OneHanesPlace
800-671-1674
E-mail form on site

Footwear • Specialty • Underwear

You're bound to leave One Hanes Place with a full shopping cart. The site carries a full line of women's underwear, sleepwear, and clothing by manufacturers like Hanes, Playtex, and Bali. If you haven't shopped at this site before, make sure you click the link for first-time visitors before you order. You'll get a sense of how the site is arranged and how to order. Although OneHanesPlace caters primarily to women, check out the underwear and clothing for men and kids too. Add hosiery to your order. Prices are great and the more you buy, the more you save.

⭐ Recommended $ Price   Selection   🎁 Convenience   😊 Service   🔒 Security

★ onlineshoes.com
Onlineshoes.com

888-786-3141
customerservice@onlineshoes.com

Footwear

Offering over 45 brands, expert customer service, and a deep selection of sizes and widths for both men and women, Onlineshoes.com is the place to start your shoe shopping excursion. Its line of shoes offers shoes for all purposes — athletic, walking, dress, casual, outdoor shoes, boots, sandals, slippers, and industrial. The site has ongoing sales on brand footwear of 20–30 percent off. Free shipping sweetens the deal. Sign up for Onlineshoes.com Shoe Mail and receive e-mail notification of upcoming sales and promotions.

★ organic-clothing.com
Feeling Goods

877-349-2102
sales@feeling-goods.com

Specialty

Feeling Goods is an organic department store. Shop at Feeling Goods for clothes that are free of toxins, pesticides, and poisons. If you consider that approximately one-third of a pound of chemicals were used for every conventional cotton T-shirt that's in your wardrobe right now, you'll see why organic clothing may be a better alternative! The site carries men's shirts, pants, shorts, and underwear and women's jackets, jumpers, and skirts. You'll also find a convenient unisex department — great for gifts. Expect to pay slightly more for your organic items. Saving the earth and yourself is worth it.

paulfredrick.com
Paul Fredrick

800-227-8162
pfcustserv@paulfredrick.com

Accessories • Career • Casual • Formal • Outerwear

Paul Fredrick offers men a business wardrobe with a small *b*. Its excellent selection of business attire is combined with a casual, breezy look to make you look professional without a snobbish or boring business air. The design collections are timeless, yet have a stylish look. The clothes you buy now will look great next season and beyond, and won't succumb to the latest fashion trend for men. The site also sells knit shirts, sweaters, sport coats, and trousers that adapt to new business casual dress styles — an ideal combo of comfort, price, and just plain good looks.

pendleton-usa.com
Pendleton Woolen Mills

800-649-1512
webmail@penwool.com

Career • Casual

Pendleton Woolen Mills offers a lot more than the flannel shirts and blankets we have come to know them for. Although the classic woolens are still available, the company now sells stylish sportswear for men and women in made from non-wool materials. However, the careful attention to detail and care that marked Pendleton's fine woolen clothing and textiles is still in evidence in its other lines. The site is arranged by category; jump to menswear, womenswear, or blankets and home, and start shopping. Or go to one of Pendleton's online catalogs by clicking that catalog's image. As you browse through the individual catalog pages, click on specific items to see more information and add them to your shopping cart.

polo.com
Polo

888-475-7674
customersupport@polo.com

Accessories • Career • Casual • Designer • Footwear • Outerwear • Sleepwear • Specialty • Underwear

Polo is known for its stylish, preppy look. The clothes for sale here don't disappoint, with fresh-faced models wearing all the latest and greatest looks of the season. The site is arranged by category. Start with men, women, children, shoes, and so on to view the items available. Prices at Polo are high so pay attention to the running tally on your online shopping cart. (On a recent visit, I saw a men's shirt for around $70 and a women's cashmere sweater for $465.) One way to keep prices down is visit the Sale room. While the markdowns aren't extensive, you'll still save some money. Read the Style Guide for Ralph Lauren's take on what's hot and what's not.

 Recommended   **Price**   **Selection**   **Convenience**   **Service**   **Security**

prisonblues.com
Prison Blues

800-784-7689
prsnblu@yoshida.com

Casual

Prison Blues clothes are not meant to be fashionable. This site sells "tough as nails" jeans, shirts, and jackets made by the inmates of the Oregon Department of Corrections. These clothes are the same high-quality, durable, no nonsense clothes worn by the inmates. The clothes have found a following among loggers, construction workers, bikers, and others who depend on their clothes to hold up under tough conditions. Read stories from Prison Blues wearers on this site. In addition to providing clothes for folks on the outside, the Prison Blues program has been beneficial to the inmates. Get all the details about this fascinating project at the site.

⭐ qboutlet.com
QB Outlet.com

877-210-2687
sales@qboutlet.com

Footwear

Name-brand footwear at 70–80 percent off! That's right. Most men's and women's name brands can be found at QBOutlet.com, and at a discount. The ease of navigation and the ability to search for the exact shoe you're looking for make this site a winner. You can search by brand, by class, by style number, or keyword search — you can even search by your size! The site also has live online customer support. The only caveat is that QB Outlet.com is a closeout store, so if you see a pair of shoes you like, buy them — they might be gone tomorrow.

ravistailor.com
RavisTailor.com

66-1-9878717
ravi@ravistailor.com

Specialty

Based in Thailand, RavisTailor.com offers clothing made just for you. As part of your initial order, you'll fill out an extensive form that lists several different body measurements. Directions and pictures on how to measure are provided. Next you'll select your garment and fabric. You can choose from suits, pants, shirts, jackets, and more. Orders are completed in 7 to 10 working days and delivery generally takes 3 to 4 working days. Shipping is completely free.

revolveclothing.com
Revolve Clothing

888-442-5830
sales@revolveclothing.com

Accessories • Casual • Designer

You're gonna need your Platinum card to shop at revolveclothing.com. Its casual clothing for men and women is definitely NOT at a casual price. For example, take the Ripper, manufactured by Paper Denim & Cloth. The Ripper is for the fashionable who don't want to wait six months to realize the shabby-chic look. The Ripper comes pre-distressed, bleach-splattered, and paint-splotched with an eye-catching hole already in the back pocket. Price? $153! Hey, it takes dough to look shabby. But you DO get what you pay for — free shipping, free returns, price match guarantee, and all products guaranteed to be in stock.

sheepskin.com
Cloud Nine Sheepskin

425-776-1650
service@sheepskin.com

Accessories • Casual

The cornball humor and the soft slippers at this site grow on you after a while. Like the little lamb says on Cloud Nine Sheepskin's home page, check out the "unbleatable" selection of sheepskin slippers. There's nothing like the feeling of surrounding your feet in soft sheepskin after a long day at work or play. What makes this online retailer "ewenique" is its one of-a-kind designs. The company creates its own original and exclusive designs and offers them at industry-leading prices. You can also access helpful, knowledgeable Customer Service Representatives. Don't miss the specials and closeouts.

⭐ sheplers.com
Sheplers

800-833-7007
service@sheplers.com

Accessories • Casual • Footwear

Sheplers offers the world's largest collection of western wear for men and women. You'll find cowboy boots, cowboy hats, men's and ladies' jeans, western shirts, western suits, western belts and buckles, western decor, as well as other western clothing items. Whether you're a real cowboy or just want to look like one, Sheplers is the site for you. Sale prices on many current items make them easily affordable. If you're ordering in quantity, say for a team or group, volume pricing can be arranged,

 Recommended   Price   Selection   Convenience   Service   Security

shirtcreations.com
Shirt Creations

877-742-7328
info@shirtcreations.com

Career • Casual

Custom shirts for men and women are the name of the game at this site. You can supply the site with your measurements and Shirt Creations will make up your shirts for you. However, you can create your custom shirt as you order. Here's how: First, choose your fabric, such as zendaline or broadcloth. Next, pick a color, collar, pocket, monogram (if desired), and cuff style. Then, fill in remaining details, including sleeve length, your height and weight, and more. That's it! In a short while, your custom shirt will arrive at your door.

shirtmall.com
Gilbert-American.com

800-373-8140
E-mail form on site

Casual

If you're looking for custom T-shirts for your entire school, team, club, class, special event, reunion, graduation, and so on, Gilbert-American.com is the place to find them. The site makes ordering really simple. It's as easy as 1-2-3. First, choose from over 1,600 of the company's sample designs. Gilbert-American.com will make the modifications you request, or use your design idea. Second, place your order. Third, receive and distribute your T-shirts. The minimum order is 24 items, but you can mix and match T-shirts, sweatshirts, and so on, to reach the minimum. Pricing is really low, with free shipping and no setup or art charges.

shizknits.com
Shizknits.com

415-826-9075
betsy@shizknits.com

Accessories

You probably have never seen a hand knitted beer cozy. Now you can have your own custom embroidered one. Artist Betsy McCall offers a variety of unusual, hand knitted hats, shawls, scarves, and other whimsical items on this site. Take a look at the "Horny Hat." You can get it with a matching pair of "Carpal Tunnel Sleeves." Don't take literally the name of the "Eyelash Shawl." There is a note of practicality in these items coupled with a sense of humor. The "Abstract Expressioknits" bear that out. So the next time you need a gift for someone who has everything, you know where to look.

Shopbop.com
Shopbop.com

877-746-7267
service@shopbop.com

Accessories • Athletic • Casual • Designer • Specialty • Swimwear • Underwear

A bevy of designers are gathered under the Shopbop.com banner, all just waiting to provide you with the latest and greatest women's clothes, shoes, and accessories. Smart Shopbop shoppers know it's best to visit The Look section to see what goes with what and view the current styles before they make a purchase (and a possible fashion gaffe). Visit What's New to see the most recent items for sale. Want to see celebrities in Shopbob.com clothing? The Press section will satisfy that whim and direct you to the Shopbop.com pages where you can buy what they are wearing.

★ sizematters.com
SizeMatters.com

866-244-8255
customerservice@sizematters.com

Accessories • Athletic • Career • Casual • Footwear • Outerwear

This online retailer offers the latest Big and Tall fashions for men. Actually the online arm of Torre, Inc., the nation's largest men's clothing store for Big and Tall sizes, SizeMatters.com carries sportswear, outerwear, shoes, and accessories. You'll also find some great pieces in leather. Shop by department, designer or brand, or type in the keyword of the item you want to buy. Not sure of your size? The handy sizing chart makes it a breeze to figure out exactly which size to order.

sneakerslippers.com
SneakerSlippers.com

888-660-2185
sales@sneakerslippers.com

Footwear

Okay, which is it? Sneakers or slippers? Why, they're both! Slippers that look like sneakers. SneakerSlippers.com also sells a variety of standard slippers for men, women, and kids. The site carries the NixesSlippers, which are animals for your feet, such as bunnies, Eeyore, pigs, elephants, pandas, moose, monkeys, and the infamous pirate dog. During March Madness for you basketball fans, you can dress up your feet in cool NCAA sneakerslippers. By the way: For a warm and fuzzy feeling, if you have a question, SneakerSlippers.com offers live online help.

 Recommended　 Price　 Selection　 Convenience　Service　Security

sovaleather.com
Sova Leather

No phone number listed
customer@sovaleather.com

Accessories

If it's made out of leather, Sova Leather has it — handbags; women's and men's wallets; briefcases; organizers; handpainted, signature bags; luggage; evening bags; belts; purses; and ties and scarves. Many of its leather goods are made in Italy. The leather goods on the site are sold at a discount and are of good quality. Shipping is one low rate, no matter how large (or heavy) your order. Pay for your purchase with credit card, check, or PayPal.

stockingshq.com
Stockings HQ

No phone number listed
customercare@stockingshq.com

Footwear • Specialty

"No tights. No compromise. The stocking revolution starts here!" That's the tagline of Stockings HQ. The site is true to its name — a headquarters for stockings! This site sells feminine, sexy, classy nylons like thigh-high, fishnets, and suspender stockings. But that's not all. Learn the history of women's stockings, and join in on the discussion with other stocking lovers on the discussion boards and chat room. Then browse through the classy selection of feminine footwear in standard and plus sizes. Although the store is in England, you can buy in U.S. dollars. The company offers a 110 percent price guarantee, and you can return the stockings even if you've opened the package.

swim-n-sport.com
Swim 'n Sport

800-497-2111
E-mail form on site

Swimwear

Swim 'n Sport sells swimwear for women, men, juniors, and children. It sells bikinis, one-piece, and two-piece swimsuits. Its beach fashions are not just for women with "model" bodies. It sells swimwear for every kind of woman — plus size, junior, designer, tan-thru, and more. After you've selected the perfect swim suit, check out the dynamite selection of cover-ups and wraps. Round out your look with accessories like bags, hats, and shoes. Read the online magazine for beauty tips and facts — not necessarily about swimming or sports, but fun to read nevertheless.

swimsuitsjustforus.com
Swimsuits Just for Us

407-389-0592
questions@swimsuitsjustforus.com

Casual • Specialty • Swimwear

Swimsuits Just for Us brings you fashionable, quality plus-size swimwear.
Shop for swimwear at this site in four ways: by style (one-piece, two-piece,
or even for mastectomy swimwear), by bra type (underwire or soft-cup), by
body type (triangle, hourglass, inverted triangle, rectangle, or circle), and
by brand. The site also carries a small line of "resort wear" — cover-ups,
sarongs, skirts, and shorts — for the full-figured woman. Going on vacation
or need your order in a hurry? No problem. Although Swimsuits Just for Us
charges one flat rate on standard shipping, you can arrange for next day
delivery on most orders.

talbots.com
Talbots

800-992-9010
customer.service@talbots.com

Accessories • Career • Casual • Footwear • Outerwear • Swimwear

Talbots sells classic, with the emphasis on *classic*, apparel, shoes, and
accessories for misses, petites, women's, women's petites, and now, for kids
and men. For more than 50 years, the name Talbots has been synonymous
with high quality, elegant merchandise. The site is nicely organized, which
is very helpful in finding the category of product you are looking for, and
even offers you the ability to buy an entire outfit at once. Combine these
features with style guides and live online customer service, and you have an
online store done right.

★ thecatspjs.com
The Cat's Pajamas

510-525-7111
sales@thecatspjs.com

Sleepwear

Meow! The Cat's Pajamas designs fun, kitschy women's sleepwear that
you've probably seen on TV shows such as *Will & Grace*, *Dawson's Creek*,
and *Dharma and Greg*. So now you can watch these shows in the character's
PJs. These are not your everyday pajamas, as the selection of PJ prints
bears out. Sushi, Asian Holiday, Scooters, Water Ski Show, Japanese Koi,
Strawberries, and Ballet Class are just some of the different designs you can
have imprinted on your PJs.

★ tie-dyes.com
Tie Dyes.com

802-649-1836
richard@tie-dyes.com

Casual

As the saying goes, "if you remember the 1960s, you weren't there." Well, Tie Dyes.com remembers them very well. This site carries a great selection of tie-dyed T-shirts, Afghans, sarongs, tapestries, leggings, ladies dresses, lab coats, shorts, girl's dresses, scrubs, tank tops, even golf shirts, all tie-dyed in vibrant colors. Each and every tie-dye is different, so you won't see your design on anyone else. Wondering how to care for your tie-dyed garment? A complete care guide is available at the site.

★ ties.com
Ties.com

888-686-8437
info@ties.com

Accessories • Designer

If you're looking for ties, you've come to the right place. Ties.com has ties — over 2,000 of them! You can shop for ties by color, category, designer, pattern, or price range. And get this: The company has a 110 percent guarantee. If, after buying a tie from this site, you find the same item at a lower price on another site within 30 days, simply e-mail them with your order number and the location of the cheaper product. You'll be credited with 110 percent of the difference between that price and Tie.com's.

title9sports.com
Title 9 Sports

800-342-4448
E-mail form on site

Athletic • Footwear • Swimwear • Underwear

Okay, here's your Civics lesson for the day. Remember Title IX? It was a piece of legislation included in the Education Amendments of 1972 that requires schools that receive federal funds to provide girls and women with equal opportunity to compete in sports. Title 9 Sports takes this idea very seriously, which you see on its About Us page. With that in mind, Title 9 Sports offers a great selection of athletic apparel for the sports woman. The clothing and accessories are grouped by sports activity — Yoga, Running, Swimwear, and "Fashletics," a combination of general sports. If you're some-what of a couch potato, read the short bios of the model athletes. You'll feel inspired to get in shape.

travelsmith.com
TravelSmith

800-950-1600
E-mail form on site

Accessories • Career • Casual • Footwear • Outerwear • Sleepwear • Specialty • Underwear

If you're a constant traveler, you need TravelSmith. Normal everyday clothes, whether for casual wear or business, are not made to stand up to the abuse that they get from being worn, shoved into a suitcase, and then worn again later. TravelSmith has created a line of easy-care, lightweight, packable clothing and luggage. The natural, high-performance, wrinkle-resistant fabrics look great after being stuffed in a suitcase or worn on the red-eye. The range of sizes and selection of travel wear is tremendous.

t-shirtking.com
T-Shirt King

800-493-7887
E-mail form on site

Casual

If America has any claim to unique fashion, it's the T-shirt, a piece of clothing worn by just about everybody. T-shirts run the gamut of style and are a very personal piece of clothing. T-Shirt King covers that gamut by offering an "Online Database of The Best T-Shirts in the World." The company sells T-shirts in a variety of categories — funny, music, comics, sports, nature, car, pet, cultural, fantasy, sci-fi, and kids' T-shirts. You can search by keyword or category. Check out the offerings *for M*A*S*H, Animal House, Brady Bunch, Caddyshack,* Black Sabbath, and more.

tummiesmaternity.com
Tummies Maternity

410-358-0116
tummiesmaternity@aol.com

Specialty

Conservative maternity clothing is the rule at Tummies Maternity. This site offers modest but fashionable dresses, formal wear, lingerie, plus sizes, sets and suits, tops, bottoms, and swimwear for the discreet pregnant woman. Its selection is modest, like the clothing, but the lines it carries are from the leading maternity designers, such as Mommy Chic, Japanese Weekend, Olian Maternity, Duet Designs, Tummi, Belly Basics, Mama Pavlova, Noppies Nature, Maximum Mama, Metro Mom, and Ran Designs.

 Recommended   Price   Selection   Convenience   Service   Security

⭐ uglies.com
Uglies.com
877-878-4592
E-mail form on site

Underwear

"You're so ugly, you make onions cry." "You're so ugly, you have to trick-or-treat by phone." Okay, okay, enough of the ugly jokes. But when it comes to ugly, this retailer is no joke. Uglies.com offers its famous Uglies boxer shorts and super roomy, super comfortable Puglies — the perfect solution for bummin' around the house, or wherever you feel like bummin'. Believe me, these products are ugly! All Uglies feature a unique five-panel "No Wedgie" design for ultimate comfort. Now that's not so ugly, is it?

ujena.com
Ujena
800-448-5362
ujena@prodigy.net

Athletic • Casual • Swimwear

Need a swim suit? Ujena is a great place to buy sexy bikinis, one-piece suits, and casual two-piece styles. The company pioneered the mix and match two-piece suit and offers several mix and match options on the site. You'll also find sexy dresses, suitable for an evening at your town's hottest club. The athletic wear sold here is skimpy and tight — just the thing to get you noticed on the field or baseball diamond. Prices don't seem too high at first glance, until you realize that most items at Ujena cover only a few square inches of flesh.

universalgear.com
Universal Gear
800-204-1844
info@universalgear.com

Athletic • Casual • Designer • Footwear • Sleepwear • Swimwear • Underwear

The look here is hot for men, with brand names like Diesel, Body Body Wear, Jocko, and Adidas leading the way. Start with underwear and build the look, layer by layer. Younger guys will probably be more inclined to shop here than older ones: I can't imagine my Uncle Al groovin' on a pair of Pistol Pete Zip Up jeans. Expect to drop some serious money for your hot outfit, because these stylish clothes do not come cheap. Fortunately, the sale rack has sweaters, shirts, jeans, outerwear, and accessories at up to 75 percent off.

victoriassecret.com
Victoria'sSecret.com

800-970-1109
E-mail form on site

Casual • Footwear • Sleepwear • Swimwear • Underwear

Shopping at the online catalog at Victoria'sSecret.com is fun. Filled with famous faces modeling beautiful lingerie, it's easy to forget that the items for sale here serve a purpose. Yet, if you're looking for a bra or need a slip or chemise, you're bound to find what you need at the site. Browse the casual clothing and business attire, too. Sign up for an account at Victoria's Secret.com and enjoy express checkout and other perks. The site doesn't charge for shipping on orders over $100.

⭐ vintagewedding.com
A Vintage Wedding

800-660-3640
dbarr@tampabay.rr.com

Specialty

A Vintage Wedding has a classic collection of vintage wedding dresses, bridal accessories, and groom's clothes. You'll also find vintage lingerie, and stoles, wraps, and capes. The collection is one-of-a-kind, so don't wait to order if you see something you like. Some of the gowns are quite old. On a recent visit, I saw a dress from 1890. Generally, the older the dress, the higher the price. Be sure to match your measurements to the listed measurements for the clothing at the site, because off the rack sizing wasn't around when most of the gowns at A Vintage Wedding were designed.

wearitall.com
WearItAll.com

888-932-7481
service@wearitall.com

Accessories • Casual • Designer • Footwear

Psst!! I'll share a secret with you, but don't tell anyone else! Some of today's hottest, hippest stars are buying their clothes from the designers and stores collected at WearItAll.com. Wardrobe masters are coming to WearItAll.com too. The site makes it fun to shop for tops, bottoms, dresses, accessories, shoes, cosmetics, and miscellaneous items with its clever menu shaped like an elevator. Click your floor (category) and see all the related fashions for sale. WearItAll.com has some wonderful clothes for kids too. Visit the site to see who's wearing the great clothes available from this site, and then pattern your look after your favorite star.

 Recommended   Price   Selection   Convenience   Service   Security

worldofwatches.com
WorldofWatches.com
800-222-0077
customerservice@worldofwatches.com
Watches

WorldofWatches.com has a lot going for it! First, you can save up to 60 percent on brand-name watches. Second, this online retailer knows how to use the technology of the Internet. Yes, you can shop by brand and style, but you can also shop within a price range for a watch. If you don't know much about watches, then use the site's online watch glossary to educate yourself before you spend hundreds of dollars on a timepiece. This company also ships internationally.

zales.com
Zales
800-311-5393
E-mail form on site
Jewelry • Watches

The name *Zales* is synonymous with jewelry. I like this site for a number of reasons. First, it offers a buyer's guide to help you understand the terminology used in describing jewelry. This guide contains some of the basic information you should know before buying any jewelry. Second, you can help others figure out what to buy you by storing a list of your favorite jewelry on the site and then e-mailing it to someone. Finally, Zales' reminder service can make sure you never forget an important date again by e-mailing reminders to you.

★ zootsuitstore.com
Zootsuitstore.com
800-408-8933
service@zootsuitstore.com
Accessories • Formal • Footwear • Vintage

Zootsuitstore.com, run by Siegel's Clothing Superstore of San Francisco, offers a distinctive look for men. The ever-popular Zoot suit, characterized by an oversized jacket with large lapels, padded shoulders and baggy, cuffed pants, is available in a variety of colors, fabrics, and styles. In fact, you can send in your own fabric and measurements and the Siegel's tailors (some of these guys have been designing Zoot suits since the 1930s) will make up a suit just for you. Siegel's outfits most of the retro-swing bands in the United States, Asia, and Europe and provides Zoot suits to movie stars, rockers, and rappers. Zoot suits are cool!

Care for Your Clothes

You scrimped and saved and finally bought a really great piece of clothing you adored. Then you wore it a few times, and put in your weekly wash load. What came back? An unrecognizable rag that was too tight, stretched way out of shape, or worse, dyed pink from the single red sock that accidentally ended up in the same wash load. Sadly, just about everyone has a similar story to tell.

Relax! With a little care and attention, your clothes can stay fresh and new looking for a long time. All it takes is a little pre-purchase planning, clean and tidy habits, and some laundry savvy.

The best time to think about caring for your clothes is before you buy them! Read the care instructions in each garment and don't be swayed by how good something looks when it's new. Unless you are prepared to pay hefty dry cleaning charges, steer clear from clothes that must be sent to the cleaners. (That beach wrap on the sale rack labeled "Dry Clean Only" probably isn't such a great buy.) Easy care items are always your best bet. Choose clothing that's washable, preferably made from materials that resist stains and wrinkles.

Dirty laundry builds up fast. Don't let the pile overwhelm you. If you use a good sorting system before your clothes hit the wash water, there's less chance of a rogue, dark sock finding its way into your wash of white delicates. Creative Spaces (creative spacesusa.com) and Organize-It (organizes-it.com) have an excellent selection of laundry bins, hampers, and sorters that will make this job easier. Keep socks together with a clever locking device from Sock Locks (sock-locks.com).

The newest washers and dryers make laundry chores a breeze. Read about all the latest ones at Maytag.com (maytag.com) and use the company's Web site to order new laundry appliances from a store near you. Thor Appliances (thor appliances.com) makes portable, built-in and stackable washer and dryer pairs that are ideal for small homes and apartments.

Unfortunately, even the greatest washing machines aren't a match for really tough stains. Without extra help a bad stain can signal a death sentence for some garments. However, with a little work, many spots can disappear. Of course, the best cure for stains is prevention. Don't wear white when you eat pasta or drink grape juice or red wine. Always place a napkin in your lap when you eat; if you're a really messy eater, tuck it under your chin. (If you think this seems silly, women can drape an old shawl or scarf over their shoulders, men can use a dark sweater.) Cap your pen or marker before you wave it around.

Visit Dilmaghani's Interactive Stain Removal Chart (dilmaghani.com/care/stains/removalchart.html) for a good online source for learning how to remove over 150 common household stains. Select the stain type on left to find out the best removal method. A description of the various methods and cleaning types can be found in the Removal Supplies list to the right. Still need help? British Murgatroyd the Butler has a printable stain removal guide at manning-and-manning.com/murgatroyd/stains.htm.

Many commercial products are designed to bust the most stubborn stains. OxiClean (oxiclean.com) carries sprays, powders, and treatments — some delicate enough for use on baby clothes or personal items. Wash Away Laundry Stain Remover is available from Doitbest (doitbest.com). Tried and true products are sometimes the most reliable. Magic Wand Stain Remover, available at The Added Touch (addedtouchstore.com), has been wowing people for 25 years. Legions of people swear that rubbing a stain with the product wand will make the stain disappear like magic.

Which laundry detergent you choose is largely governed by personal choice. Although you can't buy anything at the Web site, visit Tide.com (tide.com) for news and money-saving offers regarding the popular product. Sun & Earth (sunandearth.com) sells a line of environmentally-friendly detergents. Of course, you can make your own detergent with a recipe from the Frugal Shopper (thefrugalshopper.com/articles/detergent.shtml).

Whatever detergent you select, don't use too much. Surprisingly, too much detergent can leave stains! Be sure that you're using the right water level and temperature for the washload. The correct water temperature and cycle are important — the Permanent Press or Delicate cycle is always a good choice for clothes so they're rinsed in cool water.

Use the Delicate cycle for anything you really treasure, or if you're washing it for the first time. If it's still dirty, you can run it through the washing machine again. For really delicate items, consider hand-washing. Teddy Girl (teddygirl.com) offers a product called Lingerie-Mate for lingerie and hand washables that leaves clothes clean and sweet smelling. In a pinch, you can use a few drops of your favorite shampoo.

Make sure that the lint screen of the dryer is clean each time you add a new load to be dried. Otherwise, you're overtaxing your dryer and will be calling the repairman in the near term! Anti-static dryer sheets are a great addition to most dryer loads. Drugstore.com (drugstore.com) carries a wide variety of popular dryer sheets, including Bounce and Snuggle. Alternatively, check out the reusable chemical free dryer sheet system at Static Eliminator (staticeliminator.us).

Remove clothes from the dryer as soon as possible. Fold or hang everything and put it away. Use good quality hangers to ensure the shape of your clothes is preserved. Find metal, wood, and padded hangers at Clothes Hangers (clotheshangers.com) or Best Hangers (besthangers.com). If necessary, iron or press to remove wrinkles. A Rowenta iron or steamer, available at Allbrands.com (allbrands.com) is an excellent choice.

Home drycleaning kits are a popular alternative to sending clothes out to be cleaned. The Rocky Mountain Fabricare Association tested a few kits and has provided their findings online. Read the Association's opinion at RMFA.org. If you decide to buy a home drycleaning kit, Walgreens.com (walgreens.com) has them at reasonable prices. You'll also find the kits at USAhardware.com (usahardware.com).

Always treat your clothes with respect. With just a little attention and tender loving care, they'll last you a lifetime.

Chapter 6

Auctions and Classifieds: Trading with the Natives

● ●

As if the vast selection of products and services at the online stores were not enough to fulfill your heart's desire, another and surprising universe of shopping exists that almost matches what you can buy from the online merchants on the Web. I'm talking about the auction sites and classified ads that act as a virtual garage sale or flea market.

Did I say "surprising"? That may be an understatement. Just try to find these at your local retailer: 50 magazine pictures of Liberace, Elvis' dental records, seeds from a 933-pound pumpkin, even some North Carolina snow! But collector's items like these are only the tip of the iceberg when it comes to auctions and classifieds. You can find the more mundane items, too, like sports memorabilia, refurbished computer items, outrageous deals on CDs, Hawaiian vacations, airline tickets, automobiles — and the list goes on.

Thousands and thousands of people not unlike you hawk the personal items they find in their closets, basements, and garages, and make them available to you at great prices. You can then either buy these items outright or bid for them in an auction-style environment. You'll find merchandise similar to that sold by the online merchants but with the opportunity of purchasing them — new or used — at dramatically lower prices.

Take eBay (ebay.com), the granddaddy of all online auctions. With over 30 million users and 6 million listings, it offers merchandise from your fellow Netizens — from Arts and Antiques to Z-Diamond Studs to everything in between. But auction sites are not the only place to trade with the natives. The Yahoo! Classifieds (classifieds.yahoo.com) offer the same kinds of merchandise you find in the classified ads of your local newspaper. But that's not all. Some well-respected online merchants are a combination of online retailer and auction site, so you can get the best of both worlds. These companies offer products for bid with the safety and service that come with a traditional online retailer.

Many of the listings in this chapter have no Price, Service, or Security ratings. That's because the price of an item offered at auction or through a classified ad can range from very low to very expensive. Most auction or classified sites do not offer any kind of customer service nor any guarantee that your purchase is safe. Be sure to read Chapter 3 and the sidebar at the end of this chapter to learn the ins and outs of buying safely from auction sites.

Here are some resources that may come in handy when you're shopping the auctions and classified ads on the Web. To look up common auction terms, go to `auction-lynx.com/terms.html`. Read the latest auction news at `auctionbytes.com`. You'll want to check out the tips and suggestions for buyers at `thebidfloor.com/buyers_tips.htm` and `fl.essortment.com/onlinecomputer_pxp.htm`. Buyers and sellers can read the Federal Trade Commission's advice at `ftc.gov/bcp/conline/pubs/online/auctions.htm`.

Key Word Index

Classifieds

You can find lots of classified ads selling just the merchandise you were looking for. Look for this keyword to find them.

General Auctions

Sites that contain this keyword refer to general interest auction sites that sell a huge variety of items in a number of different categories. You can find good deals at some of the smaller general auction sites, which don't have the exposure of the top few.

Specialty Auctions

If you're only interested in a particular type of product or category, and you're looking for a good selection of those items to bid on, then the specialty auction sites is where to go.

antique-photography.com
Antique-Photography.com

No phone number listed
admin@antique-photography.com

Specialty Auctions

Antique-Photography.com is a shutterbug's delight. This online auction site offers vintage and fine art photography, equipment, books, and photography ephemera. Some examples of the items up for bid are authentic stereoviewers and slides, old cameras, real pre-1940 photo postcards, and daguerreotypes, ambrotypes, and tintypes. If you're looking for something in particular and don't see it at the site, you can post a Want List for others to view, and vice versa. The site also offers a Recommended Reading list so you can find out all you ever wanted to know about the history of photography.

★ auctions.amazon.com
Amazon Auctions

No phone number listed
E-mail form on site

General Auctions

Amazon entered into the online auction fray later than eBay, but it, too, has a good selection of products up for bid. Some of the Amazon auction categories include Coins and Stamp, Home and Garden, Travel and Real Estate, and of course, Books. One nice addition to the online auction experience is the Amazon.com A-to-Z Guarantee. If you use the credit card you have on file with Amazon, it guarantees the condition of the item you buy and its timely delivery. This feature adds a little more safety to your purchase than most auction sites.

auctions.yahoo.com
Yahoo! Auctions

No phone number listed
E-mail form on site

General Auctions

Yahoo! Auctions may be a Johnny-come-lately to the Web, but it still manages to compete with the likes of eBay. You'll find a very large selection of items for bid, but not as many of the strange and wacky products you see on eBay. Like eBay, Yahoo! does a good job of educating the first-time bidder on what auctions are — from finding an item to winning the auction. The site also offers a useful glossary of bidding terms. Yahoo! has begun a new type of auction in which the bids start at 99 cents with no reserve price, which means that some lucky bidder might be able to win an auction for that amount.

⭐ autotrader.com
Auto Trader

No phone number listed
E-mail form on site

Classifieds

Ready to dump that old heap and get a new set of wheels? Auto Trader is one of the biggest classified ad sites on the Web for used and new cars offered by individuals. Buyers can search for cars in various distances from their ZIP code, from a 25-mile radius to nationwide. The search tool also allows you to choose the criteria for filtering ads by new or used cars, price, make/model, year, or mileage. The Auto Trader site provides free and extensive information on all aspects of the car-shopping process; you can get a car's history, apply for financing, find out about safety features of the car you want, and even read the latest car reviews.

bargaintraderonline.com
BargainTraderOnline.com

No phone number listed
E-mail form on site

Classifieds

At BargainTraderOnline.com you can choose from over 80,000 classified ads and bargains. This site is a collection of high-traffic Web sites, compiling those companies' ads on its site and receiving millions of visitors each week. You can buy any type of used car or other vehicle, or even vacation timeshares or general merchandise. You can either browse BargainTraderOnline's categories of ads (including animals, collectibles, electronics, personal goods, and real estate) or use the site's search engine to find what you're looking for.

bidville.com
BidVille.com

No phone number listed
E-mail form on site

General Auctions

BidVille is similar to other general auction sites, but in its case, you can use your credit card on its secure Web site to pay for an item. If you're not satisfied with your purchase, then you have recourse by disputing the charge with your credit card company. This takes some of the risk out of buying from individuals. You have to register to place a bid or buy an item from the BidVille site, but by doing so you can easily track your auctions, review your bidding history, and look at feedback you've left.

 Recommended   Price   Selection   Convenience   Service   Security

childrensbookmarket.com/Auction/Auction.asp
Children's Book Auction

No phone number listed
admin@childrensbookmarket.com

Specialty Auctions

ChildrensBookMarket.com is a great place to find old, rare, and bargain books for children. It has all the children's book categories covered and includes activity books, animal and pet books, beginning readers, fiction, geography and culture, picture books, mythology and folklore, and cartoon and comics. Besides some very detailed description of the books, many with pictures, you also have a choice of six auction formats — Standard, Fixed Price, Dollar, Trade/Barter, Blind, and Multiple Item bidding.

classifieds.yahoo.com
Yahoo! Classifieds

No phone number listed
E-mail form on site

Classifieds

Yahoo! must be the biggest classifieds site on the Web today. Search by ZIP code to view only the classified ads in that particular area. This feature makes searching easier because you're not inundated with hundreds of ads at a time. You can browse by category or specific item. For example, browse pets and then only dogs and cats. Because you will be looking at ads in your local area, you have the option of going to see the product being advertised before you buy it. If you buy outside your area, just like buying from sellers at an online auction site, remember the safe shopping rules discussed in Chapters 2 and 3.

collectorauctions.com
Collector Auctions

765-764-1516
sales@stoutauctions.com

Specialty Auctions

Remember that toy train you received for Christmas long ago? Did you sell it or give it away when you "grew up"? Maybe you want to relive your child-hood by buying another like it. The Collector Auctions site may be able to help you out. This company specializes in collectible trains and accessories, desirable toys, and racing memorabilia. It offers for bid both scale trains and toy trains along with model railroad accessories and magazines. It also has a small selection of collector NASCAR items up for bid. All aboard!

digitalauction.com
Digital Auction

No phone number listed
custserv1@digitalauction.com

Specialty Auctions

For the consumer electronics buff, or for those who just want their house and car to rock, the Digital Auction site can provide a number of sweet deals on personal electronics gear. The site is simple and direct and works like the average auction site in which individuals sell to other individuals. You can choose from many categories of products, including PC systems, laptops, hard drives, CPUs, memory, modems, video cards, wireless accessories, digital cameras, printers, and scanners. Happy bidding!

ebang.com
eBang.com

No phone number listed
information@ebang.com

Specialty Auctions

Looking to find items like a Ruger mini-14 40 round magazine, a Viking axe, and other unique weapons? eBang.com offers guns, knives, archery items, and antique weapons, among other things. Besides the products, what makes eBang.com a distinctive auction site is that it offers three types of auctions — English Auctions, where the highest bidder wins; Vickrey Auctions, where the highest bidder obtains the item at the price offered by the second highest bidder; and Dutch Auctions, where bidders can bid on whole lots of the same product at the same time.

★ eBay
eBay

No phone number listed
E-mail form on site

General Auctions

eBay is the auction site that started it all. With millions of items available for auction each day, eBay is the biggest online auction site in existence. If you're looking for an item to buy, no matter how unusual or obscure, you can probably find it at eBay. Though it cannot support or service the products it offers for bid, it does have a comprehensive customer service department if you have problems or would like questions answered. Turnaround time for e-mail requests is 24–48 hours. A recent addition to the site is eBay Live Auctions, where you can bid in real time on live auctions happening on the floor of some of the world's greatest auction houses.

★ Recommended   Price   Selection   Convenience   Service   🔒 Security

erock.net
eRock.net

916-723-5621
admin@erock.net

Specialty Auctions

eRock.com is an online music auction site with 20 rock memorabilia categories, including posters, concert tickets, magazines, records, and more. Other categories include the Beatles, Elvis Presley, Kiss, the Rolling Stones, and General Rock Artists. You may find merchandise such as a mint condition "Introducing the Beatles" record album starting at $2,500, or a 1987 mint condition Tennessee 1-Elvis license plate starting at $9.99. You can find all kinds of unique memorabilia in this house of rock.

heritagecoin.com
Heritage Coin

800-872-6467
E-mail form on site

Specialty Auctions

If you've lost your lucky Indian penny from your childhood, Heritage Coin can get you another. Heritage Coin is a large dealer and auctioneer of rare coins and currency. You're dealing with a retailer so if you win a bid, you pay Heritage immediately. If you don't see what you're looking for, fill out a private Want List and Heritage's system will automatically alert you when the item comes in. One unique feature this site offers you is the multiple ways to bid. You can bid by postal mail, e-mail, fax, online, in person, by phone, and by fax.

oldandsold.com
Old And Sold

248-545-1787
info@oldandsold.com

Specialty Auctions

Old And Sold is an online auction service specializing in quality antiques. Items include general antiques, furniture, accessories, clothing, books and ephemera, pottery and porcelain, dolls and collectibles, antique glass items, and postcards and greeting cards. The Antiques Digest area contains thousands of articles related to antiques and collectibles and how to apprise them. Or you can submit an appraisal request to Wilcox & Hall Appraisers, which has been operating as an appraisal and antique restoration service since 1959. If you're in the mood to talk antiques, post a message in the discussion board in the Chat Cafe.

shopgoodwill.com
ShopGoodwill.com

714-547-6308
E-mail form on site

General Auctions

If you want to get a good deal and help the disadvantaged, then consider bidding and buying at the Goodwill auction site. Revenues from auction sales fund education, job training, and job placement programs for people with disabilities and other disadvantages. Goodwill may be a do-good site, but the same rules and risks of online auctions apply. It has no control over the quality, safety, or legality of the items advertised, nor control over whether or not sellers will complete the sale of items they offer. That said, just like in Goodwill's brick-and-mortar stores, you can find some neat stuff. One person's trash is another's treasure!

stealitback.com
StealitBack.com

949-234-0204
E-mail form on site

General Auctions

Founded and managed by former police officers, StealitBack.com offers items that are abandoned or no longer needed as evidence from police property rooms using an online auction method. Examples of the categories of product you can bid on are automotive accessories, bicycles, clothing, collectibles and memorabilia, computers and electronics, and jewelry. You can search for items by name, category, or the price you want to start bidding at.

ubid.com
uBid.com

888-900-8243
E-mail form on site

General Auctions

uBid offers the best of two worlds — an online retailer and an auction site. You can choose to purchase a product outright, at a fixed price, through its Superstore, or you can bid on and buy products directly from uBid's own warehouse. The best part is that most bids start at $1, so you can get brand name items at large discounts. Or bid on and buy products from uBid-Certified Merchants — uBid-approved third-party merchants who sell products on their sites. To ensure uBid buyers the ability to shop in a private and secure environment, every uBid Certified Merchant must go through a thorough application process.

 Recommended Price Selection Convenience  Service Security

usplotsforsale.com
US Plots For Sale

No phone number listed
No e-mail address on site

Classifieds

Usplotsforsale.com is an example of why online shopping never ceases to amaze me. If you're considering getting a jump on a rising real estate market, then how about checking out the classified ads for burial plots? That's right — you can browse through classified ads for your state and pick up a plot that suits your needs from individuals "dying" to sell them. US Plots for Sale offers a classified listing of cemetery plots across the United States where you either buy or sell burial plots and mausoleums online.

★ winebid.com
WineBid.com

888-638-8968
info@winebid.com

Specialty Auctions

One of the better shopping experiences on the Web is browsing and shopping for wine. It can be an epicurean delight. But one step better is buying wine at prices lower than you'll find at your local grocery store. Founded in 1996, WineBid.com is the largest Internet auction for fine and rare wines — all of which you can bid on and perhaps buy at a great price. You can search by producer, price, vintage, and even by collection or case. Quality is job one for this company. All wines it auctions are inspected and stored in its climate-controlled warehouse in Napa, California. Because you buy directly from WineBid, your purchase is protected as with a traditional retailer.

A Shopping Excursion — Going. . .Going. . .Gone! How Not to Get Burned at Online Auctions

Online auctions are a popular way to find great deals on the Web, but unfortunately they also top the list for the most Internet consumer complaints to the FTC. The auctioneer's "Going, going, gone!" can apply not only to the product just sold, but to the money just stolen from your wallet if you're not careful when buying from a seller at an online auction. The majority of complaints involve sellers who fail to deliver the product, and those who misrepresent their merchandise by selling fake or counterfeit items.

The vast majority of online auction transactions are completed safely. But even with legitimate auction sites, keep the following safety tips in mind to avoid becoming an FTC statistic:

- Know the auction site. Each site has its own rules for bidding and buying. There are no standard rules for auction sites, so read and understand them before bidding.

- Know the product you want. An informed online shopper is a successful online shopper. Do your homework. Research the product you're bidding on to make sure what the seller is offering is what you want to buy. Just as important, use the Web to find out the real worth of the item. Check other auction sites and classified ads for the price others are selling and buying the product at. Eppraisals.com (eppraisals.com) has hundreds of experts in nearly three hundred categories of antiques and collectibles on hand to provide online appraisals. Don't overbid!

- Know the seller. Many auction sites have a rating system for their sellers. Read them. Do you see a lot of negative, even neutral comments? If so, it could be a red flag. Has the seller sold these types of items in the past? For how long? The answers to these and other questions can give you an impression of the seller and whether you should do business with him or her.

- Use a safe payment method. I highly recommend you use a credit card with all purchases. If the seller cannot process a credit card, you and the seller can use a third-party service like PayPal (paypal.com). Consider using an Internet escrow service for full purchase protection (see Chapter 3).

If you do get burned after all your precautions, your first step is to make every effort to contact the other party yourself and attempt to work out the problem with the seller. You did get the seller's contact information as discussed in Chapter 3, right?

Remain civil, but if reasonable attempts fail, there are steps you can take. For example, if you've bought an item off eBay, they have a fraud protection program that may help. Another option is to use SquareTrade, which provides a forum to work out disputes.

Keep these safety tips in mind, and your online auction experience will be both rewarding and safe.

Chapter 7

Babies and Children: Shopping Is Child's Play

- -

*I*n the planning stages, a family shopping excursion seems like a great idea. Unfortunately, if you're packing a diaper bag, bottles, baggies of snacks, and a few clothing changes for baby, even the simplest trip gets overwhelming in a hurry. Babies get "shopped out" quickly and don't try to hide their displeasure. Add a whining toddler or teenager who's hard to please, and your trip to the mall or discount store can feel like climbing Mt. Everest.

An Internet shopping trip makes more sense. Inclement weather and heavy traffic never get in your family's way. Your family can shop whenever and wherever they want on the Net. Forget the local food court with its overpriced fast food and semi-clean tables. Pack a picnic basket and gather 'round the computer. Shopping for baby and children's items has never been easier.

Every child is an individual! Accordingly, the listings in this section cover a broad range of sites that deal with interests and merchandise just for kids. You'll also see lots of sites that sell gear and products that grownups need. Raising a child these days takes a lot of "stuff," and you can find most of it in the following pages.

When you're shopping for baby and children's items, don't be dazzled by a super-low price. If you're considering buying a heavy or bulky item, like a stroller or high chair, compute the shipping and handling costs and the charge for insurance at a few sites and then determine who's offering the best deal.

Key Word Index

Apparel

The Apparel sites carry clothes for infants to teens. The sites offer a smattering of everything from hip and happening to custom-made historical clothing.

Baby Gear

You can find essentials like strollers, car seats, and carriers at the Baby Gear sites.

Baby Gifts

The Baby Gifts sites offer baskets of goodies to one-of-a-kind baby gifts. Some of the selections are so adorable and cuddly — like cashmere blankets and sweet stuffed animals — you may want to order one to give away and one to keep for your inner child!

Baby Needs

The Baby Needs sites offer those items that babies can't do without — baby food, formula, diapers, and the like.

Footwear

From infant booties to genuine cowboy boots, shop at the Footwear sites for shoes for the kids.

For Teens Only

The For Teens Only category is a very special selection of sites for those from 13–19. Other age groups may not appreciate the content or merchandise.

Health and Fitness

Keeping kids healthy and active isn't easy these days. These sites can help.

Kids Room

Redecorate your kid's whole bedroom or buy a few pieces of furniture or accessories from the amazing selection of children's furniture stores in the Kids Room group.

Parenting Aid

The Parenting Aid sites carry tools to help parents perform their difficult job. Videos, online courses, and motivational aids are just a few of the tools that you'll find.

Party Time

Let the Party Time stores help you plan the perfect birthday party or other special event.

Safety

Keeping kids safe is the number one priority of the Safety sites.

Special Needs

The sites in the Special Needs section sell items for children with special needs, such as autism and related disorders, as well as items for special physical needs.

Toys and Books

Fun and games are available at the Toys and Books sites, some with an educational slant.

Uniforms

Shop for school uniforms from the convenience of home at the Uniforms stores.

1greatgift.com
1 Great Gift

800-611-3226
info@giftedbasket.com

Baby Gifts

1 Great Gift has been creating baby gift baskets since 1989. This company's goal is for your basket to be remembered for a lifetime. To that end, the folks there prepare your gift in a special container and tie it with a beautiful bow. For the gift inside, choose from a wide variety of specialty items, including blocks, a personalized CD, clothing, and, for little girls, a baby-to-bride book. A Sibling Basket is also a great idea. Your thoughtfulness will be the toast of the town when your basket from this site is delivered.

7starparties.com
Seven Star Parties

877-697-7827
sales@7starparties.com

Party Time

Long after the last candle's been blown out and the last piece of birthday cake has been consumed, a birthday party will be remembered by the party bags given to each departing guest. Seven Star Parties offers party bags for girls and boys, and also sells a unisex model. The bags are surprisingly affordable — some bags cost less than $2 — and contain four great items. The Girl's Bag is available in two styles and contains a makeup bag filled with fun, safe items — a light-up yo-yo, a ball, a necklace, and so on. The Boy's and Unisex Bags contain similar age-appropriate items.

abc123kids.com
abc123kids.com

609-452-2039
grace@abc123kids.com

Kids Room

Who said furniture for children has to be boring? abc123kids.com has broken through the boring barrier with a clever collection for kids ages three and up. Children with lots of imagination will love the Flying Colors line, with a bright chair shaped like a dinosaur and a bookcase shaped like an airplane. Slightly more traditional children (and parents) will prefer the Natural Wood Collection, with a storage bench, adjustable desk, double-sided easel, and rocking chair. Other collections are equally as innovative. Rugs, floor pillows, lamps, and other accessories enhance the furniture collections.

 Recommended   Price   Selection   Convenience   Service Security

★ abercrombiekids.com
Abercrombie Kids

866-777-1892
E-mail form on site

Apparel

From Alaska to Florida, and all points in between, kids love the Abercrombie look. Abercrombie Kids makes getting the full line of cool clothes and accessories easy for kids all over. Shop at the site for boys or girls. Just like the Sale section at the Abercrombie & Fitch Web site, the Sale section in this site for kids contains some hefty markdowns. Visit the Lifestyle section to download a screensaver or background image for your computer. Want to be the next Abercrombie model? Details are at the site.

alloy.com
Alloy.com

888-452-5569
cs@alloy.com

Apparel

Girls who love entertainment glitz and glamour will be attracted to Alloy.com. Shop at this site for the hot and happening styles. Clothes are arranged by category, style, or brand, which makes browsing through the collection easy. If you find something you like, you can check out right away or add it to your Wishlist for consideration later on. On another portion of the site you'll enjoy being shocked by the latest gossip about the hot star of your choice, reading your love horoscope, and posting your deepest problems to the message boards.

babogknitwear.net
Babóg Knitwear

00353 91 735 869
E-mail form on site

Apparel

The children's items sold at the Babóg Web site are knitted in-house in Galway, located on the western side of Ireland. You can't buy an already-knit sweater directly from the site. To get one, you must first pick the child's sweater from the pictures shown. The sweaters range from traditional to contemporary. Next, you pay for your sweater. At checkout you'll be asked for size information. In two to four weeks, a beautiful hand-knit baby sweater will arrive at your door. Sure, it's a leap of faith, but the results will amaze you.

babycakes.com
Babycakes International
No phone number listed
babycakesintl@aol.com
Baby Gifts

Babycakes International was founded in 2001 to showcase the original Warm-N-Toasty sleep sack, which comes in fleece or flannel. Other gifts are available here, too, including hats, slider bracelets, CDs, musical toys, a baby handprint kit, and some adorable plush toys. Because this site promises "10% of our net proceeds will be donated to the Autism Society of America," you may spend a few extra dollars on your baby gift. Why not? It's great to benefit as many people as possible with a single investment.

babyeinstein.com
The Baby Einstein Company
800-793-1454
customerservice@babyeinstein.com
Toys and Books

Baby Einstein approaches learning from a child's point of view. The people in this company understand that babies and toddlers are naturally curious. Accordingly, the educational toys and media this company sells are designed to stimulate a child's sense of wonder and imagination. You can shop by Theme, such as Animals, Art, Nature and Science, Age, or Product Type. If you're not sure about an item, the site's Product Demonstrations section can help you decide whether it's appropriate. Visit the Family to Family section to find out what other parents think about Baby Einstein products.

babyfurnitureshop.com
BabyFurnitureShop.com
856-809-1600
No e-mail address on site
Kids Room

Unless you're a decorator, or you have a good eye, figuring out what goes with what can be difficult. The nursery pieces that looked so great in the store or the catalogue often don't look right when you get them home. BabyFurnitureShop.com does the hard work for you. Shop here for nursery furniture arranged in groups. For example, order a crib and dresser group or a crib, changer, mattress group, and so on. The groups are arranged by manufacturer and often are priced lower than if you bought the pieces individually. If you don't need a group, you can purchase nursery and children's room furniture by the piece.

Recommended Price Selection Convenience Service 🔒Security

baby-jogging-strollers.com
Baby Jogging Strollers.com
800-721-7444
info@baby-jogging-strollers.com
Baby Gear

The quest for fitness for parents can seem impossible. Even buying a baby jogging stroller is a difficult mission. The strollers come in so many makes, models, and styles that deciding which one is right for you can be hard. Baby Jogging Strollers.com's 4-step Jogger Stroller Selector survey takes the guesswork and headache out of choosing a stroller. After you've completed the survey you'll be presented with Baby Jogging Strollers.com's recommendations and some alternative choices. Order the one you want and in a few days, you and your baby can hit the streets or track with confidence, knowing you've made the right choice.

babyonthefly.com
BabyontheFly.com
253-332-0848
service@babyonthefly.com
Baby Gear

"Think Of It As...A Carseat With Landing Gear." That's the way the purveyors of the amazing Sit'n'Stroll baby travel system describe their product, and they're absolutely correct. You see, Sit 'n' Stroll is an all-in-one car seat, stroller, booster, and airplane seat. It converts in a few simple steps. The Sit'n'Stroll is FAA-Certified, USDOT, and LATCH-Compliant, and designed for forward- or rear-facing use. Because the device is rated for children weighing from 5 to 40 pounds, it will "grow" with your child. An optional sunshade makes the device a must-have for parents who travel.

babyride.com
Babyride.com
800-721 7444
info@babyride.com
Baby Gear

Babies are on the move! Shop here for bike trailers, car seats, and strollers. The selection is great and prices are moderate — a dynamite combination in anyone's baby book. If you're a fan of Aprica strollers, you'll be glad to know that most of the Aprica line is available here at a discounted price. Aprica blends Japanese ingenuity with high-fashion Italian fabrics, resulting in a lightweight, compact unit whose looks belie its durability. Expect items ordered from Babyride.com to ship within three to five business days.

barethreads.com
Bare Threads

512-306-0824
customer_service@barethreads.com

Apparel

Silk isn't usually considered as a suitable material for children's clothes. After viewing the adorable garments at Bare Threads, you may think of silk in a whole new way. The unique garments sold here are crafted from raw silk. This easy-care fabric, called silk noil, can be machine-washed at any temperature and machine- or line-dried. This easy-to-navigate site offers jumpsuits, jackets, T-shirts, tank tops, and front button shirts available for babies, boys, and girls. Pick from a broad range of colors and then select a silk screen image for a really special look.

benettondiapers.com
Benetton Baby Diapers

888-254-8433
contact@benettondiapers.com

Baby Needs

The plain white diaper has been kicked in the butt. United Colors of Benetton, long known for brightly colored fashions, now has a line of disposable "diaperwear" that can't help but appeal to its youngest customers. Shop by diaper type, including swim, double, and pull-ups, or make your selection based on size. You can also pick up wipes, booties, and other essential baby paraphernalia while you're shopping.

birthdayinabox.com
Birthday in a Box

800-989-5506
customerservice@birthdayinabox.com

Party Time

The name tells it all at Birthday in a Box: Shop here for all the supplies you need for your child's next birthday party. Choose from one of the many age-appropriate themes or select a personalized package. A standard "box" for eight includes invitations, coordinated tableware, matching helium-quality balloons, favors and wrapping, and food and decorating suggestions. Of course, you needn't buy a complete kit; you can pick and choose the items you want. The owners started the site back in 1996 with the goal of making party planning fun and enjoyable for parents. Have questions or comments? The Birthday in a Box folks would love to hear from you.

 Recommended   **$** Price   Selection   Convenience   Service   Security

birthdaypartygameslady.com
Birthday Party Games Lady

800-558-1966
thebplady@aol.com

Party Time

The Birthday Party Games Lady offers a more cerebral approach to birthday-party planning than most of the party sites on the Internet. Instead of selling napkins, plates, and the like, she sells a complete plan — almost like a blueprint — for one of four themed parties. Each party consists of an elaborate game that will keep children engaged from the moment they walk through the door. Choose from the Detective, Survivor, Medieval Madness, or Harry Potter Birthday Party Games packages, each designed for a specific age group. Preparation time and supplies needed are minimal; bring the food and you're good to go.

bobuxusa.zoovy.com
BobuxUSA

800-315-3039
customerservice@bobuxusa.com

Apparel • Footware

A baby's feet need to last a lifetime. Inferior shoes or the wrong shoes can cause serious problems later. Bobux claims to have the perfect shoes for babies under 2. This company's amazing shoes are made in New Zealand from soft natural leather (called Eco-Leather). The unique ankle design makes the shoes easy to slip on and then remain in place. The shoes have soft soles and are lined with all-natural materials. Visit the site to learn more about this Kiwi import, and sign up for a drawing for a free pair of shoes.

boomerskids.com
Boomerskids.com

520-323-2441
boomerskidz@yahoo.com

Apparel

Boomerskids.com is the place to go for dress-up clothes for children. In fact, this site offers a year-round collection of "wedding wear" that can't be beat. Shop here for flower girl dresses in a range of sizes for infants to teens. Some of the dresses are plain, some fancy, but all are impressively elegant. Head coverings and shoes accompany the collection. Boys' suits and tuxedos are available, too. There are even a few mother-daughter dresses for a look that's sure to create a stir. The Showstopper Collection features dresses and costumes designed for young beauty pageant contestants.

britaxusa.com
BritaxUSA.com
800-721-7444
No e-mail address listed
Baby Gear

Britax USA is the American arm of a British company that has been manufacturing children's safety products for over 30 years. The company uses five crash sleds to meet global safety standards. The result of that testing is used in all its products sold in the United States, ranging from rear-facing infant seats to seatbelt-positioning boosters for older children. Many of the car seats and strollers sold at the site also have side impact protection, a feature not found in most similar child safety products. Visit the site to learn more about Britax USA and order one of the superlative seats, strollers, or infant carriers.

buggybuddy.com
buggybuddy.com
888-279-2533
tjwaldroup@aol.com
Safety

Did you know that 22,500 shopping cart injuries occur each year? The makers of Buggybuddy developed an amazing little device to help keep infants and children safe and comfortable in a shopping cart. The simple device is made of soft cotton material with a pad in the back, sides, and seat. A soft wide belt in the front attaches to the back with Velcro. The ingenious device holds babies upright in the cart seat. It restrains older kids from standing up and falling out.

caretrak.com
CareTrak
800-842-4537
caretrak@caretrak.com
Special Needs

The Care Trak systems can make life easier for parents of children with Down's syndrome, traumatic brain injury, or autism. Because children with these problems often wander away, Care Trak systems monitors their location. All Care Trak systems require the potential wanderer to wear a one-ounce water-resistant wrist or ankle transmitter that triggers an alert when the child leaves the pre-set range. Care Trak makes it easy for other family members to stop acting like police and function normally. Care Trak can tie in with your local police department.

 Recommended   Price   Selection   Convenience   Service   Security

cavenders.com
Cavenders

866-826-4865
custserv@cavenders.com

Footwear

In a world of fakes and phonies, Cavender's sells genuine cowboy boots for kids. The popular Texas chain has been selling great-looking clothes, accessories, and shoes and boots to kids and their parents for over forty years. The boot collection is extensive. From traditional Western boots to roper boots and work boots, you'll find the perfect boot here. Moms and Dads can find boots here too. Prices are surprisingly inexpensive; expect to pay under $50 for a pair of Western boots in children's sizes.

cbookpress.org
Children's Book Press

866-481-5827
webmaster@kidscan.com

Toys and Books

Children's Book Press, CBP for short, is a nonprofit publisher of multicultural and bilingual children's picture books. The first books that were published by CBP focused on Native Americans, but now the collection encompasses other ethnic groups as well. The books available at this site are arranged by ethnic group: African American, Asian American, Latino Chicano, and Native American. Multicultural Anthologies are available, too. You can also see the latest books that have been published. Teachers can find online teaching resources. Quantity discounts are offered to school and public libraries and nonprofit and corporate organizations.

⭐ childcarriers.com
ChildCarriers.com

800-742-0869
info@childcarriers.com

Baby Gear

Carrying a baby around in your arms gets awfully tiring after a while. Why not load your child into a backpack-type carrier or a front pack that allows the baby to see your face? These styles and more are available at the stellar ChildCarriers.com. This company specializes in fit. A Fit Chart on the site ensures you're getting the right carrier. Need more help? Phone support is available during business hours. Free shipping is available on all purchases over $79.99 and there's a "no questions asked" return policy if you're not completely satisfied with your carrier.

child-safety-gates.com
Child Safety Gates.com

610-539-9050
info@child-safety-gates.com
Safety

Need a gate to keep your child or toddler from getting into trouble? Child Safety Gates.com can help you find the gate you need, and show you how to install it properly. Shop by brand or price, or use the optional Baby Gates Selector Tool to find the right gate. Simply answer the five-question form with responses that most closely match your requirements. Then click "See Results," and the gate that best fits your needs is displayed. Installation kits and tips are available to ensure your gate stays just where you want it.

childsafetystore.com
ChildSafetyStore.com

561-272-8242
sales@childsafetystore.com
Safety

ChildSafetyStore.com takes its business very seriously. This company's products are hand-selected by a panel of parents and "professional child-proofers" (their exact term!) who use the same items sold here. Shop by Product, Room, or Brand or use the Product Search feature to find exactly what you need. Considerable thought has been put into the product descriptions at the site; many contain reviews by customers or the Baby Proofers team. Links to related products are also displayed when applicable. Sign up for the site newsletter and receive special promotions and coupons.

combistrollers.com
CombiStore

888-422-6624
questions@combistrollers.com
Baby Gear

CombiStore has one of the most comprehensive baby gear sites on the Internet, with a huge selection of strollers, high chairs, and rockers from which to choose. It even carries diaper bags and backpacks. However, the big draw is the Combi Acoustic Canopy Stroller. This stroller has audio speakers built directly into small pockets on both sides of the stroller's canopy and wired to the back canopy pouch. Plug in a CD or MP3 player, and your child can enjoy a concert during the stroller ride. Most orders ship out on the next business day.

 Recommended   Price   Selection   Convenience   Service   Security

cozycashmere.com
Cozy Cashmere

800-303-0417
info@ cozycashmere.com

Baby Gifts

Why not give baby a gift you would love to receive yourself? A cashmere blanket from Cozy Cashmere is cuddly and warm. The ultra-soft blanket is manufactured from the highest quality Italian cashmere. You can use it in the crib, stroller, baby carrier, or swing — anywhere baby needs the warmth and security of a blanket. Order the blanket in Baby Blue and Soft Pink. The company will personalize your package or add a special greeting and wrap the package elegantly to match the fabulous gift inside.

crib.com
Little Miss Liberty Round Crib Company

310-281-5400
customerservice@crib.com

Kids Room

In this world, there are cribs and then there are Cribs. That's right, folks, Cribs with a capital "C." The Little Miss Liberty Round Crib Company makes and sells the "original United States of America round patented crib." (Two European designers also sell the same-shaped crib.) Visit crib.com to see this amazing new baby bed. Every Little Miss Liberty Round Crib includes a high-density, waterproof foam mattress, and a dome kit. You'll also get a free mobile wand. Bedding and accessories are extra, but fortunately they're available at the site, too.

cwdkids.com
CWDKids

800-242-5437
E-mail form on site

Apparel

CWDKids is an Internet veteran. Since 1997, the company has been wowing customers with great brand-name clothing from Flapdoodles, Mulberribush, Hartstrings, Sweet Potatoes, Sara's Prints, and other fine manufacturers. Seasonal clothing and accessories for children are sold here. The site is arranged logically and is easy to navigate; handy links direct you to the Boys, Girls, and Family sections. Don't miss CWDKids Outlet for some of the best markdowns on the Internet. On a recent visit, I found a boy's designer belt marked down from $15 to $3.99.

cyberpatrol.com
CyberPatrol
866-806-4042
sales@cyberpatrol.com
Parenting Aid • Safety

CyberPatrol means business! The software package shields children from harmful Web site content. CyberPatrol also can prevent a child from divulging too much personal information during a chat or instant messaging session. Set up the Time Management feature for specific times when your child can access the computer—perfect for when you can't be in the room while your child's online. CyberPatrol is compatible with most ISPs, including AOL, and can be set up for multiple users. If your kids are hackers, CyberPatrol's log files will let you see when they try to crack the system.

cygnetcomm.org
Senior Year–The Game
530-743-0500
cygnet1522@comcast.net
For Teens Only

Being a teenager these days isn't easy. Teens are faced with some hard choices about drugs, alcohol, sex, and tobacco. Senior Year–The Game is a board game that helps teens see the consequences of some of these choices in a friendly, non-threatening way. The premise is simple: A space alien comes to earth to find out why some teens act irresponsibly. Along with 2 to 6 other players and an adult, the alien and the players begin as freshman and work their way through high school. Along the way, they face hard decisions. The first player to graduate wins.

designadiaper.com
Design a Diaper
877-739-4993
stacie@designadiaper.com
Baby Gifts

You can't go wrong with a diaper-themed baby gift, and Design-a-Diaper is standing by to put together a gift that's sure to please. A Diaper basket holds disposable diapers personalized with the baby's name or a phrase or saying of up to two lines in the color of your choice. The jumbo basket hold 45 diapers, the regular basket holds 30 and offers a combination of sizes (cleverly called Number One and Number Two). Each basket comes with a specially wrapped keepsake diaper and handwritten enclosure card. Other diaper gifts are available, too.

dickies.com
Dickies

877-425-7575
schooluniforms@dickies.com

Uniforms

Dickies has long been known as a maker of tough work clothes and bib overalls. It's only natural then, that this American company would move into the production of school uniforms. After all, school kids are often as hard on their clothes as construction workers. Dickies uses durable materials and stain release finishes that can take punishment; the uniforms sold here are designed for durability and ease of care. The site is organized for easy navigation and simplified ordering. You'll find some interesting facts and figures on the benefits of uniform programs and suggestions on starting a program at your child's school.

drlivingstons.com
Dr. Livingston's

406-993-9670
doc@drlivingstons.com

Apparel

What was old is now new at Dr. Livingston's: The tie-dye look rules at this site. Brightly colored T-shirts, rompers, onesies, and hats for infants and toddlers are available. Both long- and short-sleeved T-shirts are here for older children. Moms and Dads, you can buy tie-dye shirts in your sizes, too. The site makes navigation a snap. Use the helpful menu at Dr. Livingston's to find the group for which you're shopping — infants, kids, women, or men. There's even an entry for socks.

earthsbest.com
Earth's Best Baby Food

No phone number listed
E-mail form on site

Baby Needs

If you're looking for a high-quality baby food that's made from organically grown food, you're in the right spot. Earth's Best Organic Baby Food claims that it's the only full line of organic baby food made from foods grown without the use of any pesticides or fertilizers. Not only that, but the food is made from whole grains, fruits, and vegetables that have been cooked to preserve nutrition and flavor. Don't worry about additives; Earth's Best never adds a speck of salt, refined sugar, modified food starch, or artificial flavoring. Earth's Best full line of baby food is available at the site.

elitecarseats.com
EliteCarSeats
800-721-7444
info@babyride.com
Baby Gear

When you order a car seat from EliteCarSeats, you know you're getting the best. Why? Because Elite Car Seats claims, "we will not sell a car seat that we would not use with our own children." In keeping with this promise, this company only sells a few select brands and models of car seats. Visit the site to buy a car seat for your baby. Use the chart on the site to determine which type of car seat you need for your child. Learn about the LATCH system (Lower Anchors and Tethers for Children) and what it means to you.

elizabethstewartclarkandcompany.com
Elizabeth Stewart Clark Historic Clothing
No phone number listed
E-mail form on site
Apparel

One of the wonders of the Internet is the realm of possibilities it offers. This site, Elizabeth Stewart Clark Historic Clothing, is a perfect example. Without the Net (and this book) how would you have known where to find custom-made authentic Victorian clothing for your children? The clothes are sewn to your child's measurements, so get out the tape measure. Order well in advance because it takes around six weeks for the clothing to be completed. If you prefer, you can order a pattern and, in true Victorian fashion, stitch the clothes yourself.

elliecards.com
ellie cards
858-509-9003
info@elliecards.com
Special Needs

elliecards are a complete set of picture cards that are used to supplement communications for children with autism or speech disorders. The elliecards system was developed by parents of special needs children who needed some way to bridge the communication gap between them and their children. The carefully thought-out system consists of laminated cards that are placed in an easy-to-use binder. Each card is a photo of an everyday life item. The photos are less abstract than pictures and more easily identified by a young child. Several packages containing various combinations of elliecards are available.

 Recommended   Price   Selection   Convenience   Service   Security

enablingdevices.com
Enabling Devices

800-832-8697
info@enablingdevices.com
Special Needs

Enabling Devices, originally known as Toys for Special Children, has been focused on the needs of children with disabilities since 1976. The toys and products produced by the company are designed to improve the quality of life for those with disabling conditions. You'll find a variety of toys here including activity centers, bead chains, blocks and puzzles, bubble blowers, and much more. All the toys are arranged by category, making them easy to find and view. Unfortunately, you can't order directly online at this time; you'll need to call in your order.

★ eternalmoments.com
eternal moments

913-638-2130
info@eternalmoments.com
Baby Gifts

Time flies so fast. Why not send a unique keepsake of the day baby was born? At eternal moments, you can do just that. Displayed as the first page of a newspaper, the 11×17-inch Babyville Times contains up to 40 pieces of information about the day the baby was born. You can even send the company a digital picture of the baby to be included on the page. Decide on the format you want: unframed, mounted on poster board, and so on, and then click and order. After you enter your payment method, you'll be asked to add the personal information that will be used to make up the articles.

★ fitteen.com
FITteen.com

No phone number listed
teentrainer@comcast.net
For Teens Only

FITteen is dedicated to helping teens get fit and learn about diet and exercise. Fitness is important for teens because the habits they develop now will last long into adulthood. The site is a treasure trove of great information about exercise and workouts. Click Ask the Trainer to ask about information on a specific workout. Information about nutrition is covered, too, with links to recipes, eating plans, and food logs. Shop at FITteen for cool hats, shirts, and other workout gear imprinted with the FITteen logo. The items look cool and best of all, the profits support this commendable site.

fleecefarm.com
Fleece Farm

800-776-5319
sales@fleecefarm.com

Apparel

Children hate few things more than the feel of a stiff, scratchy shirt. Fleece Farm understands that. The clothes sold at this site will never scratch because they're made of 100 percent cotton, and most items are made of soft, touchable sweatshirt-feeling fleece. Visit Fleece Farm for shirts, sweatshirts, bike shorts, and more. It also offers a selection of comfortable baby clothes for infants. The easy-care Basic Whites can be bleached and popped into the dryer so you needn't worry if your child makes a mess. A huge selection of silk screen designs complement the Fleece Farm collection. Adult sizes in selected items are available, too.

footbeats.com
Footbeats

860-745-2009
info@footbeats.com

Footwear

Who would have guessed that you can buy shoes for all your children without taking a step? Footbeats offers an amazing selection of shoes for children from a variety of manufacturers. From baby's first shoes to name-brand sneakers, Footbeats has the shoes for your child. The layout of the site makes navigation easy and finding the right pair of shoes at the right price is a straightforward endeavor. Sites like this one are sure to leave traditional shoe stores shaking in their shoes.

frenchtoast.com
FrenchToast.com

800-373-6248
service@frenchtoast.com

Uniforms

Free shipping and special discounts make FrenchToast.com a great place to buy school uniforms. Shopping here is a breeze. Items are arranged by size, and if your school has registered with the site, a handy search tool shows you the items you must purchase for this year's school wardrobe. Know the item number of the item you want to order? Enter it in the quick order box and your order's almost done. Join FrenchToast.com for information about sales alerts, new product updates, and special offers.

funkyshop.com
Funkyshop.com

727-789-2824
info@funkyshop.com

Toys and Books

If you're over 19, you're probably going to hate Funkyshop.com. But hey, that's okay, because the target market is teens — especially kids who favor the punk look. You can find a lot of special effects for hair at this site, although if you're not ready to go all the way, try Dye Hard, Manic Panic's wash-in, wash-out hair dye. For a longer-lasting effect, semi-permanent dye in colors that range from Atomic Turquoise to Vampire Red is sure to get someone's attention. The site also sells real and fake body jewelry (don't ask!), punk clothes, and accessories.

⭐ gentlylovedclothing.com
GentlyLovedClothing.com

No phone number listed
sales@gentlylovedclothing.com

Apparel

One of the most confounding things about babies is that they grow so fast. Sometimes, spending hard-earned cash on baby clothes just doesn't seem reasonable. Well, it makes great sense if you buy clothes from this site. The items aren't new, but they've had to pass a rigorous approval process (the site owner's) to be offered for sale. Browse by size to see what's in the current catalog. Some items sell quickly, so be prepared to buy it when you see it! Prices are about half what you would pay for the same new piece of clothing in a department or specialty store. And shipping is a flat rate of $3.95.

giveashare.com
GiveAshare.com

866-291-9918
customer_service@giveashare.com

Baby Gifts

Start your baby on firm financial footing with a single share of stock from one of several companies shown at the site. Of course, the price of the share is dependent on the actual trading cost of the stock, so you may want to study the stock market if you're really serious about this gift. You'll also pay related service and registration fees. The gift includes framing and matting of the stock certificate. You can choose your frame and the wording on the plaque. The stock certificate is real; the baby is a registered stockholder in the company whose name appears on the certificate.

healthtex.com
Healthtex

800-554-7637
E-mail form on site

Apparel

Healthtex is one of those brands parents know they can trust. Well-made clothes in a range of sizes and colors, comfortable fabrics, and low prices have inspired loyalty for years. Not content to rest, Healthtex has added a new feature to its kid's clothing line that's sure to have parents clicking back to this site multiple times. Called "Kidproof" and added to select Healthtex lines, the revolutionary knit fabric protection keeps clothes looking fresh and new, even when they've been washed over and over. Learn about Kidfresh and see all the latest baby and children's fashions at the site.

iftheshoefitsetc.com
If The Shoe Fits

256-739-0262
info@iftheshoefitsetc.com

Footwear

The old saying "if the shoe fits, wear it," definitely applies to this site. If the Shoe Fits works hard to satisfy every customer. Its broad range of merchandise — from dress shoes to dance shoes and everything in between — is sure to satisfy the fussiest parent. Don't miss the hand-painted clogs. Rain gear, dance bags, hair accessories, and a great assortment of socks round out the selection. The site also offers a size chart that also converts European sizes to American sizes.

infashionkids.com
In Fashion Kids

908-371-1733
infashionkids@aol.com

Apparel

Don't be put off by the organization (or lack of organization) at In Fashion Kids. You can find lots of good clothing here, but sometimes you have to wade through a lot of links and text to find it. The prices are great and the selection is really unique. For example, on a recent visit I found ladybug-themed rain slickers, boots, and matching backpacks for girls, and several Eton suits and other dress clothes for little boys. Need a Halloween costume? Check out the extensive collection sold here. Buy a costume now and, if necessary, put it away for next year.

 Recommended Price Selection Convenience Service 🔒 Security

⭐ injoyvideos.com
InJoy Videos
303-447-2082
custserv@injoyvideos.com
Parenting Aid

If you learn best by seeing rather than reading, InJoy Videos can provide some great parenting assistance. These videos span a variety of parenting topics, including age-appropriate play for several age groups, safety at home, and circumcision. Many of the videos are available in both English and Spanish. The Five Essentials of Successful Parenting, one of InJoy's newest videos, comes as a five-video set and offers invaluable assistance to new and experienced parents. Videos on other important topics, including a video series for teens (and parents), are available at the site.

innopharm.com
Diaper Goop
501-225-8683
trogers@diapergoop.com
Health and Fitness

Sometimes simple is better. The only product for sale at this site is a soothing balm called Diaper Goop. No big television or magazine ad campaigns are planned for Diaper Goop. In fact, it's been a closely guarded secret by customers who are afraid if the product gets too popular that demand will exceed the current supply. Diaper Goop soothes inflamed bottoms better than most products that cost twice as much. You can buy it in select pharmacies and drug counters, or order it from the easy-to-navigate site. My personal suggestion is order double what you need. It's great! It works!

jrayshoes.com
J-Ray Shoes
800-342-6321
lynn@jrayshoes.com
Footwear

Since 1955, J-Ray shoes has been selling quality children's shoes to thousands of satisfied customers. This company specializes in hard-to-find sizes, especially non-standard widths. Shop here for shoes to complement classic and heirloom clothes. Or order a pair of Bear Feet shoes for your child. Bear Feet shoes are flexible and designed to mold to the shape of a child's foot, and come in a variety of styles and sizes. Special orders are welcome; contact J-Ray for details and delivery times.

kbtoys.com
KBToys.com

888-443-8366
customerservice@shop.kbtoys.com

Toys and Books

Way back in 1922, a few brothers named Kaufman opened a small confectionary store. Their goal was based on sound business practice: Give customers great service and superior selection and offer good value. The rest is history. The store thrived, grew into the KB Family of Stores, and, of course, opened KBToys.com. The owners' dedication to service at their online location is just as strong as it was in their candy store. The site is easy to navigate, and it's organized with you — the customer — in mind. Online purchases ship fast. If you're unsatisfied with your KBToys.com order, you can return or exchange it at a local KB Toys store.

keds.com
Keds.com

800-680-0966
E-mail form on site

Footwear

Few things feel as good as slipping into a comfortable pair of canvas shoes. The Keds.com Web site carries a wide selection of stylish and comfortable footwear for infants, toddlers, and older boys and girls. Scrolling through the online catalog, you will notice several unique shoes, including the Color Me Sneaker, which comes with five washable markers that lets your child draw and decorate the shoes over and over. Now how fun is that?

kidscanpress.com
Kids Can Press

866-481-5827
webmaster@kidscan.com

Toys and Books

Started in 1973 by a small group of women, Kids Can Press is a leading publisher of children's books. Visit the site for all the latest Franklin the Turtle books and stickers, or download some pages of the famous turtle to color at home. Kids Can Press is also home to Elliot Moose, and his books and some special pages devoted to him are located at the site. Don't miss the selection of craft books. With the selection of picture books for wee ones and novels for older children, Kids Can Press shows they know what kids like to read.

 Recommended   Price   Selection   Convenience   Service   Security

kidsfightingchance.com
Kids Fighting Chance

800-479-9933
customerservice@kidsfightingchance.com

Parenting Aid

Parents and children need to watch Kids Fighting Chance together. The video teaches children how to avoid dangerous situations, fight off attacks, and escape kidnapping attempts. Lifesaving techniques are covered, including how to use a backpack, jacket, or bicycle as protection or create a way to escape danger. Many more important tips and tricks are taught. There's a good chance that right now your child doesn't know any of the methods covered on the video. Practice the techniques over and over. Hopefully, your children will never need these new skills. If they do, your relatively low investment will have paid off.

kidstockmontana.com
Kidstock

877-753-4436
info@kidstockmontana.com

Apparel

Let Kidstock of Bozeman, Montana, outfit your child in style. The folks in Bozeman are a steady, sensible lot. They don't fall victim to fashion trends. Shop here for well-known brand names and sensible styles. The children's clothes are high quality and will probably last for more than one season. A Shelled Snowgear snowsuit by Molehill Mt Equipment is a great investment in your child's warmth and safety during the winter months. Shop by product or brand, or enter an item in the Search box and see if you get lucky.

lego.com
LEGO.com

800-453-4652
E-mail form on site

Toys and Books

Back in 1932, the LEGO Company was formed by a carpenter-turned-toymaker. His belief, "Only the Best is Good Enough," has been the guiding principle behind the company. Shop at LEGO.com for anything from a starter set of the building blocks to a complicated kit with thousands of pieces. Some of the kits are amazing; with a little patience and fortitude, you can build a train, tracks, and a model of Grand Central Station with the aid of kits. You can also purchase figures and accessories online. At LEGO.com, you're limited only by your budget and your imagination.

lilypadbaby.com
Lilypad Baby

No phone number listed
customerservice@lilypadbaby.com

Baby Gifts

A personalized baby gift speaks volumes. It shows that you've put some time and thought behind your offering and that you care. Your young recipient and parents needn't know that your gift came from Lilypad Baby, where with a few mouse clicks and keystrokes, a personalized gift can be dispatched quickly. Shop here for personalized baby bibs, baby gift sets, burp cloths, and baby blankets that are fashionable and functional. Bibs and burp cloths are designed with different fabrics on the front and back and are completely reversible. Gift prices start at around $15.

limitedtoo.com
Limited Too

866-458-3866
ltd2@toobrands.com

Apparel

Totally awesome. How else can you describe this site, with rockin' tweenage models wearing and selling all the great looks shown in the popular fashion mags? The site also features accessories like carryall bags, jewelry, and belts. Because the look is seasonal, the site and the stock change often. Most of the clothes carry the house brand label, but the Justice label, a slightly higher priced line, is sold as well. As an added bonus, you can apply online for a Limited Too credit card.

luckybrandjeans.com
Lucky Brand Kids

800-654-9777
luckygirl@luckyville.com

Apparel

What kid doesn't want clothes from Lucky Brand Dungarees? The Lucky Brand is really popular with school-age children and teens. Shopping here is just like shopping at one of Lucky Brand Dungaree's cavernous mall stores; find the section you want and then browse through the racks (links). Check out the Featured Collection for the latest looks for baby. Need a gift? The Lucky Brand folks thoughtfully have arranged a selection of their clothes and accessories just perfect for sending to a small recipient who will coo with delight when the package arrives.

 Recommended   Price   Selection   Convenience   Service   Security

milliondollarbaby.com
Million Dollar Baby

323-728-8988
info@milliondollarbaby.com

Kids Room

Million Dollar Baby is a great example of a company that's good at what it does — sell baby furniture. Currently, this company sells to independent specialty stores and doesn't compete with large chains. That's great for us Internet consumers because we get to shop at its online Factory Outlet Store. The offerings vary; on any given day you may find cribs, youth beds, rockers, and more. Typically, prices are low. Don't get discouraged if the store is empty when you visit. Furniture sells fast here. Check back often and be prepared to buy when you see something you like.

missem.com
MissEm.com

713-861-5445
missem@missem.com

Party Time

Instead of a plain-vanilla birthday party, how about something different for your child or teen this year? Miss Em has a few suggestions that are fun and exciting, but won't break the bank. There's a Storybook dress-up party, with hand-sewn, easy-care costumes such as Belle, Dorothy, and Little Red Riding Hood. Who wants to play Peter Pan? Peter Pan, Tinkerbell, Wendy, and Captain Hook costumes can be sewn to suit. Older kids will love the Slumber Pal Packs. Each pack holds an autograph T-shirt, flashlight, stickers, tattoos, and rhinestone body art. Check out the rest of her ideas at the site.

mngk.com
Move and Groove Kids

800-886-8801
munki@movengroovekids.com

Health and Fitness

At mngk.com, you can learn how to get your kids in shape through Munki, the star of a 26-minute Move 'N Groove Kids video. Munki leads his students through a fun dance and fitness routine that contains different movements and lots of action. The routine starts with a warmup and moves into a series of dance and aerobic moves. The video ends with a relaxing cool down. Program developers Deborah Damast and Sara Lavan have been teaching Creative Movement in New York city for more than 10 years and the video is an extension of their impressive skill.

moppetboutique.net
Moppet Boutique

866-466-7738
customerservice@moppetboutique.com
Kids Room

The owners of Moppet Boutique aren't corporate fat cats who are only in the furniture business to make money and don't care about the welfare of your children. They're parents, and that focus gives their furniture collection a unique slant. The furniture sold here is unusual (though often expensive). If you're tired of seeing the same old furniture everywhere you look, check out Moppet's castle loft beds, theme loft beds, and tent bunk beds. For something slightly less radical, a Hello Kitty heart-shaped computer chair is a great way to dress up a room.

mytoybox.com
MyToyBox.Com

866-682-8697
customercare@mytoybox.com
Toys and Books

The simplicity of MyToyBox.com's excellent toy store makes it a great place to shop for well-made toys, games, and some furniture and accessories. This company carries the complete line of Thomas the Tank Engine Wooden Railway products, as well as Thomas the Tank Engine books, games, puzzles, videos, clothing, and accessories. BRIO Wooden Railway toys and Lionel train sets are also available. If Groovy Girls are more to your liking, the entire collection awaits you. From time to time the site runs great clearance sales, so check back often.

namepaintings.com
namepaintings.com

877-739-4993
info@namepaintings.com.
Baby Gifts

Tropical scenes evoke a sense of happiness and peace, and namepaintings. com captures that feeling in the unique gift it offers. Imagine a tropical scene that spells out a baby's name. Pretty nifty, eh? Kazi Ahmed and his wife Cindy think so. In fact, you may have seen them at work in Key West, Vancouver, Hawaii, or San Francisco. A tropical name painting makes a great baby gift. It's unique (you can almost guarantee that yours will be the only one baby receives) and it will be a cherished memento. Visit the site to learn more about this unusual art form and see some samples.

 Recommended Price Selection Convenience Service  Security

★ naturerangers.com
Nature Rangers

877-429-2124
info@naturerangers.com

Apparel

The Nature Rangers store offers clothing and gear that's designed specifically for small hands and bodies. A long-sleeved pullover T-shirt with a special moisture-wicking lining sized for infants is more than an infant shirt, it's technical gear. Clothing is sized for kids from infants to about age 14. In addition to good shopping, the site is filled with great tips and information. Check in at the Visitor Center and read the latest Nature News or consult the Trip Planner for great vacation ideas.

netkidswear.com
Netkidswear.com

732-203-9677
info@netkidswear.com

Kids Room

Shop with confidence at Netkidswear.com. The site is the online department of Childrenswear Centres, a chain of children's megastores located in New Jersey. The furniture at this site is high quality. Items are usually in stock or can be obtained quickly. Check out the Wood & Wicker collection for a distinctive, elegant look. Handpainted children's rockers are heirlooms in the making and surprisingly easy on the budget. If you're a first-time buyer, read the Customer Ratings to find out what other shoppers had to say about their own purchasing experiences.

netnanny.com
Net Nanny

425-649-1100
sales@netnanny.com

Parenting Aid • Safety

Net Nanny is a software package that allows you to control your child's online experience. You can block specific sites from tender eyes, or use keyword blocking. Additional products include Chat Monitor, which monitors and filters online chat and instant messaging programs. Unlike some other monitoring software, Net Nanny products are so easy to install and configure that you won't need to ask your kids for help! Some of the newest software in Net Nanny's line benefits the whole family. Pop-Up Scrubber prevents annoying pop-up windows on Internet Explorer, and Ad-Free blocks a wide range of ads, spyware, and tracking cookies.

nickjr.com
nick.com

866-271-5860
E-mail form on site

Toys and Books

All the characters that kids love to watch on the Nickelodeon Channel are available in toy form. A shameless merchandising ploy to be sure, but what else do you expect from the official Nickelodeon Store? All the network's top players are here, including Dora the Explorer, Little Bill, and stuff from Blue's Clues. Of course, the perennial favorite, Sponge Bob Square Pants, gets ample representation, too, with many toys and games bearing his likeness. Happily, the toys and games sold here are reasonably priced and well made, and kids really like them.

notabeanbag.com
Not-A-Beanbag.com

616-361-1100
info@not-a-beanbag.com

Kids Room

Though the chair featured at notabeanbag.com looks like a beanbag, it's not. After I read through the information about the soft cushiony foam that fills the chair and conforms to your body, I realized this chair is much more. The Polymorphic Poof chair designers claim it's the "The Most Comfortable Chair on Earth...Maybe Even the Universe." The Polymorphic Poof chair is durable and comes in a wide variety of styles and sizes, including couch and pillow size, and even in fruit shapes. The chair is ideal for kids because unlike its pellet-filled lookalike, this chair will never produce the dreaded "bean bag blowout" mentioned on the site.

oralgiene.com
Oralgiene

800-933-6725
oralgiene@oralgiene.com

Health and Fitness

Kids and toothbrushes go together like oil and water. You can tell a child to brush, but chances are that the toothbrush will make only glancing contact with the teeth. The Time Machine battery-powered toothbrush changes all that. Colorful gears and blinking lights show through the clear case and make brushing extra fun. The 60-second timer shuts off automatically, so kids know when it's time to stop brushing. Dentists, hygienists, and orthodontists endorse this amazing brush, which comes with a one-year warranty.

 Recommended   Price   Selection Convenience Service   Security

oshkoshbgosh.com
OshKosh B'Gosh

800-692-4674
consumer@bgosh.com

Apparel • Footwear

For the last hundred years or so, OshKosh has been outfitting the American heartland. The clothing line has come a long way since its signature bib overall days. (You can still order them.) Shop here for infant, toddler, and boys and girl's play and school clothes. Some of the infant clothing is categorized as unisex, making for easy selection of styles and colors and matching shoes and socks. There's even a section for adults. You'll need to set up an account before you order so give yourself plenty of time for your first purchase.

pacifeeder.com
Pacifeeder

714-357-6777
info@pacifeeder.com

Special Needs

When you see what's for sale at this site, you're going to want one for every parent you know. The handy device, called a Pacifeeder, holds a baby bottle in place while the child sucks from a nipple attached to the end of a length of flexible clear tubing that runs to the bottle. Pacifeeder is for children from ages 3 to 24 months who drink from a bottle while on the go. Attach the Pacifeeder to a car seat, stroller, baby backpack, carrier, or just about any type of baby seat and the baby can happily and safely enjoy his or her bottle. Pacifeeder works with most conventional baby bottles.

parentingclass.net
ParentingClass.net

No phone number listed
E-mail form on site

Parenting Aid

ParentingClass.net offers online classes for parents going through a divorce or separation. The classes, which were designed by certified parenting instructors, are designed to help separating parents build a healthy relationship with one another while remaining parents to their children during this stressful time. To that end, the class includes a section on the various stages of divorce and how to design a co-parenting plan that works. The entire program is conducted online. Certificates for those who successfully complete the course and pass the final test are available — especially important if a parenting class was ordered by the court.

petiteamiefurniture.com
Petite Amie Furniture.com

619-544-9853
sales@petiteamiefurniture.com

Kids Room

Did you ever notice that most baby and children's furniture is made from wood or other hard material? Yet, kids like to be comfy and would enjoy curling up in an easy chair. The solution? Petite Amie Furniture.com, of course. This company's specialty is making kid-sized upholstered furniture that's just right for your child. Just select furniture from the online catalog and choose the fabric. You can mix and match fabrics; a chair can have one fabric on the skirt and another on the body. You'll need to call the site or e-mail your final order.

pipsqueakers.com
Pip Squeakers

866-722-4535
pipsqueakers@earthlink.net

Footwear

Pip Squeakers are the ideal shoes for babies. The flexible soles and roomy toe boxes are just perfect for growing little feet. However, the squeak in the shoe is what makes Pip Squeakers so special. Each time baby takes a step the shoe makes a noise. The makers claim that this squeaky noise helps enhance the development of a child's sense of hearing. More importantly, the squeak alerts parents that baby is on the move. Several different styles are available.

poopockets.com
Poo Pockets

No phone number listed
kimi@newconceptions.com

Baby Needs

Disposable diapers are convenient, sure, but the litter they leave behind is choking the earth, claim some environmentalists. Even if you're not a member of the Green Party, your baby might be sensitive to the plastic or other chemicals in disposables. PooPockets are one-size cotton diapers that present a healthy and environmentally friendly alternative. You can buy them pre-sewn or order the pattern and whip them up yourself. Each PooPocket is made with elasticized leg gussets, resulting in superior leakage protection. PooPockets fit all babies comfortably. Use by placing the PooPocket into a diaper cover with velcro-type closure and fastening.

 Recommended   Price   Selection   Convenience   Service   Security

pottycharts.com
Lee-Bee Motivational Charts
888-467-6889
info@lee-bee.com
Parenting Aid

In most households, chores turn into battles. Parents know that motivating children is one of the hardest parenting tasks. Lee-Bee has a tried-and-true method for motivating kids. Whether you're working on potty training (always a difficult time), chores, homework, or something else you've assigned, take a look at the Lee-Bee Motivational Chart system available at this site. The simple system comes with a chart, stickers, and magnets. Fill in the chart with your particular duties or chores and watch what happens. Read the details at the site and order this inexpensive life changer.

preemiediapers.com
Green Mountain Diapers
800-330-9905
kimi@newconceptions.com
Baby Needs

Finally, a site that sells diapers just for preemies! Premature babies are tiny. Wrapping a baby doll-like body in a big diaper is difficult and, worse, often uncomfortable for the child. Green Mountain sells cotton diapers for preemies and small babies. It specifically uses cotton over disposables because measuring output with a cloth diaper (often a medical necessity with a premature baby) is easier. This company also believes cotton is more comfortable on a tiny baby's tender skin. If you need baby items for a baby weighing less than 6 lb. 10 oz., Green Mountain is the place to shop.

preschoolians.com
Preschoolians
800-998-1322
info@preschoolians.com
Footwear

These shoes are definitely designed to get your child off on the right foot. Preschoolians creates shoes for every stage of toddler development, from pre-crawling to crawling, to first walking and finally to advanced walking and play. Preschoolians makes sizing and selecting the right shoes for your toddler easy while at the same time offering several attractive styles and colors. Preschoolians' guarantee and return policy further make buying shoes online an attractive option.

promdress.net
ThePromSite.Com

No phone number listed
E-mail form on site

For Teens Only

For most teens, the prom is "the" event of the school year. Even avowed prom-haters secretly hang on to every detail about the mythical party. ThePromSite.Com is devoted entirely to prom details —how to get there, what to wear, the party afterward, and so on. Click the Embarrassing link to read stories of hapless prom goers — they will make you laugh out loud. Post your own prom stories. You can also purchase a copy of The First and Original Book of Prom. Made up of the best 316 stories submitted to ThePromSite.Com, the book is a meaningful read for parents, prom goers, and educators.

proschooluniform.com
Pro School Uniform.com

No phone number listed
info@proschooluniforms.com

Uniforms

Pro School Uniform.com covers all the bases. From sweat clothes to boys' tuxedos, this site has clothes for every school and extracurricular activity in the year. Choose from pants and shorts, skirts and skorts, and a wide variety of shirts and tops. Finish your shopping with a backpack and every kid's favorite, a big bag of socks. Pro School Uniform.com can be your site for one-stop, back-to-school shopping. While you're shopping, check out the Adult Wear page. Now Dad and junior can dress like twins.

puddlesboots.com
Puddles Limited

866-721-6246
sales@puddlesboots.com

Footwear

Puddles Limited comes to you from the Isle of Man, where it rains almost every day of the year. Small wonder then, that this company offers one of the best collections of rainwear for children. Children will hope for downpours, just so they can wear cleverly themed boots and raincoats from this site. Shop here for Zebra rain clogs, Stegosaurus boots, giraffe shoes, and bee umbrellas. Buy an entire set — boots, slicker, and umbrella — by theme or mix and match the characters you like. Puddles Limited is "your one stop shop for all your rainy day needs." The site also offers feet measurement tips.

 Recommended   Price   Selection   Convenience   Service   Security

quietquilt.com
Quiet Quilt

760-918-9555
marniebe@pacbell.net

Special Needs

Some children with autism crave deep pressure; in fact, it's the only thing that helps these kids to relax. A mother whose son is on the autistic spectrum found that weighted blankets and vests soothed her son. Yet none of the commercial products she found was really helpful. The solution? The nimble-fingered mother got out her sewing machine. After much trial and error, the Quiet Quilt was developed. The amazing creation is the perfect solution if your child needs something heavy around him. The Quiet Quilt comes in a full size and a lap size, suitable for taking on car trips and in stressful situations.

rockingcrib.com
RockingCrib.com

847-490-5388
rockingcrib@yahoo.com

Kids Room

Anyone who has soothed a crying baby back to sleep knows that a rocking motion lulls the baby into calmness. Wouldn't it make sense to buy your child an automatic rocking crib that could rock him or her to sleep? The Rocking Crib is a full-size crib that comes in several styles. When you put your baby down for a nap or for the night, push the Unlock button and turn on the timer. The cost is roughly equal to a comparable non-rocking model.

roomstogokids.com
Roomstogokids.com

888-709-5380 Option 1
onlinesupport@roomstogokids.com

Kids Room

Children's bedrooms are for much more than sleeping. Because your children spend so much time in their rooms, why not create an environment where they can play, study, and entertain their friends? Roomstogokids.com can help you create those special places. This site features great looks and accessories for kids' rooms. Make sure you enter your Zip code in the Zip Code Check box to determine whether your address is in Roomstogokids' extensive delivery area. You can search for a complete room or buy pieces individually. Check out Roomstogokids.com's great credit terms if you can't pay right away.

safeandsecurebaby.com
Safe and Secure Baby

888-802-2229
info@safeandsecurebaby.com

Safety

Safe and Secure Baby is a personal business to Adena and Harold Surabian, the owners. "Nothing is more important than the safety and protection of your children," they claim. Accordingly, they offer a great selection of products designed to keep kids safe. Your best bet is to shop by category; click a category on the left and a list of related subcategories appears in the center. You may have to click two or three times to find what you want, but there's an impressive collection of products assembled at this baby safety superstore.

safetyape.com
Go Ape Over Safety

800-915-4653
info@safetyape.com

Parenting Aid • Safety

When kids feel threatened or frightened about information that's being presented, they often stop paying attention. Information about safety for children doesn't need to be scary. SA (pronounced *Say*), the Safety Ape, and his nephew, Willie, have just the right tone on the instructional safety material offered at this site. The two characters croon their way through important safety issues including bicycle, water, and fire safety; fall prevention; poison; seatbelt safety; and gun safety. Kids love the songs; you'll catch yourself singing them, too. Order an audiocassette or CD and get a corresponding coloring book.

schoolunif.com
SchoolUniforms.com

800-372-6523
info@frankbee.com

Uniforms

SchoolUniforms.com means business. The site is run by the Frank Bee Company and is readily translated into five languages. The Frank Bee Company provides uniforms to some of the most prestigious schools in the United States and is ready and able to outfit your child, too. You'll find the requisite khakis and polo shirts here, but you'll also find a great selection of blazers and suits for boys, girls, and adults. Gym clothes, underwear, and shoes are also available. For the forward-looking, the site offers academic gowns and regalia. (It doesn't hurt to dream.)

 Recommended   Price   Selection   Convenience   Service   Security

school-uniforms-hair-bows.com
School-Uniforms-Hair-Bows.com
866-955-5229
info@school-uniforms-hair-bows.com
Uniforms

If your daughter has long hair, you already know that hair bows are an important part of her school uniform. Many schools require girls to wear their hair up. Bows are a great addition to a uniform, and at some schools they are mandatory. School-Uniforms-Hair-Bows.com has a collection of pre-made bows ready to go. If you don't see what you need, this company can make a custom bow from a swatch of material. You can find scrunchies and headbands, too. Also available are ties for girls, boys, and adults. Add to that a selection of novelty items and back-to-school shopping is complete.

selfesteemclothing.com
Self Esteem Clothing
323-889-4300
info@selfesteemclothing.com
For Teens Only

Self Esteem Clothing seems a bit gimmicky at first. Teaming pop psychology with a positive message with a hip line of trendy clothes is a marketer's dream. Yet, the concept works. The site is a hit with teenage girls from all over the world. A message board receives daily postings, girls share their most embarrassing moments without shame, and emotional original poetry is posted for all to see. Young women are encouraged to feel good about themselves here. The feel-good attitude is reflected in the fashions. Kicky and fun, they range in sizes from XS to 3X. Shoes and purses are available, too.

shoeboxtasks.com
Shoe Box Tasks
888-268-6355
information@shoeboxtasks.com
Special Needs

The Shoe Box Tasks site offers simple work activities. These elementary jobs are designed to be opening points for children with autism who are leaning how to work. The tasks are also useful for children who have been diagnosed with mental retardation. Individuals with developmental delays, visual or motor impairments, and even very young children who have no impairments at all have also used the tasks. Each specially designed, carefully constructed task helps the child who is performing the work overcome organizational difficulties and gain new strength and confidence.

shoesforkids.com
ShoesforKids.com

800-879-8260
questions@shoesforkids.com

Footwear

Shoesforkids.com is a site dedicated to providing quality footwear for children. Select footwear from several categories, including casual and school shoes, uniform and classics, dress and party, and sandals and boots. To solve the mystery of how shoes are bought online without trying them on first, the Shoesforkids Web site provides a FAQ section that addresses fitting and online purchase concerns. The FAQs also include interesting general information on children's shoes such as how long we as parents can expect a pair of shoes to last before we are again logging on to buy another pair. Shoesforkids.com offers brand-name footwear with a great shipping and return policy.

shoofly-baby-shoes.com
Shoofly Shoes

303-775-2555
info@shoofly-baby-shoes.com

Footwear

Instant heirlooms are created at Shoofly Shoes. The handcrafted infant shoes with designs of animals and bugs, boats and trains, flowers, holiday themes, sports and shapes are so adorable that you'll have a hard time letting your children wear them out in the rain. In fact, you might want to buy a pair for wear and a pair as a keepsake. (Fortunately, they're inexpensive!) Enter your baby in Shoofly's gallery and let the world see her wearing her Shoofly shoes.

slumbersounds.com
Slumber Sounds

866-575-2229
service@slumbersounds.com

Health and Fitness • Parenting Aid

Does the sound of a crying baby make you feel helpless? It can, especially if you can't do anything to soothe the poor tyke, no matter how hard you try. Slumber Sounds understands. They're specialists in products and information for your crying baby. The signature three-track CD has quieted countless babies. The first track plays a mother's heartbeat, the second track plays traditional nursery melodies, and the third track plays simple background music. Listen to a sample of the music at the site. Other products include an Ookie doll, colic remedies, and herbal massage oils.

snoedel.com
Snoedels

877-766-3335
customerservice@snoedel.com

Baby Needs

Snoedels are almost indescribably adorable. They are small puppet-like toys that are used as comforts or sleep aids by babies. The people who produce each one, mostly mothers themselves who call themselves Snoedelers, have carefully thought out every aspect of the design. Snoedels are made of only the finest natural raw materials. The head is made from wool and the body is made from 100 percent cotton flannel. Take note: Snoedels do not have any faces so that the babies can imagine the faces of their parents on the sleep aid. Snoedels come in a few different sizes and colors.

★ soundprints.com
Soundprints

800-228-7839
info@soundprints.com

Toys and Books

Children of all ages love the Soundprints collection. Made up of storybooks, read-along audiobooks, and plush toys, Soundprints leads children through a trip of wonder and excitement. The picture books present fascinating natural science and historical facts cleverly woven into charming and thrilling stories. Shopping at this site is a pleasure. The books are arranged by series, with detailed descriptions providing just the right amount of information. Some books come with stuffed animals. Be sure to click the Special Offers link to take advantage of the special values that Soundprints offers its Internet customers.

southernchild.com
Aunt Polly's

864-222-0131
hotcornbread@earthlink.net

Apparel

Your first response to this site will most likely be "Aunt Polly must be kidding," but when you get deeper into this site you'll realize that she's dead serious. Not too many other places sell "partisan playwear" for children, so it's great that Aunt Polly's fills the niche. The partisan playwear here consists of children's clothing that has embroidered elephants (Republican) or donkeys (Democratic) across the front. Aunt Polly's also features a line of South Carolina pride items. All clothing is sized for young children.

store.enfamil.com
Enfamil Home Delivery

800-222-9123
askmeadjohnson@bms.com

Baby Needs

Mead Johnson, the makers of the popular baby formula called Enfamil, have established a simple way to purchase Enfamil in case lots. You can order any of the product's various types at the site: Enfamil with Iron, Enfamil Prosobee, and Enfamil Lactofree LIPIL to name a few. Nursette bottles are available, too, and just in case you need them, Mead Johnson is offering a few other baby and nutritional must-haves. Orders are shipped by FedEx. Ordering baby formula online makes sense. With a few mouse clicks and a credit card, you'll never run out of formula in the middle of the night again.

stuffedark.com
Stuffed Ark

800-530-6391
info@stuffedark.com

Toys and Books

Sometimes a Web site makes you stop dead in your tracks and say "Ahhhh." Stuffed Ark is just that site; the animals sold here are so lifelike and cute that you're bound to want one for your very own (I did). Children love them, too. Just about every animal from A to Z is represented; from armadillos to zebras, the collection is amazing. You can even find specific breeds of dogs and cats. If you're looking for a baby gift, check out the Baby Stuff section, where some animals have special features, such as proof-stitched baby-safe eyes.

sunproof.com
MasqueRays Sun Proof Fashions

877-786-7848
info@sunproof.com

Apparel

Exposure to the sun's damaging rays now can cause problems with a child's skin later. MasqueRays Sun Proof Fashions protects your child from the dangerous rays of the sun. The clothing, manufactured in Fiji and Australia, is rated UPF 50+. (Australian UPF ratings for clothing are similar to American SPF ratings for sunscreen.) A baby romper, swim shirt, and short are available in infant sizes. Older children will delight in the selection of sun suits, shirts, and shorts. Floppy brimmed hats round out the collection.

 Recommended   Price   Selection   Convenience   Service   Security

talkingpinatas.com
Talkingpinatas.com

866-798-5600
customerservice@talkingpinatas.com

Party Time

Whack! Whack! Whack! Kids love to swing away at a treat-filled piñata. Make the swing even more fun with a talking piñata. Choose a piñata that speaks when it's hit or when it detects motion. A wide variety of shapes and styles are available. If you don't see what you're looking for, use the site's Search feature to find the style that's right for your party. Generally the piñatas say "Wow! You're so lucky," "Let's have a party," or "Youch! Awesome hit!" Alternatively, purchase a non-talking piñata and an electronic talking device and put together your own talking piñata.

totsinmind.com
Tots in Mind

800-626-0339
info@totsinmind.com

Safety

Tots in Mind has some innovative products to keep babies and toddlers safe. Consider this company's original, cozy Crib Tent. The tent fits over the top of a standard crib and prevents children from falling or climbing out. The Baby's Bug Net System, a two-piece insect-proofing system, keeps nasty bugs away from tender skin, but allows air and sunlight in. The portable Playard Tent can be used indoors or outside and keeps babies secure and safe from unwanted visitors like the family pet. Visit the site to view all the products in the line, order items or replacement parts, and download manuals and written instructions.

trendytootsies.com
TrendyTootsies.com

541-548-6688
customerservice@trendytootsies.com

Footwear

If you're looking for a unique baby shower gift, check out TrendyTootsies.com, which offers hand-crafted shoes for toddlers. Each pair of shoes is hand-painted, making them an ideal keepsake and almost assuring that these shoes will one day find themselves bronzed and sitting out for display. You can choose from a number of hand-painted designs, from tractors to golf to watermelons. These shoes will draw so many compliments you may be left wishing they came in adult sizes.

truelovebaby.com
True Love Baby

No phone number listed
info@truelovebaby.com

Baby Gifts

True Love Baby is a great place to shop for baby gifts. The selection is extensive and items in a wide range of prices are available. If you're looking for a personalized gift, consider an adorable piggy bank. (It's never too early to save for college.) Beware: The plush toys available here are so charming you may want one for yourself. Click the links on the handy menu bar until you find the gift you want to send. True Love Baby makes it easy to welcome the new arrival.

waresofthewildwest.com
Wares of the Wild West

877-864-6937
No e-mail address on site

Footwear

No children should be out rustlin' up a herd of cattle without first visiting Wares of the Wild West. This fun site provides children and parents with the footwear and accessories of the Wild West. The site provides Western-style footwear for infants, toddlers, and children including Western Crepe Soles, Classic Western boots, Buckaroo Boots, and of course, Wingtip Boots. The site makes navigation a breeze. Use the handy menu at Wares of the Wild West to find the group for which you're shopping — boys, girls, or infants, for example. Best of all, prices are marked down every day of the year.

weeexercise.com
Wee Exercise

407-833-0044
info@weeexercise.com

Health and Fitness

A child is never too young to start a fitness program. Wee Exercise activities start your child on a road to fitness and can be part of a healthy playtime you enjoy together. The four-part program promoted at Wee Exercise is designed to supplement a baby's natural development through challenging physical activities. Purchase the program on video or DVD. Supplement your exercise program with a fuzzy rug, bouncy ball, or Baby Bumbo Seat. Is your baby an Exercise Master? E-mail a photo, and the judges just may pick your darling as the next "Baby of the Quarter."

 Recommended Price Selection Convenience Service Security

★ wildzoo.com
Wild Zoo

888-543-8588
wildzoo@teleport.com

Kids Room

If you expect the computer to be used as an educational tool, make the computer environment as comfortable as possible with a child-sized computer desk or table from Wild Zoo. Don't force your young child to access the computer from an adult-sized desk or table. The child-sized desks here are modified easily and are designed to grow with your children. The buddy desk has a bench seat built for two. Complete the playroom set with coordinating play tables. Wild Zoo's furniture is made in Oregon and simple to assemble. It comes with white or natural tops and your choice of trim in eight colors.

winterfootwear.com
Winterfootwear.com

800-279-0194
customer_service@winterfootwear.com

Footwear

Have cold feet? The folks at Winterfootwear.com will take the chill out of the air. The footwear available at Winterfootwear.com is specifically targeted toward keeping little feet warm and toasty in even the coldest weather. There is a bit to learn about purchasing quality winter footwear, and this site provides the information you need to know before buying those boots. Winterfootwear.com has a few different styles and colors from which to choose when selecting winter boots in youth sizes.

wowdolls.com
Wow Dolls

No phone number listed
info@wowdolls.com

Toys and Books

Her body is unattainable, her looks are out of the reach of most women, and her love life — with or without Ken — is something to dream about. She's the one and only Barbie. Mattel's Barbie doll has been a big seller since it hit the toy stores years ago. Wow Dolls sells only Barbie dolls. Some of the dolls are collector's items and are somewhat pricey. For example, the Crystal Jubilee Barbie, created for Barbie's 40th anniversary by Bob Mackie, sells for around $199. The site also offers Barbie dolls from the current line.

Preparing Your Home for a New Baby

Bringing home the new arrival is the biggest day in a family's life. New parents are often nervous and worried. Relax! The baby is coming to live in your house. As long as you provide a warm, safe environment with lots of love, your baby will be fine.

Babies need an incredible amount of gear and supplies. Start your shopping a few months in advance of the planned arrival date, because babies have a way of coming early sometimes. However, you don't need to run from store to store to get your house equipped. Shop comfortably for all your baby needs on the Internet.

Start with baby's crib. A round crib from Little Miss Liberty Round Crib Company (crib.com) is the latest and greatest. If you want a more traditional style, an automatic rocking crib from RockingCrib.com (rockingcrib.com) promises to lull a crying baby back to sleep.

A car seat is a necessity (as well as the law) for trips in the car. Visit SafetyBeltSafeUSA (carseat.org) for information on car seats and how to install them. When you're ready to buy one, visit EliteCarSeats (elitecarseats.com) and order the seat that's right for you.

You'll need a child carrier and stroller, too. The child carrier lets baby stay close but keeps your hands free. The stroller is great for walks in the park or other excursions. ChildCarriers.com (childcarriers.com), with its emphasis on correct fit and great customer service, is an excellent site to buy your carrier. BritaxUSA (britaxusa.com) offers strollers with side impact protection.

Everyone knows that babies need diapers. Sew your own cotton diapers with a pattern from Poo Pockets (poopockets.com) or cover baby's bottom in a burst of color from Benetton Baby Diapers (benettondiapers.com). Finish dressing with soft, comfortable onesies and matching socks from Healthtex (healthtex.com).

You've made a great start, but don't breathe that sigh of relief yet. Point your browser to Mapping Your Future — Prepaid Tuition Programs and College Savings Plans at mapping-your-future.org and start planning your baby's education.

Chapter 8

Computers and Electronics: Get Wired and Stay Connected

Years back, a popular cartoon series depicted a space age family whizzing around on flying saucers and using fantastic gadgets to perform everyday tasks. Although no one's piloting a saucer to the mall quite yet, many of the computers and electronics in our daily lives surpass those on the show. Each generation of computer hardware is more powerful than its predecessors. A simple telephone device like Caller ID — one which most of us now take for granted — displays the identity of the caller on an incoming call.

Electronic devices are everywhere. Folks talk on cell phones in all types of public places. Your local restaurant keeps tabs on your dinner order on a special software system. Need to check an address or make an appointment? Pull out the PDA! DVD players and GPS systems are affordable add-ons in most new cars. You can even automate your home. The list goes on and on.

This chapter includes a variety of electronic devices, including some cool computers and amazing gadgets. We've also included cameras and audio and video equipment.

TIP

The Consumer Electronics Association has developed a rating system to evaluate and compare your home's technological capabilities. Take a few minutes to rate your house before you install an expensive new electronic appliance or upgrade to home automation. Find the rating system at ce.org/techhomerating. A database at the same location contains qualified installers who can assist you with upgrades and repairs.

Key Word Index

Cameras

Snap pictures with equipment from the Cameras sites ranging from the latest digital cameras to Kodak Instamatics.

Computer Hardware

We're talking computers, printers, monitors, and all the stuff that needs to be assembled and set up for a computer to work properly. You'll also find networking hardware at these sites if you decide to branch out.

Computer Software

Without programs, your computer is nothing more than an expensive hat rack! Start with a basic operating system and buy business programs, games, educational software, or programs that do just about anything you want your computer to do! Purchase your software in shrinkwrapped boxes or download it from these Computer Software sites and use it immediately.

Electronic Games

Have a blast with computer games and video games and gear sold at the Electronic Games sites.

Electronic Gear

The collection of Electronic Gear sites offers cables, batteries, cases, cleaners, and all the accessories needed to keep your electronics equipment in good working order.

Gadgets and Gizmos

The sites with the Gadgets and Gizmos keyword offer some useful items, and some not, and some that everyone wants regardless of their usefulness. Watch that your friends don't get a case of "gadget envy"!

Home Entertainment

Full home theatre systems, DVD players, and the latest televisions are the high end of the electronics sold at the Home Entertainment sites.

Spy and Surveillance

You'll feel like Agent 007 when you shop at the sites with the Spy and Surveillance keyword. However, along with the spy merchandise, you'll find personal and home security products and many other items designed to keep you safe.

Telephones

From cell phones to land-line phones, talk is cheap (almost) at the Telephone sites. The cellular phone sites include the applicable plans.

101phones.com
101Phones.com

877-374-6635
info@101phones.com
Telephones

The question, "Need a phone?" greets you on 101Phones.com's home page. Answer affirmatively, and you'll be glad you've come to this site. Orders made before 4:00 p.m. are processed and shipped on the same day, and free shipping is part of the great customer service customers can expect at this site. The phone selection is vast; choose from corded, cordless, multi-line, conference-type, video, designer, novelty phones, and more. You can also find headsets, batteries, antennas, and other accessories. Orders can be processed online or, of course, over the phone.

101usedvideogames.com
101 Used Video Games

541-574-4400
info@101usedvideogames.com
Electronic Games

Save big money on the second-hand video games for sale at the 101 Used Video Games site. Many times the cost of two used games is less than the cost of one new one. When you're done with those games, trade 'em back! Need a Dreamcast Aftermarket Steering Wheel or memory card? How about adapters for your Gameboy, Genesis, or Nintendo 64 system? This site carries them, and more. Parents will appreciate the Entertainment Software Rating Boards for all the games sold at the site. 101 Used Video Games ships internationally.

123cctv.com
123 CCTV

800-480-0477
123cctv@123cctv.com
Spy and Surveillance

At the 123 CCTV site you can buy a complete video surveillance system. It has cameras, monitors, and all the equipment in between. You can use hidden cameras with your system or ones that are apparent and let people know they're being watched. The site has cameras for outside use, too. 123 CCTV sells complete systems. All you have to do is choose the number of cameras you want and the folks who run the site can configure and ship a system to you. The site also carries switchers, power converters, and recorders that can record for 40 days. Just in case all this is too much for your budget, or you just want some extra deterrent value, dummy cameras are available, too.

1home-security.meridian1.net
#1 Home Security Surveillance Equipment Systems
No phone number listed
customerservice@1home-security.com
Spy and Surveillance

Ever wonder where you could buy a Taser Gun? Well, look no further. #1 Home Security Surveillance Equipment Systems has them available on its Web site, as well as stun guns and stun batons. The site even has a page where you can check to see whether there are restrictions on these items in your locality. If these items are a bit much for you, you can always consider the telescoping steel baton. This baton delivers no shock, but it can still deal quite a blow. The site also carries an assortment of cameras disguised as everyday objects and various recording devices.

21stcenturyplaza.com/1spy
#1 Spy, Security and Surveillance
No phone number listed
No e-mail address on site
Spy and Surveillance

In today's world, it pays to have a third eye watching your back — an electronic eye. That's where #1 Spy, Security and Surveillance comes in. This company sells state-of-the-art surveillance and counter surveillance equipment to help keep you, your family, and your company safe from interlopers. Hidden cameras, voice and telephone recording devices, scanners, and locksmith tools are all available, along with books and videos that will teach you everything from "Acquiring a new ID" to "Wiretapping and Electronic Surveillance." If covert intelligence is your game, the #1 Spy, Security and Surveillance site is right up your alley.

adobe.com
Adobe
800-833-6687
E-mail form on site
Computer Software

Many different roads will send you to the Adobe site, because it makes many different types of software. The company is famous for its graphics programs, which come in varying degrees of difficulty. With a little practice you'll be able to get the red eye out of photos and even doctor them to unrecognizable heights. Adobe also makes a number of other programs, too, including those for Web and print publishing, and the famous Acrobat series. The company allows you to try out most programs for 30 days. You can download a full version and install it, and pay for it any time during the trial.

 Recommended Price Selection Convenience Service 🔒 Security

advanced-intelligence.com
Advanced Intelligence

0116627445300
adva@ksc9.th.com

Cameras

Advanced Intelligence of Thailand has the world's smallest wireless video camera. The camera can operate through a pinhole ½" in diameter. Included in the audio surveillance equipment is a cell phone that can be set to disguise your voice so that when you make a call, the person who answers doesn't know it's you at the other end. Plenty of other listening devices and a bug detector that lets you know whether someone is listening to you are also available. For answers to questions about specific products, be sure to check the FAQ. Worldwide shipping is available.

allabouttheaccessories.com
All About The Accessories

847-628-0670
sales@allabouttheaccessories.com

Gadgets and Gizmos

No, you can't buy an iPod or Dell Axiom at the All About The Accessories site. However, you can buy some of the coolest cases and accessories that you'll find anywhere. Whether your iPod is a full size or an adorable mini, shop this site for cases and color skins. The skin cases dress up your iPod or Axiom but also protect it from scratches and other damage. If you're a traditionalist, the MaClear case is a good bet, while military fans will like the camouflage pouch. Car chargers and related accessories round out the reasonably priced accessories found at this site.

★ allelectronics.com
All Electronics

888-826-5432
allcorp@allcorp.com

Electronic Gear

You don't need to be a computer geek or an electronic engineer to find the formula for success at the All Electronics site. Sure, this company sells some very technical electronic parts and there's a good chance that most folks (including myself) won't have an inkling as to what they do. However, the site also offers more familiar electronics, such as flashlights, extension cords, headphones, and even some oddities, like a lighted Exit sign. Prices are unbelievably low on most items. Our advice: Go through the online catalog and pick out the items you know. Stock up and save.

asontv.com
AsonTV.com

858-454-2815
E-mail form on site

Gadgets and Gizmos

You've seen the ads for the clever gadgets on late night and cable television. How many times have you missed out because you couldn't find a paper or pen to write down the phone number? Fret no more. All those gadgets are at the AsonTV.com site. You'll find the Forever Flashlight, Laser Straight, Euroblaster, and too many great gadgets to name. Products are guaranteed for 30 days, so take a chance if something looks intriguing. Get a free gift if you spend more than $100. The site ships internationally.

★ atomicpark.com
AtomicPark.com

888-322-4250
customerservice@atomicpark.com

Computer Software

Most times, buying software is an impersonal experience. You search, you click, you buy. The AtomicPark.com site introduces you to Gabby Mashburn, Senior Sales Associate, and makes your software-buying excursion more intimate. Gabby has a right to tout his company. The selection of software is excellent. Most of the top developers, including Microsoft, Adobe, Corel, Computer Associates, ACT, Veritas, and Intuit are represented here. Prices are average. However, Web orders have a "30-Day Happiness Guarantee" and free shipping. Sign up for AtomicDeals!, an e-mail newsletter that provides special offers, deals, and news about new releases. Soon, you'll be calling Gabby with your thanks.

bestbuy.com
Best Buy

888-237-8289
E-mail form on site

Home Entertainment

This site is the online location of the retail giant Best Buy. Of course, you can shop here for all the great electronics bargains you find inside a bricks-and-mortar Best Buy store — televisions, home theater equipment, computers, appliances, and so on. The site serves another purpose, though; use it as a virtual stop on your way to the store. The weekly circular is always online, so you can develop a game plan before you hit the store. The site offers store shoppers other conveniences, too. Order online and then save shipping charges with an in-store pickup.

 Recommended   Price   Selection   Convenience   Service   Security

★ bhphotovideo.com
B&H Photo-Video

800-972-5999
webmaster@bhphotovideo.com

Cameras • Home Entertainment

Billing itself as "The Professional's Source," B&H Photo-Video has the best selection of photo and video equipment you'll find anywhere. The simple category menu gives few clues to the gems that lie buried beneath it. Clicking a category link displays subdepartments within departments, including every type of imaging product and accessory and all the related supplies. B&H offers over more than 130,000 items, and all are available for shipment. Don't miss the used equipment section. B&H accepts trades or buys equipment outright, providing you with the chance to get a great deal.

bluehillsinnovations.com
Blue Hills Innovations

715-234-3303
info@bluehillsinnovations.com

Electronic Gear

Hey, there's nothing exciting about cables or connectors for your GPS or PDA. Yet, without these necessary helpers, your expensive electronic appliance cannot be connected to your computer. And you know that hunting for a missing cable is an exercise in frustration. Most times, you find all sorts of other things (including stuff you didn't know you had) but the cable or connector remains lost. So buy extra cables now from Blue Hills Innovations, and make your life easy. For a few bucks each, you can afford to indulge on all the connectors and cables you need.

brookstone.com
Brookstone.com

800-846-3000
customerservice@brookstone.com

Gadgets and Gizmos

Brookstone is a favorite stop in countless malls across the United States; the groovy gadgets are fun to handle and you can get a great pick-me-up in the expensive massage chair. The online shop carries all the same gadgets you'll find in the store. (The massage chair is available for purchase, as well. However, virtual sitting isn't nearly as satisfying as the real thing!) Shop by price, shop by top gifts, or shop by category. Don't miss the Outlet Store. Brookstone gathers all of last year's leftovers and a few one-of-a-kind items and offers them at the site at reduced prices.

buy-used-video-games.com
Buy Used Video Games

801-942-6633
info@buyusedvideogames.com

Electronic Games

Old video games don't die, they go to Buy Used Video Games to be recycled into someone else's game collection. All video games that are sold at this site have been cleaned and tested. They come with a 30-day guarantee that they work, so you can be confident that the product you're buying will perform as it is supposed to. A link to the Entertainment Software Review Board, the rating body for the Electronic Game industry, is a must visit for parents. Availability is updated daily, ensuring the ever-changing catalog is reasonably up-to-date.

★ cabletiesplus.com
CableTiesPlus

800-926-5981
info@cabletiesplus.com

Electronic Gear

Take a good hard look behind your computer or television. What do you see? (No, not dust bunnies!) Cables. Cables that seem to have taken on a life of their own. Tame those cables with the excellent products from CableTiesPlus. Choose from cable ties in various weights and strengths. Or try an expandable sleeve. The sleeves are designed for flexibility and expand to fit over irregular shapes and different sizes of connectors and end-fittings. You'll also find all the tools you need to get the job done. Win the war against cable. Neat is good.

cambridgesoundworks.com
Cambridge SoundWorks

800-367-4434
info@cambridgesoundworks.com

Home Entertainment

A lot of sound and audio equipment is out there in the marketplace and, unfortunately, price alone doesn't always dictate quality. Making a mistake and purchasing components that aren't compatible or that you don't need is very easy. That's why Cambridge SoundWorks is such a great place to shop. Its site's Hook It Up section not only holds all the information you need to figure out just what to buy, but how to connect all the pieces together. Radios, stereos, and audio and home theater equipment are for sale at this site. Shipping on all purchases is free.

 Recommended   Price   Selection   Convenience   Service Security

cellular-battery.com
Cellular-Battery.com

425-898-9923
sales@cellular-battery.com

Telephones

The rechargeable batteries used in cell phones are an expensive necessity. Without them, the devices won't work. That's why shopping at Cellular-Battery.com makes great sense. The site sells batteries for most major models, including Sanyo, Touchpoint, Qualcomm Kyocera, Nokia, Audiovox, and more. The batteries are discount priced and come with a six-month warranty and a 30-day money-back guarantee. Best of all, you'll be getting a Ni-MH battery, which means your battery has a high capacity and can be charged anytime. (Battery capacities are measured in Milliamp hours, or mAh, which determines the length of standby and talk time that the battery provides.) The company also sells discounted cell phone accessories, like hands-free kits, cases, faceplates, and antennas.

charlottecamera.com
Charlotte Camera

800-832-4224
customerservice@charlottecamera.com

Cameras • Home Entertainment

The Charlotte Camera site is one that you'll want to bookmark. Sure, the prices on the new and used camera equipment are great. But the site also carries a comprehensive stock of photo equipment and accessories to go along with your camera. Whether you need a tripod, extra lens, or something as mundane as film, you can get it here. The reason to hang on to this site, however, is for the educational value it offers. Joe Ciarlante, a professional photographer, writes a monthly column packed with tips, tricks, and helpful hints about photography. The topics vary, but the columns will help anyone trying to take a better picture. Several older columns are stored at the site.

⭐ chimecity.com
CHIME CITY

800-641-4111
webmaster@chimecity.com

Spy and Surveillance

CHIME CITY provides an inclusive list of door chimes, door bells, driveway alarms, security cameras, security devices, and security mirrors for residential and commercial customers. Need to jolt your employees? Consider one of the fake security cameras available here. The non-functioning security camera keeps people on the straight and narrow. Rex, the radar-sensing electronic watchdog, is an excellent way to detect burglars and intruders. Of course, Rex's bark is worse than his bite, but the bad guy won't know that. Check out all the great security tools at the site.

⭐ chumbo.com
Chumbo

800-343-7530
service@chumbo.com

Computer Hardware • Computer Software

Chumbo considers itself the ultimate source for hardware and software on the Internet. Shopping at this site is easy. Choose Hardware, Software, or Electronics from the tab at the top of the page, or browse the categories on the left to find what you want. You'll find a great number of useful products here, and most at considerable savings. Bravo to a company that has figured out how to make computer hardware and software shopping a reasonably painless experience.

circuitcity.com
CircuitCity.com

800-843-2489
E-mail form on site

Computer Hardware • Computer Software • Electronic Gear • Home Entertainment •Telephones

Circuit City sells a vast array of electronic merchandise, including TVs, camcorders, portable electronics, phones, satellite systems, and much more. Scroll through the site slowly because a lot of information is packed into one small space. In fact, the online megastore has so much going on that it's easy to miss a special, sale, or rebate of the week. You can usually snag a good deal on most items sold at CircuitCity.com, but shopping around before you order is best. Circuit City's return policy is generous. If you return an item purchased online, a credit will be issued to the credit card used for the original purchase.

 Recommended   Price   Selection   Convenience   Service   Security

compucruz.com
Compucruz

408-360-0480
sales@compucruz.com

Computer Hardware

The computers for sale at Compucruz's site are geared to the needs of graphics artists and Web designers. Each computer is built for speed, with lots of memory and loads of hard drive space. The base model is called "Monster in a Box," and when you read the specs, you'll see the name is well deserved. The machine screams, no doubt about it! If you're not sure about Compucruz computers (not exactly a household word), the impressive testimonials from photographers, illustrators, and satisfied customers on the site may influence your decision. The price might sway you, too — Compucruz computers are surprisingly affordable.

counter-surveillance.com
Great Southern Technology, Inc.

800-732-5000
No e-mail address listed

Spy and Surveillance

Is someone eavesdropping on your private conversations? While we may believe that "bugs" are the stuff of spies and narcotics agents, increasingly common are business rivals, suspicious spouses, and others listening in on what we think are private conversations. Counter Surveillance specializes in devices to detect these bugs. With police-grade listening devices selling for as little as $30, you can't be too careful. Neither can others, so you may want to follow this site's plans to go into the business of counter surveillance. The folks at this company should know what they are talking about. Their own offices were bugged.

customphones.com
Custom Phones

800-783-6385
info@customphones.com

Telephones

Why not make your telephone part of your décor? Or find a unique phone that's comfortable to use? You're bound to find just what you need at Custom Phones. The company carries over 1,300 working telephones of varying shapes, styles, and vintages. The antique phones have been rewired to work with today's complex wiring but retain their vintage look and feel. Folks with disabilities can choose amplified phones, big buttons styles, remote controlled speaker phones, and other helpful phone devices. If you don't find the phone you want, contact Custom Phones. The folks who run the site will make a custom phone for you.

cyberteria.com
Cyberteria.com

877-792 4009
E-mail form on site

Home Entertainment

"Why shop with us?" asks this leading dealer of plasma televisions and electronics. You have to agree that any retailer must be mighty sure of itself to pose this question to potential customers. Check out the ten answers posted at the site but don't stop there. Look at the list of satisfied customers and read the company's Dun and Bradstreet information. Still not convinced? Browse the extensive product list. From cables to video games, Cyberteria.com delivers the goods. Extended warranties on many products are available for a nominal charge.

⭐ deepshark.com
Deepshark.com

860-283-8895
shark@deepshark.com

Electronic Games

John "The Shark" Clark wanted to get the best games into the hands of gaming enthusiasts in the most cost-effective way he could. So in January of 2003 he founded Deepshark.com with the goal of becoming the largest game rental provider in the world. Deepshark.com operates with a simple concept. For a fixed monthly fee customers can rent as many video games as they want and keep them as long as they want. There are no late fees. Deepshark.com supports the major platforms and offers a full range of games, so you won't be disappointed with this unique concept.

 Recommended Price Selection Convenience Service 🔒 Security

⭐ dell.com
Dell

800-915-3355
E-mail form on site

Computer Hardware • Computer Software

Shopping at the Dell Web site is a great experience. Finding the computer or laptop that's right for you is a snap. Dell runs specials and giveaways from time to time, so it may be a good idea to monitor the price on the computer you want for a while to ensure you're getting the best deal. (This strategy can backfire sometimes, too, if you don't buy when prices are low.) If price is a major consideration, check out the refurbished computers. They are sold with warranties, and usually will save you several hundred dollars.

⭐ desktopdarkroom.com
Desktop Darkroom

888-398-9934
sales@desktopdarkroom.com

Cameras

Desktop Darkroom recently celebrated its fifteenth anniversary. During that time a lot has changed in digital photography and desktop computers. Desktop Darkroom has seen those changes and incorporated them into its support and product line. The result is not only a site for digital photography needs, but also a resource for technical information. Its News page will keep you up-to-date with changes in digital photography and inform you about rebates and special offers on products. On the subject of products, this site has plenty to satisfy the needs of the beginner or professional digital photographer.

d-store.com
d-store

No phone number listed
closeouts@d-store.com

Cameras

d-store specializes in closeout digital photography equipment and supplies, so don't expect the page-after-page of specials you find on the other camera sites. Also don't expect the expensive, high-end equipment that dominates many camera sites. At the d-store site you find a selection of digital cameras from the lower-priced and simpler end of the market. Because most of us like to point, shoot, and enjoy our pictures anyway, this type of selection is just fine. Check the Specials page often and pick up bargain-priced accessories.

dynamism.com
Dynamism.com

800-711-6277
sales@dynamism.com

Computer Hardware • Gadgets and Gizmos • Home Entertainment

Japan is an acknowledged leader in the electronics market. The hot items in Tokyo don't hit the streets of the United States for months. Why wait? Notebooks, slimtops, and PDAs by leading Japanese manufacturers are available at Dynamism.com. The computers have been Americanized; English versions of the Windows operating system have been installed and the keyboards are English with Japanese subtitles on the keys. The gadgets are the most fun. Items like TV-wristwatches, the iDuck (a light-up USB memory stick), and the latest digital cameras and PDAs will make you the envy of your friends. Instructions have been translated into English.

ebgames.com
Ebgames.com

877-432-9675
help@ebgames.com

Electronic Games

It's obvious from the selection and service that the folks who run Ebgames.com love electronic games as much as you do. Choose from several different hardware platforms, including Playstation and Playstation 2, PC games, Xbox, PSP, Nintendo DS, Game Boy, Game Cube, and more. Order online and have your game delivered to your door, or order it on the Web site and pick it up in an EB Games store. The stores are located across the United States; use the handy store locator at the site to find one near you.

electronicsdirect.com
ElectronicsDirect.com

305-513-9522
info@electronicsdirect.com

Home Entertainment

ElectronicsDirect.com sells CodeFree DVD players. Unlike conventional DVD players, these handy machines don't come with internal lock protection, which means you can watch movies from all around the world. CodeFree DVD players accept protected DVDs as well. Of course, the CodeFree designation makes the players more expensive than conventional ones. However, the ground shipping offered by this company will help to offset the cost. Additionally, if you find a lower price listed with one of its competitors, ElectronicsDirect.com claims it will match the lower price.

 Recommended   Price   Selection   Convenience   Service   Security

encoresoftware.com
Encore

310-768-1800
E-mail form on site

Computer Software • Electronic Games

Encore is a leading interactive publisher in the PC, CD-ROM, and videogame markets. Daredevil, Sacred, Desert Rats vs. Afrika Korps, SpellForce, and Soldner are some of the company's more popular games. You'll find them for sale here, along with a collection of educational software for both kids and adults. Check out the interesting collection of utility software. The wide variety of titles ensures that there's a program for every member of the family; for example, Secret Formula Beauty Makeover, Safeworld PC Nanny Cam, and the High Impact Email Marketing program, along with the seemingly at odds Spam Blocker.

frugalphotographer.com
The Frugal Photographer

No phone number listed
sales@frugalphotographer.com

Cameras

Do you have an old camera that you don't want to give up? Are you having a hard time procuring film for your camera? If you answered affirmatively to either of those questions, a trip to The Frugal Photographer is in order. David Foy, the devoted photographer who runs this site, is devoted to bringing you the best stock of unusual and hard-to-find film. The stock changes constantly, so order when you see what you need. On a recent visit, 126 Instamatic film and Macophot 120 film were available.

gadgetbargains.com
Gadget Bargains

888-376-6399
help@gadgetbargains.com

Gadgets and Gizmos

Gadget Bargain's goal is "to deliver a wide selection of the latest gadgets at BARGAIN prices," and the aspiration is more than realized. The gadgets at this site are fun and inexpensive. You can easily order one for yourself and one to give as a gift. Or throw caution to the winds and send for a few gadgets. You'll find items like automatic card shufflers, levitating tops, and the Spongebob Squarepants Talking Cookie Jar. Of course, you'll find some serious stuff here, too, such as pasta makers and showerheads. All in all, this site is fun to look at and definitely worth doing business with, if you choose to order.

gadgetuniverse.com
Gadget Universe

800-429-0039
infocenter@egadgets.com

Gadgets and Gizmos

The thing about gadgets is that some are functional and some are not. Gadget Universe carries them all, and it's up to you and me to decide what we're going to do with the darned things when the package arrives at the door. For example, the Sit-Up Sally Singing Deco Set, a doll that exercises with you, might give you a case of buyer's remorse. On the other hand, there are loads of great stuff at this site, including a Mosquito Repeller Wrist Watch, Wireless Reversing and Parking Sensor, and a Magic Steam Press that you'll wonder how you ever lived without.

gamefly.com
GameFly

888-986-6400
support@gamefly.com

Electronic Games

Buy a game or rent it? At GameFly you can do either. Order the game you want and try it free for ten days. At the end of the trial period, either send it back, start paying rent, or pay the "Pre Played" and keep it. One big problem here is that in some cases, the game may not be available for purchase. (This occurs primarily with new releases.) Choose your platform and click to your selection. New releases have their own page so you can see what is upcoming, often before it's available.

gamerecyclery.com
Gamerecyclery.com

No phone number listed
admin@gamerecyclery.com

Electronic Games

Gamerecyclery.com invites you to sell your old, outdated games and equipment. You can apply the amount you get to the purchase of merchandise or request cash. Of course, your game doesn't have to be old for you to sell it. Maybe you just want to move on to another game. In that case you can still get some value from the one you no longer want. The selection of new games at this site is as complete as any you'll find, so you may as well trade in. Don't forget Gamerecyclery.com also buys movies.

★ Recommended   Price   Selection   Convenience   Service 🔒 Security

gateway.com
Gateway

800-369-1409
E-mail form on site

Computer Hardware • Home Entertainment

Gateway offers reliable computers to home and business users. You can buy one of its pre-packaged deals or configure your own. The company offers several different models of desktops and laptops, so if you're not sure which one to buy, you may want to call a Gateway sales rep. (Alternatively ask someone not associated with the company who knows the difference between hard drive space and RAM.) Gateway also sells home entertainment equipment. Check out the selection of plasma televisions, too.

getconnected.com
GetConnected

800-775-2506
help@getconnected.com

Home Entertainment • Telephones

What a great idea! This site matches up customers with providers of cellular phone plans, TV satellite plans, or TV satellite receivers. Here's how it works: You tell GetConnected where you need service. This company searches its files and informs you what services are available in your area. (Due to the many different technologies and carriers, service availability varies by location.) Compare the offers and plans and choose the one that best suits you. You'll also have the chance to order corresponding equipment, such as phones and accessories. Then complete your order. That's it! Fast, convenient, and easy.

giftsandgadgetsonline.com
Gifts and Gadgets Online

800-244-4387
info@giftsandgadgetsonline.com

Gadgets and Gizmos

Electronic gadgets are fun; there's no doubt about it. But all too often, today's clever purchase feels like tomorrow's folly when the light of day dawns on your gizmo. Not so with the gadgets offered by Gifts and Gadgets online. Everything at this site is well designed, fun, and useful. For example, the clever Follow Me gadget is actually a transmitter that attaches to any valuable, such as a briefcase, laptop, or handbag. Carry the tiny receiver (which can be used as a key chain) with you. The receiver will beep as soon as your valuables are more than 15 feet away. Good stuff!

⭐ gizmocity.com
GizmoCity.com
202-332-8862
customer@gizmocity.com

Gadgets and Gizmos

The name GizmoCity.com may conjure up images of useless doodads, but the gizmos at this site are aimed at saving you time or keeping you safe. Consider the Electronic Deer Alert, which beeps when deer or other animals approach your vehicle from 1,500 feet away. This "gizmo" can save you (and the animal) serious harm. Or how about a Wireless Garage Door Monitor that alerts you when your automatic garage door opens? You won't spend another night with the door wide open to the world. Maybe the owners should consider changing the name of this great site!

gpsforyou.com
GPS for You
207-232-4208
service@gpsforyou.com

Electronic Gear • Gadgets and Gizmos

You'll never be lost again with a GPS unit from the GPS for You site. GPS, short for Global Positioning Satellite, keeps millions of folks on track. The GPS unit gets its bearings from the overhead satellite and pinpoints your exact location. Start by reading the information assembled at the site, and then decide which system is best for you. In addition to all the best GPS units, you'll find accessories like cases, belt clips, and antennas. Mapping software provides detailed views of specific locations. Sign up for the free monthly newsletter for the latest news and articles on GPS technology and products.

hammacherschlemmer.com
Hammacher Schlemmer
800-321-1484
customerservice@hammacher.com

Gadgets and Gizmos

Hammacher Schlemmer is no penny-ante operation, folks. This company has been providing top-notch service to the upper crust for many years and now, courtesy of the Internet, it can extend its reach to everyone. The gadgets at this site are definitely on the highbrow side. For example, you'll find a Portable Clarity-Enhancing Phone Amplifier, Mosquito Halo, and Large Image Television Videophone System, among many other items. Everything here is guaranteed for life, which tells you something about the quality of the products. The catalog is as well designed as the products. Enjoy!

⭐ Recommended $ Price 🛒 Selection 🎁 Convenience ☺ Service 🔒 Security

hpshopping.com
hpshopping.com

888-999-4747
E-mail form on site

Computer Hardware

The hpshopping.com site is the retail outlet for HP and Compaq home and home office products. Shop this site for computers, such as the HP Pavilion, Compaq Presario, and pocket PCs. You'll also find printers, scanners, digital imaging products, printing supplies, and accessories. Most equipment has several models available. If you're not sure which model to buy, hpshopping. com can determine which one is best suited to your needs. Simply answer the Find By Usage questions associated with the equipment type and you'll be presented with the best match for you. Alternatively, use Find by Features if you have an idea of what you need.

ibm.com
IBM

800-746-7426
E-mail form on site

Computer Hardware • Computer Software

Practically everyone on the planet has heard of IBM. At the IBM Shop, all the latest and greatest IBM computers are available. IBM runs special Web-only deals. Selected systems ordered before 3:00 p.m. ship the same day you order them. You can also order monitors, hard drives, and storage units. IBM makes software, too, such as WebSphere, which allows you to use your voice to interface with your portable devices! Although it doesn't make printers, third-party printers are available at IBM's site, as well.

lanblvd.com
Lanblvd.com

877-246-7059
sales@lanblvd.com

Computer Hardware • Electronic Gear

In the not-too-distant past, computer networking was reserved for businesses. However, with the rise in popularity of broadband service, many non-technical folks are finding themselves in the dubious position of home network administrator. Not to worry. We can't promise that sites like LanBlvd.com make computer networking a cakewalk. However, with the products this company offers — proper cabling, routers, NIC cards, and maybe a firewall — you should do just fine. Feel overwhelmed? Extra help is available in *Wireless Home Networking For Dummies* and *Home Networking For Dummies,* 2nd Edition, both available at dummies.com.

lgdsuperstore.com
Let's Go Digital

888-447-0011
customerservice@lgdsuperstore.com
Home Entertainment

Digital cameras! Home audio! Plasma televisions! Camcorders! And those categories only scratch the surface of the extensive product list offered at the Let's Go Digital site. This electronics superstore works as an agent for its customers and doesn't carry any stock of its own. Accordingly, it can pass its low pricing directly to consumers. Prices are low, sometimes as much as 50 percent below retail. Shipping costs on bigger items are spelled out, so you'll know in advance exactly what you're going to pay. Open Box specials are deeply discounted. However, buyer beware. The specials may be damaged, dented, or DOA (Dead On Arrival) units and cannot be returned.

★ lomography.com
Lomographic Society International

No phone number listed
myorder@lomography.com
Cameras

"Don't Think. Just Shoot." The motto of this interesting photographic society sums up its philosophy. Learn the 10 Rules of the Lomographic Society International and buy a camera at the site. The Frogeye camera will do just fine. The sturdy camera is designed for underwater use and will capture an image from as far as fifteen feet away. The Frogeye comes with carrying case, batteries, and a mini-blower. Who knows? With your new camera firmly in tow, you could be the Lomographic Society International's next member.

mailbug.com
Landel Mailbug

408-360-0480
support@mailbug.com
Computer Hardware

Mailbug is a handy service for people who want to send and receive e-mail, but don't want to use a computer. The Mailbug terminal exchanges e-mail with any valid e-mail address. It's very easy to use, making it a great tool for senior citizens. Best of all, because there's no computer attached, Mailbug can't transmit computer viruses. If you have a phone line, you're already set up to use Mailbug. Here's how the system works: For one low monthly fee, you get an e-mail address, message service, and the terminal, which you'll need to connect to your phone line. That's it!

 Recommended   Price   Selection   Convenience   Service   Security

mcafee.com
McAfee Security

888-847-8766
E-mail form on site

Computer Software

McAfee Security sells software to protect your computer. You can buy the software in a bundle, or you can purchase individual programs. Because new viruses appear all the time and hackers find different ways to enter your personal computer, most times, you'll purchase both the initial program and a subscription service that enables you to download security updates. The McAfee folks constantly work behind the scenes to produce new updates in answer to current threats. McAfee also has some good system backup products available. Few people plan for the worst, but it happens. Put McAfee on guard now.

newegg.com
Newegg.com

800-390-1119
sales@newegg.com

Computer Hardware • Computer Software • Home Entertainment

Computer components abound at the Newegg.com site. The parts and components from this site are from top manufacturers, so you needn't worry you're getting second-rate or used parts. Over 84,000 unbiased customer reviews can help you decide what to buy. You'll also find computer software, games, and cameras. Shopping by category gives you access to the catalog, but you can shop by manufacturer's brand if you know what you want. Check the clearance section for bargains. If you can afford to take the chance, refurbished items are a great deal.

onecall.com
One Call

800-340-4770
E-mail form on site

Cameras • Home Entertainment

Make one visit (call) to the One Call site for home entertainment equipment, cameras, camcorders, and more. Buying from One Call makes sense. Financing is available on many products at this site, an option that's not available at most online stores. One Call is an authorized dealer for every brand it sells. (Manufacturers are picky about authorizing dealers.) If something goes wrong or you have a question about your new equipment, One Call knows what to do to resolve the problem. Read about its excellent rating at the Better Business Bureau, and get a look at its fabulous in-stock inventory.

outpost.com
Fry's Outpost

877-688-7678
service@outpost.com

**Cameras • Computer Hardware • Computer Software •
Electronic Games • Home Entertainment • Telephones**

Fry's Outpost has some great deals on computers. The selection is tremendous, and the prices are amazing. You'll find some no-name brands, but also a fair number of well-known manufacturers here. Shop for a specific brand of computer or peruse the catalog to see what's available. Both Windows and Macintosh computers are sold. In addition, you'll find electronics, printers, networking gear, computer software, telescopes, cameras, home entertainment equipment, and much more. Shipping is free on all items over $500.

pacificpowerbatteries.com
Pacific Power Batteries

800-326-7406
sales@pacificpowerbatteries.com

Electronic Gear

It's happened too many times. The discount store has batteries for your flashlight, but not your laptop computer. The next store you visit has batteries for another device you own, but not the one you need. Before you know it, your quest for batteries has cost hours and a tank of gas. No more! Pacific Power Batteries has "Batteries for Everything." Finally, one-stop shopping for all your battery needs. Want to learn about batteries? An education awaits you in Battery School, where you'll find out the proper care and maintenance of automotive batteries, deep-cycle batteries, and common battery types.

pcclub.com
PC Club

831-429-9134
E-mail form on site

Computer Hardware

The advantage to shopping at the PC Club Web site is clear: This substantial Web site is the online arm of the PC Club chain of stores, with around 60 retail locations in the United States. The online computer superstore carries laptop and desktop computers, modems, monitors, including LCDs, motherboards, and many types of multimedia equipment. If you're planning to set up a network at home, all the right stuff is in stock. A lively group posts in the PC Club Computer Forum. You'll find answers to many questions — asked and unasked — and may make a few new computer pals.

 Recommended Price Selection Convenience Service Security

photoalley.com
PhotoAlley.com

877-690-0177
customercare@photoalley.com

Cameras

If digital photography is up your alley, then you need to make the trip to PhotoAlley.com. The Compare Digital Cameras page displays in spreadsheet form the key features of many cameras to help you make your buying decision. After you have your camera, click the Learn button and take a multipart course in digital photography. When you think you're good enough, post your work on the Feedback page and see what comments come back. Even if your pictures aren't works of art, get a Ceiva Digital Photo Receiver and transmit pictures of the kids to grandma.

★ plasmadisplaysystems.com
Plasma Display Systems

877-675-2762
info@plasmadisplaysystems.com

Home Entertainment

Television technology is changing rapidly, and there's no time like the present to get on board. The new plasma displays and LCD monitors come in a variety of sizes. You can get one to fit on your desk or hang on your wall. The Plasma Display Systems site carries more than thirty models from top manufacturers like Sony, Panasonic, NEC, and Pioneer. Additionally, it also carries a full line of speakers, cables, converters, cards, and mounting gear to ensure your new plasma display system is complete. Need help designing a custom system? Give the company a call before you order.

portabledvdstore.com
All About Portable DVD Players

866-383-8646
info1@portabledvdstore.com

Home Entertainment

All About Portable DVD Players is a comprehensive source for all things relating to portable DVD players. Come to the site to purchase brand-new, factory-sealed, portable DVD players and accessories, or just learn about most issues relating to portable DVD players. All purchases qualify for free shipping. Want to try out a portable DVD player? No problem. The site offers DVD player rentals. Your low rental fee includes the player, UPS 3-Day Select shipping to you, and return shipping. (Hint: Rent a DVD player the next time you take the family on a long car trip. No more squabbles!)

printerwarehouse.com
Printer Warehouse

800-814-5410
service@superwarehouse.com

Computer Hardware • Computer Software

Remember all that talk about the paperless office? Hard copy is here to stay. Printer Warehouse has all the printers you need to print anything, by top manufacturers. Choose a printer for Windows, Mac, or other operating system environment. How about a printer that's designed for labels, or one for photos? Printer Warehouse also sells refurbished printers, and printer accessories and supplies.

quail.com
Quail Electronics

800-669-8090
sales@quail.com

Electronic Gear

What's your "Power IQ"? Are you aware that appliances and electronics that work in one country may not work in another? Quail Electronics is a manufacturer of power cords, power strips, power adapters, and cord sets. Read the Reference Info section to learn about electricity and power needs. When you're ready to buy, choose a cord set for North America or an International model. If you're not sure what you need, use the International Cord Locator to determine what configuration the country you specify requires.

radioshack.com
RadioShack

817-415-3200
E-mail form on site

Computer Hardware • Computer Software • Electronic Games • Electronic Gear • Gadgets and Gizmos • Home Entertainment • Spy and Surveillance • Telephones

With 7,000 retail stores, RadioShack is a respected household name. The company has expanded in recent years and moved into the major electronics marketplace. You'll still find some Tandy brand equipment, but other manufacturers, including Compaq, Sony, Emerson, and Olympus, make up most of the brands here. The online catalog is vast, but searching takes a while. Check out the online coupons for some real price busters. One of RadioShack.com's best features is its extensive listing of product manuals. Print the ones you've misplaced and save them. It's comforting to know that the instructions aren't lost forever.

 Recommended Price Selection Convenience Service Security

ritzcamera.com
Ritz Camera.com

877-690-0099
contact@ritzinteractive.com

Cameras

Ritz Camera.com is the Internet representative of a 1,300-store chain. In fact, you might have a Ritz Camera or Wolf Camera store in a mall near you. As you may expect with a mass merchant, a wide range of merchandise is available here. The site carries inexpensive point-and-shoot cameras to professional, single-lens reflex cameras to professional studio equipment. Individual products are presented with a list of suggested accessories and detailed descriptions. Even if you don't buy your camera equipment from this site, stop by for the considerable free education that's offered on the pages.

★ roberts-rent-a-phone.com
Roberts Rent-a-Phone

800-964-2468
E-mail form on site

Telephones

If you're traveling internationally, you may want to include this site in your pre-travel plans. Roberts Rent-a-Phone rents cellular phones that work outside the United States. A handy coverage chart at the site shows all the coverage locations. After you place your order, your rental phone will be delivered prior to your departure. Roberts can also deliver to some locations in Europe. Rental charges are from your day of departure until the day of return. Although the service is expensive, you'll know up-front exactly what you'll pay and, best of all, you'll be assured of having cellular service when you need it.

securityplanet.com
Security Planet

509-582-6262
sales12@securityplanet.com

Spy and Surveillance

Your security is of prime importance at Security Planet. This company features a wide variety of products to keep you safe. Stun guns, stun batons, air tasers, m-tasers, and pepper spray in several sizes are offered at this site. If you're not sure what you need, detailed information is provided on all the products to help you decide. Security Planet respects state and local laws and won't knowingly sell devices where prohibited. Customers must be over eighteen. Security Planet is known and respected worldwide. Individuals, businesses, nonprofit organizations, and police forces are current customers.

sharperimage.com
Sharper Image

800-344-5555
care@web.sharperimage.com

Gadgets and Gizmos • Home Entertainment

As you're cruising through the extensive list of gadgets and gizmos available at Sharper Image, you have to ask yourself, "Do I need that? Really?" Otherwise, you're going to be in hock up to your eyeballs. Why? Because everything for sale at this site is so cool, from the ever-popular Ionic Breeze to a vacuum cleaner that never loses suction. The same great customer service to which Sharper Image customers have been accustomed is available to online shoppers: generous return policies and lots of markdowns. Watch for Web-only sales.

simplywireless.com
SimplyWireless.com

888-449-8484
customer_service@simplywireless.com

Telephones

Many really neat cellular phones are flooding the marketplace right now, but not every phone works with every cellular service. This site matches phones to plans. Choose a phone you like, or choose a carrier. Based on your zip code, SimplyWireless.com will find the plan or plans that match. After you've selected one, accessorize your phone with all the latest and greatest headsets, cases, and antennas. Canadian residents can take advantage of this great service, too.

★ softwareoutlet.com
SoftwareOutlet.com

714-979-6800
customer-support@softwareoutlet.com

Computer Software

The logic behind the SoftwareOutlet.com site is a standard business model: Buy in big lots and pass the savings on to the consumer. SoftwareOutlet.com buys software products from stores that go out of business, manufacturer and distributor closeouts, direct from the manufacturers, and sometimes, even auctions. The programs sold at the site are brand new. This company even produces some programs itself. You'll find software for both Windows and Macintosh computers. All the popular programs are available, and most are discounted substantially. The $5 Store has the best bargains. You'll also find computer accessories and a limited selection of hardware.

 Recommended Price Selection Convenience Service 🔒 Security

soundpros.com
Soundpros.com
877-894-6751
info@soundpros.com
Home Entertainment

Don't waste time or money on inferior sound equipment! Although Soundpros.com is too classy to come out and say so, that message resonates at its site, which offers home audio, car audio, and home theater equipment by the industry's top manufacturers. Detailed information on the site's featured products tells you everything you need to know about the equipment. Prices aren't rock bottom, but they're fair. If you're looking for a bargain, check out the site's specials.

spy-cam-surveillance-equipment.com
Spy Cam Surveillance Equipment
No phone number listed
No e-mail address on site
Spy and Surveillance

How would you like a surveillance device that starts recording when you pick up your phone and stops when you hang up? Or maybe you're in the market for a camera that looks like a smoke detector or a singing fish? You can get these products and many more items, too, at Spy Cam Surveillance Equipment's Web site. You can even find a credit-card-sized, tapeless audio recorder, as well as books dealing with lock picking and e-mail encryption. Just in case you think someone is listening in to your conversations, you can get a variety of devices that can detect bugs.

★ spysource.net
Spy Source
847-803-9001
info@spysource.net
Spy and Surveillance

Don't think you need a Nanny Cam or a security camera? Think you can trust your employees when your back is turned? Not necessarily. "What you don't know can hurt you," say the folks at Spy Source. Shop this site for all the security products you need to make sure that your best interests are protected. Whether you're looking for covert video cameras, room recorders, computer-monitoring devices, or other security tools, you'll find them here. You can even purchase a voice changer for times you need a vocal disguise. (Consider the possibilities of that one!)

store.apple.com
The Apple Store
800-692-7753
E-mail form on site
Computer Hardware • Computer Software

The Apple Store is the official store of Apple Computer, where you can buy Macintosh desktop computers and the latest iBooks and Powerbooks. Need a printer or scanner? If you order it from this site, you're assured it will work with your Mac. Check the software titles, including desktop programs like Microsoft Office to games, graphics programs, and utilities. You can also find iPods here, the MP3 players that have taken the world by storm. If you spend time on the Internet, consider a membership to .Mac. For one annual fee you get a powerful collection of software and services tailored to your needs.

★ store.palmone.com
Palm Store
800-890-9043
E-mail form on site
Computer Hardware • Gadgets and Gizmos

Everyone seems to have a Palm, the handheld appliance that contains a date book, address book, to-do list, and a memo book. The Palm not only organizes your business and personal life, but it allows you to play a game of chess or connect to the Internet. All the Palm handheld models are available at the Palm Store, along with accessories and software. You'll even find some instructional books on using your Palm. The GPS Navigator is a super accessory for Palm handhelds. It can customize steps for door-to-door directions, and help keep you from wandering around, lost, ever again.

superwarehouse.com
Super Warehouse
800-824-5410
service@superwarehouse.com
Cameras • Computer Hardware • Computer Software

The Super Warehouse is really super. With so much great computer hardware and software to choose from, you'll find everything you to need to put together a computer system, or upgrade the one you have. Shop by product, including Cables, Storage, Hard Drives, Laptops, Networking, Systems, and Scanners. Alternatively, shop by brand. Super Warehouse has set up branded "stores" so you can see all the products by one manufacturer, making it easy to put together the system you want. Digital cameras, PDAs, and projectors round out the hardware selection. Need software? You'll find it here it, too. What a great place to shop!

 Recommended   Price   Selection   Convenience   Service Security

symantecstore.com
Symantec

541-335-5000
E-mail form on site

Computer Software

A lot of bad dudes are cruising the Information Superhighway. Hackers, Trojans, folks who seem innocent enough but are phishing — these days, even experienced computer users need help. That's where Symantec comes in. These folks are the good guys in white hats. Their anti-virus software is designed to protect your computer against the viruses that unleash confusion in the computing world. Symantec makes other protection products, too, like Internet security and firewall software. The money you spend on protection may be your best investment of the year. Tax software and some disk management utilities are also available.

telephones.att.com
Advanced American Telephones

800-222-3111
E-mail form on site

Telephones

Advanced American Telephones designs and produces phones for one of the biggest telecommunications companies in the industry, AT&T. The products available at this site include cordless telephones, corded telephones, integrated and stand-alone answering systems, and accessories including headsets and batteries. Manuals can be downloaded directly to your computer, ensuring you'll know just how to operate all the latest features. The site has a glossary of phone terms and FAQs where you can learn all about the latest advances in telephone technology. With a little knowledge under your belt, you can put together an impressive package for your home.

televalue.com
TeleValue.com

800-522-0322
sales@televalue.com

Home Entertainment • Telephones

TeleValue.com carries telephones, electronics, and home entertainment components. You won't find any surprises at this site; the stock is pretty much standard to what you'll find at most electronics sites (and bricks-and-mortar stores, for that matter). One handy search feature distinguishes TeleValue.com from its competitors. Within each category, you can specify a price range and brand to narrow your selection. Choosing the one you want from the resulting list of qualifying products is a breeze. Spend $75 and get free shipping.

⭐ theliquidateher.com
The Liquid Ate Her

541-463-0700
sales@theliquidateher.com

Computer Software

The funky name (it used to be Abracadata) and simple interface nearly hides the great programs available at The Liquid Ate Her site. For around ten bucks, you can snag a game or home design program that will keep you occupied for hours. Programs are available in Windows and Macintosh format and don't require advanced computing degrees to set up and run. Model railroad programs enjoy the greatest selection but beware — some of the programs won't run under the latest versions of Windows. Many of the programs can be downloaded directly from the site.

thephonesource.com
Phone Source

207-774-4488
custsvc@thephonesource.com

Telephones

You won't get any static when you shop the Phone Source site. This site is a great resource for all your telephone needs. You'll find one, two, and multi-line telephones. Cordless phones in 900 MHz, 2.4 GHz, and 5.8 GHz are also available. The site offers accessories such as headsets from famous makers including Plantronics and GN Netcom. Special-needs phones for hearing and visually impaired and special-purpose products such as elevator phones, hotline courtesy phones, and emergency call boxes are available, too. Fully functional novelty and antique phones round out the collection.

tucows.com
Tucows

810-720-1155
E-mail form on site

Computer Software

Tucows has been a trusted source for software since 1993. Three types of programs are available from its site: commercial software, shareware, and freeware. All the programs have been tested, rated, and reviewed by Tucows' software experts and are available for download. Search for a program by platform (Windows, Macintosh, Linux, Palm, and so on) or go directly to the Software Store. Narrow your search to the type of program you want, such as game, virus checker, or utility, and choose from the list that appears. Most times, you'll download the program, install it, and have it up and running in short order.

 Recommended   Price   Selection   Convenience   Service   Security

tweeter.com
Tweeter.com

866-690-2370
E-mail form on site

Home Entertainment

Your current TV is going to look mighty shabby after you've seen the latest and greatest at Tweeter.com. LCDs, flat panels, widescreens, and even tube TVs are always on sale. There's even a wireless TV if you want to carry your set with you. Lucky for us, the WiseBuy deals offer lower prices on many top-of-the-line video appliances. Online shopping guides and articles arranged by brand help narrow down the decision on just what to buy. Still can't decide? Call a helpful associate during business hours. This company wants you to be pleased as punch with your new equipment.

uniquephoto.com
Unique Photo

800-631-0300
E-mail form on site

Cameras

The bricks-and-mortar component of Unique Photo has been around since 1947 and prides itself on customer service. Unique Photo presents its range of cameras, film, and accessories in well-organized, easily searchable pages. Occasionally an item has the comment "We Offer the Best Price" or "Give Me a Better Price" shown with it. It is left to you to verify these claims. Add to the cameras plenty of memory sticks, cards, and other accessories, and anyone, novice or professional, can equip himself or herself here.

vgfanatic.com
VG Fanatic

866-610-1981
sales@vgfanatic.com

Electronic Games

If you're new to the world of video gaming, VG Fanatic could be the best place for you to get started. Unlike many other game sites, VG Fanatic gives detailed descriptions of games and plenty of information on hardware. If what brought you to video gaming is your children, be sure to check out the parents guide under help topics. It will help you to understand how games are rated and how to choose games that are appropriate for your child. Of course, VG Fanatic has new and used games with trial periods and buy-back policies.

★ winbook.com
WinBook

800-254-7806
E-mail form on site

Computer Hardware

WinBook is no stranger to the computer arena. The company is a subsidiary of Micro Electronics, which has been selling personal computers for twenty years or so. Winbook is best known for its notebook computers, and you can order one of several models at this site. You get a lot for your money — most WinBooks are packed with included features like CD-RW and floppy drives that are optional on other manufacturer's laptops. Shop here for inexpensive desktop computers with the same great WinBook features. Check out the accessories, too. Monitor mounts, carrying cases, and extra memory are reasonably priced. The site's Web Specials will save you serious cash.

zones.com
Zones.com

800-248-9948
customerservice@zones.com

Computer Hardware • Computer Software

Put a diehard Windows user and a Mac user in the same room and watch sparks fly. At Zones.com, no one gets hurt, because the two factions are separate. Mac users have their own MacZone.com just for Apple computers. Windows computer users shop at Zones.com. Personal computer users will find systems, accessories, and software. Check out the prices on memory upgrades, because they change weekly. If you're buying equipment for business, some special deals are available for you, too. Check the Rebates page to see whether you're eligible for extra savings.

★ Recommended $ Price 🛒 Selection 🎁 Convenience ☺ Service 🔒 Security

Automating Your Home

Have you thought about automating your home? Home automation makes your life easier and more comfortable. It can make your home more secure and bring you peace of mind. Best of all, the end result is fun!

Your home automation project should be driven by three major elements: imagination, time, and budget. If you're lacking resources on even one of the three, consider starting small. Perhaps you can program a lamp or another appliance with a remote. Or, you may want to jump in with both feet by wiring your whole house and bringing everything online. It's up to you.

Learn about home automation before you begin the project. SmartHome has a great online article located at smarthome.com/ homeautomation.html that will provide you with lots of valuable information. SecurityGateway. com (securitygateway.com/page.asp?c= career_ov_home) also will help you to get started.

Do it yourselfers might be scared off by the article in Digital Home Magazine (digitalhomemag. com/custominstall/howdoisetitup_ automation.shtml) and decide to call in a pro. No problem. The FutureHome Guild installer directory (fhome.com) lists home network installers, digital home consultants, home control specialists, and small office network installers in the U.S., Canada, United Kingdom, Australia, and New Zealand.

X10 Technology is the easiest and most inexpensive way to get started with home automation. Here's an example of how this technology works after it has been set up. Say you want to turn on a lamp in another room. You press the remote, which sends out a radio frequency signal to an X10 Transceiver Module that's plugged into a regular wall outlet. The X10 signal travels across your existing wiring until it reaches the X10 Lamp Module and switches the lamp on. (All this takes an instant.) Voilà. Your room is bathed in light. Pretty cool, eh?

Now it's time to start shopping. X10 Wireless Home Automation (x10.com) is a great place to purchase home automation equipment. This company carries all the X10 remotes, transceivers, and modules you need. Hometech Solutions (hometech.com) is another excellent resource. Both sites carry basic kits and components that will ease you into home automation. Contact a technical representative at either site if you're not sure where to start.

There are other avenues on the road to home automation. SENSAPHONE (sensaphone.com) is a monitoring device that can be set to alert homeowners of water or gas leaks, power failures, or intruders. Purchase SENSAPHONE at the Home Security Store (homesecurity store.com).

The WaterCop system (watercop.com) automatically turns off the water when a leak has been detected, preventing small leaks from being major floods. Absolute Automation (absolute automation.com) carries the system.

Automation is really amazing! All this discussion is bound to have made you hungry. How about a pizza? Depending on your location, you can order online at Papa John 's Pizza (papajohns.com). Some things never change, though. You'll still have to pay the pizza delivery guy for the order.

Chapter 9

Drinks: Wetting Your Whistle

· ·

Did you ever wonder how drinks other than water came about? Who was the first person to say, "I wonder what the grape juice that sat too long in the jug tastes like?" They must have been brave souls, and without them we wouldn't have the selection of wines, beers, and liquor we have today.

The same goes for coffee and tea. Who were the wonderful pioneers who first thought of boiling beans and leaves in water to see what the resulting concoction tasted like? What about Dr. John S. Pemberton of Atlanta, Georgia? What made him think of adding sweet syrup to seltzer water — thus creating the first soft drink, Coca-Cola?

Yes, we owe a lot to these early groundbreakers. So if you find yourself thirsting for a beverage, check out the listings that follow and get a buzz from either the spirits or the caffeinated beverages that are offered to the online consumer today.

As the saying goes, "Choose your poison."

But before you decide to knock back a few, pick up that six-pack of soft drinks, or settle down with a steaming cup of coffee or tea, browse through the following online resources. Check out internetwineguide.com/structure/ww/winelinks.htm or internetwineguide.com/structure/abwine/abwine.htm to choose the appropriate wine for the occasion. To make the perfect cup of coffee or tea, go to coffeeguide.com or fantes.com/tea_guide.htm. For more about liquor and mixed drinks, see kuro5hin.org/story/2002/7/31/1246/16836.

Key Word Index

Beer

Lager, pilsner, bock, ale, stout, or porter — every country has at least several dozen varieties, and you can start your pub crawl at sites with the Beer keyword.

Coffee

Many people cannot begin their days without first partaking of a hot cup o' joe. Whether you like yours black or heavily flavored with lots of creamer, the sites with this keyword can point you to some of the best coffee out there.

Drinking Accessories

This keyword points you to sites with accessories to enhance your drinking experience. Glassware, gift sets, and coolers are just a few of the offerings.

Liquor

The sites that sport this keyword will lift your spirits with the liquors they offer. However, due to various state laws, many of them may not be able to ship across state lines, so be sure to read the shipping policies of these stores.

Soda

In the history of the beverages we drink, soda didn't arrive on the scene until the mid-1880s. Today it is one of the most popular drinks available for both kids and adults.

Tea

The choice of drink for not only the genteel, but also for much of the world's population. Not as "crass" as its coffee cousin, the types of tea match or exceed the types of coffee that exist in the world.

Wine

Whether you're a wine connoisseur or you just enjoy wine with dinner, the wines offered by merchants with this keyword sell wines priced for any budget. As with liquor, many of these stores may not be able to ship across state lines, so be sure to read the shipping policies of these stores.

301wines.com
301 Wine Shop & Club
707-445-0311
wines@carterhouse.com
Wine

301 doesn't refer to the number of wines available at this site. The 301 Wine Shop & Club offers a very nice selection of red and white wines, dessert wines and ports, champagne, and sparkling wines. Searching for a wine is easy: Just choose your category, for example, White Wine, the type, such as German Riesling, and then add your selection to your shopping cart. No descriptions of the wine accompany the name, so be sure you know your wine before you buy. One unique category the site offers is the selection of organic wines.

★ 800spirits.com
877 Spirits
877-774-7487
info@877spirits.com
Liquor • Wine

877 Spirits sells not only liquor and wine but also "spirited gifts." The company can deliver gift baskets — containing champagne, fine wines, liquor, and even cigars and chocolates — to raise anyone's spirits worldwide. Its prices are reasonable; for example, the Picnic in the Park gift basket is $72 and contains wine, cheese, summer sausage, and crackers in a picnic basket. If you like collector drinks, you can order a bottle of Hennessy Paradis Extra for $337 or a Remy Champaign Cognac for a mere $464.

alltea.com
alltea.com
415-382-1146
customer-support@alltea.com
Tea

The folks who run alltea.com started the site because they love tea and the Internet, and their devotion shows. The site is one of the most comprehensive tea sites on the Web. Browse the site by tea brand or tea type, or use the search feature to find exactly what you want. The Bulk section offers the best deals, with huge savings per cup. Look through the Accessories section for a gift for yourself or someone else. Or join the Tea of the Month Club, offered in six-month increments, and choose from caffeinated or herbal selections.

ambrosiawine.com
Ambrosia

800-435-2225
customerservice@ambrosiawine.com
Wine

Ambrosia is not your usual online wine store. It offers a free, personal e-mail service called the Inner Circle that offers personalized wine selections to fit your taste, it lists its Top Ten wine choices, and it offers different Wine Clubs for every taste and budget. You can search and shop by your favorite Napa Valley winery, by price, by specialty group, or by Ambrosia's highest rated wines. If California Napa Valley wines are your favorite, you can't go wrong with this online merchant's wines.

bedfordwines.com
Bedford Wine Merchants

888-315-8333
wines@bedfordwines.com
Wine

Bedfordwines.com is not a fancy online store; however, the site offers the online visitor a solid selection of wines. Although the company specializes in American regional wines, it also offers wines from France, Italy, Spain, Portugal, Australia, and New Zealand. You will also find a small selection of older and rare wines. The site also carries many different types of wine, including Cabernet, Merlot, Pinot Noir, and Zinfandel. Be sure to read its disclaimer about shipping wines out of the state of New York. These people are serious about wine quality, and they will hold your wine at no additional cost and ship it when temperature conditions are more suitable.

beeronthewall.com
Beer On The Wall

888-840-2337
giftshops@wizardempire.com
Beer

Microbreweries have become big business over the last decade. Beer on the Wall offers the beer connoisseur a wide selection of these microbrews in its online store. Beers run about $2 each. If you want to try some different brews before you decide on one, check out the 6- and 12-sample packs. Or customize a 6-pack with an assortment of beers. Another fun service is the custom label feature: You can have the wording on any beer label changed to say whatever you want.

 Recommended   Price   Selection   Convenience   Service   Security

bengalbay.com
BengalBay.com

No phone number listed
customerhelp@bengalbay.com

Tea

BengalBay wants to be your online "CommuniTea" for tea. The site features a selection of tea and related accessories designed to appeal to tea lovers everywhere. Check out the In the News section for interesting articles and pertinent facts about the benefits of tea drinking. For example, did you know that drinking at least one cup of tea a day could cut your risk of heart attack because tea contains flavonoids, organic compounds that can neutralize harmful chemicals that damage? You can find many more tea-related facts at the site.

beveragesdirect.com
Beverages Direct

630-534-6849
E-mail form on site

Soda

If you're a "tea totaler" or just enjoy a soft drink on those hot summer days, Beverages Direct can set you right up. Not only does its site carry some brand-name soda, such as Dr. Pepper, 7-UP, Diet Rite Cola, and Mountain Dew, but it also offers a very wide selection of lesser-known and regional soft drinks, such as Dog N Suds Root Beer, Green River Gourmet Soda, and Route 66 Root Beer. For a stronger caffeine buzz, you can also choose from an assortment of energy drinks and caffeinated water.

coffeekraze.com
Coffee Kraze Café

914-893-3778
info@coffeekraze.com

Coffee

Freshness counts at the Coffee Kraze Café. This company roasts its coffee in a special roaster, and then packages the coffee and ships it within the same 24-hour period. In addition to the vast selection of blends, dark roasts, gourmet flavors, reserves and organics, and specialty flavors available at this site, you'll find Torani syrups and many coffee accessories. Order a Perfect Pot pack for a variety of ground coffee pouches, each designed to make one perfect pot.

gevalia.com
Gevalia

800-238-5432
customer_service@gevalia.com

Coffee • Tea

Gevalia Kaffe has been a European favorite for over 140 years. Its online shop brings the Gevalia experience to everyone. With more than 30 varieties of coffee and 13 varieties of tea, you're sure to find a beverage to suit your palate. If you don't see a flavor you like, the folks at Gevalia will be happy to custom-blend one that's just right for you. Check out the online catalogue for sweets, housewares, and coffee accessories. If you love coffee and convenience, join one of Gevalia's Coffee Delivery Programs for a delivery that arrives every six weeks or so. You receive a free gift when you sign up.

herbal-green-tea.com
Herbal Green Tea.com

No phone number listed
info@herbal-green-tea.com

Tea

Your health. Without it, everything else in life is meaningless. The folks at Herbal Green Tea want to keep you healthy or, at the every least, prevent you from sliding further downhill. How do they propose to do this? Why with Green Tea, of course. The site sells a variety of herbal green teas in bag and capsule form. If you're not a believer, or want to know more, there's a mountain of information about the benefits of green tea at the site.

⭐ javajim.com
1st-Line Equipment

888-933-5947
sales@1st-line.com

Coffee

A coffee bean without the right equipment is, well, just a coffee bean. Add a grinder, coffee maker, maybe a milk frother or cream whipper, and, voilà, you get a great cup of coffee! 1st-line Equipment is dedicated to providing coffee- and espresso-related equipment, machines, parts, service, and accessories. The site offers everything you need for making coffee, including a variety of Italian espresso makers, regular coffee makers, press pots, milk steamers, and several types of grinders. There's also a wide assortment of coffee, flavorings, and syrups. Tech support is offered on some of the complicated coffee makers and equipment for appliance-challenged customers.

 Recommended   Price   Selection   Convenience   Service   Security

kalanicoffee.com
Kalani Organica

800-200-4377
kalani@kalanicoffee.com

Coffee • Tea

Did you ever stop to think that your regular cup of java was brimming with unseen chemicals? Sadly, many coffee growers use synthetic pesticides, herbicides, and fertilizers to grow their beans. The end result poisons the earth and often produces lousy-tasting coffee. Kalani is different. Since 1992, this company has worked with specialty growers to produce shade-grown, organic coffee. The results are spectacular! The rich Arabica blends available at this site are so fresh and pure that you'll have trouble stopping at one cup. Even the decaf is delicious *and* chemical-free. A selection of tea is available too, as are accessories like coffee grinders, French press pots, and teapots.

★ klwines.com
K&L Wine Merchants

800-247-5987
E-mail form on site

Wine • Liquor

K&L Wine Merchants claims to "bring the world's finest wines at prices you won't find anywhere else." This company's selection of wine and spirits is superb and its prices are reasonable. It offers wines from the western United States, Bordeaux, Burgundies, Rhone Valley, Champagne, Sauternes, more from France, and a comprehensive collection of Italian wines. It also has a number of old and rare wines. Be sure to check out the Port and wine accessories. Before you buy wine or liquor to be shipped to your home state, read the information provided on the Web site.

★ marktwendell.com
Mark T. Wendell Tea Company

978-369-3709
hejohnson1@marktwendell.com

Tea

If there's a superstore of tea, then the Mark T. Wendell Tea Company could be it. This company features a fine selection of gourmet teas and accessories. The company offers a line of 35 of its own unique blends and an even greater number of imported teas. Many of the imported teas are exclusive to this company. You can find green teas, black teas, organic teas, and Oolong teas, plus decaffeinated and ice tea blends. Gift certificates are also available for purchase.

morningkick.com
Morning Kick

No phone number listed
inquiries@morningkick.com

Coffee • Tea

Morning Kick understands the psychology of coffee. This company knows that coffee isn't just a drink made from roasted and ground beans. A great cup of coffee can be comforting, confidence boosting, and pleasurable. Accordingly, Morning Kick has put together a selection of gourmet and flavored coffees to suit any mood you might have. You can buy just the beans or select the grind that works best with your coffee maker. You can also find a selection of spicy chai teas and some savory treats, such as strawberries dipped in chocolate, and roasted chestnuts. The site features some great brewing tips and recipes submitted by its customers.

★ morrellwine.com
Morrell

800-969-4637
customerservice@morrellwine.com

Liquor • Wine

If you need wine or liquor, Morrell has it. Peruse this online retailer's Wine List and find reds, whites, rosés, sparkling, and even dessert and fortified wines, like Port, Sherry, and Madeira. Use the site's search box to find what you're looking for, or, if you have questions — and who doesn't when it comes to wine — you can chat with a Wine Pro in real time online! The site also offers Kosher wines. La heim!

natashascafe.com
Natasha's Cafe

888-901-8412
E-mail form on site

Coffee

Shopping at Natasha's Café is a lot like shopping at an international bazaar. The mishmash of strange and exciting items keeps you browsing for a long time. Looking for a coffee divination set? You'll find one here, complete with the instruction book (thank goodness!), a small ibrik, demitasse cup and saucer, and a 1/2 pound bag of Turkish coffee to get you started. There's also a collection of coffee and spice mills, demitasse cups and spoons, and a wide range of ibriks. (For the uninitiated, ibriks are Turkish coffee pots.) You can even buy dented ibriks at a discount. Greek and Turkish coffee round out the selection.

 Recommended   Price   Selection   Convenience   Service   Security

papanicholas.com
Papa Nicholas

888-727-2645
info@papanicholas.com

Coffee

Papa Nicholas knows his beans. He's been selling coffee beans since 1982. Today, his online store offers you a choice of roasts from mild (coffee blends from around the world) to dark (for those who like a stronger coffee). You can buy the beans if you want to grind them yourself, or you can buy coffee already ground. Papa also sells a line of specialty and decaffeinated coffee. You can even build your own in-home café by saving up "Papa Points" and using them to purchase everything you need, from grinder to brewer to mugs.

parkaveliquor.com
ParkAveLiquor.com

212-685-2442
No e-mail address on site

Liquor • Wine

Visiting this online retailer is like peeking into the liquor and wine cabinet of the rich and famous. This site carries a premier selection of fine wine and spirits, and you can easily get lost in the broad selection. You can get help, though. Using the site's search engine you can browse its extensive listings by product name, type, wine region, or Scotch (this site has one of the country's largest selection of single malt Scotches) and whiskey. The courteous and knowledgeable salespeople can answer any questions you may have. Cheers!

peets.com
Peet's Coffee

800-999-2132
webmail@peets.com

Coffee

In 1966, Alfred Peet opened his first store and coffee roastery in Berkeley, California. Since then, scores of loyal customers, nicknamed "Peetniks," have made Peet's an institution. Why? Peet's roasts each of its 32 coffees by hand, and ships them the same day to ensure freshness. In fact, Peet's coffee comes with a freshness guarantee; if your coffee order doesn't meet your standards for any reason, Peets will replace it or refund your money. You can order not only coffee, but also a variety of hand-blended teas from Peet's online store. If you have a busy schedule, set up a recurring delivery to make sure you never run out of your favorite Peet's blend. Send your friend a gift from the site while you're shopping.

popsoda.com
POP The Soda Shop

480-994-4505
phd@popsoda.com

Soda

POP The Soda Shop offers over 200 non-alcoholic beverages from all over the world. The owners saw a lack of alternative, imported, and gourmet sodas and decided to offer them in one online store. You can not only find brands like Coca-Cola and Dr. Pepper, but also gourmet and alternative brands, like Brainalizer, DOA, Moxie Original, and Ginseng Up. So if you have a taste for the exotic in your soft drinks, or if you want to expand your soda palate, check out POP's.

sacredgroundscoffee.com
Sacred Grounds Organic Coffee Roasters

800-425-2532
sacred@tidepool.com

Coffee

Coffee is sacrosanct at Sacred Grounds. In addition to providing its customers with the perfect cup of the roasted brew, the Sacred Ground management team is working hard to save the earth. The coffee sold here is certified 100 percent organic, and even the roasting operation carries a certification from Quality Assurance International. You can read about the growing and roasting process and get a taste of Sacred Ground's political views as well. Prices are a bit higher than at the supermarket, but the site contains a nice selection of coffee, coffee accessories, and even some tea blends.

sensationalteas.com
Sensational Teas

541-753-2835
information@sensationalteas.com

Tea

Make your tea-drinking experience more enjoyable and exotic by drinking your tea from a YiXing (pronounced ee-shing) teapot, just as millions of Chinese have done for centuries. The small units serve as both pot and cup; tea is brewed and drunk from the spout while it's still hot and fresh. A complete collection of YiXing teapots is available at Sensational Teas. These beautiful teapots are handmade in China and surprisingly affordable. There's also a collection of fabulous Tetsubin teapots from Japan. Sensational Teas offers tea samples for around a dollar, providing an inexpensive way to try out new and exotic tastes.

 Recommended   Price   Selection   Convenience   Service   Security

sherry-lehmann.com
Sherry-Lehmann

212-838-7500
inquiries@sherry-lehmann.com

Wine • Liquor

Sherry-Lehmann has over $10 million of fine wine to choose from and offers helpful, knowledgeable assistance via the company's wine experts. If you aren't sure of the type of wine you would like or if you want to try something new, use the wine sampler option. The wine inventory is huge, and not everything the company has is listed on the site. If you are searching for a variety of wine not listed, you can send an e-mail to the company specifying the kind and amount you need, and someone will contact you with a price. The site also offers wine accessories such as glasses and decanters. If you live in New York state only, you can purchase from the site's selection of fine liquor.

specialteas.com
SpecialTeas

888-365-6983
service@specialteas.com

Tea

specialteas.com just might be your cup of tea if you're a tea lover. The first feature you see on its shopping page is a wonderfully designed site search engine. You can search the wide selection of teas by type (like Black, Chai, Fruit Blend), origin (like Ceylon, Nepal, Kenya, China), estate (Kenilworth, Temi, Soom), added flavor (apple, rum, chocolate), characteristic (nutty, malty, red-wine like), grade (full-leaf, pressed, twig), or price. If you're a real tea aficionado, this site is your nirvana.

starbucks.com
Starbucks

800-782-7282
E-mail form on site

Coffee • Tea

Who hasn't heard of Starbucks? With stores on almost every U.S. corner and in such far-reaching locales as Indonesia and Qatar, Starbucks has become a household name. If you can't handle the crowds, shop online instead. You can order Starbucks signature coffee, whole beans or ground, as well as several flavors of tea. Consider buying a Starbucks card for the times you need a caffeine fix and actually visit your local Starbucks. Similar to a debit card, you can use the card in any Starbucks; you can check your balance and reload it from your online account.

stubbyglove.com
Stubbyglove

No phone number listed
stubbyglove@stubbyglove.com

Drinking Accessories

What do you do when you're sitting around in the outback, enjoying a cold beer? You come up with ideas like this one: the Stubbyglove, which keeps your beer cold and your hand warm. You can order a fingerless or full-fingered glove, and the site also offers a six-pack sling, worn over the shoulder, made out of the same material. Who else but a beer-drinking Australian would think up something like this? To place an order, fill out an order form and the company will send you directions on how to pay for your Stubbyglove.

teaconcepts.com
TeaConcepts.com

No phone number listed
E-mail form on site

Tea

To make your tea-drinking experience a formal affair, check out TeaConcepts for beautiful, elegant, and unique teapots and tea cups. In the teapot category, you'll find genuine Russian teapots, bone china and earthenware teapots, Chinese YiXing teapots, and traditional Japanese teapots; each category offers several pattern choices. In addition to the teapots, teacups, and other tea accessories, the site offers a decent selection of everyday teas.

tealuxe.com
Tealuxe

888-832-5893
E-mail form on site

Tea

Besides its regular tea list of black, green, herbal, organic, Chai, and Oolong teas, TeaLuxe offers informational resources for the tea drinker. If you want to know what other people are drinking and recommending, check out the TeaTenders Top Ten list for the site's most popular teas. Or fill out the Tea Questionnaire, which recommends a short list of teas based on your answers. If you already know what you want, you can do a search from the home page by Name, Category, Description, or even the Bin Number for a quick order. The site also offers gift sets and other tea-related merchandise, as well as a bulletin board that readers can use to post questions, answers, and recipes about tea.

 Recommended   Price   Selection   Convenience   Service   Security

teatime.cc
Carnelian Rose Tea Company
360-573-0917
tea@carnelianrosetea.com
Tea

You'll come away full of tea knowledge after a visit to the Carnelian Rose Tea Company's fact-filled site. The site provides a glossary of tea terms, a searchable index of teatime recipes, and a great section of tea-brewing basics. There's also an active message board where tea lovers discuss their favorite teas. You can order a variety of teas at this site. If you're new to tea drinking, or want to try out a new flavor, the helpful descriptions next to each tea name will aid your selection. Need additional assistance? There's live help available during business hours.

tea-time.com
Tea-Time
650-328-2877
teabears@tea-time.com
Tea

Tea-Time operates a large and thriving retail establishment in Palo Alto, California. Its online business is an offshoot of the successful brick-and-mortar store. Internet customers reap the benefits of both worlds, because the tea and tisanes (made from dried fruit and flowers) sold here are always fresh. Check out Tea-Time's extensive selection of pots and kettles. According to the Tea-Time folks, the right teapot or kettle is an important component of the tea-drinking experience. Can't find what you're looking for? Send a "t-mail" (Tea-Time's version of e-mail) for a quick response.

tote-a-keg.com
Tote-A-Keg
866-491-0792
E-mail form on site
Drinking Accessories

For those serious beer drinkers who have longed for a way to easily travel with a keg of cold beer on tap, Tote-A-Keg has granted your wish. This company offers a portable keg that keeps your beer cold and pressurized and dispenses a cold beer with a traditional foamy head — just like a real keg. Created by an amateur brewer from Chicago, the keg is a thermos with a tap that's topped with ice and then sealed with a lid. It looks similar to a large, dispensing drink cooler. CO_2 keeps the beer pressurized. You can get a Tote-a-Keg for any size keg of beer. Let the party begin!

⭐ wine.com

Wine.com

877-289-6886
customercare@wine.com

Wine

Wine.com claims to have "a flavor for every palate." The company backs up that claim with a selection of wines from around the world that numbers more than 2,500 domestic and imported premium wines. If you want to learn more about wine than just the price, you can also find extensive information on wine basics — the different types, winners and appellations, and how to drink wine and serve it. Don't forget to check out the selection of gift baskets and wine accessories. You can even join one of the wine clubs. As for actually buying the wine, be sure to read the site's shipping rules, because each state has its own regulations for having wine shipped directly to its residents.

⭐ wineenthusiast.com

Wine Enthusiast

800-356-8466
custserv@wineenthusiast.net

Drinking Accessories

Wineenthusiast.com is for the serious wine connoisseur. This site offers everything you need for wine storage — accessories, cellars, racks, coolers, stemware, and more — but no wine. You can also find gift sets, gourmet foods, and even beer accessories, like the "half-yard" — a large glass decanter with a wooden stand that holds 20 ounces of ale. The site even has an outlet store where you can save big on sale items. You can use the site's search engine to shop by item, brand name, or keyword. The site also offers tips on how to store and preserve wine. If wine is your passion, then this is your store.

 Recommended   **$** Price   Selection   Convenience   Service   Security

A Shopping Excursion — Setting Up Your Home Bar

Whether you build it yourself, retain the services of Bob Vila, or just set aside a small space in the recreation room of your home, you can have your very own home bar, and the following sites can help make it functional.

For basic bar supplies, like tongs, corkscrews, coasters, towels, stools (and other larger bar fixtures), blenders, pourers, and other utensils, check out the following sites:

- ShoppingBrains (shoppingbrains.com/home_bar/home_bar_starter_kits.html)

- Deuster Company (deusterco.com)

- A-Best Fixture (a-bestfixture.com/store/bar.html)

For beer bar glasses, bar signs, beer mirrors, and other supplies, check out:

- The Pub Shoppe (thepubshoppe.com), which can decorate as well as equip your home bar.

- Tango (tango-shatterproof.com), which sells shatterproof glassware that's available with custom imprinting.

If you're looking for something other than common bar items, then you can deck out your bar with some of these cool beverage accoutrements:

- Cool cocktail shakers: The Classic Shaker Company (cocktailshaker.com) offers shakers designed and crafted by the world's best silversmiths and glass blowers.

- The Quaffer (quaffer.com): a patented shot glass with a built-in chaser.

- Kegerators and wine storage units: Check out the Beverage Factory (beveragefactory.com) for these and other items.

After you have your bar set up, take a look at these sites to learn how to mix the drinks:

- BarBack (barback.com) is a software program that contains over 24,000 mixed drink recipes available at the click of your mouse.

- Real Beer.com has a beer education page (realbeer.com/edu/index.php) where you can find everything you could ever want to know about beer.

If you would rather have a book for your drink recipes, check out some of the top bartending guides at cocktails.about.com/library/reviews/aatpbartendersguides.htm. They include the following:

- *The Bartender's Bible,* a great guide to setting up your home bar

- *The World Encyclopedia of Cocktails,* which has a short section on glassware and terminology

- *The Ultimate A-to-Z Bar Guide,* which has trivia and quotes

What's an after-dinner brandy or cognac without a good cigar? For great advice on choosing the right one, check out the About Guide (cigars.about.com) to cigars.

Finally, what drinking establishment doesn't have a drinking trivia test? Print this Beer Trivia test (comedy-zone.net/triviazone/humans/page3.htm) and have it available for your guests.

Cheers!

Chapter 10

Entertainment: Keeping Yourself Amused

• •

*E*ntertainment was largely a by-product of geography in past generations. Folks went to neighborhood movie theatres and attended home games of their sports teams. Celebrations and special occasions were marked with a dinners in a local restaurant.

Today, entertainment is more global in nature. You needn't settle for the film selection at your local movie house or the menu at the pizza shop around the corner anymore. The world is your playground. There's so much to do! Sporting events, concerts, and movies compete for your attention. Love to eat out? Every town has a full complement of restaurants.

This chapter covers many of the ways you like to be entertained. From watching movies to making music, eating out to cooking lessons — you'll find them here.

The Internet Movie Database (imdb.com) is the number one resource for anything related to movies and film. Use the comprehensive directory to track down trivia or find answers to questions; the site's search tools make it easy to do so. See what's tops at the box office this week, and see what new releases are coming and when. You'll also find movie and TV news and all the hot gossip about your favorite celebs. There's more, much more to see and do on this amazing site devoted to the movies.

Key Word Index

Audiobooks

The sites in the Audio Books category carry books that let you listen to the story instead of read it — great for long trips in the car!

Books

Shop the Books sites for reading material in a wide variety of price ranges. You'll find new books, bestsellers, and even a few old and specialty books.

Eating Out

Everyone loves to go out to dinner! You can locate restaurants all over the United States with the sites listed with the Eating Out keyword.

Leisure Time

Shop the Leisure Time sites for toys, puzzles, and whatever else you like to do for fun in your leisure time.

Listening to Music

DVDs, CDs, tapes, records, and MP3s — the Listening to Music sites carry the tunes you love singing along to.

Magazines

You can subscribe to one magazine or many from the collection of Magazine sites assembled in this chapter.

Making Music

From sheet music to instruments, the Making Music sites will help you make a joyful noise.

Movies

The Movie sites feature the greatest flicks from Hollywood and around the world. You'll find movies ranging from classics up to today's hottest titles, available for rental, purchase, or download.

Reservations

Make reservations at your favorite dining establishment directly from the Reservations sites. You'll never wait on hold or be told to call back during business hours.

Self-Enrichment

The sites in the Self-Enrichment category will help you gain wondrous knowledge about yourself, the world, and a vast variety of subjects.

Tickets

At the Tickets sites, you can order tickets online for the best seats. You'll save time and often gain entrance to events that are already sold out.

alibris.com
Alibris

510-594-4500
feedback@alibris.com

Books • Listening to Music • Movies

Visit Alibris for your book, movie, and music needs. Great prices and attractive shipping deals make this site an easy place to shop. The site's chief claim to fame is that it is the Internet's number one source for finding rare or out-of-print books. The claim is not an idle one; in fact, Alibris can track down obscure titles and deliver them to your doorstep. (It did so for me more than once.) Enter as much information as you can into the Alibris Book Fetch database. If your book is located, it'll let you know by e-mail.

alllearn.org
AllLearn

646-825-5200
info@alllearn.org

Self-Enrichment

In September 2000, Oxford, Stanford, and Yale formed AllLearn, short for Alliance for Lifelong Learning. Faculty from all three universities developed the coursework. AllLearn classes utilize traditional elements, such as books and expert teachers, as well as electronic media such as multimedia CDs, videotapes, streaming media, message boards, and live chats. Classes repeat year round and range from ninety-minute faculty forums to ten-week courses. Courses range from ancient history to current events. Students get the feel of a real college experience and learn valuable information. AllLearn credits don't count towards a degree.

alltix.com
AllTix

888-609-8499
tickets@alltix.com

Tickets

This full-service ticket broker offers worldwide options and event tickets. Through AllTix, you can purchase great seats for Broadway, for sports (basketball, baseball, football, hockey, soccer, and tennis), concerts (Britney Spears, Eric Clapton, John Mayer, Dave Matthews, and Shania Twain), and extra-special events like the U.S. Open tennis tournament. Or order a gift certificate to let the recipient choose the event. You can sell your extra or can't-use tickets here as well as sign up to be on the mailing list so you can be alerted about hot new events.

 Recommended   Price   Selection   Convenience   Service   Security

almanac.com
The Old Farmer's Almanac

603-563-8111
E-mail form on site
Books

Since 1972, The Old Farmer's Almanac has published useful information for people in all walks of life, including recipes for cooks and chefs, tide tables for boaters and fishermen, sunrise tables and planting charts for gardeners and farmers, and weather prognostications for average citizens and professional meteorologists. The acclaimed book is available at this site in several regional versions. You needn't share the source of your newfound knowledge. Astound your friends with your accurate weather predictions and homespun lore.

★ amazon.com
Amazon.com

800-201-7575
info@amazon.com

Audiobooks • Books • Leisure Time • Listening to Music • Magazines • Making Music • Movies • Self-Enrichment

Amazon.com started out as a bookseller, but the company keeps expanding. Along with books, CDs, and movies, you can furnish your home, buy clothes, take care of your health and beauty needs, and more. Amazon.com is darn good at what it does! Book buyers can read reviews, excerpts, and get great pricing and fast shipping. Listening to a tape or CD before you buy helps you decide whether you like it. If you don't have an Amazon.com account yet, get one. Online shopping doesn't get better than this.

apollosaxes.com
Apollo's Axes

800-827-9196
sales@apollosaxes.com
Making Music

Even good music stores often stock a fairly small inventory of instruments. Apollo's Axes, by contrast, features an unbelievable range of instruments from all over the world, including many you may never knew existed. It's the place for hard-to-find exotic instruments as well as a broad variety of more common ones like guitars and drums. Shop for gongs, mandolins, bouzoukis, mandolas, piccolos, recorders, bagpipes, Crumhorns, accordions, and all manner of flutes. The company offers a free newsletter and gift certificates, as well as a number of great accessories.

apple.com/itunes
iTunes

408-996-1010
E-mail form on site

Listening to Music

With more than 700,000 songs to preview, buy, and download, the iTunes site offers music to match just about everyone's tastes. The bulk of the tunes are the popular type, with a lot of space in the online catalog devoted to the hot young stars of the day. Still, with just minimal effort you'll find soundtracks, music for kids, folk tunes, and more. Windows and Mac users are supported and, of course, iPod users are openly courted at this site. There's a charge per downloaded tune, but in the end, it's a small price to pay to keep the computer gendarmes from your door.

★ arhoolie.com
Arhoolie

510-525-7471
info@arhoolie.com

Books • Listening to Music • Making Music

Run by a handful of passionate musicians and music lovers, Arhoolie produces some of the music sold at this site. Whether the music is its own production or someone else's, the sound at this site is "down home." You'll find the best Appalachian, Tejano, Zydeco, and blues sounds on CD, and some really good rock and roll. There's also some gospel CDs that will literally knock your socks off. The folks who run this site have a charitable foundation devoted to the preservation of the "vernacular music." People like you and me are lucky to find indie sites like Arhoolie who work hard to keep the old great sounds alive.

audible.com
Audible

888-283-5051
greatideas@audible.com

Audiobooks

Audible harnesses the power of technology. More than 18,000 titles are in the Audible catalog, and that number is growing! Audible users download books, articles from magazines and newspapers, and radio programs. The downloaded files can be transferred to PDAs, pocket PCs, and MP3 players, or saved to CDs. Audible has low prices for shoppers and even lower prices for members. The AudibleListener club has two tiers of membership and offers a free gift. This wave of the future is worth checking out.

 Recommended   Price   Selection   Convenience   Service   Security

audiobooks.com
Audiobooks.com
No phone number listed
E-mail form on site
Audiobooks

The experience of listening to a book is not the same as reading one. Adding voice, sound effects, and even music complements the text and makes the words come alive. Audiobooks.com presents an array of choices. Bestsellers and older titles are available. Most books can be purchased abridged or in full-length (unabridged) versions. In many cases, you can select CD or cassette. Audiobooks.com also offers a unique service called Pay Per Listen. You can download many books at a fraction of the cost of purchasing the media. Pay Per Listen is not for everyone. Read the extensive Help files at the site and see whether it will work for you.

audioqueue.com
AudioQueue
No phone number listed
info@audioqueue.com
Audiobooks • Self-Enrichment

Whether you're looking for the latest bestseller or a self-help book, turn to AudioQueue. Here's how the service works: Sign up at the site and provide your credit card information. Next, browse through the list of available titles and pick as many titles as you'd like to hear. For one monthly fee, you can check up to four tapes at a time out of the AudioQueue library. As soon as you return a tape, the next tape on your queue will be sent right to your door. You can add or delete tapes from your queue list anytime. Pretty cool, eh!

bargainbookstores.com
BargainBookStores.com
No phone number listed
custserv@bargainbookstores.com
Audiobooks • Books

"Why pay more?" Spend a few minutes browsing the overstock and out-of-print titles for sale at BargainBookStores.com, and you'll wonder the same thing yourself. Books at this site are generally discounted way below retail — sometimes by as much as 90 percent. Some of the books aren't first run, and others have a bit of cosmetic damage. Still, the text inside is just fine and the money you save can go towards another book or maybe even two more. The site also offers a collection of calendars, videos, and audiobooks. Check back often for weekly specials and an ever-changing inventory.

barnesandnoble.com
Barnes & Noble.com
877-275-2626
E-mail form on site

Audiobooks • Books • Magazines • Movies • Self-Enrichment

Barnes & Noble is one big superstore of a site. The biggest danger that you'll face when shopping here is that you'll burn out too fast. Besides books of every size, shape, type, price range, and vintage, the site offers movies, music, calendars, paper, games, and gifts. Sign up for a membership and get a discount if you don't mind paying a hefty fee upfront. Take a class at Barnes & Noble University; the class is free but there's a good chance you'll need to buy a book or materials for the course from the site.

baronbarclay.com
Baron Barclay Bridge Supplies
800-274-2221
baronbarclay@baronbarclay.com

Leisure Time

Do you like to play bridge? Bridge players claim the cerebral game keeps their minds supple. While there's no scientific proof that the game improves brain function, many people play at competitive levels well into their golden years. The cards and supplies at this site are designed for bridge. Along with tables and chairs, you'll find instructional books and software. You can also order the full Baron Barclay Bridge Supplies catalog through the mail. Subscriptions to Better Bridge Magazine can be processed directly from the site; sign up today for this important periodical.

baysidepress.com
Bayside Press
636-257-3970
info@baysidepress.com

Making Music

Music educators, look no further! The Bayside Press Web site boasts instrument material for the piano and the guitar, mandolins and mandolas, banjos and dulcimers, percussion, harmonicas, and autoharps. From its extensive catalog, you can choose from various formats (books, videotapes, DVDs, and audio tutorials) and multiple styles (classical, Celtic, blues, bluegrass, jazz, and more) to provide valuable assistance in training programs and private lessons. Besides concert videos, the site also offers a selection of books for solo, duet, or ensemble performances, as well as manuscript papers, and chord and reference texts. Free shipping on orders over $25.

★ Recommended   Price   Selection   Convenience   Service   🔒 Security

bbc.co.uk/learning/courses
BBC Learning
08700 100 222
E-mail form on site
Self-Enrichment

Learn online with a British flair. The British Broadcasting System has several courses available in its BBC Learning program. The course catalog is not extensive, but the available classes are perfectly developed and informative. A companion BBC store sells products that relate to some of the online lessons. Study gardening, robot-building, oceanography, or learn to speak French, Italian, German, or Spanish. The foreign language classes are the best. Even beginners will be tossing off phrases, albeit in a British-tinged accent, after one session. You'll need to consult the Web site for course schedules and fees.

bitsandpieces.com
Bits and Pieces
800-884-2637
info@bitsandpieces.com
Leisure Time

The talented product team at Bits and Pieces has been satisfying millions of folks with unique gifts and puzzles for over 20 years. If you're looking for a challenge, you'll be thrilled with the collection of brainteasers, secret boxes, electronic and computer games, mechanical banks, books, and puzzles offered at the Bits and Pieces site. Need a diversion? The site's Puzzle Arcade is a great place to spend a few minutes. Be careful though! When you're playing free interactive games like Yali, Labyrinth, and Kismet, it's easy to lose track of time.

blockbuster.com
Blockbuster.com
888-523-5278
E-mail form on site
Movies

Ask anyone where to go to rent videos and you'll hear, "Blockbuster." The online store doesn't offer rentals, but you can purchase videos and DVDs. Sign up for My Blockbuster and get an e-mail newsletter filled with news on store and online promotions and special offers. You can also keep track of up to one hundred of your favorite movies with the site's Wish List service. Frankly, a lot of the options here seem like window dressing. Most useful feature: You can log in with your laptop and find the nearest Blockbuster when you're on the road.

boardgames.com
Boardgames.com
908-429-0202
bgsales@boardgames.com
Leisure Time

Boardgames.com offers more games than you can shake a stick at, as my grandma would say. The site is named aptly; with over seventy varieties of Monopoly for sale as well as a section for Murder Mystery Games, you're going to find something you want to play. The bigger question is, once you've browsed the catalog and given in to temptation, where will you put all those boxes?

booksamillion.com
BOOKSAMILLION.COM
800-201-3550
support@booksamillion.com
Audiobooks • Books • Magazines

BOOKSAMILLION.COM, or BAMM for short, is a book-lover's paradise. The site has hundreds of thousands of books, audiobooks, calendars, magazines, and related accessories for sale. Price is a key selling point. Look for the Compare Prices links as you browse the online catalog. Consistently, you'll see that BAMM has the lowest price. If you're planning to do some serious shopping, join the free Millionaire's Club for extra discounts and e-mail notification of sales and special offerings. Pop into the Joe Muggs café for some great tasting coffee. In a day or so, you'll be sipping your cup of java and enjoying your books when your order arrives.

booksontape.com
Books on Tape
800-521-7925
E-mail form on site
Audiobooks

If price is your only guideline, Books on Tape may not be your first choice for an audiobook. On the other hand, the site offers so many other features that the higher prices charged here tend to become slightly less significant. Books here come in a variety of formats — CD, cassette, and MP3 — and the catalog is extensive. You're sure to find a title or two you want to hear. If you're not sure, a short audio sample may influence your decision. You can choose to either purchase a book, or rent it for a 30-day period.

⭐ Recommended $ Price   Selection   🎁 Convenience   😊 Service   Security

boosey.com/pages/shop
Boosey & Hawkes Music Shop

44 (0)20 7291 7255
musicshop@boosey.com

Making Music

Boosey & Hawkes enjoys a reputation as a key classical sheet music retailer. Whether your passion lies in Haydn or Handel, Bach or Strauss, Rachmaninoff or Shostakovich, you'll find what you want at this site. This company also features chamber music bestsellers, a different spotlighted composer each week, masterworks scores, holiday choral music and choral canticles, polyphonic studies, and exam syllabi. Browse the selection of music for schools, recorder instruction, and music notation software, along with an extensive sheet music database. You can go beyond classical and locate desired materials for jazz piano, pop/rock guitar, and youth orchestra.

ccvideo.com
Critics' Choice Video

800-993-6357
vcatalog@ccvideo.com

Movies

Critic's Choice features over 50,000 movie titles from the hottest releases to old classic films you would be hard pressed to find elsewhere. Movies are available on VHS or DVD format. For your convenience, the site arranges movies by theme. For example, during the summer months, all baseball movies may be grouped in the Baseball Room, in later months another sport or theme will occupy a similar room. The Critic's Choice Video Collection contains handpicked classics culled from movie and television greats. The site features in-depth profiles of many Hollywood stars.

cduniverse.com
CD Universe

800-231-7937
manager@cduniverse.com

Listening to Music • Movies

The universe at this site is much bigger than just CDs, with movies and games occupying a big chunk of real estate. CD Universe's nice, easy design is a relief after some of the more complex music sites. Searching works just like it's supposed to: Use the listed categories or enter a name, keyword, or phrase into the search box. A nice touch allows you to order a new CD before its actual release date and then ignore the throngs in the mall on the day it hits the stores. (Sorry, the CD ships on the actual release date.)

citysearch.com
Citysearch

No phone number listed
E-mail form on site

Eating Out

Citysearch is a local service, providing up-to-date search information on local businesses from restaurants to retail, from travel to professional services. Need to find a restaurant suitable for a graduation party? Ask Citysearch. Where is a good dry cleaner? Citysearch knows. When is the touring company of a Broadway show coming to town? Citysearch can tell you. While Citysearch does not service every locality, it comes close! Log in to the site and see whether your area is covered. Citysearch even handles international areas. Citysearch partners with other travel sites, enabling you to make travel reservations online.

clownschool.net
Academy of Performing Arts in Clowning

No phone number listed
clownschool@sc.rr.com

Self-Enrichment

Like to make people laugh? Looking for a second income? Have you ever considered clown training? A series of online classes, such as The History of Clowning, The Clown Look, The Clown Skills, Job Opportunities, and Humor's Effect on Stress, are included in the course, and can be ordered individually or as a package. Each class, led by clown Flutter Ficklebottom and pals, takes about four to six hours to complete and ends with a multiple-choice exam. Not sure? Take the first class for free and see what you think. That's a serious offer — no clowning around.

columbiahouse.com
Columbia House

No phone number listed
E-mail form on site

Listening to Music • Movies

There are deals aplenty at Columbia House, and, for the most part, they're the same deals that the letter carrier delivers to your door. Join the Movie Club, CD Club, DVD Club, or the other members-only clubs that happen to be available at the time you visit. Although the clubs do offer a good deal for the first-time buyer, read all the fine print before you sign up, and be sure you understand exactly what you'll need to buy for the term of your contract.

 Recommended   Price   Selection   Convenience   Service   Security

★ commonreader.com
A Common Reader

800-832-7323
service@commonreader.com
Audiobooks

The books in A Common Reader's online catalog cover a wide variety of topics. Fiction, non-fiction, collections of art, letters, and diaries — the list is endless. However, all the books have been chosen for one reason. In its own way, each book is the type of book that you would be happy to pass on to a friend. A Common Reader has a strict set of rules for the books included in its catalogs and most of the time, this company is right on the money. The book choices are inspired! The catalog has been expanded and now includes music and movies.

compuhigh.com
CompuHigh.com

866-859-0777
E-mail form on site
Self-Enrichment

A high school diploma is important. Without one, you can be pigeonholed into low-paying jobs or passed over for promotions. This site provides the opportunity for you to earn your high school diploma. It is not a diploma mill! CompuHigh is the online division of Clonlara School, a fully accredited private school. Although you work at your own pace, you must complete the online coursework and related projects. You can meet with your teachers. When you graduate, you will be issued a diploma and transcripts that are accepted by universities and colleges. It's never too late.

cyberdungeon.com
Cyberdungeon.com

800-267-1511
clerck@cyberdungeon.com
Leisure Time

There are parallel universes out there. In one, elves live, dwarves roam, and trollocs incite panic. In another, history is rewritten as the Axis and Allies powers fight World War II. Although these games revolve around pretend scenarios, the players can get totally absorbed. Cyberdungeon.com is a popular destination for those who love role-playing games, war games, miniatures, and accessories. If you're not ready for a group, many of the games are single-player versions. When you're ready to role-play in a group, log on to the site's message boards. Role-playing games are fun!

deliverme.com
DeliverMe.com

866-346-3777
contact@deliverme.com

Eating Out

DeliverMe.com matches diners and restaurants. Simply enter the city and state, choose an optional food type — Burger, French, Café, Kosher and so on, and click Go. In a moment a list of matching restaurants appears. Click a restaurant name for more information or a map. Unfortunately, the list at DeliverMe.com isn't always very current because restaurants open and close so frequently. Your best bet is to call the restaurant before you go. Looking for a personal chef? Search for one at DeliverMe.com. The site also features links to Web-based gourmet shopping and services.

digitalcity.com
America Online City Guide

No phone number listed
E-mail form on site

Eating Out • Tickets

AOL's CityGuide is the granddaddy of local search services. The site delivers information about local restaurants, entertainment venues, community resources, and news in cities and metropolitan regions all across the United States. Using CityGuide is easy. On your first visit you'll be asked to select a city. On subsequent visits, that location will appear as your home page, but you can easily pick another city and view its events and calendar.

★ dinnerbroker.com
DinnerBroker.com

888-432-8288
support@dinnerbroker.com

Eating Out • Reservations

DinnerBroker is an online restaurant reservation service that gives you three great options. Discount Reservations rewards you for reserving a table at off-peak hours with a discount of anywhere from 10 to 15 percent of your meal price. If you book Standard Reservations, DinnerBroker makes all the arrangements. Use Prime-Time Reservations to get a table during times that are typically booked up. A small fee is charged for this service, but it's worth the convenience. Discounted and standard gift certificates from the restaurants are available, too. DinnerBroker covers areas all over the United States and Canada; check the site for participating restaurants.

 Recommended   Price   Selection   Convenience   Service   Security

discountmagazines.com
DiscountMagazines.com

No phone number listed
info@discountmagazines.com

Magazines

A subscription to a popular magazine for $5.95! That's the angle at DiscountMagazines.com. The list of available magazines is by no means as full as some of the other magazine vendors on the Internet, but you have to agree that the price is amazing. Length of subscription and number of issues varies. There's also a collection of low-priced magazines, not as low as $5.95, but good deals in their own right. Read the FAQs at the site before you order, and then follow the instructions carefully. These folks seem to know what they're doing, and they do it well.

doubletimejazz.com
Double-Time Jazz

800-293-8528
dtjazz@doubletimejazz.com

Listening to Music

It's all about the tunes, baby, it's all about the tunes. Some of the best recorded jazz can be found at Double-Time Jazz's site. Unfortunately, the folks who designed this site didn't make it easy for you to find it. The clunky three-frame design and the non-intuitive search features may make you want to give up before you score pay dirt. If you're a true jazz fan, accept the occasional dead link as a rock in the road and keep searching. The original recordings and rare live performance CDs by real jazz greats are worth it.

★ dummies.com
Dummies.com

877-762-2974
consumers@wiley.com

Books

Is there a better reference series in the world? We think not! Of course, *For Dummies* books aren't written for intellectually challenged people at all. Instead, they're expressly designed for frustrated and hard-working folks like you and me who want to learn how to accomplish a task or meet our goal as quickly as possible. *For Dummies* books are, by design, light on jargon, and heavy on good, solid, practical information with a dash of humor thrown in for good measure. Shop this site for all the *For Dummies* books in the series and maybe pick up an extra copy or two of this one.

emusic.com
eMusic

858-777-7639
E-mail form on site

Listening to Music

Want to download music to your computer that's safe and legal? Visit eMusic. The site has hundreds of thousands of songs in MP3 format from established musicians. If you're new to downloading, the optional Download Manager makes it easy to keep track of your tunes and burn CDs. You'll need to sign up for an account and provide your credit card information before you can download any music. You'll be charged for every song you download. Try out the service for free. You can download up to fifty MP3s, and if you decide to cancel, the songs are yours, no strings attached.

everyticket.com
EveryTicket.com

800-928-7328
seats@everyticket.com

Tickets

Why limit your options when you can use a buyer's service like this one that promises tickets to "every sport, every concert, every theater nation-wide"? At EveryTicket.com you can perform a nationwide search or browse the site's schedule of hot events, which range from classical theater to NASCAR racing. This company offers extras, too, such as a 5.9 percent cash discount, gift certificates, plus full Customer Care services. Through the service you can also sell tickets you can't use. Get free FedEx shipping for swift delivery.

fictionwriters.com
Fiction Writer's Connection

800-248-2758
BCamenson@aol.com

Self-Enrichment

No more excuses! Tell the story that's been inside your head for years. Your novel could be the next potential bestseller. Unfortunately, getting published is more than typing a manuscript and sending it to publishers. In the real world, getting a novel published can take the collective efforts of a devoted group of people. Fiction Writer's Connection provides help with novel writing and information on finding agents and editors and getting published. Free critiquing of your work is a benefit of membership. If you can survive the comments and incorporate the suggestions, there may be hope for your book.

 Recommended   Price   Selection   Convenience   Service   Security

findagreatrestaurant.com
FindAGreatRestaurant.com

310-829-7712
info@findagreatrestaurant.com

Eating Out • Reservations

Want to find a great restaurant? Start at FindAGreatRestaurant.com and choose your city. Next, click the cuisine you want. Here's where it gets tricky. Member Restaurants, if any exist in the category, offer 360-degree virtual tours and links to menus and online reservations. (These establishments pay for the service.) Non-member Restaurants are listed by name and address. You may need to click several times before you find a Member Restaurant. Still, the overall value of the information and the fun of the occasional virtual tour make this experience almost as good as a rich dessert.

★ folkofthewood.com
Folk of the Wood

888-209-8434
folkwood@zianet.com

Listening to Music • Making Music

If folk music is your favored genre, the Folk of the Wood site is just for you. This site carries all the traditional folk instruments such as banjos, dulcimers, fiddles, harps, basses, mandolins, dobros, and 6- and 12-string guitars. Choose from new, used, and "previously sold but still new" instruments and an assortment of tools for the acoustic artist. Browse the selection of books and videos. Of special note is the company's 500 percent policy, the MP3 listings, the FAQ database, and the free acoustic lesson offerings, covering beginner to advanced topics in a range of instruments.

gamepuzzles.com
Kadon Enterprises, Inc.

410-437-2163
kadon@gamepuzzles.com

Leisure Time

Years ago, the same folks who run the gamepuzzles.com site designed Quintillions. That game is still sold and has achieved cult status among its legion of players. Odds are many of the puzzles sold at this site will be equally as popular. The site is so vast that you'll do best to take the First Timer's Tour on your initial visit. When you get the hang of things, you'll be ready to purchase your own puzzles or play in the online Puzzle Parlor. The parlor is completely addictive! Time flies when you match wits (and lose!) against the puzzles waiting there.

greattickets.com
Great Tickets

800-701-6561
No e-mail address on site

Tickets

Specializing in selling premium seating and locating tickets for sold-out performances, this broker service grabs your attention with its list of hottest events. Look for options by city — with more than two dozen cities listed, from Boston to Los Angeles. Order for Broadway, sporting events, as well as the most sought-after concert tickets. Most of the company's offerings are U.S.-based but it also brokers for events around the world. Get your tickets by FedEx.

harpsonly.com
HarpsOnly.com

800-823-4233
info@harpsonly.com

Making Music

Featuring a straightforward selection of excellent harps and music books, this harp specialty venue strikes just the right chord. This site has both Celtic- and contemporary-style harps, and its line of rosewood lever harps are each individually crafted, not from a kit, and arrive fully assembled and pre-strung (you get an extra set of strings). Select from a range of strings (19–36) and octave ranges, in sizes from 31 to 50 inches, including some with cam-style levers. Browse the harp savings packages and accessories like chromatic tuners and metronomes. The online FAQs can help you with tuning and changing a string.

hickeys.com
Hickey's Music Center

800-442-5397
info@hickeys.com

Making Music

When you need more than just sheet music (though this site has that, too), take a look at Hickey's, a site that offers instrument rentals, manuscript paper, recordings, instruments, textbooks, software, and repair services. Find composer, language, and range folios, too, and accessories such as metronomes, electronic tuners, and music stands. No matter what genre you seek, you can search by artist or collections, by arrangements (woodwind, brass, string, and vocal catalogs), by type (chamber, jazz, orchestral parts, and scores), and by instruments (piano, organ, guitar, percussion, or voice).

 Recommended   Price   Selection   Convenience   Service   Security

★ icdchess.com
Your Move Chess and Games
800-645 4710
icd@icdchess.com
Leisure Time

This mega-chess site has been online since 1996 and, alas, it looks like it could do with some modernization. However, don't be put off by Your Move Chess and Games' outdated look and feel; its claims of being the Internet's biggest chess site probably are true. Chess boards, sets, pieces, tables, and related chess paraphernalia are all available here. You'll even find a selection of chess clocks to keep you on track. Of course, you can join the computer chess club, and spend some time talking to other chess players in the message forum. If you're still game, check out the supplies for mah-jongg, backgammon, cribbage, and a host of other games, too.

iseatz.com
iSeatz.com
877-317-7763
E-mail form on site
Eating Out • Reservations

The iSeatz.com folks have big plans for their online restaurant reservation service. In years to come, restaurants all over the country may be signed up as affiliates, and you'll be able to reserve the best table in town directly from this site. Right now, however, only a few establishments are part of the iSeatz family. Restaurants are arranged by region; check your area and see where you can go with this completely free service.

jewishmusic.com
JewishMusic.com
800-827-2400
info@jewishmusic.com
Books • Listening to Music • Making Music

JewishMusic.com fits nicely into a niche that few sites can fill. Jewish music resonates at this site, in the form of CDs, videos, music books and Judaic books, and even computer software. The music is a mixed bag, ranging from classic Yiddish oldies to contemporary hits. Click the Top 50 Albums to see what others are buying. The Listening Station is a great way to preview some of the music at the site, although you must have RealPlayer installed for the music to play properly. To score a good deal, click the Sale button and follow the links to savings.

juststrings.com
JustStrings.com
603-889-2664
csrv@juststrings.com
Making Music

Any store can sell guitar strings, but it takes a special place to obtain strings quickly for virtually any type of stringed instrument. At JustStrings.com, as the name says, the focus is exclusively on strings; you can search by instrument or manufacturer and buy strings singly, by set, or in bulk. You can swiftly locate a complete set of strings for all instruments within each instrument section online. Do you have a dulcimer, autoharp, sitar, ukulele, zither, or tambura? This site carries strings for those instruments. JustStrings.com also offers gift certificates, tuners, and a musician's atlas.

landofmags.com
LandofMags.com
800-284-1833
customerservice@landofmags.com
Magazines

You can take advantage of some great deals on magazine subscriptions at LandofMags.com, but you need to read the fine print and order in advance. Check out the low prices on the 1,300 magazines here and choose your titles from the extensive list of categories. After you've ordered, don't get impatient. Magazine subscriptions can be slow to start and take anywhere from 6 to 12 weeks to begin. Some publishers preprint their magazine labels up to two months in advance, and orders are entered manually. Your subscription officially starts with your first magazine.

lifematters.com
LifeMatters
888-255-9757
E-mail form on site
Self-Enrichment

Is it time for a mental tune-up? Are you working more and enjoying life less? At today's breakneck pace, lots of people feel this way. Not to worry. The folks at LifeMatters may be able to assist you. They offer a number of online classes and videos and DVDs that they claim will help you take charge of your life and well-being. The action-oriented information is presented in a positive way, and covers life topics such as parenting, fitness, relationships, and stress-related disorders. Books and audiotapes are available, too, and there are some nifty gifts for kids.

 Recommended   Price   Selection   Convenience   Service   Security

limu.com
Limu.com

No phone number listed
E-mail form on site

Self-Enrichment

Limu, based in the heart of London, offers students the opportunity to learn about subjects and skills ranging from the academic and professional to the fun and hobby-related. You can join an existing class or sign up for a new class in over 400 subject categories. Courses meet in Limu's Interactive Classroom, which offers live voice and text chat and a virtual drawing board. Transcripts of your live sessions in the classroom are available afterwards. If you're an expert in your field or have a skill you'd like to share, you may consider teaching a class at Limu. Details are at the site.

lowestcostmusic.com
LowestCostMusic.com

No phone number listed
E-mail form on site

Making Music

If you get happy when you find a music shop that has dozens of selections, then you'll be ecstatic when you visit LowestCostMusic.com, which boasts more than 113,000 individual pieces of sheet music, along with tablature, books, videos, and beyond. Locate play-alongs for drums, guitars, bass, piano, vocal, band, choral, orchestra, dobis, and mandolins. Search by title, artist, band, or arranger. The folks here can also help you find what you need, from "The Songs of John Lennon" to books like *Recording and Producing in the Home Studio*. As a nice extra, orders more than $25 get free shipping.

★ magazineline.com
Magazineline

800-968-7323
customerservice@magazineline.com

Magazines

Magazineline is one of the better magazine services on the Internet. Most services offer two types of magazines: general interest magazines that everyone's heard of and obscure titles that appeal to only a handful of readers. The titles at this site are edgier and younger, more in line with what people really want to read. Magazineline claims that if you find a lower introductory price from a "publisher-authorized source" on a magazine ordered here, your subscription price will be refunded. We say take advantage of the great selection, good prices, and free gifts, and look forward to a full mailbox.

magsonthenet.com
Mags On The Net

877-261-8589
E-mail form on site

Magazines

MagsontheNet makes it hard to leave without buying a few magazine subscriptions for you or someone you know. Want to send a subscription as a gift? Choose from one of seven gift cards. Special seasonal deals offer unbelievable pricing. In June, it's Graduation Time, in December, Holiday Gift Giving, and other months feature similar discounts. MagsontheNet offers subscriptions to over 200,000 different publications, so you're bound to find at least one you want to read. However, if the one you like isn't there, a handy e-mail link ensures you'll let the folks who do the ordering know.

mathprep.com
Math Courses Online

No phone number listed
rick@omegamath.net

Self-Enrichment

Poor math skills affect so many adults. It's never too late in life to improve those skills and get a handle on mathematical concepts. The classes at Math Courses Online — Basic Math and Pre-Algebra through Geometry — are aimed at those who want to expand their math knowledge. Classes are self-paced and conducted entirely online. There's no extra book to buy and all tests are included in the low class price. Test results are immediate, so you can make sure you're ready to progress to the next chapter. A certificate of completion is available on request, after you pass the final exam.

milehighcomics.com
Mile High Comics

800-676-6423
backissue@milehighcomics.com

Books

Chuck Rozanski, the owner, started Mile High Comics in 1977, and the art form has been his passion ever since. You'll find comic books of all vintages and conditions, and some that are quite expensive. Don't wait to purchase if you see a comic book that you want: Many of the comics are one of a kind or collector editions. In fact, contact the site if you want to sell or trade comic books from your personal collection. Join the free NICE (New Issue Comic Express) Club for extra discounts and services.

 Recommended   Price   Selection   Convenience   Service   Security

★ movielink.com
Movielink

No phone number listed
service@movielinkhelp.com

Movies

Movielink lets you download movies from the Internet and watch them on your computer. The service has some built-in limitations — you need a broadband connection, mucho hard drive space, and a good video card and computer monitor. The fee is minimal (less than the cost of a movie ticket), and you can choose from several hundred titles. You have 30 days after download to watch your movie, and you must complete the viewing within 24 hours of when you first click Play. Because you don't need to be connected to the Internet to watch your movie, the service is ideal for laptop users.

movietickets.com
MovieTickets.com

561-998-8000
E-mail form on site

Tickets

Want your own personal box office? Replace the time spent in line with a few mouse clicks. MovieTickets.com lets you order tickets for a movie tonight or for one that has not yet opened in your city, guaranteeing you a seat. The site also shows you weekend box-office sales to give you a handle on what's the hottest flick, along with movie release dates and premiere cities. Locate tickets and show times by city or zip code. Browse the selection of music CDs, movies on DVD, and game releases for popular platforms.

★ music123.com
Music 123

888-590-9700
E-mail form on site

Making Music

Whether you're a pro musician, DJ, teacher, or enthusiast, you'll want to check out the Music 123 site. From guitars, keyboards, and amps, to drums and percussion equipment, to band and orchestra instruments (all types, including marching, woodwind, and brass), this site is bound to have what you seek. Accessories include custom guitar picks and interface hardware, as well as software for notation and scoring, multitrack recording, and education. Lighting is just part of the DJ gear offered here. Find sheet music, too, including digital sheets you can purchase and download on the spot.

musiciansfriend.com
Musician's Friend

800-391-8762
E-mail form on site

Making Music

One visit to this virtual shop explains why it calls itself the world's largest online music gear company. Besides extras such as special financing and helpful product reviews, Musician's Friend offers all types of guitars, drums and drum sets, keyboards, and a range of accessories (strings, stands, you name it). Electronic gear abounds at this site, as well, with amplifiers and effects tools, digital music workstations, live sound and recording equipment, and tuners. Sign up for the free weekly newsletter to learn about specials. Get free express shipping on orders of $199 or more.

musicnotes.com
Musicnotes.com

800-944-4667
service@musicnotes.com

Making Music

Shop traditionally through Musicnotes.com's selection of more than 260,000 music books and materials, or take advantage of its more than 20,000 digital sheet music titles for instant purchase and download. For the latter, consider signing up for the Digital Discount Club, which gives you a 10 percent discount on all your sheet music for a year (great for frequent music shoppers like teachers, musical directors, and pro musicians). Need guitar guru sessions? Musicnotes.com can help you out in that area, too. You can browse the inventory by instruments, style, or genre, or get the Free Music Notes viewer so you can consult the site's inventory anytime.

★ mysterylovers.com
Mystery Lovers Bookshop

888-800-6078
info@mysterylovers.com

Books

You don't need to be a detective to figure out why readers return to Mystery Lovers Bookshop. The site carries a great collection of past and present mysteries. Don't miss the Recent Arrivals for the latest whodunits. Divided by paperback and hard cover, the directory contains a review for each book on the list. If you can't decide what to read on a dark and stormy night, click Staff Picks and see what the help likes best. The next time you're in the vicinity of Oakmont, Pennsylvania, stop in at the store and say "Hi."

 Recommended   Price   Selection   Convenience   Service   Security

netflix.com
Netflix.com
800-585-8131
privacy@netflix.com
Movies

Over two million members already are enjoying Netflix's more than 20,000 DVD movie library. The service is simple. Make a list of the DVDs you want and Netflix will send you three. Return one in the postage-paid envelope and Netflix will ship you another. That's all there is to it. The three-at-a-time program is available for one flat monthly fee. There are no additional charges. There are no late fees or due dates — even shipping is free. You can watch as many movies as you like. A free Trial Offer is available for new customers.

nostalgiafamilyvideo.com
Nostalgia Family Video
800-784-3362
E-mail form on site
Movies

Sure, it's a snap to run down to the local video store and find all the current releases. But what do you do when you have a hankering to see a really old movie? Go to Nostalgia Family Video, of course. You'll find films from the '30s, '40s, and '50s here, along with several old TV shows. Search by actor, title, or keyword, or browse through the various categories. Each description includes a plot summary, running time, and other pertinent information. DVDs are also available. As an added bonus, the site is chock-full of trivia about old stars and the movies that made them famous.

officeplayground.com
Office Playground
800-458-1948
info@officeplayground.com
Leisure Time

Whether you're a manager or file clerk, you need to have some fun time at work each day. Office Playground can provide all the toys and stress relievers to help you take a few moments of well-needed relaxation. If you're stressed (and who isn't?), consider a calming Zen Garden, a squishy Sumo wrestler squeeze toy, or some wind-up sushi for a few laughs. Or go in the opposite direction and purchase a Voodoo Doll. Of course, the pins you stick in the doll won't really harm the intended recipient. It's just fun, and incredibly relaxing, to let your imagination run wild, one pin at a time.

onlinegolflessons.com
Online Golf Lessons

No phone number listed
golfpro@onlinegolflessons.com

Self-Enrichment

Online Golf Lessons offers a great way to improve your golf game. The lessons are broken down into 15 short segments. In each segment, Matt Kluck, the certified PGA pro who designed the revolutionary course, provides audible instructions and clear, easy-to-follow pictures. The segments cover everything from the correct way to grip the club to the best putting stroke. Purchase a subscription to access the lesson segments. The total cost isn't very expensive and can work magic with your game. Try your first lesson for free.

opentable.com
OpenTable.com

800-673-6822
E-mail form on site

Reservations

Next time you want to make dinner reservations, stop hunting for the phone book and turn to OpenTable. More than 1,750 restaurants nationwide are signed up for the online reservation service, and more will come online in the future. Restaurants are arranged by region. Search the list by restaurant name, price range, or cuisine. Reservations can be made anytime; diners are never placed on hold or told to come back during business hours. You don't need to be a member of OpenTable to make a reservation here. However, members earn OpenTable Dining Rewards each time they use the service.

playpianotoday.com
Piano Lessons Unlimited

No phone number listed
author@playpianotoday.com

Making Music • Self-Enrichment

Have you always dreamed about sitting down at a keyboard and banging out your favorite song? If so, you may want to try Piano Lessons Unlimited's innovative piano and keyboard lessons. The lessons are provided in a number of different formats (video DVD, video CD-ROM, and downloadable video or audio), and you can begin learning whenever you want using this company's rhythmic patterns technique to train you to play any song by ear. In no time, you can master fingering techniques and play virtually any kind of music. Try the site's free online demo.

 Recommended   Price   Selection   Convenience   Service Security

⭐ powells.com
Powells.com

866-201-7601
help@powells.com

Audiobooks • Books

A smaller and more personal bookseller than the megastores, Powells.com provides personal touches that are attractive to customers. Where else will you find a store cat named Fup who freely recommends books? Browse through the Hosted Bookshelves or spend some time looking through ordered aisles. Prices at this site are good and service is first-rate. You'll need to set up an account for purchases. Powells.com ships within the U.S. and internationally.

recordedbooks.com
Recorded Books

800-636-3399
customerservice@recordedbooks.com

Audiobooks

Don't have time to read? How about listening to a recorded book instead? Never dry or boring, each audiobook is narrated by professional actors with years of stage and screen experience. You can purchase your audiobook, but rentals are less expensive and equally convenient. You'll have 30 days to listen to your audiobook. When you've finished, simply drop your book into the mail in the postage-paid return envelope that was included with your shipment. Hundreds of fiction and non-fiction titles are available.

samedaymusic.com
SameDayMusic

866-744-7736
experts@samedaymusic.com

Making Music

Do you need your music equipment quickly? The folks at SameDayMusic offer same-day shipping on select items (and a $50 cash payment if they don't ship your item that day). Choose from a wide selection of classical and bass guitars as well as other stringed instruments and drums. Amplifiers, effects equipment, guitar parts, and string-related books, videos, and CD-ROMs round out the selection. Tempt yourself with the keyboards and MIDI gear, digital pianos, and Theremins. Locate an assortment of computer music hardware. Get recording gear, studio monitors, studio racks and workstations, DJ essentials, and both wireless systems and PA speakers as well.

savvydiner.com
Savvy Diner

No phone number listed
comments@savvydiner.com

Eating Out • Reservations

Savvy Diner isn't the biggest restaurant reservation service on the Internet, but it has some definite plusses. Establishments earn their way onto Savvy Diner's pages from recommendations by local concierges and the guest services staff at better hotels. These recommendations keep the list at this site small, but ensure that the restaurants are first rate. To use the reservation service, choose your Savvy City from the home page and then select your restaurant from the list displayed. Look over the menu and then fill in the form to make your reservation. That's it! The service is free.

selfhelpguides.com
Self Help Guides

No phone number listed
support@selfhelpguides.com

Books • Self-Enrichment

The Self Help Guides offered at this site pack a lot of punch. Each guide delivers information on how to improve your life, learn a new skill, or master a new task. The Self Help Guides are only the start of the process. You'll need to work through the information, make the necessary changes and, perhaps, change your lifestyle. Each guide is specific and succinct and sticks to the subject. The developers advise buying only one or two at a time, so you can stay focused on the guide's topic. Topics range from self-help to technical skills.

sheetmusicco.com
The Sheet Music Company

440-232-2131
E-mail form on site

Making Music

Offering free budget shipping on sheet music orders of just $25 or more, The Sheet Music Company is a great resource for musicians. Get sheet music for Broadway shows, swing/jazz/blues, R&B, wedding/religious/contemporary Christian, movies, TV and film scores, holiday themes, pop and rock, as well as country and classical music. Teach yourself or others to play piano via the site's selection of instructional piano methods, including studies by Bastien and Hal Leonard. Search by instrument or artists. The site can also provide you with guitar tabs and sheets for woodwind, brass, and stringed instruments.

 Recommended Price Selection Convenience Service Security

sheetmusicdirect.com
SheetMusicDirect.com

414-774-3630
na_info@sheetmusicdirect.com

Making Music

Take the waiting and the driving out of shopping for sheet music with a site that has been selling virtually nothing but "legitimate, copyrighted, 100% digital sheet music" since 1997. Just purchase and download from SheetMusic Direct.com's collection of more than 10,000 titles (more added weekly) so you can print the results on your PC or Mac-connected printer. Also download the free sheet music viewer, Scorch2, through which you can view and listen to your music as well as alter the instrumentation and even transpose that music into a different key. The site offers a free newsletter, too.

sheetmusicplus.com
Sheet Music Plus

800-743-3868
info@sheetmusicplus.com

Making Music

Looking for something unusual? Look no further than Sheet Music Plus, which boasts more than 366,000 sheet music titles, songbooks, scores, tabs, and methods. Featuring special arrangements for guitars, pianos, flutes, clarinets, violins, saxophones, trumpets, and percussion instruments, you can also educate yourself through various "Teach Yourself" materials or order a gift certificate for a music-loving friend. Browse through genres (pop, classical, Christian, and jazz), by age group, and by artist or band. Sheet Music Plus ships worldwide, with U.S. budget shipping for just $2.99.

★ sheetmusicsuperstore.com
Sheet Music Superstore

504-250-2369
sales@sheetmusicsuperstore.com

Making Music

Finding what you need isn't hard in a virtual shop with more than 250,000 items in inventory. From piano instruction to digital sheet music downloads, to song- and play-along books and DVDs as well as VHS tapes, you've just begun to browse Sheet Music Superstore's wares. This company has bass and guitar tablatures, material for orchestra/bands/ensembles, guitar and bass accessories, and choral and vocal works. Used guitar gear, CDs, and reference books are also available. If you still manage to miss something, send a request and the folks here will try to fulfill it.

⭐ shootersedge.com
Shooter's Edge

No phone number listed
shootersedge@shootersedge.com

Leisure Time

The Shooter's Edge site scores a bull's-eye with a collection of darts, flights, shafts, and accessories. No matter what your style or where you play, you'll find darts that are right for you. Detailed product descriptions make it easy to decide. When applicable, replacement parts are included on the same page as the darts, ensuring that you always know just what equipment to buy. Do you want to practice your skills? An electronic game at the site will help you hone your skills before you meet your mates again.

solenergy.org
Solar on-Line

No phone number listed
info@solenergy.org

Self-Enrichment

The sun is an untapped energy source, and the folks at Solar on-Line can help you harness its power. The courses at this site cover photovoltaics, which, simply put, means that voltage can be produced by radiant light. The three classes offered are fairly scientific, so if you're planning to goof off, don't waste your time or money. Those planning a home-remodeling project and people who care about the earth will find the classes challenging but worthwhile. Expect reading assignments, practical exercises, and quizzes. A Certificate of Completion is awarded to everyone who shines.

⭐ songsearch.com
Songsearch

909-792-0087
song@songsearch.com

Listening to Music

Songsearch is off the beaten path for music sites, but you'll be glad you ventured afield when you visit here. The site carries over 600,000 album titles of mostly hard-to-find and imported music. If you're looking for a song you heard in a movie but haven't been able to locate it anywhere else, there's a good chance Songsearch has it. Enter the movie title in the site's search box or browse through the complete listing of movie soundtracks. The site's full category list is extensive and intelligently arranged. Songsearch ships internationally.

⭐ Recommended   Price   Selection   Convenience ☺ Service 🔒 Security

sonicrec.com
Sonic Recollections

503-236-3050
orderdesk@sonicrec.com

Listening to Music

Weird and collectible music ends up at the Sonic Recollections site. Established in 1991, the company built its reputation as a purveyor of reel-to-reel tapes, CDs, and vinyl records. The items sold at Sonic Recollections are used and often have been subjected to a fair amount of abuse by their former owners. However, the company's unique grading system makes it easy for shoppers to determine the condition of every item. Same day order processing and shipping and low prices makes Sonic Recollections a great place to shop for music you'd be hard pressed to find elsewhere. On a recent visit, I found records by Sammi Smith and Jerry Lee Lewis.

soyouwanna.com
SoYouWanna.com

No phone number listed
info@soyouwanna.com

Self-Enrichment

Life's little mysteries are explained at SoYouWanna.com. Finally, a place that teaches all those things that weren't covered in school. Wanna be a movie extra? Wanna give yourself a great manicure? You'll find these, and countless other topics, covered in a clever, surprisingly helpful way. The SoYouWanna Store displays an index of products related to each article. For example, the manicure article has product links to nail oils, beauty bargains, and "colors with a conscience." If only the rest of life could be so easy to figure out.

spilsbury.com
Spilsbury.com

800-285-2619
service@spilsbury.com

Leisure Time

Wander over to this site the next time you're looking for something to do. All the toys, games, books, puzzles, gags, and crafts have been hand-tested by the Spilsbury staff. The resulting collection doesn't include some of the useless stuff found at other sites. You'll find items that are thoughtful or just plain fun. Spilsbury always runs a few specials for Internet customers, so check them out before you complete your order. Need a gift? The site's Gift Finder takes the work out of the selection process.

stantons.com
Stanton's Sheet Music

614-224-4257
greatservice@stantons.com

Making Music

When you're looking for scores, come to the "Sheet Music Specialists" who have been in business for more than 43 years. This company features print music for all types of instruments and genres, and covers your bases whether you need materials for instrument or vocal solos, marching bands, orchestras, ensembles, or methods. How many places can you go to find music for handbells or chromatic harmonicas? This site also has what you need for guitars, organs, keyboards and pianos, string bass, French horns, violas, euphoniums, trombones, tubas, oboes, bassoons, and more.

stubhub.com
Stub Hub

866-788-2482
E-mail form on site

Tickets

This third-party vendor provides you with the opportunity to buy, sell, find, and compare tickets for special events and popular venues. For example, buy tickets for great interleague games or for any major league baseball team's games. But you can also locate tickets for other major sports such as hockey, football, and basketball, for shows, family events, speaking tours, classical music and opera, ballet and dance, TV shows, as well as parties and exclusive engagements. Most events are U.S.-based, but you can browse through choices for cities such as San Juan, Montreal, Vancouver, and Toronto, too.

techkits.com
LNS Technologies

707-448-3750
info@techkits.com

Leisure Time

The term toy is relative. What one person plays with may seem like work to another. Such is the case with the kits offered by LNS Technologies. Admittedly, the kits at this site aren't for beginners. A rudimentary understanding of electronics and a few basic tools are required. You can purchase kits such as the following: Jumbo 6-Digit LED Clock, RF Meter/Bug Detector, Vocal Special Effects, Hall-Effect Compass, Electronic Parrot, Animal Sounds Piano, Gas Sensor Alarm, or Anti-Gravity Levitator. All parts, including circuit boards, are included.

 Recommended   Price   Selection   Convenience   Service Security

tennisone.com
Tennis One

408-778-0638
admin@tennisone.com

Self-Enrichment

To play like a pro you have to see how the pros play! An annual membership at Tennis One gives you access to ProPortraits, special discounts from selected shops, and more. You'll also get unlimited use of the ProStrokes Gallery, where you can watch more than 700 digital movies of the strokes of the world's best players. Freeze the action, or go frame by frame at regular speed or slow motion, as you watch the best players in the world on the court. The Lesson Library holds more than 500 lessons from top tennis teachers. Net yourself a free one-month trial membership.

thebanjohut.com
The Banjo Hut

877-947-5550
thebanjohut@thebanjohut.com

Making Music

Why buy a banjo from a place where the workers know very little about the instrument? The Banjo Hut sells nothing but banjos, including many in affordable, all-inclusive packages for either the beginner or experienced picker. Name brands include Abilene, Hondo, Johnson, Kay, and Lotus. You can order left-handed banjos and six-string instruments here, too, along with an assortment of books, DVDs, and videos detailing the topic. The folks behind this site even set up the instrument and tune it before shipping it to you (shipping on instruments is free within the continental U.S).

ticketmaster.com
Ticketmaster

305-358-5885
E-mail form on site

Tickets

Ticketmaster's site tries hard to wrap the obvious truth in reasoning and roundabout logic, but when you get to the end, the simple fact remains: If you want to go to a big-name venue, you're going to have to pay big bucks. You'll pay not only the face price of the ticket, but service charges and other surcharges tacked on by this major ticket broker. Grin and bear it. Your best bet is to register in advance with Ticketmaster. That way, all your information will be on file when you click in, and your reservation will take only a nanosecond or two.

tickets.com
Tickets.com, Inc.

No phone number listed
E-mail form on site

Tickets

If you have an event that you want to see, you can likely find a ticket for it at the Tickets.com site. Whether you need tickets for business or pleasure, in the U.S. or in Canada, Britain, Hong Kong, or Australia, this company can sell you seats for a whole range of sporting games, concerts, the arts, and family-oriented specials. Find events other sites might not list, including Playboy's 50th Anniversary Tour, Lord of the Rings: The Symphony, and American Idols Live, and links to travel/accommodations.

trygames.com
Trygames.com

415-255-3060
info@trymedia.com

Leisure Time

Check out Trygames.com for downloadable games that you try out before you buy. Choose your game from the online catalog. Games are arranged by categories, such as Action, Classic, Sports, or view the most downloaded games or newest releases. Click to download a game you like and follow the on-screen instructions to save and install the game to your computer. Play the game through the trial period. Click the Buy It Now button in the game to complete the transaction during the trial period. Unless you buy it, you won't be able to play the game or another tryout version after the trial period ends.

universalclass.com
UniversalClass

800-355-5582
customercare@universalclass.com

Self-Enrichment

If you don't have a specific enrichment course in mind, cruise over to the UniversalClass site and look through its offerings. UniversalClass offers hundreds of different online classes in a wide variety of subjects. You can choose from such serious topics as Debt Management 101 to crafty topics like Scrapbooking on a Shoestring. How can this company offer so many diverse classes? Simple. UniversalClass provides the forum and tools for anyone to hold an online class. The class content is audited by UniversalClass reviewers before the class is posted, but some classes are better than others. Still, classes here are inexpensive and for the most part, worthwhile.

 Recommended   Price   Selection   Convenience   Service   Security

usdiners.com
USDiners.com

866-346-3777
service@usdiners.com

Eating Out

"Where can we go to eat?" That question gets asked a lot in my house and probably gets asked in your house, too. Fortunately, you can find an easy answer at USDiners.com. Start your search for restaurants in your desired area by clicking the state on the map that appears on the site's home page. Continue your search by city or cuisine type, or by price. You can be on your way to dinner in no time. Just keep in mind that the service charges restaurants to be included, so the list is by no means complete.

usrg.com
United States Restaurant Guide

No phone number listed
No e-mail address on site

Eating Out

The USRG guide rates and reviews restaurants, based on information provided by qualified volunteers. Check out Restaurants A-Z for the complete listing for a city and then get specific recommendations from the Best lists. Travelers will appreciate the city maps. If you don't see a place you like, check out the Nearby Cities link for a list of restaurants close by. Those restaurants that share menus and recipes with diners get special mention on their respective city pages. Join USRG and rate and review restaurants yourself. You'll get personalized views of cities, the streets, and the restaurants, and the satisfaction of knowing you helped other diners.

★ videocollection.com
The Video Collection

800-538-5856
E-mail form on site

Movies

You'll have to practice self-control at The Video Collection's site; otherwise, your buying spree is going to be costly. The collection here is so extensive that it's hard to know where to start. Years of great television from A&E, The History Channel, The Discovery Channel, PBS, HBO, and more are available on video. Visitors can find films of every vintage and genre using the categories list or search tool. First-time buyers receive a discount. Join the Video Star club and receive a discount for life. What's that you say? You need DVD format? No problem. DVDs are also available for many of the titles.

videoflicks.com
Videoflicks

800-690-2879
orders@videoflicks.com

Movies

Videoflicks has been taking care of American and Canadian movie lovers since 1995. Prices on the site are shown in U.S. dollars but Canadian shoppers can convert the currency with a single click. The movies here are not first run. Rather, the site specializes in hard-to-find and out-of-print movies. Movies are available in VHS and DVD. Use the Search feature to find your favorite movie titles. If you don't see what you want, send the site an e-mail with your wanted movie titles and the folks there will let you know when your titles come in.

waterbug.com
Waterbug

800-466-0234
No e-mail address on site

Listening to Music

Even though you won't find the old show called "Hootenany" on any of this year's prime time television network schedules, folk music is alive and well. There's a throng of people who love the genre, and their legions are growing. Stop over at Waterbug for contemporary and traditional folk recordings from a variety of new folk performers. Waterbug has a great way to try out the music offered at its site — three sampler CDS, each lasting about 70 minutes. You can buy one for a nominal $5, or Waterbug will give it to you practically for free if you make a purchase.

zagat.com
Zagat Survey

800-333-3421
E-mail form on site

Books • Eating Out

Benefit from what other diners have said about restaurants and hotels with the reviews at Zagat Survey. Typically you set one location as your home site, but you can read the reviews from other locations as well. Your best bet here is to subscribe to the site. Although you can read the reviews as an anonymous user, your free subscription entitles you to lots of extras. Zagat subscribers get a free new e-mail newsletter called ZagatWire that contains all the latest restaurant news and gossip. Subscribers also can use the super Zagat search feature and buy travel books and related items at a discount.

 Recommended   Price   Selection Convenience Service Security

Let's Celebrate!

Declare next weekend "Celebration Saturday Night." You don't have to have a definite reason, such as a promotion or good grade on an exam. Sometimes it's exciting to plan a celebration just for fun's sake.

Of course, every day is a holiday somewhere in the world. It's perfectly acceptable to make someone else's celebration your own! You'll find out who's celebrating what in the charming book titled, *The World Holiday Book: Celebrations for Every Day of the Year* by Anneli Rufus. Although the book is out of print, you can find it at Borders.com (borders.com) and Abebooks (abebooks.com).

To get in a festive mood, hang a celebration flag or banner for all to see. A great selection of flags is available at CelebrationFlags.com (celebrationflags.com).

It's time to plan the big event. Include a few friends in your plans. This celebration is going to rock! Decide what you would like to do. See a play or concert? Attend a sporting event? Have a sumptuous meal at a restaurant? Before you decide, it's important to know what's happening in your local area. Check the City Guide (digitalcity.com) to find out what's going on.

TicketPro.com (ticketpro.com) or Ticket Solutions (go.tickets4u.com) can work magic if you need tickets fast. Try them even if the event or venue is listed as sold out. Picking a restaurant can be a problem. Turn to The Appetite Network (appetitenet.com) for help. The site has restaurant, dining, and travel information from around the U.S. and around the world.

If you're planning on consuming alcoholic beverages during the evening, consider making one member of your party the designated driver. Mothers Against Drunk Drivers (madd.org) has some chilling statistics on their Web site about drinking and driving. A stylish alternative is to hire a limousine for the night. You'll look cool and stay safe. ABC Chauffeured Limousines (abctrans.com) has links to chauffeur services worldwide and will arrange for a limo for your special night.

Need a new outfit for the big night? You'll find some really great-looking clothes at affordable prices at J.C. Penny (jcpenney.com). For a more hip and happening look, cruise on over to Bluefly (bluefly.com).

You're all set for your celebration. Start counting down to the big night! Why not preserve your memories of the fun-filled time? Purchase inexpensive disposable cameras from Ecamera (ecamerafilms.com) for all the evening's participants. Ecamera can develop the pictures, too. Then store the photos in an album from AlbumSource.com (albumsource.com). Now go out and make your celebration a night to remember!

Chapter 11

Flowers and Gifts: Reminders and Remembrances

*I*f the Web has a vast abundance of anything, it's gifts and online merchants that sell them. Remembering someone or thanking someone is the bond that binds relationships together, whether they are friendships, family, or lovers.

Gifts come in all shapes and sizes, but they are primarily reminders and remembrances offered through greeting cards, flowers, personalized articles, and the unique gift. I've included the well-known and not-so-well known greeting card companies that offer pre-designed sentiments and also those that you can customize yourself. The flower shops offered for your consideration run the gamut from the familiar bouquets and roses to exotic floral arrangements. Personalizing a gift elevates it in the eyes of your recipient and tells that person he or she is one of a kind.

Then there's the unique gift, the one that says you looked far and wide to give something that was different and unusual for that special person. You'll find a selection of stores for those, too. Finally, you have to wrap and send your gift. I've included a selection of online stores that supply standard and creative wrapping paper and mailing supplies.

Now I have a couple gift-giving tips for you. Many online gift shops will wrap and send a gift for you. When this option is offered, take advantage of it. It solves the problem of not only getting the gift wrapped nicely, but also of getting it there on time to meet a specific occasion. (In other words, you don't have to wait for a gift to get to you so you can wrap it, just to send it out again for delivery for those geographically distant recipients.) If a credible merchant makes a delivery promise, it normally keeps it. To keep track of special gift-giving dates, sign up for an e-mail reminder service, such as the one offered for free at memotome.com.

Here are some Web sites that can help you when choosing and mailing a gift. For gift ideas for all occasions, plus etiquette and mailing tips, check out the Giving Center site (givingcenter.com). Everyone knows that the traditional wedding present for twenty-five years is silver and for fifty years gold, but did you know steel for the eleventh? Read the entire list at weddingtips.com/annv.html. For advice on giving flowers, see comedyzine.com/tips_101.html; for advice on flower care, see 800florals.com/care. For USPS packaging tips, go to geocities.com/holt_howard/holthoward/shipping_hints.html.

Key Word Index

Cards

The first greeting card was a Christmas card created in England over a hundred years ago. You can now send a greeting card for almost every occasion imaginable with sites designated with this keyword.

Flowers

Say it with flowers. You can't go wrong giving flowers from the retailers with this keyword.

Gifts

The retailers with this keyword offer the kinds of gifts you would normally see in your everyday gift shop. The online stores listed offer a wide selection and lots of choices.

Personalized

With the technology of the Web, you can personalize practically any gift, and the merchants listed with this keyword are happy to help.

Unique

Some gifts go beyond the call of the average, everyday gift shop. Find online retailers with this keyword to purchase some unique and unusual gifts.

Wrap/Mail

After you buy the gift, you have to wrap it — and may have to send it. These sites offer everyday to out-of-the-ordinary gift-wrapping and the materials to send it.

allnautical.com
AllNautical.com

888-577-4518
questions@allnautical.com

Unique

Sail into AllNautical.com if you're looking for a special gift for a special someone in your life, or for that certain someone who has everything. The selection of beautifully detailed model boats would make a great gift for a fisherman at heart or for someone who is interested in the ocean. AllNautical.com also sells lighthouses, Chelsea clocks, fine art, nautical jewelry, nautical gifts and decor, and much more to bring the peacefulness of the ocean to you. Some of the prices are on the pricey side, but the items are beautiful and well made.

alohafreshflowers.com
Aloha Fresh Flowers

888-884-5662
service@hitrade.com

Flowers

Are you planning to have a luau and would like to order genuine Hawaiian leis for your guests? Are you thinking of sending your loved one flowers, but don't want to send the traditional bouquet of roses? Are you feeling the Hawaiian blues? You can choose from an incredible variety of exotic tropical Hawaiian flowers and beautiful Hawaiian orchids at the Aloha Fresh Flowers site. The flowers are guaranteed to arrive fresh and beautiful. Aloha Fresh Flowers not only provides you superior quality with a personal touch, but it brings Hawaii to you.

associatedbag.com
Associated Bag Company

800-926-6100
customerservice@associatedbag.com

Wrap/Mail

Associated Bag Company is a packaging store that offers competitive prices and quality supplies. Whatever your packaging needs, you can meet them with this company's selection of bags, boxes and bubble wrap; envelopes, mailers, and labels; packaging and pallet wrap; tape, adhesives, and 3M tape; shipping room supplies, janitorial supplies, and product liners — and the list goes on! You can even get free samples to make sure what you order will work for you. Your order ships the same day as long as you order by 7 p.m. Central Time. Now that's service!

atomicmuseum.com
National Atomic Museum Store

505-245-2137
info@atomicmuseum.com

Unique

The National Atomic Museum Store offers gift items that illustrate the historical development of atomic energy and nuclear physics in the twentieth century. "Ho-hum," you say? Not so. How about an Einstein coffee mug that says "Get a half-life" or a non-operative Civil Defense radiological survey meter used to detect radioactivity? How about a set of historic atom bomb blueprints, or a Cray Supercomputer circuit board in an oak frame? Along with these and other unusual items, you can also find T-shirts, desk toys, movies, books, and other assorted oddities for the science lover.

autotags.com
Custom License Plates

937-275-7667
customer_support@autotags.com

Personalized

Car buffs will appreciate the customized vanity tags and engraved license plate frames at autotags.com. So if the BRN2SHP plate is already assigned to another driver by your department of motor vehicles, you can still express yourself with a vanity tag on your front bumper. Keep in mind that these vanity tags are not a legal substitute for official plates issued by your state. There is no online ordering, so you must print out and mail the order form posted on the site. No credit cards are accepted but the company does offer a 100 percent satisfaction guarantee.

baby-gifts-gift-baskets.com
Baby Gift Baskets & Gifts

866-557-1388
service@baby-gifts-gift-baskets.com

Gifts • Personalized

Here's a different site for gifts — baby shower gifts. At Baby Gift Baskets & Gifts you can find some great baby shower items all wrapped up and ready to go. Welcome the new arrival with unique baby gift baskets and personalized newborn gifts, like a decorative toy cradle filled with layette goodies, or a baby bassinet basket, or a Noah's Ark diaper cake. You can also find gifts for the expectant mom, gifts for twins, as well as gifts for the older baby or child.

 Recommended   **$** Price   Selection   Convenience   Service   Security

⭐ bestmonthlyclubs.com
Best Monthly Clubs

218-879-3414
service@bestmonthlyclubs.com

Unique

Why send one gift when you can send 12 — one every month. This feature is what's unique about gift-of-the-month clubs. And Best Monthly Clubs has chosen the best of the gift-of-the-month clubs. Clubs include Best Tea of the Month Club, Best Jelly of the Month Club, Best Cookie of the Month Club, and many others. When you buy, the company sends a card announcing the gift, and you can include a message of your choice. You can also send a free online "ecard" if you prefer. These clubs are a nice way to send your best on a monthly basis.

bostonblossomsflorist.com
Boston Blossoms Florist

888-417-7673
sepi@bostonblossomsflorist.com

Flowers

Located in the heart of Boston, Boston Blossoms Florist offers a well-organized site that enables you to choose the flower arrangement from categories organized by occasion. This company's flowers are high quality blooms that are sure to please the recipient. Boston Blossoms Florists delivers nationwide and internationally and takes care of its own by offering free delivery to all areas of Boston. It's open seven days a week, offering same-day delivery for orders placed before 3 p.m. Eastern Standard Time, and it backs its flowers with a 100 percent satisfaction guarantee.

brassbinnacle.com
The Brass Binnacle

800-737-2142
sales@brassbinnacle.com

Unique

The Brass Binnacle is a store with a nautical theme where you can buy gifts for the entire family. Its wide selection ensures that you can find a gift for anyone with the sea in his or her blood. The categories of gifts include barometers, ship's compasses, globes, maps, boat lanterns, pub signs, shelf sitters, telescopes, ship's telegraphs, sundials, and even harpoons! In the unlikely case that this site doesn't offer what you're looking for, you can contact the company and it can usually find the item for you. Now that's service! Your satisfaction is guaranteed, and each purchase includes a gift card.

bzzzybee.com
Bzzzy Bee Embroidery

901-493-9102
bzzzybee@bellsouth.net

Personalized • Unique

Bzzzy Bee Embroidery offers a unique gift idea — monogrammed embroidery. This company specializes in custom monogrammed wedding, shower, and baby gifts. If you don't want monograms, you can personalize your item any way you choose. The site offers baby bibs, guest towels, accent pillows, cocktail napkins, diaper covers, and personalized picture frames, and much more. The prices are surprisingly reasonable for such a personal customized item. You even have a choice of lettering styles. The store is easy to navigate but offers little in customer service information. It's best to call the company first and find out what its shipping and returns policies are.

customphotonotes.com
Customphotonotes.com

No phone number listed
ronichas@aol.com

Personalized

Customphotonotes.com is a company that creates unusual note cards, invitations, and announcements using your personal photographs. You can get your photo printed on metal, magnets, or even tile to create a special "I love you" or "thank you" gift. Let Customphotonotes.com incorporate your photos to help express your true feelings to your loved ones. Just e-mail a photo and fill out the online order form, and Custom Photo Notes takes care of the rest!

fleurspermail.com
Fleurs Per Mail

800-791-9557
E-mail form on site

Flowers • Unique

There are flowers and then there are *flowers*. You can buy the real kind that stay fresh for a few days, but for real-looking flowers that stay bright and fresh all year long, you need silk flowers. Fleurs Per Mail sells exquisite silk flowers for any occasion and for home decor. The site is easy to navigate and well-organized, and the site search tool lets you search by keyword, color, or flower. You can even sign up for a free newsletter. Why send roses that last only a few days when you can send silk roses — six silk open roses and six silk buds in a ceramic vase, or an arrangement featuring silk stargazer lilies and silk roses? This great gift idea will last and last.

★ Recommended $ Price   🛒 Selection   🎁 Convenience   ☺ Service   🔒 Security

flowerspotusa.com
FlowerSpotUSA.com

888-287-2475
florist@flowerspotusa.com

Flowers

Flower Spot USA is a family-owned business that has been sending flowers for 115 years nationwide. The family is involved in the daily operations to make sure that every order is handled properly and the flowers are delivered fresh and in a timely manner. You can shop by price, product, holiday, or occasion. The site also offers tips for plant and flower care. So if you're looking to cheer up a friend, wish one of your co-workers well, or put a smile on your loved one's face, fresh flowers from Flower Spot USA will make your message clear!

flowerswhisper.com
FlowersWhisper.com

800-231-7592
E-mail form on site

Flowers • Gifts

If you can't figure out what someone needs or wants, or if you want to avoid the problems associated with buying personal items like clothes for someone else, just log on to FlowersWhisper.com, and order from the variety of gift baskets, fruit baskets, plants, or flower arrangements. Shop by product or occasion, and be sure to check out the daily special and the "Guys' Guide to Giving Flowers." The site also offers free same-day delivery for online orders placed before 2 p.m. in the recipient's time zone.

fridgedoor.com
Fridgedoor.com

617-770-7913
chris@fridgedoor.com

Unique

If you or someone you know likes kitchen magnets, check out Fridgedoor.com. This company's goal is to be the single largest store for all things magnetic. You can shop by magnet brand and via subject categories, including 3-D, sounds, animals, celebrities, sports, classic TV shows, comic and super heroes, foods, drinks, flowers, humor, movies, music, and more. If you can't find the magnet you're looking for, you always have the option of creating a custom magnet. The site also offers magnetic supplies like magnetic paint, as well as materials to make your own magnets. If you're in a hurry, the site offers three-day, two-day, and next day shipping options.

giftmama.com
GiftMama.com

No phone number listed
support@giftmama.com

Unique

For those men who want to give a really special gift to their loved one, but have trouble finding something meaningful and thoughtful, the Gift Mama can help you. This site is geared toward men who want and need this type of help. GiftMama.com isn't an actual store, but the site does point you to the well-known online merchants who sell the products that Gift Mama offers to you. Suggestions are grouped by Flowers, Jewelry, Occasions, Lingerie, and Gift Baskets to name just a few categories. The site even offers relationship advice, ideas for fun dates, and tips on romance. The site also points you to a place you can order love letter templates, so you can write the perfect love letter to accompany your perfect gift.

★ gifts.com
CatalogCity.com

831-649-2489
E-mail form on site

Gifts

Malls have gift stores, but Gifts.com is a mall of gifts. This site offers every service necessary to help you find that right gift for any occasion. Gifts are organized by him, her, kids, birthdays, techies, and even teachers. The site's gift reminder service can help you keep track of those important gift-giving occasions, and you can also store a wish list of items you're interested in on the site. A sample of the categories of gifts available to you includes collectibles, gifts for the home, outdoor living, home improvement, and video and DVD. You can also use the search utility to find sale and catalog items.

 Recommended   Price   Selection   Convenience   Service   Security

gifts24.com
Gifts 24

800-443-8724
service@gifts24.com

Unique

If you're looking for a different kind of gift, something a little out of the ordinary, you can find it at this site! Gifts 24 carries items most people probably have never seen or even thought of, such as toasting glasses that are made to be placed on top of cakes. The site carries items such as light-up salt and pepper shakers, hand-crafted jewelry, rubber ducky sink stoppers, castle switchplates, and even more unique items than you can imagine. Items are grouped by general categories such as Themes, Special Occasions, Topical, and Holiday, and are grouped again into subsections and even sub-subsections to really help you narrow your search. Alternatively, you can use the extensive search tool to search by characteristics such as age group, occasion, personality type, and special interests. You will then be on your way to finding some incredibly unique gifts.

★ giftvalues.com
GiftValues.com

888-577-4518
info@giftvalues.com

Gifts • Personalized

GiftValues.com is a great site for "office type" gifts, such as really nice pens and pencils, appointment and address books, day planners and business card holders, bookmarks, key chains, and money holders. You can even personalize many of these items. You will be surprised at the quality products that are offered at these low prices. GiftValues.com is able to offer such low prices because it is part of a company that directly sources a wide variety of luxury goods. You can search for gifts for $5 or gifts for $10, or you can use the search box to find what you're looking for, or use the categories list on the home page.

grenvillestation.com
Grenville Station

888-510-7467
baskets@grenvillestation.com

Gifts

Grenville Station, based in Canada, offers an excellent selection of gift baskets and flowers for any occasion. You can find a housewarming basket containing cheesecake, coffee, crackers, and other treats. Or how about a monkey-themed birthday basket for your little one that contains banana-flavored cocoa, banana candy, a monkey mug, and a plush monkey? An American shopper can get a bargain because the prices of these gift baskets are in Canadian dollars and represent a significant savings for American customers. If you're a Canadian living in the U.S., you can send gifts to family, friends, and business associates in Canada, saving the hassles and cost involved with cross-border shipping, customs, duty, and Canadian taxes on the assessed value of the gift. You can customize any pre-assembled gift on this site for the recipient or this company will create a completely custom gift just for you.

★ hallmark.com
Hallmark

800-425-5617
E-mail form on site

Cards • Flowers • Gifts

Joyce C. Hall, founder of Hallmark Cards, Inc., wrote: "If a man goes into business with only the idea of making a lot of money, chances are he won't. But if he puts service and quality first, the money will take care of itself. Producing a first-class product that meets a real need is a much stronger motivation for success than getting rich." This philosophy is why Hallmark has always produced quality products and quality customer service. Many shoppers are already familiar with the brick-and-mortar Hallmark stores, but the online version maintains the same quality and selection. The site is well-organized and easy to use, and offers cards, ecards, flowers, and other gifts.

★ harmonydesigns.com
Harmony Designs
888-293-1109
info@harmonydesigns.com
Personalized • Unique

Harmony Designs uses hand-crafting along with printing technology to create beautiful, personalized keepsakes and gifts. Some of the different products that Harmony Designs offer include magnets, paperweights, bookmarks, and keychains. Customers can create their own products online, and in turn, create a unique and special gift for a loved one. The site also accommodates retailers who want customized items, and offers them a quantity discount. You can browse the site by subject, and you can personalize gifts using an image you submit or other items, a mint-condition postages stamp, for example.

kraftwraps.com
KraftWraps Incorporated
800-436-2021
info@kraftwraps.com
Wrap/Mail

After you buy a gift, the next step is to choose your wrapping, which can be just about as difficult as choosing the gift. KraftWraps Incorporated has an ample selection of wrapping products for all occasions, so you can be sure to find the perfect wrapping product along with matching accessories! The site offers gift bags, wrap, bows, gift cards, tissue paper, all in a variety of patterns and colors. Remember that the wrapping can be just as exciting to see as the gift itself.

kschweizer.com
K. Schweizer
800-595-1688
service@kschweizer.com
Personalized • Unique

Do you like the feel of a one-of-a-kind gift, exquisitely crafted of fine materials and beautifully designed? Who doesn't? K. Schweizer offers you a classy, elegant, unique place to unleash the writer within. Check out the sumptuous collection of leather journals, from the Milano Journal, to the ultimately touchable non-leather journals like the rustic Lama Li Journal from Nepal. Beyond journals and notebooks, this site also sells albums and scrapbooks, exquisite pens (check out their Venetian Glass Pens), stationery, and other writing accessories. You can even personalize some of the journals.

leanintree.com
Leanin' Tree
800-525-0656
info@leanintree.com
Cards

In 1949, Leanin' Tree greeting cards sold its first Christmas cards through the mail to western farmers and ranchers. This company has now grown to offer over 3,000 unique greeting cards today. Leanin' Tree's greeting cards feature lovely designs and are all original creations of independent artists. You're sure to find the cards you need in this company's extensive collection. You can search the site by occasion, subject, or both. The site also offers gifts such as journals, magnets, mugs, posters, and ornaments.

lifeflashes.com
LifeFlashes
650-349-9132
info@lifeflashes.com
Unique

LifeFlashes is not an online shopping site in the traditional sense, but it does offer a gift that says "one-of-a-kind." This company takes your photos, video clips, and mementos and turns them into a miniature motion picture or photo montage complete with titles, music, and special effects. The movie prices are $250 and $450 depending upon the length of the movie and the number of photos you use. It also offers custom pricing to fit your individual needs. The process takes about two weeks, but the result is a lasting memento sure to please and surprise everyone at that next special event.

★ lillianvernon.com
Lillian Vernon
800-901-9402
E-mail form on site
Gifts • Personalized

Lillian Vernon built its business on personalized gifts. This company not only offers personalized gifts that are gift-wrapped and ready to go, but it also offers categories of gifts such as collectibles, home and office, for him or her, and outdoor living. The site is easy to navigate and offers several different search options, allowing you to search by price, keyword, or by the Gift Finder — a utility that allows you to select several criteria at once to search on. If you can't decide on an item, Lillian Vernon also offers gift certificates. This site offers something for everybody, and for any budget.

 Recommended   Price   Selection   Convenience   Service   Security

littlesilverbox.com
Little Silver Box

No phone number listed
info@littlesilverbox.com

Personalized • Unique

Cookie Worth, founder of the Little Silver Box company, can make a lunchbox a conversation piece by adding a personal photo. The Little Silver Box company offers you the option of a round or rectangular tin lunchbox. You can use whatever photograph you want or even a collage, or use a special piece of artwork. You can even use one of the kids' art pieces from the fridge! Just send in your art via e-mail or regular mail. Prices range from $33 to $35 and the order takes three to four weeks (using a non-digital picture adds one or two weeks to delivery).

luxurycorner.com
LuxuryCorner.com

877-219-4437
info@luxurycorner.com

Gifts

Luxurycorner.com offers a wide selection of luxury gift items at up to 80 percent off retail. You can find such brand-name gifts as Mont Blanc pens, LLADRO porcelain, Waterford and Swarovski crystal, Montblanc and Cartier watches, and brand-name women's perfumes and men's colognes. You can have your gift wrapped for an additional $2.99, and UPS ground delivery on all orders is free (no minimum required). Be sure to check out the clearance section for even greater savings.

maisonconnoisseur.com
Maison Connoisseur

888-888-2612
maisonc@sbcglobal.net

Gifts • Unique

Maison Connoisseur sells unique luxury gift items for discriminating tastes. This online retailer offers products you may not find easily on the Web or at your local mall. The site includes antique reproductions of old-fashioned record players, antique telephones, music boxes, and other items. You can also find hand-carved museum-quality wooden rocking horses. Its gourmet gift baskets from Europe are top notch and unique, such as the chocolate ganache mice or chocolate cigars. High-tech gifts include a Digital Vista Frame or an Atomic Projection Alarm Clock. The gifts are a bit pricey, but they are definitely not run-of-the-mill.

medievalmagic.com
Spiral Virtual Shop
444-01634-401274
sales@medievalmagic.com

Unique

If you, a family member, or a friend are interested in Celtic and medieval design, then check out medievalmagic.com for some fun items. Spiral Virtual Shop designs, manufactures, and distributes all of its own collection of unique products. It offers high-quality pewter jewelry including pendants, brooches, earrings, bracelets, pentacles, and torcs. You can also find reproductions of weapons including samurai swords, chain mail, daggers, shields, and even a full armor suit! This company, based in England, ships to the U.S. and Canada.

mgcpuzzles.com
MGC's Puzzles
888-604-7654
E-mail form on site

Personalized • Unique

The MGC's Puzzles site is great for those of us who love jigsaw puzzles, or who need to buy a gift for a jigsaw puzzle lover, or who are looking for a very unique and extra special gift for someone who has everything. MGC's Puzzles handcrafts one-of-a-kind wooden jigsaw puzzles using a personal photograph or even a fine art print of your choice, with pieces ranging from 4 to more than 6,200. The ideas and reasons (even wedding proposals) for a custom-made puzzle are virtually endless. But be warned, the more pieces you choose, the higher the price of the puzzle. And they get pretty high! Nonetheless, these puzzles are extraordinary.

★ momastore.org
Museum of Modern Art
800-447-6662
orderservices@moma.org

Unique

The Museum of Modern Art online store offers new and unique gift ideas that are very bright and, of course, modern, and I might add, somewhat expensive. You can find items like curved glass tumblers for the kitchen, votive candles with colorful and interchangeable shades, and the "thin origami oblong scarf." You can search the site by category or designer. Check out MoMA's products for yourself, and you will see why they will be so appreciated.

 Recommended   Price   Selection  Convenience   Service 🔒 Security

nationwideflorist.com
Nationwide Florist

888-321-7673
E-mail form on site

Flowers • Gifts

Nationwide Florist is the leading provider of thoughtful gifts and beautiful flower arrangements, who strives to help its customers connect with the important people in their lives. Nationwide Florist offers teddy bears and balloons, a collection from Thomas Kinkade, and Lenox giftware. Some of the other gifts that are offered include gourmet baskets, chocolate-dipped strawberries, handcrafted cheesecakes, and lobster dinners that arrive as cool on your doorstep as the day they leave New England.

netique.com
Netique

703-689-3703
webmaster@netique.com

Gifts • Personalized

"Why send ordinary flowers, gift baskets, or chocolate gifts when you could send an extraordinary gift?" That's Netique's motto. You can shop by category of gifts or by price. Some of the categories include bridesmaids and groomsmen gifts, lawyer gifts, hearts and angels, gift for physicians, art glass gifts, compacts, and many more categories. You can also do a keyword search. Don't forget to read the articles with gift-giving suggestions — the "Corporate Gift-Giving Guide" and the rules of "International Gift-Giving Protocol."

okanagantouchwood.com
Okanagan Touch Wood

250-496-5922
mail@okanagantouchwood.com

Unique

If you've ever wanted a flower that was not only unique, but that would last forever, then check out Okanagan Touch Wood. This family-operated business based in Okanagan Valley, British Columbia, Canada, has been selling wooden flowers for over 22 years. These unique wooden gifts are completely handcrafted and original and make for charming decor as well as great housewarming gifts. You can also find wooden ladybug stools, door stops that have flowers "growing" from them, fridge magnets, even wooden flower-shaped wall clocks and welcome signs on the site. Prices are reasonable and the site is simple to navigate.

onceuponaname.com
Once Upon A Name

800-597-6499
linda@onceuponaname.com

Personalized • Unique

Once Upon A Name establishes the meaning of your loved one's first name, and then lists the personality traits, emotional spectrum, relationships, career, money, and life opportunities associated with that name. It then prints all the information out in calligraphy on a special lithograph background of your choosing. These keepsakes are printed in either 8.5 × 11 or 8 × 10 inches, which you can then frame and give away. The site also offers a large selection of mother and baby gifts, nursery decor, christening gowns, gifts for couples, baby jewelry, and so much more. If you're having trouble finding a really special gift, you'll be able to find it at this site.

peaceloveandme.com
Peace Love and Me

No phone number listed
lynn@peaceloveandme.com

Unique

Turn back time to those days of peace and love, Woodstock and tie-dyes. Peace Love and Me lets you turn back the clock with wildlife and sealife tie-dyes, tie-dyes for kids, incense and candles, fimo clay, and hemp jewelry. This company carries peace signs, peace stickers and bumper stickers, aromatherapy candles, door beads, and so much more to help bring back the hippie in you. You can even find some cool retro-Hawaiian wall clocks. The site also offers specials, gift certificates, and even some links to "peaceful" information.

pensxpress.com
PensXpress

732-817-0077
info@pensxpress.com

Gifts • Personalized

Do you ever notice that when you need a pen to write with, you can't ever seem to find one? The solution is to have many pens in many places so one is always available. To help you in this endeavor, PensXpress offers hundreds and hundreds of pens with a variety of styles and colors to choose from, including gripper, retractable, jumbo, and twist pens, to name a few. This site is also handy for those corporations and small businesses — ordering personalized pens with your company name can be a great gift for clients and customers that doubles as great advertisement.

 Recommended   Price   Selection   Convenience   Service 🔒 Security

primelinx.com
Prime Linx

888-847-9212
info@primelinx.com

Unique

Prime Linx's URL plates are a perfect gift for a client, associate, or friend. Your URL, in raised, chrome-plated letters, can be installed on your car in minutes using an automotive-grade adhesive. (If you would rather use a magnet to adhere the URL to the car, you also have that option.) URL plates can feature an e-mail address, domain name, telephone number, or anything you would like to be seen by the hundreds of motorists you pass on a daily basis.

puzzlering.com
Puzzle Ring Store

888-278-9953
E-mail form on site

Unique

If you've never seen or heard of a puzzle ring, then puzzlering.com can educate you on it. A puzzle ring consists of several interlocking bands made from 14K gold and silver. This company can also place precious stones in the rings. These unique rings make great gifts, and some people even use them for wedding rings. Check out the unique Russian wedding ring or Rolling Ring fashioned in 14K gold. The site doesn't have a search feature, but is organized by category, and offers the solution to putting your ring back together if you take it apart. A puzzle ring is sure to be a gift that will please your loved one!

pwflowers.com
PW Flowers

888-300-2893
websupport@primewines.com

Flowers • Gifts

PW Flowers' staff of experienced designers can put together an arrangement for you that can convey your feelings, whether the flowers are a gift for a loved one, a gift for a coworker, or for a formal event. You can search the site by category, price, or keyword search. This company ships through FTD, and guarantees all FTD orders. This company also offers same day delivery, and an international flower delivery service is also available. You can also order mylar balloons, teddy bears, and even "cheap" roses for delivery, although, oddly, these links are embedded in the tiny print at the bottom of the home page. Nonetheless, the site offers a nice selection.

redenvelope.com
RedEnvelope

877-733-3683
E-mail form on site

Flowers • Gifts • Personalized • Unique

RedEnvelope started in 1999 for the sole purpose of making gift giving simple and fun. No matter what the occasion or circumstance, the creative assortment of gifts that is offered at this site makes shopping for gifts a wonderful experience. Many of the gifts have been made exclusively for this site, and include cigars (like Cuban Honeys), assorted gift baskets (such as with a spa theme), gourmet foods (how about "death-by-chocolate" cookies?), jewelry (like a pearl hugs-and-kisses bracelet), and much more. You can shop by occasion (for example, selecting Anniversary brings up all gifts associated with that year's traditional and modern gift) or by recipient. If you're in a hurry you can use the company's Express Gift service and choose a gift for someone that will arrive the next day. The site offers customer service 24 hours a day, 7 days a week, and a personal shopper to help you find a gift from 6 a.m.–6 p.m., 7 days a week.

shop.nationalgeographic.com
National Geographic Store

800-437-5521
E-mail form on site

Unique

You've watched the National Geographic TV documentaries, and now you can buy from the National Geographic store. This store offers videos, books and clothing, maps, posters, prints, educational toys, and scientific items that make unique and useful gifts. For example, how about the weather forecast beacon that changes colors depending on what the weather will be that day (using standard weather map colors), and that pulses when rain is on the way? What a great gift for a weather buff! You can shop by product categories or by theme, including Animals and Nature, Culture and History, Geography, Photos, Science and Weather, and Travel and Outdoors. The World Music selections, which offer music from around the world, also make a nice gift for those musically inclined.

shoppbs.org
Shop PBS

No phone number listed
E-mail form on site

Unique

If you would like to share a PBS program with someone, you can buy it from the PBS store. The PBS store carries many of its programs in a variety of formats — books, DVDs, music, and VHS — in the area of arts, business and finance, history, how-to, science, sports, and travel. The site even has a special section for kids' gifts. You can have your order gift-wrapped and you can also order online gift certificates. Be sure to take a peek at the outlet shop for great deals on closeout items.

simply-sublime.com
Simply Sublime

507-256-4488
dgmunson@simply-sublime.com

Personalized

Simply Sublime sells classy items to personalize, the kind not normally found in personalized products on the Web. This store offers a very nice selection of full-colored designs on cake pans, clocks, cutting boards, serving trays, bar coasters, welcome mats, tavern signs, and many more items. These products are classy and good quality. Simply Sublime prints and personalizes every item in its own shop. You can add names, quotes, and even personal messages. These items make great gifts for bridal parties, and hard-to-buy-for people.

store.thetech.org
The Tech Museum of Innovation

408-795-6276
techstore@thetech.org

Unique

If you're looking for unusual and fascinating technology gifts that say, "Only in Silicon Valley!" then the Tech Museum is your place to shop for gifts — all of them surprisingly affordable for high-tech products. You can choose from items such as a Fantazein Moving LED clock where messages and time float in mid-air, or a clock where you read the time using binary code in blue lights, or a gear clock made entirely out of gears. The site's home and office gifts include the Fisher Space Pen, a Talking Calendar Clock, and a rug for your mouse. If you can't decide on one of the many great gift ideas, gift certificates are available for purchase online.

stuffwithnames.com
StuffWithNames.com

866-864-1107
E-mail form on site

Personalized

The products at stuffwithnames.com may not be unique, but you can have a name printed on every single one. These products make great gifts for kids, and also for baby showers and weddings. This company offers a decent collection of these inexpensive items, in the categories of military, sports, kids' toy trucks and cars, luggage tags, note boxes, zipper pulls, mugs, key chains, and magnets. If you don't find what you're looking for, contact the company and it will try to find it for you.

tastygram.com
TastyGram

866-288-2789
E-mail form on site

Gifts

You can send a gift with taste, or you can send a gift that tastes good. If you're looking for the latter, then consider the TastyGram. This company ships a wide variety of fresh foods directly from the people who make them, and these foods arrive as a "complete gift" in an attractive package, with a personalized card and a tin of mints. Gifts range from fresh meats and seafoods to gourmet desserts and a lot more. The company guarantees its products to be fresh, and the site offers an e-mail list for you to join so you can receive special offers and discounts.

theartifact.com
Artifact.com

888-965-0001
custsvc@theartifact.com

Unique

You've seen exquisite art and antiquities in museums, and now you can own them — not the real thing, of course, but excellent replicas. TheArtifact offers reproductions of ancient Greek and Roman art, Pre-Columbian and American art, ancient Egyptian artifacts, and even reproductions of dinosaur fossils. You can search its product offering by category or by product type, such as frescos, jewelry, icons, tapestries, vases, and more. These "artifacts" have a remarkable likeness to the original, and aren't as expensive as you might imagine, and in fact, are very reasonable. Now wouldn't that triceratops skull look smashing in your home office?

 Recommended   Price   Selection   Convenience   Service   Security

theflowerplace.com
The Flower Place

866-355-0023
customerservice@theflowerplace.com

Flowers • Gifts

The Flower Place has been in service since 1987 and is a premier Teleflora florist, which means that they deliver only the finest products created by the best designers. From flowers, plants, fruit and gourmet baskets, to balloons, teddy bears, Thomas Kinkade collectibles, and Teleflora Keepsakes, you can expect your flower arrangement or gift basket to be of the highest quality and delivered in a timely manner. For those of us who can never seem to remember those important dates, The Flower Place provides a reminder floral/gift service. You can also find information on flower types and keeping your flowers fresher longer.

uccellino.com
Uccellino, Inc.

847-433-9069
uccellinoinc@yahoo.com

Unique

Combining art with gift giving, Uccellino items are the personal creations of Susan LeVine. These beautiful and unusual gifts are "little inspirations that are meant to lift the spirits and open the heart" of your recipient. Each item is handcrafted by the artist and may come in its own decoratively designed mailer. For example, "Living All Possibilities" is a porcelain box with affirmation rings that can be hung from a window, used as napkin rings, or kept nestled in the box to affirm a positive thought. The boxes themselves can be used to store jewelry, mementos, or other personal items. These very unique gifts are a beautiful way to express one's feelings.

vanmorevanities.com
Vanmore Vanities

860-796-5422
vanities@vanmore.com

Gifts

Started by a soldier who wanted a way for families to show their love for their soldiers overseas, Vanmore Vanities will send a Vanigram to those serving our country — or as a loving gift for any occasion. A Vanigram consists of selected phrases from Vanmore or your own personalized saying. Your greeting is placed on a laminated gift card sent with a cute stuffed bear or other animal. The gifts are inexpensive and can be shipped all over the world.

windandweather.com
Wind & Weather

800-922-9463
customerservice@windandweather.com

Unique

How's this for a unique gift — beautiful weather instruments for the home and garden? Wind & Weather offers items for the weather hobbyist to the professional meteorologist. The Long-Range Weather Station has a sleek, Euro-style case, and the clock radio tunes into the Weather Channel for up-to-date weather information. Or for the more traditional weather watcher, check out the Tendency Barometer, patented in 1818. It displays how air pressure and temperature interact to affect weather trends. Wind & Weather also carries non-weather-related gifts for home, yard, and garden. If you sign up on the site's e-mail list, you'll be notified of sales and closeouts, too.

winecountrygiftbaskets.com
Wine Country Gift Baskets

800-324-2793
customerservice@winecountrygiftbaskets.com

Gift • Unique

Wine Country Gift Baskets has an incredible selection of baskets ranging from gourmet chocolates and foods to bath and body products to wines, and the presentation is beautiful! The Rise & Shine gift basket includes coffee, tea, or hot chocolate, biscotti or cookies, all arranged with a coffee scoop, two large mugs, and a matching napkin on a sturdy serving tray. Wine Country Gift Baskets also has gift baskets with names like "A Day Off" (which everyone deserves), "Bubbly Romance," "Ghirardelli Tower," and so many others that you just have to see for yourself.

yearbox.com
Year Box

800-491-9856
info@yearbox.com

Personalized

For the price of a regular calendar, you can have a personal 12-month calendar sent as a gift to friends and family. If you have some great shots of the kids, send a 12-month calendar with their pictures to the grandparents. You can choose either a desk or wall-size style in several different designs. Prices vary depending on quantity, but you can add captions for free, and if you upload pictures from your computer you can save $12 on the scanning fee. Calendars take about a week to get.

 Recommended   Price   Selection   Convenience   Service   Security

yougota.com
You Got A Care Package!
866-227-3722
customercare@yougota.com
Unique

The gift quandary — you can send a card or gift basket, but that's so ho-hum. You could send a funny book or a themed novelty item. But why not send a whole box full of fun and yummy items to get your point across? This concept is what You Got A Care Package is all about. For example, "got" a friend who's going through a break-up? No problem! Send her some fun "good riddance" gifts with "good cry" gifts like chocolate and ice cream. Know someone who's just had a nasty bike accident? Send a movie to celebrate the fact that he or she is going to be immobile for a while. You get the idea. Now get to this site!

A Shopping Excursion —
Finding That Perfect Gift

Here's the problem. You need to find a gift but either you don't have the time or you dread sorting through the hundreds and hundreds of stores on the Web. Even when you find a gift, though your intentions are good, the results sometimes aren't.

There is a solution.

Turn to a set of time-saving sites called *gift-finders*. Through the beauty of the Internet, you can enter pertinent information about a person and these gift-finder sites can recommend the perfect gift. These online retailers will generate a list of suggested gifts based on the criteria you select, such as gender, age, cost, product category, occasion, personality, interests, or profession.

For example, the Perfect Present Picker (presentpicker.com) can help you choose a gift two ways. First it lists the top 12 suggested gifts in the following categories — popular, choice, expensive, inexpensive, and outrageous. Second, you can use its sophisticated search engine to find the perfect gift based on a person's interest, or personality, and occasion. Click the search button and a gift will be suggested to you.

The Joy of Ireland (sparkk.com/yahoostore/giftfinder.html) uses a similar technology with a twist. Answer three questions — the age of the person, gender, and the amount of money you want to pay, and then it suggests a gift. But this

company adds a twist. The selections are fine-tuned based on your feedback. You can tell the company what you think of its choices by clicking a Feedback button.

At the Museum Shop (artinstituteshop.org/gift.asp), you can search for an elegant gift by price range, gender, or category. Spurs Direct (ssl.spurs.co.uk/thfcstore/gift_select.asp) in merry ol' England has a gift search engine where you can search its wide selection of merchandise by age (toddler to mature adult), gender, type of gift, and price. At Cutco (cutco.com/jsp/catalog/giftSelector.jsp) you can search for fine cutlery by occasion, type of recipient, and that person's cooking style.

Though not a search engine like the other sites, at Gifts24 (gifts24.com/g/home.html), you can browse gifts by occasion, interest, personality, occupation, lifestyle, sex, and age. For home and office gifts, Chiasso (chiasso.com/finder/giftfinder.asp) has organized its gifts by dollar amount ($50–$100), and by gifts for him and her.

Finally, if you plan on giving a piece of software as a gift — for kids or adults — and have a hard time figuring out what is appropriate, then check out Broderbund's software recommendation engine (broderbund.com). You can search by age, 1 to adult, or by grade, pre-kindergarten to college.

Chapter 12

Food: Dining in Cyberspace

· ·

"*F*ood, glorious food!" The lyrics of the show tune said it best. Food is more than simple nutrition. We assign great importance to what we eat and where we eat it. People love to get together over food, whether it's a quick cup of coffee and a snack or a long, lingering meal. Don't you love to go out to dinner?

Shopping for food on the Internet is fun! The variety of food sites is astounding. Many regional grocery chains have established online presences and offer home delivery. Popular restaurants have followed suit. There's a good chance that your favorite hoagies from Philadelphia can be at your doorstep tomorrow.

The sites shown in this chapter are some of the best of the thousands of Web sites that offer food online. As time passes, even more sites will offer food and food-related services. You'll find sites that offer groceries, ethnic foods, snacks, candy, and gourmet foods.

If you're planning an important dinner or event, contact a site before you order and ask about product availability and delivery times. Finding out tonight that your turkey won't arrive until next Wednesday is no help when you have six hungry guests waiting for dinner.

Key Word Index

Candy and Chocolate

The sites with the Candy and Chocolate keyword carry everything from bulk candy to handmade chocolate. Waist watchers beware!

Dessert

The meal after the entrée is covered by sites with the Dessert keyword. Standards like cakes and cheesecakes to custom fortune cookies are offered by the bulk of these stores.

Diet

If you've had a little too much of the stuff indicated by the preceding keywords, and are now trying to trim down, check out the Diet sites for help.

Ethnic

Sites with the Ethnic keyword offer food from the four corners of the globe.

Fish

The Fish sites sell anything that lives in water and can be eaten. Lobster, clams, seafood, and fish — alive, fresh, or frozen — these sites have it all.

Gourmet

Sumptuous repasts and tempting treats abound in the Gourmet sites. Look for everything from hand-trimmed, aged beef to tapenade to melt-in-your-mouth chocolate.

Groceries

A trip to an online grocery store is a lot like shopping at your corner market. Check out the sites with the Grocery keyword to see why.

Healthy Food

Most people think healthy food has to taste awful. The stores in with the Healthy Food keyword disprove that myth.

Meat and Poultry

The sites with the Meat and Poultry keyword offer meat, game, and fowl for your consumption.

Prepared Food

Who has time to cook every night? The Prepared Food sites offer prepared food that ranges from a complete meal service to one or two items.

Snacks

Stores designated with the Snacks keyword deal with satisfying the munchies. Some of these stores even offer healthy snacking alternatives.

800cheesecake.com
800Cheesecake.com

800-243-3732
steve@800cheesecake.com

Dessert

Rich, creamy, and oh-so-yummy, cheesecake is the perfect finish to any meal. 800Cheesecake.com offers some of the best cheesecake on the Internet. Order a plain cheesecake or splurge with white chocolate, super fudge chunk, or raspberry swirl. A heart-shaped cheesecake sends a great romantic message; add your own words on the top for real heart appeal. Cheesecakes are available in three and four pound sizes and are big enough to feed a small crowd. A sampler of regular and mini-sized pieces is also available.

artikochef.com
Artiko

888-278-4567
No e-mail address on site

Prepared Food

Artiko creates prepared foods and ships them to your door. Unlike some other delivery services, Artiko does not insist that you buy complete meals. In fact, Artiko's online catalog resembles the a la carte menu of a fine restaurant, with mix-and-match items for starters, entrees, and desserts. Some of the foods can be reheated and served, and some require a bit more preparation. You are free to order the foods and quantities you choose. The Artiko program is entirely customizable to meet your needs. Learn more about this interesting delivery service and read the online "chill out" magazine at the site.

a-u-l.com
AULSuperStore.com

800-791-2114
customerservice@a-u-l.com

Candy and Chocolate • Dessert • Fish • Groceries • Meat and Poultry

AULSuperStore.com is an online grocery store that offers delivery to all fifty states and some military addresses. Shop for canned goods and non-perishables at this site. Before you select an item, you'll need to tell AUL where you'll be shipping the order because the delivery address determines what products are available. Some items are available in individual units and case lots; the more you buy the more you save. If you have any questions, live help is available at the site during business hours. Recommend a friend, and get 10 percent off your next order.

 Recommended Price Selection Convenience Service Security

★ auntrubyspeanuts.com
Aunt Ruby's Peanuts
800-843-0105
info@auntrubyspeanuts.com
Snacks

Aunt Ruby is waiting to delight you with her tasty peanuts. She's been pleasing peanut lovers just like you for over fifty years. Actually, A&B Milling Company of North Carolina produces the peanuts here. "Aunt Ruby" is the owner's mother. The company purchases only the best quality Virginia-style peanuts that are known for lower fat content, large meaty size, and excellent flavor and texture. Shop here for roasted redskins, country-style peanuts, honey-roasted peanuts, chocolate peanut clusters, and much more. Samplers and gift baskets are also available.

auntviola.com
Aunt Viola's
No phone number listed
auntviola@cableone.net
Diet

Diets don't need to be all-or-nothing propositions. Sometimes, cutting a few calories or carbohydrates out of your diet can help you drop a few pounds. Try Aunt Viola's Best Doggone Caesar Salad Dressing if you're trying to cut carbs from your diet, or simply want to improve the taste of your next salad. In either case, you're bound to add your testimonial to the growing list. Nutritional information for the delicious dressing is shown at the site. You'll need to send an e-mail to place your order.

avenison.com
Adirondack Venison Company
518-643-0113
info@adirondackvenison.com
Healthy Food • Meat and Poultry

Venison is not one of those things that you commonly have for dinner. So when you eat venison, you might as well have the best. The venison from Adirondack Venison Company is unique. It doesn't have the strong, gamey flavor commonly associated with deer, and it's tender and juicy. Several cuts of venison are available including loin chops, medallions, burgers, stew and braising meat, tenderloins, and more. The Venison Cookbook is an excellent option for someone who's never cooked venison before. If you've never eaten venison, why not try it today?

aviglatt.com
Avi Glatt Kosher

866-281-4528
orders@aviglatt.com

Ethnic • Fish • Groceries • Meat and Poultry

The Avi Glatt Kosher grocery site carries kosher meats, poultry, and dairy items. It also carries a full line of deli items. It's best to be an informed shopper before you settle down to buy; there are no explanations or descriptions to help you differentiate between one product and another. If you need assistance, you'll need to call Avi Glatt Kosher or send an e-mail message. Wondering about what makes foods kosher? A clear, easy-to-follow explanation is provided at the site.

★ barryfarm.com
Barry Farm

419-228-4640
info@barryfarm.com

Groceries • Healthy Food

Barry Farm is a small, family-run farm in Ohio. From June to October, they set up shop at local farmer's markets in nearby Lima and Sidney. Unfortunately most of us can't make it to the markets. Fortunately, most of us can make it to their site. Shop here for home-grown dried beans and legumes, brans, grits and meals, and assorted other grocery products. The Baking section features healthy thickeners and sweeteners and each of the items in Condiments is made without preservatives. Let's hope the Barrys continue to farm forever.

★ bestbeef.com
Steak Central

888-978-3257
sfraum@bestbeef.com

Meat and Poultry

And you thought you knew meat? Steve Fraum, the host of Steak Central, will teach you enough to pass a meat cutter's final exam at this site. You'll learn about the different cuts of meat, their backgrounds, and what to look for when you buy. You'll also learn how to prepare, cook, and store meat properly. When you've digested all that, it's off to the Products page, where you can see exactly what's for sale. The Certified Angus Beef steaks are the best bet, but plenty of veal, lamb, and pork is also available.

bonappetit-int.com
Bon Appetit International Gourmet Food Service
800-473-3513
cs@bonappetit-int.com
Meat and Poultry • Prepared Food

Bon Appetit International Gourmet Food Service brings the best quality gourmet foods from all over the world to your door. This company features a wide variety of meat, poultry, and seafood. Its steaks are hand-trimmed, hearty portions of perfectly aged beef. It also offers veal and pork. But look out — the Chicago Baby Back Ribs carry a warning that they are addictive. Check out the poultry page and the Game Time Wings (Hot). The Steak and Lobster package is a great gift for relatives, friends, clients, or yourself. Place your order and bon appetit!

★ bulkcandystore.com
Bulk Candy Store
561-615-8646
info@bulkcandystore.com
Candy and Chocolate

The problem with most bulk stores is that you have to purchase huge quantities to get a great deal. Not at Bulk Candy Store. This company takes the opposite view with its small purchase policy. Using a dim sum-like approach to candy, you can fill your shopping cart with, say, a one pound package of Bullseyes chocolate caramels, a single package of Jordan almonds, and a big lollipop. The bigger the order, the more you save. The low prices at Bulk Candy Store encourage repeat business. Any questions? The owners of this humble candy store will be happy to help.

bulkfoods.com
BulkFoods.com
419-324-0032
vip@bulkfoods.com
Candy and Chocolate • Groceries • Snacks

This massive snack warehouse, BulkFoods.com, is bound to keep you busy for a while. The online catalog contains over 2,100 items with full descriptions, pictures, and current prices in easy-to-navigate format. In fact, the site's biggest failing is that you'll probably run out of steam before you work your way from one end of the catalog to the other. There are no minimum order requirements and a single packing charge will be applied on orders of any size. International shipping is available with some restrictions. Details are available at the site.

cafecubano.com
Café Cubano

305-251-4032
sales@cafecubano.com

Ethnic • Snacks

You can almost taste the strong, sweet Cuban coffee when you log into the Café Cubano site. (The Cuban music playing in the background doesn't hurt the effect.) This Miami-based site brings you not only the coffee of Cuba, but also an assortment of its food. Try a flan mix, some guava shells, or some membrillo. Accessories are here, too; you can even get a Cuban sandwich maker. If the coffee is what drew you to the site, check out the wide range of espresso coffees and variety of Cuban brands available. Add a Cuban Jazz CD, and look forward to the day your order arrives.

cakesacrossamerica.com
Cakes Across America

800-422-5387
cakes@cakesacrossamerica.com

Dessert

The cakes from Cakes Across America are baked by master bakers in your local area and then delivered directly to the recipient. You can customize your cake with a personal message, special frosting, or whatever you would like. Traditional chocolate or golden yellow cakes are offered, along with black forest, German chocolate, strawberry shortcake-style cakes and, of course, creamy cheesecakes. Add balloons, soft drinks, or tableware if you want. Cakes Across America is always looking for professional bakers to join its network. If you're interested, contact information is available at the site.

cakes-direct.co.uk
Cakes Direct

(+44) 01726 76805
contactus@cakes-direct.co.uk

Dessert

Want to end your meal with a traditional British dessert? Based in Cornwall, England, Cakes Direct will be happy to oblige. Both Treacle Tarts and Saffron Cakes from this site are great choices. A Slab Cake in either date and walnut or marble flavor is slightly lighter and less expensive. Throw caution to the winds with a Passion Cake or Chocolate Fudge Cake. Prices here are in British pounds. The site ships cakes internationally, so worldwide customers can take advantage of these toothsome delights. Other items on the site, such as a complete English Cream Tea, only ship to U.K. addresses.

 Recommended   Price   Selection   Convenience   Service   🔒 Security

candysapples.com
Candy's Apples

888-527-7531
12apples@candysapples.com

Candy and Chocolate

How about these apples? A candy-dipped apple is one of life's simple pleasures and, fortunately, is easily affordable. The pictures of the apples at Candy's Apples look so delicious that choosing which one you want may be difficult. Traditionalists may go for a caramel-dipped apple called the Plain Jane. The choices get more exotic from there with nut coating, candy, and chocolate coating, and various combinations of all three. Every month a special Apple of the Month is available only for that particular time. Each apple feeds about 4 to 6 people and weighs in at just over two pounds.

carbolitedirect.com
Carbolite Foods

800-524-4473
consumer@carbolitefoods.com

Candy and Chocolate • Diet

Carbolite offers chocolate bars, candy, snacks, chips, crackers, desserts, breads, and shake mixes. These products are lower in carbohydrates than similar products sold in the grocery store. You can order items individually or in cases. The case price is really low. Many of the bars and desserts are perishable, so if you live in a warm climate or you're buying during the summer months, consider ordering an insulated box with an ice pack for a few extra dollars. This box adds well-needed insulation and ensures your order won't become a puddle of melted goo.

caribcon.com
Caribbean Connoisseur

No phone number listed
custserv@caribcon.com

Dessert • Ethnic

Want to go to Jamaica but can't afford it this year? (Welcome to the club.) Oh well, a visit to Caribbean Connoisseur is almost as good as the real thing. Order some genuine Blue Mountain Coffee and rum cake to help set the mood. Then check out the seasonings and sauces — hey, mon, they're the same ones they use on the island. The site has a decent non-food section, with perfume and Jamaican cigars. If all this is a little much for you, or you're new to online shopping, Caribbean Connoisseur has a great Help section to make your purchases painless.

⭐ chipofthemonth.com
Anchor O'Reilly's Chip of the Month Club

800-313-2332
therese@chipofthemonth.org

Healthy Food • Snacks

Everyone loves potato chips! Why not give yourself a munchfest with Anchor O'Reilly's Chip of the Month Club? (It makes a great gift, too.) Every shipment contains six bags of unique flavors selected from local and regional chip makers located in North America. Order a one-, three-, or twelve-month subscription, or design the subscription to meet your needs. Expect to pay around twenty dollars a month or so for your six bags of fun. Gift packages are also available from this site and are sent with a customized card.

claxtonfruitcake.com
Claxton Fruit Cake

800-841-4211
claxton@g-net.net

Candy and Chocolate • Dessert

Get your fruitcake from the place that set the fruitcake industry standard, the Claxton Bakery in Claxton, Georgia. The fruitcakes at its Web site are a whopping 72 percent fruit and nuts. Choose between a dark fruitcake, to which molasses and raisins have been added, or the more traditional light model. You'll need to refrigerate your fruitcake after it arrives. Refrigerated fruitcakes last about four months or can be frozen for longer storage. Want to arrange a fundraiser for your organization or school? Why not sell fruitcakes? Details about how Claxton can help are available at the site.

coopgrocer.com
Co-op Grocer

No phone number listed
suggestions@coopgrocers.com

Groceries

Since 1985, Co-Op Grocer's policy of "Buy Low, Sell Low" has resulted in everyday savings of 20 to 30 percent to their customers. Do some comparison shopping before you settle down to place an order here, because some items aren't discounted. However, most of the batteries, canned goods, heath and beauty aids, cleaning supplies, drinks, and miscellaneous items found here sell for lower prices than you'll find at your local grocery or discount store. Orders are shipped by UPS ground within one to two business days after they're placed. There's a minimum $5 shipping fee on all orders.

 Recommended   Price   Selection   Convenience   Service   Security

daskalides.com
Daskalides

800-615-7177
contact@daskalides.com

Candy and Chocolate

Back in 1931, the Daskalides family opened its first confectioner's shop in Ghent, Belgium. The chocolate candies, called "pralines," were an instant success and became popular throughout Europe. The candy sent from this site is made in the United States, but follows the same strict rules set by the original Daskalides store. You can order a variety of boxed chocolates, including low-sugar and low-carb chocolate. Chocolate for home bakers, cookies, spreads, and jams round out the collection.

★ deandeluca.com
Dean & Deluca

877-852-2888
atyourservice@deandeluca.com

Candy and Chocolate • Dessert • Fish • Gourmet • Meat and Poultry • Snacks

Dean & Deluca started out as a tiny deli in New York city but grew into a popular gourmet empire. Shop Dean & Deluca's online establishment for everything from imported truffles to domestic salami. The same rule that applies to your regular grocery store excursions applies here — eat first or you'll find yourself sorely tempted by the vast array of delicious foods. Prices range from astronomical on some items to slightly more than what you would pay in your local supermarket.

★ diamondorganic.com
Diamond Organics

888-674-2642
info@diamondorganics.com

Groceries • Healthy Food

Diamond Organics works directly with organic farmers along California's central coast to bring you some of the freshest produce you can imagine. Take a few moments to read the descriptions of the fruits and vegetables; they often read like a mini-nature lesson and teach you things you didn't know. The beef from this company is all grass-fed, and the fish is line-caught. The Diamond Organics Dinner Club is a nifty idea. Each month, you'll receive recipes and ingredients to prepare a delicious organic meal for four adults. It's up to you to reveal the source of the great dinner.

diettogo.com
Diet-to-Go

866-243-3438
service@diettogo.com

Diet • Prepared Food

Sign up for Diet-to-Go and get your very own personal chef and custom weight-loss program. After you sign up for the program at the site, you select your meals from a menu. Several different plans are available, including low carb and vegetarian. In a few days, your food arrives. The meals are already prepared and contain the correct portion sizes so you don't need to make any decisions or choices when it's time to eat. Because you chose them, the meals contain the foods you want. You'll lose weight and look great.

dinnerdirect.com
DinnerDirect

888-999-3196
No e-mail address on site

Gourmet • Prepared Food

Can you boil water? If you answered yes, you can cook a dinner from DinnerDirect. The service prepares food in boilable pouches that can be ready in a few minutes. DinnerDirect offers two types of family-style heat and eat gourmet pouches: Fast Pouch Entrees, which contain gourmet main dishes, and Classic Entrees, which hold culinary-classic main courses with Madeira sauce. Consider ordering a few entrees for yourself. More importantly, send the pouches as a gift. Your older family members will appreciate having the easy-to-prepare entrees in their freezers.

enstrom.com
Enstrom

800-367-8766
E-mail form on site

Candy and Chocolate

Almonds, butter, sugar, and chocolate — four simple ingredients that combine into heaven at Enstrom. The almond toffee made by this company is so delicious that you'll have a hard time stopping yourself from eating more than one piece. The Enstrom family makes this amazing confection by hand and has been doing so for generations. Each batch weighs about seventy pounds, and they sell over a half million pounds each year. Enstrom toffee requires refrigeration and won't stay fresh indefinitely. (It usually gets eaten long before the expiration date!) The toffee is shipped in one to five pound boxes to the United States and hundreds of foreign countries.

 Recommended   Price   Selection   Convenience   Service   Security

ethnicgrocer.com
EthnicGrocer.com

312-373-1777
support@ethnicgrocer.com

Candy and Chocolate • Dessert • Fish • Meat and Poultry • Snacks

EthnicGrocer.com, a division of TransEthnic, Inc., is a provider of authentic ethnic products. The site carries products from fifteen different countries and covers an area from Latin America to Asia. Searching at this site is a snap. Type the first few letters or the entire name of the product under the Keyword Search and click Go. Or search by categories or brands, or even by country. Scan the posted recipes and order some new and different items. Don't miss the Special Sale section for great savings on closeouts and clearance.

familychef.com
FamilyChef.com

888-612-9264
support@familychef.com

Prepared Food

FamilyChef.com delivers complete meals to your door. Each meal is big enough to serve two adults. Each meal is individually prepared, fully cooked, and delivered frozen. All you need to do is heat in a microwave oven and serve. The FamilyChef.com program works like this: You buy a set number of meals in advance. Then you log into the Web site and order from the menu. FamilyChef.com prepares and sends the meals you selected. It's an excellent program for a working family. FamilyChef.com is also a great program for senior citizens or those who can't handle meal chores for themselves.

fanniemay.com
Fannie May Candies

No phone number listed
customerservice@fanniemay.com

Candy and Chocolate • Snacks

Fannie May Candies have been an important part of American life for years. Visit the Fannie May site to send candy, chocolates, and nuts to yourself and others. If you're trying to eat less, order a box of Debutants. These chocolates are slightly smaller in size but packed with the same great taste of the regular Fannie May line. Subscribe to the site's e-newsletter to learn when new candies or services will be available. During holiday times, you'll have the option to create your own custom box of Fannie May chocolates.

⭐ foodlocker.com
Foodlocker.com

888-465-1377
info@foodlocker.com

Candy and Chocolate • Dessert • Fish • Groceries • Meat and Poultry

Think of Foodlocker.com as a specialty supermarket. The virtual shelves contain hard-to-find and regional items that you would spend days tracking down locally. Foodlocker.com's only shortcoming is that occasionally quantities of an item are restricted. Shop here by food type, brand name, region, or imported products. The well-designed interface makes it a breeze to look through the available items, and the accompanying product information is both interesting and informative. The displayed prices include shipping charges to the continental United States.

freshfloridastonecrab.com
Gamby's Lobster & Stone Crab Shack

800-893-5310
gamby@gambyshack.com

Fish

Thanks to Gamby's you can have those Florida favorites, Florida Lobster and Stone Crab Claws, shipped to you the same day they are caught. This company also sells gulf shrimp and honey mustard sauce from that famous Miami institution, Joe's Stone Crab. Gamby's offers a limited number of choices, primarily the number of pounds you want to order. Still, if you want Florida Lobster (the kind without the claws) and Stone Crabs this is the place. My advice is to skip the Mrs. Smith's Key Lime Pie. It's $15 or so from this site, but considerably less from your local supermarket.

frozen-delights.com
Frozen Delights

888-957-1137
questions@frozen-delights.com

Dessert • Fish • Gourmet • Meat and Poultry • Prepared Food

Frozen Delights takes the legwork out of gourmet meals. This company scours the marketplaces from coast to coast and then freezes its gourmet finds. Shop here for chicken in lemon sauce, Maryland-style crab cakes, and toothsome Kentucky bourbon pecan pie. Some exotic meats, like buffalo and ostrich, are worth a try. You'll also find a wide variety of appetizers and soups. Frozen Delights vacuum-seals all its products in thick, freezer-safe plastic wrap to lock out oxygen and lock in flavor. For shipping, your order is packed in dry ice and protected in a recyclable cooler.

 Recommended   Price   Selection   Convenience   Service 🔒 Security

fuddyduddyfudge.com
Fuddy Duddy Fudge
877-765-2878
fuddyduddy@harborside.com
Candy and Chocolate

The ingredients in many chocolate and fudge products often suggest you're eating a fistful of chemicals rather than a savory sweet. Not so at Fuddy Duddy Fudge. For over one hundred years, this company has been using the same recipes to turn out delicious fudge, all without preservatives or chemicals. The fudge comes in a variety of flavors, including chocolate and vanilla pecan, rocky road, penuche, butterscotch caramel, tiger butter, and more. Each piece melts in your mouth.

⭐ germandeli.com
GermanDeli.com
877-437-6269
sales@germandeli.com
Candy and Chocolate • Dessert • Ethnic • Fish • Groceries • Meat and Poultry

Well Schatzie, if there's a sausage with "wurst" in its name, you'll find it at GermanDeli.com. Blutwurst, teawurst, liverwurst, bratwurst, bockwurst — the list goes on. You can buy the sausages individually, buy a sampler pack, or forego them completely and try something else. The accommodating folks who run the place will even special-order meat for you. Some zwieback from the bakery is good to gnaw on while you're scanning the German magazines you can order from this site.

⭐ glenwood.org/pecansale/pecan_products.htm
Holiday Pecans
866-729-2189
bblake@glenwood.org
Snacks

The pecans and snacks at the Holiday Pecans site have a purpose. Profits from the sale of these nuts help maintain and operate the Allen Cott School in Birmingham, Alabama. The school is an educational and treatment service for day and residential students diagnosed with autism, retardation, and other mental disorders. You'll find fresh pecan mammoth halves (the largest pecans grown) and one-pound bags of fresh pecan pieces. Various chocolates with pecans are also offered. Southern Pecan coffee, available here, smells heavenly. Some products are only available from October through December. You'll need to e-mail your order.

global-grocer.com
Global-Grocer

(+44) 1278 434355
info@global-grocer.com

Groceries

Sometimes it's hard to justify shopping online for groceries that you can purchase at the store. However, the products at Global-Grocer are worth a second look. Items are arranged by Drinks, Sweets and Chocolate, Snacks, and General Groceries. Shopping by country is even more fun. Select the country and click the Go button. When you see an item you want to buy, click the Put in Trolley button. Shipping is fastest to the U.K.; other locations take a bit longer.

godiva.com
Godiva

800-946-3482
letters@godiva.com

Candy and Chocolate

Godiva began as single shop in Belgium. Today Godiva is a multimillion dollar business offering coffee, ice cream, and liqueur. Yet, Godiva hasn't forgotten what made it great. The chocolate is fantastic: rich, satisfying, and packed with flavor. Shop online for the same fine chocolate you would find in a Godiva store. The chocolates and candy items are arranged by seasonal collection. For a few dollars, you can add a signed gift card and wrapping to your order. Create your own Godiva account for easy repeat ordering.

⭐ gourmetfoodstore.com
Gourmet Foodstore

877-591-8008
customerservice@gourmetfoodstore.com

Candy and Chocolate • Dessert • Fish • Gourmet • Meat and Poultry • Prepared Food • Snacks

If you're not careful, you can easily run up a big tab at the Gourmet Food-store. The convenient Food Finder that helps you locate all the sumptuous foodstuffs makes it too easy to shop. So do the helpful descriptions for almost every item in the extensive catalog. Be careful! Order only those items that you can't live without. Ask yourself whether you need these truffles, this foie gras, this caviar. Why not? After all, you're worth it. Besides, Gourmet Foodstore has a satisfaction guarantee. If you're unhappy with your order, just tell them and they'll resolve the problem immediately.

⭐ Recommended   Price   Selection   Convenience   Service   🔒 Security

gourmetfoodz.gourmetfoodmall.com
GourmetzFoods

877-755-4920
marion@greatlookz.com

Candy and Chocolate • Dessert • Fish • Gourmet • Meat and Poultry • Prepared Food • Snacks

GourmetzFoods is one of the many stores in the vast Gourmet Food Mall. The store carries a little bit of this and a little bit of that — mainly oils, spreads, condiments, and tapenades. It also specializes in unusual and hard-to-find gourmet items. If you see something you want, buy it while you're browsing because it might not be there the next time you go back. Or, buy a case of it. You're guaranteed to have a continued supply for a long time and save money, too. GourmetzFoods discounts case prices by at least five percent.

hammondpretzels.com
Hammond's

717-392-7532
info@hammondpretzels.com

Snacks

Pretzels are a universal favorite. The Hammond Pretzel Bakery, opened in 1930, has been a family-run business since its origins. Only the finest pretzels leave the bakery. They use high-quality ingredients, combine them in a family recipe that dates back to the 1800s, and then hand-roll and oven-bake the dough into scrumptious hard pretzels. Order your pretzels at the site and learn the nutrition facts about this filling snack. Details on both the salted and unsalted varieties are available. Hammond's will ship internationally.

★ harryanddavid.com
Harry and David

877-322-1200
service@harryanddavid.com

Healthy Food • Meats and Poultry • Prepared Food • Snacks

Can you believe that Harry and David, the two brothers who started the chain, originally sold pears by mail to save themselves from bankruptcy? Their stores have come a long way since then, and now offer the signature pears, lots of other fruit, and a complete line of gourmet foods. The online shop carries an expanded version of the great merchandise found in the stores. Check out the Gourmet Foods section for a wide variety of frozen entrees, appetizers and hors d'oeuvres, cool confections, bulk party treats, and more. Harry and David ships many items internationally: Click the International link for a list of products and countries.

homecookingforyou.com
Home Cooking For You

800-741-4827
info@homecookingforyou.com

Prepared Food

"What's for dinner?" is the last question you want to hear at the end of a busy day. This site will send dinner to you. The meals are made from high-quality meats and vegetables and do not contain preservatives or additives. Each meal is a complete dinner that can serve up to two adults. Thirty meal choices are available. You can order meals for yourself or send them as gifts. Meal gifts are perfect for new parents, college students, grandparents, or shut-ins. The dinners are more nutritious than fast food and just a bit more expensive.

homesteadhealthyfoods.com
Homestead Healthy Foods

888-861-5670
E-mail form on site

Healthy Food • Meat and Poultry

Out in Texas hill country, the Sechrist Ranch raises chicken and cows the old-fashioned way. In fact, the Texas Department of Agriculture designated the Sechrist Ranch the first certified organic ranch in that state. What this desig-nation means to you and me is that the chicken and beef from this company will taste amazing! The chicken contains less than two percent fat and is full of flavor. The beef has been grass-fed and the hearty taste bears only scant resemblance to the nasty stuff found in the supermarket. The Sechrists (or their representatives) will call you personally before shipping your order.

hometownfavorites.com
Hometown Favorites

888-694-2656
info@hometownfavorites.com

Groceries

Navigation at Hometown Favorites is tedious. (Hint: Click the Map link to locate the products for sale.) However, it's worth the trouble. Hometown Favorites has assembled a selection of hard-to-find and discontinued grocery items that can't be beat. Some of the items, such as Esper Deluxe Pepper Jelly, are regional. Others, like Smith Brothers Black Licorice Throat Drops, haven't been seen on store shelves for a long time. All are reasonably priced. Hometown Favorites won't reveal where it finds its amazing stash of good-ies. It will ship anywhere you ask.

★ Recommended   Price   Selection   Convenience   Service   🔒 Security

★ internationalbrownie.com
International Brownie

781-340-1588
info@internationalbrownie.com

Candy and Chocolate • Dessert

There's nothing quite as satisfying as a brownie. International Brownie has been the Internet's source of brownies for years. With sixteen delightful flavors from which to choose, you're sure to find one that you like. Select from the Chocolate brownies or the Blondes. If you have a nut allergy, you needn't worry, because the brownies without nuts are clearly marked. Order brownies by the pan, the dozen, or choose a sampler or gift pack. Just make sure you take time to enjoy them when your order arrives.

★ ipswichshellfish.com/ipshellfish/default.asp
Ipswich Shellfish Fish Market

978-356-4371
E-mail form on site

Fish

"Fresh from the sea, straight to your home." The Ipswich Seafood Gallery ships Ipswich Steamer clams, live lobsters, and hand-selected fish and shellfish. Traditional New England clambakes are available, too. The fish has not been cooked prior to shipping. Your order will be shipped in a cardboard shipping chest lined with insulating polystyrene within twenty-four hours after it's received. To ensure your seafood is kept at the proper temperature, the chest is lined with a leak-proof liner plus frozen gel packs or dry ice. Saturday deliveries incur an additional $15 charge.

jamaicaplace.com
Jamaica Place

No phone number listed
E-mail form on site

Ethnic • Groceries • Meat and Poultry • Snacks

Everything you can associate with Jamaica including Red Stripe Beer is available at Jamaica Place. It features a well-stocked grocery store selling items like Jamaican patties, jerk sauce, and Blue Mountain coffee. There's a selection of Jamaican health and beauty aids including castor oil and salt products. Whatever is troubling you will be cured by the contents of one these bottles. Most importantly, this site has all the Jamaican spices and sauces you need to cook authentic Caribbean dishes. If you're longing for Jamaica, you can book your trip at the site, or just click the weather button to check the local temperature.

jerrysmeats.com
Jerry's Meats & Seafoods

877-789-0789
jerrysmeats@jerrysmeats.com

Fish

The only way to get better salmon than through Jerry's Meats & Seafoods is to go to Southeast Alaska and catch it yourself. Because you can't, Jerry and his friends (see the online photos) have done it for you. All orders are shipped via Federal Express in special containers. King and Sockeye Salmon head the list. Also available are Halibut and King Crab. Order a container of the Crab Dip while you're at it. If you're not sure how to serve what you bought, then check out the page of recipes on the site for help. Get ready to enjoy your catch.

★ joesstonecrab.com
Joe's Stone Crab

800-780-2722
qanda@joesstonecrab.com

Fish

During stone crab season, lines of hungry diners stretch for blocks at the legendary Joe's Stone Crabs in Miami Beach. Beat the heat and order complete dinners or a la carte food from the company's site. For first timers, the dinners are actually the better deal because each complete package meal includes a mallet, cracking board, cocktail forks, bibs, and instructions. Remember that stone crabs are seasonal and only available during certain months of the year. From the displayed menu, choose the day you want your crabs to arrive and order. For now, sit back and dream of Miami Beach.

★ juliennetogo.com
Juliennetogo

626-441-2299
info@juliennetogo.com

Gourmet • Prepared Food

Tired of prepared food that tastes like plastic? Why not order a fine, restaurant-quality meal instead. Julienne Fine Foods and Celebrations of Los Angeles has a selection of Care Packages that are sure to please even the fussiest diners. After all, the same food served in the restaurant can be found in their freezer. Choose from their A La Cart menu for a selection of gourmet favorites. Hearty soups and stews include four mini loaves of Rosemary Raisin Bread. A complete dinner for two is an excellent choice. All that's missing is the wine and a bit of romance in the air.

 Recommended   Price   Selection   Convenience   Service   Security

kabobs.com
Kabobs

800-732-9484
ttirrell@kabobs.com

Gourmet • Meat and Poultry • Prepared Food

Having a party? Need food for guests to eat while you finish preparing the main course? Kabobs, the hors d'oeuvres specialists, can help. This company sells a variety of prepared food that can precede a meal or serve as the meal itself. The center of its collection is a variety of "kabobs" — various foods that have been threaded onto wooden skewers. The Antipasto Kabob, with tortellini, roasted tomato, kalamata olives, and proscuitto, is hand-threaded on a six-inch skewer. Meat kabobs are also available. Purchase a tray of one hundred units or purchase a case (four trays), all at wholesale prices.

konjacfoods.com
Konjac Foods USA

408-257-1813
info@konjacfoods.com

Diet • Healthy Food

The items available from konjacfoods.com enjoy almost cult-like status among some low-carb dieters. Others respond with a resounding, "Blecch." The pasta and noodles sold by this company are made from glucomannan, a natural soluble fiber, and water. The resulting product contains almost no carbohydrates and is very low on the glycemic index. The noodles and pasta are stored in seawater and need to be rinsed thoroughly before they are cooked. Steam, boil, or panfry the pasta or noodles or add them to soup and stews. Nutritious? Definitely. Are they tasty? You decide.

kosherman.com
Kosherman

973-731-6016
info@kosherman.com

Ethnic

Kosherman is a great source of everything "yiddishkeit." Shop at this site for Jewish holiday baskets, shiva baskets, and a wide variety of themed gifts. You'll also find kosher vitamins, herbs, and minerals, and other sports nutritional products. Kosherman contains links to other kosher sites on the Internet, making it easy to leapfrog to sites that carry the goods and services you need. This is one of the only sites that shows any intentional humor; the posted joke will make you laugh out loud. Read the scrolling Kosher News for a quick look at what's going on in the world.

koshermeal.com
KosherMeal.com

No phone number listed
info@koshermeal.com

Ethnic • Prepared Food

So listen, it's not so easy to be Kosher. You're committed to a set of dietary restrictions and can't pop into the nearest fast food joint, especially when you're on the road. KosherMeal.com can help you out by sending a kosher meal right to your hotel room. KosherMeal.com seems like a great idea — except the site doesn't do much to inspire confidence. There's a warning that orders "may be delayed up to twelve hours in cyberspace" and no phone number to call if your food doesn't arrive. My advice is to e-mail in advance of your order and make sure you're going to get what you pay for.

legalseafoods.com
Shop Legal

800-327-3474
E-mail form on site

Fish • Prepared Food

Now everyone can enjoy the fresh seafood that has made the reputation of this East Coast restaurant chain so revered. Food is shipped in meal packages, such as the Whole Clams and Chowder for four. You get clams, cornmeal breading, four ears of corn, and a quart of chowder. The order is shipped with cooking instructions so you can try to duplicate the restaurant's work. You can also order full meals of stuffed shrimp and chowder, lobster and chowder, scrod and chowder, steak and chowder, or for a snack, just chowder. Whatever you order, you can be sure it's fresh and legal.

lilsalseafood.com
Lil Sal Seafood

310-540-7213
info@lilsalseafood.com

Fish • Prepared Food

"Laissez Les Bon Temps Roulette!" That's what you'll say when you log in to Lil Sal Seafood. This site is your source for Cajun food. Try a Turducken, a turkey, duck, and chicken, all deboned and stuffed inside each other with sausage dressing. In addition to the 13 varieties of sausage, how about some alligator meat? Not just tail, but tenderloins and ribs, too. Lil Sal Seafood's catering department can ship a complete Louisiana crawfish, shrimp, or crab boil to you. There's plenty of other seafood, too. All orders are shipped overnight and arrive just in time for you to let the good times roll.

 Recommended   Price   Selection   Convenience   Service   Security

lobster-n-crab.com
Lobster-n-Crab.com

516-313-5309
E-mail form on site
Fish

Open Lobster-n-Crab.com and listen to the sea (if you have a sound card and speakers, of course). The wonderful sound is a good backdrop for the real showstoppers here: Maine lobster and blue crabs. The site offers a range of lobster sizes and crabs by the dozen, half bushel, and full bushel. Not sure how to prepare your crabs or lobster? See the extensive recipe page. All purchases are shipped fresh via Federal Express overnight service. When you make your selection, simply enter your zip code, click Recalculate, and the shipping charges will appear. Order now and listen to the waves crash while you eat your delectable meal.

★ lowcarb4you.com
Low Carb 4you.com

561-721-3446
info@lowcarb4you.com
Candy and Chocolate • Diet • Snacks

Low carb is a popular buzzword these days. So many food products claim they're low carb, but how can you be sure? Fortunately, Low Carb 4you.com takes the guesswork out of figuring food counts. Every item sold here has the nutritional information listed conveniently for you. When you view an item, a link to similar items appears. Shop by product type or brand. Low Carb 4you.com carries some hard-to-find low carb items, including the Asher candy bars and La Tiara taco shells. Sign up to receive the site's newsletter and occasional coupons and other discounts.

mikesnuts.com
Mike's Nut Shop

717-845-7122
info@mikesnuts.com
Snacks

The citizens of York, Pennsylvania, have been enjoying Mike's Nuts for years. The distinctive nut roaster stood outside the shop and was used in all kinds of weather. Order nuts from Mike's by the tin. If you get a serious case of the munchies, go for the five-pound size. You can find cashews, hazelnuts, almonds, peanuts, and all your favorite nuts at this site. There's also dried fruit and other mixes. Did you know that nuts are actually good for you? You can read some fascinating nut facts while you're shopping at the site.

mwbeef.com
M & W Beef Packers

800-489-8589
mwbeef@riverjordan.com

Meat and Poultry

M & W Beef Packers bring you a selection of U.S. Choice higher-grade beef cuts, aged to perfection, flash frozen, and shipped to you from North Dakota. This company offers a variety of other meats and poultry and is one of the few places where you can buy buffalo meat. Be sure to check out the recipe page for new ways to serve your steaks and other meat. Want to learn more about beef? The Beef Facts section at the site tells you lots of interesting facts about different cuts of meat and important storage information.

netrition.com
Netrition

888-817-2411
E-mail form on site

Candy and Chocolate • Diet • Healthy Food • Snacks

Netrition claims it's "The Internet's Premier Nutrition Superstore." After you've browsed its extensive catalogue for a while, you can't help but agree. All the diet and nutritional aids you need are assembled at this site, usually at lower prices than you can find anywhere else. Shop by brand or product, or just use the handy pull-down menu to jump to the area where your product is located. Netrition's product descriptions and explanations provide background information on the items and encourage you to purchase new or different products. The flat shipping rate is a great incentive for customers.

newharborlobster.com
New Harbor Fishermen's Co-op

866-883-2922
lobsta@newharborlobster.com

Fish

Fishermen from the town of Bristol, Maine, founded the New Harbor Fisherman's Co-op in 1972. Today the Co-op is owned by a group of 20 fishermen. Their lobsters are caught in waters around Monhegan Island. This site also offers crabs and steamers, but lobsters are their specialty. Lobsters are also their passion. You'll find pages devoted to how to cook and eat these savory crustaceans. There is information on the health benefits of lobster, too. Of course, all this information is interesting, but fades into the background when the first piece of claw meat meets the drawn butter.

 Recommended Price Selection Convenience Service 🔒 Security

newyorkcityfood.com
New York City Food.com

419-228-4640
orders@newyorkcityfood.com

Candy and Chocolate • Gourmet • Groceries

What a concept! Imagine if someone assembled many of the greatest food selections from New York city's restaurants and establishments and made them available to everyone. If your mouth is already watering, New York City Food.com is your kind of place. Shopping here is a mixed bag; you'll find bagels and bialys, chocolate, lox and caviar, pickles, and pasta. The name and contact information of the supplying restaurant is clearly marked on the appropriate page. Check the shipping prices before you order; next day prices can run up the tab.

nomeat.com
NoMeat.com

770-234-6931
service@nomeat.com

Healthy Food • Prepared Food

My sister is a vegetarian so I've heard the pros and cons. Frankly, it's entirely up to you whether you eat meat or you don't. Sites like this one make it easy for folks like my sister and me to share a table. The site has assembled just about every meat substitute ever created and even thrown in a few more substitutes for other foods, like milk and eggs. Some of the fake meat is surprisingly good; I've gotten hooked on the Low Fat Cedar Lake Meatless 3 Grain Pecan Patty. Take or leave the propaganda about vegetarianism at the site.

orientalpantry.com
The Oriental Pantry

978-264-4576
E-mail form on site

Dessert • Ethnic

Check your pantry. There's a good chance that you don't have all the spices and seasonings you need to create an Oriental meal. Alternatively, your Oriental spices are too old and outdated to be effective. It doesn't matter. The Oriental Pantry can supply just about any Oriental spice or seasoning you can name. Chinese hot chili oil, pure saffron, five-spice powder, or any of the hard-to-find flavors that distinguish Oriental cooking are available for you. Need some new recipes? They're here, too, along with a great selection of cookbooks. Finish your meal with a custom fortune cookie.

⭐ petrossian.com
Petrossian Paris
800-828-9241
customersupport@petrossian.com
Gourmet

Ah, caviar. Nothing tastes quite like it. If you're going to eat it, get the very best with an order from Petrossian Paris. The company claims it's the premier buyer and importer of Russian caviar worldwide. The caviar sold here is exquisite. Each variety of the rich and delicious caviar will thrill you with its texture, color, and size. (Of course, it's also expensive, but you already knew that.) The site offers other delicacies, including smoked fish, foie gras and pâté, rich chocolates, specialty teas, and coffee.

⭐ pfaelzerbrothers.com
Pfaelzer Brothers
800-621-0202
E-mail form on site
Dessert • Meat and Poultry

Back in 1923, the Pfaelzer Brothers were selling their exceptional meats in Chicago from a horse-drawn wagon. Today, their company sells them throughout the United States via the Internet. Already famous for its carefully aged beef, tender pork, and succulent lamb, Pfaelzer Brothers also offers poultry, seafood, and game. You can order appetizers, desserts, or complete meal packages. Looking for just the right gift? How about one of the Monthly Gourmet Gift Plans or a gift certificate? The site is organized for easy use, making Pfaelzer Brothers a top choice to be your Internet butcher.

pheasant.com
MacFarlane Pheasants
800-345-8348
No e-mail address on site
Meat and Poultry

Anyone can slap a hunk of beef on the grill: Why not invite the gang over for a really unusual meal? MacFarlane Pheasants sells pheasant meat in several different varieties. Choose from smoked pheasant, breast meat strips, frozen and uncooked (recipes are available), and multiple bird packs. If pheasant isn't exotic enough for you, rabbit, wild boar, ostrich, buffalo, and quail are also featured. For something completely different, MacFarlane Pheasants invites you to a pheasant shoot on its farm in Wisconsin. There, you'll have the chance to meet your dinner before you eat it.

 Recommended   Price   Selection   Convenience   Service   Security

plankfish.com
Plankfish

877-798-5988
info@plankfish.com

Fish

Plankfish? No, it's not a species of fish, it's a method of preparation. A Native American delicacy, plankfish is a fish fillet cooked and served on a cedar plank. Place your order, and your plankfish will arrive, frozen, via second-day air. Thaw it, cook it on the grill or bake in the oven, and enjoy. The traditional plankfish is chinook salmon so start here if you're new to the cooking method. You'll be back soon to order the halibut and mahi mahi. You have to agree, those first Americans sure knew what they were doing.

pssifish.com
Prime Select Seafoods

419-324-0032
salmon@pssifish.com

Fish

Prime Select Seafoods brings you wild salmon from the Copper River Fishery. The fish are caught inshore with gill nets. This is not a massive, open-ocean, drift-net operation. Instead, Prime Select Seafoods is a small, family-run business. The family feels strongly about environmental issues on the river and, accordingly, they use environmentally sound methods to harvest the wild salmon. Prime Select Seafoods offers a variety of frozen, smoked, and canned salmon and cod. Also available are gift packages and related merchandise. Read about the natural resources on the Copper River from the thought-provoking details provided at this site.

rockes.com
Rocke's

877-762-5372
mail@rockes.com

Meat and Poultry

For three generations the Rocke family has brought quality meat to market. Certified Angus Beef is the big seller here, with Signature Sirloin Steak close behind. Other specialty meats, including smoked hams and turkeys and a variety of sausages, are hard to beat. Looking for a gift? A Combination Box from this site will make someone happy. So will the Breakfast Box, which includes smoked bacon, sausage, Amana pancake mix, and maple syrup. Whatever you choose, the Rockes pledge to provide excellent fresh and smoked meat products, and superior customer service.

russianfoods.com
Russian Foods.com

212-421-0017
shop@russianfoods.com

Candy and Chocolate • Dessert • Ethnic • Groceries

A trip to the virtual Russian Foods.com is a lot like visiting a real Russian market. A lot of merchandise and activity is crammed into a small space, and try as you might, you can't see it all in one visit. The Food and Grocery section is a bit confounding; some items catch your eye but, unfortunately, can only be ordered in wholesale quantities or as part as of a gift basket. Shoppers have the option of posting reviews of each of the listed items. The comments, although sometimes in unreadable Cyrillic letters, are often unintentionally hilarious.

saxxmeat.com
Saxx Custom Cutting

866-251-0855
info@saxxmeat.com

Meat and Poultry

Shopping on the Internet can be an impersonal experience, but at Saxx Custom Cutting you'll be greeted by a picture of Dean, your Saxx butcher. You'll also meet Dean's wife — she works in the office. Saxx wants you to feel like you're dealing your neighbors. Dean offers you a selection of aged U.S. Choice steaks as well as quality pork and poultry. The company offers a wide variety of sausages, all made without MSG or other additives. For a real treat try the smoked or cured hams, turkeys, and sausages. One taste, and you'll add your testimonial to the ones on the site.

★ scharffenberger.com
Scharffen Berger Chocolate Maker

510-981-4050
beantobar@scharffenberger.com

Candy and Chocolate

Back in the early 1990s two longtime friends got together and decided to produce chocolate from cacao beans. The rest, as they say, is history. Today Scharffen Berger Chocolate Maker runs a thriving business in Berkeley, California. Visit the Scharffen Berger site for deep, rich, satisfying chocolate bars. Buy them in mint, mocha, bittersweet, or semisweet. There's baking chocolate, too, for your home-baked chocolate confections. Gift items are also available. To get an inside look at how Scharffen Berger makes chocolate, take a virtual tour of the factory.

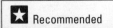 Recommended   Price   Selection   Convenience   Service   Security

schwans.com
Schwans

888-724-9267
E-mail form on site

Prepared Food

Since 1952, Schwan's has been delivering restaurant-quality frozen foods to homes across America. With convenient home delivery and a broad selection of individual products and complete meal combinations that are a snap to prepare, it's hard to pass up this service. Go to the All About Schwans page and enter your zip code to determine whether delivery service is available in your area. If you're in luck, you can sign up for this excellent service. Various credit options are available and in just a few days, Schwan's signature yellow truck will be on your street.

slackshoagies.com
Slack's Hoagie Shack

800-362-4437
E-mail form on site

Prepared Food

Slack's hoagies sandwiches, steaks, and wings are an institution in Pennsylvania and New Jersey. Now you don't need to travel to the Northeast to taste these delicious taste sensations. Slack's Care Packages bring the taste of Slack's to you. Order the Classic or Cheesesteak Classic for two hoagies, chips, Tastycakes, pretzels, and a copy of the Philadelphia Daily News. Or order a Classic Combo for a more customized order. You'll need to call your order in at this time. Are you interested in opening your own Slack's franchise? Details and compelling financial information are available at the site.

smartmeasure.biz
Smart Measure Snacks

No phone number listed
E-mail form on site

Diet • Snacks

If you're dieting or watching your food intake, you already know that limiting your portions is hard. A quick snack can turn into a major munch-out and sabotage your efforts. Smart Measure Snacks puts single servings of healthy snack items at your fingertips. Instead of reaching for the two-pound potato chip bag next time you're hungry, take out a Smart Measure Snack instead. Various flavors are available; all are delicious. The individual snack bags are available in bags of twenty or a canister of forty. If you're new to the idea or like variety, try a sampler that includes several different flavors.

smokehouse.com
Burger's Smokehouse

800-624-5426
service@smokehouse.com

Dessert • Meat and Poultry • Prepared Food

If you want smoked meat, you can't go wrong with a company that produces nearly 750,000 hams a year. Burger's Smokehouse runs an impressive operation, using acres of Ozarks land. Shop here for bacon, ham that's been smoked in a variety of flavors, and more down-home stuff like jowls. If smoked meat isn't to your liking, there's flash-frozen beef from corn-fed cattle in a variety of cuts and grinds, and lots of poultry. You can even order some rather decadent sweets, which, fortunately for us, haven't been near the smokehouse.

snackaisle.com
SnackAisle.com

603-578-0405
info@snackaisle.com

Candy and Chocolate • Snacks

Where do you go shopping when you want a snack? The answer's easy. On the Internet — SnackAisle.com, of course. Shop here for your snack favorites. You'll find potato chips, tortilla chips, vegetable chips, pretzels, popcorn, various nuts and trail mixes, and much more. There's even a Kosher section for those who observe Jewish dietary laws. If organic's your thing, the site has you covered with a variety of certified organic chips. Feeling charitable? Make a donation to give snacks to different listed charities. (You might want to call and confirm how your money will be used before you click Donate.)

snackexchange.com
SnackExchange.com

717-392-7532
sales@snackexchange.com

Candy and Chocolate • Diet • Snacks

So many snacks, so little time. Trite but true at SnackExchange.com. This site's virtual shelves are stocked with everything a snacker can imagine. You'll find gourmet handmade chocolates, dried fruit, nuts and healthy snacks, Jelly Belly jelly beans, plenty of sugar-free and low-carb candy and goodies, candy from all over the world, and much more. Best of all, you'll only pay a low, flat rate shipping fee no matter how much you order. Sign up a friend and receive a discount the next time you order.

 Recommended   Price   Selection   Convenience   Service   🔒 Security

specialfortunecookies.com
specialfortunecookies.com
408-257-1813
sales@forteconnections.com
Diet • Healthy Food

How about an extra-special Chinese fortune cookie, customized with a message or fortune created just by you? The five-by-seven-inch giant fortune cookie from specialfortunecookies.com comes in a clear plastic container and makes a dynamite hostess gift. For something less flashy, individually wrapped traditional fortune cookies in a gift container work just fine. You can add your own fortunes, or use the preprinted ones. If you're planning a big dinner party, why not send each guest home with a Fortune cookie memento that contains your special greeting? What a fun dessert.

⭐ stclairicecream.com
St. Clair Ice Cream
203-853-4774
office@stclairicecream.com
Dessert

Ice cream from the Internet? Sure, why not! Especially when it's ordered from this site. The ice cream from St. Clair is molded into exquisite shapes and colors. Holidays and special occasions are represented. You'll find ice cream that looks like American flags, various fruits, Easter eggs, turkeys, Christmas trees, seashells, and more. The flavor of the ice cream corresponds as closely as possible to its appearance. Each order is hand crafted, so order well in advance. There's a minimum on orders; you can't order one or two pieces. Of course, plan to be home the day your ice cream order arrives.

stickytoffeepudding.com
Sticky Toffee Pudding
323-549-9145
info@stickytoffeepudding.com
Dessert

Why settle for the same old dessert? Treat yourself and your guests to a British favorite. Sticky Toffee Pudding is a traditional British dessert from the Lake District in the northwest of England. Don't let the name deceive you; this is not a boring dish of pudding. Instead, you'll be treated to a light cake studded with moist dates and topped with a sticky, sweet toffee sauce. The company makes the Sticky Toffee Pudding in small batches from an authentic family recipe. All you need to do is reheat lightly in a microwave or conventional oven and serve.

store.yahoo.com/lulucakes/cakes.html
Lulu's Tennessee Treats & Warrenton, Ltd

800-232-3694
lulucake@bellsouth.net

Dessert

Lulu's & Warrenton has been baking and sending fine cakes and cookies from their Tennessee location for the last 68 years. Over that time, their line has expanded to include items like dog biscuits, chocolates, and candy, but their first love remains dessert items. The cake menu includes flavors like Southern Pecan, Triple Chocolate, Carrot with White Chocolate, Marshmallow Cloud, Tennessee Golden, Apple Cinnamon Breakfast Cake, and more. A cream cheese pound cake, glazed with hazelnut liqueur and baked in various flavors is a somewhat lighter way to end a meal. Lulu's & Warrenton ships internationally.

sweetzfree.com
Sweetzfree

No phone number listed
sales@sweetzfree.com

Diet

Sweetzfree is an amazing liquid sweetener that contains no calories or carbohydrates. All it adds is the sweet natural taste of sugar. The highly concentrated, liquid syrup base is made from sucralose and purified water. Sweetzfree dissolves instantly. Use it whenever you would use sugar or another sweetener: at the table, or in cooking or baking. Sweetzfree is available in three sizes. The one-ounce bottle is equivalent to 24 cups of sugar, the two-ounce size is equivalent to 48 cups, and the three-ounce bottle is equivalent to 96 cups of sugar. Think of the carbs and calories you'll save!

★ terrachips.com
Terra Chips

631-730-2200
E-mail form on site

Healthy Food • Snacks

Here's a "terrafic" idea for a healthy, satisfying snack. They're called Terra Chips, and one crunchy bite will convince you to throw your old chips in the trash. The original Terra Chips were made from a blend of three root vegetables. Now new varieties are joining the line. Mediterranean and Zesty Tomato Terra Chips add extra zest, and Taro Chips bring a new dimension to this exiting line of snacks. Learn more about this healthy alternative to old-fashioned potato chips and order some for yourself and your friends.

 Recommended   Price   Selection   Convenience   Service   Security

thechocolatepizza.com
The Chocolate Pizza Company
800-280-9381
info@chocolate-pizza.com
Candy and Chocolate

Chocolate pizzas beat any other type of pizza, hands down! The crust is made from milk chocolate mixed with English toffee. It's covered with pecans, roasted almonds, California almonds and drizzled with white chocolate. A side bucket of peanut butter "wings" can be added to the order. Add almond bark, chocolate-covered potato chips and pretzels, and nut crunch to your order. Chocolate pizzas have a high melt factor, so, wisely, the site does not ship between April 15 and October 15.

thehomebistro.com
Home Bistro
800-343-5588
customerservice@thehomebistro.com
Diet • Prepared Food

The chefs at Home Bistro actually trained as chefs in Paris. All the love and joy that they put into their work in France goes into the food they send to you. Accordingly, meals from this delivery service don't have the institutional look and taste that's often found in similar services. Your Home Bistro meal will make you think you're eating in a fine café. Home Bistro now prepares low-carb meals. Choose meals from the regular or low-carb menu, or mix and match the two. Gift packs and sampler packs are available — an excellent way to try out the service.

tortillas4u.com
Tortillas4u
559-441-1030
E-mail form on site
Ethnic • Snacks

The humble tortilla forms the base for so many Mexican dishes and it forms the basis for this site. In fact, the name "Tortillas4u" aptly describes what's for sale here. You'll find a wide variety of tortillas including the basic models in flour and corn and also fancier flavors like pesto garlic and tomato basil. Don't miss the California chili wraps. Additionally, you can buy a variety of chips and tortillas in shapes such as bowls, boats, and tostadas. If you feel the urge to snack in between your tortilla meals, a big bag of chicharrones (pork rinds) awaits you.

truefoodsmarket.com
True Foods Market

435-755-9266
support@truefoodsmarket.com

Groceries • Healthy Food

Looking for a healthy snack? Searching for products to improve your health? With over one thousand health-related products available, True Foods Market is the place to shop. You'll find a treasure trove of products including dried fruit, nuts, seeds, packaged meals, soups, juices, non-dairy drinks, sprouting supplies, grains, beans, and herbs. There are even several packaged entrees for the days you don't want to cook. Feeling blocked? The store's colon-cleaning products will leave you feeling better in a jiffy. Submit a request if you don't see something you want.

vegecyber.com
VegeCyber

212-625-3980
E-mail form on site

Healthy Food

There's a lot of debate about whether vegetarian diets are good for you. Even if you're an opponent of the diet, you'll have to agree that VegeCyber foods are healthy. Most contain soy protein, a well-known prevention aid for cancer and heart disease. VegeCyber offers frozen vegetarian seafood and meat substitutes. Eggless fried eggs are a VegeCyber specialty. You'll also find other sources of plant protein, such as wheat, lotus roots, and sea vegetables. Frozen products can stay fresh for three months in the freezer, even if they've been frozen and defrosted several times.

walnutcreekcheese.com
Walnut Creek Cheese

877-852-2888
customerservice@walnutcreekcheese.com

Candy and Chocolate • Dessert • Gourmet • Meat and Poultry • Snacks

If you're tired of blah gourmet food, take a trip to Amish country. Walnut Creek Cheese, located in the heart of Amish country in Holmes County, Ohio, has some delectable treats that taste as good as they look. For the most part, the cheeses and meats are made locally. Even if you're not a beef jerky fan, Uncle Mike's Beef Jerky will have you begging for more. Expect to have "reverse sticker shock" when you shop at this site because prices are really low. How low? You'll be able to throw a party.

 Recommended   Price   Selection   Convenience   Service   Security

⭐ zabars.com
Zabar's

212-787-2000
info@zabars.com

Candy and Chocolate • Dessert • Fish • Gourmet • Groceries • Snacks

Ask anyone from New York where to get the best hand-sliced nova, sturgeon, or herring. Throw in the bagels and cream cheese, too. The answer will always be "Zabar's." Fortunately for you, Zabar's now delivers all over the United States. You can order individual items from the listed departments or order one of Zabar's prepared boxes. The Taste for Two, containing bagels, lox, and cinnamon rugelach and packed in a signature tote bag, includes next-day delivery. Discover the confections that New Yorkers are raving about when you order a gourmet cake by David Glass.

Planning a Stress-Free Holiday Dinner

Holidays are supposed to be happy times. Families gather and friends come together. Unfortunately, the person preparing the holiday meal doesn't always enjoy the event. Between shopping for the ingredients, preparing the food, and then serving and cleaning up, not much time is left for holiday cheer.

The holidays don't need to be stressful. If you're the chief cook and bottle washer, tell your family in advance that this year is going to be different. Let them know that you're not spending all day locked away in the kitchen!

Start your preparation as early as possible. Plan your table decorations. Both Martha Stewart (marthastewart.com) and Sur la Table (surlatable.com) sell holiday linens all through the year. For easier cleanup, you can find nice disposable paper tableware at discount prices at PartySecret.com (partysecret.com).

On to the dinner. A simple dinner is easier to plan and serve. If you would like to include a salad, check out Diamond Organics (diamond organic.com) for fresh-picked leafy greens delivered to your door. Dress the salad with Aunt Viola's Best Doggone Caesar Salad Dressing (auntviola.com).

The main course is easy. Burger's Smokehouse (smokehouse.com) offers hams, turkeys, and a wide variety of other meats. If seafood is more to your liking, consider a feast from Lobster-n-Crab. com (lobster-n-crab.com). Of course, if your family follows the vegetarian way of eating, visit NoMeat.com (nomeat.com) for amazing meat substitutes.

Finish your dinner with a cake from Cakes Across America (cakesacrossamerica.com) and pecans from Holiday Pecans (glenwood.org/pecansale/pecan_products.htm). Ask your guests and family to assist with the cleanup. This year's holiday meal can be a breeze!

Chapter 13

Health and Beauty: Looking as Good as You Feel

Incredibly beautiful people in fantastic situations. Advertising makes it seem so effortless. The message is clear: If you use the advertised products you'll look just like the folks in the commercials! In fact, the ads imply everyone can look young, svelte, and gorgeous. Cosmetics, skin, and hair care products promise to transform men and women into near gods and goddesses.

Health and related products are in front of you all the time, too. Someone's always hawking something to cure whatever ails you. Low energy? Back pain? Debilitating facial hair? Look around long enough and you'll find a proposed cure or solution. The parade of cures for just every about ache and pain is endless.

Truth is, no magic cosmetics or creams exist that create instant beauty and youth. Nor can pills or devices guarantee perfect health and well-being. However, health and beauty aids from all over the globe can make you look and feel better. Best of all, the Internet brings them to you with a few simple clicks.

To that end, we've assembled an amazing collection of health and beauty sites for your shopping pleasure. Some offer thousands of products under one banner and have expensive corporate backing behind them. Others are mom-and-pop sites selling one or two simple items. Have fun shopping for new and exciting products in all the sites in this chapter.

 Don't take the medical advice and information you find on the Internet as gospel truth without checking with your doctor first. Along with the true facts, a lot of mistruths and wrong information is posted in cyberspace.

Key Word Index

Bath and Body

The Bath and Body sites carry soaps and lotions. You'll find everything you need to get clean and stay fresh.

Cosmetics

Makeup products of all varieties and brand names are found at the Cosmetics sites. Add a sparkle to your cheeks with a new blush, or toss out the contents of your makeup kit and start over.

Eyewear

The stores that carry the Eyewear keyword offer prescription lenses (including contact lenses) in a wide variety of styles, name brands, and colors.

Hair

A bad hair day is synonymous with doom! Keep yours looking good with products from the Hair sites. You'll also find wigs, moustaches, and (gasp!) even fake chest hair.

Healthy Living

Shop at the Healthy Living sites for organic products or for products that improve your environment.

Pharmacy

You can find all the items you'd buy at your local pharmacy, whether you're shopping at a corner drugstore or a chain megastore, in the online Pharmacy stores.

Sex

The unmentionable that everyone seems to mention is covered at sites with the Sex keyword. Shop at these sites for sex- and sexual health-related items for men and women, including condoms, menopausal aids, and more.

Skin Care

You have only one epidermis! Whether the products are for your face or body, the products sold at the Skin Care sites will keep your skin smooth and youthful.

Teeth

Dental hygiene is important. Shop at the stores with the Teeth keyword for supplies to keep your teeth healthy and your breath fresh.

Vitamins and Supplements

The Vitamins and Supplements sites offer nutritional aids in a variety of forms that claim to add needed pizzazz to your diet.

Weight Loss

At the Weight Loss sites, you can shop for exercise programs, memberships, nutritional aids, and other tools to help you lose unwanted pounds and inches.

⭐ 19dollareyeglasses.com
Zenni Optical

415-785-7003
service@zennioptical.com

Eyewear

You can't miss what this online retailer promotes — prescription eyeglasses and sunglasses for $19! Zenni Optical can sell at this price because it gets its products directly from its factories — no middlemen, and no retail overhead. All its single vision, bifocal, and progressive bifocal lenses are premium quality, high-index polycarbonate, high-impact-resistance lenses with UV protection and antiscratch coating. Full anti-reflective plus anti-radiation coating is only $4.95 extra, and memory titanium frames are only $10 more. Such a deal!

aarppharmacy.com
AARP Pharmacy Services

800-305-6992
E-mail form on site

Bath and Body • Cosmetics • Hair • Healthy Living • Pharmacy • Skin Care • Teeth • Vitamins and Supplements

There's one caveat for shopping at this site — you must be a member of AARP. Members enjoy up to a 47 percent discount and savings on prescription drugs. Non-prescription medications and other pharmacy items are similarly discounted. Shop at this online pharmacy for hosiery and undergarments, too. Need supports? This site has them. Important medical information for the senior crowd is also available, giving extra value to this well-done site.

acumins.com
Acumins

888-223-8831
info@acumins.com

Vitamins and Supplements

The phrase "What's good for the goose is good for the gander" does not apply to people! We're all individuals and have our own individual vitamin needs. Fortunately, a savvy company like Acumins is around to create a vitamin packet that's designed to fill your specific needs. The process is painless. You fill out an easy-to-use nutrition analysis at the site. In turn, Acumins takes your information and creates a vitamin packet that's made up just for you. Lots of folks have used the Acumins program and claim to feel great. You can read the testimonials of the happy customers at the site.

 Recommended   Price   Selection   Convenience   Service   Security

★ adiscountbeauty.com
American Discount Beauty

310-276-9532
info@adiscountbeauty.com

Hair • Skin Care

American Discount Beauty offers heavily discounted hair care products. You can find salon shampoos and conditioners, plus hair dyes, pomades, and color enhancers. Make sure to order beauty tools like tweezers, clippers, and scissors to finish the look. Men's hair care products are available at the site, too, including the complete Goldwell for Men line. Check out the men's replacement hair products for moustaches, beards, and chests.

alangocreek.com
Alango Creek

218-666-5880
info@alangocreek.com

Skin Care

It's immediately apparent that Alango Creek is a small family-operated business. You won't be impressed with the site design or product packaging. But you will be impressed with this company's handmade products including its Natural Old Time Cold Process method soap. It is "100% pure using only natural ingredients" and comes in a variety of fragrances. You'll also find the family's glycerin soaps, shower gels, hand and body lotions, and bath salts. The family also makes dream catchers, beaded earrings, and potpourri, which is described as "very eye appealing." Okay, so they can't write copy either, but hey, how about that handmade soap. . . .

amazingconcealer.com
Amazing Cosmetics

No phone number listed
commentsat@amazingconcealer.com

Cosmetics

The owners of Amazing Cosmetics think makeup doesn't need to be complicated. They make simple products that work — and incidentally, don't test them on animals. The product that put the company on the map is called Amazing Concealer. I'm not sure whether it's indeed "Hollywood's best kept secret," but Amazing Concealer does provide amazing coverage, concealing even the darkest of under eye circles. Other products available include Velvet Powder, Younger Looking Eyes, and blush, eye shadow, lipsticks, and liners. With the launch of this Web site, the secret's no longer concealed.

annabellina.com
Anna Bellina

770-962-8110
patricia@annabellina.com

Cosmetics • Skin Care

You'll feel pretty in pink as soon as you hit the pastel-colored Anna Bellina site. The company specializes in all natural, anti-oxidant, anti-aging skin care products. If you're looking for treatment for acne or rosacea, or simply want products designed for your dry, sensitive, or mature skin, you'll find just what you need at this site. Besides its popular Honey Rose Skin Care line, the company also carries facial cleaners, facial toners, eye treatment products, moisturizers, exfoliants, masks, and much more. Do your skin a favor — check out Anna Bellina to "revive, renew, and rejuvenate."

anti-aging-wrinkles-treatments.com
Anti Aging Wrinkles Treatments

702-947-0567
E-mail form on site

Skin Care

Snails or surgery? The choice is yours. Confused? Read on. If you want to lose the wrinkles and aren't ready for plastic surgery, then this site is for you. The main product for sale here is called Elicina Cream. It contains the natural extract of the Chilean snail Helix Aspersa Müller. This marvelous extract is what allows snails to quickly regenerate damaged skin and shell. Who knew? Forget laser surgery, dermabrasion, or glycolic peels, get rid of your wrinkles and fine lines the snail way. A jar of Elicina Cream will set you back $39, or you can buy two for $59.

atkins.com
Atkins

800-228-4467
E-mail form on site

Weight Loss

When most people hear "low carb" they immediately think of the Atkins diet. The program is a low-carbohydrate, high-protein way of eating that has helped thousands of people shed unwanted pounds. Find out the facts about the diet at the official Atkins site. Purchase Atkins products at the online store. Ketone strips, a mainstay test of the diet, are also available. You'll also find vitamins and nutritional supplements, various sugar-free products, including syrups and shakes, and other low-carb foods. Do low-carb bagels, pasta, and cereals taste as good as their high-carb counterparts? You be the judge.

★ Recommended $ Price   🛒 Selection   🎁 Convenience   ☺ Service   🔒 Security

★ avon.com
Avon

800-527-2866
E-mail form on site

Bath and Body • Cosmetics • Healthy Living • Skin Care • Teeth

This is not your mother's Avon! Gone are the days when Avon was known for second-rate cosmetics peddled door to door. Today's company features a cutting-edge line of skin care products, cosmetics to die for, and all of it available online. The signature Anew skin care line has products for all ages — if your skin needs repairing, Avon is a good place to start. If you're lucky (or young) enough to have good skin, Avon has all the products you need to protect it. Want to work for Avon? Details on employment with this cosmetics giant are available at the site.

benefitcosmetics.com
Benefit Cosmetics

800-781-2336
customer@benefitcosmetics.com

Cosmetics • Skin Care

Benefit Cosmetics began as a San Francisco Bay Area boutique and has grown into a cosmetics powerhouse with over 600 counters worldwide, including Henri Bendel in New York and Harrod and Selfridges in London. What sets this company apart is its unique line of products, which not only work, as many will attest, but whose names bring a smile to your face. From the "Honey...snap out of it" scrub and the "Bad Gal Lash" mascara to the "Touch me then try to leave" cream, feel good on the inside and out with the company's products for the lips, eyes, cheeks, and body.

★ betterlife.com
betterlife.com

800-317-7150
info@betterlife.com

Vitamins and Supplements

Even your nutritionist won't know the names of all the stuff carried at betterlife.com. This company stocks the most comprehensive collection of nutritional supplements you'll find on the Internet and does it with low prices and great customer service. Over 125 brands are stocked, an amazing feat by anyone's standards. Click the Education tab for the definition and application of each of the supplements. Each file is time stamped so you can see when it was updated with the latest information.

bluemercury.com
bluemercury
800-355-6000
team@bluemercury.com

Bath and Body • Hair • Skin Care

Seek and ye shall find cosmetics, skin care, hair care, and much more at the bluemercury site. The site carries so many products that it's easy to get lost in the massive product list and forget why you came in the first place. Products are arranged by company, such as Bliss, Bumble & Bumble, L'Artisan Parfumeur, and so on, with product categories like Fresh Skincare, Fresh Bath and Body, and Fresh Hair thrown in for good measure. Take my advice and go through the list slowly, clicking the links that interest you. You're bound to find buried treasure.

breathaid.com
Breathaid
803-432-3571
E-mail form on site

Teeth

"Do people stand far away from you in conversation? Turn their heads away when you are speaking? Kiss you on the cheek (instead of the lips)?" If you answered affirmatively to the questions asked at the Breathaid site, you've come to the right place. You're suffering from the dreaded halitosis, and Breathaid can help. The tongue cleaner, FreshBreath Kit, and the CloSysII Mouthwash, Toothpaste, & Breath Spray, sold at this site will have you kissing sweet soon again. If you want pearly whites, check out the professional teeth-whitening kit that's available, too.

⭐ clinique.com
Clinique
877-311-3883
E-mail form on site

Cosmetics • Hair • Skin Care

Clinique online shoppers have all the benefits of the department store cosmetic counter and one more. Called Club Clinique, the free membership offers loyal customers the following benefits: exclusive shopping offers, a record of past purchases, fast checkout, new product information, the ability to buy new products early, and personalized tips from Clinique's beauty experts. Plus, Club Clinique members receive e-mail alerts about Bonus Time and Special Events at local retailers. Sign up for the free membership and order your favorite Clinique products at the site.

 Recommended   Price   Selection   Convenience   Service   Security

colortration.com
Primary Color Foundations Ltd.

888-350-4505
info@colortration.com

Cosmetics • Skin Care

Have a scar or skin condition you want to cover? How about a tattoo? ColorTration waterproof foundation can help. The foundation is great for people with scars and skin conditions like vitiligo and rosacea. If you've recently had cosmetic surgery, laser treatment, or dermabrasion, you can camouflage and correct the redness and bruising with ColorTration. Under-eye circles? ColorTration's amazing covering power will astound you if you're currently using corrective makeup, concealer, or cover makeup. ColorTration is incredibly thin and totally opaque. It comes in pump bottles. See a demonstration of this cosmetic, and buy your own at the site.

condomdepot.com
Condom Depot

800-675-4286
kfidi@condomdepot.com

Sex

I'll give you one guess as to what the Condom Depot site sells! Yep, condoms, and you can buy them in small packages, 100-pack samplers, or in bulk. Make yourself a household name with an order of custom-printed condoms (250 minimum). Base your condom selection on personal preference or read through the selection of Condom Reviews from various men's magazines before you decide. Shop by brand or style. If you're the type who blushes easily, you may want to shop at this site when you're alone.

contactsamerica.com
Contacts America

877-243-8536
orders@123eyecare.com

Eyewear

Do you think the contact lens is a modern device? Not so. It's actually based on a 500-year-old inspiration of Leonardo da Vinci's. Now you can order contact lenses online at guaranteed low prices — as much as 70 percent off — from well-known manufacturers of contact lenses such as Johnson & Johnson, Cooper Vision, Ocular Sciences, CIBA Vision, Wesley Jessen, and Bausch & Lomb. You can buy all types of contacts, too, including disposable, colored, bifocal, toric, vial, and even novelty contacts. You'll need to provide a valid prescription to complete your order.

⭐ coppertone.com

Coppertone.com

901-320-2998
info@spcorp.com

Bath and Body • Healthy Living • Skin Care

What's your sun IQ? Before you buy any of the sunscreens or tanning products at the Coppertone.com site, take the quiz offered by the makers of this classic sun protection. After you've determined what you know, you'll be in a better position to decide which of the excellent products available at the site is right for you. Sunscreen should be a part of your daily skin-care regimen. If you're traveling, find out the strength of the sun at your destination with the handy UV Indicator located at the site. Watch the latest Coppertone TV ads at the site. Be sure to include "www" to access this site.

cowgirlenterprises.com

Cowgirl Skin Care

888-440-7549
info@cowgirlenterprises.com

Cosmetics • Skin Care

Yee-haw! Finally a site for the hardworking cowgirl (and those with the cowgirl spark). Do you herd horses, climb mountains, work on your garden, or simply handle the daily grind with a "can do" spirit? Well, then the Cowgirl Skincare line of creams, lip balms, and cleansing bars is for you. Hands or feet in need of moisturizing? Check out the Cowgirl Cream or the more intense Ranch Hand Cream for chapped and cracked skin. After a long day on the trail (or on the job), massage away your minor aches and pains with the Trail Boss Bar. Happy trails, ladies!

cuttinghair.com

The Haircutting School

No phone number listed
lynnsymonds@webryders.net

Hair

Before you visit The Haircutting School site, get a calculator and figure out how much you've spent on haircuts in the past year. Scary, isn't it? Now, take a look at The Hair Cutting School. For a scant amount, probably less than what you pay for one haircut at a salon, you can learn how to cut hair at home. You're actually buying a learn-at-home course that teaches the six basic haircuts from which all hairstyles are taken. You also receive professional scissors. Although the course has no official final exam, your handiwork will declare your grade to the eyes of the world.

 Recommended   Price   Selection   Convenience   Service   Security

cvs.com
CVS.com

888-607-4287
E-mail form on site

Bath and Body • Cosmetics • Hair • Healthy Living • Pharmacy • Sex • Skin Care • Teeth • Vitamins and Supplements • Weight Loss

There's so much to do and see at the CVS.com site that you'll swear you're shopping in a bricks-and-mortar CVS store. The online CVS is arranged by categories, cleverly called aisles. Browse the aisles and find the products you need. You'll find the usual mix of non-prescription medication, health and beauty aids, sexual health, personal care items, and more. There's even an aisle for Occasions and Gifts, where you can buy candy and snacks, batteries, and all those nifty gadgets advertised on TV. Drop by the Pharmacy Counter to order refills on prescription medicine and check drug prices.

dentalsourcenetwork.com
Dental Source Network

800-574-2143
E-mail form on site

Teeth

An oral workout set for your mouth is a novel idea, but it sure makes good sense! After all, fitness shouldn't stop at your neck. Each set contains a toothbrush, toothpaste, flossing appliance, and other related dental health "goodies." The sets come in various price ranges and sizes. The contents have been well thought out; for example, the X-Small set, suitable for a child, contains a three-minute timer to ensure that the teeth-cleaning process lasts longer than a swipe and a rinse. Each set is attractively packaged and makes a unique gift.

drbrandtskincare.com
Dr. Brandt

800-234-1066
E-mail form on site

Skin Care

Dr. Fredric Brandt has offices in Miami and New York and claims he is "the largest user of injectable collagen and botox in the world." He's also a clinical professor of Dermatology at the University of Miami and "a pioneer of the neck-lift." His services are in high demand and so are all his products, which are conveniently for sale on this site. Top sellers include "Lineless," an anti-oxidant, anti-aging formula and "Poreless," for treating problem skin and refining enlarged pores. Let Dr. Brandt bring out the beauty in you.

drleonards.com
Dr. Leonard's Healthcare

800-785-0880
E-mail form on site

Pharmacy • Sex • Teeth • Vitamins and Supplements • Weight Loss

Plan to linger over the massive online catalog available at this site. Dr. Leonard sells something for everyone. With over 25 entries listed under Sexual Care in Dr. Leonard's Healthcare catalog, you're sure to find the cure for whatever ails you in that usually unmentionable department. The site offers a great assortment of gels, tools, and videos to get men and women moving in the right direction sexually. Don't be put off by the fact that the catalog also offers shoes, folding canes, incontinence aids, and more. After all, this company is "America's Leading Discount Healthcare Catalog." There's even a section of Home Furnishings products that includes the incomparable Scrub 'N Flush toilet bowl cleaner.

⭐ drugstore.com
Drugstore.com

800-378-4786
aboutorders@drugstore.com

Bath and Body • Cosmetics • Hair • Healthy Living • Pharmacy • Sex • Skin Care • Teeth • Vitamins and Supplements

Drugstore.com is a department store, pharmacy, and library combined into one giant megasite. It carries just about every health and beauty aid you can think of, and the stock keeps on expanding. Drugstore.com even carries products for pets as well as for humans! Browse through categories like Medicine Cabinet, Sexual Well-Being, Personal Care, Natural Store, and more, or click directly to the Pharmacy and fill your prescription. The pharmacy accepts many insurance plans; you can check to see whether your plan is listed before you order your drugs. Don't skip the Sale section. Bargains and manufacturer's closeouts are often the best deals in town.

⭐ dudleyq.com
Dudley's

336-993-8800
E-mail form on site

Hair • Skin Care

Need a curl activator and moisturizer, pomade, or hair oil? Visit the World of Dudley! Many other hair care products are available at this site, including shampoos, conditioners, and various finishing agents. You can even buy a package of products designed specifically for your hair type. Cosmetics, hair care, and skin care products are also available. Before you shop for the first time you'll need to register and provide personal information. Dudley's operates several beauty schools and cosmetology universities throughout the United States. Learn more about this company's educational programs while you're visiting its site.

ebubbles.com
eBubbles

888-403-8701
customercare@ebubbles.com

Bath and Body • Skin Care

Want access to the best in bath and body products from around the world without having to leave your seat or spend time visiting individual Web sites? Then eBubbles is for you. This site is your one-stop shop for all your pampering product needs. You can shop easily by product to find lotions, foot and hand care, facial products, hair care, spa treatments, lip care, masks, muds, powders, and scrubs. Or shop by a list of top brands including Aquis, Cucina, Evian, I Coloniali, Inis, Roger & Gallet, Terra Nova, and many more.

eCondoms.com
econdoms.com

800-960-7797
info@health4her.com

Sex

You have to be 18 or over to enter eCondoms.com, which is the first indication that the merchandise is sexually oriented. But, hey, you knew that, because the name is a dead giveaway to what's sold here. The condom selection includes all the familiar brands and styles. Need help making a decision? Click "Ask the Condom Concierge" for some expert assistance. While you're visiting, why not check out the Bath and Body and Kama Sutra sections for a few extra products, or purchase a video or DVD. Check out the Top 10 products for a few new ideas.

⭐ edentalstuff.com
eDentalstuff.com
620-842-5567
contact@edentalstuff.com
Pharmacy • Teeth

You'll find the professional products used by your dentist at eDentalstuff. com. Actually, the site is more than just a place to buy great products. Visit eDentalstuff.com for reliable, unbiased information about dental health. The site's extensive libraries cover both conventional dental care and alternative care information. Knowledge is power, and you'll have the tools you need to make the best choices about your dental care. And, of course, you'll know what you need to buy to keep your teeth in good working order. Everything you need from breath fresheners to orthodontic accessories is available at this site.

ej-sunglasses.com
EJ's Sunglasses
800-714-9229
sunglasses@ej-sunglasses.com
Eyewear

You won't find discounts on sunglasses at EJ's Sunglasses but you will find an extravagant selection. EJ's Sunglasses carries over 70 popular brands of sunglasses and goggles such as Nike, Oakley, and Porsche Design to name just a few. These are the same sunglasses and goggles you would find in a typical retail outlet. Although EJ's offers the same prices (upwards of $150 for some) as a retail store, it brings the glasses to you with a higher level of service — a 30-day satisfaction guarantee.

endslip.com
Endslip
978-477-6397
info@durasolcorp.com
Teeth

If you don't wear dentures, move on by. You've never dealt with slipping, sliding false teeth. However, if you're one of the millions of people who wear dentures, Endslip merits some attention. The product, which comes with a 100 percent satisfaction guarantee, is designed to hold false teeth in place. Before you scoff, understand that it's made by Durasol, which also makes a concrete additive. Endslip provides a superior hold without sticky pastes or messy powders, and that won't wash away on contact with hot or cold drinks and foods. Buy some now, and save yourself some grief later.

 Recommended   Price   Selection   Convenience   Service   Security

esteelauder.com
Estée Lauder

877-311-3883
E-mail form on site

Cosmetics • Hair • Skin Care

The fragrance called Youth Dew made this superlative cosmetics and skin care company a household name back in 1953. Its products available in many fine department stores, Estée Lauder has a reputation for excellence. Shop at this site for skin care products, including the famous ReNutriv group. Estée Lauder's tanning products protect your skin any time of the year, and sunless tanners are a great way to add color. The makeup line is unparalleled for purity. You'll find everything you need to look and feel beautiful. You can also create a skin profile at the site and sign up to receive an e-mail newsletter.

eyeeco.com
eyeeco

800-574-2143
E-mail form on site

Pharmacy

Dry eyes are a problem for millions of people. The problem is caused by a myriad of reasons — LASIK surgery, contact lens use, computer use, allergies, medications, and normal aging. A product available at this site can help. Called "tranquileyes," it increases humidity around the eye and prevents the evaporation of natural tears. Each pair of tranquileyes features a sculpted eye cover lined with special foam. Purchase a tranquileyes starter kit, which contains the cover, instruction manual, two pair of foam replacement sets, container, and more. Or purchase a single, which provides a pair of tranquileyes, instruction manual, and container.

★ folica.com
Folica

888-919-4247
cs@folica.com

Hair • Skin Care

Folica.com is a superstore for hair. The site carries salon hair care products at reduced prices and a full line of professional quality hair-styling tools. If you need help choosing products, a customer service representative can help during business hours. Need a new hairstyle? Information at the site is available. Folica.com also carries skin care, cosmetics, and depilatory products. A big undertaking, yes, but this company manages to pull it off with style and grace.

★ framesdirect.com
FramesDirect.com

800-248-9427
E-mail form on site

Eyewear

I like FramesDirect.com for a multitude of reasons, some of those being 115,000 different frames available for purchase, over 65,000 models of eyeglasses to choose from, and finding and researching the best size and color options is easy. You can shop your brand of sunglasses, clip-ons, contact lenses, or designer frames using the drop-down search menus. Finally, you can fill your RX in the latest thin-lens technology at about 50 percent off retail. And you can call FramesDirect.com's expert doctors and opticians for selection advice. Service and selection make FramesDirect.com a winner.

genericvitamins.com
GenericVitamins

No phone number listed
affiliate_support@genericvitamins.com

Pharmacy • Vitamins and Supplements

Why pay one penny more than you need to for your nutritional supplements? GenericVitamins offers the same supplements found elsewhere, but at substantially lower prices. Of course, you won't see a lot of flash and dash at the site. Select your product from the Products list or check the Specials to see what's been marked down. Many packages offer a volume discount so you may want to get a group together and put in a bulk order.

gophysical.com
Mio

877-566-4636
E-mail form on site

Healthy Living • Weight Loss

Gophysical.com offers a handy gadget called a MioShape that's worn like a watch but does so much more than tell time. MioShape is a heart monitor that accurately measures your heart rate with patented sensors that work by finger touch (most other heart monitors use a chest strap). During your workout, touch the MioShape face and, presto, your heart rate and the number of calories burned are displayed. You also get a pocket-sized, sensible guide to healthy living called MioSense when you order.

 Recommended   Price   Selection   Convenience   Service   Security

greatshades.com
GreatShades.com

847-290-1691
rlidbury@greatshades.net

Eyewear

The sunglasses offered by GreatShades.com you can't buy at the mall — only factory-direct from this site. This company claims that its sunglasses are fitted with the clearest polarized lenses on earth (100 percent UV protection). But don't take the company's word for it — read the testimonials on the site. As to be expected from an exclusive retailer, the sunglasses are pricey, some just under $100, but you can buy a GreatShades T-shirt for just 25 cents.

hair2000online.com
Hair2000Online.com

No phone number listed
summer@hair2000online.com

Hair • Skin Care

Yes, the year 2000 has come and gone. But Hair2000.com is still very much a part of the Internet scene. Shop at this site for Redken hair care products that will give you the look that is popular now. Want to add streaks or full color to your hair? Several kits are available. Order appliances and rollers to give your hair height and body. Skin care products are sold at the site as well, including microwavable bleach for facial hair. You can even enter information about your hair and a stylist will analyze your input and recommend color and other products. Get today's look at Hair2000.com.

⭐ hairboutique.com
HairBoutique.com

866-469-4247
customercare@hairboutique.com

Cosmetics • Hair Care • Skin Care

Don't be deceived by the name of this great site. Sure, you'll find a great collection of shampoos, conditioners, and other products for your hair. The brands sold at the site are natural and good for your hair. Best of all, you'll be able to find them easily, because HairBoutique.com has thoughtfully arranged them so many ways. Find them by brand, category, or shampoo type, or use the site Search feature. HairBoutique.com stocks natural skin care products and bath and body products, too. A great selection of gifts is also available. Be sure to take advantage of the free shipping on large orders.

haircountry.com
Haircountry.com
800-720-1303
E-mail form on site
Hair

Don't let your hair desert you without putting up a good fight. Haircountry.com sells products that work to combat hair loss. Buy shampoos, conditioners, thickeners, and sprays that are good for the hair and give it the illusion of looking fuller. Want to know what other customers think about a particular product? Log in to the Hair Loss Forum and read the comments of others. The FAQs of Hair Loss will tell you everything you need to know to preserve your hair. If all else fails, click the Find a Doctor button. You may win a prize and get a hair replacement doc in the bargain.

health4her.com
HEALTH4HER.com
800-960-7797
info@health4her.com
Pharmacy • Sex • Vitamins and Supplements

Women will love this excellent site. Health4her.com is filled with reliable information about female health and emotional issues. The Health Library contains informative articles about key issues for women of all ages, and you can search for articles that interest you. You can buy products to relieve menopausal or PMS symptoms or to help you sleep. The site also offers a collection of nutritional products just for women. What a deal! A site for women that really delivers what it promises.

healthydeal.com
HealthyDeal.com
630-922-1137
assistu@healthydeal.com
Healthy Living • Sex • Teeth • Vitamins and Supplements

A hodgepodge of health supplies awaits you at HealthyDeal.com. The site has the look and feel of a dusty surgical supply store in a rundown part of town. Don't be deceived by the somewhat old-fashioned interface, because a dizzying array of merchandise is available at this site. You'll find blood pressure monitors, dental care, cholesterol testing supplies, fitness equipment, HIV test kits, and much more. One section is devoted to Fertility and Family Planning. If you can't find what you need, use the site's Search function. Most times, free or reduced cost shipping is thrown in as an incentive for you to buy more.

 Recommended   Price   Selection   Convenience   Service   Security

healthyenvironments.com
Healthy Environments

800-511-7732
customerservice@healthye.com

Healthy Living

The environment around you affects how you live, work, and play. So, how clean and safe is your environment? If you're like most people, the answer to that question isn't very positive. Click on over to Healthy Environments to purchase the products that will improve your space, and make you a healthier, happier person. Choose one of the air cleaners or filters at the site to purify the air you breathe. Allersoft bedding and 100-percent cotton pillows will have you sleeping like a baby. Eyes sore and irritated? Natural lighting will improve both your vision and your mood. Visit the Library section for some interesting reading.

★ lifizz.com
LiFizz

561-745-0008
info@lifizz.com

Vitamins and Supplements

The great golfer Jesper Parnevik has developed his own line of great-tasting vitamins and supplements. Called LiFizz, they are dropped into water and drunk as a beverage. The reasoning behind LiFizz is sound: Many times conventional vitamin tablets are passed through the intestinal tract before they can be absorbed by the body. LiFizz are different. Your body reaps the entire benefit they offer. Read about these amazing tablets and order them at the site. Join Jesper's LiFizz Club for convenient reorder options and a discount.

liquidmultivitaminsupplement.com
One Source Liquid Vitamin

800-267-5273
E-mail form on site

Vitamins and Supplements

Tired of vitamin pills that are hard to get down? How about a liquid multivitamin instead? One Source Liquid Vitamin offers an absorbable multivitamin that contains more than 80 vitamins, minerals, and other essential nutrients. The vitamins are affordable, because the manufacturer's only business is making and selling vitamins. This company is so sure you'll love vitamins in liquid form that it's offering a 60-day money-back guarantee on every bottle of One Source Liquid Vitamin that it ships. Why not swallow your objections (if you have any) and give the liquid vitamins a try?

losingweight.com
LosingWeight.com

No phone number listed
info@losingweight.com

Healthy Living •Weight Loss

LosingWeight.com combines products and information into a great site for those trying to drop some weight. You'll need to join the program before you can participate fully. If you're a first-timer or you're just not sure if Losing Weight.com is for you, take a tour of the site and see what the program has to offer. If you join, you'll receive personalized meal plans and feedback on your progress, plus great information on diet, nutrition, and fitness. You'll also find a warm and caring community of fellow dieters. Shop at the site for exercise and fitness aids, such as jump ropes, hand grips, and resistance bands.

medichest.com
medichest.com

203-854-0606
E-mail form on site

Bath and Body • Hair • Healthy Living • Skin Care

Remember Merthiolate? That red antiseptic burned like fire but cured skinned knees in a hurry. How about Calmol or Dippity Do? You'll find these and other "brands you grew up with" at medichest.com, "your online drugstore and more." You'll also find health and beauty aids in hard-to-locate brands at this site, such as Lavoris, Kleenite, and Gentian Violet. Mix and match your order with more contemporary products; medichest stocks 32,000 products every day. International shipping is available.

mothernature.com
Mother Nature

800-439-5506
productinfo@mothernature.com

Healthy Living

With over 8,000 natural products and 1,000 organic health and beauty aids, every day is Earth Day at MotherNature.com. Since 1995, the site has been committed to providing consumers with great service, low prices, and a super collection of natural, organic, and healthy living products. Shop by department or brand or use the well-designed Search feature to zero in on the items you want. Sign up for the MotherNature.com e-mail newsletter for weekly health news, sale announcements, and wallet-friendly coupons. The site stands behinds its products and offers a liberal return policy.

 Recommended   Price   Selection   Convenience   Service   Security

⭐ mypetfat.com
mypetfat
908-534-1348
comments@mypetfat.com
Weight Loss

At first glance, it's weird. Why would you want to walk around with a one-ounce lump of squishy fake fat in your pocket or purse? Sure, mypetfat is disgusting. That's the point. The noxious lump is representative of what's under your skin and around your organs. Armed with that vision, you can decide whether you really need a big muffin or extra helping of mashed spuds. Mypetfat's creator claims the lump of goo helped him lose 115 pounds. If conventional diets have failed you, order your own mypetfat at the site. What do you have to lose?

nads.com
Nad's
800-653-9797
E-mail form on site
Pharmacy • Skin Care

The tale and the product have made the rounds on late-night television for a few years, but buy it at nads.com instead. The story goes like this: An Australian mother developed a product to (somewhat) painlessly remove excess hair from the body of her otherwise beautiful seventeen-year-old daughter. The product became Nad's and went on to become a million-dollar seller. All the Nad's products are available at the site, from a complete hair removal kit to a Kiwi-Chamomile Smoothing Lotion. Most products include "buy one, get one free" offers.

natlallergy.com
National Allergy Supply
800-522-1448
E-mail form on site
Healthy Living • Skin Care

Dust, pollen, cats, perfume — they can make your eyes water and your nose run. Operating on a principle called "Allergen Avoidance through Environmental Control," National Allergy Supply sells products that tame your allergies. Even if you're taking allergy medication, the special bedding, covers, and cleaners available at this site will give your immune system a boost. A whole section is devoted to keeping down pet and animal dander. Asthma sufferers will enjoy the special relief section just for them. You can even buy bath and body and skin care products without chemicals and perfumes.

naturopathica.com
Naturopathica

800-792-7995
service@naturopathica.com

Healthy Living

Any site that claims "We are a destination point for embracing the pure essentials of well being," is a place that bears a visit. Frankly, unless you're already familiar with the homeopathic way of thinking, you may find some of the explanations hard to understand (I did). However, the products speak for themselves. There's a line of skin care and body care that's absolutely delicious. The selection of Bath Water Cures, actually water treatments with plant extracts, are designed to detox, rest, or renew the body. If those don't cure what ails ye', go for one of the more intense Get Well cures.

nomoregray.com
Youthair

877-566-4636
No e-mail address on site

Hair

Men, this one's for you. If your hair is going gray, but you don't want to color it, you may want to consider the product sold at this site. Called Youthair, this hair color rejuvenator and hair conditioning treatment is designed to blend away gray and restore your natural color on a gradual basis. Youthair is on the level — it's made by the same folks who make the A.I.I. Clubman hair care product line. Buy Youthair in either liquid or crème form and apply it directly to your graying hair. Now wait and see what happens! The science behind the amazing transformation is available at the site.

nutrisystem.com
Nutrisystem

800-585-5483
info@nutrisystem.com

Weight Loss

Nutrisystem has been helping people lose weight for 30 years. The program couldn't be easier — or more private. Sign up at the site, select a meal plan, and then order your food online for the next week. Choose from a preselected meal plan or pick from 28 breakfast, lunch, dinner, and snack items. The food is both delicious and nutritious and gives you a perfect portion size at every meal. Nutrisystem's online and phone counselors are available to help you with questions or when you need support. An exercise program is also included.

 Recommended   Price Selection   Convenience Service Security

nycos.com
New York Cosmetics

800-537-5301
susan@nycos.com

Cosmetics • Skin Care

Direct from the Big Apple, New York Cosmetics sells makeup to pharmacies and stores all over the United States. (Check the store locator for a store near you.) The cosmetics at its site are designed to take the rigors of New York City, like humid subway rides and extreme hot and cold temperatures and conditions. Check out the matte eye shadows in a variety of colors and the soft foundations and loose powder that provide coverage all day long. The cosmetics are typically hypoallergenic and non-animal tested. A collection of helpful Hot Tips will help keep you looking fresh for hours.

panamajack.com
Panama Jack

800-932-2431
info@ panamajack.com

Bath and Body • Healthy Living • Skin Care

Visit Panama Jack, that rakish fellow in the hat and monocle, for sun protection. The suncare line includes sunscreens and sunblocks at various SPFs. For less protection, check out the oils and bronzers. Fool everyone with a sunless tanner purchased from this site. Read the Sun Survival Guide before you purchase your sun care product. Don't forget eyeware — Panama Jack offers distinctive sunglasses in several styles and lens colors. You'll also find clothing (Panama Jack T-shirts and board shorts) and accessories (woven handbags, sea shell jewelry, and more). Need a taste of the islands? Panama Jack has its own brand of rum! You'll need to specify your location and birth date to view the alcoholic spirits.

paulayoung.com
Paula Young

800-472-4017
E-mail form on site

Hair

Turn to Paula Young for wigs. For more than 20 years, Paula Young wigs have been worn with confidence. Find your wig in a number of different ways. Select a wig made of human hair or monofilament material. Or you can select your wig by length, style, color, or brand. Have fun and consider changing your look! Read the return policy before you buy if you're not sure about keeping the wig you selected.

⭐ pennyisland.com
Penny Island
800-856-1196
info@pennyisland.com
Bath and Body • Hair Care • Skin Care

Sum up Penny Island in one word? That's easy — OATS! Who knew that besides being a good breakfast, oats are also good for your skin? They can help reduce sun damage and enhance production of collagen and skin cell renewal. The folks at Penny Island are here to "heal, strengthen, and soothe" your sensitive skin with its exclusive Oat-Amino Complex. Treat the rest of your body to oat therapy body lotions, oat body wash and shower gels, and oat bath powder.

plackers.com
Plackers.com
877-752-2537
info@plackers.com
Teeth

The dancing flossing aids on the opening page of the Plackers.com site belie the importance of the tiny product sold inside. Called Plackers, the individual flossers use Tuffloss, a patented dental floss product that's stronger than most dental floss on the market. Each Placker is small enough to fit conveniently in a pocket or purse, but is worth its weight in gold when cleaning your teeth and gums. Plackers are sold in different sizes and shapes. Visit the site to determine which one will work best for you and order a pack of Plackers today, and then "Get Flossed."

randolphusa.com
Randolph Engineering
800-541-1405
customerservice@randolphusa.com
Eyewear

As soon as you arrive at this online store, you know they're serious about sunglasses. If you're a Top Gun pilot or just want to look like one, then this is the place to buy your sunglasses. Reasonably priced hi-tech eyewear — sunglasses, ballistic eyewear, and clip-ons — is their niche. The Randolph Aviator, one of the company's premier products, is constructed to exact military standards and is standard issue for U.S. military pilots and NASA astronauts. The products at this site carry a lifetime warranty for solder joint failures, and a one-year warranty on other parts and labor. There is no warranty on lenses.

 Recommended   Price   Selection   Convenience   😊 Service   🔒 Security

reflect.com
Reflect
800-243-2288
service@reflect.com
Cosmetics • Skin Care

Let your essence shine through — with a little help from Reflect products. Instead of pulling your order off a warehouse shelf, Reflect creates each item specifically for you. Whether it's makeup, skin care, hair care, or fragrance, Reflect manufactures each product individually. You begin the process by filling out a detailed questionnaire. Reflect analyzes your answers and creates the perfect formulas. You choose both the names for your finished products and their packaging. Just sit back, and in about ten days, you'll be able to wow your friends and co-workers with your very own line.

richardsimmons.com
Richard Simmons
800-516-7106
E-mail form on site
Weight Loss

His squeaky voice, tank top, shorts, and mop of curly hair have made him a diet icon. Richard Simmons is still a giant among weight-loss gurus in America. Visit him online for the same blend of enthusiasm and optimism that has inspired legions of overweight people. Buy the Slimaway Everyday Package for a complete bundle of products Richard feels you need to take off those unwanted pounds. Or pick and choose from videos, CDs, cookbooks, and vitamins. While you're shopping, read the motivational success stories of folks just like you and chat online with others trying to lose weight.

sacrowedgy.com
Sacrowedgy.com
800-737-9295
sales@sacrowedgy.com
Healthy Living

Does your back hurt? Have you tried all kinds of treatments to stop the pain, but nothing's really helped? Well, this site offers a simple tool called a Sacro Wedgy that may be worth a try. It doesn't promise instant results, but the developers say, "The Sacro Wedgy is a "tool" to use and like any "tool," you will get out of it what you put into it." They claim that this product helps back pain in the lower region for athletes and those who suffer from diseases like fibromyalgia. Check it out and read the testimonials of satisfied customers at the site.

saltcitybathandbody.com
Salt City Bath & Body

866-858-7451
sales@saltcitybathandbody.com

Bath and Body • Skin Care

Scents rule at Salt City Bath & Body. Take your pick of bath gels, lotions, and candles with scents of apple essence, autumn blaze, fruit slices, iced pineapple, lilac and fruit, perfectly pear, secret garden, mulberry, watermelon, winter berry frost, sunflower, vanilla crème, orange passion, or holly berry. Sign up to be notified about the Lotion of the Month by e-mail. Who knows? Perhaps a new delicious scent will join the collection, making it even harder to decide. Send a gift basket from this site and make someone's day.

saveondurex.com
SaveOnDurex.com

No phone number listed
E-mail form on site

Sex

In a world where everything gets progressively more expensive, you can still get some good value for your money at SaveOnDurex.com. This company claims its prices on Durex condoms are the lowest anywhere. If you're in the market (and in the mood) this easy-to-navigate site will have you in the checkout in no time. The handy Condom Selector can help you figure out which type to buy. Shipping is fast and all packages arrive in nondescript packages bearing the return address of "Green Web Properties." Repeat customers get 10 percent off the already low prices.

saveyoursmile.com
SaveYourSmile.com

888-891-5345
customers@saveyoursmile.com

Teeth

Keep your smile gleaming with products from SaveYourSmile.com. Just about every style of toothbrush you can imagine is for sale at this site, along with high-tech flossing appliances. Is your bad breath a problem? It won't be anymore, with a little help from one of the many solutions available at the site. There's even a kid's section, so you can start your children on the road to good oral hygiene with age-appropriate brushes and toothpaste. The 100 percent satisfaction guarantee makes it easy to try new products. If you're unhappy with your purchase within 90 days, SaveYourSmile.com promises to refund your money. Now that's something to smile about!

 Recommended   Price   Selection   Convenience   Service   Security

sephora.com
Sephora

877-737-4672
E-mail form on site

Bath and Body • Cosmetics • Skin Care

Sephora's signature red carpet is familiar to millions of women who turn to the giant retailer's skin care products and cosmetics. The online store is even bigger than the retail outlet; it offers thousands of products and hundreds of brands. Take some time before you zero in on a selection. Read about the latest beauty trends, get advice and tips from the experts, or learn more about a brand at a Brand Boutique. If you're a follower of trends, see what others are buying in the Top Sellers. Sign up for samples for the products you want to try. They're free!

sheld.com
Sheldon Marketing

800-887-9130
No e-mail address on site

Healthy Living • Pharmacy • Sex • Skin Care • Weight Loss

Have you ever seen one of those late-night infomercials hawking all types of cure-alls? Well, this site is the Internet version. You won't find a stylish layout or even a warm welcome. Instead, this company cuts right to the chase, pushing a plethora of products. You can find everything from an anti-wrinkle stretch mark remover to a carb eliminator that allows you to "cheat and eat." Want premium coral calcium and trace minerals from Okinawa, Japan? Look no further. Whether you want to reduce pain with the "Herbal Hemorr-EAZE" or increase pleasure with the "Kokoro Women's Pleasure Cream," this site offers something for everyone.

shophomehealth.com
ShopHomeHealth.com

800-231-4276
customerservice@shophomehealth.com

Healthy Living • Pharmacy • Vitamins and Supplements

"The dilemma of finding home healthcare products can be frustrating," say the folks at ShopHomeHealth.com. They've put together this site to make it easier for folks like you and me to find what we need. Now, with a few clicks, finding durable medical equipment (bed rails, wheelchairs, toilet seats) in the same location as, say, acetaminophen tablets, is easy. In between are first aid supplies, linens, syringes, everything you would ever need for incontinence, ostomy supplies, and much more.

skinwisdom.com
Skin Wisdom
888-313-7546
orders@skinwisdom.com
Skin Care

If you want to combat aging, doesn't it make more sense to seal in the good instead of exfoliating the bad? This brainstorm is actually the backbone of the program created by the folks at Skin Wisdom. They've created an aloe-based skin care line that aims to accelerate skin repair by rejuvenating it, instead of using alpha-hydroxy, beta-hydroxy, and other acids to artificially exfoliate it. Skin Wisdom products contain natural ingredients like vitamin E, an antioxidant, and vitamin A that help reduce brown spots. The products are also 100 percent fragrance- and cruelty-free. Put "old" on hold with Skin Wisdom.

sneeze.com
sneeze.com
800-469-6673
info@sneeze.com
Healthy Living

Ah-CHOO! Allergies. You know the feeling . . . the tickling in your nose, the itchy eyes, the scratchy throat. Wouldn't it be great to control allergy symptoms before you needed hankies and antihistamines? Sneeze.com offers products to do just that. Shop here for air purification, filter masks, bedding and encasements, HEPA vacuum cleaners, and pure laundry and cleaning aids. Look at the section for children's bedding and toys; you'll rest easier when your kids are sleeping comfortably. After shopping at this site, you may be able to just throw away those wadded-up tissues in your pocket or purse.

spacadet.com
Spacadet.com
888-868-5477
kissjill@aol.com
Cosmetics • Hair • Skin Care

Fun and flighty! What else could you expect from Spacadet.com, packed to the gills with cosmetics, hair care products, skin care products, and other good stuff for the under-30 set. Under all the cutesy is a bit of honesty as Spacadet mentions "Colors shown on this Web site may not represent the actual color of the product or product content." Don't say you haven't been warned when you check out all the luscious lipsticks and eye shadows, foundations and powders, and other great makeup items. Earn the title of "spacejunkie" when you sign up for the site's free mailing list.

 Recommended   Price   Selection   Convenience   Service   Security

splashbathandbody.com
Splash Bath and Body

877-664-7627
splashbath@aol.com

Bath and Body • Skin Care

Bright lime and blue tones welcome you to the Splash Bath and Body site, which features fresh, handmade body products that are hip and fun. Rest assured "these are not your grandmother's soaps." You'll also find bath salts, body mists, candles, facial products, hair care products, lotions, massage oils, salt scrubs, shower gels, and bubble baths. The site even carries adorable animal scrubbie bath toys for the kids (or the kids in all of us). Don't forget your Daddy-O. Fix him up with Big Daddy Shaving Gel and Cool Daddy After Shave Lotion. Now, splish, splash, you can both take a bath.

⭐ store.yahoo.com/ghp
Healthy Legs

888-495-0105
art@healthylegs.com

Pharmacy

At the Healthy Legs site, you can find socks with a purpose! Sometimes, some of us need more than just a pair of socks. The goal of Healthy Legs is to meet that need. This company sells socks for support and for sensitive feet as well as socks for people with diabetes, arthritis, and foot pain. You can find socks for tired, aching legs; swollen legs, ankles, and feet; varicose veins; and socks for preventing foot injuries. If you have a problem with your feet or legs, the site also provides a nice reference set of links where you can educate yourself on leg and foot health.

tanita.bz
Tanita

718-336-5900
sales@tanita.bz

Healthy Living • Weight Loss

Tanita is the world leader in precision electronic scales. This company's scales blend accuracy with sleek, good looks. Several models of baby scales are available. Food and kitchen scales aren't just for chefs anymore; order one for accurate measurements in recipes and food consumption. A body fat scale is essential if you're on a weight loss or fitness program. Because the scale measures both weight and percentage of body fat, you'll know exactly how close you are to goal. Fortunately, most scales are in stock, so your order will be at your door in a few days. The site ships internationally.

travmed.com
Travel Medicine

800-872-8633
travmed@travmed.com

Pharmacy

It's a rough world for travelers. Bugs, both the insect and illness-causing variety, wait to bite. Electrical appliances and phones that work in one location often don't work a short distance away. Unforeseen occurrences can turn your trip into a nightmare. Should you stay home? Of course not! If Travel Medicine is your first destination, your trip is on the road to success. This site carries a full range of travel-related products, including insect repellants, security wallets, electrical and phone adapters, medical kits, and more. Worried about disease? Check the World Health Guide at the site before you leave home.

trimspa.com
Trimspa

800-467-3041
E-mail form on site

Weight Loss

Lots of celebrities are selling Trimspa these days and, judging from their results, the product has an effect on the war on weight. Whether you'll have the same results as, say Anna Nicole Smith, is debatable. But if you're looking for a diet aid to help you fight flab, check out the products available at this site. Trimspa comes in a few different versions, and you can even buy tasty snack bars. Read the testimonials of the other dieters at the site and make an informed decision as to whether the product is for you.

tuffbetty.com
TuffBetty Soap

503-781-9624
info@tuffbetty.com

Bath and Body • Skin Care

Two quirky sisters in Portland, Oregon, teamed up to create TuffBetty soap. The soaps this company sells are glorious. Choose from "flavors" like Coconut Almond, Lavender, and Eucalyptus and Orange. Each bar is made from natural fat and oils and is designed to cleanse your skin without drying it. If you're the outdoorsy type, you'll love the Camper Veggie Bar, made with a few drops of pure citronella oil. Don't miss the small collection of personal products. Soaps here are under $5 per bar and the rest of the collection is reasonably priced.

 Recommended   Price   Selection   Convenience   Service Security

urbandecay.com
Urban Decay

954-986-7522
onlineorders@urbandecay.com

Cosmetics

It's hip and happening. Makeup from Urban Decay will set you apart from the lemmings you know, who wear whatever fashion dictates and don't experiment with individual looks. Eye shadows in colors like Gash (dark metallic red), Shattered (bright, iridescent aquamarine), and Vert (shimmering, vibrant jade) are designed to shock. If you aren't ready for the cutting edge, Urban Decay has some "normal" shades as well. Use Urban Decay products to create an elegant or punk look. With such a wide range of colors and choices, you can create a new look whenever you desire.

★ usa.aloette.com
Aloette

800-253-3773
support@aloette.com

Cosmetics • Skin Care

A couple drops of aloe will soothe burned skin. Take its healing power a few steps further, and you have the Aloette line of cosmetics and skin care products. Actually, it makes good sense. The aloe vera plant contains a bounty of nutrients. All the products sold at this site are pure and good for your skin. Luxuriate in the shower or bath with the Aloespa line. The Aloepure Skin Care line features anti-aging, cleansing, and toning items. After you've prepared your skin, check out the full range of cosmetics available. Consider starting with a Value Package if you're new to the line.

usfloss.com
US Floss

620-842-5567
No e-mail address on site

Teeth

Let's get personal for a second. Do you floss your teeth after every meal? Tell the truth. If you're like most folks, the answer is no. Don't be ashamed — hey, it's understandable. Dental floss is cumbersome and awkward to use in a public restroom. A simple product can change all that. Called Quik Floss, it effectively removes plaque from between your teeth, and reduces inflammation and bleeding of the gums. You use each Quik Floss flosser once and then throw it away. The flossers are small and fit anywhere. Read about the amazing device and order a six-month supply at the site.

vitaminhouse.com
Vitamin House

609-695-5570
vitamins@vitaminhouse.com

Vitamins and Supplements

Vitamin House offers no-frills vitamin shopping. The site offers no fancy message boards, scrolling doodads, or flashy animation to catch your eye. In fact, you really need to do your homework before you pop in here, because you won't find many product descriptions or explanations. Still, don't give up on the site. Some of the big-name vitamin manufacturers, such as Schiff, Thompson, Natural Balance, Nature's Herbs, and more, are represented at this site, and prices are really low. The Monthly Specials offer up some great deals, and the Buy One, Get One Free offers can't be beat.

vitaminproshop.com
Vitamin Proshop

877-294-8827
info@alterna-med.com

Vitamins and Supplements

Vitamin Proshop wants to serve you. This company has received numerous Customer Service awards from Yahoo! and accolades from satisfied customers via BizRate. In fact, you can meet the folks who run the site because their pictures and bios are displayed in the Our Team section. Before you shop, read the Announcements to learn the latest Vitamin Proshop news. You may learn about a supersale, a new shipping policy, or some new products that will make you feel great. Then fill your cart with all the low-priced items you need, under the smiling gazes of the site's friendly staff.

vitamins.com
Vitamins.com

800-645-1030
E-mail form on site

Vitamins and Supplements

The vitamins sold at vitamins.com are manufactured by Puritan's Pride. From its state-of-the-art facilities, this company manufactures more than 1,000 high-quality vitamins, minerals, herbs, and other nutritional supplements. Your best bet is to set up your own personal account at the site. Reorders will be a breeze, because your regular vitamins and supplements will be recorded. Shop by category or keyword. The long category list is alphabetical and takes a while to scroll. Read the site's articles for the latest news about health and fitness.

 Recommended   Price   Selection   Convenience   Service   Security

vitaminshoppe.com
The Vitamin Shoppe
800-223-1216
E-mail form on site

Healthy Living • Sex • Vitamins and Supplements

It seems like every vitamin and mineral pill, capsule, softgel, powder, and drink has been assembled under this site's virtual roof. As if that wasn't enough, The Vitamin Shoppe now carries Sports Nutrition products like flavored whey proteins and energy bars. Watching your carbs? This site offers a comprehensive low-carb selection of bars, snacks, and shakes. If you're overwhelmed, see what others have ordered in Shoppers Favorites and then make your decision. Or if you're on a tight budget, start at the Money Saving Offers section and work through the site from there.

vmakeup.com
Victoria Jackson Cosmetics
800-848-7990
E-mail form on site

Cosmetics • Hair • Skin Care

This site is a companion to Victoria Jackson's hugely successful infomercial. If you haven't had a pen handy when the phone number flashes across the screen, here's your chance to order Victoria Jackson products. She's the makeup artist to the stars, including Ali MacGraw and Lisa Hartman. Victoria Jackson is famous in Hollywood for her "no-makeup" makeup, which she has used to create a "naturally beautiful" look. Until recently, Victoria's makeup was only available to her celebrity clients. A complete makeover video is included with your cosmetics order.

★ walgreens.com
Walgreens.com
877-250-5823
E-mail form on site

Bath and Body • Cosmetics • Hair • Healthy Living • Pharmacy • Sex • Skin Care • Teeth • Vitamins and Supplements

The first Walgreens opened in 1901. We can only imagine the thoughts of Charles R. Walgreen, Sr., the founder, if he could log in to Walgreens.com. The online store shares many of the features of the bricks-and-mortar Walgreens: great prices, a wide range of merchandise, and prompt service. You can view and print its weekly circular and coupons from the site. Refill prescriptions with a few clicks and fill your cart with treats and goodies. Visit the Health Library at the site for detailed information about health matters.

wellzymes.com
Wellzymes

800-228-1501
webmaster@enzymesinc.com

Healthy Living • Vitamins and Supplements

Shop at Wellzymes for a wide variety of nutritional supplements that are designed to make you feel better. A list at the site describes each supplement, what it's used for, and its formula. WellZymes formulas are created with you, the health-conscious consumer, in mind. The formulas are blended with herbs, enzymes, and some vitamins and minerals and are designed to deliver maximum effectiveness for overall well being and health. A detailed explanation of enzymes and homeopathics at the site will help you understand the science behind the products sold here.

Virtual Makeovers: Looking at a New You

Did you know that you can see yourself in a whole new way on the Internet? This technique, called a virtual makeover, enables sites to use your digital image or a model and show how you would look with different makeup, hairstyles, or clothes. Virtual makeovers are fun and useful, too, because they can keep you from making fashion mistakes. ("Why did I think I'd look good in bangs?") Some sites show full body virtual makeovers, others show head shots only.

If you're going to use your own image, you'll need a good quality digital camera. First learn something about digital cameras at Digital Camera Basics (digitalcamerabasics.com). When you're ready to buy, buy a digital camera at Ritz Camera (ritzcamera.com) or a discount store like Kmart.com (kmart.com).

Have a friend take a few pictures of your face as you're looking directly into the camera. (Alternatively, photograph yourself in a mirror.) Your hair should not touch your face. Don't wear any makeup, since you don't want to add makeup over makeup to your virtual makeover.

Download the best picture of yourself to your computer in JPG format. Remember the filename and location of the JPG file. You'll need to upload it to the makeover sites later on. You'll also need to follow the onscreen prompts and directions at each site to complete the makeover. Relax! The steps are easy and simple to follow.

Now, let the transformations begin!

Visit the makeover page at Substance.com (substance.com/es/mom/), the site that "has just one purpose: to bring you beauty on your terms." The site features a service called Makeover-o-Matic that lets you try on celebrity hairstyles and see yourself in different makeup. You can even save your new look or e-mail it to your friends. Register at Maybelline.com (maybelline.com) to try out their latest beauty products and shades on your own photo or one of their models. Go to MakeoverSolutions.com (makeoversolutions.com) and have a blast modeling the latest hairstyles, cosmetics, and accessories.

RimmelLondon.com (rimmellondon.com/RimmelLondon) offers a more continental look. The makeover here is extreme, but shows what you would look like wearing all the fashionable London looks of the day.

How about a new hairstyle? YourStyle-Haironline (yourstyle.nzliving.co.nz) of New Zealand and eSalon (esalon.com) offer free makeovers. If you see a look you like, print it and show it to your hairdresser. If you're wondering how you may look in a new pair of glasses or sunglasses, you can see firsthand at Glasses.com (glasses.com).

For something slightly different, why not build a 3D model of your body? You'll be able to see how you look in clothes from all sides before you buy them. Get started at My Virtual Model (myvirtualmodel.com).

Virtual makeovers can be fun. They can be overwhelming, too! Which look did you like better? Are you puzzled? Head over to Jigsaw Puzzles Online (jigzone.com) for a little online relaxation. While you're there, make your photos into your personal jigsaw puzzle. As you put the pieces together, your decision about your future new look will fall into place.

Chapter 14

Home and Garden: Shopping for Your Castle

• •

Your home is your castle. It's your refuge at the end of the day and a place to relax and unwind. You can be yourself when you're at home, with no need to put on airs or impress the boss. Home should be a safe, comfortable place.

How's your home? Do you live in a huge palace, with lush green gardens and a manicured yard? Or is your home an ongoing fix-up dungeon, with unfinished projects that never seem to get completed? If you're like most of us, you fall somewhere in the middle, dreaming of the big mansion and completing some do-it-yourself projects, but leaving others.

One thing is certain. No matter where you live, if you rent, own, or share, there's always something to buy for your home or garden. Whether it's something major like a refrigerator or something small like a new coffee maker or set of sheets, your house always needs something to keep it going. The bigger the house, the more stuff you need!

Fortunately, the Internet shines when it comes to shopping for home and garden products and supplies. Most major houseware stores have online presences, and smaller retailers sell a wide variety of wondrous merchandise. In a few short hours, you can outfit your entire home or find accent pieces from around the globe.

Find out the return policy before you order unusual cookware or a different appliance than you've used before. Experimentation is fun, but only when it doesn't turn out to be a costly mistake.

Key Word Index

Appliances

The Appliance sites carry major appliances such as stoves and refrigerators as well as small countertop appliances that make your life easier.

Barbecue

The Barbecue sites offer all the tools and equipment — except food — to make your barbecue a smash.

Bathroom

The Bathroom sites cover the most important room of the house, with everything from a deluxe commode to shower accessories and toothbrush holders.

Bedroom

Whether you view your bedroom as a refuge from the world or just a place to sleep, the Bedroom sites make it special.

Cleaning

The Cleaning sites offer tools for grime-busting, including cleaning solutions, buckets, and the like.

Furniture

Both indoor and outdoor furniture is covered in the group of stores with the Furniture keyword. You'll find sites offering full suites to small accent pieces.

Garden

You can find seeds, plants, and all the tools you need to have the best garden on your block at the Garden sites.

Kitchen and Dining

From pots and pans and everyday dishes to unique glassware and one-of-a-kind plates, the Kitchen and Dining sites can provide everything you need to cook a meal and serve it.

Laundry

The Laundry sites deal with the rather thankless task of getting clothes clean and tidy.

Linen Closet

The Linen Closet sites offer towels and sheets, along with a few odds and ends.

Swimming Pools and Spas

Order accessories and supplies for your backyard paradise from the Swimming Pools and Spas sites.

Windows

Curtains, blinds, valances, swags — if it dresses up a window, you'll find it in the Windows group of stores.

Yard

Shop at sites with the Yard keyword for patio supplies, outdoor furniture, and accessories for your yard.

100cookwares.com
100cookwares.com

866-266-4875
cust-serv@100cookwares.com

Kitchen and Dining

The 100cookwares.com site offers As-Seen-On-TV stainless-steel cookware sets that go from the kitchen to the dining table. That's not all; it also has a superior selection of copper-bottom cookware, fine china, crockpots, dinnerware, bakeware, appliances, cutlery, and just about anything any traditional cook or chef-of-the-future would need to prepare a feast or a simple dinner for two. 100cookwares.com also features a convenient section of recipes for all types of cooking. Your satisfaction with this company's products is guaranteed and a $1 delivery offer is available.

⭐ a1gardenproducts.com
A1 Garden Products, Inc.

773-429-3842
jim@a1gardenproducts.com

Yard

Does your yard make you yawn? Is your flowerbox dreadfully dry? A1 Garden Products has a wonderful array of garden accessories and a plethora of planter options. It also offers great gardening advice and helpful links to other gardening sites. You don't have to be a gifted gardener to have a beautiful backyard. The merchandise sold on this site is an eclectic assortment of outdoor amenities. So, whether you live in the suburbs or have a studio in the city, you can perk up your little piece of the world with planters and garden accessories from a1gardenproducts.com.

abbylabs.com
Abby Laboratories, Inc.

No phone number listed
sales@abbylabs.com

Cleaning

This site is divided into a selection of product lines created at Abby Laboratories: Industrial/Commercial, Plant Science, Household, Human Healthcare, Animal Healthcare, and Outdoors. Most of the merchandise provides solutions for cleaning or better health. The site is straightforward and simple to navigate. This company stands behind its products and guarantees 100 percent customer satisfaction. It also offers a section for graphic design, for those of you who are Web-savvy and need a digital artist to perk up an online project.

 Recommended   Price   Selection   Convenience   Service   Security

★ abeautifulbed.com
A Beautiful Bed

800-990-5662
E-mail form on site

Linen Closet

A Beautiful Bed is the site for those of us with a taste for the finer things in life. This company offers a wide range of ultra-high thread count sheets, bedding, and blankets with the most luxurious of fabric and color selections. Its products range from rich Italian linens to baby linens, and it also carries a sumptuous selection of drapes and curtains. Feast your eyes on all the delicious amenities with which to fill your linen closet. A Beautiful Bed also offers its clients free shipping for purchases over $350. It's easy to spend here, when everything is so luxurious!

accentfurnishings.com
Accentfurnishings.com

866-891-4430
support@accentfurnishings.com

Bedroom • Furniture • Kitchen and Dining

Accentfurnishings.com is the online store for Accent Furniture, Inc. The site features positively the best prices on top-quality home furnishings. Whether you're searching for that perfect accent piece or redecorating your entire home, Accentfurnishings.com is the site to shop. Your order is sent directly from the manufacturer, enabling the prices to stay so low. The site features a diverse selection of discounted furniture, clocks, contemporary furniture, children's furniture, and an incredible array of home accessories. Shipping is always free.

add-a-motor.com
Add-a-Motor, Inc.

888-233-6686
addamotor@cox.net

Windows

Add-a-Motor offers a nifty apparatus any couch-potato or security-minded home owner should not be without. The Add-a-Motor allows you to add remote control to your drapery and vertical blinds. This device fits your current window coverings without modification and simply plugs in. You can even plug it into a lamp timer so it opens and closes drapes without your being there, offering convenience that you will enjoy and home security when you're away. If you aren't sure this product is right for you, you can try it for a month; if you're not completely satisfied, simply return it for a full refund.

affordable-beds.com
Affordable-beds.com

760-806-1017
E-mail form on site

Bedroom • Furniture

Is your mattress lumpy? Do you need a futon for the in-laws' visit? Is it time to scrap your sheets? Well, if you answered yes to any of these questions, Affordable-beds.com has what you're looking for. The well-organized site features a wide variety of bed frames, futons, mattresses, bedding, and nightstands. It offers quality merchandise at unbeatable prices and free shipping. So, don't spend another night on that mushy mattress or in that boring bed. Visit Affordable-beds.com for super savings on beds and bedding.

altgarden.com
Alternative Garden Supply

800-444-2837
E-mail form on site

Yard

In an age where people are watching what they eat and environmental consciousness is on the rise, organic and hydroponics gardening is extremely popular. altgarden.com is the online store for the Alternative Garden Supply Co. With the new style of growing plants, many innovative techniques and products exist that one must be aware of and have access to. That's where this site comes in. Alternative Garden Supply offers grow lights, hydroponics kits, organics, fertilizers, bulbs, books, pots, flats, and many other items integral to the organic and hydroponics gardener's needs.

★ annieglass.com
Annieglass

888-761-0050
support@annieglass.com

Kitchen and Dining

Artist Ann Morhauser has taken her love for Italian relics and the belief that food tastes better on a beautiful plate and created the masterpieces known internationally as Annieglass. Annieglass products can certainly make any meal a feast for the eyes. Although Annieglass products can be found in world-class hotels, restaurants, and spas, they are equally at home on your table. The site's products are organized by item and/or series name. If you're looking for incredible plates to utilize at your next dinner party, Annieglass is, without a doubt, one of the finest choices in the world.

 Recommended   Price   Selection   Convenience   Service   Security

appliances.com
Appliances.Com
888-543-8345
E-mail form on site
Appliances

Appliances.Com was the first site to sell major brand-name appliances on the Internet. You'll find a full range of products from all around the world. Appliances.com strives to provide superlative quality products at very competitive prices. Items are arranged by category, making it easy to find the blender, toaster oven, or whatever it is that you need. The site shines in its approach to big-ticket appliances. Each appliance description contains, when available, a manufacturer's spec sheet and the product manual in PDF format, making it easy to compare before you click the Order button.

bar-b-que.com
Bar-b-que.com
847-272-8264
info@bar-b-que.com
Barbecue

Bar-b-que.com is the Internet division of the Chicago-based retail store of the same name. Since 1974 this company has been selling the finest Weber barbecue grills and other outdoor-living merchandise. The store as well as the site offer a wide selection of the top name-brand barbecuing equipment, such as meat forks, tool sets, and mitts. Also available is an assortment of grilling spices, smoking products, outdoor fireplaces and heaters, recipes, and the best barbecuing tips this side of Albuquerque. After you shop here, be prepared to want to go out and eat!

★ bazaarhomefashions.com
BazaarHomeFashions.com
877-764-0305
info@bazaarhomefashions.com
Bedroom • Linen Closet • Windows

No, don't believe the name; you're not visiting a cheesy foreign flea market! Quite the contrary, the BazaarHomeFashions.com site features a lovely line of decorative home furnishings, with an emphasis on window treatments and bedding. The Bazaar Home Fashions stores are located in West Virginia and Ohio and their product line reflects their locale. The folks who run the business have been turning houses into homes for over 20 years, specializing in products that provide charm and warmth at reasonable prices. If you like country comfort, you'll love BazaarHomeFashions.com.

bedandbath.com
bedandbath.com
No phone number listed
yourteam@bedandbath.com

Bedroom • Kitchen and Dining • Linen Closet • Windows

bedandbath.com has one simple mission, and that is to offer the consumer quality products at the best possible price, guaranteed. The company appeared on the scene in 1997 selling exclusively online, allowing it to limit overhead and keep its prices at rock bottom. The site offers all types of goodies to fill your linen closet, and a whole lot more, including window coverings, bathroom accessories, personal care products, kitchen accessories, organizational products, furniture, and candles. There is one catch: You have to be a member to enjoy the savings. Joining is fast and easy and you never have an obligation to buy.

★ bellacor.com
Bellacor
877-723-5522
customerservice@bellacor.com

Bathroom • Bedroom • Furniture • Kitchen and Dining

Are you in the dark about the latest home lighting products on the market? Bellacor can shed some light on the subject for you. The site combines access to over 500,000 lighting products and home furnishings from 700 manufacturers with a personal shopping assistant, setting bellacor.com apart from other online providers of lighting and home furnishings. The site is user friendly, with lots of great information about design, architecture, and lighting tips. Browse the categories or select a service from the Personal Shopper, Price Quote, and Project Portfolio shopping services.

bettymills.com
The Betty Mills Company
800-238-8964
E-mail form on site

Cleaning

Buying cleaning supplies is a chore. You generally have two purchasing choices: buy your supplies one at a time at the local supermarket or discount store (ensuring you'll run out soon) or lug home industrial-sized cleaning products from the warehouse club. A better option: Order the same products the pros use from The Betty Mills Company. You'll save money and have a cleaner house. Split an order with your neighbors for greater savings. If only all problems could be solved this easily.

 Recommended   Price   Selection   Convenience   Service Security

bigasstowels.com
Big Ass Towels

954-578-1083
sales@bigasstowels.com

Linen Closet

bigasstowels.com offers towels that will overflow your linen closet. This site sells oversize beach, pool, and bath towels featuring the Crown Jewel brand by Fieldcrest Cannon. The high-quality towels, made in America, are available in seven colors, and are 100 percent cotton. Of course, the real reason for shopping here is the signature Big Ass towel. The oversized towel with a plump donkey in shades wearing a towel shows how the towel got its distinctive name! Also available are Bare Ass towels (without logo), Looney Tunes, Scooby Doo, American flag and striped towels, bath mats, polo shirts, and Zen gardens.

Blankets.com
Blankets.com

206-729-4700
customerservice@blankets.com

Bedroom • Linen Closet

Blankets.com was established in November of 1999 and is located in Redmond, Washington. Just as the name indicates, the site features a large assortment of blankets and related items. Blankets.com wants to provide a high level of customer service while delivering top-quality products at low prices. The site is easy to navigate and finding that perfect blanket is just a click away. Whether you're looking for an electric blanket, Biederlack sports blanket, down comforter, Pendleton blanket, or fleece throw, Blankets.com has got you covered.

blowoutfurniture.com
Blowoutfurniture.com

713-692-7830
contact@blowoutfurniture.com

Bedroom • Furniture • Kitchen and Dining

Do you need to furnish your home but are on a tight budget? No problem! Blowoutfurniture.com, owned by James R. Eldreth, is the solution. Mr. Eldreth (his picture appears on the site) is personally involved in the business and wants to make you happy. He has been making it his business to sell quality furniture at near wholesale prices for the last 20 years. Shop here for affordable furniture for every room in the house. Moreover, talk about appealing to a mass market — Blowoutfurniture.com can be navigated in nine languages.

bodum.com
Bodum.com

800-232-6386
info@bodumusa.com
Kitchen and Dining

Bodum.com wants everyone to "give up bad design for good." A lofty ideal, true, but this company carries it off with the edgy kitchen and dining appliances and products it sells. Its merchandise is a little ahead of the curve, or may happen to have a few extra curves in its intrinsic design. The site offers everything for high-tech coffee preparation, tea service, kitchen gear, revolutionary tabletops, spare parts, and delightful gift sets for your more finicky friends and family. Bodum has come up with a product line that embodies an artful appearance while simultaneously being ultra-utilitarian.

Brassbedshoppe.com
A Brass Bed Shoppe

216-371-0400
bedshoppe@aol.com
Bedroom • Furniture

Why pay retail? You won't when you buy from Brassbedshoppe.com, America's largest discounter of solid brass and iron beds. This site sells hundreds of nationally known brands and has an enormous selection of styles. If you don't see what you're looking for, just e-mail your needs or call the office. Custom color/finish orders are never a problem. When you buy from A Brass Bed Shoppe you get a complete bed — headboard, footboard, and a heavy-duty engineered bed frame for one low price. Quality, satisfaction, and safe delivery are guaranteed.

★ burpee.com
Burpee

800-333-5808
custserv@burpee.com
Garden • Yard

Generations of gardeners have dreamed of spring over the pages of the Burpee catalog while snow blankets the ground. The Burpee Company, located in Philadelphia, Pennsylvania, has been selling seeds since 1876. Besides marketing vegetable, flower, and herb seeds, there is also a wealth of information every person who plants should be privy to. The site also features a helpful nutritional guide, tip of the day, a newsletter, and a Garden Wizard, to help you pick the perfect plant for your personality. Your garden will thank you when you fill it with Burpee seeds and plants.

 Recommended   Price   Selection Convenience   Service Security

buybathware.com
BuyBathware.Com

877-228-4927
support@buybathware.com

Bathroom

BuyBathware.com is the one-stop-shopping site for all your shower curtain, bath towel, bathroom accessories, and furnishing needs. BuyBathware.com features a cornucopia of themes: nautical looks, frogs, fish, flamingos, and more. This people-friendly site caters to those with whimsical tastes; this company believes that determining your bathroom decor should be fun whether you like southwestern designs, or just want a little Scooby Doo. Browse this site by style/design or product type and have fun pepping up your powder room or designing your master bath.

cardboardchair.com
Cardboardchair.com

No phone number listed
cust-support@cardboardchair.com

Furniture

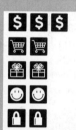

Yes, I, too, conjure up visions of my guests sitting on packing boxes. However, quite to the contrary, Cardboardchair.com brings us beautiful, comfortable, and pricey works of art that function as chairs. The company is based in Chapel Hill, North Carolina, and the chairs are produced in the U.S. from environmentally friendly materials. Cardboardchair.com's mission is to make and market the highest quality modern furniture at affordable prices. The cardboard chair and cardboard rocking chaise are beautiful and comfortable pieces of functional art. Also available on the site are cardboard tables and abstract works of art.

chefstore.com
ChefStore

No phone number listed
No e-mail address on site

Kitchen and Dining

ChefStore is the original professional cookware and chef's supply store on the Internet. The site features ultra-high quality cookware, grilling gear, kitchenware, cutlery and utensils, cookbooks and magazines, housewares, coffee and tea equipment, and tableware that world-renowned chefs and restaurants use. Discount prices make this site easy to recommend. Another bonus is the free shipping on orders over $25. If you're looking for professional culinary equipment for your restaurant or kitchen, ChefStore is your place to shop.

⭐ clasenhome.com
Clasen Home

800-366-4443
E-mail form on site

Bathroom • Bedroom • Furniture • Kitchen and Dining • Linen Closet

You can finally have the home you've always wanted, without a decorator. Clasen Home takes the legwork out of redecorating. This company specializes in fashionable bedroom accessories and linens and carries a diverse assortment of home furnishings. Treat yourself to rich fabrics, finely crafted furniture, illuminating lighting, and accessories that are sure to satisfy the most discerning consumer. Want to use your own fabric? That's okay with Clasen Home. Send them the fabric and they'll upholster it to your new purchase in just two weeks' time. Now that's service!

clean-n-brite.com
Clean-n-brite.com

877-898-8605
E-mail form on site

Cleaning • Laundry

Now you see it, now you don't. That's right, Clean-n-Brite is the As-Seen-On-TV product that removes any stain. This product is the ultraconcentrated degreaser, stain remover, and odor destroyer that eradicates the toughest stains, including red wine, pet, mildew, nicotine, oil, grass, and many more. This revolutionary product restores your belongings and household surfaces to a like-new appearance. Use Clean-n-Brite to remove years of neglect and buildup faster and cheaper than the professionals. One 2.5-pound tub provides you with a minimum of 100 gallons of cleaning solution.

clearmirror.com
ClearMirror

877-242-5327
sales@clearmirror.com

Appliances • Bathroom

Don't you hate it? That awful fog that attacks your bathroom mirror after a shower and renders the mirror useless? Not any more! ClearMirror's mirror defoggers are specially designed mirror heaters that adhere to the backs of mirrors, keeping them fog-free in the steamiest conditions. With the flip of a switch, the ClearMirror starts to heat, providing a fogless mirror at all times for applying makeup, shaving, styling your hair, or for any time you need clear vision! The ClearMirror installs easily, meets international safety standards, and is available in 12, 24, 120, and 240 volts.

 Recommended   Price   Selection   Convenience   Service   Security

clotheslines.net
Clotheslines, Inc.
830-997-6044
info@clotheslines.net
Laundry

What was once old is now new at Clotheslines, Inc. An old-fashioned clothesline is for sale at this site, with a twist. This line is designed to be hung in your garage, near the ceiling, attached to your garage door assembly. The benefits are down-to-earth: It simply saves space and money (line drying is much cheaper than using your dryer). It's perfect for families with zoning or homeowner association restrictions that prevent them from hanging a line in their yard. Installation instructions are at the site.

collapse-it.com
Collapse-It
877-236-5348
questions@collapse-it.com
Laundry • Yard

Collapse-it sells a sturdy collapsible container ideal for use as a laundry basket and other jobs around the home, office, or yard. The sturdy construction, stackability, collapsibility, and affordability make this the perfect product for all your carrying and storage needs. It is so ingenious that it is patented. Don't be fooled by imitators or knock-offs. You can only purchase Collapse-It on the official Collapse-It site. The Collapse-It is also available for commercial purchase. Your company, school, or organization logo can be printed on your order, making a great premium or giveway.

colonialimports.com
Colonial Imports
877-378-7843
info@colonialimports.com
Bedroom • Furniture • Kitchen and Dining

Is your new home in need of some old-fashioned furniture? Colonial Imports' collection is comprised of handmade rustic furniture. The antiques of the southwestern frontier and the Spanish colonial times inspired this collection. Because this company manufactures, imports, and distributes the furniture itself, Colonial Imports is able to offer the highest quality rustic furniture at factory direct prices. Shop the site for armoires, tables and chairs, bookcases, beds and nightstands, dressers and chests, desks, hutches, and assorted other items. The old-world charm of this furniture will add some Spanish appeal and a bit of the Wild West to any room.

★ Cookshackamerica.com
Cookshack, Inc.
800-423-0698
E-mail form on site
Barbecue

Cookshack, Inc. is a small business that provides a good product at a fair price. The company originated in the early 1960s and is still smoking today. Cookshack, Inc. sells home barbecue units and commercial cookers and smokers at its site. It also markets a wide variety of barbecue sauces, dry rubs, savory smoking woods, cookbooks, and a bounty of barbecue accessories. The site offers plenty of suggestions for a big rib joint owner or for someone who just enjoys some good old-fashioned barbecue in the backyard.

cowansupplyatlanta.com
Cowan Supply Atlanta
404-351-6351
ashepherd@hajoca.com
Bathroom

Folks in the know buy toilets from Cowan Supply Atlanta. The site sells TOTO and American Standard toilets to fit any bathroom. Shipping is free and all the toilets are discounted below the MSRP. If you want the latest and greatest, check out the TOTO SW834R Jasmin Washlet, the state-of-the-art in toilet technology. The Jasmin comes with a remote control to adjust the seat and water temperatures and pressure level. The Jasmin's soothing massage feature keeps you comfortable and clean. This amazing toilet will make you view your bathroom in a whole new way. If nothing else, you'll stop flushing money down the drain.

crateandbarrel.com
Crate & Barrel
800-967-6696
E-mail form on site
Barbecue • Bedroom • Kitchen and Dining • Yard

Furnish your kitchen, dining areas, and a whole lot more with the exciting merchandise at Crate & Barrel. The trendy, seasonal looks fit houses and apartments and appeal to both hip, young professionals, and established executives. Prices at the site are surprisingly moderate. Expect to pay around $30 for a folding chair and $15 for two champagne flutes. The site offers expert assistance for selecting gifts, has a gift registry for the nearly-weds, and will send gift cards.

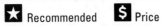 Recommended Price Selection Convenience Service Security

cuddledown.com
Cuddledown.com

800-323-6793
service@cuddledown.com

Bedroom • Linen Closet

Cuddledown.com is a family-owned business committed to making sensible products. The company began in 1973 by making just one product: down comforters. Early on, the comforters were sold to friends, but a good secret is hard to keep and word of the company's fabulous snuggly comforters spread. The company is based in Yarmouth, Maine, and its products certainly have that old-world New England appeal. The site offers a full line of comforters, pillows, featherbeds, sheets and comforter covers, blankets and throws, and a slew of other goodies to fill your linen closet.

curvware.com
Curvware

941-504-0013
mwilson@curvware.com

Kitchen and Dining

Sure it takes a while to get used to. But after you've used it for a bit, you'll never go back to regular flatware again. I'm talking about Curvware, flatware that's ergonomically molded in curvy shapes. Your first look may make you think that the spoons, knives, and forks have been caught in the garbage disposal or under the wheels of a bus, but give it a try. According to the testimonials on the curvware.com site, Curvware is the wave of the future. If nothing else, it will be a conversation piece at your next family gathering.

cyberfurniture.com
Cyber Furniture

No phone number listed
information@cyberfurniture.com

Bedroom • Furniture

Cyber Furniture is a straightforward site that sells quality fabrics, futons, sofas and chairs, leather seating, and upholstery. As a complimentary service to its cyber-customers, Cyber Furniture offers an online home fashion consultant. The consultant is there to help you find a specific piece of furniture you've been aching for or to assist in the styling of your next refurnishing project. It's easy to get started. E-mail a request for an appointment with a design specialist, and in no time, you'll be on your way to having the fashionably functional furniture you've been dreaming about.

discount-pool-supplies.com
Discount Pool and Spa Supplies

315-253-5203
E-mail form on site

Barbecue • Swimming Pool and Spa • Yard

Why choose Discount Pool and Spa Supplies? Simple — the name says it all. Discount Pool and Spa Supplies has the lowest prices on swimming pool and spa supplies, automatic pool cleaners, pumps, motors, heaters, and filters. The site sells only new name-brand merchandise. It also carries pool and spa accessories and patio and backyard gear such as floats, alarms, fencing, ladders and steps, paints, lights, grills and barbecues, waterfalls and fountains, backyard toys and games, and more. This company is committed to providing the highest level of customer service and offers free shipping on most orders.

Domestications.com
Domestications

800-577-5755
custserv@domestications.com

Bathroom • Bedroom • Furniture • Garden • Kitchen and Dining • Linen Closet

Simply speaking, Domestications.com is America's authority in home fashions. For over 15 years, Domestications has helped its customers create their dream homes with value in mind. This company specializes in the latest trends in fabrics and designs and develops original bedroom and home furnishings that are exclusively found on Domestications.com or in its catalog. So, if you're fashioning a fun bedroom for your child or a relaxing refuge for yourself, you'll find all the decorating solutions you're seeking at Domestications.

dustmitex.com
The Ecology Works

772-545-7890
E-mail form on site

Cleaning

Do you suffer from allergies or asthma? Your problem could be right under you. Visit the dustmitex.com site for a clean and natural solution for ridding dust mites from carpet and upholstery. The Ecology Works Dust Mite and Flea Control product is a scientifically formulated borate compound that dissolves easily in water and provides long-term dust mite control. It's been prescribed by doctors for patients suffering with breathing afflictions. Visit the site to order your supply and read application instructions and some effusive customer testimonials. The stuff really works!

 Recommended   Price   Selection   Convenience   Service   Security

essentiallywhite.com
Essentially White
888-259-1406
orders@essentiallywhite.com
Bedroom • Linen Closet

Essentially White is a small, family-run company located in a converted stone barn in Ontario, Canada. Its products combine the beauty and elegance of a time gone by with the quality and functionality expected today. Essentially White strives to bring its client base luxurious linens from the far corners of the globe. These elegant additions to your linen closet will enhance your abode, soothe your soul, and relax your body. Rest assured you will be in the lap of luxury with purchases from Essentially White.

everything4pools.com
Everything4Pools.com
800-552-4702
info@everything4pools.com
Swimming Pool and Spa

Everything4pools.com sells the finest quality, brand-name pool and spa merchandise at discount prices. The company continually adds to its already diverse product line and takes pride in being able to offer the biggest selection of pool and spa equipment and accessories found anywhere. If you don't find what you're looking for online, simply give the company service representatives a call and they will find it for you. Rest assured you will be set for fun in the sun, a safe summer in the pool, and soothing times in your spa when you order your supplies from Everything4pools.com.

everythingkitchens.com
Everything Kitchens
866-852-4268
info@everythingkitchens.com
Appliances • Kitchen and Dining

A butcher, a baker, or even a candlestick maker would love the Everything Kitchens site. It features every kitchen appliance imaginable and carries all the top national brands. So, if your blender is burned out, or your juicer has run out of juice, visit Everything Kitchens. Free shipping is offered on most products. A 90-day, money-back guarantee makes it easy to try new appliances, as does the claim that part of the proceeds from sales goes to charity. Want to try out a new appliance but not sure what to do with it? Check out the recipes posted at the site.

⭐ faucetree.com
Baths by Design

561-654-9681
info@faucetree.com

Bathroom

With two million products in stock, Baths by Design's site, faucetree.com, will have the bathroom or kitchen fixture you need. This site packs a plethora of bathroom supplies, including matching faucets for bidets, tub and shower sets, roman bathtubs, whirlpool tubs, toilet paper holders, soap dishes, robe hooks, towel bars, and towel rings. The site features fixtures from ALL the major brand names. Special orders, including plumbing parts, are never a problem. Most products can ship within 48 hours.

fourcornersusa.com
Four Corners USA.com

877-325-8114
sales@fourcornersusa.com

Bedroom • Linen Closet

Do you know the five philosophies for decorating the bedroom? Four Corners USA.com provides people like you and me with the answer: Rely on antiques, take an eclectic approach, take cues from country simplicity, start with chic minimalism, and insist on quality. By following these guidelines and utilizing the decorating center available on the site, anyone can put together the perfect bedroom. The site features fine bed linens, decorative throws and pillows, duvet covers, and pillow shams. Every product embodies the utmost in simple style and comfort. Fourcornersusa.com truly has finely crafted bedding products for your corner of the world.

⭐ frontgate.com
Frontgate

800-436-2105
cs@frontgate.com

Appliances • Furniture • Kitchen and Dining • Swimming Pool and Spa • Yard

You'll find the Frontgate catalog gracing upper-crust coffee tables all over the world. Now you can find the same impressive mix of high-end products online. Shop here for yard, patio, poolside, and indoor furnishings, appliances, and accessories for finer homes and luxurious lifestyles. Hey, living the good life takes a lot of work, so you need the proper equipment to relax. Spoil yourself with a special purchase, or shop this site to outfit your new mansion in Malibu. You will not be disappointed. Frontgate.com is top-shelf.

 Recommended   Price   Selection   Convenience   Service   Security

furnitureontheinternet.com
Richard Bissell Fine Woodworking
802-387-4416
rbissell@sover.net

Bedroom • Furniture • Kitchen and Dining

Is your passion handcrafted, traditional furniture? Richard Bissell Fine Woodworking features handcrafted Shaker furniture and Windsor chairs by Richard Bissell. Richard has owned and operated a small woodworking shop in Putney, Vermont since 1982. As the years passed, he developed a line of Shaker furniture and Windsor chairs. His handiwork is now available to the online world. Also offered is a selection of woodworking books, beds, tables, bookcases, chests-of-drawers, and other interesting pieces. Richard can create custom pieces of furniture for special orders.

greenshoes.com
Greenshoes
800-444-2837
customercare@greenshoes.com

Garden • Yard

Why Greenshoes? Good question! Two neighborhood kids who mowed lawns started Greenshoes years ago. After a hard day on the mowers, the lads returned home and noticed their shoes were bright green. Greenshoes' business has grown into a leading source for gardening and lawn care equipment, accessories, tools, and parts. The site sells top name-brand machines, mowers, and motors to keep your lawn green all season. Free shipping is available on all orders over $49. However, the company can't promise your shoes won't discolor after a hard day in the garden.

★ hammocks.com
Hammocks.com
866-577-3529
E-mail form on site

Furniture • Yard

A hammock is just the thing for your yard. With over three hundred hammocks in stock at Hammocks.com, you're bound to find one that works for you. Hammocks.com makes it easy. Instead of forcing customers to flip through all the hammocks in the online catalog, this company displays the top three picks in the most popular hammock categories. Or browse the site's Featured Products to see a variety of comfortable hammocks. Some models tie to trees, some need stands, and others are chair models. All are relaxing. All are fun. Outdoor furniture is also available from this convenient site.

heloise.com
Hints from Heloise

210-435-6473
heloise@compuserve.com

Cleaning • Garden • Kitchen and Dining • Yard

If you're looking to shop until you drop on this site, well, you may be a tad disappointed. On the other hand, if you drop in for some handy hints on stain busting, clutter control, or help with pets, you may get lucky. Heloise, the famous "hintologist," has a great homespun Web site filled with lots of helpful hints, recipes, and links. Kick back and stay for a while. Like what you see? Click the link to purchase Heloise's hints and advice in book, video, and pamphlet form.

heritagelacecurtains.com
Heritage Gallery of Lace

800-270-9587
info@heritagelacecurtains.com

Bedroom • Kitchen and Dining • Windows

Lace curtains make a statement of elegance, grace, and refinement. While lace curtains make any room look like a million dollars, they don't need to break the bank. Heritage Gallery of Lace offers high quality curtains and table lace products that are priced reasonably. Curtains are available in ecru or white and can be ordered in a swag pair or in individual panels. A matching valance is also available. Choose from several patterns, including English Country Rose, Heart to Heart, English Ivy, and the traditional Heirloom. Match your table lace to your window pattern or contrast the lace for a more modern look.

hici-shopper.com
Hici Patio Furniture

314-283-4228
E-mail form on site

Yard

The Hici Patio Furniture site sells ten brands of quality yard and patio furniture. It features nearly one hundred styles from which to choose and carries accessories that no yard should be without, including hammocks, umbrellas, and birdfeeders. It also offers an iron patio table and chair set that you can fold up when you're not using it. Imagine having an elegant dinner party and then being able store the dining set away the next day, when the kids want to take over the yard. For those of you who love a bargain, be sure to check out the sale and clearance sections for some real steals and deals.

 Recommended   Price   Selection   Convenience   Service   Security

httg.com
Hot Tubs To Go

410-995-6474
httg@smart.net

Swimming Pool and Spa

Hot Tubs To Go has been in the business of selling spas and supplies for your hot tub for the last 20 years. The site also offers spa chemicals, parts and accessories, gazebos, and tanning beds and lotions. For the transcendence-seeking spa-user, Httg.com also offers the full line of Spazazz Aromatherapy crystals. Be sure to check out the FAQs and Newsletters sections, which provide volumes of very useful information for current spa owners or potential purchasers.

ironworxdesigns.com
Ironworx Designs

818-395-8179
anthony@ironworxdesigns.com

Yard

Ironworx Designs is a relatively new Los Angeles-based company specializing in designing, producing, and selling the highest quality hand-made wrought iron and sheet metal products at competitive prices. The company sells table and chair sets, lounge chairs, planters, wine racks, chests and trunks. All products are available in sixteen different finishes; select the one that suits you best. A particular piece or a whole set can add rustic style and elegance to any yard, deck, or room. Purchase with confidence; every handmade item comes with a limited-time, money-back guarantee.

kitchenkrafts.com
Kitchen Krafts

800-776-0575
info@kitchenkrafts.com

Appliances • Kitchen and Dining

Kitchenkrafts.com, brought to you by Kitchen Krafts Inc., is a direct supplier of difficult-to-find food-preparation tools, ingredients, and supplies for the innovative cook. This inspirational company has been serving the home business market and the general homemaker since 1989. Its product line consists of supplies for cake decorating, home baking, candymaking, and home canning. kitchenkrafts.com also offers a wide range of tools, supplies, ingredients, books, how-to videos, and packaging products. You will be sure to find the supplies for your food-preparation business, or the beginnings of a new hobby on this stimulating site.

laundry-alternative.com
The Laundry Alternative, Inc.
888-813-9559
service@laundry-alternative.com
Appliances • Laundry

laundry-alternative.com is another site that is trying to help make life easier by offering alternative methods and products for everyday chores. The company is committed to providing you with innovative, economical, environmentally friendly laundry products that work. Its flagship item is the Wonderwash, a pressure washing machine that uses 90 percent less detergent and water than standard models. Washloads get clean in 1–3 minutes! These inexpensive, undersized units are ideal for apartment dwellers, boaters, RV owners, singles, seniors, college students, and many others. The site also offers dryers, parts, and accessories for today's laundry needs.

linenplace.com
Linenplace
973-696-3311
E-mail form on site
Bedroom • Linen Closet

Talk about user-friendly! Linenplace offers top-quality bed, bath, baby, kitchen, and dining linens. Besides being an easy site to navigate, the Linenplace site also offers informative tidbits about selecting the right thread count and distinguishing quality from ordinary products. A resource section contains a glossary, color palettes, and an expert to pose questions to. Linenplace has its sights set on educating its consumers and selling quality linens for a lot less than its competition.

★ outdoordecor.com
OutdoorDecor.com
800-422-1525
sales@outdoordecor.com
Furniture • Yard

Who needs a watch in the summer? Take a gander at a sundial instead, as you relax in a slowly swinging hammock. In the evening, you can recline in a teak lounger in the gazebo, enveloped in the soft glow of a hand-crafted lantern. Sound too good to be true? Well, you can bring nirvana to your yard from this site. OutdoorDecor.com has an awe-inspiring selection of quality yard and patio furniture, accessories, and more. This company stocks the elegant amenities you've seen but didn't know where to find. This site has the perfect pieces to create an oasis in your own backyard.

 Recommended   Price   Selection   Convenience   Service Security

outdoor-patio-furniture.biz
Outdoor-patio-furniture.biz

877-233-2723
cedar@abound.biz

Furniture • Yard

Do you like things raw? If you do, Outdoor-patio-furniture.biz has what you're looking for. This site specializes in selling outdoor yard furniture made from Indonesian Plantation Teak and western red cedar. The natural oils in this wood keep it cool to the touch even in the scorching summer months. Outdoor-patio-furniture.biz sells top-quality, long-lasting tables, chairs, swings, gliders, picnic benches, and an assortment of Adirondack furniture. All the merchandise comes with a 15-day unconditional money-back guarantee and shipping is free in the continental USA.

plowhearth.com
Plow & Hearth

800-494-7544
E-mail form on site

Garden • Yard

Does your lawn furniture look like it belongs curbside? Plow & Hearth has everything you need to perk up a patio. Your yard should be a place where you can escape from the four walls and enjoy your piece of the great outdoors. Plow & Hearth sells tasteful country living-styled yard furniture, cushions, entertaining essentials, and garden accents. The secret behind the success of Plow & Hearth is its attention to its customers' satisfaction. This company believes in treating each customer like a neighbor and guarantees all of its merchandise 100 percent.

⭐ ponds2go.com
Ponds2go.com

877-752-0889
info@ponds2go.com

Garden • Yard

Not everyone is lucky enough to live on waterfront property. However, Ponds2go.com offers the next best thing — your very own waterscape in your garden. The site offers everything one would need to put in a pond, waterfall, or fountain. The site also contains volumes of information for those who have an idea for a water decoration, but no idea how to carry it out (for example, me). Additionally, Ponds2go.com carries a sundry selection of fish and plant food, for when you've stocked your new pond with pretty pets and water-loving plants.

poolandgarden.com
PoolandGarden.com

856-468-8038
sales@poolandgarden.com

Swimming Pool and Spa • Yard

Poolandgarden.com says "just add sun and water. . ." for a perfect day in the pool or spa. This company is a factory-direct source for discount pool and spa chemicals, pumps and filters, heaters, accessories, gardening supplies and tools, arbors, trellises, and many more exciting elements to add to your yard. When the season is over and it's time to close your pool, Poolandgarden.com is the one-stop shop for winterizing equipment and chemicals. The site also sells lawn furniture, hammocks, and bird feeders.

poolladders.com
Internet Pool Ladders

248-737-1604
internetpoolladders@msn.com

Swimming Pool and Spa

What good is having a pool if climbing in and out is a major problem? Internet Pool Ladders is a leading supplier of quality pool and spa stairs and ladders. Don't take chances with your family's safety. Be sure your pool and spa ladders are secure. Walk confidently into the water on a new ladder or set of stairs you've purchased from Internet Pool Ladders. Ladders and stair sets come in many sizes, shapes, and styles. The site also offers pool and spa automatic cleaners, accessories, volleyball sets, toys, pool alarms, and above-ground pools.

queenanneslacecurtains.com
Queen Anne's Lace Curtains

800-585-5223
queenanneslace@att.net

Windows

If you want to add a dash of distinction to any room, Queen Anne's Lace Curtains has the right stuff. For the past ten years, the folks at this site have been proudly providing their customers with the finest cotton lace curtains, panels, and cut-to-order yardage available. The cotton lace is imported from Scotland and woven on Nottingham Lace looms. Queen Anne's Lace Curtains' line is selected based on enduring beauty, value, and distinctiveness in designs. The patterns vary from the traditional to the more contemporary, and the site sells only the highest quality products at the lowest possible price.

 Recommended Price Selection Convenience Service Security

⭐ replacements.com
Replacements, Ltd.

800-737-5223
inquire@replacements.com

Kitchen and Dining

Watching helplessly as a valuable piece of heirloom china goes crashing to the floor is a sick feeling. However, Replacements, Ltd. is standing by to replace the missing pieces of your tableware collections. This company stocks over 200,000 patterns of crystal and china, as well as silver flatware and hollowware. All the major manufacturers are represented at the site, including Spode, Royal Doulton, Lenox, Oneida, Wedgewood, International Silver, and others. Instructions on the site help you find the manufacturer's name and pattern name so that you can make your collection complete.

ronco.com
Ronco.com

800-486-1806
E-mail form on site

Barbecue • Bathroom • Kitchen and Dining

Why it's Ron Popiel, coming at ya, hawking his now-familiar Showtime Rotisserie, and all the other products you've seen on television. But don't guffaw — the stuff sold at Ronco.com is mostly high quality, and prices at the site can't be beat. If you can't pay upfront, don't sweat it; easy credit terms can not only be arranged, they're encouraged at this site. If the Web venue leaves you cold, never fear: You can actually watch a video clip of the Ronco infomercials online. There's a good chance you'll come away from this site wanting to buy something.

roomstogo.com
Rooms To Go, Inc.

888-709-5380
E-mail form on site

Bedroom • Furniture • Kitchen and Dining

Depending on where you live, you may have seen the television commercials for this furniture giant and caught yourself humming the company's catchy jingle. Rooms To Go is the largest furniture retailer in America, and with its reputation for high quality products, superior customer service, and speedy delivery, its site is a great pick for anyone who isn't sure where to shop. The site offers furniture and accessories for the living room, bedroom, and dining room, as well as a full line of leather furniture. Credit terms are available.

★ selectappliance.com
SelectAppliance.com
888-235-0431
customercare@selectappliance.com
Appliances • Kitchen and Dining

Russell Zipkin is the brains and heart behind SelectAppliance.com. He has been in the kitchen appliance business for 25 years. All of his experience allows him to bring you appliances to outfit your restaurant or home with multifeatured appliances that will make your kitchen a showplace and cooking a joy. SelectAppliance.com carries a line of appliances named for its founder, the Russell Range line, and a comprehensive selection of high-end professional quality brands. The site is also full of cooking tips and interesting facts, known (until now) by only a select few professional chefs.

spababes.com
Spa Babes
877-936-2223
babe@spababes.com
Swimming Pool and Spa

Spa Babes is located in Tampa, Florida, and knows just about everything about spas. If your spa is malfunctioning or making a strange noise, pack up the motor and send it over to the Tampa wizards for repair. Shop here for Spa Babes Spa Pack, a complete kit containing a controller, heater, pump, time clock, and light assembly. Also available are replacement parts for spa parts from most major manufacturers. Order a Babe Gear T-shirt with a picture of the Spa Babe emblazoned on the front.

staticeliminator.us
Static Eliminator
989-362-4116
E-mail form on site
Laundry

Do you find the price of dryer sheets shocking? Is the thought of buying one more box of static reducer sheets hair-raising? staticeliminator.us now introduces to the United States the innovative, reusable product that has all the advantages of a traditional dryer sheet, without all the chemicals. Each sheet lasts an incredible 500 loads! The patented Static Eliminator dryer sheet is 100 percent hypoallergenic, gentle on an infant's skin and clothes, and guaranteed never to spot or stain even the most delicate of fabrics. The company also sells a static eliminator dusting mitt, an antistatic keyboard mat, and an antistatic seat cushion.

★ steelform.com
Steelform.com

34 646 180 867
E-mail form on site
Furniture

Does the mention of steel furniture bring to mind the notion of angularity and rigidity? Steelform.com breaks the mold with a diverse line of modern classic reproductions from designers such as Le Corbusier, Mies van der Rohe, Charles Eames, Eileen Gray, and others. Each piece is painstakingly crafted in Italy to the same quality specifications demanded by the original artists. Since coming online seven years ago, Steelform.com has delighted tens of thousands of customers and prides itself in being a dependable source for contemporary classic furniture reproductions. Just choose your site language and currency, and then check out the products by category or by how "famous" the items are.

stemwarewithflair.com
Stemware With Flair

No phone number listed
laurie@stemwarewithflair.com
Kitchen and Dining

In 1997 the unique stemware designs of Laurie Eisenberg were prominently displayed in the windows of Henri Bendel on Michigan Avenue, in the heart of Chicago. Since then, the unique stemware has made its way to Fifth Avenue in New York City and to Union Square in San Francisco. You can now proudly own your own set of intriguingly original stemware, available from Stemware With Flair. The patented technique of combining three dimension shapes on the base of the glasses is quite realistic. For example, a martini glass has three glass olives and matches on the base, while a brandy snifter is made with a replica of a glass cigar. The stemware is whimsical and fun, and guaranteed to be the topic of discussion at your next cocktail party. Martini, wine, snifters, flutes, pilsners, margaritas, platters, and holiday designs are available at the site.

surlatable.com
Sur La Table

866-328-5412
customerservice@surlatable.com

Appliances • Kitchen and Dining

Sur La Table bills itself as "A Cook's Paradise" and it's right on the money! Whether you're a professional chef or just enjoy cooking, you'll find something at this site that you can't live without. Cutting-edge tools take the bite out of food preparation. Equally exciting is the extensive collection of tableware. After you've prepared the consummate meal, Sur La Table provides the tools to serve it with verve and style. The site also offers culinary programs, a gift registry, store listings with events, recipes, and a newsletter to keep you abreast of all the newest trends in kitchen wizardry.

swagsgalore.com
Swags Galore

631-205-1050
swagsgalore@aol.com

Windows

You can find a plethora of patterns and hordes of hardware on the swagsgalore.com site. Shop here for the large selection of discount curtains, curtain rods, sconces, shower curtains, and the hardware you'll need to install your new window treatments. The site also features a user-friendly design tips section to assist in your choosing the right treatment for every window. In addition, a measuring section gives pointers on proper measuring techniques to help you order the exact size you need.

theintimategardener.com
TheIntimateGardener.com

800-240-2771
questions@intimategardener.com

Furniture • Garden • Yard

TheIntimateGardener.com has all the outdoor furniture and accessories to turn your next garden party into an intimate affair. Why not bring your humdrum yard into high society with a few well-chosen pieces? The site offers a wide range of products perfect for year-round fun and relaxation in your yard. The site also has sections exclusively for weddings, pets, and commercial properties. TheIntimateGardener.com also features gardening supplies and accessories, home furnishings, and items for children. Something you might not know: TheIntimateGardener.com supplies prizes to a popular daytime game show where people guess the prices of items.

 Recommended   Price   Selection   Convenience   Service   Security

theshadeandshutter.com
TheShadeandShutter.com
215-561-2552
info@theshadeandshutter.com
Windows

Are you looking for top-of-the-line window treatments and coverings? Do you have discriminating taste and demand the very best in design and customer service? Look no further: TheShadeandShutter.com has been the industry leader since 1963. This company specializes in selling the world's best window fashions and designs in a diverse array of materials, colors, and fabrics. The site also features a consulting service, available to answer any design question you may have. If you're unsure about a specific fabric or color combination, this company will send you a swatch to put your mind at ease.

thetidytray.com
Simply Brilliant Products
860-928-4770
sharon@thetidytray.com
Bathroom

Is your bathroom cabinet overflowing? Do your hygienic products appear unsanitary? Well, the Tidy Tray Bathroom Cabinet Organizer can be your solution. This inspired invention was conceived and created by the sister and brother team of Sharon Belliveau and Bill Jones. After the birth of Sharon's third child, the ointments, creams, and tubes of goo were growing far beyond the capacity of her bathroom cabinet, so she decided enough was enough and dreamed up the Tidy Tray. Bill designed it, and now it's available for all of us to buy and enjoy. The tray measures 10¼" long × 2¼" wide × 1½" high.

toothbrushrack.com
Toothbrushrack.com
877-261-7526
ebrushrack@yahoo.com
Bathroom

Necessity is the mother of invention, and this is a mother of an invention for anyone who has an electric toothbrush. Toothbrushrack.com sells an ingenious item that is specifically designed to hold electric toothbrushes. No more lying down on the job for our high-powered oral care contraptions. The Toothbrush Rack's solid wood composition ensures years of use. It is offered in white and light brown and effortlessly mounts to the wall or cabinet back.

towels4u.com
Towels4u.com

No phone number listed
E-mail form on site

Linen Closet

Whether you rent an apartment or own a home, Towels4u.com offers a terrific solution when you're faced with restocking your linen closet. The user-friendly site offers quality towels and linens at 50 percent off department store and retail prices. The site also features a complete line of Christmas accessories, including stockings, tree skirts, ornaments, and seasonal banners. Towels4u.com has received a five-star customer rating, so shop this site confidently. The company also guarantees all the merchandise 100 percent.

tsunamiwave.com
Tsunami Wave

888-892-8326
info@tsunamiwave.com

Laundry

Are you sick of pouring money down the drain buying expensive laundry detergents, whiteners, stain removers, and fabric softeners? Tsunami Wave is the wave of the future. This new age, ecology friendly product utilizes sophisticated technology. Dual-activated ceramics operate in accord with magnets to improve the water's solvency. The activated ceramics increase the power of ionized water to penetrate the laundry and lift out dirt particles, resulting in clean, fresh clothes without harming the fabric fibers. The site also sells TSUNAMI Enzyme, a super-concentrated, all-natural, and biodegradable alternative to harsh detergents, bleaches, and stain removers.

uncommongoods.com
UncommonGoods

888-365-0056
help@uncommongoods.com

Bathroom • Bedroom • Kitchen and Dining • Linen Closet

Tired of seeing the same home accessories at every site you visit? You need to click over to UncommonGoods, where even the ordinary is head and shoulders above what you'll find anywhere else. Shop this site for bar ware, linens, dinnerware, mugs, coasters, and more. The stock is not extensive, so you won't get bogged down in page after page of similar-looking items. You will see fresh and exciting pieces; on a recent visit I found glass tumblers with dessert recipes written on the side and a Gauguin Bath Palette of paintable soaps for the shower.

 Recommended Price Selection Convenience Service Security

valueleather.com
Valueleather

(800 or 877) 636-7632
E-mail form on site
Furniture

With close to 300 types of leather seating to choose from, you can practically smell that new leather scent as you cruise around this site. Valueleather is THE wholesale leather superstore on the Internet. It specializes in selling leather sofas, recliners, sectionals, and chairs designed and manufactured by renowned Italian and American companies. You are certain to fall in love with the selection of seating and the unbelievably low prices available at this site. You can make online purchases in either American greenbacks or Euro dollars — the choice is yours.

villeroy-boch.com
Villeroy & Boch

888-761-0050
E-mail form on site
Bedroom • Kitchen and Dining • Yard

The Villeroy & Boch site, along with this company's product line, is fashioned for those who love a clean, elegant look. You can outfit, or build, for that matter, each room in a house and at least one outdoor space (the terrace) from this site. The company prides itself on a few select philosophies: "Credibility, quality, image, competence, elegance, harmony, design, lifestyle, innovation, and tradition." The site is uncomplicated to navigate and its layout is self-explanatory. Each category — home living and lifestyle products, building and home products, lifestyle, and professionals — is further subdivided for easy-to-find home furnishings.

wallwhale.com
The Wall Whale

866-888-8778
E-mail form on site
Swimming Pool and Spa

Spend less time cleaning your pool or spa this season and more time lounging in it. The Wallwhale takes the effort out of scrubbing the walls of your pool or spa. It creates ten times more force per stroke and gets the job done in five minutes. Self-proclaimed lazy-afternoon enthusiast, Greg Blackwell, created the Wallwhale. He knew there had to be a better way to clean the scum off his pool walls, and in 2003, the Wallwhale splashed onto the scene. The product is guaranteed to work and comes with a one-year warranty.

warehouseappliance.com
Dynamx, Inc
928-636-1955
info@warehouseappliance.com
Appliances

Dynamix Incorporated is the Internet's number-one source for propane-powered appliances, although it sells electrical appliances, too. The company was formed out of necessity say the owners; they needed a place to buy appliances that could work in less-than-perfect conditions. Most of the appliances sold at the site have been tested in the harsh Baja peninsula environment, so you can rest assured that they will work in your kitchen. You'll find refrigerators, freezers, ovens, and other appliances for use in your home, cabin, or RV. Even if you're not ready to buy, you'll come away with a lot of useful information.

Weberstuff.com
Grilling Today
866-781-0997
info@weberstuff.com
Barbecue

Weberstuff.com is the home site for Grilling Today, an authorized Five-Star Weber Grill dealer. This easy-to-operate site features the full line of Weber grills, rotisseries, and barbecuing products. The site offers home-use gas or charcoal models, Weber accessories, replacement parts, and cookbooks. Weber grills are a well-known name in barbecuing, and many people will not barbecue unless it is on a Weber. The site has a barbecue to fit every budget and your satisfaction is 100 percent guaranteed.

whiteflowerfarm.com
White Flower Farm
800-503-9624
custserv@whiteflowerfarm.com
Garden

The fruits of your labor will be apparent when you buy from White Flower Farm. The White Flower Farm is a family-owned garden center in Litchfield, Connecticut. This company has been selling annuals, perennials, shrubs, bulbs, and houseplants since 1950. The site is a unique resource for gardeners because White Flower Farm actually grows the products it sells, allowing it to select the best specimens for its consumers. The site caters to expert horticulturalists and novice dirt-diggers alike. Plenty of helpful advice is available online or is just a phone call or e-mail message away.

 Recommended   Price   Selection   Convenience   Service   Security

windowxpress.com
Window Xpressions

802-748-8633
info@windowxpress.com

Windows

Window Xpressions is known for "providing products that enrich lives," expressly a wall-mounted hanging shelving system. The product is perfect for displaying your plants in front of a window, giving your house that greenhouse-like look year round. If you don't have a green thumb, but do have plenty of knick-knacks and not enough room to display them, the Window Expression is the perfect solution. The unit is fabricated from high-quality steel and is powder coated for years of a long-lasting, wrought-iron look. Available in two sizes, Window Xpressions has a hanging unit to suit your needs.

your-kitchen.com
The Internet Kitchen

888-730-0199
returnreq@your-kitchen.com

Appliances • Kitchen and Dining

The Internet Kitchen is for the budding gourmet in all of us. It is chock-full of unusual but extremely utilitarian products. You'll find quality kitchenware of every type: cookbooks, cookware, cutlery, coffee and tea, fabric, furniture, gadgets, serveware, small appliances, and vacuum bottles. If you have been looking for a particularly interesting cookery gizmo, this site will have it. Whether the item is a new addition to your growing collection of kitchen and dining products or an auspiciously inventive gift for a culinary contemporary, you will enjoy browsing this site.

Spruce Up Your House

Every house needs a little TLC once in a while. Over time, it's easy for little house projects to get put on the back burner and big projects to get left off the schedule completely. Before too long, a number of small things start to break down. Your house starts to look shabby and unkempt.

There's no time like the present to spruce up your house. Don't worry; this isn't going to turn into a major renovation project. We're only working on the exterior!

Grab a clipboard or pad and paper for note-taking and walk through your house and yard. Look at them objectively. Note what small cosmetic repairs should be made immediately. Now check your toolbox and available supplies. Order what you need to complete the jobs from Ace (ace hardware.com) and Lowes (lowes.com).

How about paint? A coat of paint can brighten the house and give it curb appeal. Paint can also protect your house from the elements. Plan your painting project with some help from the folks at Behr.com (behr.com). This site's Exterior Painting Project Organizer will guide you through your Exterior Painting project from start to finish. Order your paint from Home Depot (homedepot.com).

Check the screens and shutters around the house. A flapping screen lets in insects and looks awful. Apexproducts (apexproducts.com) is the place to go for all your screening needs. This company carries rolls of screen cloth and insect screening and has Live Help on-site during business hours for questions. Exterior Shutter Company (exteriorshutter.com) claims "the best selection of any shutter company in the nation, shipping direct to you" and can have new shutters at your door in a few days.

See, this isn't so bad! Now move on to the yard. Dump that old mower and get a new self-propelled or riding mower from Troy-Bilt (troybilt.com). A leaf blower is a good idea, too. Visit Sears.com (sears.com) and choose the one you like. If you have a really big yard, check out the CycloneRake (cyclonerake.com) for a fast, easy cleanup. The Cyclone Rake attaches to your riding mower and converts it into a commercial-power outdoor cleanup machine. A few shrubs from Nature Hills Nursery (naturehills.com) will make your now-perfect house look like a showplace.

All done! That wasn't so bad, was it? Let's face it: Not everyone enjoys working around the house and not everyone's good at it. If you're not too skilled with a hammer or paintbrush, a helper might be a logical choice. Find a local handyman at HandymanOnline (handymanonline.com) or ServiceMagic (servicemagic.com) and then go and relax.

Chapter 15

International: Shopping the Global Marketplace

he first w in www stands for world — not just the world of information that's at your fingertips, but the shopping opportunities, as well. You can let your mouse do the walking through the world's largest shopping center and shop the stores of the world from continent to continent and country to country, without ever leaving your home.

It's not as hard to shop the world as you may think. Many sites have conversion tables to compute how much an item will cost in your home currency. In some cases, your currency may be worth more in the country you're buying from. This means you may be buying at a discount from what the natives buy at. Visit `xe.com/ucc` for a universal currency converter. Your merchandise will be shipped to your door; you can track its progress at `packtrack.com`, which tracks 58 carriers from around world. If you live overseas and receive products via an APO, FPO, or embassy address, check out `tallyshooter.com` for a directory of stores that will ship to you.

You can purchase merchandise not just made around the world, but actually buy items from Web sites in other countries. Buy exotic temptations from the Caribbean, Celtic treasures from Ireland, Tartan gifts from Scotland, European gift baskets, traditional Scandinavian clothing, Delft Porcelain from Holland, foods from Spain, cuckoo clocks from Germany, Russian military collectibles, crystal from Italy, rare teas from India, food from South Africa, art from China, themed products from Asia, and woolens from Australia. You'll find a world of shopping in this chapter!

Key Word Index

Africa

Look for this keyword to find products from one end of the African continent to the other.

The Americas

The U.S. is not the only country in the western hemisphere that sells online. Listings with this keyword will direct you to online stores in South America and Mexico.

Asia

The listings with the Asian keyword direct you to some of the most exotic merchandise on the planet. Look for online merchants with this keyword for an authentic taste of Asia.

Australia

The Australian keyword directs you to online stores from "down under," Australia and New Zealand. Be ready to find products that are made nowhere else on earth.

Europe

Many of the European countries have jumped into the world of online commerce and offer the world shopper a wide selection of products.

australianartwork.com
Clearspirit Pty Ltd
1-61-7-3398-6211
webmaster@clearspirit.com.au
Australia

G'day, mate! Shop at australianartwork.com and bring home a little bit of Australia. You can find Australian Aboriginal artwork, paintings, didgeridoos, and boomerangs — everything you need to give your home that Australian ambience. You do have to register to use the site, but where else can you find an authentic and beautiful handpainted emu egg or hand-painted boomerang?

brittany-shops.com
Brittany Shops
1-33-(0)2-98-64-38-88
E-mail form on site
Europe

Parlez-vous Français? Even though Brittany Shops is French, you can read the site in English or French. The site offers the best France has to offer, including French foods and beverages, ready-to-wear clothing, embroidery, wall hangings and tableware, health and beauty products, crepe makers, waffle makers and accessories, and cute French toys and games for kids, and from the Breton grandmother (or Mam'Goudig as the Bretons would say), tops and accessories.

chinabridal.com
China Bridal
800-870-7089
shop@chinabridal.com
Asia

If you want a touch of Chinese culture in your wedding, then China Bridal is the place to go. You can shop for Chinese bridal gowns, cheongsam dresses, clothes for men, women, and children; Chinese wedding favors; double happiness signs; phoenix crowns; and Chinese wedding invitations. You can even find gifts for your bridal party, broken into different categories — bridesmaids, groomsmen, and parents. This company ships worldwide and takes credit cards on its site. You can even post a message to the community message board to discuss your wedding plans with others.

chinasprout.com
ChinaSprout

212-868-8488
E-mail form on site

Asia

ChinaSprout's mission is to offer the best Chinese educational and cultural products on the Web. The company helps families who have adopted children from China teach these children about their rich cultural heritage. Through its online store, you can buy Chinese cultural and educational products, including books about China, children's videos to learn Chinese, toys such as monkey king costumes and Yue-Sai dolls, and clothes, including Mandarin suits and dresses. The company ships worldwide via UPS and has a return policy if you're not fully satisfied.

desertstore.com
NetStage

212-868-8488
E-mail form on site

Africa

Shop at desertstore.com, based in Saudi Arabia, for traditional Islamic clothing such as dishdasha, ghutra, iqal, abayas, jilbabs, hijabs, niqabs, and many others at discounted prices. It also sells Bedouin rugs, Bedouin jewelry, Arabian horse costumes, Arabian jambiya, daggers, and décor. It offers a 100 percent satisfaction guarantee, secure shopping, and free worldwide shipping. The clothing and other material products are beautiful and exotic. This is a great site for some remarkable merchandise at very reasonable prices.

exoticindiaart.com
Exotic India

91-11-55154124
inquiry@exoticindia.com

Asia

Exotic India Art offers western shoppers an exotic selection of paintings, sculpture, and jewelry from India. You can also find traditional Indian folk art, an online bookstore for Indian arts, cotton and pure silk Saris, and an astonishing collection of batik art works, all at reasonable prices for art. Delivery is free to all countries having diplomatic relations with India. One feature the site offers is a monthly newsletter, and you can review previous months' issues. Because the company realizes that accurately judging a work of art from an image on a screen is difficult, it offers a satisfaction guarantee with a good return policy. You can use credit cards on its site, too.

 Recommended Price Selection Convenience Service Security

★ germanworld.com
German World

1-49-9404-8032
michael@germanworld.com

Europe

When you look at the prices of the cuckoo clocks, beer steins, and collectibles from this German online merchant, you can see that you're not in a typical German souvenir store. All the Black Forest cuckoo clocks, Bavarian beer steins (pewter lid with crown on top, with a porcelain picture of King Ludwig II), and collectible ships (like a tin toy ship with a real steam engine) are all *handmade* in Germany. The products are exquisite and worthy of the cost. In addition, you can choose from cuckoo clocks with historical, beer-drinking, or hunter themes. You can order online or via fax.

★ gift-mall.com
Gift Mall

No phone number listed
store@gift-mall.com

Europe

Gift-mall.com is *the* place to buy authentic Delftware, the traditional blue china, direct from Holland. Each piece comes with a certificate of originality. Besides the Delft china, the site also offers Williamsburg porcelain beer mugs, plates, vases, bowls, and pitchers. Also be sure to check out the Little Vibes. This nifty little desk piece is a combination of movement and sound. The heat of a candle expands and contracts a bi-metal stem, causing the little brass ball to dance back and forth, which irregularly rings the chime. While you're at the site, take its online quiz on Holland to see how much you know (or don't).

gilletts.com.au
Gillett's

1-61-7-3229-6126
info@gilletts.com.au

Australia

Australia is known for its opals, and Gillett's Jewelry has some of the best. You can find opal rings for all tastes and budgets. It also sells *Lord of the Rings* jewelry with the famous elvish message inscribed, "One Ring to rule them all, One Ring to find them, One Ring to bring them all and in the darkness bind them." The site also offers live online support to answer your questions, and all products are shipped internationally via FedEx at a flat rate.

⭐ globalcrafts.org
Global Crafts
866-468-3438
support@globalcrafts.org
Africa

If you want to help those helping themselves along in the world, then check out Global Crafts, a company that specializes in African art and crafts. It offers income-generating opportunities to craftspeople in developing countries by following fair trade practices, including paying in advance and ensuring fair working conditions. You can buy Maasai jewelry, soapstone carvings, hand-woven baskets, wooden tribal masks, and other gifts. You get free shipping to the U.S. and Canada with a minimum purchase.

goodorient.com
Good Orient
No phone number listed
E-mail form on site
Asia

Here's a one-stop shop for the treasures of the east. All of Good Orient's merchandise is handpicked from various Asian countries. You can find Mandarin blouses, traditional Chinese paintings, Chinese zodiac carvings, chopstick sets, tea sets, and more. The site is organized by products for women, men, kids, home décor and gifts, and collectibles. You can use your credit card at the site, and there is a flat rate of $6.95 for standard shipping. While you're at the site, download the free Chinese name translator and translate your name into Chinese.

ilala.co.za
Ilala Weavers
(035)5620 630/1
ilala@iafrica.com
Africa

The baskets, greeting cards, wire bowls, and beadworks for sale at the Ilala Weavers site are so lovely they might take your breath away. The hand-crafted items were created by workers of Ilala Weavers, a small industry run by the Zulu people in Africa. Its mission: "To improve the income and living standard of Zulu people through their own efforts, by developing a cottage industry, guidance as to market requirements, and marketing results products." Ilala employs over 2,000 Zulu people, who work from home creating the treasures you can buy. There's no online ordering yet, so you'll need to e-mail a list of the items you want and wait for payment instructions.

 Recommended   Price   Selection   Convenience   Service   Security

in-russia.com/store
Interactive Russia
866-680-1373
admin@in-russia.com
Europe

The Soviet Union has fallen but you can still buy a piece of its society from in-russia.com/store, which ships all of its goods ordered via Internet through its Moscow office. Some of the unique products found here for you, comrade, are propaganda posters ("Long Live Soviet Constitution"), military collectibles (such as an engraved lighter with "Most Revered KGB Agent"), classic Russian and modern Russian art, kitchenware, Russian nesting dolls, even replicas of Faberge Eggs. The site offers worldwide shipping but delivery time ranges up to 30 days.

irishshop.com
IrishShop.com
011-353-1-816-1118
E-mail form on site
Europe

For a bit o' Ireland, saunter over to the Irish Shop for a fine selection of Irish goods. This online retailer offers Irish watches, posters, license plates, crystal, linen, purses, pottery, art, Claddagh, and Bodhrans. It also offers a gift selection service where you enter the type of gift — for him or her, or something for the home or office — and the price range you want to spend. Of special interest are the Titanic collectibles, which include Titanic linen napkins, a Titanic clock, and a Titanic poster. This retailer ships internationally.

⭐ madeinfirenze.it
Made In Firenze
1-39-055-701742
info@madeinfirenze.it
Europe

This Italian retailer, Made In Firenze, calls itself your Renaissance Web Store. It offers over 1,200 items from the beautiful city of Firenze, otherwise known as Florence. Here's just a sample of the merchandise available: Italian arts and crafts, Tuscan pottery, fashion bags, Zoppini Italian charm bracelets, Italian Charms, luxury trendy jewelry, Italian home décor and accents, and beautifully designed chess sets and pieces. Check out the Leonardo da Vinci Flying Machine for children that they can actually sit on.

mexgrocer.com
MexGrocer.com
858-459-0577
E-mail form on site
The Americas

Spice up your life and shop MexGrocer.com, an authentic bilingual Mexican online store selling non-perishable authentic Mexican food, household products, and Mexican cookbooks. It also sells Mexican seasonings, beverages, hot sauce, Mexican candy, and over 1,000 specialty Mexican products. You can also find cooking tips and Mexican recipes for free on the site. The company offers worldwide delivery, and your satisfaction is guaranteed. Send MexGrocer.com's gift certificates to friends and family and give them an authentic taste of Mexico.

namaste.com
Namaste.com
312-373-1777
support@namaste.com
Asia

Namaste.com is familiar to thousands of shoppers around the world. Think of it as an Indian superstore, featuring the best of Indian cuisine, culture, and clothing. Start in the grocery aisle with treats like mango pickles and Haldiram snacks. Rice and dal are always good choices, and don't forget the spices. The latest and greatest movies from Bollywood are available here, along with classic Hindustani and Carnatic classical titles. You'll also find music on DVD by a wide variety of artists. Health and beauty products are fun to browse — you may find something that captures your fancy. All in all, this site offers a good shopping experience.

norwayshop.com
Norway Shop
1-47-22-33-41-90
service@norwayshop.com
Europe

If you're Norwegian or just want to look like one, then Norway Shop can meet your needs. All sweaters, pewter, jewelry, and wood-carved products in the Norway Shop are made in Norway, and the company guarantees the quality. The clothing is pricey but original. For those of us on the other side of the pond, the site offers a sizing chart to compare European apparel sizes to those of the U.S. The site's search engine enables you to search by brand, product, and even theme.

 Recommended   Price   Selection   Convenience   Service   Security

ozwool.net
Ozwool

1-07-3314-6975
E-mail form on site

Australia

Australia is known for its sheep. The best sheepskin mats you can find come from Australian sheep. Ozwool sells a new generation of Australian sheepskins that can be used nearly anywhere, including baby and infant sleeping mats, car seat covers, wheelchair covers, floor rugs, pet mats, and underlays. These products can be washed in hot water and come in different colors. In addition, the sheepskins are designed to reduce and prevent bedsores in bed-ridden people. This company ships internationally.

provence-prestige.tm.fr
Provence Prestige

33 (0)4 90 99 08 08
webmaster@provence-prestige.tm.fr

Europe

Welcome mes amis to Provence, the charming region in France known for its food, wine, and beauty. Visit the Provence Prestige site to learn more about vacations in the Provence area and, of course, to shop. The provincial charm of the online stores is somewhat ruined by the notice, "The Chamber of Commerce and Industry rents out spaces on this site depending on availability." However, if you can get back in the shopping mode you'll find French foodstuffs, a decent collection of pottery and housewares, and some jewelry. Pick and choose items from store to store and then pay for everything at one time.

satooz.com
SATOOZ

07-3888 4044
angela@satooz.com

Africa

Although SATOOZ is located in Australia, not South Africa, it specializes in South African food and other essentials. The company ships internationally and offers a 100 percent satisfaction guarantee. Some of the South African specialties offered include Potjie Pots, Biltong and Droewors, Ouma Rusks and South African biscuits, Pronutro, Mealie Meal, Marmite, and many other items. It even offers Zam-buk ointment for the treatment of minor wounds. The site also includes a few recipes and links to other sites about South Africa.

scotwebstore.com
ScotWeb Store

1-44-131-452-8159
E-mail form on site

Europe

Hoot Mon! The ScotWeb store offers the finest Highland Dress outfits, hand-crafted jewelry, and luxurious knitwear to the global shopper. The company prides itself on the quality and authenticity of its merchandise, and promises to beat any price. The on-site Tartan finder can help you match up your Scottish name to the correct design and show you actual swatches from mills making tartans for that name. Or you can window-shop for men's cashmere sweaters, the Classic Black Prince Charlie Jacket and Vest, and even the very best bagpipes! The company will soon be unveiling an online shopping club, offering members special features and exclusive deals.

tiendaslatinas.com
TiendasLatinas.com

591-4-422-2197
E-mail form on site

The Americas

TiendasLatinas.com is the place to buy Andean gifts, including musical instruments like pan flutes and quenachos, Bolivian and Peruvian music CDs, aguayo and alpaca clothes, and handcrafted gifts like braided rugs, stuffed animals, traditional Andean games, hand-carved Charangos, Aguayo belts, and a llama rug. The company ships worldwide via certified airmail from Peru or Bolivia. The site is presented both in Spanish and English.

Chapter 16

Malls and Mega Stores: Great Shopping Under One Virtual Roof

*U*sing your mouse to surf through online shop after online shop may be fun for a while, and yes, you will find some extraordinary merchandise, but wouldn't it be nice sometimes if you could find several stores — suppose we call them mega stores — where you can find a whole range of products all in one convenient place?

Well, you can. I've put together a great selection of Internet shopping centers and department stores that fit the bill. Shopping at these mega stores provides a convenience that the average, everyday online retailer can't match. In most cases, these mega stores offer you the ability to buy a vast array of merchandise, drop it into one shopping cart, and pay for it all with just one click of your mouse.

This chapter lists department stores that you know and some you might not. I include giant mega stores that sell all manner of product, others that offer a group of stores that specialize in one product area, and others that have a regional flavor to the products they sell. I also throw in a few outlet stores where you save big on brand-name products.

So go ahead and dive in. There's not just a world of products out there, but a full universe to explore at your fingertips.

Key Word Index

Department Store

Department stores arose in the 1870s. Look for this keyword to see the latest manifestation of the department store and the wide selection of product categories offered in one store location.

Outlet Store

Bargains, bargains, bargains — that's what outlet stores promise, selling merchandise at up to 70 percent off retail. Look for this keyword to find brand-name products at steep discounts.

Regional Shopping

Shopping the world can be a lot of fun. But you can also shop the different regions of the United States. This keyword directs you to regional merchants with products of a local flavor.

Specialty Store

From environmentally-friendly products to products "as seen on TV," the specialty stores focus on one particular category of products and offer the online shopper an array of merchandise.

amazon.com
Amazon

800-201-7575
E-mail form on site

Department Store

Amazon started out selling books. However, its company executives must have read a lot of the business books Amazon carries because it's now the 500-pound gorilla of online retailers. Today, Amazon sells everything, literally, from A (Arts) to Z (zShops, which enable anyone to set up a business on Amazon). The site offers one-click purchase capability and can even make recommendations based on your past buying behavior. Amazon has written the book on being a successful online retailer and servicing the online shopper.

ashford.com
Ashford.com

888-922-9039
E-mail form on site

Department Store

Shop a selection of over 400 luxury brands and 15,000 products! That's what Ashford claims to deliver to the online shopper. Brand names, such as Prada, Burberry, Omega, and TAG Heuer, are in some cases discounted up to 60 percent, although most products are discounted in the 20–30 percent range. You can shop this site by brand, department, or price. Ashford offers not only lots of brand-name jewelry but also watches, handbags, home accents, and fragrances. It even has a small outlet shop.

asseenontv.com
AsSeenOnTv.com

866-277-3366
customerservice@seenontv.com

Outlet Store • Specialty Store

You'll feel like you're in shopper's heaven at AsSeenOnTv.com. All the products from TV practically reach out and beg for you to buy them. Shop three ways at this convenient site: by Category, such as Kitchen, Gifts and Novelties, Fitness, Personal Care, and more; by Featured Products, an area on the site where the latest and greatest products are displayed; or by the handy alphabetical index, Our Products A to Z. The index contains links to every product listed on the site, even those bonus products that never appeared on television ads. The return policy at AsSeenOnTv.com is strict, so read the product descriptions carefully before you order.

bloomingdales.com
Bloomingdale's

866-593-2540
E-mail form on site

Department Store

How popular is Bloomingdale's? Well, what other store played host to the Queen of England? If she shopped there, you might consider shopping there, too. "Bloomies," as it's affectionately called by shoppers, is as traditional a department store as you can get. It all started with the first product that Joseph and Lyman Bloomingdale sold — the hoop skirt. From there, they developed the store into a shopping destination for the well-heeled and well-to-do. The Bloomingdale's site offers all the typical department store products along with excellent customer service.

bluefly.com
Bluefly.com

877-258-3359
E-mail form on site

Outlet Store

Brand-name designer clothing selling at up to 75 percent off retail? Should bluefly.com be at the top of your apparel shopping list? You bet. You can shop its outlet stores, "Downtown," for clothing lines like Diesel, Marc Jacobs, and Joe's Jeans, or "Uptown," for designer names like Nicole Miller, BCBG, and Sergio Rossi. You can shop the whole range of products found in any department store, but without tiring out your feet walking from department to department.

★ catalogcity.com
Catalog City

No phone number listed
E-mail form on site

Department Store

Probably thousands of different catalog companies exist today, selling all manner of product. Catalog City does a fairly good job of offering the same products sold by these companies at its own online store. From the Bombay Company to Omaha Steaks to Venus Swimwear, you'll find a wide range of catalogs at this site. The best part is that as you shop Catalog City, you load your shopping cart with products from the different catalog houses, and then pay only once for all of it at checkout. If just buying the thousands of products Catalog City offers through its store is not enough, you can also click the link to a catalog's site to buy directly from the catalog retailers.

 Recommended   Price   Selection   Convenience   Service Security

coolestshop.com
Coolest Shop

541-431-0494
info@coolestshop.com

Department Store

A site that claims to be the coolest? Then you would expect some crazy, cool merchandise at this online retailer — and coolestshop.com doesn't disappoint. Check out the Cube from Loop. It has two sides that are zippered storage compartments. But that's not all. On the bottom of the cube is a secret storage compartment to hide all your stuff. Or consider the UFO desk clock or an Android watch. The site also offers cool apparel and art, as well as live customer service. Most prices include shipping — how cool is that?

coolshopping.com
CoolShopping.com

800-321-1484
shop@coolshopping.com

Department Store

CoolShopping.com calls itself the "Internet Shopping Channel," in reference to its cousins on the cable shopping channels. Looking at the site's product selection and the discounted prices, I would say that it comes close. CoolShopping.com features Oprah's Favorite Things, such as the iRobot Roomba Intelligent Floorvac and the Apple iPod. Some samples of the other merchandise offered are items for the baby, digital cameras, computers, DVDs, consumer electronics, music, toys, videos, and video games.

★ costco.com
Costco.com

800-774-2678
E-mail form on site

Department Store

You would expect Costco's Web site to mirror its warehouse roots, and it does. Costco offers many products at great prices because members buy at, or slightly above, wholesale pricing. You can buy items ranging from computers to furniture to wine. You don't have to be a member of Costco, but if you're not, you pay a little more than members do. Costco's return policy is good — you can return whatever you purchase on its site to any of Costco's warehouses worldwide. Keep in mind that product selection rotates considerably. A word to the wise — that great deal you see one day may be gone the next, never to return.

disneystore.com
The Disney Store
800-328-0368
E-mail form on site
Specialty Store

When Disney first opened a site on the Web, its slow-to-download site was a bear to navigate. Then the magic kicked in, and the redesigned site ran smoothly even on a slow connection. The Disney Store offers the Disney clothing, toys, movies, music, games, home décor, art, and collectibles that will have you wishing upon a star in no time. Shop by product type (toys, movies, clothes, home, and collectibles) or by character (Mickey, Toy Store, Pooh, Princesses, and more).

dynadirect.com
DynaDirect.com
877-438-3962
sales@dynadirect.com
Department Store

You know that thousands of products are available in today's catalogs. But shopping each catalog looking for the product you want would be virtually impossible. That's where DynaDirect comes in. This company sells the same products found in large retail chains and mail-order catalogs around the world. Its shopping categories include brand-name computer products, consumer electronics, housewares, sport items, products for the kids — even travel items to use on your trips. DynaDirect offers a good selection and average pricing, but it's a well-rounded all-in-one shop.

fingerhut.com
Fingerhut
800-603-7052
No e-mail address on site
Department Store

Fingerhut made its name by selling a wide variety of products on a monthly installment plan. The company supplied its own Fingerhut credit card to customers and gave a much wider portion of the shopping population the opportunity to buy products they wanted. If you're not looking for fancy, but just practical, Fingerhut could be the place to shop for everything from health and beauty aids to electronics to sporting goods.

★ Recommended   Price   Selection   Convenience   Service   🔒 Security

floridabymail.com
Florida By Mail
386-690-2898
info@floridabymail.com
Regional Shopping

If you would like a little taste of Florida — and not just orange juice — then Florida By Mail offers you some unique products with the flavor of Florida. Where else can you get jewelry and products made from real Floridian shark teeth? This company sells shark tooth necklaces, shark tooth jewelry, and shark tooth bolo ties. It also offers seashell jewelry and ornaments, dolphin jewelry, tasty tropical treats, and orange blossom perfume. You can even find wacky items like chocolate alligator candy and alligator bubblegum.

fortunoff.com
Fortunoff
800-367-8866
E-mail form on site
Department Store

In 1922, Max and Clara Fortunoff opened their new housewares store. Since then, Fortunoff has grown into a well-known retailer with a "vast selection of quality merchandise." That selection is now available to shoppers on the Web. Fortunoff offers what it calls "necessities to niceties" — all kinds of quality jewelry, everything for the table, home furnishings for both inside and outside the house, seasonal shopping, and fine gifts. It also offers a free gift and bridal registry.

⭐ **greenhome.com**
Green Home
877-282-6400
help@greenhome.com
Specialty Store

Are you looking for products to buy that are good for both people and the environment? Sustainable maple beds (no toxic glues, formaldehyde, or particle board), unbleached coffee cups, organic teddy bears, reused rubber carrying bags, recycled cardboard binders, and repurposed wine glasses (created from recycled wine bottles) are just some of the environmentally friendly items you find at the Green Home online store. So shop here if you want to simultaneously make your home environment healthy and reduce your impact upon the earth.

half.com
Half.com
No phone number listed
No e-mail address on site
Department Store

Before it was bought by eBay, Half.com was a store where you could buy items at half price from people wanting to sell their old CDs and videos online. Although owned by eBay, Half.com is not an auction site. If you see something you want, you just buy it outright from the seller. However, you pay Half.com, which in turn pays the seller. The selection of products for sale has grown considerably, and Half.com now sells computers and software, consumer electronics, CDs, movies, popular books — even text books — at discounted prices.

hsn.com
Home Shopping Network
800-933-2887
E-mail form on site
Department Store

The Home Shopping Network started with a novel idea — 24-hour TV product demonstrations — and became a global success. Now the company has moved to the Web. So, kick off your shoes, sit back, and browse through the bargains on products ranging from the practical to the mundane. If you missed out on that HSN special TV offer on a gold necklace or colored gemstone, or the Body by Jake Total Body Trainer, or the Wolfgang Puck cookware that your neighbor told you about, you can buy it right from the HSN site at your leisure.

macys.com
Macy's
877-797-7227
visitor@macys.com
Department Store

Macy's online store has everything you see at Macy's New York except the Thanksgiving Day Parade. Macy's is known for its fashionable clothing and gifts, created by world-class designers. You can find these same products at its online store. Choose from such product categories as men's and women's apparel, bed and bath items, housewares, jewelry, and beauty supplies. Make sure you check out the sales items, and save 20–50 percent off brand-name products.

 Recommended   Price   Selection   Convenience   Service   Security

madeinoregon.com
Made In Oregon

800-828-9673
catalog@madeinoregon.com

Regional Shopping

Made In Oregon sells products that are, well, made in Oregon. The site consists of ten Oregon retail stores all under one roof, and all using the same shopping cart so you can shop and buy with just the click of your mouse. The company also offers free gift-wrapping. A small selection of its products: the Oregon Harvest Gift Pack, which includes the bounty of Oregon's orchards, farms, and sea; Oregon Pinot Noir wine; and a Portland Palette Cookbook. The site shows off a nice selection of Pendleton woolens and Margaret Furlong Collectibles.

maikaihawaii.com
MaiKai Hawaii

866-685-2148
support@maikaihawaii.com

Regional Shopping

With a greeting on its home page that says, "aloha auinala," you know you're not on the mainland anymore. You've arrived in sunny and friendly Hawaii. MaiKai Hawaii offers unique and quality products from Hawaii and the Pacific Rim. A sample of its products includes Hawaii Snack Foods, Pure Hawaiian Hula Coffee, beautiful tropical flowers and leis, Hawaiian-style jewelry (colored coral and Tahitian pearls), and other gift ideas. Plus, you get a free gift with every order over $30.

mainegoodies.com
Maine Goodies

866-385-6238
info@mainegoodies.com

Regional Shopping

Maine is known for its beautiful shorelines, green forests, and a countryside dotted with small villages. It is also known for some of the best regional products you can buy. Maine Goodies has searched high and wide to find products made in Maine or inspired by it and has come up with a selection of goodies that will give you the essence of Maine. The site offers baking mixes, balsam-filled draft stoppers and pillows, and cooking sauces and canned goods all carrying the flavor of Maine.

neimanmarcus.com
Neiman Marcus

888-888-4757
E-mail form on site

Department Store

Neiman Marcus epitomizes a high-end department store. It covers the bases in all the categories that make a true department store — but for a price. The company's annual catalog basically tells you that if you're looking for high-quality, high-priced items, you'll find them at Neiman Marcus. Buy apparel for him, her, and the kids; accessories; jewelry; fragrances; home entertainment products; and consumer electronics. Neiman Marcus's customer service is first rate, and you can speak live to a service rep while at the site to answer any questions you may have.

★ overstock.com
Overstock.com

800-989-0135
productinfo@overstock.com

Outlet Store

Overstock.com came about as a way for merchants and manufacturers to liquidate merchandise via the Internet by offering online shoppers an opportunity to buy this same merchandise for less than retail. Today, Overstock.com offers the online shopper great deals on overstock items from retailers and manufacturers from around the country. All the products are unused, and many come with manufacturer's warranties. The site lists categories for just about any product, and all at great savings to you.

qvc.com
QVC

888-345-5788
E-mail form on site

Department Store

If you're looking for practical products at practical prices, then QVC.com is your online shopping destination. Modeled after the cable channel, QVC.com offers a selection of products seen on its TV show. In fact, if you have a fast Internet connection, you can view the television broadcast in progress in your browser and when you see a product you like, buy it online, right then and there. You have to admit the coolness of that online shopping feature. QVC also offers live online help, so if you get stumped navigating the site you can speak to a representative without having to pick up the phone.

 Recommended   Price   Selection   Convenience   Service   Security

safetycentral.com
Safety Central

707-472-0288
sales@safetycentral.com

Specialty Store

Home safety and preparedness are the reasons for the products sold by Safety Central. This online store offers hundreds of items in categories of cooking, heating, shelter, survival, personal protection and health, home and personal security — and the list goes on. If you're confused about what you need, then use the site's handy Emergency Preparedness Checklist, which lists the essentials you should have readily available for the office, car, and home in times of disaster, natural or otherwise.

★ samsclub.com
Sam's Club

No phone number listed
E-mail form on site

Outlet Store

Not to be outdone by Costco, Sam Walton of Wal-Mart fame started Sam's Club. Like Costco, it sells hundreds of limited-time products at wholesale prices. Like Costco, in order to enjoy these prices you must be a Sam's Club member (thus the word *club* is in its name). Sam's not only sells a wide range of products, but also has an auction component to its site, a photo center to develop your digital prints, and an online pharmacy. You can also access live customer service on the site. Another nifty service is the Click & Pull feature that is being rolled out across the country. Find the product you want, click on it, and pick it up at your local Sam's Club.

sears.com
Sears

800-349-4358
E-mail form on site

Department Store

From being one of the first catalog companies in the world, this retailer has become a shopping staple of the American consumer. Although specializing in appliances and tools, the Sears online store also offers products in other shopping categories, such as automotive, consumer electronics, fitness and recreation, lawn and garden items, and clothing for adults and children. Pricing is competitive, but its product quality and purchase guarantees are always first rate.

⭐ send.com

send.com

609-720-0300
E-mail form on site

Department Store

Send.com is a combination of many different sites with the same first name, such as SendFloral, SendLiquor, SendBonsai, SendGiftBaskets — you get the idea. This arrangement gives you the opportunity to shop in many different categories — the same way as in a department store — at the same time. But the feature that caught my eye was the capability of many of the Send.com stores to send items in your shopping basket to multiple recipients: perfect for holiday shopping.

⭐ skymall.com

Sky Mall

800-759-6255
E-mail form on site

Department Store

If you've ever flown on a commercial airline, you couldn't miss seeing the Sky Mall catalog in the seat pouch in front of you. Its products are different from those in the run-of-the-mill catalogs and sometimes even surprising. You'll find the latest in categories from electronics to fitness equipment. More a catalog of catalogs, this online store lets you shop through an assortment of different retailers for apparel, home living, jewelry, pet stuff, travel items, sports and fitness products, and more from Hammacher Schlemmer, Orvis, Plow and Hearth, Sharper Image, and many more.

spiegel.com

Spiegel

800-345-4500
E-mail form on site

Department Store

Spiegel is a well-known department store for women. It offers clothing and accessories for her, as well as household products for the home. You can shop Spiegel's online store the same way you shop at other retailers' sites, but you can also use its Idea Resource, which Spiegel claims is a whole new way to shop. By choosing a category, you can get expert advice on dressing, entertaining, and decorating all in one coordinated resource. Spiegel's site also includes eMarket, a mall for other companies such as Sephora, Red Envelope, and even Royal Caribbean Cruise Lines.

 Recommended   Price   Selection   Convenience   Service   🔒 Security

target.com
Target
800-591-3869
E-mail form on site
Department Store

Whether you call it Target or Tarjhay, this store appeals to everybody. More upscale than Wal-Mart, Target offers plenty of the basics, but with added flair from designers like Michael Graves and Isaac Mizrahi. Products for the home; clothing for men, women, and kids; electronics; sports; entertainment and gifts — all the typical department store categories are covered at Target, but with down-to-earth prices. If Target's selection is not enough to fill out your shopping list, you can shop one of its partner stores — Marshall Fields or Mervyns's — right from its site.

★ walmart.com
Wal-Mart
800-966-6546
E-mail form on site
Department Store

Wal-Mart has become the almost-perfect department store with a great selection, good prices, and excellent customer service. Its online store mirrors its offline stores and carries much of what is offered at them and then some. Walmart.com offers one service that other online department stores do not: You can have your photos developed by uploading them to walmart.com's photo center, and then you can pick up your photos (if you want) at your local Wal-Mart store at no charge.

wisconsinmade.com
Wisconsin Made
877-947-6233
E-mail form on site
Regional Shopping

Are you a "cheese head"? Do you want to be? Then Wisconsin Made is "made" for you. This company offers Wisconsin-made foods, music, art, clothing, and more. How about food? Wisconsin is known for its fabulous cheese such as cheddar, Swiss, and Gouda, all made at the Wisconsin dairies. By the way, you can sign up for Wisconsin Made's Cheese of the Month Club and get a different cheese sent to you every month. It also sells Wisconsin-made bratwurst, Wisconsin Ice Cream, and O & H Danish Coffee Cake. Of course, what Wisconsin store wouldn't have Green Bay Packer clothing and accessories? You can buy them here, too.

youcansave.com

youcansave.com

800-482-7530

support@youcansave.com

Department Store

YouCanSave.com claims to have over one million satisfied customers. Looking at the array of products this company sells and its prices, you could believe it. This online retailer specializes in the products you see advertised on those infomercials seen on late-night TV. How about the popular Liquid Lens Kit or the Plate Caddy? You can get them at this site. Or how about the Air Leg Massager and Emerson Switchboard? The site offers them, too. So go to bed early knowing that you're not going to miss out on some great product on late-night TV; you can just shop at this site instead.

Chapter 17

Office Supplies: Getting Down to Business

• •

The way people work is ever changing. In the not-too-distant past, most people left home to go to work. Office work was always performed in an office. When the work-day ended, everything was put away for tomorrow. The tools and machines to take work home didn't exist.

Today the lines between home and office are blurred. Tools like computers, pagers, and cell phones help people stay connected. Handhelds and PDAs help everyone coordinate schedules and due dates. Many employees telecommute — work at home — at least a few days each week. Some employees work entirely by computer and fax. There's no reason to meet with co-workers face to face.

One thing hasn't changed. Whether you work in a suite in a skyscraper or in your garage, your office is only as good as its supplies. If you don't have pens, pencils, or paper for your printer, your important business stops.

 SOHO America is an online community made up of small-office/home-office professionals who are facing the day-to-day challenges, the risks and rewards, of running a SOHO business. Learn more about the group at soho.org.

Key Word Index

Business Cards

Business cards are small paper advertisements for you. Your business card can be simple or die-cut in a fancy shape. The sites with the Business Card keyword will create a personalized business card that leaves a lasting impression.

Calendars

To stay organized and on time, the sites with the Calendars keyword offers wall calendars, timekeeping systems, and several books and systems.

Ergonomics

Ergonomics simply means the science of body comfort! Sites with the Ergonomics keyword provide chairs, furniture, and accessories designed to keep you comfortable in the office.

Office Furniture

The Office Furniture sites sell the heavy stuff — chairs, desks, filing cabinets, and the like.

Office Supplies

The Office Supplies sites offer a convenient way to shop for pens, pencils, folders, forms, and everything you need to work.

Telephone Systems

Whether you have one person or an entire corporation on staff, you need a phone system to stay connected, and the Telephone Systems sites can set you up. Who said talk was cheap?

aceprinting.net
Ace Printing Inc.

888-737-9180
info@aceprinting.net

Business Cards

Ace trumps the competition when it comes to printing business cards. Why settle for ordinary black-and-white cards when full-color cards are so affordable? You can choose an image from the site's huge library or submit a graphics image of your own for use on your cards. Ace can even scan a photograph or picture for you and place the image on your card. Your final cards will be shipped in no more than five days after your proof approval. Need your cards faster? No problem. Rush service is available for a slightly higher fee.

adirondackdirect.com
Adirondack

800-221-2444
info@adirondackdirect.com

Office Furniture

You won't go wrong with Adirondack Direct. This company has satisfied over one million customers with its stock of both office and institutional furniture. Adirondack Direct offers wholesale-priced furniture from a single source provider. This means that you will be able to order matching units and know that everything will ship together and on time. The company uses a vast distribution network with nationwide shipping points and worldwide delivery. Check out the Web Specials for current sale items. Internet shoppers receive an additional discount on all furniture purchases.

athome-atwork.com
atHome-atWork.com

866-246-3746
sales@athome-atwork.com

Ergonomics

The athome-atwork.com site carries a full line of "ergonomic solutions" for your office. You'll find the Humanscale Freedom Work Chair in several model styles and price ranges. If the somewhat staggering price of the Freedom chair overwhelms you, a selection of serviceable work chairs priced under $300 is also available. The conference and side chairs will protect your employees from injury while giving your office an interesting retro look. Don't neglect the computer carts and utility and occasional tables. Check out the accessories while you're shopping. Simple accessories like monitor lifts or keyboard trays can make the difference between injury and health.

⭐ biomorphdesk.com
Biomorph Desk
888-302-2275
customerservice@biomorphdesk.com

Ergonomics

This site offers a great idea — an ergonomic desk that's custom-built by you! That's right, the Biomorph Interactive desk is custom designed for your computer equipment and the way you use it. You put the components together online. Of course, if you're satisfied with the basic model (and it isn't shabby!) go to the Fast track single desk purchase section at the site. Otherwise, go to the Build your own set up section and select your desk, surface finish, add-ons and lighting, storage and extensions, and chair. Biomorph will contact you for final options and payment details.

businessphonesdirect.com
Business Phones Direct
866-777-7466
E-mail form on site

Telephone Systems

New and refurbished phone systems are available at Business Phones Direct. Priced to fit every size business and budget, you'll find systems from most major manufacturers at the site, including Norstar, Lucent, and Nortel. Figuring out what telephone system is best for your company's needs is sometimes difficult. Contact Business Phones Direct's sales team and explain your company's needs. Within two hours, you'll have a quote for a system customized to your requirements. Business Phones Direct will buy your existing business phone equipment from you if you purchase a new system from it.

buyofficefurnitureonline.com
BuyOfficeFurnitureOnline.com
877-583-1248
E-mail form on site

Office Furniture

You won't see pages and pages of desks, cubicles, and chairs at this online office furniture site. Instead, BuyOfficeFurnitureOnline.com works as the middleman between you and the manufacturer. If you know the furniture you want to buy, let this company know and it'll send you a quote. If you need design help, it'll develop a plan for your new office after you've e-mailed or faxed your specs. Let the company know if you want offices or workstations and your specific budgetary requirements. Pricing is typically low and installations can be coordinated nationwide.

 Recommended   Price   Selection   Convenience   Service   Security

cardconnection.com
Cardconnection.com

818-597-0137
support@cardconnection.com

Business Cards

CardConnection.com is a great source for business cards. This company has made it easy for you to design a card that's perfect for you. Its clever online design process enables you to design your card and preview it at the same time. Don't be afraid to experiment with the site's selection of font styles, ink colors, graphics, and papers. When you've finalized the design, your cards will be printed with raised lettering print. No inkjet or laser printing here! CardConnection.com offers a standard 20–30 percent discount on cards.

corporatecalendars.com
Corporate Calendars

800-660-9666
support@executivegreetingcards.com

Calendars

Competitive pricing, a vast selection of calendar styles, and fast shipping make Corporate Calendars a great place for businesses to purchase calendars. The calendars are arranged by themes, such as America, Religious, Trucking, and so on. Click a theme to see the related calendars available. Corporate Calendars also sells greeting cards and calendar cards. If you're a business owner, why not send out a twelve-month calendar card this year with your business name and address prominently displayed, instead of a more traditional holiday card that will be read and tossed in the trash?

cyberchair.com
Cyberchair, Inc.

800-242-4777
No e-mail address on site

Ergonomics

That '90s buzzword ergonomics has folks flocking to this site from far and wide to order the famous Cyberchair. With good reason: The chair is specially designed for those who work on computers. The chair is positioned higher than normal so that the user is looking down at the computer screen. The chair follows the user's movement and maintains contact with the lumbar area. Because no two people are built alike, the chair can be adjusted in various ways to fit people of all sizes and shapes. The Cyberchair comes in several styles and fabrics. Sure, it's a bit pricey, but you're worth it.

dayrunner.com
Day Runner

800-365-9327
cop.calendars.cs@meadwestvaco.com

Calendars

Day Runner organizers are powerful, flexible productivity tools that assist busy people every day. The Day Runner system is made up of a three-ring binder that holds individual modules, such as a planner, phone book, appointment diary, and a business card holder. Choosing the modules you want is up to you. Choose your binder and modules from several styles and colors. You needn't build a new system from scratch each year; simply log in and order the handy refills available online. Additionally, Day Runner stocks a full line of accessories, such as wall planners and special occasion cards.

daytimer.com
Day-Timer

800-457-5702
E-mail form on site

Calendars

Many people think the words Day-Timer are synonymous with a personal scheduling system. It's no wonder; the company's been in business for over forty years. Shop the site for your personal calendar pages, cover, and accessories. If you're new to the Day-Timer system, take a few minutes to learn how it works before you order. Day-Timer also sells a complete line of home and office supplies. Order fine writing instruments, stationery, bags and totes, travel accessories, wallets, and computer accessories at the same time you put together your Day-Timer system.

easychairworkstation.com
EasyChair WorkStation

800-810-7890
mdbailey@easychairworkstation.com

Ergonomics

EasyChair WorkStation removes the tether between workstation and computer. With this handy, ergonomic device, you can attach your laptop directly to your favorite chair or recliner. Now, you don't need to balance the computer in your lap, and you can sit comfortably as you work. EasyChair WorkStation sells a number of other components and ergonomic accessories, as well. Many of these components are designed to aid those who are wheelchair bound or disabled. The site even offers The Beneform Zero-Gravity Recliner as the base for the EasyChair WorkStation system.

 Recommended   Price   Selection   Convenience   Service   Security

enetfurniture.com
eNet Furniture

877-363-8387
customerservice@enetfurniture.com

Office Furniture

eNetFurniture is one of those easily overlooked sites. There's no flashy design and no music, only a somewhat clunky interface on the opening page. However, if you're looking for office furniture, it's worth staying. The site carries just about every piece of office furniture you can imagine. From tables and chairs to filing equipment, this company has earned its self-proclaimed designation of "The electronic mall for furniture." The prices shown for each item include shipping charges. Quantity orders get quantity discounts, so contact the site if you're buying more than a few items.

ergozone.com
Ergozone

800-695-5510
E-mail form on site

Ergonomic

Ergozone is a no-frills site that's all about comfort and safety. Browse through the convenient catalog for products you probably never thought you needed: glare filters and hoods, copy holders, backrests, seat cushions, wrist rests, and more. After looking at the items, you may decide that your current work area needs to be revamped! (I did.) You can shop by manufacturer as well; the primary ergonomics manufacturers are represented, including Biofit Engineered Products, Mediflow, and Posture Systems. Ergozone is a great place to shop if you're just starting to think ergonomically. Try a few items and see whether you feel better.

foilmaster.com
Foilmaster

973-546-7753
info@foilmaster.com

Business Cards

Let Foilmaster create an amazing business card just for you. The Foilmaster specialists use a unique process to heat-stamp the card. Choose your card stock from a wide range of backgrounds, such as enamel, leatherette, marble iridescent, and more. Next select your text from spectrum foil, gold or silver glitter, or holographic foil. The stunning foils are available in flat or metallic and the color selection is vast. Finally, choose your font and layout, and presto, your very own card will be created.

furniturewholesalers.com
Furniture Wholesalers.com

877-709-9700
info@furniturewholesalers.com

Office Furniture

Furniture Wholesalers.com says "get furnished, get busy." With its winning combination of low prices and huge stock, there's no reason to do anything else. Shop this site for all your office furniture needs: chairs, tables, desks, bookcases, filing cabinets, and more. Or order a convenient pre-packaged suite and fully furnish your conference room, boardroom, executive office, reception area, or home office. Most items are available to be shipped less than a week after a completed order. Custom orders are available, too. Your custom order will take a bit longer to ship; non-stocked colors and fabrics typically take between four and six weeks.

gapco.com
gapco.com

800-440-2368
sales@gapco.com

Business Cards

Price rules at gapco.com. Business cards are priced lower than just about anywhere else on the Internet. In fact, this company dares you to compare! For one inclusive price, your card will have one image scan, typesetting, film output, the highest quality 4-color process printing using Heidelberg offset lithography, and the highest quality high-gloss 10-point cast-coated paper. Turnaround time takes about 7 to 10 days — not bad considering all the custom work involved in your card. Need full-color postcards? You can order them here, too.

hertzfurniture.com
Hertz Furniture Systems

800-526-4677
info@hertzfurniture

Office Furniture

Hertz Furniture Systems makes shopping for office furniture fun. It helps that the furniture sold at this site is gorgeous, made of wood, and finished in warm, shining gloss. Everything from the single chairs to the office suites looks like it has been designed for an executive. Want to see the back of a chair or the side of a desk? The Virtual Gallery enables you to view some items in a 3D environment and rotate them for viewing from all angles. Check out the Swatch Patch for all the available fabrics.

 Recommended   Price   Selection   Convenience   Service   Security

homeofficedirect.com
Home Office Direct

877-709-9700
info@homeofficedirect.com

Office Furniture

If you're moderately handy with a screwdriver and a few other tools, Home Office Direct can save you big bucks the next time you furnish your home office. The site sells high-quality, ready-to-assemble home office furniture such as computer workstations, desks, and chairs. The furniture is produced by leading manufacturers like Sauder and Bestar. A few accessories like computer glare screens, keyboard drawers, and monitor drawers round out the collection. The unassembled furniture is delivered directly to your door, which is much easier than hauling cartons home from the store.

hotphones.com
hotphones.com

800-400-9884
telsales@telephones.com

Telephone Systems

The folks at hotphones.com, really Alpine Communication Systems, are serious about installing and maintaining your new phone system. Alpine is an authorized Panasonic dealer and has been in business for over 20 years. Its tech support is free and provided by Panasonic and Avaya technicians. You'll receive free installation, programming, and user manuals with your new system. As if that's not enough, you'll also get third-party Microsoft Windows programming software, PC programming cables, Quick Guides, and overlay telephone labels and software. Ground shipping is free.

ineedbusinesscards.com
1 Need Business Cards

877-273-7278
help@ineedbusinesscards.com

Business Cards

Adding an image to a business card should be easy. Almost every company that creates cards claims it can do it and yet, so many times, the resulting picture looks fuzzy or, worse, the card is completely unusable. I Need Business Cards takes the guesswork out of adding an image to your business card. First, in simple non-technical language, the site explains how the process works. Next, a utility on the Web site enables you to transfer graphics files of several different types. If the result isn't satisfactory, the company lets you know before printing your final card.

myshift.com
MyShift.com
780-992-0562
E-mail form on site
Calendars

If you own or manage a business with employees who work rotating schedules, you're aware of how difficult it is to make everyone aware of when to come to work. The crew who worked nights last week might now be scheduled for daytime hours, while last week's daytime group is expected to show up in the evening. Make it easy for yourself and the employees with a simple system from MyShift.com. Various shift trackers are available: PVC wallet calendar cards with bright, easily deciphered shifts, laminated Day-Timer shift cards, and 4.25" × 3.5" magnets marked with the shift schedule.

officedepot.com
Office Depot
800-463-3768
E-mail form on site
Office Supplies

Office Depot defined the category of office supply superstores. In similar fashion, this company is now defining the online office supply megastore. Click on a tab on the homepage and the whole site translates into Spanish. Managing an international business? Check out the international pages. Office Depot offers extensive services, many free, for small businesses. Log in for one of its Webcast seminars in the Web Cafe, or listen to on-demand Web radio. Along with all the standard supplies, Office Depot offers order tracking, order by item number, and loyalty programs.

officemart.com
OfficeMart.com
800-657-7907
E-mail form on site
Office Supplies

Officemart.com is a site meant for businesses. You can't visit its store, but with 44 warehouses this company can offer next-day shipping within the continental United States. Your best bet? Sign up for a membership and take advantage of Officemart.com's great administrative tools, such as reviewing your order history. You can maintain multiple shopping lists and order for multiple locations. This company e-mails you notices of specials and maintains a profile for you that limits who in your company can approve orders. It also offers airline miles! This site is almost as good as having an assistant.

 Recommended   Price   Selection   Convenience   Service 🔒 Security

officemax.com
OfficeMax.Com

800-283-7674
E-mail form on site

Ergonomics • Office Supplies

You can get lost in OfficeMax.Com. There are so many categories and so many items that the selection is almost overwhelming. Make a list of what you need before you visit. Otherwise, you're likely to find something you can't live without on the easy-to-use menu and add it to your cart. Menus at the site are arranged by category and by industry, so if you can't locate an item in one place, you're sure to find it on the other. Set up an account at the site for convenient reordering and access to special pricing.

office-supplies-store.com
Office Supplies Store

877-731-0008
info@officesuppliesstore.com

Office Supplies

Shop at office-supplies-store.com for standard office supplies and speedy delivery. The Office Supplies Store site is designed for simple, straightforward navigation. Choose a category from the column on the left of the page and a selection of subcategories appears to the right. Of course, you can always bypass this system and search on a keyword or go straight to your account and reorder the products you have chosen before. The Office Supplies Store site is designed to, as its mission statement says, "give rapid service with complete customer satisfaction."

phonemerchants.com
Phone Merchants

877-291-1076
phonemerchants@yahoo.com

Telephone Systems

Every office needs a phone! Phone systems, with auto answering attendants and voice mail, can help even solo office practitioners track calls. Phone Merchants carries just about every phone and phone system on the market. Fortunately, the site is arranged for ease of use; the products sold here are arranged by department (type), or you can use the Search feature to go directly to the phone or system you need. In addition to the phones, Phone Merchants carries an extensive collection of electronic products for those who are speech, visually, or hearing impaired. The site also carries ADA-compliant products made by Ameriphone.

⭐ quillcorp.com
Quill

800-789-1331
E-mail form on site

Office Supplies

Quill has come a long way since it started with a desk and two phones in Jack and Harvey Miller's father's chicken store in 1956. The site offers not only the Quill brand of office supplies, but also a wide range of products from other manufacturers. Take a few moments to set up "Reorder Reminders" that will send you an e-mail when an item should be reordered. Quill is committed to customer service and that attitude is reflected in the comments of its clients. In fact, while you're shopping here, read Quill's "Customer Bill of Rights."

staples.com
Staples

800-377-2753
support@orders.staples.com

Office Supplies

You'll find not just office supplies at the Staples site, but a whole range of services, all designed to keep your office running effortlessly. Build a list of Favorites so you don't have to search the site for items you order regularly. If you prefer going to the store to shop, log in at the site to access the weekly sale circular. Whether you shop online, at the store, or both, Staples offers a Business Rewards program that's hard to beat. Establish your own Staples account and then start earning Reward Checks and Upgrade Benefits every time you shop.

startechtel.com
Startechtel

800-564-8045
sales@startechtel.com

Telephone Systems

Startechtel sells phone systems covered by warranty from many top manufacturers, including Avaya, Nortel, Plantronics, and Panasonic. The company does not install, program, or maintain the systems outside of southern California. Instead, it puts buyers in touch with technicians who are available in the buyer's local area. Indicate that you need these services when you order. Startechtel technicians offer free technical support covering isolated voicemail and phone setup to customers. Request a free online quote for your new company's phone system on the Startechtel site.

★ talkswitch.com
Talk Switch
888-332-9322
info@talkswitch.com
Telephone Systems

Small business owners are often at a disadvantage when buying office equipment. They can either buy equipment that's intended for the home user, or for a company that's much larger. Talk Switch bridges the gap, with a small, powerful, and affordable phone system for small businesses with 1–32 phones. The all-in-one system doesn't need any additional software or add-on modules. Users can connect remotely. Most importantly, Talk Switch is easy to deploy and can be customized with Windows-based software. Getting your small office connected is a snap.

★ tide-mark.com
Tide-mark Press
860-683-4499
customerservice@tide-mark.com
Calendars

Tide-mark Press is a small publisher of distinctive calendars and books. The monthly calendars are like works of art; you may find yourself framing some of the pictures that topped the past months. Choose from such diverse calendars as artworks of various artists, scenes of Las Vegas, Atlantic lighthouses, and Mad Magazine's Alfred E. Newman. Click a small picture of a calendar to see all twelve months' worth of pictures. The site also sells beautifully constructed daybooks to help you maintain your daily schedule.

tri-pointproducts.com
Tri-Point Products
800-851-8886
tripoint@tri-pointproducts.com
Calendars

Make a date to visit Tri-Point Products when you're shopping for business calendars for your office. Your company's planning schedule will be easily readable on a large wall calendar. Both a fiscal year and calendar year model are available. The three-by-four foot calendar is laminated for write-on/wipe-off ease and comes with two special marker pens. Other calendar products available include pads of undated calendars in various sizes and several styles of heavyweight paper calendars. A clever mouse pad doubles as a calendar and keeps you up-to-date whenever you use your computer.

⭐ virtuosity.com
Virtuosity Virtual Assistant

800-771-7179
E-mail form on site

Telephone Systems

Technically, Virtual Assistant isn't a phone system. Rather, it's a computerized answering service that screens, routes, and announces all callers to you; provides the identity of new callers; and gives you the option of placing your current caller on hold while you take the new call. It also keeps a virtual phonebook of contacts that you can access by name and manages your voice mail. Your Virtual Assistant can set up conference calls. The system uses a real-sounding human voice and understands voice commands. Visit the site for a demo of this amazing assistant. You're bound to be amazed at what technology can do.

⭐ wgbc.com
World's Greatest Business Cards

877-866-5151
info@wgbc.com

Business Cards

Not all business cards need to be the same shape and size. If you handed someone a card that indicated by its shape exactly what you do, that person would be more likely to call you when he or she needed your product or service. For example, if you sell cars, your card could be shaped like an automobile. Repair computers? How about a mini-computer card for you. The bottom line is that your clever card could net you more calls than your competition. More calls mean more business! Learn more about these fascinating, although somewhat expensive, die-cut business cards at wgbc.com.

⭐ Recommended   Price   Selection   Convenience   Service   🔒 Security

Seven Simple Rules for Establishing a Home Office

Is a home office in your future? Perhaps you're thinking of setting up a home-based business, or simply saving the overhead you're incurring in the office or work space you're renting presently. Or maybe your employer is joining the growing trend and turning you into a telecommuter. Working from home can sound mighty appealing.

Before you set up shop at home, establish the seven simple rules presented next. Without them, your home office will feel like just another room in the house, and you won't get any work done.

1. Determine the days and times you will be in the office and stick to those times. Although coming in late or leaving early is easy because the office is in your home, you must remind yourself that you would follow regular hours if you worked in a regular office. If necessary, buy a big wall clock from Arc Time (arctime.com) to help you stay focused.

2. Designate a room or area of your home as your office. Make sure that everyone in your family understands this is the place where you work. Personalize your space with a sign or two from Make Signs Online (makesignsonline.com).

3. Buy the supplies and tools you need. Whether it's a computer and printer, pencils and paper, or a fax machine, scanner or other device, you must have the tools to do your job. Office Depot (officedepot.com) and Staples (staples.com) are great places to buy office supplies and accessories.

4. Get a decent phone system! Your family is not your staff and can't be trusted with important messages. You'll wonder how you ever lived without Virtuosity's Personal Assistant (virtuosity.com), a computerized phone attendant.

5. Invest in a simple filing system. Even if it's just a box or two to store your files, you must have a system to keep your papers and records organized. Quill (quill.com) has a great selection of filing boxes.

6. Don't collect paper and notes. Keep a trash-can handy and toss excess paper before it gets buried. Buy a big bright can from Office Mart.com (officemart.com).

7. Don't go overboard with new furniture. Start small and buy only the pieces you need. Going deeply into debt for a fancy suite of furniture now doesn't make sense. Cyberchair, Inc. (cyberchair.com) is a good investment for the future; the amazing chair will ensure you're comfortable as you sit at your desk.

Now you're ready to get started. Good luck in your business. You're bound to be successful!

Chapter 18

Outdoors: Shopping the Great Outdoors

· ·

Ah, yes. Communing with nature. Reveling in the clear air and clean streams, and marveling at the wildlife. That's the great outdoors!

I'm not talking about a leisurely stroll through the countryside — I'm referring to serious camping. To do it, you need tents, stoves, sleeping bags, backpacks, food, lanterns, clothing — the works. All these items are necessary for a safe and enjoyable adventure in nature. Of course, if you're not the type to rough it and just enjoy camping in your backyard with the kids, the online retailers in this chapter can help you out, too.

Shelter? No problem. Food? They have it. Clothing from top to bottom to protect you from the elements? They have you covered. These retailers offer products that will light your way and point you in the right direction, even help you find yourself if you get lost.

So, if you're going to "rough it," then put on your hiking boots and browse through the online stores listed in this chapter. Their express purpose is to seriously outfit you for whatever nature throws your way.

But before you load up that RV and head out, be sure to glance through the following informative sites for some basic information about living in the wilderness:

- ✔ Camping tips — `lovetheoutdoors.com/camping/Tips/Tips_and_Advice.htm`
- ✔ Camping tips for parents — `camp-a-roo.com`
- ✔ National camping directory — `campusa.com`
- ✔ Guide to U.S. parks and campsites — `coleman.com`
- ✔ Outdoor survival tips — `walkingconnection.com/2003ezine/features/copy/nestor2.htm`
- ✔ Camping with kids — `ivillage.co.uk/travel/famtrav/getthere/articles/0,,563209_572023,00.html`

✔ Camping with pets — `vetmedicine.about.com/library/weekly/ aa051701a.htm`

✔ State-by-state fishing license information — `fishingworks.com/licenses/ index.cfm`

✔ Mountain-biking tips — `cnn.com/HEALTH/library/HQ/01100.html`

✔ Outdoor gear guide and buying advice — `gorp.away.com/gorp/gear/main.htm`

Key Word Index

Backpacks

What you bring into the wilderness you pack on your back. Find some high-tech packs at the stores with the Backpacks keyword.

Camp Gear

Dinnerware, lanterns, camp showers, grills, sleeping bags — just a few of the offerings from the retailers with the Camp Gear keyword. They have what you need to make your outdoor adventure pleasant, comfortable, and safe.

Food

Unless you plan on living off the land, you have to think about packing food. The Food sites offer a selection of easy-pack, easy-cook foods to satisfy any hungry camper.

Footwear

The stores with the Footwear keyword offer comfortable, rugged footwear for the trails and comfy footwear for those evenings beside the campfire.

Navigation

The retailers in the Navigation category can set you up with navigation items ranging from the traditional compass to the modern GPS device. Just in case, pack that cell phone, too!

Outerwear

Coats, jackets, windbreakers, and raingear — the Outerwear sites offer often stylish clothing that protects you from the elements. You'll also find specialized apparel for hiking, mountain climbing, water sports, and other outdoor activities.

Shelter

The Shelter sites offer various types of tents to suit your camping needs. Whether you need a one-man, two-man, or two-room tent for the whole family, these sites can set you up.

2kcut.com
Millenium Cutlery

817-249-2968
E-mail form on site

Camp Gear

Pocketknives, kitchen knives, hunting knives, fishing knives, big knives, little knives, you name it, Millenium Cutlery has it. The site also offers an appraisal service, as well as a repair service so that you can extend the life and use of your knife. Do you need a sharpening stone or a pouch to carry your knife during your outdoor adventures? You can find both on the site. Search the site by brand or category, and then track your purchase with UPS tracking from the site. Be sure to sign up for the e-mail updates.

aaoutfitters.com
AA Outfitters

800-443-8119
E-mail form on site

Camp Gear • Footwear • Outerwear

AA Outfitters is a fully stocked fly fishing shop. The online catalog is jam-packed with fly rods and blanks, reels, fly lines, waders, and boots. You'll find several types of hooks and fly tying materials. Of course, you can also purchase outerwear, pants, shorts, gloves, and socks. Don't forget the bug spray for those industrial-sized mosquitoes that frequent the shallows. AA Outfitters can arrange a trip with world-class fly fishers for you. These trips are scheduled throughout the year. Imagine — a dream vacation that provides the opportunity to regale your friends with tales about the big fish that got away.

ahappycamper.com
A Happy Camper

208-736-8048
E-mail form on site

Backpacks • Camp Gear • Navigation • Shelter

Getting to your destination is half the fun, but you can enjoy getting back using an alternative route by considering a GPS unit offered by ahappy camper.com. This easy-to-navigate site also offers camping gear, including backpacks, stoves, knives, sleeping bags, and even furniture that rolls out for comfort and rolls up for convenience. The site also features Dutch ovens, enabling you to cook without having to lug around a cast iron skillet. You can even personalize the lid at this site, and get free Dutch oven tips and recipes. A Happy Camper strives for the finest quality at the best prices possible.

 Recommended   Price   Selection   Convenience   Service   Security

albionsmo.com
Albion's MO

888-843-6611
customerservice@albionsmo.com

Backbacks • Camp Gear • Navigation • Shelter

"The MO" can help any novice or experienced outdoors enthusiast. Don't know what to do or where to go? Check out the site's selection of books and guides. Although Albion's MO does have the basics for camping, it also has online suggestions on how to be prepared and what to take with you when you go. The site also has the creature comforts that campers want, such as tools, knives, first-aid kits, bags, and other travel accessories. Search the site by category, or use the Search box to find something in particular. You can also sign up for the mailing list to receive special offers.

arkatents.com
Arkatents

479-394-7893
fyi@arkatents.com

Backpacks • Camp Gear • Shelter

Don't let the rustic exterior and homespun humor of this western Arkansas-based retailer fool you. Arkatents offers a heap of information about camping and outdoor living, and the folks who run this site will share this info with you. In fact, they advise you to view their pages on outdoor safety before you buy your camping gear. Shop here for tents, kiddie pools, camo gear, and even some snow and ski equipment. The descriptions in the online catalog are easy to read and help you decide what to purchase. Feel free to call for more information; you'll receive prompt, courteous service.

★ armygear.net
Army Surplus

800-541-1839
info@armygear.net

Backpacks • Camp Gear • Food • Shelter

Many people know that military-issued equipment is durable. Die-hard campers often search local army surplus stores for military equipment. Now, anyone who wants to check out new and used military equipment can do so at armygear.net. This site offers tents, water containers, belts, backpacks, lights, footwear, cookwear, gloves, and even those "tasty" military meals. Search by category or via the Search box, and shop with confidence: This company offers a 30-day, no-hassle return policy if you're not completely satisfied.

backcountrygear.com
Backcountry Gear Ltd.

800-953-5499
bcgeartech@backcountrygear.com

Backpacks • Camp Gear • Footwear • Navigation • Outerwear • Shelter

If you want one-stop shopping for your camping gear, backcountrygear.com will do all the work for you — really! At this well-organized site, you choose a category, such as backpacks, and then look at the subcategories, such as lightweight, expedition, manufacturer, and so on. You can also view a "comparison matrix" that enables you to compare all the specifications of each backpack in a category. You can also take advantage of a gift registry for those special occasions in life — birthdays, graduations, weddings, and so on.

backpackinglight.com
BackpackingLight.com

406-522-0948
E-mail form on site

Backpacks • Camp Gear • Outerwear • Shelter

Need tips and techniques on what to do and how to do it when you go hiking and backpacking? BackpackingLight.com is a great online magazine and store with features and editorials on just about any aspect of hiking and backpacking. The writers teach subscribers how to keep it light but safe when in the outdoors. The site also offers shelter, sleep, and packing systems; product reviews; camping tips, tricks, and techniques; and even newsletters and discussion forums. BackpackingLight.com claims that because it is advertising-free it can not only "report industry trends but also drive them."

basspro-shops.com
Bass Pro Shops

1-800-227-7776
E-mail form on site

Backpacks • Camp Gear • Navigation • Outerwear • Shelter

Fishing and hunting enthusiasts will love the Bass Pro Shops site. Get the latest and greatest fishing, hunting, boating, and camping equipment, plus news releases, events updates, information on conservation and education programs, corporate incentives, hunting and fishing licenses online, vacation packages, specialty catalogs, and product reviews. What more could you want? What about gift certificates for those who love fishing and hunting? Buy one online and have it sent to your favorite enthusiast.

 Recommended   Price   Selection   Convenience   Service   Security

bentgate.net
Bent Gate Mountaineering

877-236-8428
bentgate@bentgate.com

Backpacks • Camp Gear • Footwear • Navigation • Outerwear • Shelter

If you can't come to the mountain, Bent Gate will bring it to you. Of course, we're referring to Bent Gate's great mountaineering store in Colorado. This site is the next best thing to shopping in the store. Look past the simple face of the online catalog and click through the categories until you find the items you want. Choose from an array of items, including gear for climbing, backpacking, and snow sports. You'll also find navigation tools, footwear, and even outdoor gear for your favorite canine. It's obvious someone has put a lot of time into making this site helpful. Detailed descriptions and weights (important when you're lugging something up the face of a mountain or rock) help you decide just what to buy. Bent Gate will match the price of any item you find cheaper at another Web site. Details are at the site.

blueskykitchen.com
Blue Sky Kitchen

800-821-8478
grubbox@blueskykitchen.com

Camp Gear

When you pack to go camping, do you want to take everything but the kitchen sink? Now you really can, and keep it all organized in one place. Blue Sky Kitchen has created what it calls *grub boxes*. These boxes, made from plywood and medium-density fiberboard, can hold your food and kitchen equipment all in one convenient place, so you don't have to search through all your cabinets and pull key supplies when you're leaving home, and so you don't have to search through all your gear and packs to prepare your meal when you get to your camping destination. These boxes also provide extra workspace when you're in the great outdoors. Blue Sky Kitchen has three different designs depending on your needs. If you find the finished product's price to be a little too steep, you can purchase the grub box plans and build one yourself!

bobwards.com
Bob Ward & Sons

800-800-5083
sales@bobwards.com

Backpacks • Camp Gear • Footwear • Navigation • Outerwear • Shelter

Years ago, Bob Ward started a custom gun-making and fishing tackle manufacturing company. Now it's one of the largest privately-held sporting goods stores in the Northwest. The company's slogan is "Gear Up. Get Out," and bobwards.com can help you do just that. Search the easy-to-navigate site for men's, women's, and kid's outdoor clothing; camping, fishing, and hunting gear; and golf and winter sport gear and accessories. The site also offers gift wrapping, gift certificates, and an e-mail mailing list so that you can get updates and sales info.

bumperdumper.com
Uncle Booger's Bumper Dumper

281-277-3309
No e-mail address on site

Camp Gear

Where do you stop to go to the restroom when you're in the middle of nowhere? At bumperdumper.com, you can get a product to solve this problem. With the Bumper Dumper, you can pull off the road and attach a toilet to your hitch. If you're in the woods, you can attach it to a 5-gallon bucket or prop it against a tree for more stability. If you buy the product and like it, you can show your support by purchasing a T-shirt from the site as well.

★ cabelas.com
Cabelas.com

800-237-4444
E-mail form on site

Backpacks • Camp Gear • Food • Footwear • Navigation • Outerwear • Shelter

For the last 40 years, Cabelas has been outfitting those who hunt and fish and those who love the outdoors. Its expansive site carries everything you need for the perfect outdoor experience. Shoes, clothes, and outerwear from GORE-TEX, Carhartt, and other top makers keep men, women, and kids ready for any activity. Check out the casual clothes, too. Don't miss the fishing rods, camping supplies, firearms, and boats and boating accessories. Have a lust for travel? Cabelas will book the guided outdoor hunting or fishing trip of a lifetime. What a great place to shop!

★ Recommended $ Price   🛒 Selection   🎁 Convenience   ☺ Service   🔒 Security

cactusjuicetm.com
Cactus Juice

877-554-5222
bmiller@cactusjuicetm.com

Camp Gear

Ever wonder who would be crazy enough to handle prickly pear cactus bushes? The people at Cactus Juice are. They make Cactus Juice bug repellent, an all-natural, non-toxic, kid-safe product that is also good for minor wounds and burns. Native Americans have been aware of the healing properties of the prickly pear cactus for centuries. Check out the testimonials, and read about the Miracle Gel and Total Body Lotion, also available from Cactus Juice.

campchef.com
Camp Chef

800-650-2433
E-mail form on site

Camp Gear

Camp Chef believes "that good food does not have to be sacrificed when cooking outdoors." This company offers camp stoves and accessories, adapters, griddles, leg extensions, patio covers, windscreens, pot sets, shelves, and other outdoor cooking accessories on its comprehensive site. The site also offers recipes, product warranties and manuals, and a link to a discussion forum. Now the gourmet in you doesn't have to be sacrificed in the great outdoors.

campingcot.com
K.O.T. Mfg. Co., Inc.

888-617-8675
sales@campingcot.com

Camp Gear

Do you enjoy sleeping on the cold, hard ground on camping trips? Probably not. Would you rather take along a cot, but hate to carry all that bulky equipment? Then try this cot on for size. K.O.T. Mfg. Co., Inc. has designed and manufactured a cot that folds up to the size of a newspaper and that weighs between 5.5 and 8.5 pounds, depending on the size you order. You can choose from three colors (Navy, Olive Green, and Spruce Green) and three styles (Regular, which fits heights up to 6'3"; Large, which fits heights to 7'1"; and UltraLight, which weighs only 5.5 pounds).You can quickly disassemble the cot and roll it up to fit into a carrying case. Just attach the lightweight cot to your backpack, and away you go!

campman.com
Campman

360-904-9788
sales@campman.com

Backpacks • Camp Gear • Footwear • Navigation • Outerwear • Shelter

Campman specializes in outdoor equipment for backpacking, paddling, climbing, biking, and hiking, among other outdoor activities. Search the site by product category, or use the Search tool. This company believes that you should never get into a backorder situation. Therefore, the site's inventory is updated online every four hours. Yes, every four hours. You can't beat that kind of information. So, sit back and relax in knowing that what you order is in stock and will be shipped ASAP.

campmor.com
Campmor, Inc.

800-525-4784
E-mail form on site

Backpacks • Camp Gear • Food • Footwear • Navigation • Outerwear • Shelter

This comprehensive, well-organized site offers everything you need for your outdoor adventures. From bicycles to weather gadgets, from compasses to tents and sleeping bags, you can easily find whatever you're looking for at campmor.com. The site even offers Ten Essentials Kits that contain items every camper should have on a trip. Also, check out the lightweight, yet nutritious, food selection, as well as kids' gear and clothing for your little campers. After you place your order, you can track it via the site.

clever-camper.com
Grill Thing

510-524-5798
salesinfo@clever-camper.com

Camp Gear

Remember when you used to roast hot dogs on a stick over the campfire — and remember how they sometimes fell irretrievably into the flames? Grill Thing has come up with a gadget that fits over the end of most sticks and keeps your hotdogs and marshmallows from sliding off into the fire. This gadget has a coil on the end that goes on the stick; the other end has slightly curved prongs. You can get a two-pack of this nifty device for around $4.99; however, you need to fill out the information request form on the site to find out how to purchase the item.

 Recommended   Price   Selection   Convenience   Service   Security

davepagecobbler.com
Dave Page, Cobbler

800-252-1229
cobbler@davepagecobbler.com

Footwear

Do you have a favorite pair of shoes or boots that you just don't want to throw away? But you can't part with them, can you? To get more life out of them, send your worn-out shoes to Dave Page, Cobbler. He will spruce them up, give them a new sole, and repair any holes and tears. Dave routinely repairs hiking, mountaineering, and rock climbing boots, as well as athletic shoes and even Birkenstock sandals. Just print out the order form on the site, fill it out, and send it with your payment and shoes to the address listed.

eders.com
Eder, Inc.

877-656-0808
feedback@eders.com

Camp Gear • Footwear • Navigation • Outerwear

Do you like to hunt but have little time to go to the store and check out the equipment? Use the comparison charts on eders.com to find that perfect bow, knife, or rifle for any hunting experience. The site offers several ways to search for hunting, fishing, marine, camping, clothing, and archery products. You can even get your hunting license at the same time you're checking out the online auctions for great deals. If you want to ask questions or brag, this site has live chats, as well.

ems.com
Eastern Mountain Sports

888-463-6367
customerservice@ems.com

Backpacks • Camp Gear • Food • Footwear • Navigation • Outerwear

EMS specializes in "gear and clothing for outdoor enthusiasts, from backpacks and insulated parkas to cycling gear and summer shorts." You'll find all this and more on the site, including canoeing, kayaking, climbing, cycling, fitness, and travel gear. Sign up on the gift registry so that anyone can shop for you, or give a gift card for this online store to your favorite outdoor enthusiast. To extend the life of your gear, send it in to the repair service department. You can even check out links to EMS's climbing and kayaking schools; schools are located in the Northeast, but you can sign up online. Dates and classes are listed on the site.

geardirect.com
Gear Direct

866-289-7547
info@geardirect.com

Backpacks • Camp Gear • Footwear • Outerwear

Gear Direct is a member of the Specialty Sports Network, which is a network of 90 specialty sporting goods stores in Colorado. For outdoor enthusiasts interested in skiing, snowboarding, biking, golfing, or camping, this site offers many options. You can get up to 70 percent off retail on top-brand gear. Check out the FAQs for important information about selecting skis. To find a product, search the site by either subject or manufacturer. Register a profile at the site, and receive 5 percent off all online purchases. If you want to actually go to the store and check out the equipment, Gear Direct can direct you to one or more of its member stores.

gearpro.com
Gear Pro

865-523-0066
E-mail form on site

Backpacks • Camp Gear • Footwear • Outerwear • Shelter

gearpro.com is for "technologically affluent outdoor enthusiasts." If you're technologically advanced — and have the money to spend on expensive outdoor toys — this is your site. (If you're into roughing it with just the pack on your back, you need to keep on moving to another site.) This online store can set you up with all the latest and greatest gadgets and accessories to make your outdoor excursion safe, fun, and comfortable. Check out the selection of watches that have compasses, barometers, and more incorporated into them. The heavy-duty all-terrain footwear offerings can keep you on your feet longer. When you select a category of products, a top-ten bestseller list appears, letting you know what your fellow outdoors enthusiasts are buying, too.

★ gearx.com
The Outdoor Gear Exchange, Inc.

888-547-4327
info@gearx.com

Backpacks • Camp Gear • Footwear • Outerwear • Shelter

Wouldn't it be great to hang out with a bunch of friends and just shoot the breeze about your outdoor activities? That's what the folks at gearx.com want. They believe that shopping for outdoor stuff should be relaxed, friendly, and affordable. This company sells closeouts and new and used gear. The site carries nearly 1,500 items, including books and maps, footwear, backpacks, tents, clothing, dog accessories, and rock and ice-climbing gear. The people who run this site want to give you the best quality for your money. They are such outdoor enthusiasts that they want others with the passion for the outdoors to be able to afford and have access to the same equipment. They also share their experiences and knowledge via the articles, tips, and reviews found on the site. Or ask them a question; just fill out the online form.

grandshelters.com
Grand Shelters, Inc.

866-772-2107
iglooinfo@grandshelters.com

Camp Gear

Some people love winter camping. However, until now, the best these campers could do was to use a tent or make a snow cave. Now grand shelters.com offers an alternative called the Ice Box. This affordable, lightweight, packable tool makes making a snow igloo easy. In approximately 1½ to 3 hours, depending on the size of the igloo, you can build a shelter using this innovative product. It packs all kinds of snow no matter what the type or condition. Check out the site for testimonials from impressed customers, and see comparisons of igloos versus tents and snow caves.

hatham.com
Hatteras Hammocks

800-643-3522
hammocks@thehammocksource.com

Camp Gear

Everyone knows how relaxing it is to lie down under the trees and swing back and forth in a hammock. Paul Jenkins, the founder of Hatteras Hammocks, started making hammocks as a hobby. Over time this hobby became a business. To this day all the rope hammocks he offers are still woven by hand. Hatteras Hammocks has other types of hammocks, such as quilted fabric and open-weave vinyl, as well as hammock stands and accessories. You can also view a selection of swings and swing stands, and log and hearth accessories. Be sure to check out the fun facts about hammocks via the Hammock News link.

hellynewport.com
Helly Hansen

877-666-8742
info@hellynewport.com

Outerwear

For those of you who like water sports, winter skiing, or mountain climbing, or for those who often work outside in the elements, this site offers a line of outerwear and apparel to suit your needs. You can find water-resistant jackets and quick-dry nylon pants for sailing, as well as comfortable shirts, pullovers, shorts, and other items that allow freedom of movement for any outdoor activity. The site lists a fabric chart to help you compare fabrics, as well as a LIFA chart, which shows you the various levels of moisture-wicking and warmth properties of the various weaves. If you order before 3 p.m. Eastern Standard Time, your order will be shipped to you that day. Helly Hansen also has a "Million Mile Guarantee" for all of its products. In other words, this company stands behind the durability and quality of its products. So shop with confidence at this site, and know you're getting excellent service and quality.

 Recommended   Price   Selection   Convenience   Service   Security

igloocoolers.com
Igloo Products Corp

800-364-5566
E-mail form on site

Camp Gear

Thanks in part to Igloo, people can now keep food and drinks cold outdoors. Igloo had its start making metal water coolers for construction workers. From there, Igloo introduced a 155-quart, all-plastic ice chest that could stand up to the elements and that became popular with saltwater fishermen. Today, Igloo makes a wide range of ice chests and water coolers in different shapes and sizes for both personal and commercial use. The sizes include everything from personal soft-sided coolers to large ice chests. Igloo is constantly testing new ideas to keep food at the perfect temperature for your enjoyment. It even has a new plug-in unit that can keep your food either cold or hot. Check out the site for cooler care, tips, and FAQs, and order replacement parts as well.

kampgrill.com
Kamp Products

800-536-5096
sales@kampgrill.com

Camp Gear

Ahh, the smell of food cooking over a campfire. It makes a nice image, but cooking over a campfire isn't necessarily practical. If you don't want to cook in the fire, you need something to help you cook over the fire. Kamp Products helps you avoid having to construct something every time you go camping by offering you several products you can take along instead. You'll find two different over-the-fire grills that can be folded up for easy packing. These grills come in varying sizes, can swivel, and can be adjusted up and down. You can also purchase a pot holder (that holds a pot over the fire) and a rotisserie. Roughing it has never been easier!

kidssource.com
Outdoor Kids' Source

888-672-7657
ok@mt-mansfield.com

Backpacks • Camp Gear • Footwear • Outerwear • Shelter

You love to camp. You have for as long as you can remember. But now you have kids. Has that hampered your ability to go camping? It shouldn't. Just check out kidssource.com for clothes and equipment to fit your little campers. The site offers all-weather clothing, sleeping bags, tents, backpacks and torso packs, and even snowshoes. This site shows size charts and comparison charts for its items, so you get the best fit and best value for your child. Click the link for trip planning ideas geared toward child-friendly outings. Ordering is secure, and get a free safety whistle on orders of $50 or more. Happy camping!

★ llbean.com
L.L. Bean

800-441-5713
E-mail form on site

Backpacks • Camp Gear • Footwear • Navigation • Outerwear • Shelter

In 1912 Leon Leonwood Bean, also known as L.L. Bean, founded this company because he had a passion for the outdoors. Over the last century his company has been committed to upholding his standards of "honesty and commitment to quality and customer service." On the site, you'll find clothing for men, women, and kids; outdoor gear, luggage, travel gear, and home and outdoor living products. The site's shopping services include a 100 percent guarantee, free catalogs and e-mail newsletter, and gift and tracking services. In addition to all the high-quality equipment and apparel you can buy, you can get tips on the outdoors and gear. Be sure to check out the Outdoor Discovery Schools and Outdoor Partners. This easy-to-navigate, well-organized site is a must-see for anyone interested in the outdoors.

★ Recommended $ Price   Selection   Convenience   Service   🔒 Security

mgear.com/MtnWoman.asp
Mountain Woman

800-474-9163
info@mountainwoman.com

Backpacks • Footwear • Outerwear

Finally, a site that caters to the outdoorswoman! At the Mountain Woman site, you can get the latest outdoor news and ideas with newsletters, online advice, books, travel guides, guide directories, and links to other sites. You can buy women's fitness clothing and activewear as well as gear for climbing, backpacking, and snow sports. You can make a wish list for yourself on the site, enabling friends and family to get a gift for you that you actually want. Sign up for the free e-newsletter, and chat with other outdoor enthusiasts on the site's bulletin boards.

moosejaw.com
Moosejaw

877-666-7352
moose@moosejaw.com

Camp Gear • Footwear • Outerwear • Shelter

Moosejaw is one cool outdoor site! Two young people with a passion for the outdoors founded the company back in 1992. Their love and dedication spills over to the online catalog. There's a hint of silliness here that keeps the site afloat, from the infamous column by the Dating Girl to the fact that you send e-mail messages to the "moose." There's nothing silly about the product line, however, which includes high-quality adventure clothing, footwear, and gear for men, women, and children. Sign up for Moosejaw Rewards and earn bonus points every time you shop.

mountainmiser.com
Mountain Miser

800-841-0707
comments@mountainmiser.com

Backpacks • Camp Gear • Food • Footwear • Navigation • Outerwear • Shelter

Folks in the Denver, Colorado, area have been flocking to Mountain Miser for over 20 years. Now you can, too. You'll find a wide assortment of camping equipment, outdoor gear, clothing, and accessories. The items here are the real deal — functionality is more important than appearance. The Miser Club is the way to go if you're planning to shop this site regularly. Your free membership gets you points for each dollar that you spend, and then you can redeem the points to get free gear at a later visit. Good deal!

northernmountain.com
Northern Mountain Supply

800-878-3583
mtn@northernmountain.com

Backpacks • Camp Gear • Footwear • Navigation • Outerwear • Shelter

Whether you hike, bike, climb, or paddle, you'll find great deals on outdoor gear at the Northern Mountain Supply site. The company has been providing thousands of satisfied customers with clothing, footwear, and quality outdoor gear since 1974. The collection of tents, packs, kayaks, and canoes available at the site is extensive. If you're tired of lugging heavy equipment, check out the site's selection of ultralight gear. Want to save some serious money on first-rate equipment? Don't miss Northern Mountain Supply's Killer Deals. Identified by a distinctive KD logo, the site offers discounts of up to 80 percent off on hundreds of quality items. The site is ideal for first time campers or people who spend lots of time in the great outdoors. The folks at Northern Mountain Supply can help you escape to the wilderness and have some fun.

outbackpack.com
GT Products, LLC

479-452-1893
sales@outbackpack.com

Camp Gear

What do you do when you need to "go" and there is no restroom for miles? Try pulling out your portable toilet. The one offered by GT Products is made of double-walled corrugated cardboard and weights only 1.5 lbs. The toilet and seat is rated to hold up to 275 pounds. It folds up easily for storage, yet sets up quickly. When purchased the portable toilet comes with three waste bags, toilet tissue, and a strong resealable storage bag. Worried about the cardboard getting wet and disintegrating? Don't. You can waterproof it with your car wax. This handy little item is perfect for canoeing and camping trips, offroading, hunting, and really any outdoor activity far from restrooms.

 Recommended   Price   Selection   Convenience   Service   Security

outdoorclassified.com
Outdoor Classified

800-873-6072
outdoor@outdoorclassified.com

Backpacks • Camp Gear • Footwear • Shelter

Log on to outdoorclassified.com and check out what's available in outdoor equipment and gear. Find tents, backpacks, sleeping bags, apparel, footwear, and gear such as ice picks and camp stoves. Or put your own stuff up for sale and put the money towards those new binoculars you want. Placing an ad is free, and transactions occur between the buyer and seller, with no involvement of the site. Your ad may be chosen for promotion in appropriate newsgroups, but your address will not be sold to spammers.

outdooroutlet.com
Outdoor Outlet

800-726-8106
mail@outdooroutlet.com

Backpacks • Camp Gear • Shelter

Need backpacking equipment? You've come to the right place. Outdoor Outlet sells tents, bags, and packs made by Kelty Pack, Mountain Hardwear, and Sierra Designs. Prices here are generally low. However, if you're looking to save some serious money, check out the Outrageous Deals. Every two weeks Outdoor Outlet posts quality products with really low pricing. Move fast if you see something you want, because quantities are limited and products sell out quickly. Be sure to read the Backpacker Wisdom of the Week Tip for some helpful camping knowledge.

outinstyle.com
Out In Style, Inc.

888-667-3453
sales@outinstyle.com

Camp Gear • Navigation • Shelter

Do you want to find military-issued equipment? Then go to outinstyle.com, a wholesale military surplus site. Out In Style offers special deals for shoppers. For every order over $50 the company sends the customer a free gift. Pick up some camo gear or a king-size cot at discounted prices. The company even sells law enforcement products such as bulletproof vests and lock-pick sets. Out In Style ships orders within 48 hours from the time your order is placed. The site offers live help, a sizing and color chart, and the capability to view the site in German, French, Italian, Spanish, or English.

⭐ paragonsports.com
Paragon

800-961-3030
info@paragonsports.com

Backpacks • Camp Gear • Footwear • Outerwear • Shelter

This company boasts that "savvy New Yorkers and tourists make the pilgrimage to the Mecca of Sporting Goods" known as Paragon. Offering "stores within a store," Paragon is made up of specialty shops that offer products and accessories for skating, cycling, tennis, street hockey, golf — and just about every other indoor and outdoor sport. You'll also find clothing and footwear for men, women, and youth. Paragon has 10,000 items online and 30,000 items in the store. If you want it, this company probably has it. Call the company if an item you want is not on the Web site. You also can check the status of your order online.

patagonia.com
Patagonia

800-638-6464
E-mail form on site

Backpacks • Outerwear

For those of you who are climbing adventurers yet concerned about the environment, Patagonia is the site for you. Patagonia is "committed to the core," bringing customers innovatively designed products, promoting eco-friendly practices and campaigns, and staying committed and true to the soul of the sport of climbing. The people who run this company have a passion for the outdoors and want to share it with others. They believe that equipment and gear should be durable and innovative. At the same time they believe that you should preserve and restore the environment. You can shop their store by gender, kids, or by sport (trail running, paddling, surfing, fishing, climbing, and yoga to name just a few).

 Recommended   Price   Selection   Convenience   Service 🔒 Security

performancebike.com
Performance Bike

800-727-2453
customerservice@performanceinc.com

Camp Gear • Footwear • Outerwear • Shelter

Big bikes, little bikes, fancy bikes, mountain bikes, race bikes. No matter the type, financing is available for a bike over $500 at performancebike.com. Don't forget the helmets, gloves, pumps, horns, water bottles, and so on. Check out the store locator to find a location near you so that you can actually try out the bikes. Send a virtual cycling postcard and keep up-to-date on the latest cycling news with e-tips. Search the site by category, or use the site's search box. Take a look at the affiliated custom stores — Custom Bike, Triathlete, Women's, and Outlet.

preparedness.com
Preparedness Industries, Inc.

707-472-0280
sales@preparednesscenter.com

Camp Gear • Food • Navigation • Outerwear • Shelter

Everyone knows that they need to be prepared in case of emergencies. However, do you think about being prepared when you're out in the wilderness? It is just as important to be ready in the great outdoors as it is at home or work. Preparedness Industries has what you need. This company offers food provisions, water, first aid and health products, lighting, emergency blankets, and sanitation supplies, among other things. It even has a 24-hour online order fulfillment center. Companies, schools, and other organizations can even design their own emergency kits.

rainypass.com
Rainy Pass Repair, Inc.

800-959-4626
repair@rainypass.com

Footwear • Outerwear • Shelter

What do you do when you get a hole in your tarp or tent or favorite outdoor clothing? Don't throw it away. Send it to Rainy Pass Repair. This company can repair your equipment or clothing with the latest and greatest materials. It can also clean and alter your gear. Get services on raingear, tents, sleeping bags, backpacks, skiwear, even down comforters. Turnaround is within 4–10 days, and Internet estimates are available. What a great way to save money and get years more use out of your initial purchase.

★ rei.com
REI

800-426-4840
E-mail form on site

Backpacks • Camp Gear • Footwear • Navigation • Outerwear • Shelter

Recreational Equipment, Inc. was founded in 1938 as a consumer cooperative. REI doesn't look like it did then, yet still gives members special benefits for their lifetime $15 fee. Shoppers can find anything they need for the great outdoors at varying price levels. The site offers camping/hiking gear; car racks; climbing, cycling, paddling, snow sports, cross training, and travel gear; timekeeping and navigation tools; and men's, women's, and kids' apparel. Shoppers can locate their nearest store for in-store clinics and REI-sponsored events. Not only is REI a renowned supplier of quality specialty outdoor gear and clothing, offering a broad selection of trusted gear as well as expert advice and in-depth information about products and outdoor recreation, it also actively supports the outdoors and outdoor recreation through community service.

riverconnection.com
River Connection

503-788-3077
E-mail form on site

Camp Gear • Navigation • Shelter

"Only the Best for Our Customers." That is the motto of the River Connection of Portland, Oregon. When you're on a whitewater river, you want nothing less. This site brings you a large selection of rafts and boats as well as a wide range of accessories and equipment. Camping and fishing gear are available, too. Additionally, you can check river flow conditions and obtain permits through this site. Make sure you check out the selection of life jackets. Hopefully you won't need rescue equipment, but if you like to be prepared, check out the page for it on the site.

rockydirect.com
Rocky Mountain Direct Merchants

888-377-6259
info@rockydirect.com

Backpacks • Camp Gear • Footwear • Outerwear • Shelter

Get a Rocky Mountain high! This Canadian company specializes in outdoor clothing and footwear for the whole family. You can choose to shop either in its Canadian or American section of the store. This store offers free shipping on all orders placed online and delivered anywhere in Canada or the United States. Who can beat that? The site also has a selection of tents, backpacks, and accessories, and a clothing size chart to help you out. See what others are buying with the site's top ten bestsellers list.

★ sierratradingpost.com
Sierra Trading Post

800-713-4534
customerservice@sierratradingpost.com

Backpacks • Camp Gear • Food • Footwear • Navigation • Outerwear • Shelter

The founder of Sierra Trading Post had always dreamed of owning his own business. After years of working for others, he decided to make his dreams come true. Sierra Trading Post buys name-brand overstocks and closeouts and sells the products at discounted prices. This is the place to save 35–70 percent off brand-name outdoor merchandise. Because these items are closeouts, all quantities are limited. Search the site by brand, percent of savings, or size, or do a multi-search using a variety of criteria simultaneously. If you want a particular item, jump on it when you see it. Items sell quickly.

soldiercity.com
Soldier City

877-765-2489
customerserv@soldiercity.com

Backpacks • Footwear • Navigation • Outerwear

Army, Navy, Marines, and Air Force veterans now have a place they can buy all that outdoor military-issued equipment they used during their stint. Soldier City takes pride in "Serving America's Heroes." However, this site is not limited to veterans. Anyone can shop. Soldier City has over 40,000 items from backpacks to tents, footwear to outerwear. You can even find navigation equipment and a wide range of camouflage outfits so you can blend into any kind of terrain. The site is easy to navigate and search.

tentsonsale.com
Tentsonsale.com

573-237-8328
customerservice@tentsonsale.com

Backpacks • Camp Gear • Shelter

Big tents, little tents, one-room tents, two-room tents, two-man tents, four-man tents — you can find all these at tentsonsale.com. If you need more information or have a question, you can ask Dr. Tent. The site also provides links for weather, traffic, maps, first aid, and recipes. For Boy Scouts, this company offers volume discounts and a "Try N Test" program. Prices are low because the products are direct from the manufacturer to you, and because packaging and advertising are minimized.

thetannery.com
The Tannery

617-491-0810
info@thetannery.com

Footwear

Your shoes can make or break your outdoor experience. A comfortable pair of shoes, well suited to their purpose, will send you on your way. Aching or blistered feet, or shoes that slip or slide, ruin the best plans. How about putting your feet in the (cyber) hands of the experts at The Tannery? Your best bet are the shoes by Montrail. "Function-focused," Montrail shoes are designed to fit the size, shape, and elongation of your feet. A GORE-TEX shell surrounds each Montrail shoe, keeping your feet dry. Although they're far superior, Montrail shoes cost about the same as competitor models.

trekgear.com
Trek Gear

866-873-5432
No e-mail address on site

Backpacks • Camp Gear • Food • Footwear • Navigation • Outerwear • Shelter

The people at Trek Gear want "to provide name-brand equipment at reasonable cost." They want the customers to feel that they are important and not just a number. Trek Gear has just about anything you need to live outdoors, even nutritious food for just about everyone, including your dog, as well as chocolate for those chocoholics in the crowd. The site offers a nice selection of maps and map accessories, as well as apparel and gear for camping, climbing, paddling, biking, and snow sports. Trek Gear will ship internationally and to APO/FPO addresses, and shipping is free on orders $50 or more.

uscav.com
U.S. Cavalry

800-777-7172
E-mail form on site

Backpacks • Footwear

If you want some of the "finest quality military and adventure gear," the U.S. Cavalry site is for you. This company offers backpacks, clothing, and footwear for camping and other outdoor activities, including rappelling gear, binoculars, flashlights and lightsticks, and a multitude of other products. Sign up to receive U.S. Cavalry's bi-monthly e-mail newsletters for the latest specials.

wildernessdining.com
Wilderness Dining

866-576-0642
info@wildernessdining.com

Food

Eating on the trail shouldn't be a punishment. Wilderness Dining sells food and cookware for use on camping excursions. Breakfasts and dinners come in individual, handy sealed pouches with heating instructions clearly marked. Snacks and munchies are sealed in plastic tubs. For something different, try dried vegetables. They add zip to any meal and contribute needed vitamins to your diet. Food dehydrators are available for those who want to make their own camp food. A dehydrator is expensive, so check out all the features and choose the one that's right for you.

wildernessessentials.com
Wilderness Essentials

877-759-3758
info@wildernessessentials.com

Backpacks • Camp Gear • Navigation • Shelter

When you think about the wilderness, what do you think about? Wide open spaces, clean fresh air, no hassles? Did you think about what you need to take to survive in the wilderness? Wilderness Essentials has what you need, including cooking gear and supplies, backpacks, coolers, drinking water gear, first aid and survival items, stoves and heaters, camp chairs and sleeping bags, GPS systems, and much more. This company even offers a battery-operated shower for those of you who like some of the creature comforts of home out in the wilderness. Also, check out the kids' section of the Web site. It has pint-sized equipment so you can take the kids with you on those family outdoor excursions. This site has everything you need to make your outdoor stay safe, comfortable, and fun.

wingsupply.com
Wing Supply

800-388-9464
service@wingsupply.com

Camp Gear • Footwear • Navigation • Outerwear

If you've been hunting for a great outdoor site, look no further. Wing Supply carries hunting equipment and gear for the serious hunter. Shop here for top name brands, including Rocky and Lacrosse boots, Columbia waterfowl clothing, and API and Summit Treestands. The selection of decoys is extensive — you'll find everything from doves to ducks. Motorized decoys add extra realism. Round out your expedition with realistic-sounding game calls from almost every animal and bird in the forest. Although the popularity of hunting is declining in some quarters, this site helps keep the sport alive and well. Meet other hunters and post your thoughts through the site's lively forums.

yourbasecamp.com
Your Basecamp

928-368-6800
info@yourbasecamp.com

Backpacks • Camp Gear • Food • Navigation • Shelter

According to Your Basecamp, its site is the "Last Stop Before Adventure." This Web site gives campers great information on the things they need to take with them when they go to commune with nature. In addition to this information, Your Basecamp also provides the outdoor customer a free backpack checklist, sizing chart, weight calculator, and hiking trail finder — all important items for the average camper who wants to have a good camping experience. At the site, you can buy compasses, camping food, books, lanterns, sleeping gear, repellents, coolers, pots and pans, stoves, and tents, among other things. The site also offers hiking maps, trip ideas, advice, photos, weather links, backpack-sizing information, and product reviews. This is a great site to check to ensure you're totally prepared for your trip.

 Recommended Price Selection Convenience Service Security

⭐ zodi.com
Zodi Outback Gear

800-589-2849
E-mail form on site

Camp Gear

Wouldn't a nice hot shower feel good after a day of roughing it in the wilderness? Then check out this online retailer. Zodi Outback Gear has battery-operated and solar-powered instant hot water shower units. It even sells privacy enclosures so you can feel like you're taking a shower at home rather than in the wilderness. After you feel clean and crawl into your tent for a restful sleep, it would be nice to have your tent all nice and warm. Zodi Outback Gear can help you in that area, too. The tent heaters offered at the site can keep you warm all night long. This is roughing it?

A Shopping Excursion — Camping Is Kid's Play

So the kids have graduated from camping in the back yard to experiencing the real outdoors, and they're ready for their first adventure. Equipping young children for the outdoors is different from buying camping gear for the older folks. Safety precautions should always be in place when camping with kids. So, before you set out on your shopping excursion for camping and hiking gear for children, read the Camping Safety Check Sheet for Kids (ctsafekids.org/Fact_Sheets/fact18.htm).

To prepare for taking the family into the great outdoors, check out some of the great sites that offer camping gear just for the young ranger.

CampingGurus.com (campinggurus.com/catalog/Kids_Camping_Gear_page_1_c_24.html) has a small but fun collection of kids' ponchos, bug jars with a magnifying glass, kid-sized flashlights and safety whistles, pond nets, and complete fieldtrip bug labs. You may as well teach the kids something about nature while they're experiencing it. For Coleman brand backpacks, coolers, water carriers, lighting, tents, and sleeping bags just for kids, check out SleepingBagsandTents.com (sleepingbags andtents.com).

The 4 Outdoor Fun site (4outdoorfun.com/forkids.html) offers products similar to the sites mentioned above, but also carries kids' air mattresses. BrandsPlace.com (shop.store.yahoo.com/brandsplace) sells only Coleman camping gear for the tots, including Coleman kids' binoculars, a cool radio flashlight, Illumisticks, and a Secret Sleeper QuickBed.

Outdoor Kids' Source (kidssource.com) is just that — a comprehensive source for camping gear for kids. This company sells rugged kids' camping and hiking equipment, including sleeping bags, backpacks, torso packs, snowshoes, and snorkeling equipment from leading manufacturers. It doesn't ignore the essentials either, such as child carriers, family first-aid kits, and an excellent assortment of outdoor-related books for adults and children.

Not to be outdone, the Outdoor Kids Store (outdoorkids.com) specializes in reasonably priced, high-performance clothing and gear for infants, toddlers, and kids for any type of outdoor activity. You can find winter, camping, and canoeing products; rain gear; and rock-climbing gear for kids.

Nature Rangers (naturerangers.com) has all the clothing, gear, ideas, and information to make your outdoor activity a fun and safe experience for you and your kids. This company has been helping kids (and their moms and dads) stay outdoors since 1998. Its product line focuses on families who love to camp, hike, backpack, kayak, climb, snowshoe, and ski. The site offers what you need for just about any outdoor activity that you and your family can think of. Another full comprehensive site for camping kids is AlpineZone.com (gear.alpinezone.com/kids.htm). Like Nature Rangers, it also offers just about everything you need to outfit your kids for the outdoors.

Finally, the well-known and experienced outdoors company, REI (rei.com), has a special place on its shopping site just for kids. Products range from camping gear and clothing to games and toys for outdoor fun, as well as instructional and guide books.

So go shopping, pack up the gear and family, and enjoy the wonder of nature. Don't forget to tread lightly out there.

Chapter 19

Pets: Caring for Your Animals

• •

*P*ets are important members of our families. They entertain us and make us laugh. In many homes they are treated like children — favorite children, in fact. And why not? You can whisper all your deepest secrets to your pet and know that word will never get around the neighborhood. Your pet is thrilled to see you whenever you come home. You and your pet will always love each other unconditionally.

Makers of pet products see this love as big business. From necessities like food to fripperies such as complete lines of apparel, it seems everyone wants to cash in where they can. No problem. The net result is that pet owners like you and me get to choose from an amazing collection of pet food, products, and accessories when we go shopping.

The Web sites in this chapter cater exclusively to pets. You'll find everything from food to memorials. Some of the prices will astound you. If you're a pet owner (or know someone who is) you may not be able to resist the toys and temptations offered by the collection of sites we've assembled.

Many online pet stores offer a regular replenishment service for pet food and supplies at a discount. The food is delivered to your door at intervals you specify, meaning your pet never runs short. This handy and convenient service can save you hours of shopping time in the course of a year.

Key Word Index

Birds

From big parrots to small canaries, the Bird sites cater to the avian species, offering products from cages to feeders.

Cats

Owners of felines — whether long hairs, short hairs, purebred, or alley cats — should look at the Cat sites. (Although anyone who has a cat knows that cats rule their owners!)

Dogs

Man's best friend is well taken care of at sites that bear the Dogs designation.

Fish

The Fish sites offer both fresh and saltwater varieties for your home or office fish tank, as well as food and other accessories for these colorful little swimmers.

Pet Clothing

From sweaters to Halloween costumes, the special collection of Pet Clothing sites can keep your pet fashionably dressed.

Pet Food

You can find food for every species, taste, and budget at the Pet Food sites. Match your animal type to zero in on the food you need to keep your pet healthy.

Pet Gear

The Pet Gear sites sell the equipment your pet needs on a daily basis. It may be something small like a leash, bowl, or scoop, or something big, like a dog door. Use in conjunction with other keywords to find exactly what you need.

Pet Grooming

Because your pet can't make an appointment at the local hair salon or barber shop, you're often the home groomer. Make it easy on yourself with grooming aids like combs, brushes, mitts, soaps, shampoos, and special aids from the Pet Grooming stores.

Pet Lodging

The Pet Lodging sites sell cages and carriers and whatever else is considered a home or lodging for your species of pets.

Pet Toys

All pets like to have fun. At the Pet Toys sites, you can find toys to keep your pet stimulated and active.

Pet Training

Whether you're working on advanced obedience training or keeping Rover from jumping up on company, the Pet Training sites offer a variety of training tools and aids that can help. You can find training aids for several animals in these stores.

Reptiles

Snakes, lizards, iguanas, and so on. These are pets you probably wouldn't want to cuddle with on a cold or stormy night, but the stores listed with the Reptile keyword sell supplies and food for them anyway.

Small Animals

Shop the Small Animals sites for the squirrel, ferret, bunny, or other small pet in your life.

agilityforless.com
Agility for Less

585-749-4808
creekhed@agilityforless.com

Dogs • Pet Training

Whether your interest — and your pup's — is in competition, obedience, or sheer fun, the Agility for Less site delivers canine agility equipment at reasonable prices. Access professional-type obstacle training equipment like tunnels and weave poles. Teach your dog to negotiate panel jumps, tire jumps, wing jumps, see-saws, and swaying bridges. In the process, your dog's weight will improve, his confidence will soar, and the result should be a happier, healthier canine. You don't have to be a pro trainer either, because the site also offers books and videos to teach you just what to do.

bigtopbarkery.com
Big Top Barkery

No phone number listed
bigtopbarkery@aol.com

Dogs • Pet Food

The circus theme on Big Top Barkery's site is just half the fun of this gourmet dog bakery featuring wonderful treats made from an all-natural peanut butter using only unsalted nuts. The Trufflez look luscious enough for human consumption and the Smores are crafted from a peanut butter cookie, carob bar, and cream cheese. Order a pizza cookie or a bone-shaped gift box and check out the "Pawty in a Box," which contains everything you need for a canine celebration. Careful about ingredients, this company offers goodies that are preservative-, salt-, and sugar-free. Orders ship expedited with an ice pack.

birdcages4less.com
Bird Cages 4 Less

877-247-3224
info@birdcages4less.com

Birds • Pet Food • Pet Lodging

Offering an amazing array of cages for birds both large and small, Bird Cages 4 Less provides free seven-day shipping on all orders. You can shop for both powder-coated and stainless steel cages, as well as large aviaries and adventure cages. Accessories featured include cage covers plus a range of perches, play stands, swings, and breeder boxes. Browse the selection of food, seed mixes, treats, toys, digital scales, and vitamins. Find complete owner's manuals for a variety of different birds among the site's many books. Locate helpful training tools, including a CD that can teach your bird to talk.

 Recommended Price Selection Convenience Service 🔒 Security

birdsupplies.com
Chirp n Squawk Bird Supplies

877-377-8295
birdsupplies@msn.com

Pet Food • Pet Lodging • Pet Training

This site is for the birds, literally. From tiny to large, this company has something for all types. How many places can you find a bird carseat or a specialty treat cookbook? Browse through the site's training tools, breeding supplies, care and grooming accessories, and the adoption center. Shop the selection of foods and treats, play stands, toys, cages, water bottles, and dishes. Wild birds have their own page, too. Educate yourself with the offering of books and videos, not to mention the online bird care articles.

★ borwickinnovations.com
Borwick Innovations

800-365-5657
ewinters@silcom.com

Cats • Dogs • Pet Gear • Small Animals

Borwick Innovations not only promises innovative products for your four-legged friends, it delivers them. If your pet likes to go in and out, you know the problems: interruptions, damaged screen doors, and mosquitoes and other bugs. That is, unless you invest in one of Borwick's choices of pet screen doors, including one designed to let your pet move back and forth through a sliding door. The pet doors are suited to both cats and dogs. For the humans, the site also offers wind bells and a patio table vase. While you're there, look at the CurryComb, for long- and short-haired pets.

bottomsupleash.com
Bottoms Up Leash

800-805-2001
info@bottomsupleash.com

Dogs • Pet Gear

Hip dysplasia and arthritis are big problems for dogs and their owners, but this site offers some relief. Offering a "new leash on life," Bottoms Up Leash specializes in a unique type of leash that allows you to support your canine's hindquarters as he or she moves up steps, inclines, or in regular walks, returning much needed mobility for your pet and keeping you from hurting your back. The leash, only offered online and through select vets and groomers, adjusts to support dogs from 10 to 135 pounds. You can also order a dog ramp at the site, too. Be sure to check the site's resources for senior dogs, and read the testimonials of other pet owners.

cagesdirect.com
Cages Direct

800-782-0627
info@cagesdirect.com

Birds • Cats • Dogs • Pet Gear • Pet Lodging • Small Animals

If you've shopped for a crate or cage for your animals, you know that store selection is often limited to just one or two models. But Cages Direct features a rather robust range, from dog pens and crates, to cat domains, to cages for your ferret, rabbit, or bird in an assortment of sizes and prices. Some even come in designer colors. Supplies like cage stands and covers are available, too. So are gates, bedding, dishes, and exercise kennels. The company also offers vehicle barriers to keep your pet from jumping into the front seat.

cajuncrawkitty.com
CajunCrawKitty.com

504-834-3114
daveanderson@cajuncrawkitty.com

Cats • Pet Food

Need the cure for cat snack fever? The answer just might be crawfish-flavored treats. Invented almost accidentally by a fellow whose feline-loving wife had 30 cats, his furry crew tore apart the kitchen looking for more of the good stuff. Now your kitty can enjoy these healthy fish meal goodies. The treats arrive in a bright plastic bucket. Buy one, buy three, or buy a whole case (the more you purchase, the bigger the discount). You can use PayPal as well as credit cards and eChecks at the site.

canadianexoticpets.com
Canadian Exotic Pets

No phone number listed
pam@canadianexoticpets.com

Cats • Dogs • Pet Food • Pet Gear • Pet Lodging • Pet Toys • Small Animals

Find food, supplies, pouch shirts, and totes for your pet sugar glider, chinchilla, rabbit, ferret, hedgehog, or primate at the Canadian Exotic Pets site. It offers bird food, too, along with cat and dog supplies. Whether you need cage cleaners and deodorizers, a bath house for your chinchilla, specialty cages, or exercise equipment such as wheels, these folks stock it (however, not all products are available for shipment to the U.S.; check the online list). Yet here's something special: elaborate pet portraits done in watercolor from a prized photo that you supply, with prices ranging from $100 to $475. This company takes PayPal, check, or money order.

 Recommended   Price   Selection   Convenience   Service Security

catabbey.com
CatAbbey.com

970-482-7535
lcain@mfire.com

Cats • Dogs • Pet Food • Pet Gear • Pet Lodging

Despite the name, the CatAbbey.com offers products for dogs as well as cats, focusing attention on healthy pet food made with human-grade ingredients. Herbal pet remedies are big at this site, addressing issues such as appetite, immune stimulation, calmers, and eye relief. The site carries chemical-free and ultra-gentle shampoos, and grooming and therapeutic sprays. Besides the usual carriers, leashes, collars, and toys, you can also buy whole-house air purifiers to cut down on pet allergens, kitty gyms and condos, life vests, carseats, backseat hammocks, and Chaya's Canine Naturals. If you need a bird carrier, the site has it, too.

★ cat-dog-doors.com
Cat Dog Doors.com

610-539-8736
info@cat-dog-doors.com

Cats • Dogs • Pet Gear • Small Animals

Tired of jumping up to let your cat or dog in or out of the house but concerned about the hassle of finding and installing the proper access door? Cat Dog Doors.com can help, both with its assortment as well as its intelligent online Pet Doors Selector to guide you through the right selection for your pet and your home. Shop by type and size of pet, by price, or by brand name. The site also carries containment gates for in-home use as well as vehicle barriers to keep your four-legged friend safely in place.

catpicturegallery.com
Cat Picture Gallery

610-539-8736
custserv@catpicturegallery.com

Cats • Pet Gear

For those who harbor deep feelings for felines, or if you can't get enough kitty in your life, Cat Picture Gallery is your domain. Order from an inventory of adoring and adorable cat pictures grouped by theme (cats, kittens, funny, cute), and peruse articles about the role cats have played in art throughout history. Surf the site's stock of kitty calendars, plus T-shirts and sweatshirts sold with a 100 percent guarantee. Big cats like cougars, tigers, and lions get shirt treatment, too. While you're visiting, sign up for the free cat newsletter e-zine.

cattoys.com
CatToys.com

877-364-8697
E-mail form on site

Cats • Pet Gear

Shopping for the discerning, finicky feline can make for a tough proposition. CatToys.com helps by sorting its toy selection into categories like personality (for example, couch potato, night player, or extremely active), breed, type, or brand. Some toys are outrageously cute and/or funny, like the political animals and the revenge options (poor dogs!). How about some organic catnip or cat treats such as Alaskan salmon and specials for the fussy eaters? The site offers beds, carriers, and baskets, too, including a great cuddle-and-carry basket. Take the cat nickname survey and sign up for the free newsletter.

classypets.com
Classy Pets

866-872-4785
info@classypets.com

Cats • Dogs • Pet Clothing • Pet Gear

For the pet who doesn't yet have everything comes a site boasting diamonds for your dog and pearls for your cat. The accent is on elegance at Classy Pets, from the gourmet treats so yummy you'll want some yourself, to the exclusive selection of beds, collars, leashes, jewelry, toys, and truly unique bowls and feeders. Need a cowboy hat or a slicker for your pampered pooch? This site has it, along with pet toiletries, travel accessories, and your kitty's own can of catviar. Yet most of this four-legged luxury is very affordable.

coldnoses.net
Cold Noses

508-228-5477
No e-mail address on site

Cats • Dogs • Pet Clothing • Pet Gear

One visit to the Cold Noses site and you'll understand why this unique site calls itself the exclusive Nantucket boutique for dogs and cats and the people who love them. This company offers a bit of everything, from pawkerchiefs, collars and leads, to holiday hats and catnip cuties, to gourmet dog cookies, haute feline cat goodies (check out the Kitty Kaviar), and fun and fanciful food dishes. Under People Stuff, you'll find breed-specific hats, belts that match the company's dog collars, pet carry packs, and an assortment of shirts. The site even offers St. Bernard brandy kegs.

 Recommended Price Selection Convenience Service Security

cooper-cadie.com
Cooper & Cadie

866-802-2777
info@cooper-cadie.com

Cats • Dogs • Pet Clothing • Pet Gear • Pet Grooming • Pet Training

Need natural, healthy pet supplies for your cats and/or your dogs? Find them at Cooper & Cadie, along with apparel, treats, toys, feeders and dishes, waterers, bones, and chews. Grooming tools include waterless cleaning products, while training tools feature goods for both obedience and hunting education, along with containment fences and bark control collars. The company offers treatments as well, covering hip and joint, skin and itch relief, dental, ear cleaning, and first aid. The site also has the basics, such as carriers, leashes, and bed material. You get a free Chuck-it for dogs with your first order.

dealsforpets.com
DealsforPets.com

No phone number listed
info@dealsforpets.com

Cats • Dogs • Pet Food • Pet Gear

Buying in bulk can save you money, no matter what you're shopping for. DealsforPets.com brings special deals, manufacturer overruns, and closeout values to your pets. If your pet doesn't need a 50-pack of assorted toys, maybe you can split a large order with friends. Find and buy value packs throughout the store of toys for cats and dogs, as well as treats like bacon bones, pork links, lamb and rice biscuits, and peanut butter bites. Get discounts on rawhide chews. The site also carries rabbit and guinea pig food, plus grooming and hygiene products and training pads.

doggear.com
Mickie's Place

866-968-4453
sales@mickiesplace.com

Dogs • Pet Gear • Pet Training

Don't leave your dogs behind when you go out for a weekend of adventure. Bring them along, but with safety in mind thanks to this site specializing in gear for the active outdoor canine. Beyond tools to help you get your pet into proper condition for the experience and articles offering tips, this site boasts a wide array of products that include tents and sleeping bags, beds and packs, feed bags, cold-weather apparel (coats, boots, and shoes), water filters and floatation devices (think doggy life jacket), and first aid. Find training info, too, along with a sister site for adventure-seeking humans.

doggy-gifts.com
Doggy Gifts
866-937-3647
E-mail form on site

Dogs • Pet Gear • Pet Grooming

Putting on the dog for your canine has never been easier. There's no minimum purchase at the Doggy Gifts site, and you receive free shipping on U.S. orders. The site also features a live-help shopping consultant. Shop well-known brands like Kong, Bamboo, and Breeders' Choice for toys, treats, harnesses, carriers, pet pillows, sleepover bags, flea and dematting combs, plus nail and dental care accessories. Get a supply of waste bags for your car or to carry along. Don't forget to check out the training tools and books.

exoticnutrition.com
Exotic Nutrition Pet Company
757-930-0301
exoticdiet@cox.net

Pet Food • Pet Gear • Small Animals • Reptiles

Consider the Exotic Nutrition Pet Company your trusted source for exotic mammal and reptile products. This company has inventory for all types of unique pets, from prairie dogs and sugar gliders to skunks and hedgehogs, chinchillas, squirrels of all types, plus primates, arachnids, and snakes big and small. Choose from live insects (yum) and food, treats, cages and accessories, vitamins and nectars, heaters, supplements, and exercise equipment. For those planning to acquire a rarer pet, check out the starter packages. Browse through the site's book section to learn even more.

⭐ ferretstore.com
TheFerretStore.com
800-440-3356
E-mail form on site

Birds • Cats • Dogs • Fish • Pet Food • Pet Gear • Pet Lodging • Pet Toys • Pet Training • Small Animals

For those tired of ferreting out a source of quality small pet supplies comes an online store focusing on ferrets but with something for dogs, cats, and other small animals as well. TheFerretStore.com sells sleepers, nesting material, litter and litter pans, cages and cage covers, beds and blankets, toys, feeders, bottles, and bathing accessories. Peruse the site's selection of books and magazines to increase your knowledge, and take advantage of the links — such as to pet chat forums. You'll discover discounts on sale items along with free shipping on orders of $35 or more.

⭐ Recommended   **$** Price   🛒 Selection   🎁 Convenience   ☺ Service   🔒 Security

fouronthefloorpetwear.com
Four on the Floor Petwear

888-459-9327
fourfloor@aol.com

Dogs • Pet Gear

You've got your favorite T-shirts. Now your dog can, too. Macho mutts may prefer the Superman or FBI turtlenecks, while designer doggies can slip into something from Liz Claibone or Canine Kline. The canine with puppitude is apt to drool over the muscle tee or do flips over the fashion found in Barktoria Secret (think black lace). When cooler weather strikes, consider a berber or jacquard fleece sweatshirt. But wait . . . there are great goggles, too, that protect your dog's eyes from sun, sand, and wind.

groomerschoice.com
Groomer's Choice

888-364-6242
sales@groomerschoice.com

Cats • Dogs • Pet Grooming • Small Animals

Whether you're a pet grooming professional or just want optimum results in cleaning and preening the family pet(s), you've just found a serious source for grooming equipment and accessories. From shampoos and conditioners, tubs, dryers, clippers, cleaners, cages and kennels, steps and ramps, clamps, restraints, and muzzles, Groomer's Choice has it all. The company also offers books and videos to teach you techniques (pro groomer software, too), as well as professional-grade dematting tools and trimmers.

healthypetsnw.com
Healthy Pets Northwest

503-236-8036
hpnw@callatg.com

Cats • Dogs • Pet Food

If you believe in holistic wellness, you may want to extend that belief to your precious animals with this natural alternative for pet foods and supplies. Healthy Pets Northwest sells Flint River foods (free shipping on these), dog and cat treats, natural flea remedies, ear wash, hip and joint health products, multivitamins and probiotics, along with books at its site. Consider the Bark Flower Essentials, a line of herbal treatments covering a number of symptoms, such as beech, which is used to help your pet with intolerance toward other animals, and chestnut bud, used to deter the animal from repeating bad behaviors. Check out the site's articles on pet health, too.

⭐ healthypetstore.com
Healthy Pet Store

888-294-7387
sales@healthypetstore.com

Birds • Cats • Dogs • Pet Grooming • Reptiles • Small Animals

Just as its name suggests, Healthy Pet Store's site focuses on the healthy pet by addressing the needs of dogs, cats, birds, and small animals. You can find a roomy pet iguana cage, fish aquariums, special training pools, and tortoise food. The live customer service option offers assistance in selection on the range of toys, treats, food (kosher, too), pet doors, books and magazines, bowls and feeders, plus care accessories such as shampoo, nail and coat products, ear kits, medical supplies, supplements, and odor control. You get free shipping on orders $50 and more.

hm-e.net
Horizon Micro-Environments

800-443-2498
george@hm-e.net

Birds

When you need to ship birds of any feather, you can't just stick them in a box, can you? This site boasts of itself as the live bird shippers for the U.S. Postal Service's Express Mail (overnight delivery) and features Biosecure containers with filters for shipping a whole host of fowl (adult turkeys, pheasants, doves, ducks, geese, parakeets, parrots — you name it). The filters are important because they protect both people and birds from airborne disease, dust, and dander. Non-biosecure containers can be used for eggs, adult chickens, and baby chicks. Check the site's tip files on shipping and regulations.

itchyspot.com
Itchy Spot Scratchers

904-258-8064
tiss@bellsouth.net

Dogs • Pet Gear

Whereas we can ask for help when we have an itch we cannot reach, your pet isn't quite so fortunate. How can it say, "No, scratch over there"? With this in mind comes a great tool, designed exclusively for dogs by a licensed massage therapist. However, cats and even people like it, too. The unique Y-shaped device offered by Itchy Spot Scratchers acts as both a back scratcher and a massager, offering deep relief without the need to get pet dander beneath your nails. Order small or large, for cats or dogs. A percentage of the sales proceeds goes to pet charities.

 Recommended   Price   Selection   Convenience   Service 🔒 Security

just4pooches.com
Just4PoochesCompany

908-709-4364
info@just4pooches.com

Dogs • Pet Food • Pet Gear • Pet Toys

Your dog will grin at you for shopping at the Just4PoochesCompany site when the order is delivered. You'll discover lots of healthy food (including Kosher), not to mention great toys. Yet that's just the start; you can browse the doggy aromatherapy, grooming and bath goodies, beds and pillows, flea/tick/odor control products, coat and skin care products, supplements, or dental hygiene products. For the pup on the go, you can find travel accessories, plus ramps and other access helpers along with waste disposal bags for the trip. Be sure to get a book or magazine, too.

justpawspetwear.com
Just Paws Petwear

250-545-3522
justpaws@shaw.ca

Cats • Dogs • Pet Clothing • Pet Food • Pet Gear

If your pet's favorite "paw-sition" is "whatever's comfortable," then check out the Just Paws Petwear site for a selection of cozy cat tents and pet beds to make you both very content. The site also offers "pawsitively" perfect booties and coats. In the costumes section, you'll find a wedding gown and even a tuxedo for Rover! You can also get a high-visibility mesh safety vest to help your pet be seen during walks. Under toys, you'll be delighted at the tennis ball octopus. Practical items you can buy at the site include collars and leashes, carriers, and collapsible travel dishes.

kosherpets.com
Kosher Pets

954-938-6270
corporate@kosherpets.com

Dogs • Pet Food

You don't have to be Jewish to know that Kosher food is considered healthier because of the rigorous inspection standards. This company brings these standards to dog and cat food as well, which you may find especially good for pets suffering from food allergies. In fact, Kosher Pets boasts the first and only kosher cat food. Their products are made with kosher animal protein, whole grains, essential amino acids, and probiotics. You'll enjoy the witty packaging, like kibble schmibbles and deli dog treats the company promises will bring out the mensch in your pup.

★ lafeber.com
Lafeber Premium Bird Food

800-842-6445
info1@lafeber.com

Birds • Pet Food

Doc Lafeber, a practicing vet, provides the name and the experience behind this site featuring food and toys for your favorite bird (tamed or wild). At the Lafeber Premium Bird Food site, you can buy Nutri-nuts, popcorn, and many varieties of Nutri-berries, or Nutri-Start for baby birds. Order the avi-cakes, which are special seed cakes made from cracked corn, rolled oats, and whole eggs covered with rich, thick molasses. Get vitamins, too, as well as Doc Lefeber's book on pet birds. Read through lots of good bird information including "15 Steps to a Wonderful Bird Bath Time." Whether you have a parrot, macaw, cockatiel, cockatoo, or budgie, it'll love you for checking out this informative site.

liveaquaria.com
LiveAquaria.com

800-334-3699
customerservice@liveaquaria.com

Fish • Pet Food

LiveAquaria.com, managed by veterinarians, offers quality aquatic life delivered directly to your door. Notably, the site features weekly specials, a 10-day "arrive alive, stay alive" guarantee, and free shipping on orders over $175. Yet it also boasts a wealth of live fish (marine, freshwater, brackish, and pond), invertebrates (crabs, jellyfish, sponges, and more), plants, coral, and rocks, as well as equipment and supplies. Select from a range of aquariums, pumps and temperature control mechanisms, water purification devices, lighting, parts, and both food and feeders. Other products cover your tank cleaning needs.

 Recommended   Price   Selection   Convenience   Service   Security

lonestarchinchilla.com
Lone Star Chinchilla

903-391-1248
orders@lonestarchinchilla.com.com

Pet Food • Small Animals

If you're among the many who think fur looks better on the animal than on a person, and you've dreamed of owning a chinchilla as a pet, check out Lone Star Chinchilla's site. This company ships chinchilla feed worldwide, which you can order through e-mail or phone. Yet there's more: pellets, hay, treats, wheels, bottles, pans, and special medical supplies. You can use this site to learn the details about keeping these charming animals as pets, and you can even order live animals from its exclusive stock. However, you have to pick up the animal in person (this company won't ship it).

mackiesparlour.com
Mackiesparlour.com

888-991-7884
mail@mackiesparlour.com

Pet Clothing • Pet Gear • Pet Grooming • Pet Toys

Mackiesparlour.com is a unique online pet store and boutique boasting beautiful dog beds, colorful dog bowls and feeders, collars, and carriers. You'll find quite an apparel array as well. Treat your dog to a trendy shearling coat, a hooded sweatshirt or sweater, a denim jacket, or a cute little dress. Find shirts, too, including delightful Hawaiian print designs. What about a hat or a pearl necklace to complete the ensemble? The toys are nothing to bark at either, from ducks and chicks to a yellow school bus. Finally, don't forget the treats in standard and unique flavors.

marinedepot.net
Marine Depot

714-385-0080
sales@marinedepot.net

Fish • Pet Food

Each type of aquarium has particular needs. Marine Depot focuses on those individual needs by offering key tools for every fish enthusiast, whether you're keeping tropical, saltwater, fresh-water, or reef-based systems. Frozen formula and freeze-dried nutritional packs are just part of the food selection on hand. You'll also find additives and medications, along with a comprehensive complement of aquarium sets, controllers, pumps (dosing, air, and external), heaters and chillers, an array of test kits, and key reference books and CDs to further your education and enjoyment.

★ merrickpetcare.com
Merrick Pet Foods

800-664-7387
info@merrickpetcare.com

Cats • Dogs • Pet Food

"A good man is concerned with the welfare of his animals," Proverbs 12:10. The family owners of Merrick Pet Foods display this Bible quote on their site's homepage. Attempting to practice what they preach, Merrick specializes in holistic, gourmet pet foods. This company uses human-grade products for its protein sources and fresh fruits and vegetables in its pet foods. Its canned dog foods feature such flavors as Turducken, Venison, Working Dog Stew, and Grammy's Pot Pie. Treats include such specialties as Ostrich and Rice Sausages. Your animal may eat better than you if you order from this site, but you have to agree that Merrick is trying hard to do right by our four-legged friends. Be sure to enroll your pet in the birthday club; he or she will get a card and free treat in the mail. The site offers free shipping on all orders, as well.

mreed.com
M. Reed Enterprises

209-267-1175
mreed@mreed.com

Fish • Pet Food

Tropical fish food isn't just flakes. Mike Reed, the man behind this online store, has more than two decades of experience in the business and now sells his line of highly nutritious foods online. Some of these include technically advanced formulations that are all natural and/or color- and behavior-enhancing feeds that can be found nowhere else. Such food takes the form of frozen, dry, fry, or live. You'll find fry treats, water supplements, and fish videos. He also offers complete directions on producing your own live feed, along with supplies such as a worm composting bin and live worms. Purchase in quantities of 4, 8, or 16 ounces, or 5 pounds. Prices are displayed in an easy-to-read table format.

⭐ myfriendforever.com
MyFriendForever.com

No phone number listed
info@myfriendforever.com

Cats • Dogs

The death of a pet brings emptiness, pain, sorrow, and a broken heart. The grief is deep and painful and the memory of the adored friend is too painful to let go. Why not visit MyFriendForever.com and post a tribute to your departed friend? MyFriendForever is a memorial site for pets, and allows you to post a tribute with or without a picture. After you sign up, you'll receive your own unique ID and simple link, so you can share your tribute with all the people who knew and loved your pet, too. Your beloved pet's memory will live on forever.

petco.com
PETCO.com

877-738-6742
cs@orders.petco.com

Cats • Dogs • Fish • Pet Gear • Pet Grooming • Pet Toys • Pet Training • Reptiles • Small Animals

You've probably seen Petco's commercials, but you'll find this company's shopping site great if you don't have a store nearby. Offering thousands of products for dogs, cats, birds, fish, reptiles, and small animals, Petco makes it easy to stock up on food, health care accessories, grooming supplies, and pet resource material like books and videos. There's the added bonus of an unusually large selection of items like beds, aquariums, cages, carriers, treats, training products, ID tags, and food/water dishes. Monthly specials can help you curb costs. Finally, find lots of online resources like pet-related yellow pages, an e-mail newsletter, and online discussion boards.

petexports.com
Pet Exports

+44(0)23 8076 6876
ca@petexports.com

Cats • Dogs

What do you do when you need to ship your prized pet to or from England? You visit the Pet Exports site, the home of Chilworth Pet Exports, who provide international shipping for unaccompanied pets. This company collects and ships from English airports (Heathrow among others) and Portsmouth seaport, and provides complete services including documentation, the container, vet requirements, boarding, flight arrangements, quarantine, insurance, and transportation. Let this company handle everything for you to make the process as smooth as possible. Check the site for complete details on the types of containers used.

petfooddirect.com
Petfooddirect.com

800-865-1333
pfd@petfooddirect.com

Birds • Cats • Dogs • Fish • Pet Food • Pet Grooming • Pet Lodging • Reptiles • Small Animals

With over 11,000 products in Pet Food Direct's comprehensive inventory, you can't help but find what you need for your dog, cat, reptile, bird, fish, or other small animal. This includes food and treats for all plus toys. Bird lovers can select from cages and supplies. Get your small animals a habitat, or check into getting your reptile a heater or lighting. Locate a filter or powerhead for your marine/tropical fish. Shop for beds, mats, first-aid kits, and grooming and hygiene products for the pup or kitty. Notice, too, that some products ship for free when you choose ground shipping for delivery. The site also offers a 100 percent guarantee, a Red Tag area for specials, as well as a Meals Plus program that enables you to have automatic delivery of food and supplies for your pets based on a schedule of your choosing.

 Recommended   Price   Selection   Convenience   Service   Security

petfoods.com
Country Pet Food

800-454-7387
E-mail form on site

Cats • Dogs • Pet Food

Commercial foods may be fine for many pets, but what about yours? Your dog or cat may need something more — namely, the far better nutrition found in a more natural diet. Country Pet Food offers not just any pet food. Its Countrypet line of all-meat products comes from New Zealand and is frozen into 1.5 lb. rolls. Available in chicken, lamb, or lamb and vegetable for dogs, and fish or chicken for cats, you can buy a case of all one flavor or purchase an assortment. The price includes free shipping within the continental U.S.

petfriendly.com
PetFriendly.com

800-582-1889
customerservice@petfriendly

Cats • Dogs • Pet Food • Pet Gear • Pet Grooming • Pet Lodging • Pet Toys • Pet Training

PetFriendly.com is a site by pet lovers for pet lovers. The result is obvious in the selection of products this site offers. For example, there's a flipper feeder that allows your dog to raise the lid to eat while keeping out dirt and bugs. The animal toys (for cats, dogs, and birds) are made in the U.S., usually from 100 percent cotton. Private label shampoos along with pet beds and houses are also featured. Find collars, leashes, carriers, grooming accessories, feeders, and water dispensers for both cats and dogs, as well as books for you.

petlabs.com
J & G Laboratories

877-787-7815
petinfo@jandglabs.com

Dogs

Loving our pets often doesn't translate into enjoying all the smells they produce. Facing that fact, the people behind this site have developed a special-formula odor spray to eliminate unpleasant smells. This product, called Odor Free, is not a coverup; you simply spray it on your pet's food daily to gradually stop the odors associated with urine, stool, gas, bad breath, and even a funky coat. Made from the Mojave Yucca plant and boasting a peanut butter flavor, an 8-ounce bottle offers 340 full sprays, enough for a large dog for a month. The company has a money-back guarantee as well.

⭐ petsmart.com
PETsMART

888-839-9638
cs@petsmart.com

Birds • Cats • Dogs • Fish • Pet Food • Pet Gear • Pet Grooming • Pet Lodging • Pet Toys • Pet Training • Small Animals

Consider PETsMART your pet department store, with a fairly broad selection of products "for the happier, healthier pet." Locate just about everything you want or need for your dog, cat, bird, reptile, or other small animal. Beyond the usual suspects like collars, leashes, tags and toys, dishes, food, and treats, you can buy barriers, access ramps, car seat harnesses and seat covers, and something which gives us all paws . . . er . . . pause, a pet food quantity calculator. Check out the ASPCA breed guides and resource books as well as grooming accessories. Shipping is free on orders $50 or more.

petstreetmall.com
Pet Street Mall

800-957-5753
customerservice@petstreetmall.com

Cats • Dogs • Pet Food • Pet Gear • Pet Grooming • Pet Lodging • Pet Toys • Pet Training

Now you don't have to take your pup or kitty to a mall to find a broad selection of useful items and cool extras. Start with Pet Street Mall's pet beds, cat furniture, and dog and puppy crates. Then work your way through the virtual aisles filled with pet gates, dog doors, feeders, products like training and bark control collars, smart treats, and containment fences. You'll find a wide variety of Innotek brand goods, and supplies for your fish and reptiles, as well. The company also offers a line of pet memorial products like urns, markers, and plaques, and shipping is free on orders over $40. Gift certificates are available, and you can join a Pet Lover's Club for a 5 percent discount on selected products.

 Recommended   Price   🛒 Selection   🎁 Convenience   ☺ Service   🔒 Security

puppylovegourmetbakery.com
Puppy Love Gourmet Bakery

866-541-7389
info@puppylovegourmetbakery.com

Dogs • Pet Food • Pet Gear

How many places can you shop for a birthday cake made just for your pup? Ah, but this Calgary bakery's scrumptious treats are available for cats, ferrets, and horses, too. At the Puppy Love Gourmet Bakery, you won't find added salt, refined sugar, byproducts, or additives in its baked goods. In fact, this bakery specializes in treats suitable for pets with allergies or dietary restrictions, including items that are grain-free and low carb. Order more standard dog and cat food as well, in cans, raw, or kibble form. The site also has jerky, scratching posts, pet couches, and toys.

purrfectgift.com
Purrfect Gift

650-618-1832
julie@purrfectgift.com

Cats • Dogs • Pet Clothing • Pet Toys

Purrfect Gift is a boutique created with the focus on the individuality of the pet — and pet lover. This company promises that no two gifts are ever exactly alike. Cats and dogs get equal time at this site. This applies to its trademark selection of kerchiefs for both species with a variety of cute prints along with a handy sizing chart, too. Choose from an assortment of toys and treat jars. Browse the very affordable snuggle beds. Then paw your way through the placemats on which to serve your favorite kitty cuisine. Be sure to check out the charming collectibles for owners, too.

purrfectpaw.com
Purrfectpaw.com

702-878-7297
sasha@purrfectpaw.com

Cats • Dogs • Pet Gear

Cat owners too often have to make a choice between their furniture and their cats. Now you can have both, thanks to an invention that won't require you to declaw the kitty or suffer through fruitless training. Purrfectpaw.com's clear, acrylic shields attach in seconds to the corners of most couches and chairs using narrow adhesive strips, giving you protection from cats who like to sharpen their claws. This company also offers wholesale products (minimum order: one dozen) such as dog and cat supplies, leashes, collars, toys, feeders, chews, and safety lights.

★ riverwonders.com
River Wonders

818-702-0558
sales@riverwonders.com

Fish

Not looking for the same old, same old? As direct importers of stock from the Amazon, Asia, and expert breeders, River Wonders specializes in hard-to-find "river wonders" and tropical fish. These folks also promise both exotic and beautiful fish without the middlemen. Be sure to check the site's stock list for current availability, which often includes different varieties of piranha (iridescent, too), sting rays, and even turtles. You can find freshwater fish as well, with a selection of tetras, arowanas, cichlids, and catfish. Need equipment? You can find it, too, along with both flat rate and inter-national shipping.

safepetproducts.com
SafePetProducts.com

877-231-1426
E-mail form on site

Cats • Dogs • Pet Training

Verbal commands aren't always enough to dissuade animals from bad behavior. Once they target an item or area, it's tough to get them to stop. That's where this site's unique products come in, addressing issues that allow you to gain control. At the SafePetProducts.com site, you can find SoftClaws, an alternative to declawing, which allows you to place nail caps on your cat to stop the scratching damage. Cat Stop is an ultrasonic deterrent to felines or other small animals from a yard or garden area. Scarecrow is a motion-activated sprinkler to discourage four-legged fiends, while Scat Mat says "No!" when you can't.

sheepdogwhistle.com
Sheep Dog Whistle

No phone number listed
info@sheepdogwhistle.co.uk

Cats • Dogs • Pet Training

From North Wales comes this highly specialized site featuring handmade and even personalized border collie herding and training products, such as the Commander sheep dog whistle to teach dogs how to tend the flock. The unique whistle comes with complete instructions for use. For example, train the dog to respond to one long whistle blow to stop or lie down or two short blasts to move away from the herd. This company also sells quality shepherd crooks (handsome even as decoration, too), along with dog ID tags.

 Recommended   Price   Selection   Convenience   Service   Security

spoiledrottendoggies.com
SpoiledRottenDoggies.com
877-413-8747
halloweenextreme@aol.com

Dogs • Pet Clothing • Pet Gear • Pet Toys

If you — or your canine — enjoy doggy dress-up, you can't miss this site. Whereas many online shops offer just a few costumes, SpoiledRottenDoggies. com features several different categories of costumes alone, and that's just the start of the fun. Nor is clothing limited to costumes. You can get sunglasses, biker jackets, plus some chic little hats, in sizes to fit pups large and small. Of course, you can also shop for more standard dog needs, too, such as collars and leashes, ramps, a great variety of toys and chewies, designer dog beds, bowls, and the ever-useful pet odor remover. Search the site by category or use the Search box to find what you need.

spoiledrottenkitties.com
Spoiled Rotten Kitties
954-926-5656
costumes@anniescostumes.com

Cats • Pet Clothing • Pet Gear

Anyone who says it's a "dog's life" has never visited this site for fabulous felines, featuring a mixture of the useful and the unusual. Spoiled Rotten Kitties offers cat beds so lush you'll want one yourself. It also offers uncommon goodies such as whimsical cat costumes like the Puss pirate, cat hats, and signs that remind you that while dogs have masters, cats have staff. Browse the wide selection of carriers, and then prepare to pamper your kitty with a choice of bowls and accessories, plus great treats and toys. The family-owned business behind this site offers a range of other products for dogs and people, too.

squirrelstore.com
The Squirrel Store
561-833-9948
trixierules@excite.com
Small Animals

If you love scampering squirrels, you're going to go nuts for this store. The Squirrel Store offers a gourmet selection of squirrel and other wildlife food, including black walnuts, pine nuts, and pumpkin seeds, plus specially formulated peanut butter and monkey biscuits. Then browse through the squirrel houses (big enough for a family), cages, and both cute and functional accessories like sleeper sacks and snuggle toys with a realistic heartbeat and warmer. This company even offers a squirrel travel cage — on wheels — for the tree rodent on the go. You will also find tips for keeping squirrels as pets.

supersoaper.com
Super Soaper
954-938-6270
supersoaper@pinklemonadedesign.com
Dogs • Pet Grooming

No, the Super Soaper is not a water gun, but a thoughtful way to bathe your dog in the shower. Large pet tubs, after all, can cost a lot. By combining a washer, pet shampoo reservoir, and grooming brush into a single-hand device, the job of bathing your pet becomes much easier. To install, just unscrew your showerhead, screw in the adapter, and then replace your showerhead. Then hook up the hose to the adapter, fill with shampoo, and turn on the water to begin washing. (Keep in mind that this company only accepts PayPal online.)

thepamperedpup.com
The Pampered Pup
561-833-9948
store-comments@thepamperedpup.com
Dogs • Pet Clothing • Pet Gear

This "Pawsitively Palm Beach" site is designed to help you make Rover or Spot feel like top dog. It boasts perfectly doggy pooch panache ranging from dresses, T-shirts, polo shirts, and coats, to even elegant formal wear for the canine ready for an all-star night on the town (you supply the limo). Besides fashion and canine jewelry, this site features totes and leather carriers, bowls and beds, grooming and spa accessories, collars and leashes, plus treats and toys. Be sure to use the size charts to ensure a proper fit.

 Recommended   Price   Selection   Convenience   Service   Security

timberwolforganics.com
Timberwolf Organics
863-439-0049
E-mail form on site

Dogs • Pet Food • Pet Gear • Pet Grooming

"Pet foods the way nature intended" is the Timberwolf Organics motto because it specializes in carefully formulated diets that take the whole dog's health into consideration. The result, the company says, are quality products that not only maintain weight, aid digestion, and produce a great coat, but that also reduce the dermatological stress found with commercial foods that results in scratching and discomfort. At this site, you'll find each food painstakingly described. Besides a number of different diet formulas, you can shop for meat rolls made from venison, elk, buffalo, and chicken/herbs. You'll also find supplements, leashes and collars, natural shampoos, and more.

videocatnip.com
Video Catnip
888-238-4395
orders@videocatnip.com

Cats • Pet Toys

Looking for some special entertainment that can stimulate your kitty whether you're home or not? Look no further than the bestselling "Video Catnip," a production created just for cats and available in DVD and VHS format. The program runs 25 minutes and grabs your cat's attention through a series of enchanting birds, as well as raucous chipmunks and squirrels. Cats react and respond, and some owners say their pets search behind the TV for the critters. You can also buy "Nonstop Kittens." Shipping's included in the price.

voicepals.net
VoicePals, LLC
888-543-7387
petalk@voicepals.net

Cats • Dogs

Want to leave your lonely pet a friendly, familiar voice when you're away from home or your pet is being boarded? Studies show many pets suffer deeply from separation anxiety. Your voice can help reduce that anxiety. PeTalk, an easy-to-use, inexpensive (about $30), battery-operated device, allows you to record a ten-second message that will play back once an hour or at other intervals you set. Use it to offer soothing words, reinforce commands ("Off the couch!"), and remind your beloved animal that you'll return soon. A complete FAQ on the site fills in the details.

wagwear.com
WagWear

212-623-7210
info@wagwear.com

Dogs • Pet Clothing • Pet Gear

What's the best-dressed dog wearing this year? Chances are, it may be an outfit from Wagwear, where you can purchase a sleek military style sweater or casual baseball tee. But Wagwear's smart design sense certainly doesn't stop at clothing. This company also offers the tee-pee hound lounge, creative collars, and leading-edge leashes alongside handsome dinner dishes and fun beds. Pup won't forgive you if you fail to peruse the bones and toys — and be sure to consider a backpack so he can carry his stash. The site also features links to dogs available for adoption.

whitepinedesigns.com
White Pine Designs

877-288-2008
info@whitepinedesigns.com

Dogs • Pet Clothing

When it's cold, we all like to snuggle up in a warm sweater. So why not get one for man's best friend? Offering comfy, handmade ski and sweatshirt sweaters available in your choice of knit patterns and colors, White Pine Designs also provides free shipping with your order. These sweaters aren't just doggy fashion either, because they're quite practical. Not only do they keep your pet comfortable during a chilly outing, they're made with 100 percent acrylic yarn so these sweaters can be tossed into the washing machine for quick cleaning. Check out the site's custom collars, too.

⭐ youractivepet.com
YourActivePet.com

877-288-2008
info@youractivepet.com

Dogs • Pet Gear

Whatever adventure you and your dog plan together, YourActivePet.com has the gear your pup needs to succeed. After all, you wouldn't do snow sports or hiking without adequate protection, and neither should your dog. You'll find everything from hunting and skijoring gear to backpacks, boots, coats, life jackets, and reflective vests. Explore the superb x-back harness that fits your dog like a glove but gives you complete control for nature travels with your pet. Shop for toys, bowls, and collars. For you, there's a computer journal and handbook.

 Recommended   Price   Selection   Convenience 😊 Service 🔒 Security

youronlinepetstore.com
YourOnlinePetStore.com

888-895-8412
sales@youronlinepetstore.com

Cats • Dogs • Pet Lodging • Small Animals

For those who frequently travel with their small pets, you want the type of carrier recommended by vets, animal care agencies, and airlines such as American, Delta, and United to ensure your animal's safety and comfort. For many, the choice comes down to Sherpa brand pet carriers, such as those offered from YourOnlinePetStore.com. Use the online size selection chart to shop for the right fit. One model has wheels for easy transport, while another, called an all-in-one (in medium size only), allows you to use it as a backpack, a shoulder bag, or a handbag.

Traveling with Your Pet

Is a trip with your pet in the plans? Here are a few sure tips to make sure that both you and your furry (or feathered) family member have a safe and fun time.

Advance planning is the your key to success. Most airlines have rules and regulations about animals in the air. Check as far in advance as possible and make reservations accordingly. If you're traveling by car, make sure your pet is comfortable and map out necessary comfort stops before you hit the road.

Always check with your airline for specific policies when you make your reservations. Cats and dogs will need a health certificate from a veterinarian, issued no more than 10 days before departure. They'll also need airline-approved carriers. Both Luggage Online (luggageonline.com) and CallingAllDogs.com (callingalldogs.com) offer carriers in different sizes and styles. Don't put a leash in the carrier; your pet could get tangled in it.

If you're traveling by car, never let your pet loose. Keep him on a leash or in a carrier. The clear, circular Pet Coupe, available at petcarriers.net, enables your dog, cat, or bird to see the outside as the miles fly by. Food and water are important; the Flip Feeder and Gulpy Water Dispenser from PetFriendly.com (petfriendly.com) are designed for pets on the go.

Bring along a small cat travel litter box and kitty litter, available from Greg Roberts Quality Pet Supplies (pet-dog-cat-supply-store.com) for your feline companion if you're going to be on the road for more than a few hours. Packing a few cleanup supplies in case of accidents is always a good idea. Check out The Pet Collection kit at Meguiars (meguiars.com) for dealing with the unexpected.

If you're going to need lodging, make sure the hotel accepts pets. Travel Pets (travelpets.com) has a great online directory to pet-friendly hotels. Petswelcome.com (petswelcome.com) features a similar service and enables you to make online reservations at a pet-friendly hotel.

Your trip should be a breeze! However, if you need the services of a veterinarian in a strange city, don't panic. Get online and go to Switchboard (switchboard.com). The online directory will locate the nearest vet for you.

Chapter 20

Seasonal and Holidays: Party On!

A h, the holidays. A time for family and the celebration of ritual as we pass through the year. The rites of spring and the rituals of Easter and Passover give way in turn to fireworks, cook-outs, and celebrations of independence. Those activities are followed by a harvest season of spooky critters and ghouls, the family holiday season that celebrates both hearth and home, the new year, and then the holiday of love and romance.

To re-state in less poetic prose, the online merchants listed in this chapter offer specific products that can brighten your celebration of our most popular seasonal events and holidays.

You'll find merchandise to help you celebrate the Easter and Passover holidays such as Easter decorations, egg coloring kits and Easter baskets, and Passover items. You'll find merchants that sell patriotic items for your 4th of July party and cook-out, and online Halloween stores where you can find that perfect costume, convert your simple abode into a house of horror to welcome the trick-or-treaters, and buy the paraphernalia for your Halloween party.

Ghosts and ghouls give way to friends and family and holiday lights with Christmas and Hanukkah. You'll find online merchants whose primary focus is making your holiday season as bright as it can be. Christmas trees (or Hanukkah menorahs) and tree ornaments, house decorations, and holiday supplies to help you deck the halls can be found at these online retailers.

Last but not least, you can't forget the day when you show your loved one how much he or she really means to you — Valentine's Day. If you wear your heart on your sleeve for someone and want to show it, the online merchants listed in this chapter can help you put a sparkle in that special person's eye.

Now for a few shopping and holiday tips to make your holidays more festive.

For Christmas tree tips, check out the following sites:

- Christmas tree tips — gardeningtips.org/December/feature.shtml
- Christmas safety tips — sosnet.com/safety/christmas.html
- Choosing the perfect tree — interiordec.about.com/cs/cmastreetips/a/cmastree.htm

These sites give you decorating tips for sprucing up your home for the holidays:

- ✔ Holiday decorating tips — `oldworldcraft.com/decoration_tips.htm`
- ✔ More holiday decoration ideas — `christmas.com/pe/1366`
- ✔ Simple holiday decorating — `interiordec.about.com/cs/christmasdecor/a/holidayideas.htm`

Make your holiday a ghoulish one with these Halloween tips:

- ✔ Halloween decorating tips and ideas — `fabulousfoods.com/holidays/halloween/decortips.html`
- ✔ Costume tips — `darklinks.com/dhauntfun.html`
- ✔ Halloween party archives — `calweb.com/~bertino/halloween.html`
- ✔ Carving patterns and tips — `jack-o-lantern.com/index3.html`
- ✔ Halloween decor — `interiordec.about.com/cs/halloweendecor`

Create egg-cellent Easter eggs with Easter tips from these sites:

- ✔ Egg-coloring tips — `w3.gwis.com/~ack/Egg.html`
- ✔ More egg-coloring tips — `canadaegg.ca/english/child/decorate.html`

Key Word Index

4th of July

When you're ready to fire up the grill and have a 4th of July cook-out, the online retailers with this keyword can help you get your outdoor holiday off to an explosive start.

Christmas

These merchants will help you get your house and hearth ready for the Christmas holidays.

Easter

Bunnies, eggs, and baskets mean Easter. Find what you need to celebrate this holiday at merchants who have this keyword in their listing.

Halloween

Time for ghosts, goblins, and jack-o-lanterns. It's Halloween! You can buy everything you need for Halloween from the online retailers with this keyword.

Hanukkah

Merchants with the Hanukkah keyword sell merchandise to light up your holiday and home for Hanukkah, the Jewish festival of lights.

Valentine's Day

A bouquet of roses, a box of chocolates, and candlelit dinners are all unmistakable signs of Valentine's Day. Merchants with this keyword will put romance in your heart — and in your shopping basket.

⭐ americangoldrose.com
American Gold Rose

800-458-7134
goldrose@americangoldrose.com

Valentine's Day

If you want to give someone more than just flowers, how about a rose dipped in 24K gold? American Gold Rose has been in the floral business for 25 years. Its Classic old rose is 12 inches long with leaves and sells for around $50. Some of the other golden products this company sells are a champagne rose and vase, a Victorian gold rose pin, mini gold rose earrings, and a gold rose corsage. You can order by phone, fax, online, or mail. Your satisfaction is 100 percent guaranteed.

awaywithwordsinc.com
A Way With Words

854-638-3465
info@awaywithwordsinc.com

Valentine's Day

Mindy and Paula are identical twins who have a way with words, especially when working together. These women can write a poem for any special occasion and make the words sound as if they are from you. Have them write a special Valentine's Day poem, or a toast for the bride and groom. You can even have the poems framed for a little bit extra. There's no online ordering so you'll have to contact them via e-mail or place your order by phone.

bloomingcookies.com
Blooming Cookies

800-435-6877
feedback@bloomingcookies.com

Easter

Here's an unusual gift or table decoration for Easter — Blooming Cookies, which are a selection of cookies arranged like flowers in a mug, vase, flower pot, or other container. This company has put together a special selection of Blooming Cookies for the Easter season such as the Happy Easter Kraft Box and the Bunny Box, to name a few. The arrangements are filled with an assortment of Chocolate Chip, Chocolate Chip Pecan, White Chocolate Macadamia Nut, Oatmeal Walnut Raisin, and Peanut Butter cookies. Or you may choose all of one flavor. In addition to Easter, you can choose gifts for other special occasions. Just choose the category, select an arrangement, and then order online, by phone, or by mail. How sweet it is!

 Recommended   Price   Selection   Convenience   Service   Security

bronners.net
Bronner's
989-652-9931
customerservice@bronner.com

Christmas

Bronner's brick-and-mortar store in Michigan boasts over 6,000 Christmas items. But it doesn't scrimp in its online store either. The site features many collectibles — Hummels, Precious Moments, Disney, and Department 56, to name a few. Bronner's collection of holiday items includes Christmas lights, ornaments, artificial trees, garland and wreaths, holiday decor, Nativity scenes, outdoor decor, stockings and stocking stuffers, and Christmas tree accessories. The site is well organized, and you can also order from Bronner's mail order catalog on the site.

★ christmas-depot.com
The Christmas Depot
877-353-5263
E-mail form on site

Christmas

The Christmas Depot calls itself "the Internet's premier retail Christmas site." I tend to agree. The site offers more than 10,000 Christmas-related products for your shopping perusal. You can find artificial Christmas trees, lights, garlands, ornaments, animated figures, holiday music boxes, and outdoor decorations. But it doesn't end there. If you enjoy hanging collectibles on your tree and placing them around your home every year, the site offers the full line of fine quality Village products and collectible Snowbabies from Department 56. The prices are reasonable, and you can fill your shopping stocking all at once at this Christmas superstore.

christmasdonebright.com
Christmas Done Bright
888-453-0599
lightup@christmasdonebright.com

Christmas

Most people hang up several strings of lights or place a lighted Santa on the lawn and call their front yard "decorated." But if you're one of those people who really want to light up Christmas, then welcome to Christmas Done Bright. This company supplies angels, Santas, Christmas trees, reindeer, snowmen, stars, nativity scenes, toys, and a host of animated displays — all in colorful lights. But be forewarned — buy your Christmas presents *before* you buy these lighted decorations. They're not cheap.

christmasforest.com
Christmas Forest

800-637-9627
ramona@christmasforest.com

Christmas

The Christmas Forest site offers a modest collection of evergreen wreaths and swags, which will add the scent of the northwest forests to your home at Christmas time. The site also offers an evergreen Christmas cross and the Farmer's Basket, filled with scented pine cones and forest fresh evergreens. It also has something that your holiday door should not be without — a brass wreath hanger. This product is an alternative to hammering a nail into your door and solves the problem of hanging a wreath on a metal door. The site offers free shipping to the contiguous 48 states, a 10 percent discount on orders of ten or more items, and even a fundraising program.

christmastrees.net
Redrock Farm

866-685-4343
christmastrees@direcway.com

Christmas

If you like the scent of a real Christmas tree in your home but don't have the time to lug a tree from the tree lot back to your house, then Redrock Farm of Chelsea, Vermont, can help you out. You can order a fresh balsam fir online and have this company ship it to your front door. You can get a tree up to 7 feet tall for shipping, and a complimentary tree removal bag comes with each tree. The trees are very affordable, but keep in mind that you pay for shipping based on how far you're from Vermont.

clicket.com
Clicket.com

888-798-4512
info@clicket.com

Christmas • Easter

Costumes are not only for Halloween, as Clicket.com proves. Prices for adult costumes range from around $100 to almost $500 for the premium commercial-use costumes. Still, you can buy a nice chicken or Easter Rabbit costume at a reasonable price and make your kids smile. The site offers bunny costumes for babies to tots at very low prices and some cute Christmas costumes for kids, such as snowmen, elves, and angels. Of course, adults can find a variety of Santa suits. The site offers costumes grouped by category or you can use the site search engine to find what you're looking for.

 Recommended   Price   Selection   Convenience   Service   Security

evergreenhomedecor.com
Evelyn's Evergreens
866-434-7005
evelyn@evergreenhomedecor.com
Christmas

From the green forests of Maine come a nice selection of evergreen wreaths, swags, and centerpieces for your home. Evelyn's Evergreens has over 25 years in handcrafting evergreen balsam wreaths and other products. Two recent additions to the evergreen holiday line that you may not find elsewhere are the holiday sprays and Kissing Balls. The sprays are pine and balsam gathered into a fragrant 24-inch-long cluster, enhanced with berries, holiday decorations, pine cones, and beautiful decorative bow and ribbons — and you can choose from three styles. The Kissing Ball is a 12-inch ball crafted from fresh evergreens and adorned with frosted Austrian pine cones, berries, and velvety ribbons. These products are reasonably priced and unique.

expressflags.com
ExpressFlags.com
800-804-4716
customerservice@expressflags.com
4th of July

What's the 4th of July without an American flag? If you want to show your patriotism on July 4th, then ExpressFlags.com has your flag. Choose from miniature and tabletop flags, outdoor flags, classroom banner or mounted flags, and antenna and car window flags, all reasonably priced. The flags are made of nylon, cotton, or polyester. You can even go historical by purchasing the 27 flags flown throughout the United States history. (By the way, did you know that the first official U.S. Flag (1777-1795) was a "staggered" 13-star pattern and not the Betsy Ross flag of 13 stars in a circle?) The site also offers a list of flag displaying do's and don'ts, as well free shipping on orders $75 or more.

⭐ florapacifica.com
Flora Pacifica

800-877-9741
info@florapacifica.com

Christmas

Florapacifica.com is not your ordinary Christmas wreath and swag store. Flora Pacifica sells some unique variations on the evergreen product. You can find a snowflake wreath shaped like — what else — a snowflake. It also offers a 16-inch square fresh myrtle frame wreath, a triangular swag, an evergreen mantelpiece, a fresh winter snow wreath, and a wreath made entirely out of acorns. For something other than evergreen, check out the monochromatic burgundy wreath and the all-white-flower wreath. In any case, you're sure to find something to brighten your home decor for the holidays.

giftsongs.com
GiftSongs.com

800-725-7664
contact@giftsongs.com

Valentine

Say it with flowers. Say it with gifts. Say it with words. Now, say it with music! That's right. At GiftSongs.com you can purchase a professionally recorded, digitally mastered personalized song on either a compact disc or a cassette singing your never ending devotion to the one you love. You also receive a custom-printed lyric sheet suitable for framing. The site offers different categories of special occasions. Just pick the occasion, supply the content asked for on the form, and voilà — a song made just for you and someone you love. You can hear samples of the songs right on the site, and review the lyrics. The price is only around $40 for cassettes and $50 for compact discs. What a deal!

 Recommended $ Price   Selection   Convenience   Service   Security

⭐ halloweenmart.com
Halloween Mart

800-811-4877
questions@halloweenmart.com

Halloween

Getting you and your home ready for Halloween can be a ghoulish chore. Halloween Mart can help. This store offers a wide selection of Halloween costumes and decorations at reasonable prices. As for costumes, you can dig up a selection of them for adults, children, and your pet. You can even pre-order costumes from upcoming movies to ensure you get the one you want. There is on-site sizing information, and if you have a question, you can contact one of the company's experts. Check out the special effects section, where you can find fog machines, lighting effects, strobe lights, and music and sound effects, perfect for creating a spooky atmosphere.

jack-o-lantern.com
Jack-O-Lantern.com

No phone number listed
steve@jack-o-lantern.com

Halloween

Jack-O-Lantern.com not only gives you a great selection of jack-o-lantern carving patterns that you can download and print, but also offers a complete set of carving tools so you can do a bang-up job carving that pumpkin. Each kit contains an all-purpose saw, a poker, a detail saw, and a drill. The price is only around $8. The site also carries Pumpkin Dunk'N, which will help your masterpiece last 10 to 15 days longer. You'll find pumpkin carving tips on the site, too.

judaicaplace.com
JudaicaPlace.com

877-857-5223
info@judaicaplace.com

Hanukkah

However you spell it, Hanukkah or Chanukah, Judaica Place carries just about all you need to celebrate this holiday. It has been in business for more than 20 years and boasts the largest collection of in-stock Judaic items. The Hanukkah merchandise sold at this store includes candles, Torah tapes, decorations, dreidels, menorahs of all types, kitchenware, paper goods, oils and accessories, and toys and games for the kids. It even carries a small section of chocolate and sweets. The site's features include a keyword search tool and a Top Requests list.

judaicaspecialties.com
Judaica Specialties

888-277-7897
info@judaicaspecialties.com

Hanukkah

Judaica Specialties offers unique, contemporary, and traditional Judaic merchandise for Hanukkah. You can even find a light-up Hanukkah bear or a Hanukkah piano tea pot. If you're looking for a wide selection of traditional and contemporary menorahs, this site has them. It also has a special kids section where you can buy some cute and modern-looking dreidels and other unique, reasonably priced toys. Most of the products sell for less than $25.

makeupmania.com
MakeUpMania.com

800-711-7182
info@makeupmania.com

Halloween

If you're the type of person who walks to the beat of a different drummer and want your Halloween face to be unique, then MakeUpMania.com is for you. This New York-based complete make-up store employs professional special effects artists. The site supplies you with the generic prosthetic pieces (noses, horns, burns, cuts and scars, and so on); you supply the imagination. It also sells special effects products like beards, fresh scabs, bald caps, temporary tattoos, and even thick, fake blood to give your costume that extra special "something."

maladyspoetry.com
Ma Lady's Poetry

706-863-7245
admin@maladyspoetry.com

Valentine

Sometimes, putting your feelings into words is so hard. If you just have to tell your Valentines how you feel about them but can't find the right words, then Ma Lady can help. Whether for friends or lovers, she'll craft a love poem of 1 to 6 stanzas at about $9 per stanza, and you can place an order right on her site with your credit card. An ornate keepsake card in vellum and ribbon is included. Plus, poemas en español are available.

 Recommended   Price   Selection   Convenience   Service   Security

michiganchristmastrees.com
Michigan Christmas Trees

800-999-0208

info@michiganchristmastrees.com

Christmas

Fresh Christmas trees shipped right to your door? At the Michigan Christmas Trees site you can buy a fresh Michigan Christmas tree up to nine feet in height and have it shipped to you for the holidays. Your tree is delivered via UPS to your door in 3 to 5 days. The company offers a 100 percent money-back guarantee, and orders placed before Thanksgiving receive a 10 percent discount. While at the site, don't forget to order a tree stand. You can also find fresh garland to decorate your doorway, mantel, light post, porch, or stair rail.

mileskimball.com
Miles Kimball

800-546-2255

E-mail form on site

Easter

Looking for those little toys and trinkets to fill out that Easter basket? Miles Kimball offers them, and more. How about a personalized letter to a child from the Easter Bunny? You can order it at this site, as well as wind-up walking eggs, chick jelly bean dispensers, egg string lights, and dozens of other Easter goodies. To see the Easter products offered, click on Other Holiday and then Easter in the site navigation bar. The prices are low, so you can accessorize your Easter baskets without straining your wallet.

nightmarefactory.com
The Nightmare Factory

512-858-5063

shop@nightmarefactory.com

Halloween

Fangs and teeth, scary costumes, masks, props, Halloween books and videos, magic, makeup and blood, Halloween CDs and sound effects? You can find all this and more for Halloween at the Nightmare Factory. If you're looking for specialty theme costumes, like Batman, Star Wars, and Star Trek, you can find those, too. The body parts, weapons props, creatures, and critters are especially gruesome in the site's props department. It also sells life-size cardboard cutouts of assorted Star Wars, Lord of the Rings, and other characters, plus Halloween party supplies. Prices run the gamut from less than $50 to life-size props for thousands of dollars.

⭐ ornamentbox.com
Santa's Drawers

888-528-8269
nmiley@mindspring.com

Christmas

When Christmas is over and the tree has to come down, you have to remove your precious ornaments from the tree and find the box they came in or wrap each of them in tissue paper. But this chore is no more, with Santa's Drawers. When you use this company's ornament box your Christmas ornaments nestle in individual compartments that vary in size to accommodate different-sized ornaments. Santa's Drawers are made with heavy-duty corrugated cardboard, and the drawers can be removed and carried around the tree for easy decoration and removal. You can customize the drawers to make sections larger or longer for odd-shaped ornaments. So save yourself some time and be organized for next year, and order a four-drawer, seven-drawer, or eight-drawer ornament box. Keep your lights neat and tangle-free with the light box, also available at ornamentbox.com.

ornamentz.com
Orna Mentz

302-996-0573
sales@ornamentz.com

Christmas

The Victorian-style ornaments sold at ornamentz.com each cost about the same as a box of 12 ornaments at a discount store, but they are unique and beautiful to behold. You can choose from a wide selection of exquisite and ornate tree décor harking back to the Victorian era. The site is light on information about the retailer, but the clear and sharp pictures of the different ornaments speak for themselves.

⭐ screamteam.com
The Scream Team

626-792-5444
generalinfo@screamteam.com

Halloween

You won't find your average Halloween mask at screamteam.com. The Scream Team offers you film-quality prosthetics, just like the ones used in Hollywood. These are not over-the-head rubber masks, nor the face appliqués you can find in costume and makeup shops. This stuff is professional quality, and you can get all the pieces you need to look as scary as you like, including a complete make-up kit that has everything you need to transform yourself. The faces run about $50, and the make-up kit is around $30. Detailed instructions are included in each kit.

simplyclassicgiftbaskets.com
Simply Classic

800-962-4895
E-mail form on site

Easter

Why give your family or kids a common everyday Easter basket like the kind you see in your local discount or grocery store? Give a gourmet basket of goodies from Simply Classic. Many of this company's baskets are filled with a stuffed bunny, Easter Pez dispenser and candy, chocolate eggs, Jelly Bellies, assorted candies, chocolate Easter suckers, bunny-shaped cookies, caramel and chocolate popcorn, Ghirardelli chocolates, and marshmallow bunnies. Mmm, enough sugar for the perfect Easter morning.

todayschristmas.com
Today's Christmas

800-457-0305
sales@todayschristmas.com

Christmas

If you're tired of buying a new tree every year just to drop it off at the local tree-recycling center a few weeks later, then an artificial tree from this site is what you want. Today's Christmas offers fine artificial Christmas trees by Barthelmess USA, GKI, and Santa's Own, and sends them directly to you. These unique trees have folding branches for easy setup and storage. The site offers traditional and slim-shaped trees, and an assortment of tree heights. Tree prices range from $100 to almost $1,000 — enough selection to fit any budget. You can even buy your artificial tree already pre-lit so you don't have to string lights. Now that's convenience!

valentinesgifts.com
ValentinesGifts.com

866-386-8300
service@personalizationmall.com

Valentine's Day

A Valentine's Day gift needs to be special and personal. At valentinesgifts.com you can find picture frames, albums and prints, keepsakes, and other items that you can personalize with your own romantic message for free. Prices are affordable; many gifts are under $30. By the way, the Valentine's store is just a part of a much larger Personalization Mall, filled with gifts that you can personalize for all occasions.

★ yournovel.com
YourNovel.com

800-444-3356
comments@yournovel.com

Valentine's Day

If you've ever thought how great it would be to have a romance novel written about you and your sweetheart, well now you can. At yournovel.com, you supply interesting information (like favorite radio station, cologne, pet name, eye, and hair color) about the people you want to star in the book, and this company writes and sends you a 140–190-page paperback book that's written in your choice of either a mild or steamy tone. Some of the titles are *Awake, My Love; Another Day in Paradise;* and *Love's Bounty: An Outer Banks Romance.* The price is only about $50 for each book.

 Recommended   Price   Selection   Convenience   😊 Service   🔒 Security

Ringing in a New Year!!

People around the world celebrate the dawning of a new year at different times and in different ways. Yet, whenever New Year's occurs, the day is a celebration in most cultures. "Happy New Year!" is a universal greeting in any language.

In the United States, New Year's Eve parties are a common way to mark the passage of one year to the next. The best known party is held at Times Square in New York City where millions of people brave the elements to watch the electronic ball drop at midnight. If you want to be part of the throng, New York City Vacation Packages (nycvp.com) can help arrange your trip. Alternatively, watch the famous ball drop from a live Webcam at the Times Square Alliance Web site (timessquarebid.org).

Parties at home provide a fun, safe way to welcome the new year. Get your party supplies at Plum Party (plumparty.com) or Theme Parties N More (themepartiesnmore.com). Food for your party is an important component of the night's festivities. Order a selection of appetizers from Appetizerstogo.com (appetizerstogo.com) and incomparable sweets from Black Hound New York (blackhoundny.com). Why not have your party catered? You'll find a list of local caterers at LocalCatering.com (localcatering.com).

An old Southern tradition dictates that all who consume a dish of Hoppin' John, a tasty casserole made from black-eyed peas and rice, will enjoy good luck through the coming year. Order a dried mix from Southern Connoisseur (southern connoisseur.com) and make a pot of the hearty fare to serve on January 1. If you're a whiz in the kitchen, visit Hoppin' John's (hoppinjohns.com). This Web site, owned and operated by cookbook author John Martin Taylor, features cookbooks, gourmet items (including Hoppin' John mix), sweetgrass baskets, and housewares.

New Year's Eve is a great night for celebrating in London. Crowds gather in Trafalgar Square, Piccadilly Circus, and at the base of Big Ben waiting for midnight. When Big Ben's chimes announce the midnight hour, the crowd sings Auld Lang Syne. Learn about this fascinating song and find links to the lyrics and karaoke version at robertburns.org/encyclopedia/AuldLangSyne.5.html.

The next day is New Year's Day. At noon, London hosts a street parade that travels through the central part of the city. Thousands of performers from around the world participate in the exciting event. You'll find information about the parade at its official Web site — The New Year's Day Parade - London (londonparade.co.uk).

Australia is a fun place to be on New Year's Eve. Most Australians love to party and welcoming in a new year is the perfect excuse for a grand celebration. Get a feel for the festivities in the land of Oz at the New Year's Eve Web site located at newyearseve.com.au. The warm summer weather in Australia makes New Year's Day an ideal time for a cook-out, picnic, or relaxing day at the beach. For some genuine Australian products to serve at your next bash, visit About Australia (about-australia-shop.com).

The Chinese New Year, called "Yuan Tan," takes place between January 21 and February 20. The exact date is determined by the lunar calendar. Chinese New Year celebrations are based on bringing luck, health, happiness, and wealth until the next year.

(continued)

(continued)

Chinese New Year celebrations are marked by parades, usually featuring costumed dragons that signify wealth and longevity. Firecrackers — available online at Skylighter (skylighter. com) — are believed to frighten away evil spirits. Luck is an important element of the Chinese New Year tradition. Kumquat trees are the luckiest plants of all. Purchase your own lucky kumquat tree at World Wide Plants (worldwideplants. com). Lucky Money is distributed by relatives in special red envelopes with each family name and good-luck message written on them in gold. The tokens are given on New Year's to the family's children and unmarried relatives. You can find lucky money envelopes and other Chinese New Year's gifts at Worldsearch.com (worldsearch. com/marketplace/gifts/chinese_new_ year).

New Year's is always fun. Even though the holiday occurs only once every year, you can get in a New Year's frame of mind anytime. Take a few moments and search for the New Year's words in the online Wilstar New Year Word Search puzzle (wilstar.com/holidays/puzzles/ newyearpuz.htm). Happy New Year! Every day is a new beginning.

Chapter 21

Sports, Hobbies, and Crafts: Spending Your Free Time

· ·

Seven days a week. Twenty-four hours a day. Sixty minutes per hour. These established time concepts are ones that we all share. No matter how we try to slice or dice it, only so much time is available. Work, school, or important endeavors take up most of that time.

Free time, if there's any left over after you do the things you have to do, is all your own. How do you like to spend it? Do you play sports? Do you have a favorite hobby? Or are you a "crafty" person, who enjoys making things?

The luxury of spending your free time the way you like is important. It relaxes your mind and refreshes your spirit. Usually, it also requires gear or supplies. Standing in the checkout line of a sports superstore, with the background music cranked to an unacceptable earsplitting level, cannot be relaxing. Hunting for a stenciling brush and paint in your local crafts store on a busy Saturday morning never rekindles your flagging spirits.

Fortunately, we've come to your rescue! We've assembled a sampling of sites that sell sports gear and equipment, hobby supplies, and craft goods. You'll find everything from amateur radio equipment to radio-controlled vehicles, mosaic and beading supplies to stenciling apparatus, as well as tons of sports sites selling their associated gear. Shopping online will help you free up more time for the things you love to do. With all the great sites we've put together, you may discover a new sport or craft to try.

Are you a sports nut? So is Ralph Hickok, and he's put together one of the most comprehensive sports sites on the Internet at hickoksports.com. This amazing site contains sports rules, history, quotes, and more. The site is updated frequently with new sports information.

Key Word Index

Aquatic Sports

The sites with the Aquatic Sports keyword carry supplies for sports played in water, such as swimming, diving, and water polo.

Cold Weather Sports

The Cold Weather Sports sites aren't for loafers! Skiers, snowboarders, and anyone else who loves to be outside in below-freezing temperatures can find all the gear they need to keep going. (You'll have to find your own snow, though.)

Crafts

The sites with the Crafts keyword sell supplies and kits for making things with your hands. You'll find stitchery, scrapbooking, woodworking, painting and stenciling, mosaic supplies, and more.

Fitness

Staying fit is so important to your general well being. The Fitness sites can help, by selling you everything from running shoes to martial arts supplies.

Hobbies

Shop at the Hobbies sites for gear and accessories for ham radio, models, radio-controlled vehicles, and a few other hobbies.

Individual Sports

You'll find loads of equipment in the Individual Sports stores for just about any sport that you play by yourself, including tennis, skateboarding, running, and racquetball, among others.

Sports Superstores

The Sports Superstores are just that — stores that sell everything for every sport under one virtual roof.

Team Sports

The Team Sports sites offer gear and accessories for sports where more than one person is needed to make up a team, such as baseball, soccer, and even lacrosse.

aesham.com
AES.com
800-558-0411
info@aes.com
Hobbies

Visit Aesham.com, the Web site of Amateur Electronic Supply, for all your amateur radio needs. Amateur Electronic Supply has been serving the ham community for 47 years. The site also caries radio-controlled model boats, cars, and planes, model rockets and supplies, as well as shortwave radios and scanners. If amateur astronomy interests you, check out the telescopes by Celestron, Bushnell, and Meade that AES.com stocks. This site ensures you have what you need to enjoy your spare time.

aquagoggles.com
Aquagoggles
519-743-3422
info@aquagoggles.com
Aquatic Sports

The frustration of not being able to see takes the enjoyment out of swimming for many people. It doesn't need to be like that. With a pair of goggles from Aquagoggles, you can see when you're in the water. The goggles cost $20 or so, and correct myopic vision to match your current prescription. The lenses are made of shatter-resistant polycarbonate material and can really improve your water experience.

aquajogger.com
Aqua Jogger
800-922-9544
info@aquajogger.com
Aquatic Sports • Fitness

Many people have discovered the benefits of water exercise. By exercising in the water you eliminate the impact inherent in many forms of exercise. So whether you're beginning an exercise program or are a seasoned athlete rehabilitating an injury, Aqua Jogger's site will be of interest. aquajogger.com features equipment that provides floatation and resistance essential for this form of exercise. Check out the women's and men's fitness systems, or begin with the basic system, a buoyancy belt that suspends your body at shoulder level in deep water. This site also is an information source for water exercise. There's no time like the present to get fit in such a painless way!

artcraftetc.com
Art Craft Etc.

800-537-2738
cindy@artcraftetc.com

Crafts

Art Craft Etc. supplies the wood craftsmanship and you provide the imagination to transform it into a beloved item in your home. Choose from the selection of stools, cabinets, chests, trunks, trays, tables, and more. You can find larger pieces as well, such as a grandfather clock, jelly cabinet, and Victorian secretary's desk. Be aware that some require at least some assembly upon delivery, and shipping is not included in the listed price. While you wait for your order's arrival, think about the paint, stain, and other decoration you want to apply to make the piece your own, or finish it for resale.

aspeneast.com
Aspen East Ski Shop

866-422-3739
sales@aspeneast.com

Individual Sports • Cold Weather Sports

Aspen East Ski Shop is located in Killington, Vermont. You can purchase skis, boots, and bindings, and apparel from its online store for your next ski trip. Of course, this company hopes that you will make Killington your next stop. Accordingly, in addition to the first-class ski equipment presented at the site, the Aspen folks have another unique offer. Called Season Tune, the one-time charge program enables you to turn in your skis or snowboard to the Aspen Ski Shop mechanics for all the tune-ups and alignments you need during one ski season. Of course, you'll need to be in the Killington area, and this deal applies to only the pair of enrolled skis or snowboard.

barbwatson.com
Barb Watson's Brushworks

909-653-3780
E-mail form on site

Crafts

Barb Watson's Brushworks is the type of site to inspire you to pick up a brush even if you have no prior experience. The highlight on the site is her line of primed metalware that is all set for you to apply your artistry — no additional prep required. Yet the site helps in that area as well, providing you a background in the ABCs of color, pattern packets (including flowers, still life, and veggies), and some color theory. Browse the sale items plus already painted objects you can purchase. The results can be exquisite.

 Recommended   Price   Selection   Convenience   Service   Security

bareroots.com
Bareroots

760-648-7244
E-mail form on site

Crafts

Holidays and theme-related subjects are popular at Bareroots' site, featuring sewing patterns covering all four seasons, along with love and friendship. For pillow lovers, select from designs created for each different month; these can be put together to create a special quilt or wall hanging. Need a tote or purse for your projects? You can buy those patterns at the site, as well as patterns for sewing kits, sewing machine covers, a combined armchair caddy and pin cushion, plus quilt labels. Other kits show you how to create a table runner, Christmas stockings, quilts, and pillows.

beapro.com
BeaPro.com

888-423-2776
support@beapro.com

Team Sports

Who doesn't want to be a pro ball player? If you have aspirations in baseball, BeaPro.com is your site. You can find pitching machines for any budget, as well as protective screens for pitching batting practice. With this equipment you can train at the level that professional ball players do. The site also offers training equipment for softball and a selection of bats and gloves for the serious ball player. Just don't expect a replica jersey from a major league team. Of course, if you're buying from this site, you may very well get your own major league jersey some time soon.

bigtoesports.com
Big Toe Soccer

800-444-0365
info@bigtoe.com

Team Sports

Big Toe Soccer is a big site. If it can fill two pages just with referee's shirts, just imagine what it can do in other categories. You'll find big selections of everything that has to do with soccer at this team-oriented site, including shin guards, shoes, clothing, books and videos, and clothing for referees and fans. In addition to the expected uniforms, it offers fund-raising programs and advice. You can join the Premier Club and purchase items at a discount. Check out the sale pages, too. For selection, Big Toe Soccer always scores a goal.

bitsnbobs.com
BitsnBobs

No phone number listed
dar@ratrix.com

Crafts

If you have the paint, the BitsnBobs site has the items you'll want to decorate. Many of the traditional craft themes are represented, such as pumpkins, ornaments, Santa, animals, angels, and cherubs. The mediums are varied: pecan resin, paper machè, ceramic bisque, and chalkware, allowing for a range of detail and expression to suit your whimsy. The prices are affordable even for a crafter on a budget. You can find glitter (including glass and iridescent), polyurethane, and sealer at this site as well as paint palettes (glazed or not).

blades.com
Blades Board & Skate

888-552-5233
E-mail form on site

Cold Weather Sports • Individual Sports

This unusual site deserves a visit even if you're not involved in the three sports it represents: inline skating, skateboarding, and snowboarding. The Blades Board & Skate site offers plenty of gear and supplies for the three sports. The best part of the site is the Build Your Own Board program for both skateboarders and snowboarders, which allows you to choose components for your board and purchase them as a package at a discount. Check out the footwear, too. In addition to the shoes and boots for the featured sports, you can also find casual shoes and U.S. Military-specification combat boots, just in case you need them.

bowlersparadise.com
BowlersParadise.com

888-969-2695
E-mail form on site

Individual Sports

Remember when bowling balls were black spheres with holes in them, and they all looked pretty much the same? BowlersParadise.com brings you page after page of bowling balls in all the colors of the rainbow, and of interest to serious bowlers, for all lane conditions. The site even has a unique category for bowling balls used for converting spares. If you use more than one ball, you can buy multiple-ball bags on wheels. The site offers plenty of shoes, too, and numerous accessories. It's easy to see why this site is called BowlersParadise.com.

 Recommended   Price   Selection   Convenience   Service   Security

bowling.com
Bowling.com
800-441-2695
helpdept@bowling.com
Individual Sports

Remember those rental bowling shoes — the ones that bowling proprietors used to think were too ugly for anyone to steal? After all, who wants shoes with the size on the back? Well, so many people want them that Bowling.com caters to this demand. To match, pick up a retro bowling shirt with an embroidered logo. If you're a serious bowler, as opposed to a fashionista, Bowling.com lives up to its name. A collection of balls and bags from makers like AMF and Dexter will keep you rolling strikes.

buymosaictile.com
BuyMosaicTile
888-266-7242
sales@buymosaictile.com
Crafts

Yearning to create your own wall mural or other mosaic tile projects? Want to have your friends gasp in amazement at your handiwork? BuyMosaicTile has what you need, whether you want to purchase a kit or loose tiles. The kits at the site come with everything you need to assemble the design, including tiles, backing, and mount material. (Adhesion and grouting materials are sold separately.) An approximate build time is shown with each kit, so you'll know in advance just what you're getting into. If you want to try your own design, loose mosaic tiles, tools, and materials will speed you on your way. Check out the design software and instructional videos and DVDs.

cabincrafters.com
Cabincrafters.com
800-669-3920
E-mail form on site
Crafts

It's amazing how a few good supplies can spark the imagination, isn't it? That's what you find at Cabincrafters.com, whether you want to work with wood, glass, paper machè, or faux slate. The site even has snow and water globes you can decorate yourself. Beyond that, you can locate a range of stencils, pattern packets, craft books, and a line of good Black Gold brushes in a variety of styles. Choose from several different wood projects, including clocks (you can buy the parts, too), chalkboards, trays and cabinets, plus novelty items. Also be sure to review the paint selection.

capeziodance.com
Capezio Ballet Makers, Inc.

888-227-3946
info@balletmakers.com

Fitness

When Salvatore Capezio opened his shoe repair shop near the Metropolitan Opera House in New York, he hung a sign above the door that proudly read, "The Theatrical & Historical Shoemaker." Capezio has come a long way since then, but it is still where serious dancers turn first for their needs. The online shop offers shoes, clothes, and accessories for dancers from Capezio and other brands. This site also connects users with the dance community for news, tips, and other information.

ccs.com
CCS

800-477-9283
service@ccs.com

Cold Weather Sports • Individivual Sports

Into boards? Then the CCS site is for you. The choices are easy. Choose Skate Store or Board Store from the home page. You can buy either complete packages or customize your gear by choosing from the selection of components. CCS knows its customers, too. Pages on the site are devoted to video games and an interesting e-zine, as well as tips and pictures for skaters and snowboarders. Visit the message boards or lurk in the chat room. Download cool music and stay up to date with what is going on in the skater community.

christysports.com
Christy Sports

877-754-7627
E-mail form on site

Cold Weather Sports • Individual Sports

Christy Sports is well known in Rocky Mountain ski areas as a bricks-and-mortar retailer and renter of ski equipment. With a Web presence, this company can provide the high-quality products to everyone, not just those in the West or those on a ski trip there. The Christy Sports team tests all products it sells. Not only does this approach ensure quality, it also allows product descriptions that enable customers to choose the product that is best for them. On the Web site you can also find some great bargains on off-season merchandise.

 Recommended   Price   Selection   Convenience   Service   🔒 Security

coastalkites.com
Coastal Kites, Inc.
877-544-5483
info@coastalkites.com
Hobbies • Individual Sports

The next time someone tells you to go fly a kite, you'll know just where to go. Coastal Kites is your complete source for kites of all sizes and complexities. This easily navigable site has kites from inexpensive child's toys to stunt kites that you can steer. Best of all, every kite is pictured in color with complete descriptions. Choose your kites from a wide variety of shapes and sizes. Birds, butterflies, planes, ships, fish, dragons, parafoils, and even those old box kites are represented. Order today and you'll be outside, in the wind, tomorrow afternoon.

coinwire.com
Coinwire.com
877-415-4435
sales@coinwire.com
Hobbies

Coinwire.com is for serious coin collectors! Casual browsers and those new to the hobby may be turned off by the clunky catalog and ponderous descriptions. However, you can find buried treasure at this site, if you look around. Starter sets and beginner kits for just a few dollars provide a great intro into coin collecting. For the serious collector, the coins offered in Closeouts and Hot Deals will save you big bucks and often are real finds. Orders ship within 48 hours.

coloradoskishop.com
Colorado Ski Shop
413-746-4144
E-mail form on site
Cold Weather Sports • Individual Sports

Skis and snowboards crowd the Colorado Ski Shop. The only thing that's missing is snow. You'll find skis by Alpine, Volkl, Dynastar, Rossignol, Head, Atomic, and Blizzard for men, women, and children. Corresponding poles, bindings, and boots are also available. You'll find plenty of clothing, too. Dynastar, Head, Airwalk, and Lamar make up the bulk of the snowboard stock. Occasionally, used and rental ski and snowboard equipment is offered for sale at the site, so check back often if you're looking to make a good deal.

comteksystems.com
ComTek Systems

704-542-4808
info@comteksystems.com

Hobbies

Amateur radio enthusiasts generally lead two lives. (I know — I am one!) They might appear as average joes and janes, but underneath all that is a side that loves to communicate with strangers and needs sophisticated equipment to do it. Sites like ComTek Systems make it easy, with hybrid phasing couplers, remote antenna systems, 61-hole radial rings, and stack yagi systems. If all this jargon makes sense to you, get to ComTek immediately. If it doesn't and you're intrigued, maybe it's time to study for your amateur radio license. (Hint: Learn more at arrl.org.)

crossstitchunlimited.com
Cross Stitch Unlimited

609-890-1155
shop@crossstitchunlimited.com

Crafts

Boasting an online catalog of more than 7,300 items, Cross Stitch Unlimited undoubtedly has something you need for your craft. Renowned designers are represented at the site, like Thomas Kinkade, 4 My Boys, Green Apple, and Black Swan Designs. Peruse the site's beads and buttons. You can find not only needlepoint canvasses, but a number of different types, including both printed and line drawn. The site also offers a selection of fabric, fibers, fanciful extras, embellishments, charts and leaflets, and varied notions. Obtain accessories or items such as a box or tray to adorn with your work.

debsstitchery.com
Deb's Stitchery Store

270-825-1237
sales@debsstitchery.com

Crafts

Shopping for counted cross stitch and cross-stitch patterns and sewing accessories shouldn't be like searching for a needle in a haystack. Sites like Deb's Stitchery Store make it easy, regardless of your skill level. Choose from a large number of needlework designers, including well-known names like Pegasus, Mill Hill Gallery, Indigo Rose, and Cross My Heart. Find kits, zippers, fabrics (canvas, linen, and specialty), fibers, and featured items. Among beads, there's something for all, from antique glass to bugle, frosted, crystal, and metal, along with beading needles.

 Recommended   Price   Selection   Convenience   Service   Security

delphiglass.com
Delphi

800-248-2048
sales@delphiglass.com

Crafts

Glass and tile are beautiful art mediums and Delphi, in business for more than 30 years, boasts many of the supplies you'll need for working with them. Beginners can choose from a variety of starter kits, including a special one containing all you need to create your own silver jewelry and designs just as you would mold clay. Once fired, your creation turns into pure silver. Locate unusual patterns and projects, like a panel lampshade done in Tiffany style. Don't forget to browse the offering of tiles and glass as well as the sale specials.

dickssportinggoods.com
Dick's Sporting Goods

877-846-9997
E-mail form on site

Sports Superstore

Dick's Sporting Goods is a "shop 'til you drop" site. From trampolines to treadmills and plenty of stops in between, Dick's is your supplier of recreational needs. Start with the Top Shops for featured items. If you have something specific in mind, you can go right to it on this easily navigable site. There is also a Shop by Brand capability so you can check out what's new from your favorite manufacturer. Whatever you're looking for in sporting goods, you can probably find it at Dick's. More importantly, you can find it easily.

diversdirect.com
Divers Direct

800-348-3872
experts@diversdirect.com

Aquatic Sports • Individual Sports

There's a whole other world out there, and Divers Direct can show it to you. This online store carries a great assortment of scuba gear and equipment. If you're new to the sport or not sure what to buy, click the Expert Product Tips button from each group to get more information. The Weekly specials merit a look. Save a few bucks and put them towards your next diving trip. Thinking about earning your Open Water SCUBA Certification? Divers Direct offers an online course that begins the process. After you follow the certification instructions and complete four dives, you'll be an SDI Certified Open Water Diver.

donaldpatton.com
The Patton Company

No phone number listed
donaldpatton@worldnet.att.net

Hobbies

Shop at The Patton Company site for model railroading, radio-controlled airplanes and cars, racing cars, and plastic models. The photographs have a homemade quality that may seem slightly unprofessional, and the store does not produce a print catalog. However, what it lacks in appearance, it makes up for in service. If you have a question or problem before or after you buy, contact the folks at this site for thoughtful help and serious answers that you may not get from a chain store. Our advice: Avoid the Stock Tips posted at the site.

downtownhobbies.com
Downtown Hobbies

530-889-2139
E-mail form on site

Hobbies

Downtown Hobbies stocks over 80,000 products. The owners have a passion for radio-controlled airplanes, cars, and boats, and that love is apparent in the site's online catalog. You'll find radio-controlled items in sizes and price ranges that will match your needs. Whether you're just starting out or want to enhance your collection, go Downtown the next time you need a new toy. While you're shopping, check out the Message Board and Picture Gallery to see what folks like you are up to.

dunhamssports.com
Dunham's Sports

888-801-9158
customersupport@dunhamssports.com

Sports Superstore

Way back in 1937, Dunham's Sports opened its doors as Dunham's Bait & Tackle in a little shop outside of Detroit. Now this company has become one of the largest full-line sporting goods chains in the United States. (It still sells fishing gear, but you won't find any bait online!) Dunham's features top-brand sports equipment at great prices. Its 100 percent Lowest Online Price Guarantee ensures you'll get the best deal. Here's how it works: If you find a lower price for an item that you purchased from the site within fourteen days, Dunham Sports will take 100 percent of the difference off the total online purchase price. Details are at the site.

 Recommended   Price   Selection   Convenience   Service Security

eastbay.com
Eastbay
800-826-2205
E-mail form on site
Sports Superstore

Eastbay makes shopping for sporting goods and accessories easy. The site is a veritable sports superstore, and you're sure to find all the gear and equipment you need. Locate your equipment in one of several ways: Use the site's search feature, click one of the handy tabs at the top of the page, or visit the Eastbay Specialty stores. The store within a store concept works really well and makes it doubly easy to get in and out quickly with a minimum of clicks. Sign up for the Eastbay newsletter and get e-mail notification of specials and news on new products.

ebodyboarding.com
ebodyboarding.com
877-326-2734
info@ebodyboarding.com
Aquatic Sports • Individual Sports

Bodyboarding is a gear-intensive sport. A good board is essential, as is a wetsuit. Add on swim fins, wetsuit hoods, booties, gloves, and possibly more. You could easily rack up a big tab for bodyboarding equipment that wasn't right for you, or that you didn't need. Fortunately, ebodyboarding.com has all the tools to ensure that you buy what's right. The site's Booger Picker tool helps you determine which board suits you best. Various charts and tables provide detailed information about available accessories and help you make informed decisions about what to buy. Try to top the pictures of other bodyboarders at the site.

eham.net
eHam.net
No phone number listed
webmaster@eham.net
Hobbies

eHam.net is a community site designed and operated by and run for active amateur radio operators, often called hams. The site is always bustling with activity and information. Drop in to read the latest articles, chat with fellow hams, read product reviews, or answer a survey question. If you want to find other ham operators, check the Callbook. It's updated daily with data from the current FCC database. Shop at eHam.net for books and manuals about amateur radio.

⭐ ellusionist.com
Ellusionist.com

866-244-2426
E-mail form on site

Hobbies

Want to be the talk of the office tomorrow morning? It's a sure bet if you learn magic from Ellusionist.com. This site specializes in "Street Magic." Your mastery of Street Magic will give you the power to create illusion that is simple but devastating, anytime and anywhere. Props, like the Black Tiger Deck, a standard deck of playing cards that appear to perform magic effects, are available. Order the instructions on video or DVD, or if you're in a hurry, download them to your computer. The site offers many tricks, including card tricks and even levitation! If you want to perform tomorrow, order a download tonight and get busy.

everlastboxing.com
Everlast Boxing

800-777-0313
info@everlastboxing.com

Fitness • Individual Sports

You know the name. You've seen it on the front of boxing trunks and the cuffs of boxing gloves. Now you can have gear with the Everlast name on it. Serious boxers will find punching bags, speed bags, boxing bags, heavy bags, gloves, protective cups, and mouthpieces. The rest of us will be content with cool shorts, shirts, and (ladies only) sports bras. There are even trunks like Rocky's. On a more serious note, consider training and competition equipment for gyms and home use. It all has the Everlast name behind it.

evolutionsurf.com
Evolution Surf

888-386-4249
sales@evolutionsurf.com

Aquatic Sports • Individual Sports

Surf's up at Evolution Surf. Shop this site for surfboards, as well as a wide range of swim accessories for women. Unfortunately, the annoying design of the site undermines the value of boards it offers. Different windows open, and getting back to previously visited pages is difficult. Still, the fact remains that this site is one of the best places on the Internet to buy a surfboard. Navigate through the tangle of open windows on your computer and be prepared for a treat when you get to the page that shows all the groovy boards.

 Recommended   Price   Selection    Convenience   Service   Security

fauxstore.com
The Faux Store

800-270-8871
webmaster@fauxstore.com

Crafts

Achieving rich-looking, classic faux effects in design gets easier when you shop this site. The emphasis at The Faux Store is on faux finishing and decorative painting products. To aid in selection, products bear symbols indicating whether each is best for more of a beginner, intermediate, or experienced user. Browse through Venetian gems, verdigris kits, tints, waxes, top coatings, sealers, plasters, color washes and stains, iridescents and metallics, as well as brushes and trowels. Check out the specials for some money-saving bargains — a great way to get started with this exciting craft.

fogdog.com
Fogdog Sports

800-624-2017
E-mail form on site

Sports Superstore

Looking for a gift for the athlete in your life? Look no further than the Fogdog Sports Gift Center tab. One click and you're presented with a number of general selections and easy-to-navigate pages organized by interest with popular gift items featured. If you're just looking to keep yourself supplied for your sport, this site is also a good bet. Easy navigation and a good selection make it a good source for sporting goods. Spend some time browsing the Outlet pages for bargains. So whether it's gifts, bargains, or something in between, Fogdog Sports is your site.

footlocker.com
Foot Locker

800-991-6815
E-mail form on site

Fitness • Individual Sports • Team Sports

Whether you play sports, watch sports, or cheer those who play, Foot Locker has you covered. The site is the online branch of a company that has been providing sports equipment and apparel for over 30 years. Click the sport name you want equipment for, or click the tabs on the top of the page — shoes, clothing, sports equipment, accessories, fan gear, brands, sport — to get to the equipment you need. The online return policy is generous. Items purchased through the Foot Looker site can be returned to any of the chain's 2,700 stores.

forumancientcoins.com
FORVM Ancient Coins

252-240-2457
customerservice@forumancientcoins.com
Hobbies

FORVM Ancient Coins' site carries an extensive inventory of Greek, Roman, Byzantine, Biblical, and other historical coins. Most of the coins for sale are displayed with a description and a photo, so you get a good idea of what you'll be getting. If you're not satisfied, you can return your coin to FORVM for a complete refund. The site is not only a place to buy coins, but you can hang out here as well. Drop in on the Discussion Boards and learn more about ancient coins in the Resources section.

★ getboards.com
GetBoards.com

800-754-2627
helpguy@getboards.com
Aquatic Sports • Cold Weather Sports • Individual Sports

"One if by land, two if by sea." Three if by *snow*? No, the great patriot Paul Revere didn't utter his famous quote quite this way. But who knows how history might have turned out if he had shopped at GetBoards.com before his famous midnight ride through the streets of Boston. The site sells wake boards, body boards, and surfing gear and accessories for those who love the water. Landlubbers will find just about any non-motorized device, including scooters, freeboards, carveboards, and more. Love the snow? Have a blast with skiboards, snowboards, and twintip skis. Clothes and accessories for all three environments are here, too.

gijoes.com
G. I. Joe's

800-578-5637
E-mail form on site
Sports Superstore

G. I. Joe's has the right idea. This company's slogan, "Seize the weekend," sums up why you would want to shop at this store. The site offers a great selection of sports, outdoors, and automotive gear available at very competitive prices. You won't find any surprises here; the equipment is arranged by sports category. It's easy to browse through the categories and locate what you want. Sales and free shipping offers occur with some regularity. Some of the money you spend at the site is used for charity. G.I. Joe's Foundation provides financial support for youth sports and outdoor organizations.

glassmart.com
The Stained Glass Web-Mart

800-452-7796
sales@glassmart.com

Crafts

The Stained Glass Web-Mart offers serious tools for the serious glass artist, including diamond wire and diamond band saws, grinders, circle and strip makers, and cutters. You can even order saw blades. Pick up a soldering iron as well as soldering flux and putty. Get what you need to craft a Tiffany-style lamp. Order starter kits and glass projects, plus Color Magic glass paints, glass clusters, iridescent glass nuggets, table foilers, and stepping stone molds. The site also offers bead-making materials, chipping and UV glues, and copper foil. International orders are welcome.

★ golfballs.com
Golfballs.com

800-372-2557
service@golfballs.com

Individual Sports

Golfballs.com started in 1995 selling used golf balls. Since then it has sold over 5,000,000 golf balls. Golfballs.com has also expanded its line to include a full range of golf equipment and apparel. It offers a wide range of golf balls including unusual brands and custom-printed logo balls. Gollfballs.com has a sophisticated order tracking system and can ship merchandise on a next-day delivery basis if needed. While you're there, be sure to check out the Golf Humor page. The cornball jokes won't help your game, but they will make it easier to laugh about it.

golfclubfinder.com
Golf Club Finder

714-838-4255
ronmers@golfclubfinder.com

Individual Sports

If you left your seven iron beside a green somewhere, Ron Mers and Golf Club Finder can help you find a replacement. Just log in and post a description of the lost club. The site contains pages of golf club terms so you can craft an accurate description of the club you're looking for. This site can also get you a hard-to-find club or full set of clubs. Golf Club Finder also has a large selection of golf books. If you're a golfer, make sure to bookmark this site.

⭐ golfdiscount.com
Golfdiscount.com
888-394-4653
golfsales@golfdiscount.com
Individual Sports

If you're a golfer (or a junior golfer), you can find all the golfing gear you ever wanted at Golfdiscount.com. Better yet, it's true to its name, offering low prices on top-of-the-line golf gear. It also offers a Tip of the Day to keep you coming back. Don't have a handicap? Golfdiscount.com's Handicap Club will calculate one for you. If the site's closeouts and specials don't excite you, check out the Coming Soon page. Order the latest driver before it hits the stores. This site should be a regular part of every golfer's Internet browsing.

golfjoy.com
Golfjoy
877-465-3569
info@golfjoy.com
Individual Sports

Golfjoy makes it easy for shoppers to spend less time on the computer and more time on the golf course. The Internet arm of Vegas Golf, this group prides itself on its high levels of customer trust and loyalty. The Web site, like the store, is bulging with golfing products for men, women, and juniors. On the site the task of searching for the item you want is made simple by the intuitive menus of brands and product categories. Spend some time browsing the Golf Art pages and don't forget to look at the Closeouts category.

golfoutlet.com
GolfOutlet.com
866-858-0496
customerservice@tgwmall.com
Individual Sports

Don't let the name fool you. GolfOutlet.com is more than just another place to buy golf clubs. Although it offers great prices and specials on the latest golf gear, what makes this site a must visit are its other services. Uncensored golf course reviews by regular golfers are a hoot to read and you, too, can rate courses you have played. Other features include want ads and golf message boards. Spending time on this site is almost as much fun as being on the course. Be sure to try it.

 Recommended   Price   Selection   Convenience   ☺ Service   🔒 Security

hamradio.com
Ham Radio Outlet
800-444-0047
sales@hamradio.com

Hobbies

Ham Radio Outlet claims it's the "world's largest retailer of amateur radio equipment." A look at the site gives you no reason to doubt the claim. This site searches the inventory of eight stores to give you a wide selection of products. You can also look at assortments like "open box specials" or "gift selections." One of the site's pages is devoted to used gear. However, this site is not for the uninitiated. The site offers little information to help those who don't already have some knowledge of amateur radio, but if you're a "Ham" the site has a ton of stuff for you.

hamstation.com
The Ham Station
800-729-4373
sales@hamstation.com

Hobbies

Are you ready to set up your "ham shack"? The Ham Station's site is a good place to start. This well-organized, easy-to-navigate site offers amateur radio equipment with detailed descriptions and pictures. If you're already established in amateur radio and ready to upgrade, The Ham Station will accept trade-ins. Do you want to see the super equipment used by others with whom you communicate? Click the Shacks button and then choose the country where your buddies live. You can find them by call sign as well. Send in your picture to join the ever-growing Shacks gallery.

herrickstamp.com
Herrick Stamp Company
516-569-3959
mail@herrickstamp.com

Hobbies

Whether you're a veteran philatelist or a novice collector, the Herrick Stamp Company has lots to offer. This company's huge inventory filled with quality stamps is constantly restocked. If you're looking for a bargain, buy a large lot of stamps. You just may find a rare gem tucked away at low prices — it's a chance worth taking. The Rarities Gallery holds old and valuable stamps that will be the crown jewel of any collection. Herrick can also appraise stamps for you. Follow the prompts on the site to get the appraisal service started.

hobbymaker.com
Hobby Maker

800-274-8076
info@hobbymaker.com

Hobbies

Hobby Maker caters to families. For the little ones, Thomas the Tank Engine wood model train will spark interest. Everyone can enjoy the dollhouse and miniature selections; putting them together is a real family activity. The site carries a wide variety of model kits in various degrees of complexity. With products ranging from the simple assembly of a car for a young child to a complicated creation of a sailing ship for an older one, the site can offer hours of pleasure to children. There's even a selection of Science Projects that are sure to work!

jamesmccusker.com
James T. McCusker

800-852-0076
mail@jamesmccusker.com

Hobbies

If your stamp collection centers around U.S. First Day Covers, the James T. McCusker site is a place you must visit. The experts at this site manage to ferret out the best stock around and make it available to you. Some of the buying goes on in auction format, so be prepared to bid early and often. Your best bet is to sign up to receive e-mail notification about the auctions, so you're always in the loop and never let a cover slip by. The site buys aggressively, too, so you may want to contact the folks who run it if you have stamps and covers to sell.

justbats.com
JustBats.com

866-321-2277
support@justbats.com

Team Sports

JustBats.com is aptly named. You won't find a lot of baseball gear on this site — just bats! (If you're looking for gloves, try the site's sister location, JustGloves.com.) With no fall-back product, the bats at this site have to be first rate, and they more than meet expectations. In fact, the site claims that some Major League baseball players get their bats from this site. Use the well-organized Bat Directory to find the bat you need. All the top manufacturers are represented, as well as bats for seniors, fast- and slow-pitch softball, and more. Even notorious fungo hitters can find the right bats.

jwhitecricket.com
JWhiteCricket.com

516-867-1608
customerservice@jwhitecricket.com

Team Sports

Are you a gully or a slip? Perhaps you're a mid-on. Even if you're a long leg or a square leg, you'll want to check out JWhiteCricket.com. Of course, if you're a batsman, bowler, or wicket keeper, you probably already know about JWhitecricket.com. If you do play cricket, and much of what was once the British Empire does, you have an online source for all your gear. Many people think cricket was the forerunner to baseball, and the game is enjoying a resurgence of popularity in some parts of the U.S.

karatedepot.com
KarateDepot.com

877-216-2669
csupport@karatedepot.com

Fitness • Indiviual Sports

"Ah, Grasshopper, look deep beneath the sliding menus to find the essentials you need." Oops, sorry. The pictures of people kung-fu fighting on the opening pages of the KarateDepot.com site transported me back to that ancient television show. But there's nothing ancient here. Only lots of quality equipment, gear, and apparel for karate, jujitsu, tae kwan do, and other forms of the martial arts. The weapons descriptions spark your imagination; even if you've never picked up an Escrima Stick, you'll want to after spending time browsing the site. With $2.95 flat-rate shipping, martial arts enthusiasts and dreamers like me are free to order and play.

kitesonline.com
Kitesonline.com

888-713-9223
info@kitesonline.com

Hobbies • Individual Sports

If it has to do with wind, and it's made of fabric, you'll find it at Kitesonline. com. This company offers many kites to choose from, ranging from small inexpensive ones for the beginner to large complex ones to challenge the expert. Enthusiasts can also find sport kites for harnessing the wind to power skis, a buggy, or a surfboard. If kites aren't your thing, the site also carries decorative flags and windsocks. For something really different, take a look at the lawn sails and wind wheels. What are lawn sails and wind wheels? You'll just have to go to the site and find out.

kitestailstoys.com
Kites, Tails & Toys

877-861-8750
info@kitestailstoys.com

Hobbies • Individual Sports

Kites, Tails & Toys is all about service. Click on the Easy to Fly Kites link and find a selection of single-line kites that will get you in the air in a hurry. These kites are also attractive, colorful, and in some cases complex flying shapes. The 7' Kite Combo Value Pack gives you a seven-foot multicolor delta kite and everything you need to fly it. The Magical Sled Kite folds up to become its own carrying case. The Rainbow Tri-plane is a sure attention getter. Read the onsite instructions to learn how to make a kite from a paper bag.

lacrosse.com
Great Atlantic Lacrosse Company

800-955-3876
gacustserv@sportsendeavors.com

Team Sports

Lacrosse, once the province of a few Eastern Team Sports schools, has moved mainstream. Unfortunately, many of our bricks-and-mortar sports retailers have not caught up. If that's what you've found in your search for lacrosse gear, a visit to lacrosse.com is in order for you. You'll find all the gear you could want, plenty of books and videos, and services such as a wish list and a frequent buyer club, called Club Lax. This company even offers custom stick stringing. The Power Rankings section allows you to see the rankings of the best U.S. high school lacrosse players.

lacrosseunltd.com
Lacrosse Unlimited

877-932-5229
info@lacrosseunlimited.com

Team Sports

Here is a lacrosse site that, like you, just won't quit. Lacrosse Unlimited offers page after page of lacrosse gear and apparel. Check out the custom stick pages. Have your stick strung in team colors: If you're feeling funky, a Rasta color scheme makes a great personal statement. You'll even find a section devoted to women's equipment — finally, a store that doesn't expect women to use lacrosse equipment made for men! Lacrosse teams get special consideration at this site. Contact the site for more details about what it can do to outfit your team. If you have a young lacrosse player, be sure to visit the Camps page.

 Recommended   Price   Selection   Convenience   Service   Security

libertystreet.com/StampMng.htm
Liberty Street Software

905-566-5082
info@libertystreet.com

Hobbies

Liberty Street Software does not sell stamps. Rather, it sells software for managing your stamp, coin, and currency collections. This company applies the same technology to the home and office by offering software to manage your home or commercial assets. You can download the software or have it shipped to you. The products allow you to record images and descriptions. Documenting your valuable collection is wise not only for your own benefit, but also for insurance purposes or proof of ownership. This tool is truly valuable for the serious collector.

liquidgolf.com
Liquid Golf

800-903-6376
customerservice@liquidgolf.com

Individual Sports

Golfers try to avoid liquid at least until the nineteenth hole, but they won't want to miss the Liquid Golf site. With its vast array of merchandise and its low price guarantee, there's a lot to recommend at this great golf site. Check out the special departments for ladies and lefties. If you already have clubs, but want new ones, trade-ins are accepted. Simply click the Trade-in button to determine the value of your used clubs. Liquid Golf offers an e-Z Pay plan on purchases over $500. It can bill your credit card in three installments, making it easier to get those expensive new clubs you want.

★ martialartssupplies.com
MartialArtsSupplies.com

877-223-4528
E-mail form on site

Fitness • Individual Sports

Learning to defend yourself is a good idea in today's uncertain times. It's also a great way to stay fit! MartialArtsSupplies.com offers a large selection of sparring gear, such as protective headgear, body protectors, and a variety of gloves and footwear. The site also has training bags and a multitude of belts and patches. If you really get into this kind of thing, you can buy a complete Ninja suit. Even if you're not at Black Belt level yet, you'll impress the heck out of your friends when you smash a breakable tile or brick you obtained from this site.

mcsports.com
MC Sports

888-801-9159
E-mail form on site

Sports Superstore

Sometimes a big sports superstore can put you on sports overload. Even though you've planned to buy a specific item, the sheer volume of so many sports items coming at you makes you leave the site without making your intended purchase. MC Sports makes shopping easy. Its home page is clean and uncluttered. Simply browse the handy categories to find the equipment you want. Better still, visit the Info Center and take advantage of MC Sports' Buyer's Guides. You'll find great information and advice about equipment and gear. Check out MC Sports Hot Picks for extra savings on seasonal items.

midwest-sports.com
Midwest Sports.com

800-334-4580
info@tennisshop.com

Individual Sports

If racquet sports are your racket, then the Midwest Sports.com site is for you. This site carries gear for not only tennis, but also racquetball, squash, and badminton. Racquets, apparel, shoes, and accessories are all shown in great abundance. A whole page is devoted to strings, and why not? Expert racquet stringers are on staff. Your game can benefit by your shopping at midwest-sports.com, no matter what your level of play. With its selection of tennis clothes, at least you will look good on the court even if you don't play that well. So check out this Web site and get prepared for your next match.

militarycoins.com
Militarycoins.com

703-924-1774
info@militarycoins.com

Hobbies

Militarycoins.com's site is a great starting place for the collector of contemporary military coins. The company's recent alliance with Northwest Territorial Mints ensures that coins it sells will be made in the United States. Militarycoins.com sells coins representing all branches of the United States military, as well as the White House, Skunk Works coins, and a few miscellaneous designs. Download a free Windows background for your computer from the site while you're visiting.

 Recommended   Price   Selection   Convenience   Service   Security

modells.com
Modells.com

866-835-9129
E-mail form on site
Sports Superstore

Since 1889, those in the know have been saying "Gotta go to Mo's." Now that Modells is online, you can say it, too. Like other big sports superstores, Modells.com sells a wide range of gear and equipment for most sports. Prices at the site are generally low, and specials and deals make them even lower. Modells.com offers customers a convenient Learning Center for current information about sports and sporting goods. The Center is arranged by individual sports and contains buyer's guides, sizing charts, and other information you can use to make a decision before you buy.

mvp.com
MVP.com

866-690-2381
E-mail form on site
Sports Superstore

Not only can you get your sports gear at the MVP.com site, you can get the uniform of your favorite team, too. The home page may suggest a Fan Gear site, but a closer look reveals a serious sports site. The item descriptions include an abundance of technical information. For example, the Senior League baseball bat displays product specs, features and benefits, a comparison chart, and more. So browse your sport, but keep your eyes open for that commemorative item. Also spread around the site are bargains on reduced price items.

ngcgolf.com
NGC Golf

800-285-3900
customerservice@ngcgolf.com
Individual Sports

Would you like a golf ball that goes so far that it "could make some golf courses obsolete"? How about a driver whose "secret metal may hit too far for some par fours"? You can find these and many other items with similar claims at the NGC Golf site. You may have a hard time choosing between irons made of an armor-piercing metal and a set with bulge and roll faces. If you do, you may be a candidate for the irons with the "floating sweet spot." The golfer who likes to play late in the day can order a golf ball that lights up. See these and many more unusual items at NGC Golf.

niketown.com
NikeTown.com

800-806-6453
E-mail form on site

Fitness • Individual Sports •Team Sports

If only a real metropolis called NikeTown existed, where every resident had really cool shoes, the best equipment, and always looked wonderful. Shop at the NikeTown.com site for the same great shoes and accessories worn by the movers and shakers in the sports and entertainment world. The site carries all the latest shoes for men, women, and kids. Best of all, most sizes and colors are in stock, so you can have the shoes you want. Site visitors can also find equipment and a great selection of clothes. Set up an account for quick and easy shopping.

nordictrack.com
NordicTrack

800-220-1256
E-mail form on site

Fitness • Individual Sports

NordicTrack has long been a pillar of the home-fitness equipment industry. The NordicTrack cross-country skiing machine has spawned a host of cheap imitators, but nothing is as good as the real thing. You can buy one for yourself at this site. In addition, you can buy treadmills, elliptical machines, and steppers, as well as stationary bicycles and strength-training machines. Many of the machines can be programmed to provide a specific type of workout, and some machines contain heart monitors. Apparel and nutrition pages round out the selection.

oceanicworldwide.com
Oceanic Worldwide

510-562-0500
info@oceanicusa.com

Aquatic Sports • Individual Sports

Bob Hollis, the founder and owner of Oceanic Worldwide, is passionate about diving. He's been involved in the sport for a half-century and has been in the business since 1972. In addition to the standard diving gear offered everywhere else, Oceanic sells many custom-designed and unique items not found elsewhere. Oceanic-designed dive products typically carry warranties. According to Bob Hollis, "Our aim is to create products that will exceed the needs of divers and also naturally extend the freedom of diving." Good deal!

 Recommended   Price   Selection   Convenience   Service   Security

oldclubs.com
Old Clubs

214-678-1070
E-mail form on site

Individual Sports

Old Clubs' online auction site was created by golf addicts for golf addicts. You can pick up last year's hot driver at a bargain price or convert your putter collection to cash. In addition to the auction pages is an online store featuring a wide range of golf items. While you're at it, check out the Bargain Bin with clubs priced under $20. Site visitors also have opportunities to chat with other golfers and check out links to many golf-related sites. This site helps northern golfers get through the winter months and the rest of us stay in touch with the game.

oshmans.com
Oshmans

888-801-9163
vicepresident@oshmans.com

Sports Superstore

Oshman's has been satisfying discerning buyers of sporting goods equipment since 1919. Now it's your turn! If you live near an Oshman's store, read the weekly sale brochure online. Online shoppers get deals of their own — free shipping is offered on select items, and sale prices on the site are not always available in the stores. Hit the Info Zone for buyer's guides, sizing tips, and athlete's tips before you buy an expensive piece of equipment. A few minutes of your time upfront can save you wasted time and money down the road.

peterglenn.com
Peter Glenn of Vermont

800-818-0946 ext.159
sales@peterglenn.com

Aquatic Sports • Cold Weather Sports • Individual Sports

Peter Glenn's slogan used to be "Go for the Snow," but the Web site goes much further than that. Shop the site for cold weather sports gear, and then check out gear for cycling, hiking, backpacking, and kayaking. You'll also find equipment for wakeboarding and waterskiing. Think of this site as a place to shop for "outdoor adventure sports." Skiing equipment is still the house specialty. Even in the off-season the site has a great selection. The merchandise in other sports is first rate, but the descriptions are short and may leave you with unanswered questions. Don't miss the Travel section if you're thinking about a sports-related trip anytime soon.

pinemeadowgolf.com
PinemeadowGolf.com

503-236-0531
privacy@pinemeadowgolf.com
Individual Sports

PinemeadowGolf.com sells golf "clone" clubs. This company manufactures the clubs itself, and ships them directly to you. In most cases, the clubs are much less expensive than their branded competition. Clubs are available for both men and women. PinemeadowGolf is so sure that you will like its clubs that it offers you a 30-day money-back guarantee on any standard order, as well as in-store credit toward a future purchase on any customized order. Golfers may want to swing by this site and check out the online catalog.

potomacsupplies.com
Potomac Supplies

800-426-5723
jagrove@erols.com
Hobbies

Potomac Supplies' site is great for stamp collectors. Items ordered online are subject to a 20 percent discount. Shop the site for mint sheet albums and files, first-day covers, stock books, and more. Several different catalogues are available and can be purchased in paper or CD format. Consider the Stamp Collectors Database (SCDB) for Windows software for your computer. The software is compatible with most versions of Microsoft Windows and is an excellent way to track and catalogue your collection. Shipping is free on orders $100 and over.

puma.com
Puma

No phone number listed
customerservice@puma.com
Fitness • Individual Sports • Team Sports

If you're looking for solid, dependable shoes and clothes at very reasonable prices, you'll be more than happy with the stock at Puma. Unfortunately, by the time you wend your way to the online store, there's a chance that you'll be so frustrated that you'll be unable to appreciate what a great deal is offered on the shopping pages. Puma's expertise in shoe design obviously doesn't extend to Web site design — the pages are hard to navigate, slow loading, and totally mystifying at times. My advice: Keep heading toward the shoes. They're the best deal in town!

 Recommended   Price   Selection   Convenience   Service   Security

⭐ racquetballcatalog.com

RacquetballCatalog.com

866-443-2777

lisa@sportsandgear.com

Individual Sports

The RacquetballCatalog.com site has everything you need for racquetball. It also sells products for tennis, handball, and squash, but racquetball is the number one specialty. Shop this site for racquets, of course, but also for racquetball shoes, protective eyewear, videos, and books. If you're in the market for a new racquet, you will appreciate RacquetballCatalog.com's demo program. You may try as many as four racquets for a nominal charge plus the cost of shipping. What a great way to find the racquet that works for you!

rchobbies.org

R C Hobbies Online

866-681-1441

rchobbies@sbcglobal.net

Hobbies

Hey, kids, this must be the place! That is, if you're looking for radio-controlled models. Cars, boats, airplanes, helicopters — R C Hobbies Online has them all. You can buy a slow-flying airplane to get started or a realistic combat aircraft to really test your radio control flying abilities. For boats, too, come this way. The site offers simple models that the kids can use in the pool to ones that require a serious commitment of money and time. The site also has pages for general hobby items and model trains, but radio control hobbies are RC Hobbies' specialty.

⭐ roadrunnersports.com

Road Runner Sports

800-636-3560

E-mail form on site

Individual Sports

Serious runners and casual joggers both will enjoy the Road Runner Sports site. The selection of shoes is unequaled, and if finding the right size is a problem, the Road Runner Shoe Dog will fetch a pair or two that match your personal specifications. (The Shoe Dog fetched me a perfect pair and I'm tough to fit!) Discounts and special offers always come into play. For added discounts, join the Run America Club. Created by Road Runners, your annual membership entitles you to extra discounts, a subscription to *Fitness Runner* magazine, product testing, and much more. Details are at the site.

royaldesignstudio.com
Royal Design Studio

800-747-9767
sales@royaldesignstudio.com

Crafts

With stenciling, you can take ordinary surfaces and convert them into something with extraordinary appeal. Royal Design Studio's online shop features stencils and stencil products, interior decorating information, and paint supplies. Among its gallery of stencils you'll discover laces, paisleys, scrolls and swags, brocades, tiles, and oriental themes. Order from the selection of glazes, gilding supplies, plasters and textures, etching and metal effects, and top coats and sealers. Besides what's available online, order a copy of its 120-page portfolio of stencil design applications to further jumpstart your imagination.

ruggers.com
Ruggers

877-784-4377
customerservice@ruggers.com

Team Sports

Rugby is growing in popularity in the United States. It is popular as a recreational or club sport, and many colleges and universities field teams. It is played by women as well as men. Ruggers.com offers hard-to-find rugby gear. Shirts, shorts, boots, and protective gear are all well represented at this site. Equipment and balls are also available. To improve your game, consider something from the selection of books and videos. If you're looking for something unique, check out the international jerseys.

runningshoes.com
RunningShoes.com

800-390-1256
info@runningshoes.com

Fitness • Individual Sports

RunningShoes.com is a no-nonsense site for runners who would rather run than shop. In one fell swoop, runners can purchase shoes, apparel, accessories, and nutritional items needed to pursue their sport. Not all manufacturers are represented at the site, so you may be disappointed if you're looking for swooshes or stripes. Still, leading brands such as Asics, Brooks, and New Balance, as well as hard-to-find makes like Mizuno and Saucony have enough shoes and clothes to keep most runners happy. Don't check out without considering a pair of wild print running shorts. The retro-look shorts will turn a few heads when you jog by.

 Recommended Price Selection Convenience Service Security

sahobby.com
San Antonio Hobby Shop, Inc.

650-941-1278
No e-mail address on site

Hobbies

The radio control enthusiast can find loads of stuff at the San Antonio's Hobby Shop site to keep busy. Cars, planes, and boats are all well represented, with products for beginners and expert levels. As an added bonus, each product description includes the features, assembly requirements, and what other items may be needed to get up and running. Need new tools? The tool section is a model lover's dream. Featured are tools designed for the precise work that model assembly and maintenance requires.

scrapbookgiant.com
Scrapbookgiant.com

810-639-2328
questions@scrapbookgiant.com

Crafts

Scrapbooking is one of the hottest and most personalized crafting fields today. Whether you're just getting started or eager to delve farther into your craft, the Scrapbookgiant.com site offers what you'll want and need. This site boasts hundreds of stickers, as well as kits, albums, layout packages, cutters and trimmers, embellishments, laser-cut designs, and both die cuts and die-cut paper. Check out the site's selection of pens and markers, punches, cut offs, adhesives, heritage packages, page toppers, and theme-related material. Accessories are covered, too, including storage systems. Military folks get a 20 percent discount.

scrapbookingmall.com
Scrapbookingmall.com

801-792-7030
info@scrapbookingmall.com

Crafts

The Scrapbookingmall.com site is at least as much of a scrapbooking resource as it is a store, because you can locate supply stores by state and brands sold, as well as find information and assistance. Browse the site's stickers and borders, die cuts, papers, pens and markers, punches, heritage kits, glue markers, and major theme-related designs. You can also order great accessories like a master scrapbook organizer. Oddly, this company also offers bunk beds and playhouses, both finished and unfinished, along with bunk bed designs and kits. Kids will adore these.

scrapbook-magic.com
Scrapbook Magic

713-557-9966
tdacke@houston.rr.com

Crafts

If you believe you don't have time to preserve your special memories through scrapbooking, think again once you visit Scrapbook Magic's online shop. This company specializes in simplified scrapbooking solutions to let you get started quickly and easily. With most of its kits priced at $6 and under, shopping is also affordable. Check out the theme kits, which are pre-packaged and ready to assemble with all the latest and greatest embellishments plus instructions. Also buy albums as well as cutting mats and tools. Finally, this company's products are all made in the USA and archive-safe.

skateboard.com
Skateboard.com

619-243-1882
customer_service@skateboardinc.com

Individual Sports

Skateboards are made up of three components: decks, trucks, and wheels. The Skateboard.com site has what seems like an endless selection of these items. For the skateboarder wanting a custom board, this site is heaven. You'll also find technical information and news from the skateboard world. This site also has the selection of T-shirts and baggy shorts that are the uniform of the skater. The shoe selection is aimed in that direction, too, but for the older ones among you, the classic Vans in black-and-white check are available.

skateboards.com
Skateboards.com

831-462-3120 ext. 16
dk1@skateboards.com

Individual Sports

Skateboards.com is a Web site with a tremendous selection of complete boards and components for the skateboarder who either wants a custom board or needs to replace broken parts. The site doesn't offer a lot of hand-holding or support, though. The online catalog is arranged by part name, and you won't find product descriptions or any information telling you what parts you need or how to put a skateboard together. Your best bet is to purchase a complete board from this site if you don't know the lingo, or e-mail or call for help before you're stuck with a bag of parts you don't know what to do with.

 Recommended   Price   Selection   Convenience   Service   Security

skiandsnowboardhouse.com
SkiandSnowboardHouse.com
888-271-7500
sales@skiandsnowboardhouse.com
Cold Weather Sports • Individual Sports

A directive on the home page of this site implores you to "add SkiandSnowboardHouse.com to your favorites list!" Good idea! After you've spent some time at this site, you will want to come back again and again. With its low prices and great line of gear and apparel, this site could easily become your source for skiing and snowboarding gear. The site is easy to navigate and logical and intuitive in its presentation. Check out the Hot Deals on Cool Gear section. You'll save a few bucks that can be put toward your next equipment purchase.

★ snowshack.com
SnowShack
877-669-7422
sales@snowshack.com
Cold Weather Sports • Individual Sports

Spend a little time on the SnowShack site and you'll swear snowflakes are falling. The descriptions of skis, ski gear, snowboards, and blades make you lust for snow. The site carries a full line of outdoor winter sports equipment. The lighthearted catalog (Stuff to Keep You Warm, Stuff for Kids, Stuff for Snowboarders, and more) makes it fun to shop here. Each product is explained in terms a layperson can understand and if additional equipment is needed, it's listed. Men's, women's, and children's sizes are available in clothing and equipment. Refer five friends to the site and get free shipping.

soccer.com
Soccer.com
800-950-1994
custserv@sportsendeavors.com
Team Sports

Serious about soccer? At Soccer.com you can find the exotic gear that only the foreign players seem to have. Try finding Kelme or Joma shoes at the local sporting goods store. How about a Marcott Chest Protector Bra or padded Diadora Goalkeeper Pants? You can find all that and more at this site! You can also check on events in the soccer world and get the television schedule for soccer broadcasts in your local area. If you've ever wondered what soccer equipment your favorite player endorses, there's a good chance you can find out at this site.

⭐ soccerstore.com
SOCCERSTORE.com

800-566-5536
E-mail form on site

Team Sports

Are you a "Soccer Mom"? Or are you, perhaps, a "Soccer Dad"? You, as well as your soccer player will want to visit SOCCERSTORE.com's site. This site has a wide range of equipment, apparel, and footwear. Youth league coaches and parents should check out the Coaching pages to find a selection of books that can help your perspective of the game. Also take a look at the replica uniforms and the DVDs and books. All make great gifts for a soccer player. This site also offers a top-notch collection of shoes that can satisfy the needs of any player.

solowatersports.com
Solo

360-805-1000
No e-mail address on site

Aquatic Sports • Individual Sports

Okay, picture this: You've waited all week to go water skiing, and today's the day. Everything's perfect. The weather is beautiful, the water is smooth as glass, but you can't go because your driver and spotter both canceled at the last minute. Unfortunately, this scenario happens all too often. Well now you don't need to depend on others anymore! With the aid of the nifty device sold at the Solo site, you can water ski or go wakeboarding whenever you want. Called SOLO, the personal ski machine "lets you go it alone!" Read all the details about this radical device at the site.

speedo.com
Speedo

888-477-3336
service@speedousa.com

Aquatic Sports • Individual Sports

The word *Speedo* has become synonymous with abbreviated men's bathing suits. Of course, those classic men's competition suits are represented at Speedo's site, but visitors also find a broad line of swim and active wear for men, women, and children. Speedo also features high-tech competition suits designed to give you the edge in the pool. The innovative suits are made of low-friction fabrics and are available in a variety of styles, including full body suits. You'll leave your competition behind after the first lap.

⭐ Recommended $ Price   Selection   Convenience   ☺ Service   🔒 Security

★ sportchalet.com
Sport Chalet
888-801-9162
E-mail form on site
Sports Superstore

If you live in North California, there's a good chance you're already familiar with this sports superstore. Sport Chalet's greatest strength is the incredible degree of service it provides to customers. Buyer's guides lead you through the process of selecting new equipment and help you decide what to buy. When you buy something new, consult the Sport Chalet Owner Guide section to get the most from your new sporting equipment. If you need help later on, Sport Chalet will always be there to assist you, whether it's a question about equipment or the sport itself. Good deal!

sportmart.com
Sportmart
877-528-8326
vicepresident@sportmart.com
Sports Superstore

Looking for a good, dependable place to buy your sports equipment? Try Sportmart. You'll find a wide range of equipment at great prices. Shop by category or use the site's search engine to find the equipment or gear you want. Paintball fans can find some good buys at this site. The Optics and Telescope Department is surprisingly well stocked, and super deals can be had on almost every offering. Sportmart provides a handy order tracker so that you'll know the date your stuff will arrive.

stencils4u.com
Heart of the Home Stencils
888-675-1695
E-mail form on site
Crafts

At the Heart of the Home Stencils site, you can discover how easy it is to use stencils to decorate with paint and get exceptional results. With stencils, you can turn any old wall into a beautiful expanse and transform a canvas into a rich, eye-appealing floorcloth. Shop this online retailer to locate everything to get you started, including products and supplies such as brushes, scrubbers, and painter's tape. Browse stencils by categories like Americana, nursery, kitchen, garden, and the alphabet. Complete online help offers tips, plus you can order helpful books and videos. Peruse the suggestions for creative projects you can apply to your design situation.

stitching.com
Needlecraft Showcase

901-458-6109
amys3808@aol.com

Crafts

When you want a site that has all your needlework needs sewn up in a neat little package, visit the Needlecraft Showcase site. This site serves more as a online sewing resource than a shop. Post and read messages on the message boards to share project ideas and ask questions. Surf through the bounty of links to other sites to order products and find additional design ideas. Download free charts and projects. This site serves as a portal for all of your knitting, needlepoint, and cross stitch needs.

stuff4scrapbooking.com
Stuff 4 Scrapbooking

866-273-2653
E-mail form on site

Crafts

Although scrapbooking is the main focus at the Stuff 4 Scrapbooking site, look beyond and you can locate card-making materials and envelopes as well as specialty papers. This site carries albums, adhesives, stickers, punches, and organizers. Visitors also can find matting materials, craft scissors, embossing tools and embellishments, templates, rub-on transfers, die cuts, paper crimpers, and roller paper crimpers. Looking for folk art kits? Get them at this site, too, along with quality card stock, collage paper, adhesive Vellum, and designer and brand paper (M&Ms, Scrabble, and Clue, to name a few). Free shipping is available on orders of $100 or more.

swimgym.net
Swim Gym

305-273-1129
swimgym@swimgym.net

Aquatic Sports

Swim Gym offers merchandise for the competitive and recreational swimmer. Additionally, the site is a great resource for diving, water polo, and synchronized swimming equipment. Choose your store from the online store list and then choose the items you want. You can mix and match items from different stores; for example, Lane Lines from Competitor Warehouse and Split Timers from Accusplit. You'll need to mail, fax, or e-mail your order. If you know someone who can't swim (including yourself), the Swim Gym instructional video will have everyone in the water in no time flat.

 Recommended   Price   Selection   Convenience   Service   Security

swimtowin.com
PA Sports, Inc.

650-328-8555
service@swimtowin.com

Aquatic Sports

Don't let the name of the PA Sports site intimidate you. At swimtowin.com, you'll find a lot of fashion. Sure, this site has competition suits in the latest designs and materials, but you can find board shorts for men and attractive one- and two-piece suits for women. Pages of the site are devoted to water toys and sandals. If you're a competitive swimmer, you won't be disappointed. In addition to a great suit selection, plenty of goggles and training aids are available. No matter what your level of swimming proficiency, you may remember the floral swimming cap your mother or grandmother wore. You can get that at this site, too.

tenniscompany.com
The Tennis Company

888-276-1727
support@tenniscompany.com

Individual Sports

The Tennis Company has a page of testimonials on its site, and you may want to add your own comments to it after you shop at this site. The Tennis Company is a full-service tennis pro shop on the grounds of the San Diego Tennis & Racquet Club. Its dedicated staff is expert in filling the equipment needs of players at all levels. The folks there evaluate equipment before they decide to stock it, so you can have confidence in the quality of the products this company offers. Products include racquets, shoes, clothing, tennis bags, hats and visors, and a multitude of accessories. Before you make a decision, read the product reviews on the site. The descriptions provide a lot of technical detail, but the reviewers also explain the terms used. Not only will you know what to buy, you'll know why you bought it.

tennisexpress.com
TennisExpress.com

713-781-4848
karen@tennisexpress.com
Individual Sports

If you're looking for anything that has to do with tennis, you can get it at the TennisExpress.com site. You'll see more racquets than you thought existed and more shoes than you can shake a racquet at. Visitors can find apparel to suit any taste and instructional books and videos for the beginner or expert. Accessories such as sunglasses and nutritional products are also available. You can even find tennis-themed salt and pepper shakers for your kitchen and an Anna Kournikova poster for your wall. Don't you wish it were this easy to buy a better game?

tennisracketpros.com
Tennis Racket Pros

888-983-6647
E-mail form on site
Individual Sports

You won't find the latest tennis fashions at the Tennis Racket Pros site. In fact, you won't find any tennis clothes at all. Tennisracquetpros.com is a serious tennis site for the serious tennis player. Its selection of racquet frames is extensive and top of the line. Four pages of the site are devoted to strings. The shoe selection reflects performance, not appearance. The site offers a number of ball machines (not especially useful for the social player). The kid's pages feature high-quality racquets and training aids. A selection of racquetball and squash racquets is also available. Tennis pros, or those players who want to improve their games, will do well to visit this site.

tenniswarehouse.com
Tennis Warehouse

800-883-6647
info@tennis-warehouse.com
Individual Sports

Add the Tennis Warehouse site to your browser favorites. It's your "everything tennis" site. It offers all the major brands and a few not so well known. Are you wondering about the polar moment of inertia of your racquet? That and other technical tennis terms are explained at the Learning Center. Are you considering a new racquet? Check out the Demo Program. If you're happy with your old racquet, then the link to the Racquet Finder can help you buy a few more of them. Just try not to spend more time on this site than you do on the court.

 Recommended   Price   Selection   Convenience   Service   Security

⭐ theathletesfoot.com
The Athlete's Foot

888-801-9157
E-mail form on site

Fitness • Individual Sports •Team Sports

Started in Pittsburgh in 1971, The Athlete's Foot now has more than 750 stores in over 45 countries. Shop online for shoes, clothes, accessories, and sports equipment. The online catalog is clear and crisp and offers shipping information about each item. View the site's Comparison Chart to see how your choice stacks up against similar models. Fit Tips provide much needed information about getting the best fit. Shopping for a team? Call or e-mail to find out about The Athlete's Foot volume discount policy.

thegolferscloset.com
Palm Beach Golf Center

800-472-1196
E-mail form on site

Individual Sports

Men and women golfers can stock their closets with golf clothes and shoes from the Palm Beach Golf Center. Golf gloves and hats are available, too. The site even has a page for plus-size golfers. The site is well organized and easy to navigate. With free standard shipping on gloves and apparel, expect your order in about three days. Subscribe for a weekly e-mail of specials. You can also create your own favorites on the site to make ordering of things you buy regularly simple. New Items and On Sale pages are always worth visiting. After all, there's no reason to look shabby when you're on the course.

⭐ the-house.com
The-House

866-243-6932
info@the-house.com

Cold Weather Sports • Individual Sports

Do you know what snowboard is right for you? Start with this formula: Multiply your height in inches $\times 2.54 \times 0.9$ to find the suggested board length in centimeters. Confused? You need to consider your age, overall physical condition, weight, and so on, too. Plus, the terrain and conditions can play a role in your board selection. In any case, you can find great discounted snowboards at The-House's site. If you know which board you want, order it! Or, take advantage of the great customer service offered by the knowledge-able folks at The-House. Either way, you'll get the board that's right for you.

themagicwarehouse.com
The Magic Warehouse
877-946-2442
sales@themagicwarehouse.com
Hobbies

"If you're just starting out in magic, you've come to the right place." So say the wizards at The Magic Warehouse's site on the Beginners page. What follows are well-organized, informative pages of tricks and effects you can order. Besides the Beginners page, visitors can find pages for children's magic and many others. Want something different? Try the Hot Wallet. You just take out the wallet and open it, and flames shoot out. Close it, reopen it, and it is a normal wallet. Even if you don't become a magician, you'll be noticed when it's your turn to pay the check.

thesportsauthority.com
Sports Authority
888-801-9164
E-mail form on site
Sports Superstore

The Sports Authority is a familiar name to countless shoppers. With hundreds of stores in the United States and Japan, lots of folks are familiar with the sport superstore's great deals on equipment and clothes for almost every sport you can name. The online store is even bigger than the bricks-and-mortar stores, with free shipping deals and Web promotions added as extra enticements to shop online. Click the Outlet Authority for super good deals on older or one-of-a-kind equipment.

thestore.adidas.com
thestore.adidas.com
800-869-5248
E-mail form on site
Fitness • Individual Sports

Navigating around thestore.adidas.com's site is a bit like running a cross-country race through the woods — you may find a lot of unusual twists and turns until you finally get to the latest and greatest Adidas gear and apparel, including shoes, clothing, and accessories, at the site. In fact, many times you'll find new items online before you see them in your local store. (On a recent visit I found a pair of snazzy golf shoes that weren't expected in my local pro shop for a few months.) Sign up to get notified when new items are added to the site.

 Recommended   Price   Selection   Convenience   Service   Security

the-swim-store.com
The Swim Store

800-214-6285
No e-mail address on site

Aquatic Sports

Whether you're a casual swimmer or planning to swim the English Channel one day, The Swim Store has all the swim gear and apparel you need. This company's supply of competitive swimwear is unequaled, with men's and women's suits from Speedo, Arena, TYR, and Dolfins. Also available is gear for swimmers and triathletes, including goggles, caps, kickboards, hand paddles, masks, swimmer radios, stop watches, tempo trainers, stretch-cords, zoomers swim fins, books, videos, and more. Lifeguards are covered, too, with suits and clothing and heart rate monitors, in case the worst happens. This comprehensive water sport site has much to recommend it.

thetrickery.com
The Trickery

973-657-0446
howard@thetrickery.com

Hobbies

How did he do that? That's what you're supposed to think when you see a magic trick. The Trickery's site will make your friends say the same about you. This site is well stocked with magic tricks and gear necessary to create the magic effects that defy explanation. Making a coin disappear from an open palm may be advanced, but at this site you can buy tricks and instructions that will have you doing simple magic in no time. This site is a complete online magic store for the beginner or professional magician.

⭐ tileshack.safeshopper.com
Tile Shack

405-273-1747
mosaics@tileshack.com

Crafts

For those whose favored medium is vitreous tile — whether you're a beginner or a seasoned artist — comes this family-owned and operated online shop bearing all your needs. Browse Tile Shack's collection of tiles, stained glass, millefiori, and mixes. Find tile kits and bases and choose from unique pre-cut glass, including those already shaped as moon, stars, and flowers. Because you need tools as well, peruse the site's inventory of cutters, grids, mosaic mounts and mesh, grouts and adhesives, and safety products plus the project storage solutions. The site offers free shipping on orders of $100 or more.

totaltabletennis.com
Total Table Tennis

800-869-5248
info@totaltabletennis.com

Individual Sports

Table tennis is the name of the game at Total Table Tennis. Shop its site for tables, robots, and accessories. Tables come in a wide variety of styles and price ranges. Some tables are approved by the USA Table Tennis Association and can be used for tournament play. Order a Newgy-made robot to improve your play. (Extra benefit: Robots never laugh when you miss a shot.) Finish your order from Total Table Tennis with glue, scoreboards, clothing, and any other accessories you need to be a winner on the court. The site ships internationally.

tourlinegolf.com
Tourline Golf

800-530-5767
E-mail form on site

Individual Sports

If you think you can't afford new clubs, think again. Tourline Golf specializes in used golf clubs. Its stock comes from PGA professionals at clubs and courses across the country. Tourline Golf can put a set of high-quality demo clubs in your bag for substantially less than new ones would cost. So if you're in the market for another set of clubs, or just want to see what's available, browse on over to Tourline Golf and start saving some money.

usmint.gov
The United States Mint

800-872-6468
E-mail form on site

Hobbies

Of course, the primary function of this all-important branch of the United States government is to produce the paper money and coins that keep commerce flowing. Of secondary importance is the service it offers to hobbyists and collectors. If coin collecting is your hobby, start at The Mint for uncirculated state quarters, uncut currency, and special commemorative coins. Most of the coins are sold in sealed packages, and are ideal for gift giving. Prices are surprisingly reasonable and service is fast and efficient.

  Recommended $ Price ⚲ Selection 🎁 Convenience ☺ Service 🔒 Security

vikingwoodcrafts.com
Viking Woodcrafts

800-328-0116
viking@vikingwoodcrafts.com

Crafts

Viking Woodcrafts may already be familiar to you as a distributor of decorative supplies. More than 1,000 books and 1,500 pattern packets are available at its site, along with books, brushes, unfinished surfaces, and artist supplies and accessories. You have several surface mediums to choose from, including glass and porcelain, slate, stoneware, resin, metalware, paper machè, and unfinished wood. Find material to work on scrapbooking, miniatures and replicas, shelves and cabinets, stools, clocks, toys and games, and signs. The site features sales and clearance specials, as well as the usual paper, stamps, stencils, paints, and rub-on transfers.

vsathletics.com
VS Athletics

800-676-7463
sales@vsathletics.com

Team Sports

Finding good track and field gear has always been a challenge. You're not likely to find javelin boots or a vaulting pole at a mass market sporting goods store. These and many other hard-to-find items are available in abundance from VS Athletics. At its site, you can find all the specialized variations there are in shoes. You can also purchase implements such as shots and discuses. Starting blocks and timers and hurdles are available, too, as well as plenty of sale items. So if you're a track and field athlete, make a visit to this site part of your training routine.

windpowersports.com
WindPower Sports

702-220-4340
info@windpowersports.com

Hobbies • Individual Sports

If you're a beginning kite flyer, the WindPower Sports site is a good place to start for an abundance of kite-flying information and gear. If you're experienced, why go anywhere else? WindPower Sports has a wide variety of kites for all skill levels. Offerings include not only traditional kites, but also sport kites that can be used with a buggy, mountain board, or skis to pull a person by wind power on land. Use one of these large kites with a surfboard, and become a participant of one of the newest water sports around.

workoutwarehouse.com
Workoutwarehouse.com

800-201-3729
salesinfo@iconfitness.com

Fitness

If you don't have time to go to the gym, or you don't want to, why not set up
your own home fitness center? Workoutwarehouse.com can help you. This
site specializes in several brands of fitness equipment and carries both
cardio and strength-training equipment as well as accessories. Begin your
fitness journey with a treadmill or stationary bike. Move up to ellipticals and
steppers as you get more experience. Graduate to multi-exercise strength-
training machines. Check out Workoutwarehouse.com and you will be on
your way to having your own private "we never close" gym.

worldwideaquatics.com
World Wide Aquatics

800-543-4459
E-mail form on site

Aquatic Sports

Water lovers unite! World Wide Aquatics has all the equipment and gear you
need to keep you in the water and out of the mall. Whether you're a triathlete
or a water polo player, you'll find everything you need at this site. Along
with suits and sunblock, the site offers balls, water polo caps, kickboards,
fins, and more. A full range of water exercise gear is also available, for those
who work out in the pool. The owners of the site are swimmers themselves,
and they'll be happy to work with you to provide any equipment you need.

wrestlersexpress.com
Wrestlers Express

800-759-8326
mail@wrestlersexpress.com

Team Sports

Wrestlers Express isn't the site for those guys who sling each other around
the ring in corny costumes and in the roles of good and bad guys. Nope, this
site deals with equipment for serious Freestyle and Greco-Roman wrestlers.
The site has a big selection of singlets, shoes, and apparel. Protective gear
such as earguards and kneepads (always a good idea when your opponent is
trying hold you down to win) is available. Consider the anti-bacterial skin
cleanser or skin protector spray; one spray lasts four hours, keeping dirt
and grime in perspiration or on unclean surfaces from coming in contact
with the wrestler's skin.

★ Recommended Price Selection Convenience Service 🔒 Security

yoga.com
Yoga.com

866-266-9642
staff@yoga.com

Fitness

People are drawn to yoga for different reasons. Some take up yoga for the calm and serenity it offers, others for the fitness yoga brings, and others try it because it's the hip and trendy thing to do right now. Whatever your reasons for practicing yoga, one thing is certain. You have to have the right gear. Shop at Yoga.com's site for yoga mats and props, and comfortable clothes that can easily accommodate yoga postures. Pick up a yogatard or two. Instructional videos and music will complement your training, and afterwards, you can buy a book devoted to the topic. Site visitors can also find pages devoted to Pilates, natural healing, massage, and meditation.

★ yogaforegolf.com
YOGA fore GOLF.com

No phone number listed
paul@yogaforegolf.com

Fitness

Paul Toliuszis (rhymes with delicious) is one cool dude. He's both a scratch golfer and a yoga instructor. Paul developed a program, which he sells at his YOGA for GOLF site, to enhance a golfer's performance through yoga. He offers serious yoga classes, not just a few stretches, meant expressly for golfers. Paul sells three video classes: YOGA fore GOLF, Senior YOGA fore GOLF, and Power YOGA fore GOLF. Each is a complete sixty- to seventy-minute yoga class. Even though a golfer will see improvement almost immediately, Paul cautions that significant gains will be made only through regular practice. Paul's videos are available through this site.

Let's Go to the Super Bowl

Every major team sport has a championship game or series. The Super Bowl, the National Football League's annual championship, is more than a game. It's an institution. The day on which the game is played is referred to as "Super Bowl Sunday." People travel thousands of miles for the extravaganza. Other folks hold big parties in their homes or attend catered events that cost thousands of dollars.

This year, plan early for the Super Bowl. The pre-game festivities go on for days and the post game party is a blast. Get in the mood by visiting the official Web site of the National Football League (nfl.com). Get pumped with Super Bowl details and history at Superbowl.com (superbowl.com).

The best way to go to the game is to purchase a complete travel package that contains hotel accommodations and tickets. TSE (tseworld.com) and Premiere Sports Travel (sportstravel.com) are experienced at handling all the arrangements. If you wait until the last minute for tickets, try Maxim Tickets (maximtickets.com). You'll pay a premium, but may end up on the fifty-yard line.

If you're like most of us, you'll be watching the kickoff from home. Why not treat yourself to a new flat-screen TV from Electronix Webshop (electronixwebshop.com) so you can be sure to see every play of the game. (Before you buy your new television, read some great buying tips and advice from PCworld.com at yahoo.pcworld.com/yahoo/bguide/0,guid,34,page,2,00.asp.

You'll also need some fan gear — a jersey or helmet — to get yourself ready. SportsFanfare.com (sportsfanfare.com) has a great selection of fan gear and brings the game home to you. Order an NFL football at Wizard Sports (wizardsports.com) to get you in the mood.

Did you know Pepsi is the official drink of the National Football League? Visit Pepsi World (pepsi.com) to see the latest ads and download music. There may even be a surprise or two on the site for you. You'll need to order some Pepsi for Game Day. Order both Pepsi and pizza at Pizza Hut (pizzahut.com). Depending on your location, your order can be delivered to your door at half time.

After the game it's natural to feel a bit let down about the season's being over. Click over to the Arena Football League (arenafootball.com) and meet the teams and players of this league. There's still plenty of football left!

Chapter 22

Transportation: Traveling Round and Round

• •

Most historians credit the ancient Mesopotamians with the invention of the wheel at about 4000 BC. That simple disc revolutionized the world in many ways. The wheel made life easier. It also gave people the ability to move from one place to another.

The road beckons in today's society. We're a mobile bunch. We leave home for work, school, or recreation. We're as likely to drive to the grocery store for a single quart of milk at midnight as we are for a weekly grocery shopping for the family. Our cars rule!

The Internet is a great place to shop for all types of vehicles and travel-related accessories and devices. Want to buy a car online? No problem. Need to shop for parts for your RV? You'll find them online. How about a new scooter or bicycle? Visit several sites and compare prices and features before you buy. No matter where you're traveling, begin your journey online, and find the best deals and equipment.

The listings in this section cover a wide range of sites that deal with car purchases, accessories, and parts. You'll find sites that can help you get financing for that new car. We also include sites that sell parts and accessories for recreational vehicles and motorcycles. Scooters and bicycles are covered in this chapter, too. You're bound to say, "Hey, I didn't know I could buy *that* online," when you see sites like those presented in this chapter.

If you're buying a bike or scooter that requires assembly, make sure you have the tools and expertise to handle the job before you order. A box of parts that looks like a science experiment gone bad may not turn out to be the great deal you originally thought.

Key Word Index

Apparel

The Apparel sites carry clothes and uniforms that are car, cycle, or motorcycle themed, such as matching his-and-her leather motorcycle jackets, or bike shorts.

Automobile Broker

Visit the Automobile Broker sites if you want to purchase a car online. The brokers offer different services, so you'll need to determine which one best meets your needs.

Auto Financing

Unless you have a suitcase of cash under your bed or a big stash in the bank, you're going to need the services of the sites with the Auto Financing keyword when you buy your next car.

Auto Parts

You can find parts and accessories for your car at the Auto Parts sites. These are items you generally find in an auto parts or tire store.

Bicycles

From mountain bikes to recumbents to electric-powered bikes, the Bicycles stores sell bicycles and related gear.

Motorcycle Accessories

The sites with the Motorcycle Accessories keyword carry accessories to spiff up a motorcycle or its rider. Shop for anything from helmets to sissy bars.

RV Accessories

At the RV Accessories sites, you'll find a wide variety of accessories for your RV or motorhome, from a simple device that reroutes odors from the holding tank to hitches, awnings, and even replacement parts.

Scooters

There's the Razor. There's gas, electric, and push scooters. There's even a bicycle scooter! Shop for the aforementioned models and other scooters at sites with the Scooters keyword.

acscorp.com
Automobile Consumer Services, Inc.
800-223-4882
help@acscorp.com
Automobile Broker

Automobile Consumer Services, Inc. (ACS) says it was the first online car-buying service, with its "Buyer's Agent" service for individuals. For $29, your Buyer's Agent will research and negotiate a competitive purchase price (typically near dealer's cost) for the vehicle of your choice. (If the Agent can't produce a vehicle for the specified price, your money is refunded.) Or, if you would prefer a free service, use the site to build the new vehicle you want and be referred to a local dealer. Fleet, leased, and used car sales services are also available.

airdynamicracing.com
Air Dynamic Racing
760-291-1781
questions@airdynamicracing.com
Auto Parts

Air Dynamic Racing caters both to individual car owners and businesses from its California location. As an established warehouse distributor, this company features great customer service, low prices, and fast shipping. Prices at this site are generally low. For example, on a recent visit, a Performance Two kit that included a V4 cold air intake, performance bolt on headers, and a volution high-performance exhaust muffler was marked down to around $230. Similar markdowns will be available when you shop. Bulk discounts are available to speed shops and retail stores; call to set up the details.

★ allamericanleathers.com
All American Leathers
800-891-5221
E-mail form on site
Motorcycle Accessories

All American Leathers has been in the leather business since 1972, and prides itself on knowing what works and what doesn't. This company shares that knowledge at swap meets, Bikeweeks, and on its site, where you can buy riding jackets, vests, chaps, and headwear, all American made with premium leather. Wholesale orders are also accepted. Shipping is UPS ground, and all items are 100 percent guaranteed. The site also includes interesting details about leather, odd American laws, information about shows in which the company is participating, and Bikeweek history.

amvtwin.com
American V Twin

407-903-0058
E-mail form on site

Motorcycle Accessories

The American V Twin site features selected biker accessories from the company's retail stores in Massachusetts and Florida. The online catalog features products from belts and buckles to helmets, flags, and headwraps. Gift certificates are available. All major credit cards, plus PayPal, are accepted. You can also place orders by calling the company. Free shipping is available within the continental U.S. for orders over $100. A 30-day, no-hassle return or exchange policy ensures customer satisfaction.

autobytel.com
Autobytel.com

888-422-8999 ext. 3050
consumercare@autobytel.com

Automobile Broker

Whether you're looking for a new or used car or just researching your options, check out the fast, professional, and reliable Autobytel.com. When you search the site for used cars, the results display each vehicle's details, distance from your location, mileage, and price in an easy-to-compare format. After you find the car of your choice, you can easily contact the seller (you don't actually purchase through this site). Or, to keep a list of your favorite cars, sign up for a free "wishlist" — part of "My AutoByTel," where you can also get recall notices and service reminders for the cars you own.

autoloan.citifinancial.com
CitiFinancial Online Auto Loan

877-782-8239
E-mail form on site

Auto Financing

CitiFinancial Online Auto Loan has designed a program that can help you get the vehicle of your dreams from an authorized dealer. It's important for you to understand the program and follow each of the steps carefully. You'll need to fill out the online application before you commit to purchasing your car or truck, and submit any additional documentation requested by the lender. Upon approval, you'll receive a check that can be activated at an approved dealership. After you've chosen your vehicle, the dealer will forward the completed documents to CitiFinancial and wait for authorization to deposit the check. When the authorization is received, your loan is complete.

★ Recommended Price Selection Convenience Service 🔒 Security

autoloans.us
AutoLoans.Us

No phone number listed
information@autoloans.us

Auto Financing

AutoLoans.Us helps people with bad credit get financing for new and used vehicles. The online credit application takes less than three minutes to complete, and is completely free and secure. The severity of the person's credit problems dictates how high the interest rate will be, but the site boasts that 100 percent of those who apply are accepted. After you submit an application, a financial services representative will call you to discuss your options and arrange for financing. Note that completing an online application does not obligate you to receive financing through the site.

autopartstreet.com
B & B Auto Parts

800-425-1227
partsdept@bbautoparts.com

Auto Parts

If you know which auto part you need, head over to B & B Auto Parts for fast, easy, no-frills parts and service. Enter the details about the vehicle in question, and then select the specific part needed. Or, search the main catalog by part type. An e-mail address, online Contact Us form, and toll-free number puts you in quick contact with customer service reps if you need assistance choosing a particular part. This company also maintains a store in New York City, where it has over 40 years experience in the auto parts industry.

autopurchasebyweb.com
AutoPurchasebyWeb.com

No phone number listed
customerservice@autopbw.com

Automobile Broker

The "Car Configurator" feature of AutoPurchasebyWeb.com makes finding the new car of your choice easy, wherever it may be within the United States. After you choose the options you want, the system locates the vehicle and displays two prices: the Dealer's Invoice Price and the Manufacturer's Suggested Retail Price. You negotiate the purchase price (somewhere in between those two) and get financing through the site, and then the vehicle is delivered to you. Customer service reps are available toll-free at all stages of the process. After the purchase, this site even reminds you when the vehicle needs service!

axtionsystems.com
AXtion

888-521-6688
support@axtionsystems.com

Scooters

AXtion provides high-quality boards, blades, scooters, and "axcessories." The scooters at this site range from inexpensive children's models to adult scooters with large step boards, patented front and rear suspension systems, and combination hand and foot brakes. Choose from a variety of colors and price ranges. Whether you're making your way around campus or just riding for fun, you're sure to find a scooter that meets your needs. Don't miss the collection of gliderboards and all-terrain boards. Live dangerously! It's never too late to take up a new sport.

bestairhitch.com
BestAirHitch.com

270-779-9182
E-mail form on site

RV Accessories

BestAirHitch.com, the brainchild of an RVing couple from Kentucky, sells and installs TravelSaver Air Ride Hitches and accessories for fifth-wheel trailers. Recently the company added BrakeSmart controllers, ElecDraulic hydraulic disc systems, and LED lights to its roster. Classified listings for used parts and accessories are also posted. Click the Schedule link to see whether Steve and Jo will be RVing through a town near you soon. Note that hitch prices do not include freight charges from Stoughton, Wisconsin.

bestofbents.com
Best of Bents

303-463-8775
info@bestofbents.com

Bicycles

Best of Bents is the largest dealer of recumbent bicycles in the Rocky Mountain region. Its slogan, "Bicycles for the Pedally Insane" is a tongue-in-cheek jab at folks who are not familiar with the low-slung recumbent model. Recumbent bicycles are gaining in popularity and are represented at this site by quality manufacturers such as Bachetta, Big Cat, and Penninger. Best of Bents even offers a three-wheeled racing trike. (For the record, this model looks nothing like the adult trikes you see at retirement communities!) Read the on-site classifieds and score a used recumbent, or post one for sale.

 Recommended   Price   Selection   Convenience   Service   Security

bikepartsusa.com
BikePartsUSA

877-727-8731
info@bikepartsusa.com

Bicycles • Scooters

BikePartsUSA's site is the discount store for those who enjoy two-wheeled contraptions of all types and sizes. Not only can you find bicycle helmets, seats, tires, baskets, computers, and all the obligatory accessories, you can even buy a special dog leash that will attach Fido to your bicycle so you two can enjoy more quality time together frolicking through suburbia. The site offers more than 9,000 bicycle-related items from 150 manufacturers. You can search by product category or by manufacturer. Tricycles, recumbents, and even motorized scooters are also available.

bikerbags.com
Biker Bags

No phone number listed
E-mail form on site

Motorcycle Accessories

Biker Bags offers an extensive catalog of every type of bag a biker could want — fork bags, saddlebags, windshield bags, sissybar bags, purses, pouches, and plenty of others in between. The site touts that everything is "40% below retail on 100% genuine leather." Join the site's mailing list to receive additional discounts via e-mail throughout the year. Its Custom Catalog feature acts like "wish lists" do on other sites, making it easy to provide friends and family with a list of all the bags you want. The Specials change often so check back frequently for an even greater deal.

bikesdirect.com
BikesDirect.com

No phone number listed
sales@bikesdirect.com

Bicycles

BikesDirect.com has been selling bicycles on the Internet for more than ten years. Shop at the site for all the latest road, mountain, comfort, cruiser, and hybrid bicycles. Shop around before you shop this site so that you can appreciate the really low prices on the bikes. All bikes sold here are shipped free within the continental United States. Your bike will arrive 90 percent assembled, but BikesDirect.com advises that you may want professional assistance to put the rest together. However, if you feel you can handle the remaining assembly, instructions and pictures are at the site to assist you.

⭐ bikesmart.com
BikeSmart.com
866-600-2453
info@bikesmart.com
Apparel • Bicycles

BikeSmart.com has an offer you can't refuse. BikeSmart.com's registered customers get 10 percent off the site's regular low prices for life. Considering the already reduced prices and the vast amount of merchandise offered in the online catalog — bikes, frames, components, and accessories — that's an astounding offer. But it gets better. Special, hard-to-find parts and accessories are included in the offer, too. Sale items in both the regular and special order catalogs are excluded. If you have a mountain or road bike now, or are considering buying one in the future, register at BikeSmart.com today.

⭐ boostcaraudio.com
Boost Car Audio
818-771-9180
E-mail form on site
Auto Parts

If you like to blast hip-hop or sing aloud to opera, or you fall somewhere in between, cruise over to Boost Car Audio's site. This audio superstore can transform your car's audio system. Amplifiers, speakers, CD players and changers are available, as well as woofers, subwoofers, equalizers, and a vast range of other audio equipment. The site also sells car security systems. Each alarm purchase includes a car-wiring diagram, specific to your vehicle, to assist you on your installation. After all, now that you've spent your hard-earned dollars on audio upgrades, you need to protect your investment.

buttbuffer.com
The Butt Buffer
866-859-5699
E-mail form on site
Motorcycle Accessories

The Butt Buffer site sells exactly what the address implies — items to buffer your butt, "to make your next ride the most comfortable you've ever had." The developers of the Butt Buffer have found a way to "alleviate the stiffness, soreness, and lower back pain" from long rides. Available in all sorts of colors and styles, there's sure to be a Butt Buffer for the motorcycle enthusiast in your life. Want to try before you buy? A list displays locations where you can try one yourself.

 Recommended   Price   Selection   Convenience   Service   Security

buyautoparts.com
BuyAutoParts.com

888-907-7225
sales@buyautoparts.com

Auto Parts

BuyAutoParts.com has it all — wholesale car parts, truck parts, and parts for vehicles dating back to 1961! The online catalog is searchable by vehicle year, make, and model, or by part number. Orders totaling $50 or more qualify for free ground shipping in the continental U.S. Because this company maintains warehouses on both coasts and in between, your order arrives quickly. Wondering why your brakes squeal or how to check your engine oil? BuyAutoParts.com even maintains a Learning Center section with articles answering this and other common questions about car maintenance.

campingworld.com
Camping World

866-694-1580
info@campingworld.com

RV Accessories

Camping World offers an extensive online catalog of all things related to RVs and camping. In fact, this "RV and Camping Supercenter" has been around since 1966, with 30 locations nationwide, and is now the world's largest retailer of RV accessories, supplies, and services. Departments include Outdoor Equipment, Upkeep and Storage, Systems, Interior, and On the Road. Orders over $75 qualify for $1 shipping. Store locations offer repair and service. Or, if you're interested in learning more about RV service and repair, Camping World even has an RV Institute in Bowling Green, Kentucky.

caraddons.com
CarAddons

800-338-8637
E-mail form on site

Auto Parts

CarAddons is a division of Trail Blazers, a retail auto and truck accessories store with locations in Kentucky and West Virginia. Use this site to shop for all kinds of products for your car, including everything from oil filters, tachometers, and camshafts to pet dividers, car covers, and window tints. You're guaranteed to find the best price from CarAddons, or the product is free! Live help is available six days a week via a toll-free phone number. Ground shipping within the continental U.S. is free. Have a truck? Buy truck accessories at the sister Web site: truckaddons.com.

carbuyingusa.com
CarBuyingUSA

No phone number listed
service@carbuyingusa.net

Automobile Broker

CarBuyingUSA helps consumers buy and lease cars without the hassle of negotiating with car salespeople. Simply call or e-mail the company to receive a free estimate. After discussing your options with the company representative, you can decide whether to begin the search for your new car using the CarBuyingUSA service. After you agree to use its service, a 2 percent fee applies to the invoice price of the car, but the site guarantees to get you a low price on your new vehicle, including that advisory fee. (Fees for used cars are 2 percent of wholesale or $250, whichever is greater.)

carcontracts.net
CarContracts.Net

801-475-6420
support@carcontracts.net

Automobile Broker

Selling your own car can be a hassle, especially if the person you sell it to has "buyer's remorse" and tries to get out of the deal. CarContracts.net sells vehicle purchase agreements and bills of sale for nominal fees. These contracts offer legal protection for the buyer and seller, including warranty provisions, a defects disclosure, as well as funding and arbitration provisions. Simply input the details of your contract, pay by credit card, and print the contract. Both parties sign the form to make it legal, and you can breathe a sigh of relief.

carsdirect.com
Cars Direct

800-431-2500
advisor@carsdirect.com

Automobile Broker

As "America's #1 way to buy cars online," the Cars Direct site has been rated number one by *Forbes, Time, PC Magazine,* and Yahoo! Internet Life. The site is loaded with all the new car specials you see advertised elsewhere by the dealers themselves. Cars Direct helps new car buyers by negotiating a good price with a local dealer, from whom you will then purchase the vehicle. It helps used car buyers by offering printable lists of vehicles meeting your specifications, with dealer contact information. You can also research cars, sell your car, finance a car, and get trade-in quotes.

 Recommended   Price   Selection   Convenience   Service   Security

creditsoup.com
CreditSoup.com

No phone number listed
E-mail form on site

Auto Financing

CreditSoup.com connects auto lenders and borrowers. The CreditSoup.com procedure is simple, easy, and fast. Start by providing a few personal details, such as your name, zip code, and e-mail address. For privacy purposes, you'll need to enter a personal password. Next, you'll be asked to complete a short questionnaire about your financing needs and preferences. (Don't worry, the site is secure.) CreditSoup.com will use the information you provide to identify the lenders that match your needs. Depending on the lender, you can fill out an online credit application or ask to be contacted personally.

★ custom-wheels-car-rims.com
Custom Wheels and Car Rims

800-901-6601
sales@custom-wheels-car-rims.com

Auto Parts

The highly polished (no pun intended) Custom Wheels and Car Rims site sells custom wheels and car rims for almost any vehicle made today. Packages are available that ship with four custom wheels and four tires, fully mounted and balanced. Search by vehicle type for what works with your car, or select the specific type of wheel or rim you're looking for. With a Low Price Guarantee, great warranties, quality customer service, and free shipping (within the continental United States) to boot, it's no wonder this company has garnered such respect from customers.

cycleies.com
International Ecological Systems, LTD

866-742-6274
info@cycleies.com

Bicycles

Plug into the latest trend with an electric bicycle from the International Ecological Systems site. Why not? Electric bikes are fun to ride, easy to operate, and provide hours of riding pleasure. If you're using your bicycle for transportation, an electric bike makes good sense. You can use the bike with the battery-powered motor, on pedal power, or with a combination of both methods. Electric bikes are easily charged, don't make noise, and are ecologically friendly. You don't need a special license, permit, or insurance to ride an electric bike. However, riders must be 18 years of age or older.

discountrvparts.com
Discount RV Parts

866-721-5048
customerservice@discountrvparts.com

RV Accessories

Discount RV Parts stocks parts, supplies, and accessories for your motor home, travel trailer, fifth-wheel, or pop-up camper. All parts — from hubcaps and generators to awnings and hitches — are shipped to your location. Search the catalog by part, category, or page number to display a page from the site's companion printed catalog. To buy a product online, locate the product's blue part number and enter it in the Price Check box before clicking GO. Want to rent a motorhome? A link to a companion site is available at the Discount RV Parts home page.

⭐ dyersonline.com
Dyers RV

866-713-3429
customerservice@dyersonline.com

Motorcycle Accessories • RV Accessories

Dyers Trailer Sales, in Rochester Hills, Michigan, offers "big company convenience" with "small business product knowledge." The online catalog offers everything from plumbing and sanitation to covers, hitches, and tie downs. Motorcycle and snowmobile products are also available. An advanced search tool makes it easy to locate just what you're looking for. Or, if you know the product code, click the Quick Order link to add it to your cart. Weekly Web specials highlight hot products at great prices. You can even sign up to have the weekly specials list e-mailed directly to you.

fancyscooter.com
FancyScooter.com

888-910-8999
info@fancyscooter.com

Bicycles • Scooters

FancyScooter.com imports scooters directly from China. You'll also find mopeds, mini-motorcycles, dirt bikes, ATVs, and electric bikes. Prices at this site are low, because FancyScooter.com handles all the importing and cuts out the middleman. The scooters sold at the fancyscooter.com are legal for street riding in most states, although you should check with local authorities. The scooters are designed to reach maximum speeds of 30 to 40 miles per hour, making them a great way to get around town. Online scooter manuals offer valuable assistance to new owners.

 Recommended   Price   Selection   Convenience   Service   Security

⭐ gearlink.com
GearLink
727-447-4007
E-mail form on site
Apparel • Bicycles

The array of merchandise and training aids at GearLink's online store is astounding. You can purchase a complete road, mountain, or triathalon bike, or buy the frame. Dream Cross Bike Frames are available, as are car and bike racks, helmets, saddles, pedals, and other components. Visitors can peruse a complete line of clothing and shoes for men and women. If you can't train outdoors, consider a virtual reality trainer. The device is designed to simulate road conditions and will give you a great workout from the comfort of home.

helmetshop.com
The Helmet Shop
800-630-6434
info@helmetshop.com
Motorcycles

The Helmet Shop sells not only helmets — in all shapes, colors, and sizes — but also bike accessories like covers, bags, and gloves on the Internet and in its Daytona Beach (Florida) retail store. The company boasts it is "the original discounted helmet and accessory store with unbeatable prices." The store's Wish Lists are useful for creating gift suggestions to share with friends and family. Sizing charts are available to aid in online ordering. Frequent customers can benefit from signing up for a free, secure shopping account with this store to save shopping information and aid in speedy checkout.

hiwheel.com
Rideable Bicycle Replicas
510-769-0980
info@hiwheel.com
Bicycles

The cycles from Rideable Bicycle Replicas won't get you to the finish line first, but they will get you a lot of attention. In fact, be prepared for people to wave and smile as you pass by. Rideable Bicycle Replicas manufactures spoked, big-wheeled cycles, using materials and techniques that are virtually the same as those used in the late nineteenth century when these cycles were popular. The high wheelers, also known as Penny Farthings, provide maximum strength while keeping the original antique look. You'll also find reproductions of three-seat courting cycles and some rickshaws.

instantcarloan.com
Instant Car Loan
No phone number listed
E-mail form on site
Auto Financing

1-800 Communications, Inc. uses its Instant Car Loan site to help customers with credit problems find loans for new and used cars. The "one-minute" application is free and doesn't obligate you to receive financing through the site. After completion of the application, an auto loan expert will review your credit history and then contact you to discuss your options. With no obligation and no fees, anyone struggling to find financing has little to lose from checking out this site.

jacmacscooters.com
JacMac Scooters
904-260-7553
jac@jacmacscooters.com
Scooters

Jacmac Scooters is a real scooter shop located in Jacksonville, Florida. Jac, the owner, makes sure each Internet customer gets a high level of service. "When you order from me, I will hold your hand for as long as you need me to," says Jac. The site is like a kid's dream come true, with karts, scooters, and racers from Tanaka, BladeZ, and other manufacturers. Need an engine? You can order one from this site. A number of Tanaka owner's manuals are available as well; these are must-haves if you're planning to upgrade or customize your current equipment.

lambertenterprises.8k.com
Lambert Enterprises, Inc.
919-402-0900
keepit11@aol.com
RV Accessories

Lambert Enterprises's Keep-It-Up Battery Maintainers, patented in the U.S. and Canada, are used to keep your motorhome's engine fully charged. Since 1996, the devices come standard on all motorhomes built by Monaco. For owners of older rigs, Lambert offers the battery maintainers direct-to-consumer through its site. Color-coded wires have been pre-attached to make installation easier. Originally created for Monaco motorhomes, the devices are also being used on some models by other manufacturers. No-hassle ordering is available by calling the company at its North Carolina offices. All products are shipped by UPS next-day.

 Recommended   Price   Selection   Convenience   Service   Security

myautomatch.com
Auto-Match, Inc.

888-827-4610
sales@myautomatch.com

Automobile Broker

Auto-Match, Inc. is different from a traditional car dealer because the company stocks only the cars requested by consumers. To get started, complete its Vehicle Specification and Authorization (VSA) form to have a customer service representative begin looking for your vehicle. After it's been located, you're alerted by telephone and offered the best price possible. At this point, all contact between you and the dealer is made in person or over the phone. You can either pick up the vehicle in Auto-Match's Colorado or Florida locations, or have it delivered to a dealer near you.

nashbar.com
Bike Nashbar.com

800-888-2710
custserv@nashbar.com

Bicycles

If you're a hardcore cycling enthusiast, racer, or competitive athlete, the Bike Nashbar.com site is for you. Although you can't buy a bicycle at this site, you can buy everything you need to put one together or just replace the parts on your old two-wheeled friend. Choose from a wide selection of mountain bike forks, stems, and seatposts, as well as helmets of just about any size, shape, and color. Bike Nashbar.com also sells cycling shorts, jerseys, and dozens of accessories. For the ambitious cyclist, bicycle frames are also available so you can assemble your own custom ride.

nationalcycle.com
National Cycle, Inc.

877-972-7336
info@nationalcycle.com

Motorcycle Accessories

Since 1937, National Cycle has been a top quality retailer of bike accessories, providing everything from windshields and spotlight bars to hand deflectors and saddlebags. Select your bike type and see what products are available before you order. Need tech support? Call, e-mail, or fax in your question for assistance. National Cycle shows off its products at many local bike shows. See the calendar of events at the site to determine when company reps will be in a city near you. National Cycle is not limited to sell only in the United States; it has lists of distributors throughout the world.

newcarslowestprice.com
NewCarsLowestPrice.com

800-432-1327
call8004321car@msn.com

Automobile Broker

NewCarsLowestPrice.com boasts that it offers the world's only Money-Back Guaranteed Lowest Price for consumers looking to buy or lease a new car or truck. Here's how it works: You pay a flat fee for the site's service and specify the vehicle you're looking for. The site's professional vehicle buyers locate your car and notify you of its price. If you agree to the price and buy the vehicle, it is delivered to a dealer for your inspection and pick up. If they are unable to find you the car you want at the price you want, your money is refunded. Everybody wins!

not-just-parts.com
NotJustParts!

478-956-5535
sales@not-just-parts.com

RV Accessories

The NotJustParts! site offers (as the name implies) not just parts, but also custom accessories for your truck, motor home, RV, camper, or utility trailer. You can search the online catalog by manufacturer, part number, or keyword. If you can't find what you're looking for, just request it! A customer service representative will be in touch to help you locate the part in question, and a money-back guarantee makes sure you're satisfied. A list of helpful how-to's includes tips on hitching up your trailer, trailering tactics, and a safety checklist. Free classifieds are also available right from the site's home page.

⭐ pepboys.com
Pepboys.com

215-430-9000
E-mail form on site

Auto Parts

Manny, Moe, and Jack were three of the original Pep Boys back in 1921, and the company is still going strong in locations all across the country and at Pepboys.com. The Web site contains an online catalog of the store's accessories, tires, and wheels. You can search by brand, keyword, part number, or by vehicle type. You can purchase additional products in any of the Pep Boys stores. (Click the Find a Pep Boys link to locate a store near you.) Free ground shipping is available on all orders shipped within the continental United States.

 Recommended   Price   Selection   Convenience   Service Security

⭐ rainkap.com
RainKap Ltd.
888-758-6066
info@rainkap.com
RV Accessories

RainKap Ltd. helps RV owners alleviate a common problem — black streaks on RV siding — by "routing dirty rooftop water away from RV siding and window mounts." The product, called RainKap, is available in four lengths, which are cut to fit a particular RV and easily installed in place of an RV's existing trim molding. A free sample is available, and a 90-day money-back guarantee ensures customer satisfaction. RainKap is an amazing device. The streaks are a dirty job, and RainKap is there to eliminate them.

roadloans.com
RoadLoans
888-276-7202
loanhelp@roadloans.com
Auto Financing

RoadLoans specializes in financing and servicing new and used vehicle loans for customers with less-than-perfect credit. Actually the Internet direct-lending division of Triad Financial Corporation, RoadLoans has helped thousands of consumers get into the car or truck of their dreams since its launch in June 2000. You can obtain financing from RoadLoans for new or used vehicles purchased from a franchised dealer, or to refinance your current auto loan. Visit the site to fill out the online loan application, or use the Payment Calculator to figure out what you can afford.

sidewalkerusa.com
SidewalkerUSA
626-618-0237
info@sidewalkerusa.com
Scooters

Is it a scooter with a big seat? Is it a bike that looks like a scooter? You'll be asking yourself these questions when you see what's for sale at the SidewalkerUSA site. No matter what you decide, you'll agree that these hybrid bicycle-scooters are amazing. The hybrids offer some great advantages: Riders don't experience seat pain, and the upright position is easy on the spine. The scooters go anywhere a bicycle can go. Bicycle-scooters are durable and have proven themselves under tough riding conditions. They also look way cool.

sunnyparkrv.com
XTREME VENT

888-877-8360
customerservice@xtremevent.com

RV Accessories

SunnyparkRV is another company seeking to alleviate the woes of RV owners. In this case, the problem is that stinky holding tank odor. The solution? An XTREME VENT. SunnyparkRV's product replaces your existing holding tank vent cap and directs the air flow to the outside of the vehicle — away from your nose. The XTREME VENT is available in white, gold, or graphite and is suitable for motor homes, fifth wheels, travel trailers, campers and boats, or anywhere a water holding tank is used. Installation is fast and easy; in fact, the simple instructions appear online. XTREME VENT comes with a lifetime warranty.

superduperscooters.com
SuperDuperScooters.com

800-686-3886
E-mail form on site

Scooters

SuperDuperScooters.com is, well, superduper! There's not a lot of flash or glitz. Visitors find no exploding scooters or cranking audio, just solid products and good value. The site's free shipping offer is a great money saver. Shop here for electric, gas, and kick scooters from manufacturers like Rad2Go, Razor, and BladeZ. Great product descriptions tell you exactly what you're getting. Don't miss the companion sites: SuperDuperHoops.com and SuperDuperGames.com for similar good deals.

tirerack.com
The Tire Rack

888-541-1777
custsvc@tirerack.com

Auto Parts

The Tire Rack started as a retail store in 1979 in Indiana, where the company quickly earned a reputation for award-winning customer satisfaction and warranty support. Its site was created in 1996 to give customers a place to research products and buy tires, wheels, suspension products, and brakes online. The Upgrade Garage section enables you to plug in your specific vehicle's information and see all the products available for customizing it. You can even save the information by personalizing the site with a free Tire Rack account. Gift certificates are also available.

topendmotorsports.com
TOP END Motor Sports
203-467-9774
topendms@aol.com
Apparel • Auto Parts

TOP END Motor Sports sells parts for your car's engine, exterior and interior, as well as parts for your brakes and suspension. Additional promotional products are available, and include clothing, magazines, video games, and even computer desktop wallpapers, all for the car enthusiast. Members of this site can subscribe to an online newsletter, participate in discussions about cars and racing, receive technical support, and even post classified ads. (You don't have to be a member to view the ads.) Membership is free. Live support is available through AOL Instant Messenger.

unicycleclub.com
Unicycle Club
336-998-3579
patty@unicycleclub.com
Bicycles

Admittedly, most folks don't own a unicycle and don't have plans to buy one. However, according to information found at this site, unicycling is a great way for children to build coordination and confidence. The Unicycle Club can help you start a unicycle club in your child's school and fix you up with one of the of the quirky devices. Prices are low — generally under $100 — and unicycling looks like a blast for kids of all ages. You'll also find several instructional videos to help you get started.

velosophy.com
Velosophy
866-218-2453
info@velosophy.com
Apparel • Bicycles

Velosophy operates a bike shop in Cooperstown, New York. This company's obvious love for cycling is apparent on this classy site, where you'll find a great selection of bicycles. Shop for cycles from Kona, Jamis, and Cannondale. You'll also find bike components, accessories, tools, and parts. The stock is so complete that you can find a wheelset for your Titanium steed, a new seat for your mountain bike, or a brand-new bike to add to your collection. Clothing from Cannondale and Louis Garneau will make you look like a pro! Need new cycling shoes? Buy them at this site, and score free socks with every pair.

virtualbank.com
VirtualBank
877-998-2265
info@virtualbank.com

Auto Financing

Need a car loan? VirtualBank's revolutionary approach to banking makes applying easy. Log in to the Virtual Bank Lending Center and choose Auto. Then use the convenient pull-down menus to pick your Product (new or used car), Term (number of months), and the amount of money you want to borrow. Indicate the U.S. state and whether the application is filed individually or jointly. Now review your choices and click Calculate. You'll be forwarded to the ePartner Network and asked to complete an application. After approval you'll be contacted by an auto loan expert to review your approval terms.

whaccessories.com
Wild Hair Accessories
623-581-1994
info@whaccessories.com

Motorcycle Accessories

Wild Hair Accessories offers products for sportbikes and Streetfighters. Its site is a good source of information about the current trends in Europe. (A portion of the site is in German.) Learn about the new Streetfighter craze and how it is taking Europe by storm. The Streetfighter, or Fighter for short, is a drastically changed motorcycle with a powerful engine. Wild Hair Accessories is the only source in the United States for TÜV approved items from respected German manufacturers. Shipment is available worldwide, with rates varying according to the size of the item and the location to which it's being shipped.

★ womanbiker.com
WomanBiker.com
877-962-4537
info@womanbiker.com

Apparel • Motorcycle Accessories

This New Hampshire company seeks to find the most exciting bikewear for women from across the globe. The clothes offered by WomanBiker.com are designed for function and style. Custom sizes are available; this company understands that real women don't always fit into tiny molds. The site's extras make shopping for bikewear fun and easy. For example, the Wind Chill Chart will tell you how cold you'll feel on a motorcycle at varying degrees. Do you want to order matching outfits with your husband or boyfriend? WomanBiker.com carries a full line of his and her clothing.

 Recommended Price Selection Convenience Service 🔒 Security

wrenchscience.com
Wrench Science
866-497-3624
sales@wrenchscience.com

Bicycles

The idea behind Wrench Science's site should be called "virtual bike" because you'll build a customized bicycle online. Using the site's special software, you can put together a frame, fork, and components. The software ensures that the parts you choose will work together. It also keeps a running tally on what you spend, and shows you the total weight of the pieces you've selected. You can save your choices and work on them later, or buy the bicycle you've built when you're done. Need help or want to discuss different options? During business hours, Wrench Science reps are standing by to help.

zscooter.com
Z Scooter.com
626-618-0237
info@zscooter.com

Scooters

A scooter can't be beat for zipping around town. Z Scooter is constructed of high-quality T6 aluminum and is a light, yet sturdy machine. The scooter has a sleek, modern design with a flat, rear fender braking system that means business. Add a lighted wheel, a bell, or inexpensive color grips to your Z Scooter. Don't forget a storage bag to hold your new scooter when it's not in use. Check out the amazing new Z Scooter and view photos of Z Scooter tricks and feats at the site.

Nothing Smells as Good: Buying a New Car Online

Buying a new car online may seem radical to some buyers. However, some sound business reasons exist for considering this new way to purchase an automobile. First and foremost, the price! Online dealers don't need to maintain glitzy showrooms, huge staffs, and other related expense. The savings go directly to you. You save in other ways, too. A site that operates nationally has greater buying power than a small local dealer. The result? More cars ordered equal lower prices, and you get the break.

Your online purchase will be faster, too. You won't need to drive from dealer to dealer, looking for one that sells the car you want. Instead, you can build your car online, adding the options that you want. No smooth-talking salespeople will attempt to convince you to add features that jack up the price (and the commission).

Buying a car online has some downsides. You'll need to pick your car up at a dealership, because regulations prohibit it from being delivered to your door. You'll also need to make the payment and insurance arrangements yourself. Finally, you won't have the opportunity to test-drive your car before you buy it.

Before you begin searching for the car of your dreams, do a little paper work. Figure out how much you can afford to pay. Unless you're planning to pay for the car with cash, the time you spend now can result in thousands of saved dollars later on. Learn your credit score. Sites like Equifax (equifax.com) and 1 Free Credit Report (1-free-credit-report.com) can tell you what your potential lenders will know about you.

Next, consider how you're going to finance the car. Online financing is the way to go. If your credit score is good, consider financing from E-Loan (eloan.com) or Capital One (capitaloneautofinance.com). Credit score not so good? Household Auto (householdauto.com) is a bit more expensive, but also a bit more lenient.

How about insurance? You can't drive without it in most states. Again, a little prep work will save you time and money in the end. Because you're in charge of handling your auto insurance, get a copy of your driving record before you start shopping for coverage. You can get the record from your state, or from your current agent. Progressive (progressive.com), Geico Direct (geico.com), or Electric Insurance (electricinsurance.com) are good starting places to look for insurance on your new vehicle.

After you arrange the money, you're ready to rev up your mouse and start shopping. CarsDirect.com (carsdirect.com) is the best place to buy a car on the Internet. Select your make and model and get your quote. You'll be entitled to all manufacturer's rebates and special sales programs offered by the dealers. Alternatively, visit InvoiceDealers.com (invoicedealers.com) to receive a no-obligation quote from new car dealers in your area. Similar services are offered by AutoWeb (autoweb.com) and Car.com (car.com). Find the car you like and click and order.

When your car arrives, impress your friends and family with your new Web-savvy wheels. A new driving cap from HatsintheBelfry (hatsinthebelfry.com) will make you look like a professional driver. Or go all out and hire a chauffeur for the day. Services like WeDriveU (wedriveu.com) provide fully insured and certified chauffeurs who drive for you in your car. Happy motoring!

Chapter 23

Travel: Getting Away from It All

● ●

Ah! Taking the time to recharge the spirit and enjoy some well-earned rest and relaxation at faraway places and exotic locales, or visiting out-of-town family and friends on special occasions and holidays can be easier than you think. Whether you want to reserve a flight, rent a car or a hotel room, book an exciting cruise, find a tour to exotic places, or buy travel gear for your trip, the online merchants listed in this chapter are your passport to adventure and travel. You'll find online retailers to provide airline, car, and hotel reservations for those on a budget, as well as for those who can go first class. This chapter provides not only listings for accommodations beyond the ordinary hotel room (think vacation rental properties), but also listings of organized tours that expose you to new and out-of-the-ordinary locales that you would normally not think of putting in your travel plans.

But travel is not just planes, trains, and automobiles and where to stay when you get there. You have to address the questions of what to wear and what to bring, and choose the items and products suitable for travel. This chapter lists online merchants for that kind of merchandise, too.

Before you head out on your travel trek, here are some travel resources to help you plan your next trip. The tips4trips.com site provides 1,000 travel tips on a variety of subjects. For travel safety tips and resources, you can visit kevincoffee.com/safety_tips_index.htm. For the official word on safety, the U.S. State Department's travel notices can be found at travel.state.gov. The kids will appreciate the suggestions at fodors.com/familytravel. To find out more about getting domestic travel documents for your pet, go to petsonthego.com/resourcesdomestic.html. For accommodations once you and your pet arrive at your destination, you'll want to visit petfriendlytravel.com. These sites, plus the merchants that follow, will help you truly get away from it all.

Key Word Index

Air Travel

You can find some great deals on airline tickets at the sites with the Air Travel keyword. Search for your time and day, choose a flight, and reserve your ticket — all without ever leaving your home.

Car Rental

After you get to your destination, you'll need a set of wheels. The Car Rental sites can help you rent anything from a subcompact to an RV.

Cruises

Travel listings with the Cruise keyword can guide you to a high seas adventure.

Lodging

Whether you're looking for a budget hotel or an expensive resort, the Lodging sites can make your stay comfortable and pleasant.

Property Rental

If you would rather rent a condo or home when traveling, the Property Rental sites can direct you to available property to use when traveling for business or vacation.

Tours

Travel sites with the Tours keyword offer tours for young and old, and range from the near and familiar to the far ends of the earth.

Travel Gear

The Travel Gear keyword designates merchants that specialize in travel wear that can make your trek more comfortable and economical.

airfareplanet.com
Airfareplanet.com

503-345-0410

sales@airfareplanet.com

Air Travel • Car Rental • Cruises • Lodging

Now you can find discounted international travel with Airfareplanet.com's site. This company offers 500 destinations in 116 countries. Airfareplanet.com also offers one day of free parking at most major airports. (Hey, every little bit helps.) If you choose to go to Europe, consider buying a European rail pass good for 15 days to 3 months, depending on the length of your stay, from this site. Other site features include package vacations; cruise vacations; flight, hotel, and car deals; and even a vacation auction section where you can bid on accommodations all over the world.

airgorilla.com
AirGorilla.com

619-435-2147

help@airgorilla.com

Air Travel • Car Rental • Cruises • Lodging

Do you want to fly one way or round trip, or have the option of flying to multiple cities? AirGorilla.com enables you to choose flights based on how you want to fly, while keeping your fares low. AirGorilla.com can also help with booking your car rental, hotel, cruise, and package vacations at a discounted rate. The site also features Travel Tools that allow you to confirm your flight, buy travel insurance, as well as get the latest travel news.

alamo.com
Alamo

800-462-5266

crelations@alamo.com

Car Rental

Alamo was the first car rental company to offer unlimited free mileage. Thank you, Alamo!! It was also the first to focus on the leisure traveler, offering affordable travel deals to those of us who do take a break on occasion. Alamo's philosophy is "providing a fun, low-cost, high-value rental experience." The site features tools that allow you to book your rental, check the weather at your destination, and even get driving directions. The site also runs exclusive Internet deals. Because it's now the official car rental company for Disney, you can even order your Disney tickets in advance via a phone number on Alamo's site.

allcruiseauction.com
All Cruise Auction

No phone number listed
allcruiseauction@allcruiseauction.com

Cruises

Have you always wanted to take a cruise but figured that you would never be able to afford it? Well now you can, because at All Cruise Auction you can bid on cruises from all the major cruise lines. It's just like bidding on eBay or uBid. You make a bid, and watch to see whether someone outbids you. When the auction ends, the top bidder gets the cruise. The nice thing about using this site is that the price you pay includes port charges, taxes, and government fees. If you have a cruise package that you cannot use, you can also use All Cruise Auction to find a buyer with its Reverse Auction option. The site also features a Top Ten Cruise Auctions list, an FAQ section, and a discussion board where you can talk with other "cruisers" about the various cruises and cruise lines.

avis.com
Avis

800-230-4898
E-mail form on site

Car Rental

Avis is the second largest car rental agency in the United States. The company is dedicated to service, as indicated by its "We Try Harder" slogan. Avis was the first car rental agency to be located at the airport to be more convenient to the travelers. Although business travelers make up a significant portion of its customer base, the company offers specials to leisure travelers, too. The site features many specials as well as tools that let you make your reservation, check the weather and maps of your destination, and view Avis's partner sites in the hotel, airline, and other industries. You can also enroll in the My Avis program to receive special deals and other bonuses.

★ bestfares.com
Bestfares.com
800-880-1234
E-mail form on site
Air Travel

Bestfares.com helps you find the lowest published airfares online. You can choose from Internet-only fares, snooze-you-lose fares, senior specials, and last-minute deals, among other categories. You can even have hot deals e-mailed to you. Become a member of bestfares.com and receive members-only fares that are discounted even more, as well as discounts on car rentals, accommodations, and cruises. After you book your reservations, use the site's resources links, which feature various handy travel tools, such as a money exchange tool (if you're traveling out of country) to figure out how much money to take. The site also offers many informative articles on travel in general.

budget.com
Budget
800-527-0700
E-mail form on site
Car Rental

Do you like to drive new cars, especially luxury cars or SUVs? Then Budget's site is the right place for you to check out car rentals. The age of 90 percent of the cars on any Budget Car rental lot is less than nine months old. Periodically, Budget sells its "old" fleet to keep the fleet fresh. Over one-third of Budget's fleet is specialty and luxury vehicles. If you want to travel in style, check Budget's site to find just the vehicle you want, and then make your reservation online. Be sure to click the Specials link to find ways to save, and sign up for the e-mail service to be first to find out about future specials. If you're a frequent traveler, check out the programs described on the site for even more benefits.

christinecolumbus.com
Christine Columbus
800-280-4775
annette@christinecolumbus

Travel Gear

Annette, a seasoned traveler, discovered long ago that no matter how well she thought she had planned, she always came across an unforeseen problem. She began to make notes of the things that were forgotten, or lessons she had learned. Over time, she put her knowledge and that of others together to create the Christine Columbus Web site. The site is geared toward women travelers, but men will benefit from the site's travel tips, as well. The philosophy of Christine Columbus is, "The better prepared you are, the better time you will have, regardless of what occurs." Christine Columbus has tips on traveling, printable checklists, and a catalog of travel-related gear for women travelers. Find items such as backseat entertainment organizers, inflatable back pillows, lightweight luggage, and collapsible travel cups, among other things. The site also offers gift certificates, perfect for the woman on the go.

cruise.com
Cruise.com
888-333-3116
No e-mail address on site

Cruises

Have you ever wanted to take a cruise on "The Love Boat"? Through Cruise.com, you can have that chance. Maybe not the Princess Cruise line as in the show, but you can find a specialized cruise; for example, cruise themes include those for expectant mothers, kids, luxury, singles, special needs, and weddings. Which category do you fit in? This site can help you find the right cruise for the right price. Just search by cruise line, destination, and month, and input the number of days you want, and the cruises matching your criteria are shown to you. You can book your reservation, if desired, from any of the choices. The site also has a list of travel suppliers, cruise reviews and guides, and cruise menus.

★ Recommended   Price   Selection   Convenience   Service   🔒 Security

cruisedirectonline.com
Cruise Direct Online

800-365-1445
No e-mail address on site

Cruises

Cruise Direct Online prides itself on giving you, the customer, "total service." Cruise Direct Online even has a 5 to 10 percent additional discount on already competitive rates for cruises both close to home and far away. The site is quite comprehensive, so expect to spend a good amount of time browsing around. You can shop and compare the cruises with the online cruise ship ratings and cruise reviews. If you need more help deciding on a cruise, the site offers a Personal Cruise Travel Advisor, who will contact you at your convenience. You also can get the free newsletter called "Last Minute Details." Who couldn't use information like that before a trip out to sea?

⭐ discounthotels.com
Hotel Discounts & Discount Hotels

866-294-8886
support@discounthotels.com

Lodging

Would you like to save 70 percent on your hotel reservation? Of course you would! Discounthotels.com has negotiated rates with savings up to 70 percent off with many national chain discount hotels. Just scroll down to the bottom of the home page and choose a state or city for a list of hotels. The next time you want to get a room in a discount hotel and the hotel chain tells you it's sold out, check out discounthotels.com. Sometimes this company can book a room for you that appeared to the hotel as being sold out. Remember the saying, "It's not what you know, but who you know." That could very well be true with discounthotels.com. Check out the FAQ page to find out more about the process.

dollar.com
Dollar Rent A Car

800-800-3665
E-mail form on site

Car Rental

Dollar Rent A Car could be known as just another car rental agency, but it distinguishes itself from the others with its commitment to "exceptional customer service." You can get a rate quote, or make your car rental reservation online. After you make a reservation, you can view, modify, or cancel it at anytime, right on the site. Dollar.com also offers Travel Tools on its Web site, including a vacation weather finder, so you can pack accordingly for your destination; travel maps so you don't get lost; a list of great drives for frequent renters; and e-bags luggage so you can have the exact luggage you need. You can even make air and hotel reservations from Dollar's site so you don't have to go to another Web site to make reservations. Be sure to check out the online specials for great savings before you book.

enterprise.com
Enterprise Rent A Car

800-261-7331
E-mail form on site

Car Rental

The philosophy of Enterprise is "to provide customers with exceptional service, give employees respect and ample career opportunities." Through the years that is exactly what it has done to become the largest car rental company. Years ago Enterprise decided that its market niche was the hometown renters rather than the airport travelers. It even developed the trademark of "We'll pick you up," to demonstrate its commitment to its customers. This company will pick you up from work or home, take you to the rental lot, then take you back home or to work after you return the car. View the cars available online, and then make your reservation. If you're in the market for a used car, check out the former rentals for sale in your area — just type in your zip code to view a list of vehicles.

 Recommended $ Price   Selection   Convenience   Service   Security

⭐ expedia.com
Expedia, Inc.
800-397-3342
E-mail form on site

Air Travel • Car Rental • Cruises • Lodging

Expedia is the fourth largest travel agency in the U.S. It also is one of the leading online travel services. Not only can you make reservations for airlines, cars, hotels, and cruises, but you also can get travel alerts. The site offers maps and information about your destination, and also offers packages that let you order "trip extras" such as theater tickets or theme park passes. Expedia.com also offers a direct link to passport information for those of you traveling abroad.

geoportals.com
Geoportals.com
No phone number listed
nnarine@geoportals.com

Air Travel • Cruises • Lodging • Tours

Geoportals.com is a unique travel resource. This site is a collection of sites organized so that you can find information quickly and easily. Through the categories on this site, you can search the Internet for the best deals and even be routed to a rival site if it has the better deal. Search for bargain fares; frequent flyer and business travel programs; budget vacations; golf, outdoor, or ski trips; cruises; adventure or cultural events; and bargain accommodations. Have you ever wanted to do a volunteer project while you were on vacation? Now you can. Geoportals can find the right situation for you.

hertz.com
Hertz
800-654-3131
E-mail form on site

Car Rental

Hertz has done a lot of firsts in the car rental industry. It was the first to have in-car cell phones, on-board navigation systems, and a multilingual site to name a few. Hertz not only rents cars for business and leisure travelers, it has expanded its business to include equipment rental to construction and industrial companies, to provide third-party liability claims administrators, and to provide rental cars for people whose cars are being repaired. You can view available car types online, and make or change a reservation. Hertz also offers online specials and car rental clubs that offer members exclusive benefits.

hotwire.com

Hotwire.com

866-468-9473
E-mail form on site

Air Travel • Car Rental • Cruises • Lodging

Hotwire.com lives up to its slogan, "Fly. Sleep. Drive. Cheap." You simply enter your travel dates and departure and arrival cities into the appropriate fields. Hotwire searches its inventory to find the lowest rates, at which time you can make your purchase. After completion of the purchase, you then find out which airline (or car rental company, or hotel) you will be using. Save money even on short-notice purchases. Hotwire.com's travel partners allow Hotwire access to unsold inventory which means big savings for you. If you still have doubts, check out the testimonials on the site from satisfied customers.

i4vegas.com

i4vegas.com

800-442-4002
info@i4vegas.com

Lodging

Are you planning a trip to Las Vegas anytime soon? Do you know where you want to stay? Check out i4vegas.com to get seasonal specials. Every hotel in Las Vegas is featured on this site, from the ritziest, most expensive hotels to the dirt cheap hotels. i4vegas.com gives a full description of the rooms, the restaurants, and the added value bonuses for the hotel. Just enter your check-in and check-out dates, the number of rooms, and then sort by name or price to see a list of hotels and their prices. The site also has a strip area map so that you can determine how far a hotel is from the Vegas attractions you want to see.

letravelstore.com

LeTravelStore.com

800-713-4260
gear@letravelstore.com

Travel Gear

If you're an independent international traveler (or would like to be one), LeTravelStore.com can make sure you travel safely, comfortably, and securely by offering a wide selection of travel gear and accessories. This site has all the packing devices you will need from luggage to backpacks, and briefcases to shoulder totes. Take a look at the selection of organizers, travel guides, toilet kits, and much more for your travels, whether near or far from home. Be prepared for your trip in the finest style.

 Recommended   Price   Selection   Convenience   Service   Security

⭐ **luxurylink.com**
Luxury Link Traveler
888-297-3299
help@luxurylink.com

Cruises • Lodging • Tours

Do you have an unlimited amount of money that you do not mind spending on a luxury vacation? Have you ever wanted to take a vacation like those shown on "The Lifestyles of the Rich and Famous"? Then luxurylink.com is for you. This company prides itself on being the "premier luxury travel resource." It specializes in gourmet escapes, intimate hideaways, spa and golf outings, active and adventure trips, and even family vacations. You also can pull up the tour calendar to see what is going on when and where and make your plans accordingly.

⭐ **magellans.com**
Magellan's
800-962-4943
E-mail form on site

Travel Gear

Magellan's has a philosophy that you should get "superior products *and* world class service." This philosophy is reflected at its site, which offers travel-related gear and accessories, including clothing, health and beauty items, appliances, luggage and packing organizers, and wallets and money belts. Do you see items you want but need to wait to buy them? Create a wish list on the site, and the next time you visit the site you won't have to search for the items. Magellan's also offers travel tips, packing tips, and "Good Information to Know" when you're traveling.

miles4sale.com
Miles4Sale.com
866-630-8717
E-mail form on site

Air Travel

Do you need just a few more frequent flyer miles to be able to fly free on your next vacation? Do you want to give the gift of travel to someone you love? You can at Miles4Sale.com, without having to spend time in the air on flights. At this site, you can buy miles for yourself or as a gift. You can buy miles for America West, American Airlines, or Delta. The miles are available in 500 mile increments, up to 50,000 (sometimes more, depending on the airline), and you can use the miles any way you want (upgrade, free tickets, and so on).

nationalcar.com
National
800-227-7368
E-mail form on site
Car Rental

National's colors are green and white. Thus, it has the Emerald Club for frequent car renters and the Emerald Aisle for priority service. The Emerald Reserve Service allows you to rent any car other than an intermediate car and have it waiting for you on the Emerald Aisle when you arrive. The QuickRent service allows you to bypass the counter and go straight to the car class you reserved. Even if you don't belong to National's clubs, you can still reserve a car online, or change or cancel a reservation. Internet specials are a regular feature, and you can also sign up for exclusive e-mail offers.

★ orbitz.com
Orbitz.com
888-656-4546
E-mail form on site
Air Travel • Car Rental • Cruise • Lodging

Orbitz.com offers more than just online travel services for airline tickets, car rental, and cruise and hotel reservations. It has a section dedicated to Travel Watch, which keeps customers informed of weather, travel conditions, and other travel-related issues in real time. At the site, you can check out airport guides, airline guides, city guides, overseas travel, and currency. Each of these areas can be helpful when you're trying to plan either a business or leisure trip. Orbitz.com also has a section dedicated to News and Features. In this area you can find the latest travel news and flying forecasts, and travel tips. Registered Orbitz members receive even more benefits.

passports.com
Passports
800-332-7277
info@passports.com
Tours

Are you a teacher who wants to take high school or college students on a trip abroad? Are you a student who wants to go abroad? Passports is known as "America's favorite student travel company." The people at Passports.com set up trips for teachers and students to any number of destinations for varying lengths of time. Choose one of the pre-planned itineraries, or create a custom one with Passport's help. Teachers can earn free trips, cash stipends, and cash bonuses, among other things. See the site for details.

 Recommended   Price   Selection   Convenience   Service   Security

placestostay.com
CnG Travel Group

866-224-9765
custserv@placestostay.com

Lodging

Placestostay.com is dedicated to finding you distinctive lodging for your leisure travel. Choose from bed and breakfasts, inns, and resorts, including smaller, independently owned properties off the beaten path. Do you have an idea of where you want to go, but don't have a definite place you want to stay? Use the geographic search tool on this site to help you decide where to go. All hotel prices are in the local currency so that you know how much money to take along. Check out the discounted section for great deals.

★ points.com
Points.com

866-340-3717
E-mail form on site

Air Travel

Become a member of Points.com and you can register all your frequent flyer miles and points from your favorite loyalty programs, such as eBay Anything Points, Nesteggz, and American Airlines. Then, for a nominal fee, you can transfer the points between carriers to use any time you want. Register for the Points*plus* Membership and get Auto-Exchange benefits. This service automatically transfers your points between accounts either monthly or quarterly depending on how you set it up. If you're extremely busy and want to save money, this is the way to go. All you pay is the low-cost membership fee.

★ priceline.com
Priceline.com

800-774-2354
E-mail form on site

Air Travel • Lodging

Priceline.com has changed its format. It is still a low price leader in Internet airfares. However, now you can choose your airline. No more of the mystery of whether you will get a ticket on an airline that you would prefer not to be on. You still can name your price as you did before. Priceline.com also offers name-your-price deals on car rentals, hotels, cruises, and vacation packages. Be sure to read Priceline's city guides online, and sign up for e-mail specials and alerts. You can even see William Shatner's latest Priceline.com commercial on the site.

resortsandlodges.com
Resortsandlodges.com

651-578-0307
custserv@resortsandlodges.com

Lodging

Where do you want to go for your vacation? What do you want to do when you get there? These are important questions to answer before booking reservations anywhere. No matter what your preference and/or budget, Resortsandlodges.com can help. This company can help you set up a ski weekend, a family vacation, or a romantic getaway just about anywhere worldwide. You can browse the site by location, activity, or property type. The options are extensive. The site offers top locations and top categories of interest if you need help deciding on a destination.

sidestep.com
Side Step

408-235-1700
E-mail form on site

Air Travel • Lodging

Sidestep.com is a travel search engine. You enter the information about your trip — the dates, times, departure city, and arrival city — into the appropriate fields. The search engine uses your criteria to search dozens of sites (airfare, rental car, and hotel) for the best deals and compares the rates side by side. When you're ready to buy the airline tickets or make the hotel reservations, you go directly to the seller's Web site to make the transaction.

smarterliving.com
Smarter Living

617-886-5555
feedback@smarterliving.com

Air Travel • Car Rental • Cruises • Lodging

Are you getting ready for a really big adventure, but don't know where to start? Try getting the travel information or advice you need by checking out smarterliving.com. Smarter Living does not sell tickets. However, it does "give independent, objective advice on how to make the best travel decisions." If you become a member of Smarter Living, you can receive additional discounts from the top travel companies that this company works with. Membership is free; you receive a weekly e-mail newsletter as part of your membership. The site is updated daily with the latest discounts and specials.

 Recommended   Price   Selection   Convenience Service Security

studentuniverse.com
Student Universe
800-272-9676
E-mail form on site
Air Travel • Lodging • Tours

Do you have a child away at school? Are you a student away from home? Then use studentuniverse.com to help you travel at great savings. Studentuniverse. com has special rates for students only. Everybody knows college students usually don't have much money. Their parents usually don't have much more if they are paying for the school. This site keeps this in mind and offers affordable airfare. Student Universe also sets up trips abroad for groups of students. Students wanting to travel Europe on the cheap can purchase rail passes on this site, and book a bed in a hostel. The site also offers travel guides, online tools, and travel insurance.

travelgearoutlet.com
TravelGearOutlet.com
877-700-2362
info@travelgearoutlet.com
Travel Gear

TravelGearOutlet.com is the closeout division of LeTravelStore.com. If you need a good quality suitcase, daypack, wallet, pouch, toiletry kit, packing folders or cubes, all at affordable prices, then check out this site. TravelGearOutlet.com offers discounts on closeouts and discontinued products, styles, and colors. So save a few bucks now on the packing devices, so you have more money to spend when you get to your destination.

travelocity.com
travelocity.com
888-709-5983
E-mail form on line
Air Travel • Car Rental • Cruises • Lodging • Tours

Whether you're a seasoned traveler or a first-timer, Travelocity.com can help you plan your trip. You can make flight reservations, car rental reservations, hotel reservations, and get a guide to your destination city, all on this site. If you use the TotalTrip service, you get special rates when you book your hotel and flight together. Also, you can get great advice and other guides to help you plan your trip. Sign up for the e-mail newsletter so you can track fares to your favorite vacation spots, and find out about and take advantage of great last-minute deals. The site offers an extensive FAQ section to answer all your questions.

traveltools.com
Travel Tools

317-876-5594
cservice@traveltools.com

Travel Gear

Are you a business traveler, or do you know one? You know how hard it is to pack just for the trip, but what about the work you have to take with you? How do you keep it organized during your trip? Travel Tools has the solution. This company offers briefcases, travel electronics, rolling tie cases, and auto office accessories, to name just a few items to help you business travel successfully. If you like to mix business with pleasure, or need to entertain a business prospect, check out the convenient travel case for your golf clubs. The site offers men's and women's gifts, and lists the top site sellers if you need help deciding on a product.

travelweb.com
TravelWeb.com

866-437-8132
E-mail form on site

Lodging

Do you know where you're going to stay when you reach your destination? Do you know anything about the hotel? Take the mystery out of searching for a hotel on the Web by checking out Travelweb.com. This site claims to have the largest network of discounted hotels to choose from, and gives a detailed description of each. Travelweb.com is a quick and easy method of finding and reserving a room in a quality hotel at a price you can afford. You can also book your air or car reservations through its affiliates via links from this site.

tripreservations.com
Prestige Travel, Inc.

800-255-0372
No e-mail address on site

Lodging • Tours

Tripreservations.com can help you plan a trip to one or more of the gambling cities of Nevada (Las Vegas, Mesquite, Laughlin, or Reno/Lake Tahoe). You can search for hotel accommodations, shows, golf, and tour information for any of the hotels in the area. Prices are guaranteed to be the lowest available published rate. This company is an American Express Travel Services Representative, so you can make your reservation with confidence. Now get ready to play those slots!

 Recommended   Price   Selection   Convenience   Service   Security

walkabouttravelgear.com
Walk About Travel Gear

800-852-7085
sales@walkabouttravelgear.com

Travel Gear

When you travel, are you on a tight budget? Do you want to do a lot of the sightseeing by yourself with no organized groups? The founders of Walk About Travel Gear are always on a budget and try to economize wherever they can. They have found unique items that come in handy when traveling in parts unknown. Ever thought about the possibility of a fire in your hotel or whether it even has smoke detectors (especially in some of the less-developed travel destinations)? Now you can take along your own portable one. What about the water — is it safe? This site offers portable water purification systems, including a "survival straw." Other useful products include a collapsible travel cup, personal alarm systems, security belts, mini-compasses, bug repellents, and other items for the traveler.

A Shopping Excursion — Family Travel

Have kids? Still travel!

Just because you have a family doesn't mean traveling with the kids — and your pets — has to be a chore. All kinds of resources on the Web can help you pack, plan, reserve, and execute a fulfilling family vacation, but without the headaches.

First, stop in at the Family Travel Forum (familytravelforum.com). For just $3.95 a month, you get access to the latest family travel deals, safety alerts, news of great events and festivals, learning vacations, and seasonal travel opportunities — plus exclusive discounts on family travel vacation packs. If you would rather not pay a monthly fee for information, then travel on over to the Family Travel Network (familytravelnetwork.com). It's the nation's oldest and largest free online site devoted exclusively to family vacations. The Family Travel Network is an online magazine and Web site that provides family travel information, tips, and resources to parents, grandparents, kids, travel professionals, and others.

About Family Travel (about-family-travel. com) specializes in custom-made vacations for families. This company even provides self-catering apartments for families so you can have that home away from home. GORP Outdoors (gorp.com/gorp/eclectic/family.htm) is both a how-to and where-to for information on taking children hiking, camping, fishing, biking, and wildlife viewing.

The About Guide to Travel with Kids offers the Top 6 Family Resort Destinations (travelwithkids. about.com/cs/familyresorts/tp/ topresortplaces.htm) and the Best Family Beach Vacations (travelwithkids. about.com/cs/familyresorts/l/ blbeachresortAZ.htm) around the world. Also, read about some of the Best Family Vacation Spots (travelwithkids.about.com/cs/ vacationideas/l/bltpvacations.htm).

Don't forget the family pet — your vacation wouldn't be complete without him or her anyway, as many places have now come to recognize.

Pets On the Go (petsonthego.com) lists 30,000 pet-friendly B&Bs, inns, hotels, resorts, and private rentals, open to people who vacation with pets. If you do bring the pet, read the tips on the site for planning for emergencies when traveling with pets.

If you just have a dog, then DogFriendly.com (dogfriendly.com) lists and describes thousands of dog-friendly places throughout the U.S. and Canada, from lodging to outdoor restaurants, parks, beaches, attractions, and more.

With the online resources available to you nowadays, you can plan all the details of your next family vacation before you go, and use the vacation to do what you're supposed to do — relax.

Chapter 24

Zany Fun: A Look at the World Wide Weird

• •

*L*aughter is the best medicine. A few chuckles turn around even the most dreadful day. A shared giggle with a friend keeps you smiling for hours. A good hard laugh makes you feel happy and actually lowers your blood pressure!

Of course, humor is strictly a matter of taste. The standup comedian that has you howling may leave your office colleagues shaking their heads. Of course, that same group probably chortles through a sitcom that you find only mildly amusing. Fortunately, such a wide range of material exists in the world that everyone can find something funny.

We've cast our "net" far and wide through the Web and hauled in some products to make you smile. Some are rib-ticklingly funny, some are unusual and others, well, they're just plain tasteless! The products in this chapter share one common theme however: They're all in good fun!

Visit Pop Goes The Culture (`cultureschlockonline.com`) for a humorous look at the cinema, people, trends, and fads that shape our modern world.

Key Word Index

Around the House

The listings with the Around the House keyword offer products for your home that although useful, are not your run-of-the-mill decor. However, you may be surprised at what may strike your fancy.

Funny Money

Sites that sell pads of million-dollar bills and other non-legal tender are the highlight of sites with the Funny Money keyword. Surprisingly, some funny money has real value in the business world.

Jokes and Gags

Exploding golf balls, hand buzzers, squirting flowers, and all the usual stuff populate this keyword. Fortunately, the joke won't be on you when you shop at the Jokes and Gags sites.

Novelties

You'll have fun with the items sold at the Novelties sites. Look for things like talking presents, bonsai kits, and loads of silly stuff.

Pranks

Practical jokers unite! Your family, friends, and neighbors better watch out when you're finished shopping at sites with the Pranks keyword.

Tasteless

The merchandise sold at the sites with the Tasteless keyword is tacky and not always in the best taste! You'll find macabre items like furniture made from caskets, practical jokes, and lighted toilet seats.

Wearables

Proclaim your funny bone with the items purchased from the stores with the Wearables keyword. From T-shirts with rude sayings to hats and belts, you'll find them at these sites.

3dglasses.net
3DGlasses
800-821-5122
3dglasses@rainbowsymphony.com
Wearables

It's a snap to change your outlook on life, with a pair of 3D glasses from this site. 3DGlasses has many different glasses available, including decoder, rainbow, anaglyph, polarized, and more. You can even order glasses to watch a solar eclipse. The glasses are great party favors. If you own a business, the glasses make a great giveaway with your business name and a custom message imprinted on the side. A free pair awaits visitors to 3DGlasses. Details are at the site.

amazingflygun.com
Wonderfully Weird
+27 (0)21 426 1987 (South Africa)
help@amazingflygun.com
Around the House • Novelties

Wonderfully Weird has come up with something we all need — a gun that shoots flies! No more messing around with rolled-up newspaper, flyswatters, or the occasional shoe. The flygun is a plastic gun that shoots a spring-powered swatter at flies (and mosquitoes). The purveyors of this fine insect-destroying weapon claim that it really works. The record, supposedly, is 30 flies in five minutes. Because the fly doesn't get squashed with this device, there's no yucky cleanup. For around $7 (and cheaper the more you order), you can't beat it!

bonsaipotato.com
Bonsai Potato
800-345-5359
sensei@bonsaipotato.com
Novelties

"Zen — without the wait!" At Bonsai Potato you can order a kit that contains everything you need to learn the shortcuts to patience and achieve inner peace — using the common potato. Here's what you get: pruning shears, tweezers, a state of the art mini-replica of an ancient version of an actual Bonsai Potato altar, and a hilarious 32-page book explaining the rich tradition of the art of the Bonsai Potato. All you supply is the potato. Check out the site's gallery of Bonsai Potato art. Come on! Where else can you find inner peace so fast!

carprank.com
CarPrank.com

No phone number listed
carprank@brightwebsite.com

Pranks

The gag's pretty simple — place the trick cup that's available from CarPrank.com on the roof of your car and drive away. The cup looks like a soft drink cup from a fast food joint or convenience store. People will honk, wave, and otherwise indicate to you that the cup's up there. The cup is easy to install, easy to remove, and guaranteed to not blow off your car. Call me diabolical, but I say take the joke one step further: Why not place the cup on the roof of someone else's car, like your little brother or that nosey neighbor, just before they drive away? Now that's a serious prank!

casketfurniture.com
Casketfurniture.com

800-789-9395
mhp@casketfurniture.com

Around the House • Tasteless

CasketFurniture.com's mission is "to reduce the burden of high-priced funerals with a unique alternative." The alternative is to use your casket as a piece of furniture. Whether as a couch, shelf, or end table, this company's products are designed to blend into most contemporary interior designs. Remember, every piece of casket furniture can also be transformed into a high-quality casket at your time of need. If you would like something on a smaller scale, how about a casket-shaped business card holder, or casket-shaped speakers? Don't forget your faithful dog or cat — the site offers pet-size caskets and urns for them, too.

cybercal.com
Cybercalifragilistic Interactive

800-713-7701
staff@cybercal.com

Novelties

If you're a computer nerd or just want your desk to look like you're one, then this online retailer of computer novelties is your ticket. Cybercalifragilistic Interactive sells computer-shaped sugar cookies, computer-themed cat and mouse jewelry, and novelty items made from recycled circuit boards. It also offers a small line of computer-themed infant and toddler T-shirts, and a Wel.com doormat. These one-of-a-kind products are definitely worth a look. You can order online, or via phone, fax, or postal mail.

 Recommended   Price   Selection   Convenience   Service 🔒 Security

cycoactive.com/blender
Tom Meyers, Art/Not Practical

206-323-2349
E-mail form on site

Around the House

If you like to have the latest and greatest in kitchen gadgetry, then you'll like the useful product offered by cycoactive.com — the BlenderPhone. The "ringer" is the blender motor, which pulses like a telephone bell. To answer the phone, pick the pitcher up out of the base and put the phone, connected to the pitcher, up to your ear. To hang up, replace the pitcher in the base. Warning — BlenderPhone is not cheap. It will set you back around $300 because they are handmade one at a time. You really didn't think these things were mass-produced, did you?

despair.com
Despair, Inc.

877-337-7247
E-mail form on site

Novelties

You're probably familiar with those sickening motivational posters that hit the business world about 10 years ago — you know, the ones about striving for the best and success in an organization? Well, Despair, Inc. takes a more realistic approach to motivation — demotivation posters. You can also find Underperformance awards, demotivating stickie notes, pessimist's mugs, and notecards with themes like Mistakes, Elitism, Mediocrity, Procrastination, and Cluelessness. In the Elitism category is a card stating "It's lonely at the top. But it's comforting to look down upon everyone at the bottom." You can review past year's demotivation collections through 2000, and you can join the site's Wailing List. So pull down your Dilbert cartoons and spread a little office despair with some demotivation products.

ducttapecreations.com
Duct Tape Creations

No phone number listed
comments@ducttapecreations.com

Wearables

Make a fashion statement in products made from, you guessed it, duct tape! Before you turn away from the Duct Tape Creations site, consider the facts. Unlike similar products, articles made from duct tape are built to last. They won't tear, they're virtually indestructible, and if lost in water, they float! Wallets are available in trifold, bifold, and checkbook style. A belt is a good choice, too. Simple styles are a safe bet, but for fancier occasions, the rhinestone buckle can add glitz. Backpacks, tote bags, and purses are also available, and you can even order a duct tape rose. One word of caution: Because all orders are handmade, your order may take two to four weeks to process.

easymillions.com
EasyMillions.com

360-574-2400
sales@easymillions.com

Funny Money • Jokes and Gags

Of course, the million dollar bills at EasyMillions.com are not legal tender. However, you can easily imagine what just one of them could buy. Available by the pack, you can impress the world as you peel them off and hand them out to everyone in sight. On a more serious note, the bills make a great sales tool. The bills can be customized and used as business cards. (Your customers won't toss this card in the trash!) "Thanks a Million" cards and matching envelopes are also available.

elifesize.com
eLifesize

800-216-9728
E-mail form on site

Around the House • Novelties

You can find life-size cardboard cutouts at eLifesize's site. The cutouts work great as advertising tools. Put one outside your shop or store and draw a crowd! If you're having a party, the cutouts make great silent guests (they don't eat or drink) and work as fabulous icebreakers. Shop for your cutout by name or category. Most of the cutouts are silent, but some have sound capabilities. Most cutouts are around 6 feet tall, but some smaller desktop models are available. Send a photo, and the eLifesize folks will create a custom cutout just for you.

 Recommended   Price   Selection   Convenience   Service   Security

⭐ eprank.com
ePrank

866-467-7265
E-mail form on site

Pranks • Tasteless

Decisions, decisions. Should you buy a fake insulting parking ticket to put in your pal's car window, or would the fake busted window (actually made of plastic cling) shock him more? Shopping at ePrank is like that — with so many great gags assembled at one site, sometimes making a choice is really hard. Select from Adult Pranks, Bathroom Pranks (totally gross!), Car Pranks, Classic Pranks, Money Pranks, and more. Remote-controlled pranks provide the opportunity to watch the action and control the direction of the joke. Just don't expect any kudos when it's revealed you were the one behind the curtain.

flypower.com
FlyPower

800-884-7667
wings@flypower.com

Novelties

Great minds throughout history have been fascinated by the possibilities of harnessing insect energy. Now you can, too, using fly power. The FlyPower Construction kit includes all the material you need to construct two fully functional airplanes utilizing a common housefly as the engine. I kid you not. These people are serious. If you don't believe me, read the History of Fly Power and Fly Facts to see that this can actually work. Get this kit (around $6 or so) and impress your friends and stun your family.

funnyundies.com
FunnyUndies.com

239-768-3116
sales@funnyundies.com

Wearables

Novelty underwear awaits you at FunnyUndies.com. How funny the boxers, thongs, and bikinis are that are sold here is pretty much up to you, because you supply the message that's embroidered on the underwear. Not sure what to say? You're not alone. Visit the on-site Photo Gallery and Hall of Fame to see what others have come up with. Messages can be embroidered from stock embroidery or you can request custom lettering. Undies are available for men and women. Take some time and read the funny stories at the site. You'll laugh yourself silly.

gagsplus.com/funnymoney/index.shtml
Gags Plus

866-843-8386
E-mail form on site

Funny Money

The new U.S. State quarters are on sale at Gags Plus — well, not exactly. At first glance the quarters appear to be the real deal. After all, the quarters have the same size and weight as the real ones. In fact, these fake quarters have been pressed on real quarters. On closer examination, the pictures on the coins aren't quite right. The California quarter shows Arnold choking Davis; the Texas quarter shows President George W. Bush astride a horse; and many of the other pictures depict crude scenes. Buy them individually or collect the set. Just take care not to spend one.

johnny-light.com
Johnny-Light

888-566-5483
info@johnny-light.com

Around the House • Tasteless

How many times has someone in your home forgotten to lower the toilet seat? Countless marriages have ended in divorce because one partner disagrees with the other's seat treatment, and who knows how many fall-ins in dark bathrooms have occurred? Now a simple, yet effective device can end the problem. Called Johnny-Light, it lights up the toilet bowl at night when the toilet seat is raised and goes off when the toilet seat is lowered. Batteries are included with every order. Installation is a breeze; you can read the instructions at the site. Imagine, no more strife!

lacoroner.com
Skeletons In The Closet

323-343-0760
E-mail form on site

Tasteless

Skeletons In The Closet is run by the L.A. County Coroner's Office to generate revenue for county-run projects. Coroner toe-tag keychains, boxer shorts called "undertakers," beach towels, T-shirts, tote bags, baseball caps, and office products are for sale at this site. Each item displays a unique Los Angeles County Coroner design such as a skeleton in Sherlock Holmes attire, a chalked-out body outline, or the L.A. County Coroner seal. Send a gift from Skeletons In The Closet for pure shock value; imagine the recipient's face when a package marked "Coroner's Office" arrives at the front door.

⭐ madmartian.com
Mad Martian

No phone number listed
E-mail form on site

Novelties • Wearables

No, the eyeball-themed stuff for sale at Mad Martian isn't from the red planet, it all just looks like it's out of this world. With almost 200 "eye-tems" for sale at this site, you're bound to see something you want. Eyeball mood rings tell the world the emotional state of the wearer, while eyeball ties and hats add a rakish look to any outfit. The orbs also adorn mugs, keychains, candles, and toys. Check out the Shirt Shop for non-eyeball-themed T-shirts, mugs, and mousepads.

mcphee.com
Archie McPhee

425-349-3009
mcphee@mcphee.com

Around the House • Jokes and Gags • Wearables

Archie McPhee's site is one that doesn't take itself too seriously. Named after a gent who knew how to have fun, the company has been selling silly toys, gifts, and wearables for more than 20 years. The categories in the online catalog — Amusements, Lifestyle, Lounge, Fashion, Tiki Island, Enlightenment, and Paradise Pals — give little clue to the irreverent gems you'll find. Don't expect a total gross-out. Some of the décor items are surprisingly elegant and reasonably priced, too. Sign up for the Cult of McPhee e-mail list and get a slew of members-only benefits.

nakedaprons.com
NakedAprons.com

618-394-9344
info@nakedaprons.com

Wearables

Well now that we have your attention. . . . NakedAprons.com offers real aprons with pictures printed on them. Michelangelo's "David," Botticelli's "Venus," and a "Naked Fat Man" (for which no one takes credit) are featured on this site. You'll also find fully clothed people on the front of the aprons sold at this site. If people aren't to your liking, consider buying an apron with glasses of beer or wheels of cheese on it. You can also find aprons decorated with animals and even Santa Claus. All aprons are crafted from easy care materials and functional. An apron from NakedApron.com makes a great hostess gift.

noveltieswholesale.com
NoveltiesWholesale.com
800-283-3442
lottofun@charter.net
Funny Money • Jokes and Gags •Wearables

NoveltiesWholesale.com doesn't waste bandwidth with pictures, colors, or other fancy Web page elements. Instead, the site cuts right to the chase with a simple page of links leading to just about every joke and gag you can name. Hand buzzers? Exploding pens? Whoopie cushions? You can find all these items and more at this site. Prices are really low, and you can purchase small quantities if you like. Because shipping is a flat rate of $4.95, it pays to gather everything you want in a single order. The site ships internationally.

pushindaisies.com
Pushin Daisies
No phone number listed
cadavercat@pushindaisies.com
Tasteless

This site is really macabre! Owned and operated by a licensed funeral director, Pushin Daisies is a mortuary novelty shop. Shop at this site for death-related products ranging from the comical to the weird. Pushin Daisies offers chocolates, from caskets to body parts. Dead rose bouquets make a statement without words. Things get genuine rather quickly though. Embalmer's kits, body bag/cremation pouches, toe tags (printed and plain), and funeral windshield stickers for sale at this site are "the real thing." Have a fascination with death? Talk with other like-minded individuals on the site's message board, appropriately named Coffin Talk.

revengeunlimited.com
Revenge Unlimited
No phone number listed
E-mail form on site
Tasteless

If you've ever wanted to get even with someone, or ever wanted to give someone a really good gag gift, then check out the offerings of Revenge Unlimited. This company offers the perfect revenge items, like a bouquet of dead roses (around $40), as well as books on getting revenge, such as *Get Even 2: Even More Tricks from the Master of Revenge*. Or you can choose a tool for getting even, such as Blue Mouth gum, a Dribble Mug, or a Gag Winning Lottery Ticket. These non-aggressive, all-in-good-fun pranks can help you blow off a little steam, and give everyone a good laugh.

 Recommended Price Selection Convenience Service  Security

sendblackroses.com
The Black Rose Floral Company
818-705-8407
inquiry@sendblackroses.com

Tasteless

Tired of turning the other cheek? Want to convey the message that's really in your heart? Consider a gift of roses from The Black Rose Floral Company. The black rose is a powerful symbol in cultures all over the world. Send a black rose gift to poke fun at a milestone birthday, express a heartfelt loss of love and affection, or stick it to the person who stuck it to you. Whatever your sentiments, your gift won't soon be forgotten. Roses are available in silk, natural, or dried and can be sent singly or in arrangements or centerpieces.

slouchtowels.com
The Slouch
979-775-5837
customerservice@slouchtowels.com

Around the House

The Slouch is a beach towel — but no ordinary beach towel. The Slouch covers your entire lounge chair from top to bottom and stays that way because of a pocket that holds on to the chair. The Slouch is made of your choice of terry cloth or terry velour, and you can personalize your Slouch, too, by adding your name, initials, or a logo. The site offers some tongue-in-cheek before and after shots of chairs with and without the Slouch. The price for this little bit of poolside heaven is around $50.

⭐ stupid.com
Stupid.com
631-274-0393
apple@bellsandwhistles.com

Around the House • Jokes and Gags • Novelties

Make sure you're alone when you browse the online catalog from Stupid.com. You're going to laugh out loud at some of the funny stuff available here, no doubt about it. The doormat that reads "Nice Underwear," the motion-activated talking toilet soap dispenser that yells "Hey, don't forget to wash your hands!" when someone walks by, and the nightlights that are shaped like knights in shining armor are just a few examples of the great items assembled at this site for your enjoyment. Don't miss the candy (Wurmz and Dirt, Toothache Candy, and more) and all the Stupid Toys. This site is not so stupid, after all.

sushiclock.com
Sente

No phone number listed
sushiclock@yahoo.com

Around the House

Like the sushi this clock is named after, the clocks made by Sente are all handmade. Priced between $35–$50, these unusual clocks actually work. They are battery-powered, with second hands and quartz movement, and the hours are simulated pieces of sushi sitting in a round sushi-style serving tray. Sushi Clocks are black inside with a red rim, and you can choose from two different side patterns. You can also buy a dim sum clock (12 pieces of dim sum sitting in a round bamboo dim sum tray) or a manju or doughnut clock (mmm, doughnuts). You can order online, or via check or money order. The site also has a listing of sushi cookbooks, rice cookers, and dim sum cookbooks.

talkingpresents.com
Talking Presents

866-265-0552
info@talkingpresents.com

Novelties

Finding a special gift can be difficult sometimes, especially if you don't have a lot of money to spend. The tried-and-true gifts of flowers, cards, and candies just don't cut it sometimes. So why not send a gift that talks? Talking Presents sells some wild and crazy talking items, or ones that let you record your own message. The site offers a talking parrot that repeats everything you say and a condiment holder that yells, "Cheeseburger, cheeseburger, cheeseburger, ketchup, mustard, relish, get your fixin's here!" Or you can buy the talking teddy bear that speaks the message you record, the Talking Alligator Cookie Jar, and the ever-popular Remote Fart Machine. You can search for products by category or by price and you can enter a monthly drawing for prizes, too.

 Recommended   Price   Selection   Convenience Service Security

teethbydnash.com
Teeth By Dnash

914-525-7777
dnash@dnash.com

Wearables

Just how serious are you about getting a set of vampire fangs? You could mosey on down to the nearest discount or novelty store or click over to Teeth by Dnash. The fangs here are made just for you and designed to last for years. Start the process with top and bottom study molds of your mouth from your dentist. You'll also need to decide whether you want to match your existing tooth color, or order a sinister shade like red or black. Your new teeth will arrive shortly. A word of caution: Biting a non-consenting person is illegal and considered assault in all 50 states, so ask before you bite.

thejokestop.com
The Jokestop

909-816-7399
shop@jokestop.com

Pranks

If you live in Southern California, you may have already partaken of the comic wares of The Jokestop. The pranks available at this site are aimed at golfers, because everyone knows how seriously they take their sport. Four prank golf balls are available: Jetstreamer, which ejects 15 feet of spiraling, streaming ribbon on impact; Unputtaball, which wobbles away from the hole when tapped with a putter; Exploder, which explodes into a puff of smoke when struck with a club; and finally, the Phantom, which breaks down into a watery mist when hit. Hilarious! Hint: Don't try these out on your boss at the company golf outing.

themilliondollar.com
The Million.com

No phone number listed
get@themillion.com

Funny Money

I think it was Senator Dirksen who said, "A billion here, a billion there, and pretty soon you're talking real money." It may not be real money at this online retailer, but you can buy your own personalized million or billion dollar bill. The cost — just 50 cents plus shipping, of course. It's not U.S. currency but it has the same size, look, and feel of the real thing. You can even personalize your bill with your own signature the bill. You can use your credit card via PayPal, or you can pay via check or money order.

theprankstore.com
The Prank Store

503-391-1173
jerry@theprankstore.com

Pranks

If you're known as a prankster, The Prank Store is going to push all your buttons. The site carries some of the best practical jokes, prank items, and gag gifts on the Internet. The items here are organized by category so you'll have no trouble finding the prank or gag you want. The Prank Store carries a few tasteless bumper stickers that adhere to any metal surface and can be reused. The shocking stapler is good for a few laughs when an unsuspecting office mate tries to use it. For added laughs, lend an unsuspecting victim your Shock Pen. If you want to be really gross, order a Bubba Booger key-chain. Pressing Bubba's nose produces nasty results!

wiztees.com
WIZtees.com

805-449-2022
No e-mail address on site

Tasteless • Wearables

If you're the type who loves to see others blanch when they read the slogan on your T-shirt, this site is perfect for you. With T-shirt categories like Rude, Stupid, and Suggestive, WIZtees.com can provide you a T-shirt that will raise a few eyebrows wherever you go. Some of the sayings aren't too bad. For example, the Attitude T-shirt that reads "take my advice . . . I'm not using it" may get a few chuckles as you go past. On the other hand, you may need a dose of courage to wear "KEEP STARING I MIGHT DO A TRICK." Shipping is free on all orders.

wyb.com/jokes.html
Would You Believe

800-700-3828
wyb@wyb.com

Jokes and Gags • Tasteless

Some of the corniest jokes and gags — more than 400 in all — await you at the Would You Believe site. The site is a practical joker's playground: Fake doggie doo, squirt pens, and bogus parking tickets are only a sample of what you'll find. The gags are arranged by categories, such as Bang and Shock, Cuffs and Locks, and Surprising Snakes. The Bathroom Humor category should be avoided by anyone with a shred of taste! Happily, the joke won't be on you when you order from this site. Prices are low and shipping is fast and reliable.

 Recommended   Price   Selection   Convenience   Service   Security

⭐ zymetrical.com
Zymetrical

804-758-4444
sales@zymetrical.com

Pranks

Zymetrical is a great source of pranks, gags, jokes, and novelties. The prank items are both realistic and inexpensive, with items like Disappearing Ink, a Squirt Pen, and Squirt Cigarette priced reasonably. Even the Dribble Glass (always good for a few chuckles) is priced low and can be used again on new, unsuspecting victims. Pick up a Shock Computer Mouse if you suspect an unauthorized user is working on your computer when you're away. Someone borrowing your cell phone without permission? Play "gotcha" with the Shock Cell Phone Lighter. Ah, the possibilities are endless.

Touring Amusement Parks

Everyone loves going to the amusement park. Some people like the big theme parks, with thrill rides, shows, and loads of attractions. Other folks favor smaller parks, where the crowds are smaller and the lines are shorter but the rides aren't always on the cutting edge. No matter which type of park you favor, a trip to the park is always an exciting event.

The soaring ticket prices at some parks may shock you. Look for coupons in the local paper or supermarket to help offset the cost. Maybe your employer has an annual picnic or park day with discount passes. If you go to the park frequently, season passes are the way to go.

Did you know that amusement parks became popular in the United States after the 1893 World's Columbian Exposition in Chicago? Learn more about their history, and where the country's oldest amusement parks are located at the Web site of The National Amusement Park Historical Association (`napha.org`).

Six Flags (`sixflags.com`) is a popular amusement park destination for many families. With locations throughout the United States and Mexico, Spain, and Canada, you're bound to find a Six Flags near you. You can purchase a season pass online. Alternatively, buy your tickets online and print them from home. You'll never need to wait in line at the gate.

Florida is home to several great amusement parks. Walt Disney World (`disneyworld.disney.go.com`) has four theme parks and two water parks, hotels, restaurants, and ticket plans to meet any budget. Universal Studios Florida and its sister park, Islands of Adventure (`themeparks.universalstudios.com/orlando/website`) is another fabulous destination. Visit Universal to watch the movies come to life and enjoy thrill-packed rides. Like Disney, Universal is a full-fledged resort. Busch Gardens (`buschgardens.com`) serves up rides, adventure, and nature. You can buy tickets online at all three parks' sites.

If a theme park vacation isn't in the cards this year, don't despair. Right now, we're going to take a virtual tour of five very different American amusement parks. Keep in mind that your computer may need special software such as Real Player or QuickTime. Don't worry; the site will let you know if you don't have the software installed. Most times, it will point you in the right direction to get and set up the software you need.

Ready for some fun? Good! Let's go.

Our first stop is Fun Forest Amusement Park (`vrseattle.com/html/vrlist.php?cat_id=135&lang=`) located in Seattle, Washington, at the base of the Space Needle. After you've seen all the sights at Fun Forest, it's time to mosey on over to the Super Slide Amusement Park in Bismarck, North Dakota. Super Slide (`giantdipper.com/virtualgd.html`) is a small, low-tech park. Fortunately, there aren't any lines. Check out the slide.

How about a water park? Knights Action Park and Caribbean Water Adventure (`knightsactionpark.com/park_tour.html#`) in Springfield, Illinois, will keep your family amused for hours.

Our fourth stop on the tour takes us to Hershey Park (`hersheypa.com/attractions/hersheypark/rides/new_attraction/virtual_movie.html`) in Hershey, Pennsylvania. The clean and green family amusement park opened its doors in 1907. Ride the roller coaster, if you dare!

Our final stop on our amusement park tour leads us to Cedar Point (`cedarpoint.com/public/inside_park/webcam/index.cfm`) in Sandusky, Ohio. This famous park is located on a peninsula that juts out into Lake Erie. Watch the action at the park via the live Webcams.

All that touring can make you hungry for some candy. How about a big lollipop? Really big! You'll find the best lollipop in the world at Great Big Stuff (`greatbigstuff.com/chupa`). Enjoy!

Part III
The Part of Tens

The 5th Wave   By Rich Tennant

LARRY'S
LUNCH TRUCK

MENU

SAY HI!

"Can someone please tell me how long 'Larry's Lunch Truck' has had his own page on the Web?"

In this part . . .

Ah, the Part of Tens! In this part you find valuable information such as ten ways to protect yourself and your purchase when shopping online, ten places to turn when you have problems with a purchase, ten places for product and merchant reviews, and ten ways to find the best prices on the Web.

Use this Part of Tens as a checklist when you shop online.

Chapter 25

Ten Ways to Protect You and Your Purchase When Shopping Online

● ●

In This Chapter

▶ Know what you want and from whom you buy

▶ Always use a credit card

▶ Look for security

▶ Guard your privacy

▶ Look for a third-party endorsement

▶ Look for guarantees

▶ Know your total cost

▶ Use an escrow service

▶ Beware of phishing

● ●

As you've seen by reading through this directory, the Web is filled with an abundance of fantastic shopping sites that can meet almost every personal need or desire. But this wonderful shopping opportunity does come with risks. Threats to your wallet and personal information are everywhere on the Net. And they're not so easily seen for what they are. They can hide behind flashy-looking, professional Web sites, in online classified ads, in unsolicited e-mail, in newsgroup postings, and in chat rooms.

So how do you protect yourself and your purchase when shopping online?

Here are ten ways to protect you and your purchase. Keep them handy when doing your shopping excursions and abide by them. They can save you a lot of money and heartache.

Know What You Want

Until the day when you can reach into cyberspace and actually touch the merchandise you must understand that the Web is virtual world with virtual products. Before you click that Buy button, you should have done your homework. The more you know about what you're going to purchase, the less chance your purchase will go sour, needing to be exchanged or returned — or heaven forbid — leaving you stuck with an unhappy purchase. This homework rule goes double for any item you buy through auctions or classified ads. The Web has an extraordinary set of search and research tools at your disposal so you can gather the information you need to make a successful purchase. Use these tools. Become informed before you buy.

Know the Merchant

The Web is great for leveling the playing field. In other words, you'll not only see the well-known merchants with an online presence, but also the not-so-well-known. Buying from Amazon or The Gap is a no-brainer. You know these merchants have a solid reputation and that purchasing from them is safe. But what about that interesting-looking site with that unique product line, the merchant you never heard of? A reputable company should offer many different ways to contact it — phone number, fax number, street address — not just an e-mail address. Having several different types of contact information is helpful if you have a problem with your order, or just need to ask a question before you buy. Next, research the merchant. Use the Web sites listed in Chapter 1 to see whether other buyers and organizations like the Better Business Bureau have any negative comments about what this company sells and the way it sells it.

Always Use a Credit Card

Only use a credit card when purchasing online — not a debit card, check, cashier's check, or money order. The reason is simple. If you have a problem with a merchant, you always have recourse with a credit card. Just tell your bank you're dissatisfied with your purchase and have it reverse the charges. When you pay any other way, the merchant has your money and the leverage. If the company doesn't accept credit cards, then figure out how much you really want that product and how much risk you're willing to take in regards to sending payment first. Do as much research on the merchant as possible to make sure it's reputable.

Look for Security

Any real merchant that collects a credit card for payment has a secure way to accept your card on its site. Most often you can find a statement assuring you of credit card security on the home page or some customer service page on the Web site. If you don't see this assurance stated clearly on the company's site, contact it and confirm site security before using your credit card.

Guard Your Privacy

Right up there with credit card security is guarding your personal privacy. You want to know what kind of personal information the merchant is collecting and holding on you and what it intends to do with it. Every viable merchant has a privacy policy somewhere on its Web site — most often you can find a link to its privacy policy from the home page. Read the policy fully. Find out whether the company shares your name and personal information with third parties. If it does, you'll become a good candidate for spam.

Look for a Third-Party Endorsement

Merchants most certainly toot their own horns. But some go the extra mile and acquire a third-party endorsement of their site and how they do business. Being a member of the Better Business Bureau is a good example. Other companies register themselves with third-party survey companies such as BizRate, which rates shopping sites for consumers. These third-party endorsements add to your shopping peace of mind. See Chapter 1 for others.

Look for Guarantees

Satisfaction guarantees are very popular, and you'll find them on the better shopping sites. Satisfaction guarantees are not product warrantees, or exchange polices that may have stipulations regarding what you can exchange and when. A true 100 percent satisfaction guarantee means just that. Return the product for any reason. No questions asked.

Know Your Total Cost

Be aware of the shipping and handling surprise! You should be presented with the final, total cost of your order — including shipping and handling, applicable taxes, and any costs of special requests like gift wrapping — *before* the merchant asks for your credit card number. After your number goes through, if you change your mind about the product, getting a credit may be a hassle.

Use an Escrow Service

Buying something at auction is THE riskiest kind of online shopping. You're buying from your fellow natives — individuals, not verifiable merchants. And most often, you're sending them money in the form of a personal check, cashier's check, or money order before you receive the product you purchased. The best way to protect yourself in this case is to use an Internet escrow service like I describe in Chapter 3. You send your money to the service, which holds your money until you receive the product, and pays the seller when you're completely satisfied.

Beware of Phishing

You buy a product from a merchant. You get an unsolicited e-mail from that merchant asking you to verify some personal information such as your credit card number or your PIN number, or maybe even your social security number. You reply, and the next thing you know your bank account has been vacated. This is called a *phishing* scam in which consumers receive an e-mail, supposedly from a merchant or their bank, requesting personal information. A credible merchant will NOT ask for sensitive personal information using an e-mail message. If you get one, report it to the merchant or your bank immediately.

Chapter 26

Ten Places to Turn When You Have Problems with a Purchase

....

In This Chapter

▶ Better Business Bureau

▶ U.S. Postal Inspection Service

▶ Square Trade

▶ WebAssured

▶ Netcheck Commerce Bureau

▶ Planet Feedback

▶ David Horowitz's Fight Back

▶ National Consumer Complaint Center

▶ Internet Fraud Complaint Center

▶ National Fraud Information Center

....

*Y*ou made your purchase. It arrives at your door. You open it up and — there's a problem. It may not be what you ordered — it's the wrong size, color, or item. Or worse yet, you purchase an item and it never arrives!

You can protect yourself and your privacy by using the services of the Web sites I present in this chapter. And if you have a complaint against a merchant, these sites will be more than happy to help with that, too.

Better Business Bureau

The Better Business Bureau (bbbonline.org/privacy/dr.asp) is the granddad of all business complaint organizations. If you think that a company has treated you unfairly, you can file a complaint online with the BBB. This organization contacts the merchant to help resolve the issue.

U.S. Postal Inspection Service

If you bought the product online and it was delivered by mail, you can complain to the U.S. Postal Service (`usps.com/postalinspectors/fraud/MailFraudComplaint.htm`). You can post a complaint, but keep in mind that although the Inspection Service can't resolve routine business disputes between companies and their customers, it can act against a company or individual if a pattern of activity suggests an attempt to defraud consumers.

Square Trade

If the merchant you did business with is a member of Square Trade (`squaretrade.com`), and you have dispute with this merchant, Square Trade will intercede between the buyer and seller to settle disputes, whether the seller is an online merchant or an individual seller on eBay or another auction site.

Web Assured

A merchant subscribing to WebAssured (`webassured.com/address/complaint.cfm`) promises a high standard of conduct in dealing with customers. Web sites carrying the WebAssured seal promise that you get exactly what you order. Better yet, even if the merchant isn't a member of WebAssured, consumers can still sound off via the Automated Dispute Resolution System.

Netcheck Commerce Bureau

NetCheck (`netcheck.com/complaint.htm`) has assisted the public in receiving refunds totaling an estimated $2 million. This company handles complaints on any Web site worldwide concerning fraud, refunds, copyright infringement, false advertising, spam, or unsolicited bulk e-mail.

Planet Feedback

At Planet Feedback (`planetfeedback.com/consumer`), you can sound off on a public bulletin board about a transaction you had with a merchant, and the whole world can see it. Other online shoppers may chime in with their own opinions as well.

David Horowitz's Fight Back

At well-known journalist David Horowitz's Web site (fightback.com), you can get consumer support and resolution of your problem for a small fee. David has much experience in educating consumers to stand up for themselves against merchants. He has been instrumental in getting consumer protection laws on the books.

National Consumer Complaint Center

The National Consumer Complaint Center (alexanderlaw.com/nccc) provides a method for promptly communicating consumer complaints to United States government agencies that are interested in investigating and taking action for consumers.

Internet Fraud Complaint Center

The Internet Fraud Complaint Center, the IFCC (ifccfbi.gov/index.asp), is a partnership between the Federal Bureau of Investigations and the National White Collar Crime Center. The IFCC provides a convenient and easy-to-use reporting mechanism that alerts authorities of a suspected criminal or civil violation.

National Fraud Information Center

The National Fraud Information Center (fraud.org) provides a handy online form (68.166.162.20/repoform.htm) for you to fill out for reporting Internet or telemarketing fraud. You can also call in the suspected fraud via a toll-free number found on the site.

Chapter 27

Ten Places for Product and Merchant Reviews

*Y*ou've shopped the World Wide Web and found that one product in a million, and it looks too good to be true — and it just may be. So before you lay out the bucks for your intended purchase, do a quick check with the Web sites presented in this chapter and see whether that product or merchant you chose is a lemon.

Consumer Reports Online

Consumer Reports Online (consumerreports.org) is published by Consumers Union, an independent, nonprofit testing and information organization. Since 1936, CU's mission has been to test products, inform the public, and protect consumers. This organization is a comprehensive source for unbiased advice about products and services.

Consumer Search.com

An extensive site for product reviews, ConsumerSearch.com (`consumersearch.com`) reviews hundreds of product reviews, analyzes and ranks them, and then distills the information you need and recommends which products are the best.

Rate It All

With more than a million ratings across thousands of topics, RateItAll (`rateitall.com`) is one of the most extensive and diverse online databases of opinions, ratings, and reviews in the world. It lists comments and suggestions from real consumers about hundreds of topics.

Epinions

Epinions (`epinions.com`) does not decide what content to post and what not to post. Epinions is a platform for people to share their experiences — both good and bad — with other consumers via reviews, ratings, and comments.

BizRate

One of the first organizations to rate online businesses, BizRate (`bizrate.com`) collects merchant and product ratings from more than one million online buyers each month, making BizRate's merchant ratings some of the most reliable on the Web.

ePublicEye

ePublicEye (`epubliceye.com`) registered merchants display the "monitored 24 hours" seal prominently and link it to the ePublicEye Customer Satisfaction Database. Consumers may file a report of their experiences with a registered business any time, day or night, seven days a week. The reports, once confirmed, are recorded instantly and are immediately available to other consumers.

Ethical Consumer

Ever wondered whether the manufacturer you're buying from is making its products in an ethical way? You can easily find out by checking with Ethical Consumer (ethicalconsumer.org). It has the facts on manufacturers and companies concerning child labor, global warming, and even arms trading.

Good Housekeeping

The Good Housekeeping (magazines.ivillage.com/goodhousekeeping) Seal of Approval has been around for almost 100 years. That seal goes to the best products that this magazine has reviewed. If a product bearing the seal proves to be defective within two years of purchase, Good Housekeeping will replace the product or refund the purchase price.

CNET

If it's electronic, CNET (cnet.com) reviews it. Chock-full of product reviews, news, and shopping guidance, CNET's site is the best on the Net to get the scoop on consumer electronics.

Audio Review

What CNET doesn't cover in the audio department, Audio Review (audioreview.com) does. This site lists reviews on speakers, amplifiers, home theater systems, portable audio products, TVs, and headphones.

Chapter 28

Ten Ways to Find the Best Prices

· ·

In This Chapter

▶ Get Connected

▶ EveryBookstore.com

▶ Value Find

▶ CheapestRate.com

▶ ShoppingList.com

▶ TotalDeals.com

▶ PriceSCAN.com

▶ Froogle.com

▶ mySimon.com

▶ PriceGrabber.com

· ·

A good shopper always looks for the best deal. And the Internet makes finding deals so easy. If you're looking for a Web site that points you to bargains on or off the Web or for a way to comparison shop millions of products with a click of the mouse, then the Web sites presented in this chapter can send you in the right direction.

Get Connected

Get Connected (`getconnected.com`) covers the realm of telecommunication products. This site offers the largest selection and lowest prices on wireless phones and plans, high-speed Internet, long distance phone service, and satellite television available anywhere online (subject to availability in your local area).

EveryBookstore.com

If you're looking for the lowest price on books, EveryBookstore.com (`ebs.allbookstores.com`) is a "no bells and whistles" Web site for fast and easy comparison shopping at more than 30 online bookstores, starting with the big names like Amazon.com and Barnes & Noble, to the somewhat smaller stores on the Web.

Value Find

Value Find (`valuefind.com`) searches for millions of new and used products, and compares prices from vendors, auctions, and classified ads. This site also lets you compare two merchants side-by-side so you can find the best values.

CheapestRate.com

CheapestRate.com (`cheapestrate.com`) shops the Web for the lowest cost product or service. The site lists the best company for each category and evaluates it by price, quality, service, delivery, response times, and ease of using the site.

ShoppingList.com

ShoppingList.com (`shoppinglist.com`) is an online guide to offline sales and covers a wide range of stores and products across the U.S. Enter your zip code to see the current offline ads for stores in your area. This site provides a great service for finding deals at your local stores.

TotalDeals.com

TotalDeals.com (`totaldeals.com`) can save you money online with coupons, coupon codes, free shipping, sales, freebies, rebates, and more. You can even print coupons on your own printer at home for groceries and local businesses.

PriceSCAN.com

PriceSCAN (`pricescan.com`) tracks down deals regardless of whether or not the vendor has a Web site. PriceSCAN's staff gathers product and pricing information from vendor's magazine ads, catalogs, and daily faxes. They also receive pricing data submitted directly by vendors. This information is entered into a searchable database that you can use to save money.

Froogle.com

Froogle (`froogle.google.com`) is a service from Google, that wonderful search engine. Using Froogle makes finding information about products for sale online easy by focusing entirely on a very specific task — locating stores that sell the item you want and sending you directly to the online merchant where you can make a purchase.

mySimon.com

mySimon (`mysimon.com`) is one of the most popular comparison-shopping agents on the Net today. Simon shops hundreds of merchants and millions of products to find the one you desire with the lowest price.

Price Grabber.com

PriceGrabber.com (`pricegrabber.com`) takes the convenience of comparison-shopping one step further than other shopping bots. Right on its home page, the best deal on the three most popular items in each of its many product categories is highlighted.

Index

● *C* ●

• I •

• J •

• K •

• R •

Notes

Notes

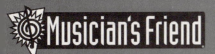